OXFORD MONOGRAPHS ON MUSIC

FOUR AND TWENTY FIDDLERS

Four and Twenty Fiddlers

The Violin at the English Court
1540–1690

PETER HOLMAN

CLARENDON PRESS · OXFORD

Oxford University Press, Walton Street, Oxford OX2 6DP

Oxford New York
Athens Auckland Bangkok Bombay
Calcutta Cape Town Dar es Salaam Delhi
Florence Hong Kong Istanbul Karachi
Kuala Lumpur Madras Madrid Melbourne
Mexico City Nairobi Paris Singapore
Taipei Tokyo Toronto
and associated companies in
Berlin Ibadan

Oxford is a trade mark of Oxford University Press

Published in the United States
by Oxford University Press Inc., New York

© Peter Holman 1993
Reprinted 1994, 1995
New as paperback edition 1995

British Library Cataloguing in Publication Data
Data available

Library of Congress Cataloging in Publication Data
Holman, Peter.
Four and twenty fiddlers: the violin at the English court,
1540–1690/Peter Holman.
p. cm.—(Oxford monographs on music)
Originally published: Oxford : Clarendon Press : New York : Oxford
University Press, 1993.
Includes bibliographical references and index.
1. String ensembles—16th century—History and criticism.
2. String ensembles—17th century—History and criticism. 3. Music—
England—16th century—History and criticism. 4. Music—
England—17th century—History and criticism. 5. Great Britain—
Court and courtiers—History—16th century. 6. Great Britain—
Court and courtiers—History—17th century. I. Title.
II. Series.
[ML756.H64 1995] 787.2'0942'09031—dc20 95-41445
ISBN 0-19-816592-7

Typeset by Best-set Typesetter Ltd., Hong Kong

Printed in Great Britain by Biddles Ltd
Guildford and King's Lynn

IN MEMORY OF MY MOTHER
LUCY HOLMAN (1915–1987)

Four and twenty Fidlers all in a Row,
And there was fiddle fiddle,
And twice fiddle fiddle,
'Cause 'twas my Lady's Birth-day,
Therefore we kept Holiday,
And all went to be merry.

Wit and Mirth; or, Pills to
Purge Melancholy
Thomas D'Urfey, 1699

Preface

THE origins of this book go back more than twenty years, to a moment one day in June 1969, at the end of the summer term of my second year at King's College, London. Thurston Dart asked me what academic work I was going to do during the holidays, and I answered on the spur of the moment that I wanted to investigate the origin of the violin in England. My main motive must have been to please him, for Dart had virtually invented the subject. He was the first person to question the received opinion—which went back to Roger North and Thomas Mace—that the violin was little known in England before the Restoration. In a series of influential articles, editions, and recordings in the 1950s and 1960s he suggested that some of the so-called viol consort repertoire, including music by Orlando Gibbons, John Dowland, John Coprario, and William Lawes, had been written for violins rather than viols, or for a mixture of the two. Thus his response to my proposal was unexpected, to say the least: he was sure I would only find enough pieces of evidence to be counted on the fingers of one hand. Whether he intended it or not, his words brought my natural obstinacy to the fore: I went straight to the library, and managed to cover a sheet of paper with references before I went home that night.

At first the subject seemed straightforward enough: it would take the form of a history of the English court violin consort from its inception on 1 May 1540, when a group of six Jewish string-players from Venice received posts at Henry VIII's court. An obvious end to the study presented itself when I discovered that almost exactly 150 years later, on 2 May 1690, William III ordered a retrenchment in the royal household that had the effect of removing the court from the centre of English musical life. After that the royal band, the descendant of Henry VIII's violin consort, became a part-time institution whose members spent most of their time working in London's commercial theatres and concert halls. In that form it survived, on paper at least, into the twentieth century.

However, over the years the project has become rather more than a history of an institution. Indeed, I now find it easiest to define its boundaries in negative terms. I have not attempted to deal in detail with the physical development of the violin: I am not qualified to comment on the technical aspects of its construction, and in any case such comments would have little validity, for no English violin-family instruments seem to have survived from before the middle of the seventeenth century. Violins are not usually depicted accurately enough in sixteenth- and seventeenth-

century pictures to be of any use in this context; we often cannot be sure
that the pictures are of English provenance, and it is impossible to tell
whether the artists intended to depict English instruments.

I have not attempted to deal with the technical aspects of violin-
playing. I am not a violinist, and no English treatises on violin-playing
survive from before the 1690s. What little can be deduced from English
treatises on viol-playing is discussed in David Boyden's classic book *The
History of Violin Playing from its Origins to 1761* (London, 1965; 2nd edn.,
1990), as is the information contained in Continental violin treatises—
which may or may not be relevant to England. I have, however, tried to
bring Boyden's account of the origin of the violin up to date in my first
chapter, taking into account the mass of important new material relating
to fifteenth- and early sixteenth-century instruments and instrumental
music that has come to light since the 1960s. We can now be reasonably
sure that the violin was developed in the decade 1495–1505, and that the
process was accomplished in a workshop within the orbit of the courts of
Ferrara and Mantua. More important, we are now beginning to understand the historical and musical context from which the violin emerged;
we are beginning to be able to answer the questions 'how?' and 'why?', as
well as 'where?' and 'when?'.

The book is not a work of analysis in the conventional sense: the reader
will not find bar-by-bar commentaries on the harmonic and melodic
structure of the early English violin repertoire; it mostly consists of simple
dances, and does not need a garrulous guide. Instead, I have approached
the music largely through its textures and scorings—issues, usually
neglected by analysts, that are of crucial importance to the understanding
of early instrumental music. Indeed, one of the main themes of this book
is that the disposition of the parts of a piece of early violin music is often
a clue to its instrumentation, and to the identity of the ensemble for
which it was written. In recent years the revival of 'original' instruments
has tended to run ahead of our understanding of how they were used in
ensembles. It is not uncommon to hear 'authentic' performances of
Purcell in which Baroque instruments are beautifully and stylishly played
in combinations that only came into being decades after the composer's
death. The history of the violin has often been equated with the history of
the soprano member of the family, and with its solo repertoire. But,
in common with other instruments, the violin was mainly played in
ensembles or consorts throughout the sixteenth and early seventeenth
centuries, and in England a significant solo repertoire did not develop
until after the Restoration. For that reason my emphasis throughout has
been on the violin as a family, and on its ensemble repertoire.

When David Boyden wrote his book in the 1960s it was possible to fit a
comprehensive history of the violin 'from its origins to 1761' between two

covers. To take account of all the research published since then, a Boyden for the 1990s would have to be in many volumes. But it no longer seems important or even desirable to write general histories of particular instruments. The need now is for focused studies of particular times and places, relating archival material to the surviving musical repertoire; to some extent my model has been the admirable recent books on music in particular fifteenth-century cities, such as Lewis Lockwood's *Music in Renaissance Ferrara* and Reinhard Strohm's *Music in Late Medieval Bruges*. The English court is an ideal vehicle for a study of this sort. The Tudors and earlier Stuarts maintained one of the largest musical institutions in Europe, and controlled it with a labyrinthine bureaucracy that recorded every transaction in minute detail—and in numerous copies. England has largely escaped the repeated wars, invasions, and civil strife that resulted in the destruction of so many archives on the Continent, and the Public Record Office houses the most complete government records in Europe, possibly in the world.

It is odd, therefore, that archival research into music at the Tudor and Stuart court, so flourishing in Victorian and Edwardian times, never really revived after the Great War. When I began my research I had to rely almost entirely on publications such as Willibald Nagel's 'Annalen der englischen Hofmusik von der Zeit Heinrichs VIII. bis zum Tode Karls I.' (1894), Henry Cart de Lafontaine's *The King's Musick* (1909), on articles in *The Musical Antiquary* (1909–13), and on contemporary government publications such as the *Calendar of State Papers, Domestic Series*, the *Calendar of Treasury Books*, and the *Letters and Papers, Foreign and Domestic, of the Reign of Henry VIII, 1509–47*. These volumes were cited by all the standard histories of English music, biographies of English composers, and studies of English musical sources, so when I finally began to work in the Public Record Office it came as a shock to find out that they were mostly inaccurate, incomplete, and thoroughly misleading. The situation has since been transformed by the publication of Andrew Ashbee's admirable *Records of English Court Music* [RECM]—in part a revision of *The King's Musick*. But in general English music is still less well served by archival studies than the music of most European countries. One of my aims is to show that seemingly 'dry as dust' documents can contribute a good deal to our understanding of music of the past, and often have a direct bearing on how we should perform it.

Part of the problem is that we have tended to undervalue the role of the court in the musical life of Tudor and Stuart times. The court did not just employ more musicians than any other institution in England—there were nearly a hundred by the end of Henry VIII's reign. It also employed most of England's prominent composers, and was the source of most new ideas—or the main route by which new ideas from the Continent reached the wider musical community. The history of the violin in England illustrates the process particularly clearly. The violin probably reached England for the first time in the luggage of the string-players who arrived at court from Venice in 1540 (Ch. 4). It gradually spread outside the court, to professional musicians in aristocratic households, in the theatre, and in waits groups (Ch. 6); amateurs only took it up in large numbers in the 1650s and 1660s (Ch. 11).

At first the violin was used almost entirely for dance music—professional string-players would have used the viol for contrapuntal music, and for accompanying the voice—but a repertoire of contrapuntal music was created for it in James I's reign by Orlando Gibbons, Thomas Lupo, and John Coprario; significantly, they all worked at court in Prince Charles's household (Ch. 9). Again, the new forms they created, such as the fantasia suite, were not taken up generally by composers outside the court until the Civil War. A new type of dance music in three or four parts with two violins came into England from Germany in the 1620s; it seems to have been brought to court by Maurice Webster, and it was developed there by Charles Coleman and William Lawes before being taken up by waits and theatre musicians outside (Ch. 11). At the Restoration the royal violin band was enlarged to become the Twenty-four Violins in imitation of the French Vingt-quatre Violons; its composers, such as John Banister and Matthew Locke, began to use French genres such as the overture and the branle—which were rapidly taken up in the London theatres and elsewhere (Chs. 12, 13, and 14). Finally, the Restoration court ode and its derivatives (such as the annual odes on St Cecilia's day) became a mainstay of London's burgeoning concert life in the 1690s (Ch. 17).

Many people have helped me over the years with information, advice, encouragement, and criticism. In the early stages I was in constant contact with David Lasocki, who was in London working on his dissertation, 'Professional Recorder Players in England, 1540–1740'. David virtually educated me in the techniques of archival research, and gave me a great deal of information; many of the references in parish registers and wills were found by him. More recently, Andrew Ashbee has been a constant source of advice and information. In particular, he gave me access to many references before they appeared in *RECM*, and allowed me to read each volume at proof stage. It is to Dr Roger Prior of Belfast University that we owe the discovery that many of Henry VIII's court musicians were Jews; his knowledge of Elizabethan Jewry enabled me to understand many puzzling features of the early history of the court violin consort. He has been generous with his advice and criticism. Robert Spencer allowed me access to manuscripts in his private library, and has regularly supplied me with valuable information. Herbert Myers read successive drafts of the first chapter, and improved it greatly with his perceptive and detailed comments. I owe many of the references to violinists outside the court to Lynn Hulse, who is researching music in Elizabethan and Jacobean aristocratic households. She also put me in touch with a number of historians, including Dr David Starkey, Dr Pauline Croft, and Lord Russell of the Tudor Seminar at the Institute of Historical Research, University of London. David Starkey's help, given in person and in his published writings, has been crucial in helping me to understand the place of music in the court scene. Gordon Dodd, custodian of the Viola da Gamba Society's *Thematic Index of Music for Viols*, encouraged me at an early stage, and has patiently answered my queries over the years. I am grateful to Bruce Phillips of Oxford University Press for encouraging me over a long period, and to Bonnie Blackburn, my editor, for her invaluable help.

I am also grateful to the following for reading portions of this book in draft, or for providing me with help in various ways: Lisa Agate, Margaret Downie Banks, Clifford Bartlett, Anne Batchelor, David Blackwell, Stephen Bonta, Roger Bowers, Malcolm Boyd, Donald Burrows, the late John Buxton, Mark Caudle, Tim Crawford, Paul Denley, Peggy Dixon, Mary Edmond, Jack Edwards, Warwick Edwards, John Elliott, Suzanne Eward, David Fallows, John Ferris, Kristine Forney, Nigel Fortune, Johan Giskes, Penelope Gouk, Basil Greenslade, Dominic Gwynn, Ian Harwood, Robert D. Hume, Lewis Jones, Michael Lowe, Calum McCart, Rosamond McGuinness, Margaret Mabbett, Judith Milhous, John Milsom, Karel Moens, Paul O'Dette, Christopher Page, Andrew Parmley, Ian Payne, Lionel Pike, Andrew Pinnock, David Pinto, Curtis Price, John Pringle, William Prizer, Rowland Ross, Ian Spink, Piet Strychers, Robert Thompson, Ruby Reid Thompson, the late Michael Tilmouth, Peter Tourin, Tony Trowles, Jonathan Wainwright, Andrew Walkling, Peter Walls, John Ward, Pamela Willetts, Bruce Wood, Christopher Wool, and Neal Zaslaw.

I have received unfailing help by post or in person from the staff of many institutions, including the following: the Bodleian Library, Oxford; the British Library, Reference Division; Cambridge University Library; the library of Christ Church, Oxford; the library of the Duchy of Cornwall; Edinburgh University Library; the Euing Music Library, Glasgow; the Greater London Record Office; the Guildhall Library, London; the library of Hatfield House; the Institute of Historical Research, University of London; Biblioteka Jagiellońska, Kraków; Kent Archives Office, Maidstone; the library of King's College, University of London; the University of London Library; the library of Longleat House; Murhardsche Bibliothek der Stadt Kassel und Landesbibliothek;

the National Library of Scotland, Edinburgh; the New York Public Library; the Public Record Office, Chancery Lane; the Rowe Music Library, King's College, Cambridge; the library of the Royal College of Music, London; the Sibley Library, Eastman School of Music, Rochester, NY; Universitetsbiblioteket, Uppsala; Westminster Abbey Muniment Room; Westminster City Libraries, Archives Department; the School of Music Library, Yale University.

Over the years my colleagues in The Parley of Instruments have rehearsed and performed most of the music mentioned in this book; I have greatly benefited from their enthusiasm, advice, and criticism. We have been able to record much of the repertoire thanks to Ted Perry of Hyperion Records, and Hugh Keyte, Chris Sayers, and Graham Dixon of BBC Radio 3. My daughter Louise helped with translations and the index, and checked most of the references; I am grateful to her and the rest of my family for their constant support and encouragement. The book would never have been finished without it.

P.H.

Colchester
January 1993

I have taken the opportunity of this reprint to correct a number of small errors. I am grateful to Andrew Ashbee, Richard Charteris, Duncan Druce, Christopher Field, Paul Hopkins, Christopher Morongiello, Ian Payne, Anthony Rooley, Jonathan Wainwright, and Bruce Wood for drawing them to my attention.

Colchester   P.H.
July 1995

Contents

List of Plates

Between pages 226 and 227

List of Figures

List of Tables

List of Music Examples

Note to the Reader

ARCHIVAL documents and other original written sources have been transcribed without changing spellings, capitalization, or punctuation, though I have not retained the distinction between italic and roman type in printed documents, except when it is required by modern conventions of setting out play-texts. Also, 'y' used as a thorn (as in 'ye' and 'yt') has been rendered as 'th', and the interchangeable letters 'i' and 'j', 'u' and 'v' have been modernized. Contractions have been expanded within parentheses; editorial additions are within square brackets. Wherever possible, I have quoted from original sources, especially when the correct identification of instruments is in question; readers should be alert to the possibility that quotations taken from secondary sources may have been modernized.

Proper names outside quotations are mostly given in the form used in *Grove 6*, though there are some cases where I have preferred the form used by the individual concerned in autograph documents: 'Dietrich Stoeffken', for instance, rather than 'Theodore Steffkin'. Many musicians mentioned in the book are too obscure to have an accepted modern form of their name, and I have often had to make an arbitrary choice between several alternatives; significant variants appear in brackets after their first appearance. For simplicity's sake, I have mostly preferred Anglicized forms of the names of immigrants—'Albert of Venice', for instance, rather than 'Alberto da Venezia'. To keep the length of the book within manageable bounds, I have not put together full biographies of the violinists who served the English court; they will appear in the *Biographical Dictionary of English Court Musicians*, to be published in conjunction with *RECM*.

The music examples are simple quotations from the given sources rather than critical editions, so obvious errors have been corrected without notice. Changes to time signatures, key signatures, clefs, and note-valves are indicated by the use of prefatory staves. In the text pitches are indicated using the system in which the open strings of the modern violin family are *C G d a*, *c g d' a'*, and *g d' a' e''*. Clefs are indicated using the system in which the modern treble, alto, and bass clefs appear as g2, c3, and F4.

In sixteenth- and seventeenth-century England the year was normally reckoned in official documents from Lady Day (25 March) rather than 1 January. Thus '1634' covers what we think of as 25 March 1634 to 24 March 1635; I have rendered dates between 1 January and 24 March using the form '1634/5'. The 'Old Style' or Julian calendar was still used in England until 1752, which means that after 1582, when Pope Gregory XIII instituted the 'New Style' or Gregorian calendar, dates in English documents were ten days (eleven after 1700) behind those on the Continent. In some cases it is not clear whether Englishmen abroad or foreign visitors in England were using Old or New Style.

Official documents often use regnal years, which were reckoned from the date of the sovereign's accession. Henry VIII came to the throne on 22 April 1509, so 6 Henry VIII covered 22 April 1514 to 21 April 1515. The accession dates of Henry VIII's successors were: Edward VI, 28 January 1547; Mary, 6 July 1553; Philip, 25 July 1554; Elizabeth, 17 November 1558; James I, 24 March 1603; Charles I, 27 March 1625; Charles II (calculated from the death of his father), 30 January 1649; James II, 6 February 1685; William and Mary, 13 February 1689. Payments to courtiers were often made on, or reckoned from, the four 'quarter days': Lady Day (25 March), St John the Baptist or Midsummer Day (25 June), Michaelmas (29 September), and Christmas (25 December). The date given for payments or appointments is the one that appears on the particular document quoted; it is not necessarily the date when the recipient actually received payment, or when the monarch signed the appropriate warrant, for transactions frequently took several weeks to pass through the court system (see Ch. 2).

I have retained the old system of English currency throughout the book. There were twelve pence (*d.*) to the shilling (*s.*), and twenty shillings to the pound (£).

Abbreviations

(based on those used in *Grove 6*)

AcM	*Acta musicologica*
AnnM	*Annales musicologiques*
CMc	*Current Musicology*
CMM	Corpus mensurabilis musicae
CSPD	*Calendar of State Papers, Domestic Series*
DDT	Denkmäler deutscher Tonkunst
DTÖ	Denkmäler der Tonkunst in Österreich
EDM	Das Erbe deutscher Musik
EM	*Early Music*
EMH	*Early Music History*
Grove 6	*The New Grove Dictionary of Music and Musicians*
GSJ	*The Galpin Society Journal*
HMC	Historical Manuscripts Commission
INV	a portion of a manuscript written from the end with the volume inverted
JAMIS	*Journal of the American Musical Instrument Society*
JAMS	*Journal of the American Musicological Society*
JLSA	*Journal of the Lute Society of America*
JRMA	*Journal of the Royal Musical Association*
JVGSA	*Journal of the Viola da Gamba Society of America*
LSJ	*The Lute Society Journal*
MA	*The Musical Antiquary*
MB	Musica Britannica
MD	*Musica disciplina*
ML	*Music and Letters*
MLE	Music for London Entertainment
MMg	*Monatshefte für Musikgeschichte*
MMR	*The Monthly Musical Record*
MQ	*The Musical Quarterly*
MR	*The Music Review*
MSD	Musicological Studies and Documents
MT	*The Musical Times*
NA	*Note d'archivio per la storia musicale*
OED	*The Compact Edition of the Oxford English Dictionary*
PRMA	*Proceedings of the Royal Musical Association*
RBM	*Revue belge de musicologie*

RdM	*Revue de musicologie*
RECM	*Records of English Court Music*
ReM	*La Revue musicale*
RIM	*Rivista italiana di musicologia*
RMARC	*Royal Musical Association Research Chronicle*
RMFC	*Recherches sur la musique française classique*
RMI	*Rivista musicale italiana*
SIMG	*Sammelbände der Internationalen Musik-Gesellschaft*
SMw	*Studien zur Musikwissenschaft*

LIBRARY SIGLA

(following the RISM system as used in *Grove 6*)

GERMANY

D-B	Berlin, Staatsbibliothek Preussischer Kulturbesitz
D-Hs	Hamburg, Staats- und Universitätsbibliothek
D-Kl	Kassel, Murhardsche Bibliothek der Stadt und Landesbibliothek
D-LEm	Leipzig, Musikbibliothek der Stadt
D-Mbs	Munich, Bayerische Staatsbibliothek

SPAIN

E-SE	Segovia, Catedral

IRELAND

EIRE-Dm	Dublin, Marsh's Library
EIRE-Dtc	Dublin, Trinity College

FRANCE

F-Pn	Paris, Bibliothèque Nationale

GREAT BRITAIN

GB-Bu	University of Birmingham, Barber Institute of Fine Arts
GB-Cfm	Cambridge, Fitzwilliam Museum
GB-Cu	Cambridge, University Library
GB-Drc	Durham, Cathedral
GB-En	Edinburgh, National Library of Scotland
GB-Ge	Glasgow, Euing Music Library

GB-Lbl	London, British Library, Reference Division
GB-Lcm	London, Royal College of Music
GB-LEc	Leeds, Public Libraries, Music Department, Central Library
GB-Lgc	London, Gresham College / Guildhall Library
GB-Lkc	University of London, King's College, Faculty of Music
GB-Lpro	London, Public Record Office
GB-Mr	Manchester, John Rylands University Library
GB-Ob	Oxford, Bodleian Library
GB-Och	Oxford, Christ Church

ITALY

I-FZc	Faenza, Biblioteca Comunale
I-MOs	Modena, Archivio di Stato
I-Rc	Rome, Biblioteca Casanatense

THE NETHERLANDS

NL-Lt	Leiden, Biblioteca Thysiana

POLAND

PL-Kj	Kraków, Biblioteka Jagiellońska

SWEDEN

S-Uu	Uppsala, Universitetsbiblioteket

UNITED STATES OF AMERICA

US-AUS	Austin, University of Texas
US-LAuc	Los Angeles, University of California, William Andrews Clark Memorial Library
US-NH	New Haven, Yale University, School of Music Library
US-NYp	New York, Public Library at Lincoln Center, Library and Museum of the Performing Arts
US-OAm	Oakland, Mills College, Margaret Prall Music Library
US-R	Rochester, Eastman School of Music, Sibley Library
US-Ws	Washington, DC, Folger Shakespeare Library

1

'Quagmires of History and Terminology'
The Origin of the Violin

THE early history of the violin is a notoriously difficult subject. In 1875 George Hart wrote that it remained 'more hopelessly obscured than the identity of the "Man in the Iron Mask"', while Gerald Hayes observed in 1930 that the violin was 'one of the very few important instruments of which it can be said that at a given date it was not at all, and shortly afterwards it is found fully-fledged in active life'; as late as 1965 David Boyden was moved to remark that 'most accounts of the "inventor" of the violin and the precise date and place of its origin bog down in the quagmires of history and terminology'.[1]

There are a number of reasons why the subject has got bogged down. The most obvious is that research has traditionally focused on surviving instruments. But few genuine sixteenth-century stringed instruments exist—there seem to be only a handful from before 1550—and those that do are likely to have undergone many changes over the centuries. Violin-family instruments will have been updated in the eighteenth and nineteenth centuries to cope with changing musical demands, and an alarming number of the specimens on which theories of the evolution of the violin have been based in the past are now turning out to be forgeries.[2] The lira da braccio is a particularly suspect area, for it was thought in Victorian times to be an important ancestor of the violin.[3] The one at the Royal College of Music in London with the label 'Joan Karlino Brescia 1452' is certainly a fake, while Karel Moens has recently proposed that the famous 'Vendelinus Tieffenbrucker' lirone at Vienna, supposedly made in Padua around 1590, is actually a composite instrument cobbled together out of two cellos.[4]

---

[1] G. Hart, *The Violin: Its Famous Makers and their Imitators* (London, 1875), 37–8; G. Hayes, *Musical Instruments and their Music 1500–1700*, ii: *The Viols, and other Bowed Instruments* (London, 1930; repr. 1969), 160; D. Boyden, *The History of Violin Playing from its Origins to 1761* (London, 1965), 6.

[2] See L. Libin, 'Early Violins: Problems and Issues', *EM* 19 (1991), 5–6.

[3] See e.g. A. Hajdecki, *Die italienische Lira da Braccio* (Mostar, 1892; repr. 1965).

[4] L. C. Witten, 'Apollo, Orpheus and David: A Study of the Crucial Century in the Development of Bowed Strings in North Italy 1480–1580, as seen in Graphic Evidence and some Surviving Instruments', *JAMIS* 1 (1975), 48; K. Moens, 'Der frühe Geigenbau in Süddeutschland', in

A second problem is that research into the early violin has mostly been conducted by dealers, restorers, and collectors. They may have handled more old instruments than anyone else, and they certainly have a better eye for craftsmanship than academic scholars. But they often have a vested interest in reaching a particular conclusion, and most of them have little experience or interest in exploring and evaluating the sources of documentary evidence. Our received history of the early violin depends to an alarming extent on a small pile of 'facts' that have gradually accumulated as they have been repeated parrot-fashion from book to book. The result is about as illuminating as a history of Roman Britain would be were it to be based on the efforts of enthusiasts with metal detectors. David Boyden's account of the early violin is important because he was the first person to make a serious attempt to place the instrument in its social and musical context. But he was limited by the small amount of archival material that was available in the 1960s, and he made little effort to place the violin in the context of the general development of instruments and instrumental music.

Most of Boyden's conclusions about the origins of the violin were based on pictures. In particular, he used several paintings by Gaudenzio Ferrari in churches near Milan to suggest that 'the earliest type of violin' (by which he meant an instrument similar in shape to the modern violin, but with three strings) was developed in northern Italy in the 1520s. He drew attention to a small three-string violin in the *Madonna of the Orange Trees* at Vercelli, painted *c*.1529–30, and a fresco in the cupola of 'Saronno Cathedral' (actually Santa Maria dei Miracoli at Saronno) which includes three three-string violins of different sizes.[5] The Saronno fresco remains the earliest picture of the complete violin family, but subsequent research has brought to light violin-like instruments in Ferrarese frescoes of the first decade of the sixteenth century. A four-string 'viola' appears in a mixed group with two viols, a rebec, and a viola da mano in the fresco *The Coronation of the Virgin*, probably painted between 1510 and 1515 by Michele Coltellini or Ludovico Mazzolino in the church of Santa Maria della Consolazione (Pl. 1(*a*)), and another fresco, painted by Garofalo or his assistants at the Palazzo di Ludovico il Moro between 1505 and 1508, shows a small violin-like instrument.[6]

F. Hellwig (ed.), *Studia organologica: Festschrift für John Henry van der Meer zu seinem fünfundsechzigsten Geburtstag* (Tutzing, 1987), 349–52.

[5] Boyden, *History*, frontispiece and pl. 2; see also E. Winternitz, 'The School of Gaudenzio Ferrari and the Early History of the Violin', in G. Reese and R. Brandel (eds.), *The Commonwealth of Music: Writings on Music in History, Art, and Culture in Honor of Curt Sachs* (New York and London, 1965), 182–200; id., 'Early Violins in Paintings by Gaudenzio Ferrari and his School', in *Musical Instruments and their Symbolism in Western Art* (London, 1967), 99–109.

[6] M. Remnant, *Musical Instruments of the West* (London, 1978), ill. 42, 45; see I. Godt, 'A Major Angel Concert in Ferrara', *Musei ferraresi, bollettino annuale*, 12 (1982 [actually 1984]), 209–17 and B. G. Vigi, *Ferrara: chiese-palazzi-musei* (Ferrara, 1991), 71.

Pictures are our main guide to the complex set of developments that brought the violin into being. But they have their drawbacks. One is that paintings of angel musicians, such as the Saronno fresco, tell us more about the appearance of their musical instruments than about the way real musicians on earth might have played them. More generally, pictures reinforce the traditional idea that instruments should be defined by their shape. A bowed instrument in a painting is accepted as a violin if its body shape conforms sufficiently to our notions of what an early violin should look like—notions that have been fashioned mainly by the subsequent history of the violin, and the development of its 'classic' shape. Not only is this perilously close to being a circular argument, but it also places an unreasonable emphasis on what seems to have been the most variable aspect of bowed instruments at the time. The early sixteenth century was a period of rapid change and adventurous experimentation in instrument-making, and it is not surprising that a number of shapes were tried for the violin before the 'classic' one emerged victorious in Italy around 1550; in northern Europe non-standard variants were in use well after 1600. The 'classic' shape of the viol prevailed even later—in the middle of the seventeenth century. Before then some Italian viols were made in a figure-of-eight shape, while German instruments often had a complex festooned outline, and a surprising number of viols throughout Europe were shaped like violins.

It is perhaps more useful, therefore, to define the early violin more by how it was played and how it was used than by its appearance. This is certainly how Philibert Jambe de Fer, the author of the earliest detailed description of the instrument, distinguished it from the viol in his *Épitome musical* (Lyons, 1556).[7] He ignored its shape beyond mentioning that it was 'smaller and flatter in form' than the viol. It was made in three sizes; it had only four strings; it had no frets; it was tuned in fifths; it was much harsher in sound than the viol; it was held on the shoulder; it was played standing; it was 'commonly used for dance music'; and it was used largely by professionals—'few persons are found who make use of it other than those who, by their labour on it, make their living'. The viol, by contrast, had five or six strings, was fretted, was tuned in fourths (or fourths with a third), and was held on or between the knees, or on a stool. Also, it belonged to a better class of society: it was an instrument 'upon which gentlemen, merchants, and other persons of culture pass their time'.

Once we begin to see the violin with Jambe de Fer's eyes, some of Boyden's quagmires become a little firmer under foot. The essential structure of the violin body—a hollow box with indented sides made up

---

[7] F. Lesure, 'L'*Épitome musical* de Philibert Jambe de Fer (1556)', *AnnM* 6 (1958–63), 341–86; G. J. Kinney, 'Viols and Violins in the *Epitome Musical* (Lyon, 1556) of Philibert Jambe de Fer', *JVGSA* 4 (1967), 14–20.

of a belly, a back, and connecting ribs—was not new: it appears in many fifteenth-century pictures of the vielle or medieval fiddle.[8] (For obvious reasons, it is impossible to tell from pictures whether vielles had been developed with arched backs, or with a soundpost and bass bar; but the same is true of early violins.) Nor was there much new about the way individual instruments were played. The typical vielle had no frets, was held on the shoulder, and was played standing up. It usually had five or more strings (one of which could be a drone running off the fingerboard), rather than the three or four of the violin, but a three-string tuning in fifths was well established on the other main medieval bowed instrument, the small pear-shaped rebec. It is often said that the violin, in Boyden's words, 'adopted the body shape of the lira da braccio and the three strings and the fifth-tuning of the rebec'.[9] But the theory that the violin acquired its classic shape from the lira da braccio is questionable, for it is based on the evidence of instruments that have turned out to be forgeries, or have been dated too early. It is at least as likely that the 'classic' shape was borrowed for the lira da braccio from the violin—or that it was applied to the two instruments at the same time.[10] And the violin clearly did not come into being merely because a three-string tuning in fifths was applied to the vielle. Three-string vielles sometimes appear in fifteenth-century pictures—a good example was painted by Albrecht Dürer shortly after a trip to Italy in the winter of 1494–5—and Johannes Tinctoris gave 'three simple strings tuned to a pair of fifths' as the most common tuning of the instrument in his treatise *De inventione et usu musicae*, written between 1481 and 1483.[11]

There is, however, one important feature of the violin that has been virtually ignored in the debate over its origin: the instrument differs from the vielle and the rebec in that it was made from the first as a family in several sizes. To appreciate the importance of this development we need first to examine the origin of what we might call 'the consort principle'. In

---

[8] For the vielle, see in particular M. Remnant, 'Fiddle', *Grove 6*; ead., *English Bowed Instruments from Anglo-Saxon to Tudor Times* (Oxford, 1986); C. Page, *Voices and Instruments of the Middle Ages* (London, 1987), 111–33; H. M. Brown, 'The Trecento Fiddle and its Bridges', *EM* 17 (1989), 308–29; I am grateful to Herbert Myers for allowing me to read his unpublished 1977 paper 'The Construction of a Fifteenth-Century Fiddle'.

[9] Boyden, *History*, 30.

[10] See the sequence of instruments illustrated in Witten, 'Apollo, Orpheus and David', 5–55; for the lira da braccio, see E. Winternitz, 'The Lira da Braccio', in *Musical Instruments and their Symbolism*, 86–98; B. Disertori, 'Pratica e tecnica della lira da braccio', *RMI* 45 (1941), 150–75; H. M. Brown, *Sixteenth-Century Instrumentation: The Music for the Florentine Intermedii* (MSD 30; Rome, 1973), 39–46.

[11] F. Anzelewsky, *Dürer* (London, 1980), pl. 75; A. Baines, 'Fifteenth-Century Instruments in Tinctoris's *De Inventione et Usu Musicae*', *GSJ* 3 (1950), 19–26; the date of the treatise is established in R. Woodley, 'The Printing and Scope of Tinctoris's Fragmentary Treatise *De Inuentione et Usu Musice*', *EMH* 5 (1985), 245.

sixteenth-century art music virtually every melody instrument was made in co-ordinated sets of several sizes. But this had not always been so: there is no sign of the consort principle in the early Middle Ages. Pictures of the period, of course, show instruments of many shapes and sizes, but it should not be assumed that they have a structured relationship to one another, any more than it can be assumed that paintings of angel 'orchestras' are a reliable guide to the composition of earthly ensembles. Rather, the luxuriant diversity to be seen in medieval pictures suggests the sizes (and therefore the pitches) of instruments were unstandardized, which in turn reinforces the idea that minstrelsy in the early Middle Ages was focused on solo performance.[12] As polyphony invaded the various genres of secular music during the later Middle Ages, so the solo minstrel gave way to the ensemble, and the single instrument to the set. Some instruments, such as the shawm, the recorder, and the flute, were already in existence, so there must have been a moment when those types were made for the first time in several sizes.

It is obvious that there is a connection between the spread of the consort principle and the spread of polyphony into secular music. A number of medieval instruments had some sort of device for producing drones, which clothed monophonic melodies with an automatic accompaniment. And some, such as the bagpipe and the hurdy-gurdy, were so wedded to the drone principle that they were not suitable to be developed in sets; they gradually dropped out of use in art music, but continued to be played by folk musicians. A family of instruments, its three or four sizes pitched a fourth or fifth apart, mimics a polyphonic vocal consort—which exploits the natural difference in pitch between adult males and children or women, and between low and high voices in these categories. So it is reasonable to assume that in at least some cases the application of the consort principle marks the point when an instrument made the transition from monophony to polyphony.

The consort principle seems to have originated with the shawm. The shawm came into Europe in the thirteenth century as a member of the ceremonial loud wind band of the Arab world. It seems that it was first made in more than one size in the middle of the fourteenth century, when a tenor-range instrument called 'bombarde' began to be used alongside the ordinary treble-range shawm—'bombarde' is first recorded in a musical context in 1342.[13] Significantly, the bagpipe with its drones began to disappear from the loud wind band (or *alta capella* as it became known) in the early fifteenth century—the period of the first unequivocal references to polyphony played on wind instruments—such as the three

---

[12] An idea pursued fruitfully in Page, *Voices and Instruments* and *The Owl and the Nightingale: Musical Life and Ideas in France 1100–1300* (London, 1989).

[13] H. W. Myers, 'Slide Trumpet Madness: Fact or Fiction?', *EM* 17 (1989), 383–4.

Posaunen that played 'together in three parts, as one ordinarily sings' at the Council of Constance of 1416–17, or the motet played by shawms at the wedding of Charles the Bold in 1468.[14] The *alta capella* seems to have been essentially an improvising ensemble: when it played for the basse dance it consisted typically of a bombard, which provided a plainsong-like cantus firmus, around which a treble shawm and a slide trumpet wove florid stereotyped counterpoint.[15]

The consort principle may have been applied next to the 'flute' and the douçaine, if we are right to interpret a reference of 1426 to four 'grans instruments de ménestrels', four 'fleutes', and four 'douchaines' as sets of instruments in several sizes; they were made in Bruges by Loys Willay for the Marquis of Ferrara on behalf of Philip the Good.[16] Bruges was evidently a centre for making and playing 'flutes', for another set of four was purchased from Pierre de Proost in the same year, a quartet played at the wedding of Margaret of York and Charles the Bold in 1468, and a 'coker'—a set—was purchased for the town's wind-players in 1481.[17] It sounds as if the Bruges flute quartets used sets of several sizes of instrument, though it is not clear whether they were end-blown or side-blown. There are more fifteenth-century pictures of recorders than flutes, and several sizes of recorder seem to be shown in the painting *Mary Queen of Heaven* (*c*.1485) by the Master of the St Lucy Legend.[18] Three sizes of recorder were certainly in existence by 1511, when they appeared in Sebastian Virdung's *Musica getutscht*, and there are three sizes of transverse flute in Martin Agricola's *Musica instrumentalis deudsch* of 1528.[19] The douçaine is likely to have been made in sets at an early date,

---

[14] K. Polk, 'Instrumental Music in the Urban Centres of Renaissance Germany', *EMH* 7 (1987) 172–3; J. F. R. and C. Stainer (eds.), *Dufay and his Contemporaries* (London, 1898), 16.

[15] For the *alta capella*, see K. Polk, 'Wind Bands of Medieval Flemish Cities', *Brass and Woodwind Quarterly*, 1 (1966–8), 93–113; id., 'Municipal Wind Music in Flanders in the Late Middle Ages', ibid. 2 (1969), 1–15; E. A. Bowles, 'Iconography as a Tool for Examining the Loud Consort in the Fifteenth Century', *JAMIS* 3 (1977), 100–13; P. Downey, 'The Renaissance Slide Trumpet: Fact or fiction?', *EM* 12 (1984), 26–33; Polk, 'Instrumental Music in the Urban Centres', 159–86; id., 'The Trombone, the Slide Trumpet, and the Ensemble Tradition of the Early Renaissance', *EM* 17 (1989), 389–97; R. W. Duffin, 'The *Trompette des Menestrels* in the Fifteenth-Century *Alta Capella*', ibid. 397–402. For the basse dance, see in particular D. Heartz, 'The Basse Dance: Its Evolution *c*.1450–1550, *AnnM* 6 (1958–63), 287–340; F. Crane, *Materials for the Study of the Fifteenth-Century Basse Dance* (Brooklyn, 1968).

[16] R. Strohm, *Music in Late Medieval Bruges* (Oxford, 1985), 92.

[17] J. Marix, *Histoire de la musique et des musiciens de la cour de Bourgogne sous la règne de Philippe le Bon (1420–1467)* (Strasburg, 1939; repr. 1974), 105–6; K. Polk, 'Voices and Instruments: Soloists and Ensembles in the Fifteenth Century', *EM* 18 (1990), 192.

[18] Remnant, *Musical Instruments of the West*, 116.

[19] J. Godwin, 'The Renaissance Flute', *The Consort*, 28 (1972), 70–81; B. Thomas, 'The Renaissance Flute', *EM* 3 (1975), 2–10; H. M. Brown, 'Notes (and Transposing Notes) on the Transverse Flute in the Early Sixteenth Century', *JAMIS* 12 (1986), 5–39; H. W. Myers, 'Renaissance Flute', in J. T. Kite-Powell (ed.), *A Practical Guide to Historical Performance: The Renaissance* (New York, 1989), 37–41.

since it seems to have been a soft variant of the shawm, with a cylindrical rather than a conical bore.[20]

Bowed instruments seem to have made the transition from monophony to polyphony in several stages spread over a considerable period. There is no doubt that they were essentially monophonic instruments for most of the Middle Ages. As late as the fifteenth century the great majority of vielles and rebecs appear in pictures either with a flat bridge or no bridge at all. (I use the word 'bridge' to mean a wedge inserted between belly and strings; I use 'string-holder' for the bar, attached to the belly, from which strings run, as on the lute and guitar.) Either way, the player would have had no option but to sound the strings simultaneously, unless he was able to tilt the bow to isolate the top or bottom strings, a task well-nigh impossible on the large number of vielles shown with only a shallow waist or no waist at all, particularly since they are often played with a large and unwieldy bow. Bowed instruments with drones persisted remarkably late in some parts of Europe. There are several pictures of bridgeless viols from Elizabethan England (see Ch. 3), and a lira da braccio with a flat bridge appears as late as 1625 in two of the versions of Jan Brueghel's *Allegory of Hearing*.[21] There are a number of vielles in fourteenth- and early fifteenth-century pictures that appear to have arched bridges, though it is by no means certain that the purpose of the arching was to enable the player to pick out single lines—it could have been merely to allow him to vary the notes in a chord.[22]

It also remains to be demonstrated that fourteenth- or early fifteenth-century pictures of vielles with arched bridges are necessarily evidence that bowed instruments were used in polyphony. The case of St Caterina de' Vigri (1413–63) and her violeta may be relevant here.[23] The small four-string instrument, preserved today in her tomb in the convent of Corpus Christi at Bologna with, it seems, its original fittings, has a gently arched bridge. Yet Caterina was a religious rather than a musician—she founded Corpus Christi in 1456 and was its abbess until her death—and she does not seem to have belonged to that sphere of musical life that cultivated polyphony: an account of her life mentions that she asked for 'a violeta to play and praise with' during an illness, which sounds as if she

[20] For the douçaine, see B. Boydell, *The Crumhorn and other Renaissance Windcap Instruments* (Buren, 1982), 403–7; N. Buckland, 'Styll Shalmes', *FoMRHI Quarterly*, 19 (Apr. 1980), 42–57; id., 'Further to the "Styll Shalmes"', ibid. 25 (Oct. 1981), 24–5; H. W. Myers, 'The *Mary Rose* "Shawm"', *EM* 11 (1983), 358–60.

[21] L. van Dijck and T. Koopman (eds.), *The Harpsichord in Dutch Art before 1800/Het klavicimbel in de Nederlandse kunst tot 1800* (Amsterdam and Zutphen, 1987), ill. 56, 56a.

[22] Cases of apparently arched bridges in trecento pictures are discussed in Brown, 'Trecento Fiddle'; the issue is also discussed in Myers, 'Construction'.

[23] M. Viella, 'The Violeta of S. Caterina de' Vigri', *GSJ* 28 (1975), 60–70; I am grateful to Lewis Jones for information about the instrument and its bridge.

used the instrument to accompany herself when she sang monophonic *laude*.

Bowed instruments certainly do not seem to have been used much in composed polyphony until shortly before 1500. It used to be thought that the central repertoire of fifteenth-century secular music, the Franco-Netherlandish chanson, was mostly intended for a high voice accompanied by low-pitched instruments. The lower parts were said to be invariably untexted in the sources, and their angular writing was thought to be 'instrumental' in character; they were frequently played on vielles, rebecs, or even viols in the 1960s and 1970s. But the notion that the style of the writing in medieval music is a clue to its intended scoring was exploded by Lloyd Hibberd in the 1940s, and is now discredited.[24] Dennis Slavin has recently pointed out that the tenor and contratenor parts of early fifteenth-century chansons are texted more frequently in the sources than has been recognized, and has drawn attention to the unwritten conventions governing the extempore addition of text to untexted parts.[25] Moreover, a good case has now been built up from documentary evidence that fourteenth- and fifteenth-century chansons were most commonly performed just by three or four voices—a case that has received eloquent practical support from the work of Christopher Page's ensemble Gothic Voices.[26]

If composed secular polyphony was most often performed in the fifteenth century with voices alone, what role would there have been for bowed instruments? Many of them must still have been used for monophonic music. In *De inventione et usu musicae* Tinctoris wrote that the viola *cum arculo* was used 'over the greater part of the world' for 'the recitation of epics', and the lira da braccio (essentially a late type of vielle used in humanist circles) is solid evidence that such improvised vocal music was accompanied with a chordal technique: it usually had several bourdon strings running off the fingerboard, and is often depicted with a flat bridge. It is also likely that professional musicians in northern Europe continued to use drone techniques: there are references to solo players of the *Geige* (a word used at the time for several types of bowed instrument;

---

[24] L. Hibberd, 'On "Instrumental Style" in Early Melody', *MQ* 32 (1946), 107–30.

[25] D. Slavin, 'In Support of "Heresy": Manuscript Evidence for the *a cappella* Performance of Early Fifteenth-Century Songs', *EM* 19 (1991), 178–90.

[26] H. M. Brown, 'Instruments and Voices in the Fifteenth-Century Chanson', in J. W. Grubbs (ed.), *Current Thought in Musicology* (Austin, Tex., 1976), 89–137; C. Page, 'Machaut's "Pupil" Deschamps on the Performance of Music: Voices or Instruments in the Fourteenth-Century Chanson?', *EM* 5 (1977), 484–91; C. Wright, 'Voices and Instruments in the Art Music of Northern France during the Fifteenth Century: A Conspectus', in D. Heartz and B. Wade (eds.), *Report on the Twelfth Congress* [of the International Musicological Society] *Berkeley 1977* (Kassel, 1981), 643–9; C. Page, 'The Performance of Songs in Late Medieval France: A New Source', *EM* 10 (1982), 441–50; D. Fallows, 'Specific Information on the Ensembles for Composed Polyphony, 1400–1474', in S. Boorman (ed.), *Studies in the Performance of Late Medieval Music* (Cambridge, 1983), 109–44.

see below) in German town archives throughout the century, and solo string-players still occur in English court accounts in Henry VII's reign (see Ch. 3).[27] But German town archives suggest that professional string-players worked most commonly in pairs: Keith Polk has found dozens of references to duet teams of either two bowed instruments, two lutes, or lute and bowed instrument, and many of them apparently offered all three combinations.

Duet teams did not necessarily play polyphonic music. The lute duet was well established in the fourteenth century, and there are many references to pairs of vielle-players still earlier, when drone techniques are almost certain to have been used. An example, picked at random, is the pair of German *Geige* players Henry and Conrad recorded at the English court between 1299 and 1306.[28] Nevertheless, there is evidence that a type of polyphonic improvisation had been developed for pairs of lutes and vielles by the middle of the fifteenth century. Its best-known exponent was the *chitarino*-player and lutenist Pietrobono, who served at the Ferrarese court on and off between 1441 and his death in 1497.[29] By 1449 he had formed a team with a *tenorista*, and Tinctoris described their method of performance in *De inventione et usu musicae*: 'some teams will take the highest part of a piece and improvise marvellously upon it with such taste that the performance cannot be rivalled'.

It seems that they played polyphonic chansons on two lutes with plectra, Pietrobono decorating the top part and his colleague providing the tenor; arrangements along these lines, but with the second lute playing the two lower parts using finger technique, were published by Francesco Spinacino in 1507.[30] It has even been suggested recently that the florid two-part arrangements of vocal music in *I-FZc*, 117, the Faenza Codex, conventionally thought to be for keyboard, are for lute duet or lute and harp, and come either from the repertoire of Pietrobono himself, or that of Leonardo del Chitarino, who was at Ferrara in 1424—the manuscript seems to be of Ferrarese provenance.[31] This Leonardo has

[27] K. Polk, '*Vedel* and *Geige*—Fiddle and Viol: German String Traditions in the Fifteenth Century', *JAMS* 42 (1989), 504–46; see also id., 'Voices and Instruments'.

[28] C. Bullock-Davies, *A Register of Royal and Baronial Domestic Minstrels 1272–1327* (Woodbridge and Dover, NH, 1986), 37–8, 68–9.

[29] L. Lockwood, *Music in Renaissance Ferrara 1400–1505* (Oxford, 1984), 95–108.

[30] P. Danner, 'Before Petrucci: The Lute in the Fifteenth Century', *JLSA* 5 (1972), 4–17; D. Fallows, 'Fifteenth-Century Tablatures for Plucked Instruments: A Summary, a Revision, and a Suggestion', *LSJ* 19 (1977), 7–33.

[31] T. J. McGee, 'Instruments and the Faenza Codex', *EM* 14 (1986), 480–90; the traditional view that the manuscript is for keyboard has been reasserted in J. Caldwell, 'Two Polyphonic *Istampite* from the Fourteenth Century', *EM* 18 (1990), 371–80, who nevertheless proposes that two dances are intended for vielles; for Leonardo, see Lockwood, *Music in Renaissance Ferrara*, 16, 100, 315; transcriptions are in D. Plamenac (ed.), *Keyboard Music of the Late Middle Ages* (CMM 57; Rome, 1972).

been tentatively identified with the lutenist Leonardo de Alamania, who was at Brescia between 1409 and 1419, and there is certainly some evidence that the florid lute-duet style was German in origin.[32] Tinctoris wrote that 'in this many Germans are exceedingly accomplished and renowned', though he recognized that Pietrobono was the supreme exponent. It is also significant that Pietrobono was known mainly as a *citarino*-player, the small lute-shaped instrument called 'gittern' in English and *quintern* in French and German, for the combination of *quintern* and lute was a favourite one in Germany, and is specifically mentioned as early as 1404 in a Cologne document.[33]

A similar type of polyphonic improvisation was also played on vielles. Again, our main witness is Tinctoris, writing in *De inventione et usu musicae* about the famous Flemish brothers Jean and Charles Fernandes: 'at Bruges, I heard Charles take the treble and Jean the tenor in many songs, playing this kind of viola so expertly and with such charm that the viola has never pleased me so well'. A manuscript at *E-SE* contains some textless two-part versions of well-known chansons, consisting of a florid version of the top part and the tenor. Six are attributed to Tinctoris, and Reinhard Strohm has suggested that they come from the repertoire of the Fernandes brothers.[34] The Bruges performance apparently took place in 1482, but the practice of improvising polyphony on pairs of vielles probably goes back to the early fifteenth century. Strohm has suggested that Jean Fernandes was the Jean Ferrandes who worked as a duet team with Jean de Cordoval at the Burgundian court from 1433 to 1456; they are listed variously as vielle-players, lutenists, or just players of *bas* instruments.[35]

Men such as these were far from being unlettered minstrels, and were increasingly associated with composed music. The Fernandes brothers, for instance, were professors of the University of Paris, and became its rectors in 1485. Conrad Paumann (*c.*1410–73) was an organist and a composer as well as a lutenist and a vielle-player, and may have had an important role in introducing the polyphonic duet idiom to northern

[32] A. Atlas, 'On the Identity of some Musicians at the Brescian Court of Pandolfo III Malatesta', *CMc* 36 (1983), 14–16; McGee, 'Instruments and the Faenza Codex', 485, 489–90.

[33] L. Wright, 'The Medieval Gittern and Citole: A Case of Mistaken Identity', *GSJ* 30 (1977), 8–42; H. M. Brown, 'St. Augustine, Lady Music, and the Gittern in Fourteenth-Century Italy', *MD* 38 (1984), 25–65; Polk, 'Voices and Instruments', 180, 187.

[34] H. Anglés, 'Un manuscrit inconnu avec polyphonie du xvᵉ siècle conservé à la cathédrale de Ségovie (Espagne)', *AcM* 8 (1936), 6–17; Strohm, *Music in Late Medieval Bruges*, 88–9, 142–3; Polk, 'Vedel and Geige', 521; the pieces attributed to Tinctoris are in *J. Tinctoris, Opera Omnia*, ed. W. Melin (CMM 18; Rome, 1976), 76–7, 106–7, 137–46.

[35] Marix, *Histoire*, 267–73; A. vander Linden, 'Les Aveugles de la cour de Bourgogne', *RBM* 4 (1950), 74–6; Polk, 'Vedel and Geige', 521.

Italy.[36] But *bas* instrumentalists did not invent the art of improvising florid counterpoint against a cantus firmus, for it was essentially the same as that long used by *haut* wind bands, and it was probably borrowed from them as the dividing-line between the two classes of musician broke down in the course of the fifteenth century.[37]

The vielles used by the Fernandes brothers must have had arched bridges. Indeed, Tinctoris, thinking perhaps of their instruments, wrote that the strings 'are stretched in a protuberant manner so that the bow (which is strung with horsehair) can touch any one string the player wills, leaving the others untouched'. But he did not mention that the vielle was made in more than one size (even though he wrote in detail about the two sizes of shawm), and the type of improvisation represented by the Tinctoris pieces in the Segovia manuscript only needs a single size of instrument. They have a maximum overall range of eighteen notes (notated c–f''), and would therefore have fitted in first position (I think we can take it that vielle-players had not developed position changes) on two five-string instruments tuned, say, c g c' g' c'' or two four-string instruments tuned in fifths (Ex. 1.1). The text of a Florentine carnival song of *c.*1490 mentions Germans playing 'rubechine' and 'gran rubechaze', and this has been taken to mean that 'at least two sizes of bowed instrument' had been developed by then.[38] But the 'gran rubechaze' are said to be unsuitable for dances ('non può far bel calatine'), so the difference seems to be one of function as well as size. It is more likely that the author intended a contrast between two types of instrument—the small rebec (particularly associated with dance music), and the larger-bodied vielle—rather than two sizes of the same family. Similarly, the references to 'rubebe', 'rubechette', and 'rubecone' in Simone Prudenzani's poem sequence 'Il Sollazzo' are not necessarily to a structured consort—or to a polyphonic ensemble at all.[39]

The need for bowed instruments in several sizes would have become pressing when musicians turned from improvising in pairs to playing composed music in three and four parts, and that seems to have happened in Italy shortly before 1500, particularly at the courts of Mantua and Ferrara. Once again, the impetus seems to have come from German wind-players. During the 1480s and 1490s scribes in Naples, Florence, and a number of northern Italian towns began to copy manuscripts of Franco-Netherlandish chansons in textless versions. In time northern

---

[36] W. Prizer, 'The Frottola and the Unwritten Tradition', *Studi musicali*, 15 (1986), 3–37; Polk, '*Vedel* and *Geige*', 520–1.

[37] On this point, see Polk, '*Vedel* and *Geige*', 526–7, 542–3.

[38] T. J. McGee with S. E. Mittler, 'Information on Instruments in Florentine Carnival Songs', *EM* 10 (1982), 452–61; Polk, 'Voices and Instruments', 190; Polk, '*Vedel* and *Geige*', 540.

[39] Brown, 'Trecento Fiddle', 327.

Ex. 1.1. Johannes Tinctoris, 'Le souvenir', bb. 1–7, unnumbered MS at *E-SE*, fo. 203ᵛ (from Tinctoris, *Opera omnia*, ed. Melin, 137)

European composers on the spot added new pieces to this repertoire of 'songs without words', some based on old chansons, others freely written.[40] The original chansons would have been performed north of the Alps mostly just with voices, but the intention in Italy was clearly to provide material for instrumental ensembles.

In one case, *I-Rc*, 2856, the Casanatense Chansonnier, the ensemble in question has been identified. Lewis Lockwood has shown that the ranges of some of its pieces were narrowed, presumably to fit the ranges of wind instruments; he suggests that it is the manuscript referred to as

---

[40] L. Litterick, 'Performing Franco-Netherlandish Secular Music of the Late Fifteenth Century', *EM* 8 (1980), 474–85; ead., 'On Italian Instrumental Ensemble Music in the Late Fifteenth Century', in I. Fenlon (ed.), *Music in Medieval and Early Modern Europe: Patronage, Sources, and Texts* (Cambridge, 1981), 117–30.

'Cantiones a la pifarescha' in Ferrarese inventories of 1480 and *c*.1494, and that it was compiled for the *piffari* at Ferrara, 'perhaps as a tribute to their virtuosity, and also to give a special touch to the festivities of Isabella d'Este and Francesco Gonzaga in 1480'.[41] The Ferrara wind-players were led by Corrado de Alemagna from 1441 to 1481, and included other Germans at various times. There were also Germans in the *piffari* at Florence, Milan, and Mantua; by Francesco Gonzaga's time (ruled 1484–1519) the Mantuan *piffari* could read music, had arrangements of polyphonic vocal music in their repertoire, and played stringed instruments as well as winds.[42]

The sudden emergence of the Italian repertoire of 'songs without words' probably provided the impetus for the development of bowed instruments in more than one size. It was the first sizeable repertoire of written instrumental ensemble music, and it was a serious medium that attracted composers of the calibre of Josquin des Prez and Heinrich Isaac. But there was a problem. In humanist circles, where we might expect such music to be appreciated, wind instruments were regarded as inferior to strings, following the authority of classical authors such as Plato and Aristotle, and the example of the myths that feature Apollo and his lyre triumphing over the pipe-players Pan and Marsyas.[43] Wind instruments, with their indecorous warlike and phallic associations, were considered doubly unsuitable for court ladies. By tradition the chief musical symbol of manly magnificence, a band of *haut* instruments, did not form a part of their households. Instead, as Keith Polk has pointed out, they tended to patronize *bas* ensembles such as lute-duet teams.[44] It is not surprising, therefore, that Isabella d'Este, the greatest female patron of music of her time, should have gone to some lengths to promote stringed instruments at the expense of winds in her Mantuan circle. She commissioned a cycle of seven allegorical paintings for her *studiolo* in which stringed instruments are consistently associated with virtue, spiritual love, and harmony, while wind instruments are associated with vice, sensual love, and strife.[45] On one occasion she brusquely rejected the offer of a bone recorder from her favourite instrument-maker, Lorenzo

[41] Lockwood, *Music in Renaissance Ferrara*, 142–3, 224–6, 266–72; see also A. S. Wolff, 'The Chansonnier Biblioteca Casanatense 2856: Its History, Purpose, and Music', Ph.D. diss. (North Texas State University, 1970); Johannes Martini, *Secular Pieces*, ed. E. G. Evans (Recent Researches in the Music of the Middle Ages and Early Renaissance, 1; Madison, Wisc., 1975).

[42] W. F. Prizer, *Courtly Pastimes: The Frottole of Marchetto Cara* (Ann Arbor, Mich., 1980), 3; id., 'Bernardo Piffaro e i pifferi e tromboni a Mantova: strumenti a fiato in una corte italiana', *RIM* 16 (1981), 183–4; Polk, 'Instrumental Music in the Urban Centres', 181–3; Prizer, 'North Italian Courts, 1460–1540', in I. Fenlon (ed.), *The Renaissance* (Man and Music; London, 1989), 148.

[43] For an extended discussion of this point, see W. F. Prizer, 'Isabella d'Este and Lorenzo da Pavia, "Master Instrument Maker"', *EMH* 2 (1982), 112–16.

[44] Prizer, 'North Italian Courts', 145; Polk, 'Voices and Instruments', 180, 188.

[45] Prizer, 'Isabella d'Este', 115–16.

da Pavia.[46] And, apparently, she was determined to find an alternative to wind instruments for the new repertoire of instrumental music. The result was the viol consort.

The origin of the viol remained obscure until recently. It used to be thought that the Renaissance instrument was descended in a direct line from the so-called 'medieval viol', the large waisted bowed instrument that is played vertically in twelfth- and thirteenth-century pictures, often placed on the lap like the treble viol. But all attempts to bridge the intervening centuries failed, and there matters rested more or less uneasily until Thurston Dart, in a characteristic flash of intuition, suggested that the viol was the result of a cross-fertilization between the Spanish vihuela de mano and the vielle; that it was, in essence, a bowed guitar.[47] It was left to Ian Woodfield to find the evidence in Spanish pictures, to refine the theory somewhat, and to explain how the instrument got to Italy.[48]

Briefly stated, Woodfield's thesis is that the viol came into being when the vihuela de mano acquired its bowed playing technique from the Moorish rabab (not the vielle, as Dart thought) in or around Valencia in the middle of the fifteenth century. At that time, like bowed instruments in other parts of Europe (and elsewhere, for that matter), it was made in a single size, and must have been played with drone techniques, for it is usually shown with a flat bridge, or no bridge at all. Its one novel feature (apart from the vertical playing position, which also came from the rabab) was that it was much larger than other bowed instruments. Or rather, it had a long guitar-like neck with a long string-length, which meant that much lower notes could be played on it than on the soprano-range rebec or the alto-range vielle.[49] (I hope I have disposed of the idea that vielles were made in more than one size; I shall deal with the notion of a fifteenth-century rebec consort in due course.)

A less satisfactory aspect of Woodfield's thesis is the idea that the viol arrived in Italy as a result of the migration of Catalans to Rome in the wake of the election of Rodrigo Borgia to the papacy in 1492. True, the first evidence of the viol in Italy seems to be a reference in a letter of 6 March 1493 describing a group of Spaniards from Rome playing *viole* 'almost as large as myself' at a Sforza family celebration in Vigevano near

---

[46] Ibid. 113.

[47] T. Dart, 'The Viols', in A. Baines (ed.), *Musical Instruments through the Ages* (Harmondsworth, 1961), 184.

[48] I. Woodfield, 'The Origin of the Viol', Ph.D. thesis (London, 1977); id., *The Early History of the Viol* (Cambridge, 1984).

[49] For the relationship between pitch, length, and thickness of gut strings, see the bibliography in S. Bonta, 'Catline Strings Revisited', *JAMIS* 14 (1988), 38.

Milan.[50] Also, a fresco in the Borgia apartments in the Vatican, commissioned by Alexander VI after his election, includes a long-necked vihuela de mano.[51] But even if the 1493 letter refers to bowed rather than plucked *viole*, which is not certain, two swallows do not make a summer. Most of the early references to the viol in Italy come from Mantuan and Ferrarese sources—including the 1493 letter, written by the Ferrarese chancellor Bernardino de' Prosperi to Isabella d'Este. No doubt some viols were brought to Rome by the Borgias and their entourage, but others must have come in the luggage of Jewish musicians fleeing from Spain to Italy following Ferdinand and Isabella's expulsion of the Jews in 1492. We shall see in later chapters that most if not all the string-players who came from Italy to the English court in the 1540s and 1550s were Sephardic Jews, whose families had earlier moved from the Iberian peninsula to northern Italian towns. In these liberal and independent centres they were relatively safe from the Inquisition, which actively persecuted Jews in Rome and the Papal States.

It may be that Isabella d'Este was personally responsible for having the Spanish viol converted from a single-size drone instrument into one made in several sizes with arched bridges. She certainly knew enough about music and musical instruments to be able to give detailed instructions to the instrument-makers who worked for her. In July 1497, for instance, she ordered a lute from Lorenzo da Pavia that was to be 'good and medium-sized, that is, neither too large nor too small'.[52] She added, 'we require you to make it of such a size that when it is strung, it will have [will be pitched?] two steps higher ["che 'l habia due voce più alte"] than the viola you made, which is a little low for our voice'.

Isabella's viol consort seems to have come into being in March 1495 when she ordered three instruments variously called 'viole' and 'viole ovver lire' from an unnamed maker while on a visit to Brescia; in June she sent her lutenist Giovanni Angelo Testagrossa to inspect them and negotiate a price.[53] It is clear from subsequent correspondence that they were bowed rather than plucked, and were made in two sizes: in 1499 she ordered her Brescian agent to have another 'viola grande' made, the size of the larger ones in her consort. The Ferrarese painter Lorenzo Costa may have had these instruments in mind when in 1497 he painted viols of two sizes with arched bridges in an altar-piece for the church of San

---

[50] Woodfield, *Early History*, 81–2.

[51] Prizer, 'Isabella d'Este', 101–2; Woodfield, *Early History*, 82–3; for the vihuela de mano, see D. Gill, 'Vihuelas, Violas, and the Spanish Guitar', *EM* 9 (1981), 455–62.

[52] W. F. Prizer, 'Lutenists at the Court of Mantua in the Late Fifteenth and Early Sixteenth Centuries', *JLSA* 13 (1980), 18.

[53] Id., 'Isabella d'Este', 102–4.

Giovanni in Monte in Bologna.[54] Their distinctive body shape, with two corners linking a broad lower half to a narrower upper half, can also be seen on a vihuela de mano and a lira da braccio in an intarsia panel made between 1506 and 1508 for the door of one of Isabella d'Este's cabinets, and on a viol played by an angel in a painting by Garofalo at Modena; Laurence Witten has suggested that some surviving instruments with the shape are Brescian in origin.[55]

Whether or not the 1495 instruments really did make up the first bowed consort, there is little doubt that the viol was chosen as its basis because it had a significantly longer string-length than the vielle or the rebec. A consort made up of an existing Spanish viol with an arched bridge and two larger bass-range instruments a fourth or fifth lower would have easily encompassed the three-part repertoire of 'songs without words'.[56] Of course, a bowed consort with a similar overall range could have been assembled earlier by combining, say, two vielles and a rebec. But most 'songs without words' would have had to have been transposed up by as much as an octave to fit their TBB- or ATB-range parts on SAA-range instruments. And this would have been no use in music that combined a soprano- or alto-range voice with lower instruments, as in the polyphonic frottola. Indeed, the frottola may be the first genre developed specifically for viols. It seems to have originated in Mantua in the 1490s, and was based on earlier types of improvised song performed by lute-duet teams. Just as improvised instrumental duets gave way to composed three-part music, so the improvised accompaniment of the frottola (divided between the singer and his *tenorista*) gave way to three composed untexted lower parts.[57] The likelihood that these parts were intended for viols is increased by the fact that Isabella d'Este had 'an integral and indispensable role' in the frottola's origins and development, according to William Prizer; many early frottole were probably written for her to sing.[58]

Isabella's home town, Ferrara, was also an early centre of viol-playing. The arrival of Agostino della Viola at the Ferrarese court in 1497 seemingly changed the existing duet team of Andrea and Zampaulo della Viola into a trio; a fourth della Viola, Jacomo, is first recorded in 1499.[59]

---

[54] Woodfield, *Early History*, 88.

[55] Prizer, 'Isabella d'Este', 105–7; Woodfield, *Early History*, 92; Witten, 'Apollo, Orpheus and David', 19–28.

[56] For early viol tunings, see H. M. Brown, 'Notes (and Transposing Notes) on the Viol in the Early Sixteenth Century', in Fenlon (ed.), *Music in Medieval and Early Modern Europe*, 61–78; Woodfield, *Early History*, 140–54; K. M. Spencer and H. M. Brown, 'How Alfonso della Viola Tuned his Viols, and how he Transposed', *EM* 14 (1986), 520–33.

[57] Prizer, 'The Frottola and the Unwritten Tradition', 8–12.

[58] Id., 'North Italian Courts', 143–7.

[59] Lockwood, *Music in Renaissance Ferrara*, 325–6.

On 19 March of that year Lorenzo da Pavia wrote to Isabella d'Este that Alfonso d'Este was in Venice and wanted to order five 'viole da archo' made 'in all the possible sizes [*modi*] in the world'.[60] There are two points of interest here. The phrase 'in all the possible sizes in the world' suggests that a third size of viol, presumably soprano-range, had been added to the existing tenor and bass by 1499. This would have enabled viol consorts to play any vocal polyphony, including the five- and six-part chansons with an overall range of three octaves or more that Josquin and his contemporaries were beginning to write. It is significant that Alfonso himself played in 'una musica de sei viole' during the celebrations for his marriage to Lucrezia Borgia in 1502.[61] Alfonso's example seems to have prompted other members of his family to take up the viol. Isabella d'Este wrote to her half-brother Giulio on 14 May 1499 that she had begun to play the *viola*, that she had been practising for two days, and hoped to 'play tenor to Don Alfonso' when she next went to Ferrara.[62] Cardinal Ippolito d'Este, their brother, also played the viol, as did Lucrezia Borgia, if a viol-like instrument on a medallion of her struck shortly after her marriage is evidence of her own musical interests, rather than those of her husband.[63]

The other point is that Alfonso d'Este and his family seem to have been the first aristocrats to play consort instruments. Put another way, the emergence of the viol consort marks the moment when ensemble instruments began to be cultivated outside the professional sphere. Amateurs had hitherto cultivated music largely as a solitary activity, using solo instruments such as the harp or the vielle. Baldassare Castiglione wrote in *Il cortegiano* (Venice, 1528) that a courtier might sing to a stringed instrument ('cantare alla viola'), play all keyboard instruments ('tutti gli instrumenti di tasti'), and participate in a four-part viol consort ('quattro viole da arco'); for much of the sixteenth century the viol remained the only socially acceptable consort instrument.[64] In some countries it remained the preserve of professionals until much later; it was only generally taken up by English amateurs after 1600 (see Ch. 6).

We can now understand why the first evidence of the violin comes in Ferrarese pictures shortly after 1500. I have argued that the viol consort was developed for Isabella d'Este and her circle so that 'noble' strings could replace 'ignoble' winds in polyphonic ensemble music. The same humanist agenda probably produced the desire for a second family of bowed instruments that could replace wind instruments on the dance

[60] Prizer, 'Isabella d'Este', 104.
[61] Woodfield, *Early History*, 87, 89.
[62] Prizer, 'Isabella d'Este', 104.
[63] Id., 'North Italian Courts', 150; Woodfield, *Early History*, 89.
[64] O. Strunk (ed.), *Source Readings in Music History*, 5 vols. (London, 1981), ii. 94.

floor. The process paralleled the development of the viol consort in that two sizes, soprano and bass, were extrapolated from an existing single-size instrument. But because the model was the alto-range vielle, smaller than the Spanish viol and played on the shoulder, the violin consort as a whole was smaller and livelier in articulation than the viol consort. The families were initially distinguished either by qualifying *viola* with diminutives and augmentatives, or by adding the phrases 'da braccio' and 'da gamba'. Thus violins were often referred to as *violette* or *violini*, while viols were called *violoni*. It should be emphasized that these words applied to violins and viols as a class, irrespective of the size of individual instruments. *Violino* did not come to mean a soprano violin, or *violone* a contrabass viol, until much later.

The evidence, such as it is, suggests that the impetus for the creation of the violin family came from Ferrara rather than Mantua. On 20 December 1511 'maestro Sebastian da Verona' was paid to look for timber for making 'violette' for the Ferrara court, and for repairing its 'viole e violoni'.[65] We cannot be sure that these 'violette' were violins, but it is likely in view of the fact that they are juxtaposed with 'viole' and 'violoni'—which may have been viols and plucked instruments respectively. A clearer case is provided by a Ferrarese inventory of the same year:

	Viole	Lauti
Una viola, zoè un basso	No. 1	
Una viola, zoè un tenore	No. 1	
Viole da gamba, numero sei, con sei archetti	No. 6	
Due lauti, uno con la cassa, uno l'altro no		No. 2
Quattro violoni alla napolitana		No. 4[66]

The first two instruments on the list can be identified as violins by a process of elimination. They were clearly not plucked *viole* because they were the tenor and bass members of a consort; nor were they viols, which are described as 'Viole da gamba'. William Prizer has suggested that the 'violoni alla napolitana' were vihuelas, the instrument referred to in Mantuan sources variously as 'viola spagnola', 'liuto ala spagnola', 'viola ala napolitana', or just 'spagnola'.[67]

It is not clear whether the tenor or bass *viole* in the document belonged to the first violin consort, or whether it was made by Sebastian

---

[65] *I-MOs*, Libri d'amministrazioni dai singoli principi, no. 781, fo. 161ᵛ; I am grateful to William Prizer for this reference.

[66] Prizer, 'Isabella d'Este', 110.

[67] Ibid. 110–12.

of Verona. It is certainly not impossible that the earliest violins came from the same workshop or workshops that produced the first viol consorts. After all, Brescia has traditionally been thought of as the earliest centre of violin-making. But it is probably significant that the violin and the viola in the Ferrarese frescoes have four corners, and are quite different in shape from the two-cornered Brescian instruments. Either way, we can be fairly sure that a violin consort was in use in Ferrara in the first decade of the sixteenth century.

Little is known about how the violin consort spread outside the Este–Gonzaga circle, for there are few reliable references to it until it is found widely distributed on both sides of the Alps in the second quarter of the century. In part, the problem is that the violin, the preserve of professionals, figures less prominently in the correspondence and literature of the time than the viol, which was played by members of the literate classes. Another problem is that northern Italy was repeatedly invaded and fought over by French and Imperial armies in the early sixteenth century, so it was not a promising environment for the creation and survival of documents. And, with a few exceptions, Italian archives have not been searched by musicologists as thoroughly as those in northern Europe.

There is also the recurring problem of terminology. We have no means of knowing whether the many unqualified references to *viole*—such as the 'quattro suonatori di liuto, viole e altri strumenti' who appeared in a Bolognese triumphal car in 1512, or the *viole* heard in a play during the Roman carnival of 1519—are to violins or viols.[68] French is less ambiguous in this respect. The word 'viole' existed in the fifteenth century, when it seems to have been a generic word for stringed instruments (see Ch. 3), and there are supposedly references to 'joueurs de violon' as early as 1490 in the Lorraine archives at Nancy.[69] But French musicians and scribes seem to have used *viole* and *violon* consistently to distinguish viol from violin the moment the two instruments arrived in France. There was no need in French to qualify *viole* as *viola* was qualified in Italian.

It is not surprising, therefore, that the largest body of unambiguous early references to the violin is in the accounts of the dukes of Savoy, who ruled Savoy and Piedmont from Turin, for they were written in French until 1558.[70] There is a payment to a group of 'vyollons' from Vercelli as early as 1523, and dozens of professional groups across northern Italy

---

[68] E. Elsner, 'Untersuchung der instrumentalen Besetzungspraxis der weltlichen Musik im 16. Jahrhundert in Italien', Ph.D. diss. (Berlin, 1935), 85; Prizer, 'Lutenists at the Court of Mantua', 28.

[69] A. Jacquot, *La Musique en Lorraine* (Paris, 1882; repr. 1971), 22–3.

[70] S. Cordero di Pamparato, 'Emanuele Filiberto di Savoia, protettore dei musici', *RMI* 34 (1927), 229–47, 555–78; *RMI* 35 (1928), 29–49.

were evidently using violins by the 1540s and 1550s, often in small towns such as Abbiategrasso, Desenzano, Rovereto, and Peschiera. A large town like Milan might support several groups: one day in December 1544 four violinists entertained the duke of Savoy during the day, and four others in the evening. In general, the Savoy accounts give the impression that by then the violin was the most popular instrument among professional groups—wind instruments are rarely mentioned—and that even quite humble classes of musician were using it.

The violin also appeared in France itself at an early date. David Boyden drew attention to a woodcut done in Paris in 1516 which shows four hybrid instruments of different sizes played by 'the most celebrated string quartet in history', Plato, Aristotle, Galen, and Hippocrates.[71] They are shaped more or less like violins, with a three-string alto and a four-string tenor, yet only the soprano is played *da braccio*—the rest are held vertically. However fanciful the details, the picture shows that consorts of bowed instruments were known in France in the second decade of the century. A group described variously as 'viollons, haulxboys et sacquebuteurs', and 'violons de la bande françoise' had already been established at the French court by 1529.[72] The six have French names—Jehan Henry, Pierre de La Planche, Pierre Champgilbert (Camp Guillebert), Jehan Fourcade, Nicolas Pirouet, and Jean Bellac (Veillac)—and may therefore have come into contact with the violin while accompanying the French court on its forays south of the Alps. But the instrument was also brought to France by travelling groups of Italians. Paule de Malan, Nicolas de Lucques, and Dominique de Lucques were members of the French court violin consort in 1533; in 1538 'Thimodio de Luqua et ses compaignons, joueurs de viollons', were serving the Venetian ambassador in Paris; in 1543 Vincent Maudin, Cyprien Renelio, Michel Sauzel, and Marc-Antoine Gayerdel (who joined the English court violin consort in 1545; see Ch. 4) were 'violons' in the service of the Cardinal of Lorraine; and in about 1555 a violin consort led by Baldassare de Belgiojoso (Balthasar de Beaujoyeulx) is said to have arrived from the Milan area.[73]

The same pattern was repeated in German-speaking countries. By 1600 many courts and large towns employed violin consorts, some of which included Italians or used Italian instruments. The group at Munich was founded by four members of the 'Bisutzi' family in the 1550s, and

[71] Boyden, *History*, 12–13.

[72] H. Prunières, 'La Musique de la chambre et de l'écurie sous la règne de François Ier', *L'Année musicale*, 1 (1912), 244–5.

[73] V. Gai, *Gli strumenti musicali della corte medicea e il museo del Conservatorio 'Luigi Cherubini' di Firenze* (Florence, 1969), 66; Prunières, 'La Musique', 245; D. Heartz, *Pierre Attaingnant, Royal Printer of Music* (Berkeley and Los Angeles, 1969), 82; Boyden, *History*, 38.

was enlarged around 1568, probably for Duke Wilhelm's marriage to Renée of Lorraine.[74] The five newcomers, who included three members of the Morari family, may have been part of Renée's entourage; the court at Nancy acquired a set of violins as early as 1534.[75] Italian 'Geiger oder Musici' were at the Viennese court by the 1560s (including three members of the Ardesi family from Cremona), at Weimar in 1569, at Innsbruck in the 1570s and 1580s, and at Hechingen in the Black Forest from 1581.[76] Italian instruments mentioned in inventories include a set of Brescian 'geig' at Augsburg (1566), 'Ein Italiänisch Stimwerckh von Geigen, darinn ein discant, drey tenor und ein Bass' at Baden-Baden (1582), and 'Fünf venedische geugen' at Hechingen (1609).[77]

Geigen is another thorny terminological problem. Around 1600 it was used in opposition to *Phyolen* or *Violen* to distinguish violin from viol (though *Violen* could also mean violins; see Ch. 7)—as in the Baden-Baden inventory, which lists a 'phyola da gamba' as well as 'Geigen'. But *Geige* was in use long before the violin came into being, and evidently changed its meaning several times. Around 1400, Keith Polk suggests, it tended to be used for the rebec, while *Vedel* was associated with the vielle.[78] Things were more complex a century later. *Geige* had become the most common term for bowed instruments, and early sixteenth-century treatises show that it was applied to more than one type. Two bowed instruments figure in Virdung's *Musica getutscht* (Basle, 1511), the 'clein Geigen' and the 'Groß Geigen'.[79] The former is a three-string rebec, but the latter is an odd fretted instrument with huge waists and shoulders ending in sharp corners (Fig. 1.1). Only one size of each is illustrated, and while the *kleine Geige* has an arched bridge, the *große Geige* must have been a drone instrument, for it has nine strings attached to a string-holder on the belly; Ian Woodfield has suggested that it was strung like a five-course lute, with the top string single, and the rest in pairs.

In the first five editions of *Musica instrumentalis deudsch* (Wittenberg, 1528, 1529, 1530, 1532, and 1542) Agricola described four types of

[74] A. Sandberger, *Beiträge zur Geschichte der bayerischen Hofkapelle unter Orlando di Lasso* (Leipzig, 1894–5), iii, pt. 1; Boyden, *History*, 61–2; see also J. Haar, 'Munich at the Time of Orlande de Lassus', in Fenlon (ed.), *The Renaissance*, 243–62.

[75] Jacquot, *Musique en Lorraine*, 36.

[76] L. von Köchel, *Die kaiserliche Hof-Musikkapelle in Wien von 1543 bis 1867* (Vienna, 1869), 48, 52; E. Pasqué, 'Die Weimarer Hofkapelle im XVI. Jahrhundert', *MMg* 29 (1897), 138; W. Senn, *Musik und Theater am Hof zu Innsbruck* (Innsbruck, 1954), 144 ff.; E. F. Schmid, *Musik an den schwäbischen Zollerhöfen der Renaissance* (Kassel, 1962), ii. 489–90.

[77] D. A. Smith, 'The Musical Instrument Inventory of Raymund Fugger', *GSJ* 33 (1980), 42; O. zur Nedden, *Quellen und Studien zur oberrheinischen Musikgeschichte im 15. und 16. Jahrhundert* (Kassel, 1931), 28; Schmid, *Musik an der schwäbischen Zollerhöfen*, ii. 529.

[78] Polk, '*Vedel* and *Geige*', 507–8.

[79] E. M. Ripin, 'A Re-evaluation of Virdung's *Musica Getutscht*', *JAMS* 29 (1976), 189–223; Woodfield, *Early History*, 100–1; Polk, '*Vedel* and *Geige*', 508–10.

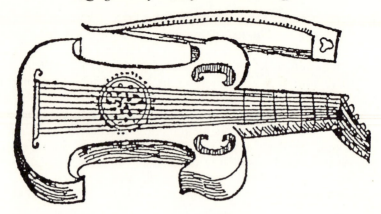

1.1. Sebastian Virdung, *Musica getutscht* (Basle, 1511), fo. B 3ʳ, illustration of *grosse Geigen*

Geige, the second, third, and fourth of which are illustrated.[80] There are four sizes of each type, *discantus*, *altus*, *tenor*, and *bassus*, with three tunings (the alto and tenor are in unison), though the illustrations of the second and third still show them without bridges and string-holders on the bellies, perhaps because the illustrator was copying Virdung's picture of the *große Geige*. The first type, 'großen Geigen', have five strings (apart from a six-string bass), while his 'ander art auff grosse odder cleine Geigen' have four strings tuned in fifths, fourths, and a third. The 'kleinen Geigen' have three strings tuned in fifths, and are said to be 'usually without frets', but frets are shown in the illustration, and the bodies, with large waists and sharp corners, are closer to *große Geigen* than to any type of violin. The fourth type, also 'kleinen Geigen', are three-string rebecs with arched bridges.

In the revised sixth edition (Wittenberg, 1545), Agricola described three types, 'grossen Welschen geigen', 'Polischen Geigen', and 'kleinen dreyseitigen handgeiglein'.[81] The first, fretted 'foreign' (i.e. Italian) viols with four and five strings must have been played with arched bridges, though the 1528 picture of bridgeless instruments is repeated. The Polish *Geigen* are not illustrated, but they are said to be played without frets, using the fingernails to stop the strings, and have three strings (with a

---

[80] Hayes, *Viols*, 156–7, 162–6, 239–41; Polk, *'Vedel* and *Geige'*, 510–12; see also E. Dann, 'Martin Agricola and the Early Three-stringed Fiddles', in E. Strainchamps, M. R. Maniates, and C. Hatch (eds.), *Music and Civilization: Essays in Honor of Paul Henry Lang* (New York and London, 1984), 232–42.

[81] A quasi-facsimile, ed. R. Eitner, is in Publikationen älterer praktischer und theoretischer Musikwerke, 20 (Leipzig, 1896).

four-string bass). The little three-string 'handgeiglein' have the same tuning, but again the 1528 picture of rebecs is repeated, with its three-string bass. The other main source of information about *Geigen* is Hans Gerle's *Musica teusch* (Nuremberg, 1532).[82] Gerle, like Virdung, has only two types, 'dem grossen Geygen', and 'den kleynen Geigleyn'. The former is said to have five or six strings with frets, and is shaped like a sixteenth-century Venetian viol, though again the two instruments illustrated do not have bridges. The latter has three strings (with a four-string bass), is tuned in fifths, is shaped like a rebec, and has an arched bridge.

What are we to make of all this? An obvious point is that we cannot assume that references to *kleine Geigen* are violins rather than rebecs in the first half of the sixteenth century, though they are more likely to be so if the players or the instruments are described as Italian. Another is that drone techniques clearly survived in Germany long after 1500; indeed, there is no evidence that any type of *Geige* was developed in more than one size before the first viols and violins appeared. Rebec consorts are often assumed to have existed in the fifteenth century, and Gerald Hayes made the point that Virdung referred to 'clein Geigen' in the plural.[83] But Virdung also referred to the harp and the lute in the plural, and thought the 'clein Geigen' useless, which suggests an obsolete instrument rather than one embodying the fashionable consort principle. The rebec was probably developed in several sizes in the 1510s or 1520s for German musicians who wanted to play polyphonic music on bowed instruments, but who preferred to stick to the simple and proven design of the rebec.

Much the same can be said of the *große Geige*. Keith Polk has recently suggested that Virdung's instrument with large waists and sharp corners (which he calls 'German viol') existed earlier than the Italian viol, and that it is the *Geige* referred to in archival sources from about 1475.[84] But, as we have seen, *Geige* is no more reliable than *viola* as evidence for a particular type of bowed instrument. Nor is there any hard evidence of the 'German viol' before 1500. The earliest picture of one seems to be in the Garofalo fresco in the Palazzo di Ludovico il Moro in Ferrara, though only the neck and the top of the body are visible.[85] There is also a print done by Hans Wechtlin in Strasburg between 1502 and 1507 that includes a three-string bridgeless instrument with a similar body, but

---

[82] A. Silbiger, 'The First Viol Tutor: Hans Gerle's *Musica Teusch*', *JVGSA* 6 (1969), 34–48; Hayes, *Viols*, 156–7.

[83] Hayes, *Viols*, 156.

[84] Polk, '*Vedel* and *Geige*'.

[85] Illustrated in Remnant, *Musical Instruments*, 31.

played *da braccio*.[86] There is certainly no hard evidence of a consort of 'German viols' before the 1528 edition of Agricola's book, and even then the issue is not straightforward, for the 'consort' seemingly consists of bridgeless drone instruments. Hans Burgmair's engraving of carts of Maximilian's musicians in his *Triumphzug* (engraved 1516–19) certainly shows three 'German viols', one of which has an arched bridge, but they are all roughly tenor size, and the small instrument played *da braccio* is more like a violin than a viol (Fig. 1.2).[87] We can argue about when the 'German viol' came into being, but the Italian viol probably provided the model for it to be developed in several sizes.

The German sources of information about the *kleine Geige* may be ambiguous and confusing, but, used with caution, they can be a useful supplement to our meagre knowledge of the sizes and tunings of early violins. The first Italian description of the violin consort was published by Giovanni Maria Lanfranco in his *Scintille di musica* (Brescia, 1533), 137–8.[88] His 'Violette da Arco senza tasti' (also called 'Violetta da Braccio, & da Arco') are made in four sizes, 'Soprano', 'Co(n)traalto', 'Tenore', and 'Basso', but have only three tunings, with the alto and tenor in unison. In other words, the consort consisted of a single violin, two violas of different sizes, and a bass. This layout, analogous to that of contemporary wind consorts, was the standard one for violins for most of the sixteenth century, though a third viola was added when five-part dance music became common after about 1550. Scorings with two violins were gradually adopted by violin bands in most countries in the course of the seventeenth century, though the French court orchestra, the Vingt-quatre Violons, retained the old layout until after 1700.

The earliest violin consorts probably consisted entirely of three-string instruments, like those in the Saronno fresco. Sylvestro di Ganassi gives three-string tunings in his *Lettione seconda* (Venice, 1543), Ch. 23, with the sizes pitched a fifth apart as in contemporary wind consorts: the bass is tuned *F c g*, the violas *c g d'*, and the violin *g d' a'*. This simple and logical arrangement (implied by Agricola's 1528 description of *kleine Geigen*), was soon complicated by the addition of a fourth string, and, it seems, by intonation problems: tuning a chain of pure fifths across several instruments produces an uncomfortable discrepancy between sharp open strings at the top, and flat ones at the bottom. For the same reason shawms were rarely played in complete sets, and tended to be mixed with

---

[86] B. Geiser, *Studien zur Frühgeschichte der Violine* (Berne and Stuttgart, 1974), ill. 54.

[87] Discussed and illustrated in Polk, '*Vedel* and *Geige*', 512–17; see A. Aspland (ed.), *Triumph of the Emperor Maximilian I* [Commentary volume] (London, 1875), 113.

[88] See B. Lee, 'Giovanni Maria Lanfranco's *Scintille de Musica* and its Relation to Sixteenth-Century Music Theory', Ph.D. diss. (Cornell University, 1961), 252–3.

1.2. Hans Burgkmair, 'Musica süess Meledey', *Triumphzug Maximilians* (1516–19)

trombones and other loud instruments; recorders were eventually made so that the set was pitched *F c f c'* rather than *F c g d'*.

In the violin consort one solution was to tune the bass up a tone, so that it was an octave below the violas. No source actually gives *G d a* for a three-string bass, but it probably lies behind the odd tuning *F G d a* given by Gerle and Agricola (in 1545) for the bass *kleine Geige*: *F* was required because it was the standard bottom note of mid-century dance music. It was probably for this reason that the bass violin acquired a fourth string earlier than the violin or the viola: Lanfranco's tunings are for a three-string violin, three-string violas, and a four-string bass. He gives them using a system of intervals between the strings rather than absolute pitches, but if we take it that the violin was tuned *g d' a'* and the viola *c g d'*, as in Ganassi, then the bass violin must have been tuned *Bb' F c g*—the tuning given by Jambe de Fer, by Lodovico Zacconi in his *Prattica di musica* (Venice, 1592), and by the majority of seventeenth-century sources.[89] Given that *G d a* had been developed as the nucleus of a four-string bass tuning as early as the 1530s, it is odd that no source gives *C G d a*, the modern tuning, before 'De organographia' in Michael Praetorius's *Syntagmatis musici tomus secundus* (Wolfenbüttel, 1618–19).[90] It does not seem to have become common until the violoncello, a small version of the bass violin developed in seventeenth-century Italy for solo playing, began to replace the bass violin in string ensembles.[91]

With gut strings, instruments that went down as far as *Bb'* would have needed a much longer string-length than those that only went down to *F*. Indeed, there seems to have been two distinct types of bass violin. Small basses were used for playing standing or walking along, slung across the chest and supported, in Jambe de Fer's words, 'with a little hook in an iron ring, or other thing, which is attached to the back of the said instrument quite conveniently, so that it does not hamper the player'. Many pictures show basses played in this way, and hooks or rings are found on some surviving instruments. A good example is a small three-string bass shaped like a Venetian viol at the Shrine to Music Museum, Vermilion, South Dakota, which has a metal loop built into an upper rib.[92] Large basses, with a string-length long enough to reach down to *Bb'*, were used for playing in fixed positions, on a stool, as in the famous

[89] For Zacconi, see D. Boyden, 'Monteverdi's *Violini Piccoli alla Francese* and *Viole da Brazzo'*, *AnnM* 6 (1958–63), 393; Boyden, *History*, 42–3.

[90] M. Praetorius, *Syntagma Musicum II, De Organographia Parts I and II*, trans. and ed. D. Z. Crookes (Oxford, 1986), 39, 56.

[91] For the development of the violoncello, see S. Bonta, 'From Violone to Violoncello: A Question of Strings?', *JAMIS* 3 (1977), 64–99; id., 'Terminology for the Bass Violin in Seventeenth-Century Italy', *JAMIS* 4 (1978) 5–42; id., 'Catline Strings Revisited'.

[92] I am grateful to Paul O'Dette and Mark Caudle for drawing this instrument to my attention, and to Dr Margaret Downie Banks of the Shrine to Music Museum for providing me with details of it.

painting said to show Queen Elizabeth dancing the volta (see Plate 3.(a)), or resting on the ground, as in an engraving of the 1568 wedding banquet at Munich (Fig. 1.3). Such instruments are often thought of as early double basses, but it is unlikely that they were tuned lower than *B♭'*, or that they doubled bass lines at the lower octave. The Munich picture shows two large four-string basses of equal size in a six-man consort; they presumably took the two bass parts of the six-part motet by Rore that was played during the banquet by six 'viole da brazzo', according to Massimo Troiano's accompanying text.[93] Troiano wrote that at court dinners 'Antonio Morari and his companions, with their violins, sometimes also with viols and various other instruments, play French chansons, motets of refined style, and some exquisite madrigals'. Some sets of violins probably included both types: an Innsbruck court inventory of 1596 mentions 'ain grossen pasz' and 'ain clain pasz' in a set of six viole 'used for dancing'.[94]

The violin and the viola acquired a fourth string around the middle of the sixteenth century. Ganassi still gave three-string tunings in 1543, as did Agricola for *kleine Geigen* in 1545. But in 1556 Jambe de Fer described a violin consort with four-string instruments, the violin tuned *g d' a' e''*, and the violas *c g d' a'*—the modern tunings. The new strings were added above the existing three, and were probably required by the steadily expanding ranges of consort music; the upper range of the violin in first position was extended from *f''* to *c'''*. *F c g d'* is given as an alternative for the viola by Zacconi, and in Daniel Hitzler's *Extract aus der neuen Musica oder Singkunst* (Nuremberg, 1623); it was arrived at by adding the new string below the existing three.[95] Instruments of this sort have come to be known as 'tenor violins', and seem to have existed for a short period around 1600—they may, for instance, have played the 'Trombone overo Viola da brazzo' part with the range *B–f'* in Monteverdi's *Sonata sopra Sancta Maria*.[96] But they do not seem to have been used in consort dance music: to my knowledge, the inner parts of sixteenth- and seventeenth-century dance music never go below *c*, the lowest note on the ordinary viola. Indeed, Praetorius gives *F c g d'* as one of the tunings for the bass violin, and small instruments strung this way may have played high-lying bass parts, though whether they were held *da braccio* or *da gamba* is a nice question.

[93] Boyden, *History*, 62; H. Leuchtmann (ed.), *Die Münchner Fürstenhochzeit von 1568, Massimo Troiano: Dialoghe* (Munich, 1980).

[94] F. Waldner, 'Zwei Inventarien aus dem XVI. und XVII. Jahrhundert über hinterlassene Musikinstrumente und Musikalien am Innsbrucker Hofe', *SMz* 4 (1916), 128–9.

[95] For Hitzler, see M. Riley, 'The Teaching of Bowed Instruments from 1511 to 1756', Ph.D. diss. (University of Michigan, 1954), 239–41; E. Segerman, 'Hizler's [*sic*] Tenor Violin', *FoMRHI Quarterly*, 27 (Apr. 1982), 38.

[96] See D. Boyden, 'The Tenor Violin: Myth, Mystery, or Misnomer?', in W. Gerstenberg, J. La Rue, and W. Rehm (eds.), *Festschrift Otto Erich Deutsch* (Kassel, 1963), 273–9.

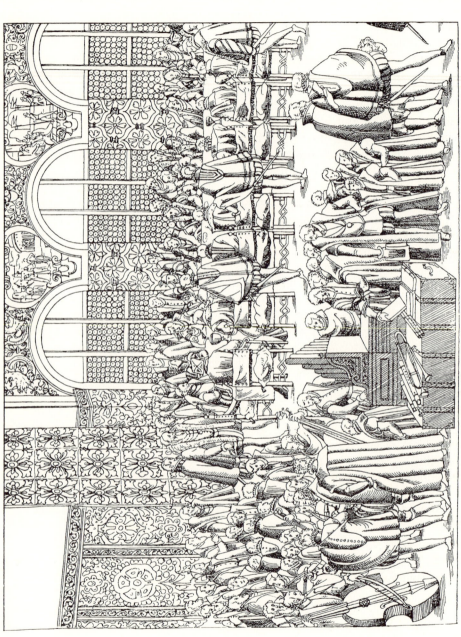

1.3. Detail of 'The Wedding Banquet in the Georg-Saal of the Munich Residenz, 22 February 1568', H. Wagner, *Kurtze doch gegründete beschreibung des...Hochzeitlichen Ehren Fests* (Munich, 1568), showing a

What did sixteenth-century violinists play? The violin was essentially a consort instrument until about 1600, so we should not expect to find solo music for the soprano member of the family. Nor should we expect to find music that specifically calls for violins. Most professional groups played several sets of consort instruments, choosing whichever was most appropriate for the task in hand: viols for contrapuntal music, violins for dance music, loud wind instruments for playing outdoors, and so on. More versatility would have been required from those who worked in town bands or at small courts than those who worked in large establishments such as the French or English courts, where four or five separate instrumental consorts were maintained. Nevertheless, highly skilled groups were often highly versatile. In 1546 Vincenzo Parabosco recommended a six-man Brescian group to the court at Parma, stating that they were most excellent performers on the 'trombetta' in 'every way it can be played', as well as sets of six 'tromboni', 'pifari', 'Corneti', 'Cornemuse', 'flauti', 'piferi ala alemana', 'viole da brazo', and some unspecified 'new and unusual' consorts; Parabosco added: 'I believe you will especially enjoy the combination of these instruments, one type with another, and combined in various ways with vocal music'.[97]

Because of this, most sixteenth-century consort music was written in a neutral style, with limited ranges so that it could be played on as many different types of instrument as possible. And when a particular piece did not fit a particular combination, it could easily be transposed or arranged so that it did. Composers only began to specify particular instruments when they began to write in idioms that favoured one type rather than another, and that did not happen until after 1600. The odd exception, such as the five-part pieces printed in *Balet comique de la Royne* (Paris, 1582), proves the rule: there is nothing intrinsically violinistic about them, and they are only hailed as 'the earliest printed violin music' because the accompanying text happens to mention that they were played on violins in the original performance.[98] Nor is there anything exceptional about the four-part 'Pavanne des dieux' in Claude Gervaise's *Sixième livre de danceries* (Paris, 1555), which is 'fait bonne pour les violons' according to a manuscript note in the only surviving copy.[99] In short, we are not going to find the violin's early repertoire by looking for pieces that specify the instrument, or by trying to formulate a set of criteria to identify 'violinistic' pieces in the consort repertoire.

[97] N. Pelicelli, 'Musicisti in Parma nei secoli XV–XVI: la capella alla corte Farnese', *NA* 9 (1932), 42–3.

[98] Boyden, *History*, 55–6; see also C. and L. MacClintock (trans.), *Le Balet comique de la Royne, 1581* (MSD 25; [Rome], 1971).

[99] Ed. B. Thomas (The Attaingnant Dance Prints, 6; London, 1972), no. 2; Heartz, *Pierre Attaingnant*, 372–3; the phrase is read as 'qui est fort bonne pour les violons' in H. M. Brown, *Instrumental Music Printed before 1600: A Bibliography* (Cambridge, Mass., 1965), 168.

However, we do have the advantage that the violin had a more clearly defined role in sixteenth-century musical life than most instruments: from the beginning it was strongly associated with dance music. This does not mean, of course, that it was never used for contrapuntal music—an instance at the Munich wedding has been mentioned—or that wind groups immediately gave up their place on the dance floor once it appeared.[100] But I have argued that the violin was developed so that the Este–Gonzaga circle could dance to strings rather than winds, and the main reason why it spread so rapidly across northern Europe was surely that it was quickly recognized as the best vehicle for courtly dance music. So, in a sense, all sixteenth-century consort dance music should be considered as potential violin music, though it is likely that only a small amount of it was specifically or exclusively conceived for the instrument.

It is surely no coincidence that the violin emerged at a moment of profound change in the history of dance and dance music. Each fifteenth-century basse dance had its own choreography, because it was geared to the length of the cantus firmus. The new dances that replaced them shortly after 1500, such as the pavan and its related saltarello or galliard, had a standard choreography, and were constructed in short repeated sections using simple patterns such as AABB or AABBCC. The new dance music was also quite different from the old. It was often in four, five, or six parts, and usually had a tune in the soprano instead of a cantus firmus in the tenor. Such music could not readily have been improvised because the inner parts did not have readily defined or discrete functions. Yet sixteenth-century pictures show that dance musicians, in common with other professional instrumentalists, did not use written music, so they must have played a composed repertoire from memory (see Ch. 4). This is probably why so little of the new dance music survives, at least in consort settings.

In fact, there are only a handful of sources that seem to contain music that the earliest violin consorts might have played. *Six gaillardes et six pavanes* and *Neuf basses dances deux branles* (both Paris, 1530), the first two books in the series of *dançeries* published by Pierre Attaingnant, contain pieces that have Italian chord-progressions such as the Passamezzo antico, or have concordances with Italian lute and keyboard sources, and were evidently fairly old by the time they were published.[101] There are also one or two mid-century manuscripts with Italian pieces that might go back to the years around 1500. *D-Mbs*, Mus. MS 1503h, a set of part-books from the library of the Augsburg book-collector Johann Heinrich Herwart

---

[100] For the use of violins in church music, see S. Bonta, 'The Use of Instruments in Sacred Music in Italy, 1560–1700', *EM* 18 (1990), 519–35.

[101] Ed. B. Thomas (The Attaingnant Dance Prints, 1; London, 1989); see also B. Thomas and J. Gingell (eds.), *The Renaissance Dance Book* (London, 1987).

(1520–83), contains four-part Italian dances, many of which still have the tune in the tenor rather than the soprano, and the antique type of cadence where the tenor descends 2-1 while the bass ascends an octave, like a fifteenth-century contratenor.[102] Another Italian collection surviving in northern Europe, *GB-Lbl*, Royal Appendix MSS 59–62, has a similar repertoire, but with slightly more modern features.[103]

By the end of the sixteenth century the violin consort must have been one of the most familiar sounds in the courts and towns of northern Europe. But in the northern Italian courts, its cradle, it seems to have been in decline. There is little sign that violin consorts were employed at Mantua and Ferrara on a regular basis in the late sixteenth century. In 1588 the Mantuan court hired *violini* from Parma and Casalmaggiore, presumably because it had no group of its own, and when a violin band was recruited for the Florentine court in 1608 it consisted of twelve Frenchmen.[104] In advanced musical circles in Italy sets of instruments such as viols or flutes came to be thought of as boring. Vincenzo Giustiniani wrote in 1628 that 'such diversion, with the uniformity of sound and of the consonances, became tiresome rather quickly and was an incentive to sleep rather than to pass the time on a hot afternoon'.[105] He associated shawms and 'bands of violins' with the lower classes: 'festivals in small towns and country districts, and also in the great cities at the festivals of the common people'. The fashion was for mixed ensembles, such as the extravagant groups that played in Florentine *intermedi*, in the *Concerto grande* at Ferrara, or in Venetian polychoral church music.[106] In mixed ensembles the violin tended to be used without the other members of the family, and soon after 1600 it was given a new role in the early Baroque solo repertoire. In the process the violin consort was neglected by Italian musicians; the lead in such matters passed to northern Europe, and it was more than half a century before Italy recovered it.

---

[102] M. Morrow (ed.), *Italian Dances of the Early Sixteenth Century* (Dance Music of the Middle Ages and Renaissance, 1; London, 1976).

[103] Ibid., 2–3 (London, 1978).

[104] C. MacClintock, *Giaches de Wert (1535–1596)* (MSD 17; Rome, 1966), 48; A. Solerti, *Musica, ballo e drammatica alla corte medicea dal 1600 al 1637* (Florence, 1905; repr. 1969), 41; T. Carter, 'A Florentine Wedding of 1608', *AcM* 55 (1983), 101.

[105] V. Giustiniani, *Discorso sopra la Musica (1628)*, trans. C. MacClintock MSD 9; Rome, 1962), 79–80 (trans. adapted).

[106] Brown, *Sixteenth-Century Instrumentation*; A. Newcomb, *The Madrigal at Ferrara 1579–97* (Princeton, NJ, 1980); I. Fenlon, *Music and Patronage in Sixteenth-Century Mantua* (Cambridge, 1980); E. Selfridge-Field, *Venetian Instrumental Music from Gabrieli to Vivaldi* (Oxford, 1975); D. Arnold, *Giovanni Gabrieli and the Music of the Venetian High Renaissance* (London, 1979).

2

'The Place of a Musicon in Ordinary'

Place and Patronage at Court

TUDOR England was one of the most centralized countries in Europe. Most of her wealth and perhaps a fifth of her population (about 4,000,000 in 1600) was concentrated in the home counties.[1] London, with a population of over 200,000, was more than ten times the size of her nearest rivals, Norwich, Bristol, and York; an extraordinarily large proportion of the nation's commercial, intellectual, and artistic life was conducted in her noisy and crowded streets. Above all, London was the seat of England's highly centralized form of government, organized around the court and the person of the monarch.

At the beginning of Henry VIII's reign most of the palaces familiar to us from the art and literature of later times had not yet been built, or still belonged to the aristocrats who built them. Of the ten owned by Elizabeth at her death in 1603 only four, the Tower, St James's, Oatlands, and Windsor Castle, were actually built by the Crown.[2] Most of the rest became Crown property as a result of the disgrace of its owner. Greenwich is a case in point. The most easterly of a string of palaces on the Thames (London's main thoroughfare until the late eighteenth century), it was built by Humphrey, Duke of Gloucester, in 1427; Henry VI confiscated it when the duke fell in 1447. Henry VIII was born there, and the palace, rebuilt around 1500, became his favourite residence, convenient for hunting and inspecting the fleet.[3] Elizabeth also spent a good deal of time there; James I gave it to his queen, Anne of Denmark, and it was eventually demolished to make way for the Royal Naval Hospital.

Travelling upstream from Greenwich, the sixteenth-century tourist would have come first to the Tower, visited by the Tudors only on

---

[1] M. Ashley, *England in the Seventeenth Century (1603–1714)* (The Pelican History of England, 6; 3rd edn., Harmondsworth, 1961), 12–13.

[2] For the royal palaces, see H. M. Colvin (ed.), *The History of the King's Works*, 6 vols. (London, 1963–82); I. Dunlop, *Palaces and Progresses of Elizabeth I* (London, 1962); B. Weinreb and C. Hibbert (eds.), *The London Encyclopaedia* (London, 1983; repr.1987); R. Weinstein, 'Early Tudor London', in D. Starkey (ed.), *Henry VIII: A European Court in England* (London, 1991), 14–19.

[3] For the Tudor palace, see S. Thurley, 'Greenwich Palace', in Starkey, *Henry VIII*, 20–5.

the eve of coronations. Passing by three occasional royal residences, Baynards Castle and Bridewell near Blackfriars, and Somerset House in the Strand, he would have come next to Westminster, and Whitehall. Whitehall was another confiscated palace. As York House it had been the London residence of the Archbishops of York until the fall of Wolsey in 1529, when it replaced the old Palace of Westminster as the chief residence of the court. John Norden called it 'a regal mansion . . . beautiful and large', but foreign visitors often found it unprepossessing; Count Magalotti, who visited it in 1669 with the Grand Duke of Tuscany, wrote that it was 'nothing more than an assemblage of several houses, badly built at different times and for different purposes'.[4] Yet the court, divided into many separate departments and administrative offices, evidently found such a rabbit warren convenient, and the area remained the seat of government after the palace was destroyed by fire in 1698 (Fig. 2.1). Nearby St James's palace, built by Henry VIII on the site of a hospital, only became an important royal residence after 1698; most of it was destroyed by fire in 1809.

Four royal residences lay upstream from Whitehall. Richmond, the old manor of Sheen, was rebuilt on a grand scale by Henry VII, who named it after his Yorkshire earldom. Elizabeth often spent the summer there, though it was neglected by the Stuarts and most of it was destroyed in the Civil War. Hampton Court, the only Tudor palace substantially intact today, was another of Henry VIII's acquisitions from Wolsey, who began building it in 1514. After Whitehall, it was the palace most consistently favoured by the Tudors and Stuarts, for it was near enough London to be within easy reach, yet distant enough to be safe in times of plague. Oatlands and Windsor, the most westerly of the Thames-side palaces, were largely used for hunting, though the annual Garter ceremonies were frequently held at Windsor, and the later Stuarts often spent the summer there. Oatlands, built by Henry VIII at great speed in 1527–8, was small and architecturally unimpressive—a German traveller described it in 1602 as a 'cheerful hunting-box'—though it had the merit of a superb elevated position on the Surrey bank of the Thames between Walton-on-Thames and Weybridge; it has entirely disappeared.[5]

The use to which the palaces were put varied according to circumstances and the preferences of individual sovereigns. Most of them, however, were kept as 'standing houses', staffed and furnished ready for a royal visit. No single building or its vicinity had the resources for an extended stay, so the court made an average of four or five 'removes' a

---

[4] Dunlop, *Palaces and Progresses*, 59–60.   [5] Ibid. 31.

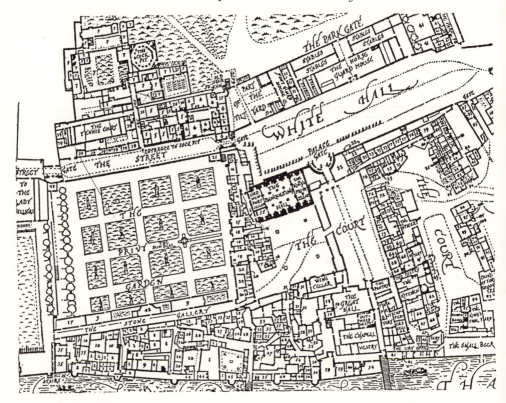

2.1. Ralph Greatorex?, detail from the *Survey of Whitehall c.*1663–70, engraved by George Vertue (London, 1747). From E. Boswell, *The Restoration Court Stage (1660–1702)* (Cambridge, Mass., 1932), 24

year.[6] During the three legal terms, the main working part of the year, it stayed close to London, though in the summer it might venture further afield—to Newhall near Chelmsford perhaps, or to Nonsuch near Cheam in Surrey—and leisurely progresses were regularly made around the great houses of more distant parts of the kingdom. Originally, the entire court moved around, but in time the main departments of government became fixed at Whitehall, and only a small group of courtiers and servants travelled with the sovereign; in Tudor and Stuart times the royal musicians often stayed behind, leaving entertainment along the route to be provided by local musicians.

[6] The movements of Elizabeth's court are summarized in E. K. Chambers, *The Elizabethan Stage* (Oxford, 1923; repr.1974), i. 1–70; see also W. K. Jordan (ed.), *The Chronicle and Political Papers of King Edward VI* (London, 1966).

The court, then, was an administrative concept rather than a single building or a locality, though its structure was reflected in the design of the standing houses.[7] They were divided into three main areas: the Stables, the Household (strictly, the service areas 'below stairs' such as the kitchen, the pantry, and the laundry), and the living areas above stairs, collectively called the Chamber. The Chamber was divided in turn into separate areas for the king and the queen (the 'king's side' and the 'queen's side'); other important members of the royal family, such as the Queen Mother or adult princes and princesses, also had their own living-quarters. All this, of course, was not just a matter of bricks and mortar. The Lord Chamberlain, head of the Chamber, had his counterpart in the Lord Steward, head of the household below stairs, just as other members of the royal family had their personal retinues of servants, organized into miniature versions of the main royal household.

The Chamber consisted of a series of connected rooms in a sequence from the most public to the most private. The visitor proceeded by way of the great hall and the guard chamber to the Presence Chamber, where the throne of state was placed and distinguished visitors were received. In the Middle Ages the sovereign lived a semi-public life in the Presence Chamber, for there was little or no distinction between public ceremony and his private life. But in the 1490s Henry VII obtained more privacy for himself by establishing a distinction between the Presence Chamber and the Privy Chamber, his private living and working areas; it was one of a series of administrative changes that were eventually embodied in Henry VIII's Eltham Ordinances of 1526, the model for household organization up to the Civil War and beyond. At first, the Privy Chamber covered all the private areas of the court; later, in the reign of James I, another distinction was made between it and a still more private area, the Bedchamber.[8] Naturally, the changes had implications for the architecture of the standing houses as well as the administrative structure of the court. The effect of the Eltham Ordinances, David Starkey has written, was 'to put a frontier within the palace and to establish an equally clear line of demarcation between those royal servants who could cross it and those who could not'.[9] The Presence Chamber (and other public areas of the court) was open to courtiers of all ranks, while the Privy Chamber was closed to all but its own small staff and a few individuals personally selected by the sovereign.

---

[7] Recent studies of the court structure are D. Starkey (ed.), *The English Court, from the Wars of the Roses to the Civil War* (London, 1987); id., *The Reign of Henry VIII: Personalities and Politics* (London, 1991).

[8] N. Cuddy, 'The Revival of the Entourage: The Bedchamber of James I, 1603–1625', in Starkey, *English Court*, 173–225.

[9] Starkey, *English Court*, 4.

The complex structure of the court was paralleled in miniature by the royal music. In theory all court musicians were members of the Chamber, but in practice they were grouped into a number of separate and semi-autonomous institutions, each with a distinct role in court life, its own personnel, its own repertoire, and its proper station in the palace. The Chapel Royal was the largest and oldest.[10] Dating from the twelfth century and consisting in Tudor times of twelve children and thirty-two gentlemen, it provided the sovereign with daily choral services in the chapels that were to be found in the main standing houses. It also served as a useful pool of singers for secular entertainments, ranging from pageants and disguisings in Henry VIII's reign to court odes after the Restoration. Doubtless, its members also contributed a good deal to informal music-making throughout the Tudor and Stuart period.

The secular musicians of the early Tudor court are best classified according to the medieval distinction between loud and soft: *haut* instruments were played outdoors or in large halls, while *bas* instruments were suitable for a small room.[11] The royal trumpet and drum band and the fife- and drum-players came into the *haut* category; the former presumably provided fanfares for entrances and exits on state occasions just as their successors do today, while the role of the latter in processions can also have changed little over the centuries. They were attendants rather than musicians: they played simple, monophonic music and did not belong to the section of musical society that was literate and cultivated polyphonic music. So a further distinction needs to be made between them and the other *haut* group at court. The shawm- and sackbut-players were musicians first and foremost: they were the English equivalents of the *alta capella*, the dance band of Flemish towns that consisted of two or three shawms improvising around a slow-moving cantus firmus provided by a slide trumpet or a sackbut.[12] Most of Henry VIII's shawm- and sackbut-players came from the Netherlands or Germany, which is not surprising since the arts of making and playing sets of wind instruments of several sizes had been first developed there, and were still novel in England. The number of them varied a good deal during the reign as

[10] See E. F. Rimbault (ed.), *The Old Cheque-Book or Book of Remembrance of the Chapel Royal from 1561 to 1744* (London, 1872; repr. 1966); W. L. Woodfill, *Musicians in English Society from Elizabeth to Charles I* (Princeton, NJ, 1953; repr.1969), 161–76; P. Le Huray, *Music and the Reformation in England 1549–1660* (London, 1967), 57–89; D. Baldwin, *The Chapel Royal, Ancient and Modern* (London, 1990).

[11] E. A. Bowles, '*Haut* and *Bas*: The Grouping of Musical Instruments in the Middle Ages', *MD* 8 (1954), 115–40; R. Rastall, 'Some English Consort Groupings of the Late Middle Ages', *ML* 55 (1974), 179–202.

[12] See Ch. 1 n. 15.

groups came and went, but an establishment of seven was fixed in the 1530s, which persisted for the rest of the century.[13]

Henry VIII's *bas* instrumentalists were a heterogeneous group. At the beginning of the reign they included a consort of four 'styll shalmes'.[14] Later they were succeeded by a consort of rebecs and/or flutes. Most of them, however, were solo instrumentalists, such as the lutenists Giles Dewes, Arthur Dewes, and Philip van Wilder, the famous blind harper William More, the Venetian organist Dionisius Memo, or the virginal-player Mark Smeaton, the musician who confessed to adultery with Anne Boleyn, causing their downfall.[15] They must have spent much of their time giving informal concerts—Memo played to ambassadors for four hours in the queen's chamber at Windsor one day in July 1517—but they would also have given members of the royal family music lessons. The aristocracy usually learned music by way of a plucked instrument, on which they could accompany their own singing as well as play solo music. All the Tudors were lutenists, while Henry himself, his sister Mary, and his daughters Mary and Elizabeth played the keyboard as well.[16] Henry was exceptionally musical: he may also have played the harp (he appears with one as King David in an illumination in his own psalter[17]), and he could certainly sing at sight and play ensemble instruments such as the recorder or the cornett. Until the reign of James I instrumental ensembles were largely the preserve of professionals. Amateurs lacked the more advanced skills they required, and it was still thought, in the words of Sir Thomas Elyot, 'that a gentilman, plainge or singing in a commune audience, appaireth his estimation'.[18]

It is clear, therefore, that the Eltham Ordinances did not have as drastic an effect on musicians as it had on some other classes of courtier. It established a distinction between the favoured few, who were granted entry to the Privy Chamber, and the majority who remained outside. But this distinction was already implied by the division of instruments into *haut* and *bas*, and it was largely a matter of common sense: instruments such as the lute and the virginals were best heard in a small, quiet room, while consorts of loud wind instruments were portable, could be played standing, and were loud enough to carry over the hubbub of conversation and the clatter of dishes in the Presence Chamber. The shawms and

[13] D. Lasocki, 'Professional Recorder Players in England, 1540–1740', Ph.D. diss. (University of Iowa, 1983), i. 21.

[14] See Ch. 1 n. 20.

[15] J. Stevens, *Music and Poetry in the Early Tudor Court* (2nd edn., London, 1979), 265–9, 281–2; for van Wilder, see J. M. Ward (ed.), *Music for Elizabethan Lutes* (Oxford, 1992), i. 1–6.

[16] See J. M. Ward, *A Dowland Miscellany, JLSA* 10 (1977), 112–15.

[17] Reproduced in P. Holman, 'The Harp in Stuart England: New Light on William Lawes's Harp Consorts', *EM* 15 (1987), 189.

[18] E. D. Mackerness, *A Social History of English Music* (London, 1964), 49–50.

sackbuts are described as 'of the Privee Chamber' in a document relating to Henry VIII's coronation in 1509, presumably because they accompanied dancing there, but once the Eltham Ordinances were in force the instrumental consorts were assigned to the Presence Chamber.[19] When two new groups, five recorder-playing members of the Bassano family and six string-players, arrived from Venice in 1540, they also joined the Presence Chamber. Several of their descendants, who were by then serving in the shawm and sackbut consort as well as the recorder consort, were said in 1634 to be 'of the presence Chamber', and as far as musicians were concerned the distinction between Privy Chamber and Presence Chamber only began to break down in the reign of Charles II.[20]

By and large, musicians do not appear in the lists of the Privy Chamber, and the individuals concerned can often be identified only through the use of courtesy titles. The lutenist Mathias Mason, for instance, was styled 'the Lute of the Privie Chamber' in a list of livery for Elizabeth's funeral, and 'one of the Groomes of his Majesties most honourable Privie Chamber' in Robert Dowland's *Varietie of Lute-Lessons* (London, 1610), while his colleague, the singer and lutenist Robert Hales, received the same title in Dowland's *A Musicall Banquet* (London, 1610) (see Ch. 10).[21] Many of the later Privy Chamber musicians were lutenists, though Philip van Wilder ran a group of 'singing men and children' towards the end of Henry VIII's reign (see Ch. 3). The keyboard-players in the Privy Chamber, such as Mark Smeaton and Sir Ferdinando Heybourne alias Richardson, tended to be more courtier than musician, heirs to a tradition that required the personal attendants of the medieval kings, as the 'Liber niger' of Edward IV put it, to 'kepe honest company aftyr theyre cunnynge, in talking of cronycles of King's and of polycyes, or in pypeing, or harpyng, synging, or other [or else] actes martialles, to help occupy the courte'.[22]

How were royal musicians chosen? Court posts or 'places', as they were generally called, were in theory the gift of the sovereign. In practice, such lowly appointments were initiated in three ways. A candidate might petition the king; a number of petitions from Tudor and Stuart musicians, some of them autograph documents, survive among the State Papers in the Public Record Office. He might be recommended by a courtier. Most

[19] H. C. de Lafontaine (ed.), *The King's Musick: A Transcript of Records Relating to Music and Musicians (1460–1700)* (London, 1909; repr. 1973), 4.

[20] W. C. Metcalfe (ed.), *The Visitations of Essex* (Harleian Society Publications, 13; London, 1878), 344–5.

[21] A. Ashbee (ed.), *RECM, iv: 1603–1625* (Snodland, 1991), 1.

[22] *A Collection of Ordinances and Regulations for the Government of the Royal Household* (Society of Antiquaries; London, 1790), 46; for Richardson, see R. Marlow, 'Sir Ferdinando Heybourne alias Richardson', *MT* 115 (1974), 736–9.

commonly, he would be appointed directly by the Lord Chamberlain, presumably on the advice of serving musicians. Sometimes the claims of rival candidates and their patrons led to conflict. When Alfonso Ferrabosco II died in March 1627/8 the Bishop of Bath and Wells attempted to have his place as a court composer given to Thomas Tomkins. The machinery had hardly been set in motion, however, when it was stopped with the note 'Staied and passed to another'.[23] The explanation was that Charles I, probably responding to a petition, had promised that Ferrabosco's four court posts were to be divided between his sons Henry and Alfonso III.

Like most court business, the outcome of such contests tended to depend more on family connection, influence, or chance than on the merits of the case. The instrumental consorts, in particular, employed members of the same family over large periods of time. Four generations of Lupos served in the court string consort, from 1540 until the Civil War; there were Bassanos for even longer in the wind consorts, for Henry Bassano did not die until 1665.[24] Such nepotism was unremarkable in a system founded on family interest, and in an age when professional musical skills were commonly passed down from father to son. It only became unacceptable when the candidate was unfitted for the job. The Earl of Newcastle, listing the abuses of government of Charles I's reign for the benefit of the future Charles II, wrote that 'An other Error was, & a great one, to [whit], that most officers were misplacet':

for hee that is fitt to bee B(isho)p of Canterbury Is not fitt to bee Generall, nor hee that is fitt to bee a generall, To bee Bishopp of Canterbury,—a Taylor to make shoes, & a Shoemaker, briches, this breeds a confution, & the king, & the Commonwealth ill served, this was so Comonly done as a merry Mutition [musician] that I knowe, desired the place of the kinges bagpiper, which is £50 a yeare, one told him, hee wonderd hee would desire Itt, since hee knew nothing of itt, hee sayd therefore hee Hopte to have itt, for they always gave places, to those That were moste unfitt, for them, as a Luteneste place, to one that playd of the viole, & a violest place to one that Playd of the Lute,—And so in higher offices which was our bayne, As sir Henery Vayne to bee made Secretary, that could Hardly write & reade . . .[25]

---

[23] Ashbee, *RECM*, iii: *1625–1649* (Snodland, 1988), 28–9; for the court financial structure, see W. C. Richardson, *Tudor Chamber Administration 1485–1547* (Baton Rouge, La., 1952); G. R. Elton, *The Tudor Revolution in Government* (Cambridge, 1953; repr. 1979); *Guide to the Contents of the Public Record Office*, 3 vols. (London, 1963, 1968); G. E. Aylmer, *The King's Servants: The Civil Service of Charles I 1625–1642* (2nd edn., London, 1974); P. Williams, *The Tudor Regime* (Oxford, 1973); Ashbee, *RECM*, i: *1660–1685* (Snodland, 1986), pp. ix–xv; Starkey, *English Court;* Ashbee, *RECM*, iii. pp. ix–xiii; Ashbee, *RECM*, iv. pp. ix–xix; Ashbee, *RECM*, v: *1625–1714* (Aldershot, 1991), pp. ix–xvi; Ashbee, *RECM*, vi: *1558–1603* (Aldershot, 1992), pp. vii–xv.

[24] See the chart in Lasocki, 'Professional Recorder Players', ii. 556.

[25] T. P. Slaughter (ed.), *Ideology and Politics on the Eve of Restoration: Newcastle's Advice to Charles II* (Philadelphia, 1984), 57.

Newcastle's criticisms were undoubtedly well founded in the case of 'higher offices', but there could be good reasons for giving a place formerly held by a wind-player to a string-player, as was often done in the reigns of James I and, ironically, Charles II. In 1608 the violinist Jeremy Hearne actually received the place once held by Elizabeth's bagpiper Richard Woodward, but there is no sign that he was made to play the bagpipe. Rather, it was a method of enlarging the string consort without changing the theoretical establishment of the royal music. A similar situation arose in January 1616/17 when the violinist Adam Vallet was appointed 'one of his Ma(jes)t(ie)s Music(i)ons for the Lute' as an expedient 'untill such time as he shall have the place of a Musicon in ordinary by the next vacancy'.[26] Such stratagems were frequently the only way that change, made necessary by the rise and decline of particular instruments or types of ensembles, could be effected in a bureaucracy bound head and foot by precedent and tradition. In the words of G. R. Elton, 'it had always been the habit of the government to use any available treasury for the purpose of paying expenses . . . The money in all the royal treasuries was available for any assignment on it, and choice was presumably governed by immediate convenience'.[27]

Elton's point is well illustrated by the odd way that court musicians were paid from the end of Henry VIII's reign to the accession of James II. In theory all of them were under the control of the Lord Chamberlain, and should therefore have been dealt with by the Treasury of the Chamber. In practice, some of them, including the recorder consort, received their wages directly from the Exchequer of Receipt, while others (including the string consort) were dealt with by the Treasury of the Chamber; this explains why the Bassanos rarely figure in the Lord Chamberlain's papers, until recently the main source of published information about Tudor and Stuart musicians.[28] The number of those musicians paid directly by the Exchequer gradually increased during the seventeenth century. It acquired new clients, for instance, when the Lutes and Voices was set up at the beginning of Charles I's reign; the new group combined those musicians who had belonged to his household while he was Prince of Wales with those who had worked in James I's Privy Chamber (see Ch. 10). Even those who continued to receive their wages from the Treasury of the Chamber became clients of the Exchequer when they acquired extra income in the form of annuities and pensions. The transfer of musicians from the Treasury of the Chamber to the Exchequer was partly an expedient designed to cope with the increasing size and cost of the royal household. But it was also a symptom of the

---

[26] *GB-Lpro*, SO3/6; see Ashbee, *RECM*, iv. 45.
[27] Elton, *Tudor Revolution*, 174.
[28] They are the basis of Lafontaine, *King's Musick*; *RECM* is a multi-volume revision of *The King's Musick* with material added from Exchequer documents and other sources.

decline of the Chamber as a political institution, and the corresponding rise or revival of the Exchequer. The relative importance today of the Chancellor of the Exchequer and the Lord Chamberlain shows that the process continued long after the period under discussion.

Like all royal servants, musicians were appointed to their places by means of warrants that carried the sovereign's authority in the form of one of the three royal seals. Each of them had a different function. The Great Seal of England, the oldest, was administered in Chancery under the Lord Chancellor and the Lord Keeper, and was used to give legal force to major court appointments and large grants of money or property. The Privy Seal, administered by the Clerks of the Privy Seal under the Lord Privy Seal and the Master of Requests, was smaller and more recent in origin; it was used for most legal business and, increasingly, court appointments. The Signet, the smallest and the most recent of the three, was administered by the Clerks of the Signet under the Secretaries of State. It was used for the sovereign's personal correspondence, and to authorize less important expenditure such as payments to musicians and other minor officials.

Small sums such as the payment of travel expenses and the cost of equipment for court use—including the purchase and repair of musical instruments—could be authorized directly by the Privy Council, and by prominent courtiers under their own seals. Furthermore, the sovereign could circumvent the normal channels by using the Privy Purse, kept by a prominent member of the Privy Chamber, the Groom of the Stool. It is unfortunate that Privy Purse accounts for the main royal household survive only for 1529–32, 1550–2, 1558–69, and 1603–5, for they are full of fascinating material relating to daily musical life at court. In October 1614 James I ordered that the Privy Purse be relieved of 'certain payments used of late to be made out of it', including payments for 'cornetts, lutes, violins and other instruments of music and for strings and repairing of them'; in fact, payments of this sort had begun to appear regularly in the Treasury of the Chamber accounts from 1607–8.[29] Privy Purse accounts also survive from the households of Princess Mary (1536–44), Princess Elizabeth (1551–2), Queen Anne (1604–18), Prince Henry (1608–10), and Princess Elizabeth (Michaelmas 1612 until her wedding to the Elector Palatine in February 1612/13). Secret Service accounts fulfilled a similar function after the Restoration; so far they have been traced for 1679 to 1710, though at least three earlier volumes from the series may have survived into modern times.[30]

[29] Ashbee, *RECM*, iv. 41, 81.

[30] F. Madden (ed.), *The Privy Purse Expenses of the Princess Mary* (London, 1831); P. C. S. Smythe (Viscount Strangford) (ed.), 'Household Expenses of the Princess Elizabeth during her Residence at Hatfield, October 1, 1551, to September 30, 1552', *The Camden Miscellany*, ii (Publications of the Camden Society, os 55; London, 1853); Ashbee, *RECM*, iv. 196–206, 207–8, 213–15; v. 270–8.

The procedure used for court appointments is set out in a memo-randum entitled 'The Method (and style) of issuing Instruments under the Great Seal', written most likely in December 1653.[31] A warrant was prepared by the Clerks of the Signet on behalf of the Attorney General for the sovereign's signature, the 'Royal Sign Manual', or his signature expressed in the form of a stamp. Once this was obtained, it proceeded through the system, carried from office to office by the individual himself, the 'party prosecutor'; he went from the Secretary of State to the Signet Office, back to the Secretary, then to the Privy Seal Office, and finally to Chancery:

The party prosecutor thereof came to the Secretary for it [the warrant], and himselfe carried it to the Signet office. where the Bill was transcribed, with a direc(t)c(i)on to the L(or)d Privy Seale, and the originall remaynes w(i)th the Clerke of the Signet: and the transcript was againe brought to Mr. Secretary to be sealed. And then that under Seale, was delivered to the party prosecuteing and by him delivered to the Clerke of the Privy Seale. who kept the transcript from the Signet for his warr(an)t and transcribed anew & directed it to the L(or)d Keeper and put it under the privy seale. That privy seale, the party prosecuteing tooke himselfe and carried it to the L(or)d Keepers Seale-bearer who, imediately carried it to the L(or)d Keeper, and the Lord Keeper at the bottom of the transcript under the privy seale wrote upon it thus Recepi: 2° die Decemb[e]r. Littleton This recepi, was the warrant for the date of the Pattent, and it always bore that date, according to the Act of Parliam(en)t. The party prosecuting then tooke the Privy Seale back with the Teste thus entred upon it, and delivered it to the Clerke of the Pattents in Chancery, who engrossed it for the Greate Seale.

When the process was complete, and each officer along the route had received his fee, the exhausted party prosecutor received his Letters Patent under the Great Seal—his certificate of appointment. At some point, often before the royal assent had been obtained, he would have been sworn in before the Lord Chamberlain or the Gentlemen Ushers Daily Waiters, and would have received a certificate to that effect. Samuel Pepys's experience of obtaining the post of Clerk of the Acts to the Admiralty in July 1660, recorded day by day in the *Diary*, shows that the process was slow, trying, and expensive; it cost him 'a great deale of money, about 40*l*' in fees.[32]

Musicians, particularly those paid by the Treasury of the Chamber, were often appointed by a simpler method: the Clerk of the Signet prepared, in the words of a document appointing the Restoration violinist

[31] *GB-Lpro*, SP18/42/5, printed in Aylmer, *The State's Servants: The Civil Service of the English Republic 1649–1660* (London, 1973), 436–7.

[32] *The Diary of Samuel Pepys*, i, *1660*, ed. R. Latham and W. Matthews (London, 1970), 192–9, 201.

John Singleton, a 'Warrant to prepare a bill to pass the Privy Signet, thereby authorizing the Treasurer of the Chamber' to pay fee and livery.[33] These 'warrants under the Signet' were often granted in the form known as 'warrants dormant', which allowed payments to be made at regular intervals without the authority of a new warrant. Appointments were made, also for no easily discernible reason, either for life or 'during pleasure'—that is, until the end of the current reign, when they were renewed or not, depending on circumstances.

The main virtue of this cumbersome system, or so it seems to us, was that it usually generated enough duplicate documents to compensate for the ravages of time; the most important series of documents relating to musicians in the sovereign's household are listed in Table 2.1 at the end of this chapter. Warrants were recopied at each office along the route, and must therefore have existed in several parchment or paper copies. The original warrants, with the king's signature, were kept by the Signet Office, whence a collection of them found their way into the State Paper Office, and eventually into the State Paper classes of the Public Record Office. Another copy was retained by the individual as his 'patent', his proof of appointment: on 13 July 1660 Pepys carried his home in triumph to his wife, 'at which she was overjoyed'.

Each office concerned with appointments also recorded the details of warrants in chronological order in a record or docquet book, or, in the case of Chancery, on parchment rolls. The docquet books of the Signet Office, a valuable, little-known source of information about royal musicians, survive from 1585 to the Civil War and beyond, apart for a missing volume for 1596–1603; there are also two stray volumes for 1541–3 and 1550–3.[34] The Privy Seal Office docquet books are less valuable, since they omit those transactions that were dealt with directly by the Signet Office; however, they survive for the years 1571–80 and 1601 to the Civil War and beyond, so they cover some years missing from the Signet Office series. We are fortunate that as many Signet Office and Privy Seal Office documents survive as they do, for, as a clerk in the Privy Seal office recorded in his current docquet book, on 12 January 1618/19 'The Banquetting house at Whitehall & the Records of the Signett & Privie Seale that were kept under the same, were consumed by fire'.[35]

When the appointment process was complete, the new musician would have been added to the records of either the Treasury of the Chamber or

---

[33] Ashbee, *RECM*, i. 23.

[34] In T. Dart, 'Two New Documents Relating to the Royal Music, 1584–1605', *ML* 45 (1964), 16–21, the first two Signet Office docquet books, *GB-Lpro*, SO3/1 and SO3/2, are described (using their former class-marks Ind. 6800 and Ind. 6801), though it is stated wrongly that the rest of the series is lost; they are calendared in Ashbee, *RECM*, vi.

[35] *GB-Lpro*, Ind. 6745; J. Charlton, *The Banqueting House, Whitehall* (London, 1964), 16.

the Exchequer of Receipt, first by copying his warrant into a docquet book, and then by entering his name into the monthly accounts. None of the Exchequer docquet books seems to survive, but there are many sets of its accounts; the most useful are the 'enrolments and registers of issues', starting in 1597. There are Treasury of the Chamber docquet books for 1628–44, but its accounts are scattered and incomplete in the Tudor and Stuart period: between 1509 and 1642 I have only found examples for 1509–18, 1518–21, 1525/6, 1528–31, 1538–41, 1542, 1543–4, 1545, 1547–8, 1548–9, 1552, 1555, 1586, 1593–4, 1605, 1611, and 1613. Luckily, there is an alternative from the beginning of Elizabeth's reign, when detailed copies of the Treasury of the Chamber accounts began to be made for annual audit at the Upper Exchequer, the Exchequer of Audit. A paper copy of these 'declared accounts' ('declared' because the auditing process involved them being read aloud in the Court of Exchequer) exists in the Audit Office classes of the PRO, but the years 1562–4, 1573–4, 1601–2, 1626–7, 1631–2, 1636–7, and 1640–1 are missing; a copy on parchment in the Pipe Office classes is complete, but it only goes up to 1627. Some of the information about musicians in the declared accounts was published early in this century, but it was taken from the Audit Office copy; also, most of the minor expenditure was omitted, including payments for travel expenses (which show that musicians in James I's reign sometimes acted as diplomatic couriers), and for the purchase and repair of instruments.[36]

The process of paying courtiers involved the use of several other types of document. When the individual or his representative collected his money he signed either a separate receipt or, more commonly, an entry in a receipt or acquittance book. Acquittance books are thus a useful source of autograph signatures; only two exist from the pre-Civil War Treasury of the Chamber, for 1570 and 1581–2, though there are four from the Exchequer of Receipt, for 1590–2, 1621–2, 1628–9, and 1629–32. There is also a set of acquittance books for Henrietta Maria's household for 1630–3 and 1636, and many separate receipts signed by Prince Charles's musicians survive, though they are now scattered over England and America.[37] Acquittance books are more plentiful after the Restoration.

Assignment books were used to record information necessary for the correct payment of wages. Many entries are copies of letters from courtiers to creditors authorizing them to collect future income as payment for debt. Other matters are also included, such as copies of wills

---

[36] 'Lists of the King's Musicians, from the Audit Office Declared Accounts', *MA* 1 (1909–10), 56–61, 119–24, 182–7, 249–53; *MA* 2 (1910–11), 51–5, 114–18, 174–8, 235–40; *MA* 3 (1911–12), 54–8, 110–15, 171–6, 229–34.

[37] Ashbee, *RECM*, iii. 244–51; iv. 216–30; v. 298.

and administrations (legal settlements of the estates of those who died intestate), obtained to ensure that arrears of salary were paid to the right individual; they are a valuable supplement to the few wills of musicians that have survived in the main collections of probate records. No Treasury of the Chamber assignment books have survived, but there are three from the Exchequer of Receipt, for 1621–42. There is a single petition book from the Treasury of the Chamber, for 1626–37; such documents—there must have been others—were used mainly to deal with complaints against courtiers, particularly for debt. Many establishment books, listing court places and their salaries department by department, have survived in the Public Record Office and elsewhere. They have often been used by musicologists, but they are of limited value: even when they give the names of individuals they tend to be inaccurate and out of date.

In Henry VIII's reign the medieval system of calculating wages on a daily basis was still used, though it was gradually replaced by monthly or quarterly payments. When the string consort first arrived at court in 1540 its members received 12*d.* a day, which was increased to 20*d.* at the beginning of Edward VI's reign, though the payments were actually made monthly.[38] Later recruits to the group were given amounts based on an annual sum—Alfonso Ferrabosco II received £50 a year when he joined in 1601—even though many of their colleagues still received wages based on 20*d.* a day up to the Civil War and beyond.[39] But even 20*d.* (£30. 8*s.* 4*d.* a year) was generous compared with other professional instrumentalists at the time. The London waits, for instance, the most prominent instrumental group in the capital outside the court, received less than half that in Elizabeth's reign, and waits in provincial towns often received only £2 or £3 a year.[40]

The problem with such comparisons is that they mean little unless other sources of income are taken into account: court salaries, in particular, were often just the tip of a profitable iceberg. They were always supplemented by an allowance for livery, and were frequently further increased by other benefits, including the practice of giving an individual more than one post. We have seen, for instance, that Alfonso Ferrabosco II held four places when he died in 1628, which a clerk in the Treasury of the Chamber tried, not without some difficulty, to sort out as follows:

Nb their Father enjoyed 4 places (viz) A Musitions place in g(e)n(e)rale   A Composers place   violls place [substituted for 'A Winde Instrumente(s) place'] and an Instructors place to the Prince in the Art of Musique. All [crossed out]

---

[38] *GB-Lbl*, Arundel MS 97, fo. 155ᵛ; *GB-Lpro*, E101/426/5, fo. 55ᵛ.
[39] *GB-Lpro*, E351/543, m. 73, see Ashbee, *RECM*, vi. 164.
[40] Lasocki, 'Professional Recorder Players', i. 122.

The Benefit of all which places did discend unto his sonnes by his Ma(jes)t(i)e(s) speciall grant.[41]

Ferrabosco was a special case, for he was brought up at royal expense after his father returned to Italy when he was a small child, and he enjoyed unusual royal favour throughout his career (see Ch. 9). But he was not the only pluralist, nor the most blatant: Thomas Purcell seems to have held the record with five or possibly six posts in the 1670s (see Ch. 12).

Court musicians could also expect a number of other benefits in kind or in cash. The most important was an annual black livery provided by the Great Wardrobe (which also supplied special red liveries for corona-tions). The Wardrobe, in theory part of the Chamber, had its own premises near St Paul's, its own master, and maintained its own financial records; they eventually became mixed up with the records of the Treasury of the Chamber in the Lord Chamberlain's classes of the Public Record Office. The earliest Wardrobe docquet books and account books, starting in 1549 and 1554 respectively, record the issue of livery in kind—clothing materials and a cash allowance for making it into a uniform—but in 1563 many court musicians, including the string consort, were given a cash payment of £16. 2s. 6d. instead, paid by the Treasury of the Chamber.[42] It was calculated as follows:

14 yards of camlet for a gown @ 3s. 4d. a yard:	£2.	6s.	8d.
3 yards of black velvet to guard the gown @ 16s. a yard:	£2.	8s.	0d.
1 fur of budge:	£4.	0s.	0d.
8 yards of damask for a jacket @ 10s. a yard:	£4.	0s.	0d.
3 yards of velvet for a doublet @ 16s. a yard:	£2.	8s.	0d.
8 yards of cotton to line the jacket @ 8d. a yard:		5s.	4d.
3 yards to line the doublet @ 10d. a yard:		2s.	6d.
for furring the said gown:		3s.	4d.
for making the same gown:		3s.	4d.
for making the said jacket:		2s.	0d.
for making the said doublet:		3s.	4d.[43]

In the reign of Charles I the Wardrobe began to pay some musicians in cash for livery, taking over this function altogether at the Restoration. There are acquittance books dealing with these transactions for 1628–9 and 1632–3, as well as an assignment book covering 1631 to 1642. Incidentally, it is often assumed that court musicians played during the funerals and coronations of sovereigns because they received liveries for them. They may have done so, but the issue of livery is not evidence one

---

[41] GB-Lpro, LC5/132, 3; see Ashbee, RECM, iii. 28–9.
[42] Ashbee, RECM, vi. 88
[43] Ashbee, RECM, i, p. xii.

way or the other, since it was given to most members of the Chamber; it was intended to be worn in the vast processions that were a feature of these occasions.

Another benefit enjoyed by some courtiers was the provision of 'diet' or free board at court, and the related 'bouge' or 'bouche'—bread and ale for breakfast together with firewood and candles. Before the reign of Charles I it seems that musicians on duty got their meals by sitting at the table of an official whose rank entitled him to more dishes than he could eat.[44] There are a few references to cash payments or 'board wages' instead of diet: eighteen court musicians are listed as receiving them in the early 1540s, while in 1576 'Anthonie Maria, and his fellowes, musitions' and 'Piero Guye, and his fellow (a musicio(n))' were among those who 'receive bourd wages daylie through oute the whole yere'.[45] 'The musicions' and 'The Consorte' were listed as receiving 'bord wages for their dyett' from 1 June 1603, and the violinist Richard Dorney received £30 board wages in April 1626, a sum inherited by his successor Simon Hopper in January 1641/2.[46] Dorney was a 'supernumerary musician', and was probably given board wages because his colleagues were beginning to receive diet on their own account: in July 1626 'certain of his Majesty's musicians' were given an 'allowance of five dishes at a meal and bouge of Court'.[47] But the new system evidently caused problems: the number of 'Musicons and Consorts' receiving '3 messes of 3 dishes of meate' was 'soe great that they cannot sitt together w(i)th any conveniency', according to a note written in 1627 by a clerk of the Lord Steward's department.[48] The matter was referred to the Board of Greencloth (the administrative body of the household below stairs), which ordered that the wind consorts 'be restored to their former allowance of 4 dishes of meate and that the newe Consorts for Voyces, Lutes, &c be likewise allowed a diett of 4 dishes and the Musicons a dyett of 3 dishes to be eaten sev(er)ally in their owne Chambers'.

Many court musicians also received substantial benefits in kind, in the form of New Year's gifts, leases on lands, licences to export and import goods, monopolies on goods and services, and privileges to exploit inventions. Gifts were exchanged as a matter of course between the sovereign and many of his courtiers on 1 January. It was actually a form of patronage because the gifts given by the sovereign were always more valuable than those received, especially from lowly servants such as musicians. The early Tudors gave money—the string consort received

[44] On this point, see Aylmer, *King's Servants*, 168–71.
[45] *GB-Lbl*, Lansdowne MS 2, no. 11, fos. 34ʳ–35ᵛ; Ashbee, *RECM*, vi. 35.
[46] *GB-Lpro*, LS13/168, 51; Ashbee, *RECM*, iii. 16, 114–15.
[47] Ashbee, *RECM*, iii. 19.
[48] Ibid. v. 2–3.

40s. in 1541 and £6 in 1544—while Elizabeth gave gilt plate (at first three and then five ounces each) in return for items such as 'iiii venyse glasses' (Mark Anthony Galliardello, 1579), 'a glas of swette water' (Ambrose Lupo, 1585), and 'a payre of perfumed gloves' (Peter Lupo, 1585).[49] Sometimes the gifts were musical, such as 'a box of Lute strynges' (Ambrose Lupo, 1579), or 'v songe books' (Peter 'Wolfe' [i.e. Lupo], 1579). James I continued the custom, though by then the musicians evidently found it difficult to think of novel gifts; in 1605 and 1606 they all gave the king pairs of perfumed gloves.[50] Other members of the royal family—such as Queen Anne, Prince Henry, and Princess Elizabeth—also gave royal musicians New Year's gifts on occasion, as did noblemen such as the Duke of Suffolk and the Earl of Salisbury.[51]

Land was usually bestowed on musicians in the form of leases for a specific period, often for long service or to alleviate hardship. Ambrose Lupo, for instance, was granted leases on lands to the value of £20 in 1590; he had served since 1540, and was described in the document as 'one of the eldest of her Majesty's musicians for the vials'—he died on 10 February 1590/1.[52] Ambrose also obtained a lease for one Cissel Gorge in May 1590, an interesting example of the influence that a favoured musician could exercise at court. [53] In the sixteenth century immigrant musicians at court often sought and were given licences to import and export goods, presumably because they had the contacts overseas to make good use of them. The string-player George of Cremona, for instance, was allowed to import 300 tuns of 'Gascoyne wine and Tholos woade' in July 1549, and 150 quarters of wheat in November 1573.[54] However, the granting of such licences did not necessarily mean that the holder was engaged in the trade himself: the licence was an exemption from the existing trade laws, and could be sold off profitably in portions to merchants.[55]

---

[49] *GB-Lbl*, Arundel MS 97, fo. 164ᵛ; *GB-Lbl*, Add. MS 59900, fo. 69; *US-Ws*, MS Z. d. 15; see Ashbee, *RECM*, vi. 38; *US-Ws*, MS Z. d. 16, see Ashbee, *RECM*, vi. 46.

[50] Ashbee, *RECM*, iv. 10–11, 12–13.

[51] For instance, Ashbee, *RECM*, iv. 206, 208, 213–14; HMC, *Report of the Manuscripts of the Earl of Ancaster Preserved at Grimsthorpe*, ed. S. C. Lomas, 66 (Dublin, 1907), 466; Library of Hatfield House, Accounts 6/30; see W. Edwards, 'The Sources of Elizabethan Consort Music', Ph.D. thesis (Cambridge, 1974), 36.

[52] HMC, *Calendar of the Manuscripts of the Most Hon. the Marquis of Salisbury ... Preserved at Hatfield House, Hertfordshire*, 9, iv, (London, 1892), 19; Ashbee, *RECM*, vi. 148; *GB-Lgc*, MS 1432/3, fo. 36ᵛ.

[53] *GB-Lpro*, SP38/1; Ashbee, *RECM*, vi. 53.

[54] *Calendar of the Patent Rolls Preserved in the Public Record Office. Edward VI*, iii: *1549–1551* (London, 1925), 115; J. R. Dasent (ed.), *Acts of the Privy Council of England*, NS, viii, *1571–1575* (London, 1894), 139.

[55] W. T. MacCaffrey, 'Place and Patronage in Elizabethan Politics', in S. T. Bindoff, *et al.* (eds.), *Elizabethan Government and Society: Essays Presented to Sir John Neale* (London, 1961), 120; see Lasocki, 'Professional Recorder Players', i. 126.

Under the Stuarts monopolies were evidently thought more profitable than import and export licences. The most notorious example is the monopoly given in October 1619 to Alfonso Ferrabosco and the flute-player Innocent Lanier to dredge the Thames. They received 1*d.* per ton for their trouble on the import and export of strangers' goods as well as the right to levy fines for annoyances in the river. Ferrabosco disposed of his share to William Burrell, but Lanier created havoc by meddling in the business, disrupting shipping and causing his partner enormous financial loss.[56] Another Lanier, Jerome, went in for strange inventions. In May 1643 he obtained a privilege for 'his owne Invention, in affixing of wooll, Silke and other materialle(s) upon lynnen cloth, and other substance(s) w(i)th oyle and such like Cimente(s) w(hi)ch he calleth Londrindiana being usefull and serviceable for hanging(s) and other occasions', while in February 1634/5 he received a tenth of the profit due to Captain Thorness Franke 'for the sole using and practizing of a way by him invented for the saving of fewell and lessening the annoyance of Smoke'.[57] Perhaps James Shirley had him in mind when he satirized ludicrous inventors and inventions in the antimasque of 'projectors' for his masque *The Triumph of Peace* of 1634.

A more useful patent, at least to musicians, was sought in May 1622 by Orlando Gibbons, the court violinist Adam Vallet, William Heather, founder of the Oxford music professorship, Thomas Day, Master of the Children of the Chapel Royal, and a certain John Clarke. It provided for a monopoly on 'the sole making of all strings for musicall Instrumente(s), called Venice, or Romish minikin, and Catlin-strings, for fourteene yeares; w(i)th a prohibic(i)on for importac(i)on of any such string(e)s.'[58] There must have been opposition to it, perhaps from vested interests among importers, for it is marked 'staid' in the Signet Office docquet book, and it never proceeded through the court system. Strings were clearly a problem: 'A corporac(i)on of the Society of Guttstringmakers into a body politique' was proposed in December 1634 and again in December 1637.[59] On the second occasion a petition was accompanied by covering letters from two groups of potential customers, clockmakers and musicians; the latter, represented by Thomas Day and the Master of the Music Nicholas Lanier, pointed out that 'Gutt strings are of an unavoidable use in o(u)r sev(e)rall occasions, and that they hath beene made formerly better than now they are'.

Royal musicians enjoyed a number of privileges by virtue of their status

---

[56] For an outline of the affair, see G. A. Philipps, 'Crown Musical Patronage from Elizabeth I to Charles I', *ML* 58 (1977), 35.

[57] *GB-Lpro*, SO3/10; see Ashbee, *RECM*, iii. 78, 82.

[58] *GB-Lpro*, SO3/7; see Ashbee, *RECM*, iv. 55.

[59] Ashbee, *RECM*, iii. 81; *GB-Lpro*, SP16/373 (80), I–III.

as courtiers. They were entitled to the courtesy title 'gentleman', and they were normally beyond the jurisdiction of the civil authorities, though they could be arrested by a Messenger of the Chamber on the orders of the Lord Chamberlain. Anyone arresting a court musician could themselves be arrested, as John Huquet discovered in July 1631. Huquet had been pursuing the violinist Nicholas Picart for a debt of £22. 10s. 1d. ever since February 1630/1. In May the Lord Chamberlain responded to his petitions in the normal way: after asking Stephen Nau (the composer and effective leader of the violin band) to mediate between the parties, he awarded Huquet the sum (which had now risen to £22.19s.) out of Picart's next wages. But Huquet ran out of patience, took the law into his own hands, and was apprehended with Gabriel Clinkard 'for arresting Mr. Picart'.[60] Court musicians could even have people arrested for offending them in apparently trivial ways. In September 1633 Griffin Jones was arrested 'upon the complaint of John Heydon, musition for the violins for abusive language given him as fidling rogue et(c)'.[61] Incidents of this sort often involved court musicians from immigrant families and the citizens of London, the arrogance of the one matched, it seems, by the xenophobia of the other. A violent dispute at the Royal Exchange on 6 February 1628/9 involving members of the Lanier family, a constable, and a crowd of onlookers, even led to an exchange of letters between the Privy Council and the Lord Mayor.[62]

Court musicians were supposed to be exempt from the taxes and duties imposed by the London parishes in which they mostly lived. In November 1573 the Lord Chamberlain wrote to the Lord Mayor to complain that 'Her Majesty's musicians had been lately molested with divers new payments and other charges'.[63] He pointed out that 'Being her servants in ordinary they had to attend daily upon her, for which reason they ought not to be chosen to any office, as Churchwarden, Constable, Scavenger, Watchman, nor charged with subsidies nor fifteenths'. In February 1639/40, when Ambrose Beeland joined the violin band, he was given a certificate:

expressing these previledges vizt that hee may not bee arrested or not to be chosen unto any Office, nor warned to attend at Assizes & not bee impannelled on Juryes not to be charged w(i)th any contributions Taxes or paym(en)te(s) but in Court only as other his Ma(jes)t(i)e(s) se[r]vantes: to bee free from watching & warding in regard of his nightly & late Attendance at Court.[64]

    [60] Ashbee, RECM, iii. 58, 60, 61.
    [61] GB-Lpro, LC5/132, 338; see Ashbee, RECM, iii. 72–3.
    [62] Lasocki, 'Professional Recorder Players', i. 134–7.
    [63] W. H. and H. C. Overall (eds.), Analytical Index to the Series of Records known as the Remembrancia, Preserved among the Archives of the City of London, 1579–1664 (London, 1878), 428.
    [64] GB-Lpro, LC5/133, 374; see Ashbee, RECM, iii. 103–4.

The document seems to be the only one of its kind, but similar privileges were probably enjoyed by most if not all court musicians at the time. In theory, as the certificate states, they were assessed for taxes at court. In practice, court musicians can have paid very little tax: they are among those exempted from subsidies in September 1587, November 1589, June 1593, June 1606, October 1610, April 1621, June and July 1624, December 1625, April 1626, June 1626, June and July 1628, May 1629, April and May 1641, February 1641/2 and June 1642.[65] The series of court assessment rolls (often compiled for subsidies for which courtiers were subsequently exempted) are important because they seem to give the actual state of the royal music on a particular day, not its theoretical establishment. But not many early rolls survive, many of them are damaged, and the information is sometimes not as accurate or up to date as it seems: Augustine Bassano, for instance, appears with the word 'mort' against his name in a list dated 20 March 1609/10, and indeed, he had died in October 1604.[66]

Royal musicians were exceptionally favoured by the standards of the time, particularly by comparison with their colleagues outside the court. Several of the immigrant families who arrived in England during the course of the sixteenth century—the Bassanos, Lupos, Galliardellos, and Laniers, for instance—bettered themselves to the point where they began to be assimilated into the landed gentry, and to turn away from music. The Bassanos and Lupos acquired estates in Essex and Kent respectively, and were granted coats of arms; a branch of the Galliardellos was also granted arms, and married into Staffordshire gentry. The Laniers were the most distinguished and enduring of these families. Later members included Sir John Lanier (d. 1692), governor of Jersey and a commander at the Battle of the Boyne, and the American poet and musician Sidney Lanier (1842–91).[67] A branch of the Lupo family, headed by two sons of Peter, Albanus (b. 1579) and Philip (b. 1582), settled in Virginia in the reign of James I, and still exists in the USA.[68] But the most extraordinary instance of musical talent of a specialized type persisting in a family over many generations is provided by Peter Goodwin, the present-day trombone- and sackbut-player working in London: he is a direct descendant of the sixteenth-century Bassanos through a branch of the family that moved from London to Derby in 1666.[69]

[65] Ashbee, *RECM*, vi. 49, 52, 58; Ashbee, *RECM*, iv. 13, 28–9, 53, 59–61; iii. 7, 9–10, 13–16, 18, 31–4, 44, 106, 107, 115, 116; v. 1–2.

[66] Ashbee, *RECM*, iv. 25; Lasocki, 'Professional Recorder Players', ii. 604.

[67] E. W. Parks, *Sidney Lanier, the Man, the Poet, the Critic* (Athens, Ga., 1968).

[68] Information kindly supplied by Michael D. Lupo of Dahlonega, Ga., and G. M. Lupo of Brooklyn, NY..

[69] P. Goodwin, 'Venice Preserved', *Philharmonia Year Book* (London, 1986–7), 59–63.

Yet court service did not always bring fortune and position. Many musicians, even some of the most favoured, such as Thomas Lupo I and Alfonso Ferrabosco II, found it difficult to make ends meet, presumably because they were expected to maintain a social position that was beyond their means as minor courtiers, especially when their income was in arrears. Lupo got into severe financial difficulties at the end of his life. By July 1627 Roger Nott was petitioning the Lord Chamberlain for a debt of £40, while at the same time William Heyricke was trying to obtain the large sum of £106. 13s. 4d. against Lupo's Exchequer annuity. On the 27th the unfortunate musician was forced to assign the sum to Heyricke out of future income. But a note at the bottom of the entry records that 'before he could subscribe his wife by violence kept him of[f] & would not p(er)mitt him'.[70] What happened as the result of Mrs Lupo's action is not recorded, but her husband was dead by the end of the year. It is appropriate to end this survey of the court and its financial structure with a scene of personal drama conjured up by an Exchequer assignment book, for it reminds us that our knowledge of the composers of the period and their music is founded on such seemingly humdrum archival material.

[70] Ashbee, *RECM*, iii. 24, 25, 26.

TABLE 2.1. *The most important series of court documents relating to musicians in the sovereign's household, Henry VIII to Charles I*

Treasury of the chamber

ACCOUNTS

1509–18	*GB-Lpro*, E36/215; copy: *GB-Lbl*, Add. MS 21481
1518–21	*GB-Lpro*, E36/232
1525/6	*GB-Lbl*, Egerton MS 2604, fo. 1^r
1528–31	*GB-Lpro*, E101/420/11 (*MA* 4 (1912–13), 179–83)
1538–41	*GB-Lbl*, Arundel MS 97
1542	*GB-Lbl*, Stowe MS 554
1543–4	*GB-Lbl*, Add. MS 59900
1545	*GB-Lbl*, Add. MS 27404, fos. 17–21
1547–8	*GB-Lpro*, E101/426/5; partial copy: *GB-Lpro*, E315/439 (*MA* 4. 55–6)
1548–9	*GB-Lpro*, E101/426/6 (*MA* 4. 56–7)
1552, 1555	*GB-Lpro*, E101/424/9
1586	*GB-Lbl*, Harley MS 1641
1593–4	*GB-Lbl*, Harley MS 1642
1605, 1611	*GB-Ob*, Rawlinson MS A204
1613	*GB-Ob*, Rawlinson MS A239

DOCQUET BOOKS

1628–44	*GB-Lpro*, LC5/132–5 (Ashbee, *RECM*, iii. 28–117)

ACQUITTANCE BOOKS

1570	*GB-Lpro*, E101/430/15 (Ashbee, *RECM*, vi. 101–6)
1581–2	*GB-Lbl*, Harley MS 1644 (Ashbee, *RECM*, vi. 127–34)

PETITION BOOK

1626–37	*GB-Lpro*, LC5/183 (Ashbee, *RECM*, iii. 20–91)

Great Wardrobe

ACCOUNTS (FOR LIVERY IN KIND)

1554–1640	*GB-Lpro*, LC9/52–103 (Lafontaine, *King's Musick*, 11–106, under former pressmarks Vols. 1–53)

TABLE 2.1. *Continued*

DOCQUET BOOKS (FOR LIVERY IN KIND)

1549–1642   *GB-Lpro*, LC5/49–51 (Lafontaine, *King's Musick*, 9–11, under
                 former pressmark Vol. 811; Ashbee, *RECM*, vi. 6–69;
                 iv. 5–69; iii. 6–116)

ACQUITTANCE BOOKS (FOR LIVERY IN CASH)

1628–9   *GB-Lpro*, LC9/376/iii (Ashbee, *RECM*, iii. 40–6)
1632–3   *GB-Lpro*, LC9/257 (Ashbee, *RECM*, iii. 67–75)

ASSIGNMENT BOOK (FOR LIVERY IN CASH)

1631–1642   *GB-Lpro*, LC9/340 (Ashbee, *RECM*, iii. 67–107)

Signet Office

DOCQUET BOOKS

1541–3   *GB-Lpro*, DL42/133
1550–3   *GB-Lbl*, Royal MS 18. C. XXIV
1585–96   *GB-Lpro*, SO3/1 (Ashbee, *RECM*, vi. 46–65)
1603–42   *GB-Lpro*, SO3/2–12 (Ashbee, *RECM*, iv. 4–69; iii. 6–118)

Privy Seal Office

DOCQUET BOOKS

1571–80   *GB-Lpro*, IND1/6743 (Ashbee, *RECM*, vi. 25–40)
1601–46   *GB-Lpro*, IND1/6744–9 (Ashbee, *RECM*, vi. 71, 73)

Exchequer of Receipt

ACCOUNTS

1509–1642   *GB-Lpro*, E405/82–182 (Ashbee, *RECM*, vi. 172–224)
1551   Library of the Society of Antiquaries, MS 209 (late copy)
1567–69   *GB-Lpro*, E403/858–62 (Ashbee, *RECM*, vi. 177–81)
1569–1608   *GB-Lpro*, E403/2259–91, the years 1572–3, 1574–5, 1582–3,
                 1588–9, 1592–5, 1600–1 missing (Ashbee, *RECM*,
                 vi. 181–240)

TABLE 2.1. *Continued*

| 1597–1643 | *GB-Lpro*, E403/1693–1755: copy 1598–1603: *GB-Lpro*, E403/866–75 (Ashbee, *RECM*, vi. 229–46; iv. 116–95; iii. 161–243) |

ACQUITTANCE BOOKS

1590–2	*GB-Lbl*, Add. MS 22924
1621–2	*GB-Lbl*, Add. MS 41578 (Ashbee, *RECM*, iv. 180–5)
1628–9	*GB-Lpro*, E405/543 (Ashbee, *RECM*, iii. 175–8)
1629–32	*GB-Lpro*, E407/10 (Ashbee, *RECM*, iii. 178–97)

ASSIGNMENT BOOKS

| 1621–42 | *GB-Lpro*, E406/45–8 (Ashbee, *RECM*, iv. 54–68; iii. 6–116) |

Exchequer of Audit

DECLARED ACCOUNTS

| 1558–1627 | *GB-Lpro*, E351/541–4; partial copy: *GB-Lpro*, AO1 (Ashbee, *RECM*, vi. 80–167; iv. 70–115; iii. 130–8) |
| 1627–42 | *GB-Lpro*, AO1/393/66–AO1/395/77, the years 1626–7, 1631–2, 1636–7 and 1640–1 missing (Ashbee, *RECM*, iii. 139–60) |

Privy Purse

ACCOUNTS

1529–32	*GB-Lbl*, Add. MS 20030 (N. H. Nicolas (ed.), *The Privy Purse Expenses of King Henry VIII* (London, 1827))
1550–2	*GB-Lpro*, E101/426/8
1558–69	*GB-Lbl*, Harley Roll AA23 (Ashbee, *RECM*, vi. 20)
1603–5	*GB-Lpro*, E351/2792; copy: *GB-Lpro*, AO1/2021/1 (Ashbee, *RECM*, iv. 232)

Subsidy Rolls (only those known or thought to include musicians)

| 1537 | *GB-Lpro*, E179/69/29 |
| 1542–3 | *GB-Lpro*, E179/69/35 |

TABLE 2.1. *Continued*

1543–4	*GB-Lpro*, E179/69/37
1546–7	*GB-Lpro*, E179/69/56
1547	*GB-Lpro*, E179/69/50
1549–50	*GB-Lpro*, E179/69/62
1563–4	*GB-Lpro*, E179/69/81 (Ashbee, *RECM*, vi. 12–13)
1566–7	*GB-Lpro*, E179/69/82 (Ashbee, *RECM*, vi. 15–18)
1570–1	*GB-Lpro*, E179/70/117 (Ashbee, *RECM*, vi. 22–4)
1576	*GB-Lpro*, E179/69/93 (Ashbee, *RECM*, vi. 32–4)
1590	*GB-Lpro*, E179/266/13 (Ashbee, *RECM*, vi. 53–5)
1593	*GB-Lpro*, SP46/43 (Ashbee, *RECM*, vi. 58–9)
1598	*GB-Lpro*, E179/70/107 (Ashbee, *RECM*, vi. 66–8)
1602	*GB-Lpro*, E179/70/115 (Ashbee, *RECM*, vi. 71–3)
1608	*GB-Lpro*, E179/70/122 (Ashbee, *RECM*, iv. 17–19)
1608–9	*GB-Lpro*, E179/70/121 (Ashbee, *RECM*, iv. 20–2)
1610	*GB-Lpro*, E179/70/123a (Ashbee, *RECM*, iv. 25–7)
1623–4	*GB-Lpro*, E179/67/71, E179/70/134a (Ashbee, *RECM*, iv. 59–61)
1624–5	*GB-Lpro*, E179/70/141, E179/70/135 (Ashbee, *RECM*, iv. 61–5)
1625	*GB-Lpro*, PS02/63 (Ashbee, *RECM*, v. 1–2)
1625–6?	*GB-Lpro*, E179/70/131 (Ashbee, *RECM*, iv. 65–7)
1626	*GB-Lpro*, E179/70/136 (Ashbee, *RECM*, iii. 13–15)
1628	*GB-Lpro*, E179/70/144, also undated rolls *GB-Lpro*, E179/70/145, E179/70/151 (Ashbee, *RECM*, iii. 34–9)
1640–1	*GB-Lpro*, E179/70/146; copies: E179/70/149, E179/70/150 (Ashbee, *RECM*, iii. 107–110)

New Year's Gifts Rolls (only those known or thought to include musicians)

1538/9	*US-Ws*, MS Z. d. 11
1555/6	Unknown (G. Hayes, *King's Music: An Anthology* (London, 1937), 53)
1556/7	Unknown (J. Nichols, *The Progresses and Public Processions of Queen Elizabeth* (2nd edn., London, 1823), i, pp. xxxiv–xxxv)
1558/9	*GB-Mr*, English MS 117 (Ashbee, *RECM*, vi. 2–3)
1562/3	*GB-Lpro*, C47/3/38 (Ashbee, *RECM*, vi. 11)
1563/4	*US-Ws*, MS Z. d. 12
1564/5	*US-Ws*, MS Z. d. 13 (Ashbee, *RECM*, vi. 14)
1567/8?	*GB-Lbl*, Add. MS 9772 (Ashbee, *RECM*, vi. 18)
1573/4	Unknown (Nicols, *The Progresses*, i. 380–1) (Ashbee, *RECM*, vi. 27–8)
1574/5	*US-Ws*, MS Z. d. 14; *GB-Lbl*, Sloane MS 814, fo. 9ᵛ (Ashbee, *RECM*, vi. 29)

TABLE 2.1. *Continued*

1575/6	*GB-Lbl*, Add. MS 4829 (Ashbee, *RECM*, vi. 31)
1576/7	*GB-Lpro*, C47/3/39 (Ashbee, *RECM*, vi. 36)
1577/8	Unknown (Nichols, *The Progresses*, ii. 65–91)
1578/9	*US-Ws*, MS Z. d. 15 (Ashbee, *RECM*, vi. 38)
1580/1	Library of Eton College, MS 192
1583/4	*GB-Lbl*, Egerton MS 3052
1584/5	*US-Ws*, MS Z. d. 16 (Ashbee, *RECM*, vi. 46)
1587/8	*GB-Lbl*, Add. MS 8159 (Ashbee, *RECM*, vi. 50)
1588/9	Unknown (Nichols, *The Progresses*, iii. 1–26, where it is said to be 'in the Lansdowne MSS')
1597/8	*GB-Lpro*, C47/3/40 (Ashbee, *RECM*, vi. 65–6)
1598/9	*US-Ws*, MS D. d. 17
1599/1600	Unknown (Nichols, *The Progresses*, iii. 445–67) (Ashbee, *RECM*, vi. 69–70)
1602/3	*GB-Lpro*, C47/3/41 (Ashbee, *RECM*, vi. 74)
1604/5	*GB-Lbl*, Add. MS 15649 (Ashbee, *RECM*, iv. 10–11)
1605/6	*GB-Lbl*, Add. MS 8126 (Ashbee, *RECM*, iv. 12–13)
1610/11	*GB-Lpro*, SP14/61/40

3

'Mynstrelles with Straunge Soundes'

Fiddles, Rebecs, and Viols at the Early Tudor Court

THE early history of string-playing at the English court is an obscure subject. Court documents of the fourteenth and early fifteenth centuries seem to use words such as *violour*, *vieler*, *vidulator*, *gigator*, *crowder*, and *fytheler* to describe individuals who were principally players of bowed instruments, though it is not always possible to match these words with the main types of instruments that occur in contemporary English pictures—those known today as the rebec, the vielle or fiddle, and the crowd or crwth. Furthermore, these terms, ambiguous enough to us already, tend to disappear from court documents in the course of the fifteenth century. After 'Cornuce Snayth, fiddler' died or retired in 1423 no other holder of a regular court post is identified by title as a string-player until the reign of Henry VIII, though 'a woman that singeth with a fidell' was paid 2*s.* in November 1495, and 'the Quenes fideler' received 26*s.* 8*d.* on 17 February 1496/7; Sydney Anglo also suggests that the mysterious 'corde' played at court by a servant of Edmund Arundel and a Spaniard in April and June 1501 was a crwth.[1] There was a category of three 'stringmynstrelx' in the first part of Henry VII's reign, though they could have been harpers or lutenists, who occur in court documents with increasing frequency at the period. It may be that some players of bowed stringed instruments are hidden behind the generic terms 'minstrel' or 'still minstrel', but harpers, shawm-players, and trumpeters continued to be named by their instruments, so on the face of it there was an actual decline in the use of bowed strings at the English court during the fifteenth century.

A possible explanation for this state of affairs is that, in England, as on the Continent, bowed instruments were increasingly seen as belonging to the outmoded, monophonic sphere of musical life. During the previous

---

[1] S. Anglo, 'The Court Festivals of Henry VII: A Study Based upon the Account Books of John Heron, Treasurer of the Chamber', *Bulletin of the John Rylands Library*, 43 (1960), 29, 31, 36; see also W. H. G. Flood (ed.), 'Entries Relating to Music in the English Patent Rolls of the Fifteenth Century', *MA* 4 (1912–13), 225–35; R. Rastall, 'The Minstrels of the English Royal Households, 25 Edward I–1 Henry VIII: An Inventory', *RMARC* 4 (1964), 1–41; id., 'Some English Consort Groupings'; Remnant, *English Bowed Instruments*.

two centuries polyphony, originally confined to sacred music, had gradually spread to secular song and then to instrumental music. We saw in Ch. 1 that the shawm was developed in several sizes in the fourteenth century—the crucial innovation—and was subsequently used with the slide trumpet (later, the trombone) in the *alta capella*, the polyphonic improvising dance ensemble of fifteenth-century northern European courts and towns. Later, the idea of making instruments in families of more than one size was applied to other wind instruments, so that by the end of the fifteenth century court and town minstrels were beginning to work regularly in ensembles rather than as solo or duet performers. There are also signs that bowed instruments were used in polyphonic improvising ensembles on the Continent in the second half of the fifteenth century, though they do not seem to have been made in sets of several sizes before the viol and violin appeared around 1500.

As has happened so often in England's musical history, these innovations took about a generation to cross the Channel. It is difficult to be sure when the *alta capella* first arrived at the English court, since a reference to a group of musicians in an account book is no guarantee that the individuals concerned actually made up an ensemble, or that it played polyphony. However, we can be fairly sure that the group of sackbuts and shawms that worked at court throughout Henry VII's reign was a polyphonic ensemble. Its members all had foreign-sounding names, and one of them, the Guillim who was described as 'one of the shakbusshes' when he left for Flanders in February 1495/6, had been paid 70s. in April 1492 for 'flotes with a case', which sounds like a set of instruments of different sizes.[2] An astonishing number of foreign groups visited the English court during Henry VII's reign, some of which must have been polyphonic wind ensembles. In 1506, for instance, 20s. was paid to 'the King of Castelles mynstrelles' on 20 February, £6. 13s. 4d. 'to the straunge [i.e. foreign] mynstrells that played afore the King' on the same day, and 40s. to 'v. straunge mynstrelles that pleyd affore the King' on 5 June.[3] Evidently, the policy of enlarging and improving the royal music by importing foreign instrumentalists did not begin in Henry VIII's reign, as is often thought, but was already well under way in his father's time.

By contrast, the few players of bowed stringed instruments recorded at the time in court documents seem to belong to another world. They were solo performers, not members of ensembles, and only one of them, the Spaniard who played on the 'corde', is identified as a foreigner. The woman who sang 'to a fidell' in 1495 probably used her instrument in the classic medieval manner to provide a chordal accompaniment to monophonic song. The same can be said of the musician who accompanied

---

[2] Anglo, 'The Court Festivals', 30, 27.   [3] Ibid. 40–1.

court dancing in Westminster Hall at Epiphany 1494 'with a subtyle Fedyll'; his partner played 'a small Tabret'.[4] Such performers must increasingly have seemed an anachronism at a court where a distinctive style of polyphonic secular song was being developed, and where even amateurs—including members of the royal family—were beginning to learn polyphonic solo instruments such as the lute and the keyboard.[5] The renewed popularity of bowed stringed instruments at court during Henry VIII's reign may therefore be a sign that they were at last beginning to be used for polyphony.

The first string-player to receive a regular post at the Tudor court seems to have been Thomas Evans. He first appears in the accounts for June 1514 (backdated to May) as a 'Rebeke' with the monthly wage of 6s. 8d.; he was one of three 'mynstrelle(s)' to be given livery by a warrant dated 13 November 1514; and he was one of three named 'mynstrelles of the qu(ee)nes chambre' who received a gift at the New Year 1518/19.[6] In 1516 Evans, 'one of the Kynges Mynstrelles', complained to Cardinal Wolsey that 'one Grigge', a servant of the Sheriff of London, had 'made assaute & affray' on him, and had imprisoned his servant John Davys 'without grounde or cause'.[7] His complaint came before Chancery on 5 October, but it was eventually dismissed for lack of evidence. We learn from the letter that he was Wolsey's 'dayly Orato(u)r' as well as a musician, and that he was 'but a Straunger havyng lytell acqueyntaunce with the same Cite' (of London); his name and that of his servant suggests that they were Welsh.

Evans was joined at court by a second rebec-player in 1518. John 'Saverneac' (Severnake) was described in his appointment warrant dated 23 October as 'of the p(ar)ties of Frannce oon of our mynstrelle(s) using to pley upon o(u)r Rebek', and was given 16d. a day or 40s. a month.[8] Severnake lived in the London parish of St Olave, Hart Street for most of his career in London: 'Pety John Frenchman' appears as early as 1522 in a list of those in the parish assessed for a subsidy, and in another subsidy document, undated but either from 1524–5 or 1534–5, he is listed unambiguously as 'Pety John Savernal, Frencheman'; Severnake was living in the parish in November 1535 when he and his wife Isabella were granted land that had belonged to the former monastic house of Holy Trinity, Aldgate.[9] Richard Rastall has identified him with the 'Pety John'

---

[4] J. M. Ward, 'The Maner of Dauncying', *EM* 4 (1976), 140.
[5] Id., *A Dowland Miscellany*, 112–14.
[6] *GB-Lpro*, E36/215, 325; *GB-Lpro*, E101/418/5, fo. 16ʳ; *GB-Lpro*, E36/232, fo. 26ᵛ.
[7] A. F. Hill, 'Thomas Evans', *MA* 4 (1912–13), 262.
[8] *GB-Lpro*, E101/418/12, no. 1.
[9] *GB-Lpro*, SP1/25, fo. 220ʳ; R. E. G. Kirk and E. F. Kirk (eds.), *Returns of Aliens Dwelling in the City, and Suburbs of London 1523–1571* (The Publications of the Huguenot Society of London, 10, i; Aberdeen, 1900), 14; *GB-Lpro*, C66/689/20 and E315/279/4; see M. C. Rosenfield, 'The Disposal

who was at court as early as 1504 in the service of the future Henry VIII, but this individual seems to have been another Little John—Pety John Cokeren, who was certainly at court by the beginning of 1510.[10] Severnake can be more plausibly identified with the 'pety John mynstrell' who figures in the Privy Purse accounts a number of times in 1530–2; this man was certainly a foreigner, for on one occasion he was paid 40*s*. 'for a Contrey man of his that gave the king a tree of wax at westm(inster) place'; Severnake was still called 'Petie John' as late as the New Year 1543/4, when he was one of a group of three minstrels who received a gift of £4.[11]

From 1518 to April 1521, when the surviving series of Chamber accounts are interrupted, Evans and Severnake were the only rebec-players at court, but by the time the accounts resume in the form of a single list for the regnal year 17 Henry VIII (22 April 1525 to 21 April 1526) they had been joined by a colleague.[12] John Pyrot, another Frenchman to judge from his name, is listed as receiving 40*s*. a month, the same as Severnake. At the time Evans was still getting only 6*s*. 8*d*. a month—an example of the discrepancies that tended to arise in a financial system governed by precedence or short-term administrative expedience. Evans, Severnake, and Pyrot are still listed as rebec-players when the surviving chamber accounts resume once again in October 1528, but Pyrot disappears for good after March 1528/9; he was evidently replaced by Thomas Bowman, with whom Evans shared his salary, by then 40*s*. a month.[13] Bowman is always listed as a minstrel rather than a rebec-player, but his association with Evans evidently continued: on 9 January 1531/2 the two shared a livery payment and a special reward of 40*s*. from the Privy Purse with the harper William More.[14] Evans and Bowman were still colleagues at the New Year 1540, when they shared 30*s*. under the title 'Quenes minstrelle(s)' with Andrew Newman—who is normally described in court documents as 'the wait'; another permutation, Newman, Evans, and More, received gifts at the New Year 1540/1 and 1543/4 as the Queen's minstrels.[15]

Several more rebec-players arrived at court around 1530. The Privy Purse accounts contain payments to 'grand guill(ia)m of the pryvay chambre' on five occasions between 11 March 1530/1 and 17 August

---

of the Property of Monastic Houses, with a Special Study of Holy Trinity, Aldgate', Ph.D. thesis (London, 1961), 113–14.

[10] Rastall, 'The Minstrels', 38; *GB-Lpro*, LC2/1, fo. 74[r]; *GB-Lbl*, Add. MS 21481, fo. 19[v], 22[r].

[11] Nicolas (ed.), *Privy Purse Expenses*, 52, 110, 114, 128, 147, 190, 234; *GB-Lbl*, Add. MS 59900, fo. 69[r].

[12] *GB-Lbl*, Egerton MS 2604, fo. 1[r].

[13] *GB-Lpro*, E101/420/11, fo. 1[r], 31[v], 88[v].

[14] Nicolas, *Privy Purse Expenses*, 187.

[15] *GB-Lbl*, Arundel MS 97, fo. 108[r], 161[v]; *GB-Lbl*, Add. MS 59900, fo. 68[v].

1532; on the first 20*s*. was spent on 'a Rebecke for great guilliam', while on the last 30*s*. was paid to 'graunde guilliam by the kinge(s) com(m)aundement for his surgery, when his was syke at London'; he was called Big William to distinguish him from another musician in the Privy Chamber, 'litle guill(ia)m'.[16] The two do not appear in the Chamber accounts for 1528–31, but they can probably be identified with the 'Will(ia)m Divayte' and 'Guillam De trossges' who first appear in a fragmentary list of courtiers assessed for a subsidy dated 4 November 1537; they also appear as 'minstrels' receiving 53*s*. 4*d*. each a month when the surviving Chamber accounts resume in February 1537/8.[17] Dufayt (Devaite, Duvet, Devett) and de Troches (de Trossges) are revealed as 'o(u)r fluyte(s)' when that consort is specifically identified for the first time in a livery warrant dated 10 December 1543; they continued as flute-players until de Troches died in or shortly before October 1561, when he was succeeded by Nicholas Lanier, the grandfather of the composer Nicholas Lanier; Dufayt died on 29 May 1573, when he was succeeded by Jacques Harden (James Harding).[18]

It seems, in fact, that the court rebec consort was replaced by (or was changed into) a flute consort in the 1540s. John Severnake appears as a flute-player in the 1543 list just mentioned and in many later documents; he died in 1557 in St Olave's parish, and was apparently succeeded at court by the flute-player James Foeinyart (Foniyart) by a warrant dated 31 December 1559, backdated to 30 December 1558.[19] Thomas Bowman died in October or November 1540, while Thomas Evans is last heard of in September 1544; Evans does not appear in the livery lists for Henry VIII's funeral and Edward VI's coronation in February 1546/7, and Robert Woodward replaced him by virtue of a warrant dated 8 April 1553.[20] Woodward is given as a rebec-player in a set of Chamber accounts dated 24 October 1555, though he appears in later documents just as 'musician'.[21] He served at least until Michaelmas 1599, and his post was used in 1608 as a means of enlarging the violin band, when it was given to Jeremy Hearne (see Ch. 8). The process of change from rebecs to flutes may well have started as early as the 1530s, for in the list

[16] Nicolas, *Privy Purse Expenses*, 114, 130, 141, 210, 245.

[17] *GB-Lpro*, E179/69/29; *GB-Lbl*, Arundel MS 97, fo. 3[r].

[18] *GB-Lpro*, E101/420/1, no. 5, but Princess Mary had already given 'The Flute(s)' a New Year's gift in January 1543; see Madden, *Privy Purse Expenses of the Princess Mary*, 104; 'Lists of the King's Musicians', *MA* 1 (1909–10), 59, 182–3.

[19] *GB-Lpro*, LC5/49, 90; *GB-Lpro*, LC9/52, fo. 40[r]; he is also mentioned in Library of the Society of Antiquaries, MS 209, 93; Library of the Society of Antiquaries, MS 125, fo. 24[r]; *GB-Lpro*, E101/424 (9), 134–5, 153–4, 195–6; *GB-Lpro*, E101/426/5, fo. 13[r]; *GB-Lgc*, MS 9051/1/221d; see Rosenfield, 'The Disposal', 185–6; 'Lists of the King's Musicians', *MA* 1 (1909–10), 58.

[20] *GB-Lbl*, Arundel MS 97, fo. 156[r]; *GB-Lbl*, Add. MS 59900, fo. 138[v]; *GB-Lbl*, Royal MS 18. C. xxiv, fo. 329[v].

[21] *GB-Lpro*, E101/424 (9), 195–6.

of New Year's gifts for 1538/9 mentioned above Severnake already appears with de Troches and Dufayt, not with Evans or the other string-players.

We can learn something of the role of the rebec at court from documents relating to masques and other entertainments. The accounts for the expenses of a pageant at Greenwich on 6 January 1512/13 mention two groups of musicians: six 'mynstrelle(s) w(i)t(h) strange sounde(s)', also called 'vi strange mynstrelle(s)', were placed on a stage mountain, while there was a separate group of four 'mynstrelle(s) for the dance' who were also referred to as 'the tamboryns and rebeke(s)'; a similar group of four 'mynstrelle(s)' who played 'the taborette(s) & the Rebeke(s)' is mentioned in the accounts of a court 'mummery' given a year later, at Christmas 1514.[22] There are also a number of references to rebecs in mixed ensembles with a plucked instrument, a wind instrument, or a drum. The ordinances of the Earl of Northumberland's household, compiled around 1510, lists 'Mynstralls in Houshold iii Viz. A Taberett A Luyte and a Rebecc' as if it were a standard ensemble; on 13 August 1514, a Venetian diplomat reported, dancing at court was accompanied by 'piva, una arpa, una violeta et un certo pifaretto' who 'played together very well'; as late as 10 June 1520 there was dancing in the English camp at the Field of Cloth of Gold to the sound of the 'tamburo et tuifolo et violeta', while a list of instrumentalists who played 'each in their turn' at a banquet on 23 June includes 'tamburi, violete et tuifoli'.[23] The exact identity of the *tuifolo* is open to question (*tufolo* can mean a terracotta tube or pipe), but violeta is most likely to mean a rebec at this period; the violeta of Santa Caterina de Vigri, for instance, is a small four-string rebec-like instrument (see Ch. 1). The identity of the rebec-players in the earliest of these references is more of a problem, for none was employed at court until Evans and Severnake received posts in 1514 and 1518. It is possible that, like young court musicians of later times, they spent a period serving without pay before receiving their coveted appointments. Perhaps they were among the 'alcuni puti che cantavano, et alcuni che sonavano di lauto, ribeba et arpicordo, che era una suavissima melodia' ('some boys who sang, and some who played the lute, rebec, and harpsichord, which made the sweetest melody') in front of Venetian diplomats on 7 July 1517.[24]

The rebec was evidently a mainstay of dance ensembles at the early

[22] *GB-Lpro*, E36/217, 183–5, 194.

[23] T. Percy (ed.), *The Regulations and Establishment of the Household of Henry Algernon Percy, the Fifth Earl of Northumberland, at his Castles of Wreslle and Leckonfield in Yorkshire* (London, 1770; new edn., London, 1905), 42; Marino Sanuto, *I diarii*, ed. F. Stefano *et al.*, xix (Venice, 1887), col. 190; ibid., xxix (Venice, 1890), cols. 240, 249.

[24] Sanuto, *I diarii*, xxiv (Venice, 1889), col. 541.

Ex. 3.1. Anon., 'Votre trey dowce regaunt plesaunt', bb. 1–8, *GB-Lbl*, Add. MS 5665, fo. 144ᵛ (from Stevens (ed.), *Early Tudor Songs and Carols*, no. 17)

Votre trey dowce regaunt plesaunt

Tudor court, but those ensembles need not have played polyphonic music. In the trios the plucked instrument could easily have provided a drone accompaniment to a monophonic melody played by the rebec and/or the pipe, while the rebecs in the rebec and tabor quartets recall the pairs of *gigatores* mentioned in English court documents as early as the beginning of the fourteenth century—when they are unlikely to have used polyphonic techniques.[25] Nevertheless, the art of improvising florid descants over cantus firmi, adopted by lute- and fiddle-players on the Continent during the course of the fifteenth century, had reached England by about 1500, to judge from a textless duo with the tenor incipit 'Votre trey dowce regaunt plesaunt' in the early Tudor songbook known as Ritson's manuscript, *GB-Lbl*, Add. MS 5665, fo. 144ᵛ (Ex. 3.1).[26] Its tenor, derived from Binchois's *rondeau* 'Vostre tres doulx regart plaisant', supports a florid upper part unrelated to the original chanson. Walter H. Kemp has argued that it is a written-down dance improvisation in the rhythm of a saltarello or pas de Brabant. A simpler example of the same

---

[25] Rastall, 'Some English Consort Groupings', 181, 201; see also, for instance, Bullock-Davies, *Register of Royal and Baronial Domestic Minstrels*, 37–8, 68–9.

[26] J. Stevens (ed.), *Early Tudor Songs and Carols* (MB 36; London, 1975), no. 17; W. H. Kemp, '"Votre trey dowce", a Duo for Dancing', *ML* 60 (1979), 37–44.

technique is the duple-time piece entitled 'Quene note' in an earlier English manuscript, *GB-Ob*, MS Digby 167, fo. 31[^v].[^27]

The arrival of John Pyrot and the two Williams at court between 1521 and 1530 increased the number of royal rebec-players from two to four or five. It is surely no coincidence that during the same period there was a fundamental change in the nature of the dances in fashion at the English court. Until about 1520 English courtiers seem to have danced to items from the fifteenth-century basse dance repertoire, such as the seven choreographies in Robert Coplande's translation of a lost French treatise on *The Maner of Dauncynge of Bace Daunces after the Use of Fraunce and other Places* (London, 1521), or the collection of basse dances written at about the same time on a blank leaf of a Latin dictionary now in Salisbury Cathedral Library.[^28]

The music, whether it was provided by an *alta capella* of shawms and sackbuts or *bas* instruments such as rebecs, would have consisted of a given cantus firmus played in slow notes, which controlled the steps of the dancers, around which were improvised one or more lines of florid counterpoint. Two pieces in another early Tudor songbook, the one known today as Henry VIII's Book, *GB-Lbl*, Add. MS 31922, show that this idiom was still current in England around 1515, when the manuscript is thought to have been compiled. John Ward discovered that the anonymous untitled four-part piece no. 91 has a known basse dance tenor as its cantus firmus: the melody is found in vihuela settings by Narváez and Valderrábano, and was known in England as 'The base of Spayne'.[^29] No. 78, a three-part setting of the popular Dutch tune 'T'Andernaken', is not known to have been used as a basse dance, but it uses the same idiom: the tune, in long notes in the tenor, is surrounded by florid lines made up largely of improvisation formulas (Ex. 3.2). The piece is ascribed to Henry VIII, but it is related to other Continental settings of the tune, and belongs more to the sphere of the professional instrumentalist than the courtly amateur, whether or not it is actual dance music.[^30] Perhaps the king's name became attached to it because it was associated with him in some way, rather than because he had a hand in its composition.

A new dance idiom came into England in the 1520s, perhaps as a result of the unprecedented diplomatic and social contacts with France at the time of the Field of Cloth of Gold. On the occasion mentioned above,

[^27]: Discussed and transcribed in J. Caldwell, *English Keyboard Music before the Nineteenth Century* (Oxford, 1973), 17–18.
[^28]: Ward, 'The Maner of Dauncying', 127–31, 137–9.
[^29]: Ibid. 131–6; J. Stevens (ed.), *Music at the Court of Henry VIII* (MB 18; 2nd edn., London 1969).
[^30]: For a recent account of the melody, see W. Edwards, 'The Instrumental Music of "Henry VIII's Manuscript"', *The Consort*, 34 (1978), 280–1.

Ex. 3.2. Henry VIII?, 'Taunder naken', bb. 1–7, *GB-Lbl*, Add. MS 31922, fos. 82ᵛ–84ʳ (from Stevens (ed.), *Music at the Court of Henry VIII*, no. 78)

when there was dancing in the English camp to *tamburo*, *tuifolo*, and *violeta*, a Venetian diplomat reported that Francis I brought along his *pifari* with a trombone 'who played excellently' for 'un ballo a la italiana'; on 17 June the French king performed a dance to *pifari* that was said to be 'a la ferarese'.[31] In 1520 such dances are most likely to have been examples of the pavan, which was beginning to sweep Europe; four pieces entitled 'Pavana alla ferrarese' appear in the very first printed collection to include pavans, Joan Ambrosio Dalza's *Intabulatura de lauto* (Venice, 1508), nos. 20–3. When the Emperor Charles V danced 'la pabana' with some of his courtiers at Windsor on 15 June 1522 during his second visit to England, Henry VIII sat it out because, John Ward has suggested, he was still unfamiliar with it; yet by the time Sir Thomas Elyot published *The Boke Named the Governour* in 1531 'pavions' were on the list of current dances with 'base daunsis', 'bargenettes' (bergerettes), 'turgions' (tordions), and 'roundes'.[32]

The choreography of the pavan was actually far from new. It was essentially a simplified version of the old basse dance with, for the first time, a standard sequence of steps—each cantus firmus of the old basse dance was a different length, and therefore had its own choreography. But the pavan and the other new dances differed fundamentally from the old in that they were composed rather than improvised: they were usually based on a tune in the top part or a chord-sequence in the bass rather than a cantus firmus in the tenor; they were cast in simple block chords rather than intertwining strands of counterpoint; and they were made up of short repeated strains—each component of the basse dance had usually been through-composed (or 'through-improvised'). Among the earliest collections of consort dance music in the new style are the two publications of four-part *dançeries* issued by Pierre Attaingnant in Paris in 1530, *Six galliardes et six pavanes avec treze chansons musicales a quatre parties* and *Neuf basses dances deux branles vingt et cinq pavennes avec quinze gaillardes en musique a quatre parties*, though two later manuscript collections, *D-Mbs*, Mus. MS 1503h and *GB-Lbl*, Royal Appendix MSS 59–62, appear to contain Italian repertoires from much the same period (see Ch. 1).

The English were slow to take up the new dance music. At the Field of Cloth of Gold they still danced to rebec, pipe, and tabor, and, as we have seen, mixed trios such as William More (harp), Thomas Evans (rebec), and Andrew Newman ('wait' = shawm?) were still to be found in the queen's household in the early 1540s. However, an English source

---

[31] Sanuto, *I diarii*, xxix, cols. 240, 244.

[32] Ward, 'The Maner of Dauncying', 139, 142; see also G. A. Bergenroth (ed.), *Calendar of Letters, Despatches, and State Papers, Relating to the Negotiations between England and Spain, Preserved at the Archives at Simancas and Elsewhere*, ii (London, 1866), 445.

contains what may be the earliest datable consort pavan, for its title seems to connect it with the contacts between England and the Imperial court in the early 1520s.[33] *GB-Lbl*, Royal Appendix MS 58 was started as a vocal part-book, but several sequences of instrumental music were subsequently copied into it, perhaps in the middle of the sixteenth century. A group of keyboard pieces, fos. 40–9, consists of the three famous original works, 'A hornepype' / 'hughe aston', 'My lady careys dompe', and 'the short mesure off my lady wynkfylds rownde', as well as seven dances that are clearly transcriptions of consort pieces: they are in three strict parts, they have no keyboard figuration, and the keyboard score is at times so badly aligned as to make it likely that the scribe was copying from individual parts; they seem to have been arranged for keyboard merely by leaving out the alto part (or in one case, the tenor).[34]

The pavan in question, 'the emprorse pavyn', fo. 47[r], could even have been the one that Charles V performed at Windsor in 1522; like a number of early pavans it is in triple time, and was evidently danced to a dotted semibreve beat instead of the semibreve beat of the more common duple-time pavan (Ex. 3.3). It is not clear whether the other six pieces are the work of the same composer, or even come from the same period. They seem to be in the same style, yet three of them are connected with dances in Continental publications several decades later: 'The kyngs pavyn', fos. 47[v]–48[r], is a version of the 'Pavane Lesquercarde', no. 31 of the *Tiers livre de danseries* (Paris, 1555) by Jean d'Estrées; the untitled fifth piece, fo. 48[v], is similar in outline to a branle in Gervaise's *Sixième livre de danceries* (Paris, 1559), no. 11; and the seventh piece, 'A galyard', fo. 49[v], is found in a five-part version in one of the collections published at Breslau in 1555 by Paulus and Bartholomeus Hessen. Whatever their origin, these simple dances are probably a fragment of the court repertoire, and may represent the sort of thing that the rebecs played in their heyday in the 1520s and 1530s.

When did the viol first reach England? Henry Peachum, in *A Pleasant Dispute between Coach and Sedan* (London, 1636), wrote that 'Beere and viols da gamba came into England both in one yeare in Henry the Sevenths time'.[35] For what it is worth, however, beer (strictly, fermented malt flavoured with hops) was also thought in the seventeenth century to have arrived in England in Henry VIII's reign. Sir Richard Baker, in his

---

[33] Ward, 'The Maner of Dauncying', 139, 140, 142; Caldwell, *English Keyboard Music*, 46–7.

[34] F. Dawes (ed.), *Ten Pieces by Hugh Aston and Others* (Early Keyboard Music, 1; London, 1951); the pieces are reconstructed in P. Holman (ed.), *Seven Dances from the Court of Henry VIII* (Corby, 1983), and in B. Thomas (ed.), *Six Dances from the Court of Henry VIII* (London, 1989); see also J. M. Ward, 'The Lute Music of MS Royal Appendix 58', *JAMS* 13 (1960), 117–25; id., *Music for Elizabethan Lutes*, i. 13–16.

[35] C. Monson, 'Consort Song and Verse Anthem: A Few Performance Problems', *JVGSA* 13 (1976), 4; Woodfield, *Early History of the Viol*, 206.

Ex. 3.3. Anon., 'The emporose pavyn', bb. 1–12, *GB-Lbl*, Royal App. MS 58, fo. 47ʳ (from Holman (ed.), *Seven Dances from the Court of Henry VIII*, no. 1)

Chronicle of the Kings of England (London, 1643), places the event around 1524, when 'it happened that divers things were newly brought into England, whereupon this Rhyme was made: "Turkeys, Carps, Hoppes, Piccarell, and Beer, Came into England all in one year"'.[36]

1524, as it happens, is close to the date that has been generally accepted until recently for the viol's introduction into England. In his classic study of early Tudor music John Stevens wrote that 'consorts of viols were, apparently, not fashionable in the English court until after about 1525', and that viol-players 'are scarcely mentioned, even as *professionals* in the royal household, before 1526'. Discussing the textless pieces in Henry VIII's Book, he went further: 'the generally accepted view that they are music for a consort of viols would be convincing if

[36] 'Turkey', *The Compact Edition of the Oxford English Dictionary* (London, 1979), 3435.

there was evidence that viols were popular at the English court earlier than the 1540s'.[37] The dates 1525 and 1526 seem to refer to the list of payments, already mentioned, for the regnal year 17 Henry VIII. Among the musicians listed on fo. 1[r] are two 'vialle(s)', 'hanse hossenet', and 'hanse heighorne', who received 33s. 4d. each monthly. This entry is not, however, evidence that they arrived in England in 1525 or 1526, as has been supposed, since the Chamber account books for the previous four years are lost. Nor, it seems, were Hossenet and Highorne the first people to play the viol at the English court.

Ian Woodfield has suggested that the viol was first brought to England direct from Spain by musicians of Catherine of Aragon, who was married first to Prince Arthur in 1501, and then, after Arthur's premature death, to his younger brother Henry in 1509. He cites as evidence the inventory of Henry VIII's possessions drawn up at his death in 1547, which contains the entry 'Foure Gitterons with iiii cases to them: they are caulled Spanish Vialles'; the implication drawn is that they were examples of *vihuelas de arco*—the original, single-size drone viol that was used in Spain before the instrument was developed in several sizes in Italy (see Ch.1).[38] Catherine undoubtedly brought her own musicians with her to England in 1501. At her first meeting with Prince Arthur she and her ladies 'called for their Minstrellis, and with right goodly Behaviour and Manner solaced themselves with the Disports of Dauncing'; the 'Princesse stylmynstrels at Westm(inster)' were paid 40s. on 4 December 1501, a few weeks after Catherine's marriage; and a group of 'the Quenes mynstrelle(s)', who may or may not have included Spaniards, regularly appear in the Chamber accounts during her second husband's reign.[39] It may also be that the Spaniard who 'pleyd on the corde' on 25 June 1501 was one of them, and that his 'corde' was actually a 'Spanish viol'. Crwths and Spanish viols would have demanded the same sort of technique, and probably sounded quite similar.

There are also a surprising number of later instances of bridgeless viols in England. They suggest that medieval bowed instruments and their drone techniques were not immediately and completely replaced by the new polyphonic bowed instruments. A design by Holbein for a pageant arch in honour of Anne Boleyn's entry into London in May 1533 shows a girl playing a viol-like instrument in a group of mixed voices and instru-

---

[37] Stevens, *Music and Poetry in the Early Tudor Court*, 5, 277; id., *Music at the Court of Henry VIII*, p. xix.

[38] Woodfield, *Early History*, 206–7; the musical entries in the inventory are edited in R. Russell, *The Harpsichord and Clavichord* (London, 1959), 155–60.

[39] J. Leland, *De rebus Britannicis collectanea*, ed. T. Hearn (London, 1770), 370; see Ward, 'The Maner of Dauncying', 138; Anglo, 'The Court Festivals', 37; for instance, *GB-Lbl*, Add. MS 21481, fo. 20[r], New Year's gifts for 1509/10.

ments representing Apollo and the Muses.[40] The drawing is only a sketch, but it shows clearly enough that the instrument's strings end at a string-holder, a bar fastened to the belly, as on the guitar or a fifteenth-century Spanish viol; there is no sign of a bridge or a tail-piece. A similar design is shown in more detail in an Elizabethan painting of a musician accompanying dancing, found on the back of a portrait of Sir Christopher Hatton.[41] His instrument is a guitar-like viol with no bridge or tail-piece; again, the strings are clearly fixed to a string-holder so that the player can only have accompanied dance melodies with continuous drone chords. Similar instruments are also found in a wood carving in the great hall of Buckland Abbey in Devon, executed in or around 1576 as part of Sir Richard Grenville's conversion of the former church into a private house, and in a sixteenth-century print of dancing of uncertain origin or date; in the latter the accompaniment is played by a violinist, a lutenist, and a musician playing a tenor-size viol-like instrument across his knees; the strings are attached to a bar on the belly.[42] It would be easy to dismiss this detail as an inaccuracy in the picture were it not for the fact that there appears to be a tail-piece on the violin.

There is circumstantial evidence that the viol consort was introduced to England around 1515 by members of the van Wilder family. Between December 1516 and December 1517 'mathewe Weldre mynstrell lewter' appears in the Chamber accounts, receiving 22s. 2d. a month until January 1517/18, when he is listed with the comment 'wage(s) n(ihi)l'.[43] No more is heard of him, so he must have died or left the court at that time. We know that Matthew van Wilder played the viol as well as the lute since he is described as 'the King's minstrel and player upon lutes and veoldes' in his appointment warrant dated 7 January 1516/17.[44] He is probably the same person as the 'Matthys de Wildre' who is listed as a *musette* player at the Burgundian court in 1501; in 1506 he and his fellow bagpipers Guillaume Terro (Terrou, Arroul) and Bertrand (Bartram) Brouart (Bruard) were among the musicians who accompanied Philip the Handsome on a disastrous voyage to Spain that ended when their ship was wrecked on the Dorset coast; they were subsequently entertained by Henry VII at Windsor.[45] Terro, for one, was not just a bagpiper, for he is

---

[40] Reproduced in R. Strong, *Holbein and Henry VIII* (London, 1967), pl. 6.

[41] Reproduced in J. M. Ward, 'The English Measure', *EM* 14 (1986), 15.

[42] *GB-Ob*, Douce Prints, E.2.6 (338), reproduced in Ward, 'The Maner of Dauncying', 134–5.

[43] *GB-Lpro*, E36/215, 510, 565.

[44] J. S. Brewer (ed.), rev. R. H. Brodie, *Letters and Papers, Foreign and Domestic, of the Reign of Henry VIII*, i, part 3, *1509–1513* (London, 1920; repr. 1965), p. lxv. I failed to find this document while working in *GB-Lpro*, but Andrew Ashbee identified it as E101/417/2 in a review of this book, *ML*, 75 (1994), 439–42.

[45] E. Vander Straeten, *La Musique aux Pays-Bas avant le XIXe siècle* (Brussels, 1867–88; repr. 1969), vii. 149, 152, 160–3.

listed as 'joueur de vyole du roy' in 1505; Brouart appears briefly in English court documents for 1508–9 as a minstrel.[46]

A second member of the family, Peter van Wilder, was appointed a 'mynstrell' at £10 a year in April 1519, backdated to February, though he is listed as a lutenist in most later documents; 'Peter luter and his wief', for instance, received four gilt spoons as a New Year's gift in January 1527/8.[47] Peter van Wilder seems to have been in some sort of royal service as early as 1515, for in 1544 he was said in the document making him an English denizen to have been 'the king's servant these 29 years'— that is, from about 1515; he presumably worked at court for a few years before receiving a formal appointment, and he can perhaps be identified with the *putino* who, a Venetian diplomat reported in a letter dated 19 May 1517, 'played upon the lute, better than ever was heard, to the amazement of his Majesty, who never wearies of him'.[48] We know that Peter van Wilder also played the viol as well as the lute. He appears as a viol-player, for instance, in the 1543 and 1547 livery documents already mentioned; the 1547 lists, relating to the funeral of Henry VIII and the coronation of Edward VI, are particularly important since they record the real state of the royal music at a particular moment, not what it was thought to be according to the theoretical court establishment.

Philip van Wilder, the third member of the family, is not found in a court document until the set of Chamber accounts for 1525/6, when he appears as 'phillip welder mynstrell' receiving 50s. a month; on 14 April 1526, however, he was given a licence to import 800 'barrels or tuns of pastel or woad of Toulouse and of wine of Gascony' tax-free, which suggests that he was already well established and in favour at court; he was certainly living in London by 1522, for the subsidy document already mentioned in connection with John Severnake lists 'Phyllyp of Wylde Frenssheman' as living in the same parish, St Olave, Hart Street.[49] For what it is worth, his four-part 'Fantasia con pause e senze pause' is ascribed to 'Maestro Phillipo di Fiandra chi visse circa l'Anno 1520. in Inghilterra, musico de Re Henrico octavo' (Master Philip of Flanders who lived around 1520 in England, musician of King Henry VIII) in one of Francis Tregian's scores, written probably in the second decade of

---

[46] Ibid. 170; Anglo, 'The Court Festivals', 43; *GB-Lpro*, LC2/1, fo. 125ᵛ.

[47] *GB-Lpro*, E36/232, fo. 38ʳ; *GB-Lpro*, E101/420/4.

[48] W. Page (ed.), *Letters of Denization and Acts of Naturalisation for Aliens in England 1509–1603* (The Publications of the Huguenot Society of London, 8; Lymington, 1893), 244; R. Brown (ed.), *Four Years at the Court of Henry VIII* (London, 1854), ii. 75; the original document is in Sanuto, *I diarii*, xxiv, col. 392.

[49] *GB-Lbl*, Egerton MS 2604, fo. 5ʳ; *GB-Lpro*, C66/649, m. 21; see Ward, *Music for Elizabethan Lutes*, i. 1–6; a recent biography, from secondary sources, is in J. Bernstein, 'Philip van Wilder and the Netherlandish Chanson in England', *MD* 33 (1979), 55–75.

the seventeenth century.[50] Philip van Wilder eventually became one of the most prominent court musicians of his time, teaching members of the royal family the lute and supervising music in the Privy Chamber; when he died in January 1552/3 his will was witnessed by John Severnake.[51]

At present we do not know how the three van Wilders were related to each other, but it is likely that Peter and Philip were Matthew's sons, and that Peter was the elder of the two. John Ward suggested in the article on Philip in *Grove 6* that a painting by Holbein of a lute-player at the English court around 1534–5 is his portrait; if this is so, then he was perhaps born just after 1500, since the picture shows a handsome man apparently in his early thirties. Peter was already at court in 1515, so he was probably born a few years earlier. In their grants of denization Peter and Philip were both said to have been born 'in the dominion of the Emperor', and Peter's document is more precise: he was born 'in Millom'.[52] Ward has suggested that 'Millom' is the present-day Belgian village of Millam, near Dunkirk and the village of Wylder; around 1500 this area was in the Burgundian Netherlands, and was therefore legally part of the Empire. Yet it was (and is) French-speaking, which perhaps explains why Philip was described in 1522 as a Frenchman. There are, however, some indications in the sources of Philip van Wilder's music that he, at least, may have spent some time in northern Italy. David Humphreys has drawn attention to a manuscript of a motet in Verona, a madrigal printed by Scotto in Venice in 1538, and two English sources of his music that describe him as an Italian.[53] Thus it is possible that the van Wilders' knowledge of the viol was acquired directly from the area where it was first developed as a consort instrument.

The case for associating the van Wilders with the arrival of the viol in England is made stronger by the fact that the references to it in court documents begin with an entry in the revels accounts for 1515, the year in which Peter apparently entered royal service. A pageant given before the king at Greenwich on 6 January included 'vi mynstrelle(s) w(i)t(h) straunge sounds as sag[buts] [shawms] vyolle(s) & outhers' dressed in blue and white damask, who presumably provided the music for a dance of four knights; a similar entry in the revels accounts for 4 March 1521/2 mentions 'mynstrelle(s) w(i)t(h) vyalle(s) and other Instrumente(s)'.[54]

Can we be sure that 'viol' meant then what it means to us? The word is

[50] *GB-Lbl*, Egerton MS 3665, pp. 56–7; *Philip van Wilder: Fantasia con Pause et senza Pause*, ed. P. Holman (Corby, 1983).

[51] Rosenfield, 'Disposal', 190.

[52] *GB-Lpro*, C82/750; see Ward, *Music for Elizabethan Lutes*, i. 2.

[53] D. Humphreys, 'Philip van Wilder: A Study of his Work and its Sources', *Soundings*, 9 (1979–80), 14.

[54] *GB-Lpro*, E36/217, 196; the word 'shawms', now erased, is taken from the précis of the document in Brewer, *Letters and Papers*, ii, part 2, *1513–14*, 1501; *GB-Lpro*, SP1/29, fo. 230ᵛ.

obviously a variant of *viole*, which is recorded in French long before the early sixteenth century. Rowland Wright's invaluable *Dictionnaire des instruments de musique*, for instance, cites instances of it in literature of 1318, 1394, and 1412; *vyell* is first recorded in English in 1483—in, significantly, a translation printed by Caxton of the French romance *Geoffroi de la tour l'Andri*.[55] In the fifteenth century *viole* appears to have been used as a generic word for stringed instruments—much as the root word *viola* was used in Italian—but once the viol and violin families reached France (or the French-speaking Savoy court) they were apparently distinguished in the modern way by the use of *viole* and *violon* (see Ch. 1). We cannot be sure that this is true of all the early instances of 'viol', for the word was still used occasionally in a generic sense even after 1600 (see Ch. 6). But the clerks in the Treasury of the Chamber (who would have been in frequent personal contact with court musicians, and would surely have adopted their terminology) certainly seem to have used 'rebec', 'viol', and 'violin' in the modern way from the later part of Henry VIII's reign (see Ch. 4), and there is no sign that the meanings of these words changed at any point.

It is surely no coincidence that the van Wilders and the viol arrived at the English court about the time that Henry VIII's Book was compiled, for the manuscript is the first English source to contain a sizeable amount of textless pieces, apparently intended for instruments. Some of them are English partsongs just written out, for one reason or another, without words. But there are a number of pieces, such as the Benedictus (no. 1) and 'La my' (no. 5) by Isaac, 'Fortuna desperata' (no. 2) by Busnois, and 'Alles regretz' (no. 3) and 'De tous biens plaine' (no. 36) by Hayne van Ghizeghem, that were corner-stones of the Italian repertoire of 'songs without words', a mixture of textless versions of old Franco-Flemish chansons and newer pieces in a similar idiom composed from scratch for instruments by composers in northern Italy (see Ch. 1). It has never been explained how and why Henry VIII's Book contains so much of this repertoire, though one possibility is that items were brought to England by the van Wilders, who played them on their viols. A work such as Cornish's 'Fa la sol' (no. 6), a fantasia-like exploration of a given pattern of notes, is clearly an imitation of Isaac's 'La my'.[56] Could it (and similar pieces by English composers in other sources) have been written for the van Wilders? They certainly mark the true beginning of English consort music.

Hans Hossenet (Harsenet, Arseneste) and Hans Highorne (Hichorne or 'great Hans'), the first specialist viol-players at the English court,

---

[55] *Dictionnaire* (London, 1941), 185; *The Compact Edition of the Oxford English Dictionary*, 3634.
[56] Edwards, 'Instrumental Music', 278–80.

appear to have been Dutch or German, to judge from their names. Indeed, Hossenet is given in a 1549 subsidy list for Greenwich as a 'douchman, of the vyolls of the kynges majestie'; in sixteenth-century English the word 'dutchman' meant a German as much as an inhabitant of the Netherlands.[57] It is not known exactly when they first appeared at court because of the gap in the surviving accounts between 1521 and 1525–6, but it is possible that they came to England in 1522 in the entourage of the Emperor Charles V. They may originally have formed a duet team of improvising musicians akin to the blind Flemish brothers mentioned by Tinctoris (see Ch. 1), but there are indications that they eventually made up a trio with Peter van Wilder, presumably to play written three-part viol music.

Ian Woodfield has drawn attention to a livery warrant dated 16 November 1531 for 'Petre Savage Hans Highorne and Hans Hosmust o(u)r Vyalx mynstrelle(s)'.[58] Woodfield suggests that this Peter Savage was 'possibly the first viol-player of English origin to enter the ranks of the King's "vials"', but he is not known elsewhere, so it seems that 'Savage' is merely a translation of 'Wild' or 'Wilder', and the reference is really to Peter van Wilder. The next year there is a livery payment in the Privy Purse accounts to 'iii of the vyalle(s)', though their names are not given; three unnamed 'vyalle(s)' were also given livery by warrants dated 9 December 1535 and 28 November 1538.[59] Finally, 'Hanse highehorne', 'Hanse Hasenest', and 'Peter de welder' are given together at the end of a group of eighteen musicians listed as receiving 'bourdwage(s)' in a document dealing with catering arrangements in the royal household for the regnal year 31 Henry VIII (1539–40).[60]

When the group of six viol-players arrived at court from Italy in 1540 they were referred to in the Chamber accounts as the 'newe vialle(s)', and were listed separately from the existing viol-players, the 'old vialle(s)'.[61] This may have been because Highorne, Hossenet, and Peter van Wilder were members of the Privy Chamber, while the new group belonged to the Presence Chamber, in company with the consorts of wind-players. As a lutenist and Philip's probable brother, Peter van Wilder is likely to have been a member of the Privy Chamber, though he does not seem to be described as such in contemporary documents. Hans Hossenet was also a lutenist as well as a viol-player, if he can be identified with the 'Haunce the luter' who received New Year's gifts from Princess Mary in 1542/3

---

[57] W. H. Mandy, 'Notes from the Assize Rolls and other Documents Relating to the Hundred of Blackheath', *Transactions of the Greenwich and Lewisham Antiquarian Society*, 1/5 (1913), 309.

[58] *GB-Lpro*, E101/420/1, no. 13; Woodfield, *Early History*, 207–8.

[59] Nicolas, *Privy Purse Expenses*, 260; *GB-Lpro*, E315/455, fo. 10ʳ; *GB-Lpro*, E315/456, fo. 8ᵛ.

[60] *GB-Lbl*, Add. MS 47516A, fo. 11ᵛ; see also *GB-Lbl*, Lansdowne MS 2, fo. 38ᵛ.

[61] For example, *GB-Lbl*, Add. MS 59900, fo. 69ʳ; *GB-Lpro*, E101/426/6, fo. 30ᵛ.

and 1543/4.[62] Hans Highorne is not known to have been a lutenist, but he was certainly succeeded by a member of the Privy Chamber at his death in May or June 1542: a livery warrant dated 22 May 1549 ordered that Thomas Kent be admitted 'unto the Rowme of one of oure vialle(s) which greate hans Dicessed late had whiche Rowme the sayde Thomas hathe occupied ever sithene the dicease of the said hannce'; in the Chamber accounts for October 1543 and September 1544 Kent is given as 'Page of the Kinge(s) chamb(e)r', and in the livery lists for the funeral of Henry VIII and the coronation of Edward VI he heads a group described as 'Singinge men and Children undre Philips(s)'—the group, distinct from the Chapel Royal, for which Philip van Wilder maintained six children 'belonging to the kinges previe chamber'.[63] Finally, Kent was listed in a livery warrant for December 1553 as a singer and one of the 'sewers of our Chambre'.[64]

The explanation for this complex and confusing state of affairs is probably that Kent and his colleagues fulfilled several roles in the Privy Chamber: as members of a viol consort, as singers, as lutenists, and as members of mixed ensembles of voices and viols. Philip van Wilder's own chansons survive with text, in wordless versions without text probably intended for viols, and, in a number of cases, in lute arrangements.[65] Van Wilder's 'Fantasia con pause e senza pause' is another example of the sort of refined consort music that may have been played by the 'old viols' in the Privy Chamber. It is an example of an unusual contrapuntal discipline that allows the four parts to be fitted together in two ways: with rests in imitative counterpoint, and without rests in continuous four-part harmony. The same technique was used by the French composer Pierre Moulu in a 'Missa Alma redemptoris mater', published in 1522.[66]

The 1550s saw a number of changes to the 'old viols'. Hans Hossenet died in or before December 1554, and was succeeded by Thomas Browne; Browne, like Kent, appears to have been a singer in the Privy Chamber as well as a viol-player, since he appears in the 1547 list of 'Singing Men and Children under Philips'—there is no evidence that he was a member of the Chapel Royal, as Woodfield states.[67] Thomas Kent is last heard of in Chamber accounts dated 24 October 1555, while Peter

---

[62] GB-Lbl, Royal MS 17. B. xxviii, fo. 86ᵛ, 110ʳ; see Madden, *Privy Purse Expenses of the Princess Mary*, 104, 140.

[63] GB-Lbl, Stowe MS 554, fo. 17ʳ; GB-Lpro, LC5/49, 24; GB-Lpro, Add. MS 59900, 138ᵛ–140ʳ; GB-Lpro, LC2/2, fo. 64ᵛ; GB-Lpro, LC2/3 (3), 118.

[64] GB-Lpro, LC5/49, 62.

[65] Humphreys, 'Philip van Wilder', 31–2; Ward, *Music for Elizabethan Lutes*, i. 5–6; Bernstein, 'Philip van Wilder', 68–75.

[66] G. Reese, *Music in the Renaissance* (rev. edn., New York, 1959), 277; H. M. Brown, 'Pierre Moulu', *Grove 6*.

[67] GB-Lpro, LC5/49, 70; Woodfield, *Early History*, 208–9.

van Wilder finally disappears after a livery document for the coronation of Elizabeth in January 1559 (not before he was once, perhaps erroneously, listed as a member of the flute consort); there is no sign that either of them was replaced permanently, but two livery lists dated 6 December 1555 give Innocent of Cremona in place of Kent, indicating that Innocent was briefly a member of the 'old viols' before joining the 'new viols'.[68] By the beginning of the new reign, therefore, the 'old viols' had effectively ceased to operate as a discrete group, since only Thomas Browne was still active, and he was promptly transferred to the 'new viols': in the Elizabethan Declared Accounts of the Chamber he is listed with them, and after the regnal year 5 Elizabeth (1562–3) his designation changes from 'musicion for the violles' to 'music(i)on for the violens', bringing him into line with the rest of the group; he died sometime between Lady Day and Midsummer 1582.[69]

The decline of the rebec consort and the 'old viols' in the 1540s and 1550s illustrates the profound impact that the 'new viols' had on musical life at court. The older groups were unable to compete with an organized and settled sextet of musicians who played complete sets of viols and violins. In the wider context of sixteenth-century music it illustrates the triumph of consorts made up of different sizes of a single instrumental family over older and more heterogeneous ensembles. It also demonstrates how quickly and thoroughly the violin replaced the rebec as the chief vehicle for court dance music.

[68] *GB-Lpro*, E101/424 (9), 195; *GB-Lpro*, LC2/4 (3); *GB-Lpro*, SP12/8 (10), fo. 14^r; *GB-Lpro*, LC5/49, 90, 260.
[69] Ashbee, *RECM*, vi. 84, 88, 132.

4

'Ministers of Pastime'

The String Consort 1540–1558

IN the summer of 1539 Henry VIII was once again preparing for marriage. In June the French ambassador reported that:

The King, who in some former years has been solitary and pensive, now gives himself up to amusement, going to play every night upon the Thames, with harps, chanters and all kind of music and pastime. He evidently delights now in painting and embroidery, having sent men to France, Flanders, Italy and elsewhere for masters of this art, and also for musicians and other ministers of pastime. All his people think this is a sign of his desire to marry if he should find an agreeable match.[1]

Unfortunately, Henry's 'agreeable match' turned out to be the fourth of his six wives, the boorish and philistine 'Flanders mare', Anne of Cleves; their marriage lasted for only a few months in 1540. But Henry's search for 'musicians and other ministers of pastime', evidently directed by Thomas Cromwell, had enduring consequences for English music, for it brought to England musicians whose families were to serve the Crown for over a century; the institution they founded only finally disappeared from the formal establishment of the royal household in this century.

The new musicians, it seems, were recruited not by sending men abroad, as the French report suggests, but through the English resident in Venice, Edmond Harvel. In a letter dated 4 October 1539, a single survivor from what was evidently a sizeable correspondence on the topic, Harvel informed Thomas Cromwell that he had:

well considerid yo(u)r lordships answer concerning the matter w(i)t(h) this state for the musiciens. Wherof nether of ther part nor myne hath ben movid any farther in the bessines for i[t] stands to be agenst the kinge(s) dignite to have made any farther sute for suche a trifle but rather contemne ther rusticite usid in the thing most vilely. But the minstrelle(s) of ther owne propre motion and for that ardent desire they have to visite the kinge(s) mag(es)t(i)e although they have ben denied of licence wich they have privately requirid of the duke and putting also any displeasure or damage [that] might ensue unto them aside, are dep(ar)tid

---

[1] J. Gairdner and R. H. Brodie (eds.), *Letters and Papers, Foreign and Domestic, of the Reign of Henry VIII*, xiv, part 1: *January–July 1539* (London, 1894; repr. 1965), 498.

toward Englond the first of thinstant monith w(i)t(h) al ther instrumente(s). They are iiii bretherne al excellent and estimid above al other in this cite in ther vertu. Wherby I hope they shalbe very grateful to the kinge(s) highnes & to yo(u)r lordship also deliting in good musike not vulgarly as I understand. Beside(s) it shalbe no small honor to his mag(es)t(i)e to have musike comparable to any other prince or p(e)rchance bettre & more variable. And bycause thes me(n) are pore & cowde not set forwarde(s) in so costeley a journey w(i)t(h)owt helpe off monye aswel for ther owne coste(s) as for conveyance of ther instrumente(s) & other necessaries I have deliverid the(m) clx crownes of gold, and providid beside(s) l(iv)res of credit for soche monye as they might nede by the waie that they be not destitutid to go forwards w(i)t(h)owt inpedime(n)t & discom(m)odit[y] which I have don aswel to gratefye to the kinge(s) highnes as also by the com(m)ission off Mr Knevet trusting that yo(u)r lordship will alow the thing wel for I have do(ne) it of a good minde, and to do his mag(es)t(i)e service therin whiche is my principal desire above al thinge(s).[2]

The circumstances behind Harvel's letter seem to have been as follows. Acting for Thomas Cromwell, he had recruited four brothers who were considered the finest instrumentalists in Venice. Harvel, of course, may have been exaggerating their prominence to justify his expenditure, but the doge reportedly valued their services enough to deny them the licence that they needed to leave the Republic. Harvel evidently felt that it was beneath his dignity as an English diplomat to intervene further on their behalf, but the musicians left Venice without a licence, assisted by Harvel's 160 gold crowns (£40) and letters of credit. The four brothers (a fifth was already in London) were members of the wind-playing Bassano family; they arrived in the spring of 1540, and on 6 April they were given court places as 'Alvixus, John, Antony, Jasper and Baptista de Basani, brothers in the science or art of music' at the rate of 2s. 4d. a day.[3]

A second group, a consort of six string-players, arrived from Venice soon after: in November 1540 'Alberto da Venitia, Vincenzo da Venitia, Alexandro da Mylano, Zua(ne) Maria da Cremona, Ambrose da Milano, and Romano da Milano pleyer[s] on the Vialles' were given places at the lesser rate of 12d. a day backdated to 1 May; Harvel was paid £66. 16s. 4d. that month on the orders of Thomas Cromwell 'for so muche money by him d[i]sburced and bestowed in and aboute the conveyance of certain mynstrelle(s) w(i)t(h) their Instrumente(s) of Venice to the kinge(s) highnes'.[4] This, of course, could refer to the £40 that the Bassanos were given, enlarged by expenses incurred after Harvel had written to Cromwell, but it is more likely to have been intended for the string-

[2] *GB-Lpro*, SP1/153, fo. 215^{r–v}.
[3] *GB-Lpro*, C/66/690, m. 38; see Lasocki, 'Professional Recorder Players', i. 24, 30.
[4] *GB-Lbl*, Arundel MS 97, fos. 131^r, 155^v.

players; after all, £66. 16s. 4d. for six musicians is roughly in proportion to £40 for four. We shall see, too, that at least one of the Milanese musicians was resident in Venice before coming to England, so it is likely that all six set out for England from Venice as a group.

By 1540 ensembles made up wholly or principally of different sizes of a single type of instrument were well established at the English court, as they were elsewhere in Europe. Groups of shawms and sackbuts (often called just 'sackbuts' in court documents) had been employed there since the late fifteenth century.[5] There was a group of 'styll shawms' (most likely, a type of soft shawm with a cylindrical bore, called douçaine in French) at the beginning of Henry VIII's reign, but by the end of the reign *bas* wind instruments were represented by a flute consort, some of whose members had once played the rebec (see Ch. 3).[6] The groups who arrived in 1540 did not, therefore, introduce the skills of consort playing to the English court. Nor were they the first to come from abroad, for throughout the reign most of the ensemble instrumentalists had foreign-sounding names, and some of them, such as John Severnake, the van Wilder family, and Hans Hossenet, are known to have come from abroad. In 1540 most of the court instrumentalists, particularly in the main ensembles (the trumpet band apart), seem to have been immigrants.

Significantly, the Englishmen, such as the lutenist Arthur Dewes, the harpist William More, and the virginal-player John Heywood, tended to play solo instruments, for the skills required for playing in polyphonic consorts had been developed abroad, and took a while to filter through to native musicians. Those who came in 1540 seem to have been chosen for their ability to improve musical standards at the English court, and to provide it with novel instrumental sounds. The Bassanos, Harvel emphasized to Cromwell, were 'esteemed above all others' in Venice, and could provide Henry with music 'comparable to any other prince or perchance better and more variable [varied]'. They were employed in England as a recorder consort, but they brought 'all their instruments' with them, and later became famous throughout Europe for making many types of consort instruments, including cornetts, crumhorns, flutes, shawms, viols, and lutes of different sizes, as well as recorders.[7] The viol had been played at the English court since about 1515, but there had never been more than three or four players at a time, and they were

[5] Lasocki, 'Professional Recorder Players', i. 21.

[6] See Ch. 1 n. 20; Lafontaine, *The King's Musick*, 4.

[7] D. Lasocki, 'The Anglo-Venetian Bassano Family as Instrument Makers and Repairers', *GSJ* 38 (1985), 112–32; G. M. Ongaro, 'Sixteenth-Century Venetian Wind Instrument Makers and their Clients', *EM* 13 (1985), 391–7; D. Lasocki, 'The Bassanos: Anglo-Venetian and Venetian', *EM* 14 (1986), 558–60; M. Lyndon-Jones, 'The Bassano/HIE(RO).S./!!/ Venice Discussion', *FoMRHI Quarterly*, 47 (April 1987), 55–61; B. Kenyon de Pascual, 'Bassano Instruments in Spain?', *GSJ* 40 (1987), 74–5.

evidently no match for an established six-man consort that presumably imported the latest Italian music, playing techniques, and instruments— including, it seems, the violin.

Little is known about Albert of Venice and his companions before they came to England. Their names suggest that they were recruited from Milan and Cremona as well as Venice, but Ambrose of Milan, for one, had evidently lived in Venice for a period before coming to England: when he was granted an augmentation of his coat of arms towards the end of his life he was described as 'Ambrose Lupus' (the family tended to use the surname 'Lupo' in England), the son of Baptist from 'Castello maiori' and 'Busto in Normandy, in the republic of Malan'.[8] 'Castello maiori' is possibly the main part of the Venetian district of Castello (as opposed to the island of Castello), and 'Busto' is perhaps the town of Busto Arsizio, north-west of Milan; it is certainly not in Normandy, though Milan was held several times by the French in the early sixteenth century. Ambrose's two sons Peter and Joseph were said to have been born in Venice, the former in a subsidy return of 1571, the latter in the document of 1600–1 making him an English subject; they both worked in Antwerp before coming to London, joining the musicians' guild there on 17 January 1555 and 20 August 1557, when they were said respectively to be 'Venetiaen' and 'Ambrosiussoone, geboren tot Venegien'.[9] If Peter was at least 20 in 1555 he would have been born in or before 1535, thus the Lupos may have lived in Venice for five years or more before moving to England.

Until recently it was assumed that the members of Henry VIII's string consort were natives of the area in northern Italy bounded by Turin in the west and Venice in the east, that is associated with the early development of the viol and the violin. But it seems that they were not native Italians at all, though Ambrose, to judge from his Milanese first name, was born in that city. On 26 April 1542 four of them, 'albertin(o) de Venysian', 'alexandri(no) de mylano', 'Joheni Maria de Cremona', and 'ambrosin(o) de myllano', witnessed the will of the former court musician who was normally known just as John Anthony or John de Antonia; he first appears as one of the sackbut-players in the list of Treasury of the Chamber wages for the regnal year 17 Henry VIII (1525–6), and he served at least until April 1531, when the surviving Chamber accounts cease once again; he was apparently the 'Antony the Sagbut' who was paid 53s. 4d. from the Privy Purse in November 1531 for 'his coste(s) going to Southampton w(i)t(h) the new sagbutte(s)', though he had

---

[8] W. H. Rylands (ed.), *Grantees of Arms Named in Docquets and Patents to the End of the Seventeenth Century* (Harleian Society Publications, 66; London, 1915), 160.

[9] Kirk and Kirk, *Returns of Aliens*, i. 451; W. Page, *Letters of Denization*, 158; G. Spiessens, 'Geschiedenis van de gilde van de Antwerpse spellieden (Deel 1: xvide eeuw)', *RBM* 22 (1968), 33.

evidently retired by the time the accounts resume in February 1537/8.[10] John Anthony, who lived and died in the London parish of All Hallows, Barking by the Tower, was said in his will to be 'de Castello'—evidently the Venetian district again—which explains why four of the string-players from Venice witnessed his will, and why he went down to Southampton with the new sackbuts in 1531, for they too were from Venice: a Privy Purse payment for 20 September 1531 reveals the names of three of them as 'loyes de Jeronom', 'Jasp(er) de Jeronimo', and 'John de Jeronimo'; David Lasocki has argued that they should be identified with three of the Bassano brothers, whose father's name was Jeronimo, and that they worked in England for a while in the early 1530s before settling for good in 1540.[11]

The crucial part of John Anthony's probate record is not the will itself, but the entry, made two days later, in the probate act book: it records the dead man's name as 'Anthonii Moyses' and Ambrose as 'Ambrosius deolmaleyex'; we have Roger Prior to thank for unravelling these names to reveal that they and their bearers were Jewish.[12] 'Anthony Moyses' is easy enough: according to a style common among Jews at the time it merely means 'Anthony the son of Moses'. The extraordinary name 'deolmaleyex', however, seems to be an inadequate attempt by an English clerk to render the name 'de Olmaliach' or 'de Almaliach'; Dr Prior points out that 'Almaliach' is a form of the Sephardic name 'Elmaleh'. Like other Sephardic Jews, members of this family would have dispersed from Spain to other parts of the Mediterranean during the Expulsion of the Jews under Ferdinand and Isabella in the 1490s. 'Lupo', the Italian form of the German 'Wolf' and the Spanish and Portugese 'Lopez', was a surname frequently adopted by Jews in Gentile society; it must have appealed to them as a suitably ironic name for a persecuted people who were often likened to wolves in the mythology of the time.

Another early member of the string consort with a hidden Jewish name is Francis of Venice, who joined the group in November 1543. In one set of documents, Chamber accounts for 1547–8, he is listed as 'Francisco Kellimo de vicentia', which may mean that he had connections with Vicenza as well as Venice; in others he is described variously as 'Fraunces Kennythe', 'Francis Kennyt', and 'Francis Kener'.[13] Roger Prior has argued that 'Kellimo' is an Italian form of the Hebrew *kelim*, which

[10] GB-Lgc, MS 9171/11, fo. 73ᵛ; GB-Lbl, Egerton MS 2604, fo. 1; Nicolas, *Privy Purse Expenses of King Henry the Eighth*, 174; GB-Lbl, Arundel MS 97, fo. 3ʳ.

[11] Nicolas, *Privy Purse Expenses*, 165; Lasocki, 'Professional Recorder Players', i. 23–4.

[12] GB-Lgc, MS 9168/9, fo. 223ᵛ; R. Prior, 'Jewish Musicians at the Tudor Court', *MQ* 69 (1983), 253–65; id., 'A Second Jewish Community in Tudor London', *Jewish Historical Studies (Transactions of the Jewish Historical Society of England)*, 31 (1988–90), 137–52.

[13] GB-Lpro, E101/426/5, fo. 55ᵛ; Kirk and Kirk, *Returns of Aliens*, i. 358; GB-Lgc, MS 1432/2; see Prior, 'A Second Jewish Community', 142–3.

can mean both a musical instrument and the voice of the *chazzan*, the synagogue cantor, while 'Kener' is a variant of *kinnor*, the Hebrew for a stringed instrument; 'Kennythe' or 'Kennyt' may be a version of *kinot*, another musical word in Hebrew, meaning 'lamentations'. Like the Lupos, Francis seems to have used a Gentile surname on occasion, since he is listed in a subsidy document of 1583 as 'Fraunces Hithcoke Italien Musitien'.[14] 'Hithcoke' seems merely to be a variant of the English name Hitchcock. Francis lived and died in the same London parish, St Alphage within Cripplegate (later called St Alphage, London Wall), as Ambrose Lupo, and may have shared the house that the latter rented from the parish from 1564 until his death in 1591, for they are listed together as 'Fraunces Francisco and Ambrose Luke musicions', 'ii of her Majestes musicions' in the entries for the parish in a subsidy document of 1582–3.[15]

It is not hard to find Jewish connections for other early members of the string consort. One of the most revealing concerns Mark Anthony Galliardello, who joined in 1545 and served until his death in 1585; in one document he is said to be 'de Bressa' (of Brescia), and he was apparently related to the 'Franchisco Galliaerdel' who was said to be 'Jacobssoone, geboren van Bressa' when he joined the Antwerp musicians guild on 20 August 1557.[16] For much of his time in England Mark Anthony seems to have shared a house in the London parish of Holy Trinity, Minories with his fellow royal musician Anthony Mary, who served in the sackbut consort from March 1538/9 until his death in 1572; in a 1568 subsidy document, for instance, they are listed as 'Markentonye Galliandine and Anthonye Maria, born in Italie, ii of the Quenenes musisions' living in the Minories.[17] Anthony Mary was also a Jew from Italy: he is described variously as a Venetian and 'de Tarinso' (possibly a version of 'de Tarviso', from Treviso); he appears in a 1571 subsidy document as 'Anthonye Maria, alias Cuson, one of the Quenes Ma(jes)ties musicians, borne in Venys'; and in his nuncupative will, made on 20 September 1572 and proved on 9 October, he is described as 'Anthonie Maria al(ia)s Cossin of the Minories'. 'Cuson' and 'Cossin' are just variants of the Ashkenazi name 'Gershon' or 'Curzon'.[18] In his will, which was witnessed by Ambrose Lupo, Anthony Mary 'gave and bequeathed the lease of his house wherin he dwelte at the tyme of his

[14] Kirk and Kirk, *Returns of Aliens*, ii. 316.

[15] *GB-Lgc*, MSS 1432/2, 1432/3, churchwardens accounts; Kirk and Kirk, *Returns of Aliens*, ii. 268; Prior, 'A Second Jewish Community', 143–4, argues that the form 'Luke' or 'Lux' is an indication that Ambrose was a native of Łuck or Lutsk in the Ukraine, but the family was apparently Sephardic rather than Ashkenazic, so it is likely to be a simple mistake for 'Lupe' or 'Lupo'.

[16] *GB-Lpro*, E101/426/5, fo. 55ᵛ; Spiessens, 'Geschiedenis van de gilde', 33.

[17] *GB-Lbl*, Arundel MS 97, fo. 65ᵛ; Ashbee, *RECM*, vi. 109. Kirk and Kirk, *Returns of Aliens*, iii. 422.

[18] Prior, 'Jewish Musicians', 256; Kirk and Kirk, *Returns of Aliens*, ii. 127; *GB-Lgc*, MS 9051/4, fo. 19ʳ⁻ᵛ.

deathe unto Mr Marke Antonio Galiardelo his frende'. 'Galliardello', with its echoes of the Italian *gagliarda* and the French *gaillard*, sounds like another example of a surname invented by Jews for the benefit of Gentile society.

The most important passage of Anthony Mary's will is the clause in which he left the residue of his estate to 'his brother Franncisco Alberties children to be devided amongste them at the discretion of Mr Marke Antonio', who is named sole executor. Given that the families of immigrant musicians frequently intermarried, and that the word 'brother' could include brothers-in-law, 'Franncisco Alberties' may refer to Francis of Venice and may mean 'Francis the son of Albert'; Francis of Venice certainly seems to be the 'Frannce(s) Albert Myllyner' who was promised 'the chief and first standing place at the court to himself', and the 'Frau(n)ce(s) Albert' who was granted a licence to export 400 tons of beer tax-free by warrants dated 20 January 1541/2 and 25 July 1542, for Francis duly received his place in the string consort in November 1543.[19] 'Milliner' at the time meant a native of Milan as much if not more than a vendor of the sort of garments that were made there, so it may be that the Kellim family, like the Lupos, had connections with Milan as well as Venice. If Albert of Venice could be shown conclusively to be Francis's father and a Kellim it would make it more likely that the whole string consort was Jewish, for his name always appears first in the lists of the group during his lifetime, suggesting that he was its leader or senior member.

At present there is no direct evidence that the Cremonese members of the string consort were Jewish. But one of them, George of Cremona, who arrived at court in the company of Mark Anthony Galliardello in 1545, is given in documents a number of times in the late 1540s and early 1550s as 'George de Combre', and on two occasions as 'George de Combre of Cremond'. [20] The word 'Combre', Roger Prior suggests, is a simple contraction of Coimbra, the Portuguese city; his family may therefore have made the same journey—from the Iberian peninsula to Italy and then to England—as the other Sephardic Jews in the string consort. Later, 'de Combre' or 'de Cremona' was anglicized to 'Comey', though its range of variants, including 'Comyn', 'Coomin', 'Conne', 'Come', and 'Comer', suggests that there was uncertainty as to exactly what form the name should take; as late as 1607–8 a subsidy document gave George's nephew as 'Anthonie Combre'.[21]

---

[19] *GB-Lpro*, DL42/133, fos. 89^r, 149^r; *GB-Lbl*, Add. 59900, fo. 87^v.

[20] For instance, *GB-Lpro*, E101/429/9, 137, 154, 196; *GB-Lpro*, E101/426/5, fo. 13^v; *GB-Lpro*, E179/69/62; Library of the Society of Antiquaries, MS 209, 94; *GB-Lpro*, E101/426/5, fos. 50^v, 56^r.

[21] Prior, 'Jewish Musicians', 258; Ashbee, *RECM*, iv. 20.

TABLE 4.1. *The founding families of the string consort: a possible reconstruction*

De Almaliach/Lupo of Milan

Baptist ┬── Ambrose ┬── Peter ────── Thomas II
      ├--- Romano └── Joseph ┬── Thomas I ──── Theophilus
      └--- Alexander   └── Horatio

Kellim/of Venice/Hitchcock

    ----┬--- Albert -------- Francis
       ├--- Paul
       └--- Vincent

Comey/of Combre (Coimbra)/of Cremona

    John Maria ----┬── George
                 └── Innocent ── Anthony ── Richard

Galliardello/of Brescia

Jacob ──┬--- Mark Anthony ── Caesar
       ├--- Paul
       └── (Francis, Antwerp musician)

-- = conjectural relationship

It is not possible at present to work out all the family relationships of the early members of the string consort because few parish records exist from before Elizabeth's reign, but it may be that all of them were members of just four families, Kellim of Venice, De Almaliach alias Lupo of Milan, Comey of Coimbra and Cremona, and Galliardello of Brescia; Table 4.1 is a tentative reconstruction of their family relationships. As migrants from Spain and Portugal to Italy during the 1490s, they could well have been among those who were responsible for introducing the viol to Italy, for the instrument seems to have travelled the same route at about the same time.

The six original members of the string consort apparently served without interruption for two years, from May 1540 to May 1542, when Romano of Milan is said in the Chamber accounts to have died; the next month, instead of recording the usual wages of 31*s.* for the rest of the group, the clerk wrote 'n(ihi)l They be gon in to their Contrey' against their names; nothing more is heard of them until they were reappointed without explanation at the same rate by a warrant dated 23 February 1543/4 backdated to 1 November 1543, with Francis of Venice and Paul of Venice replacing Romano and John Maria of Cremona.[22]

[22] *GB-Lbl*, Stowe MS 554, fos. 13ᵛ, 15ᵛ; *GB-Lbl*, Add. MS 59900, fo. 87ᵛ.

Why did they leave England so soon after arriving? Roger Prior has connected it with an incident in the winter of 1541–2 when, according to a dispatch by the Imperial ambassador Eustace Chapuys dated 29 January 1541/2, Henry VIII had 'lately ordered the arrest and imprisonment of the new Christians [converted Jews] who came from Portugal'. Chapuys added the enigmatic comment that 'most likely, however well they may sing, they will not be able to fly away from their cages without leaving part of their feathers behind'.[23] According to Prior's persuasive interpretation of the affair, Chapuys alluded to singing birds because those in prison included the string consort, who were released earlier than their fellow 'new Christians', and were allowed to leave the country until the affair died down; he also suggests that John Anthony and Romano of Milan died in prison, that the four members of the string consort witnessed John Anthony's will because they were in prison with him, and that Ambrose 'deliberately chose, at this moment of crisis, to identify himself and his deceased friend as Jews', perhaps because his Jewishness had become common knowledge and he felt that he had nothing to lose.

The Tudors seem to have encouraged Jewish musicians to settle in England. David Lasocki and Roger Prior have identified a number of other possible Jews among the court instrumentalists in addition to those already mentioned, including the Bassano family, the recorder-player William Daman, the Spanish lutenist Anthony Conti (de County), and the sackbut-players Mark Anthony Petala, Edward Petala, Peregrine Simon alias De Maion, and Anthony Simon.[24] Prior has suggested that Henry VIII encouraged them at a time when England was still theoretically closed to Jews because it was realized at an early stage in the English Reformation that Jews would make reliable servants: 'they owed loyalty neither to the Pope nor to Luther'. But some of them—Peregrine Simon and John Anthony, for instance—were already in England in the 1520s, so religion cannot have been the only motive. Jews have been renowned for their musical skills for centuries, and in the sixteenth century their network of extended families, often spread between several countries, made them the ideal people to supply European courts with the personnel for instrumental consorts. The example of the Bassanos also suggests that Jewish craftsmanship contributed not a little to the development of instrument-making in northern Europe.

[23] Prior, 'Jewish Musicians', 259–62; P. de Gayangos (ed.), *Calendar of Letters, Despatches, and State Papers, Relating to the Negotiations between England and Spain, Preserved at the Archives of Simancas, Vienna, Brussels, and Elsewhere*, vi, part 1 (London, 1890), 467; see also C. Roth, 'The Middle Period of Anglo-Jewish History (1290–1655) Reconsidered', *Transactions of the Jewish Historical Society of England*, 19 (1960), 6–7; id., A *History of the Jews in England* (3rd edn., Oxford, 1964; repr. 1978), 138.

[24] Lasocki, 'Professional Recorder Players', ii. 545–55, 584–91; Prior, 'Jewish Musicians'.

For their part, Jewish musicians were probably attracted to England as a place of refuge, safe from the Inquisition. England offered them a life of relative security, provided they were prepared to conform to the established religion. Whatever the motives on both sides, the Protestant state and its Jewish-Italian servants evidently developed a relationship of mutual benefit, for it endured in some cases over three or four generations, and was not noticeably disrupted when Catholicism briefly returned during the reign of Queen Mary, or in 1609, when there was another attempt to expel Jews from England.

The main change to the personnel of the string consort before the reign of Elizabeth came in 1545. On 1 May of that year 'Mark Antonye Gayiardell and George Decombe vialline(s)' were appointed in place of Alexander of Milan and Paul of Venice, who are last heard of when the sequence of surviving Chamber accounts is interrupted after September 1544; Mark Anthony is known to have been in France around 1542 in the service of the Cardinal of Lorraine, and it was said in the 1571 subsidy document that he had been 'borne in Italie' and had been 'sent for by Kinge Henrye theight'—an example, perhaps, of an international Jewish family network in action.[25]

Their appointment document seems to be the earliest instance of the word 'violin' in English, though there is no reason to think that the instrument arrived in England for the first time in 1545, or that Mark Anthony and George were more associated with it than their colleagues. Mark Anthony sold 'a case of violles' to the court in November 1550, and George is sometimes listed as a viol-player; furthermore, in documents of 1550–2 the whole group is described variously as 'violen players', 'violeites', 'violons', and 'violans'.[26] Most likely, the six original members of the group brought complete sets of viols and violins with them when they came to England in 1540, the former to be used for contrapuntal music, the latter for dance music. The viols in question may have been the 'chest collored redde with vi Vialles havinge the Kinges Armes' listed in the inventory of Henry VIII's possessions taken after his death in 1547; no violins are mentioned in the document, perhaps because the instruments used by the group remained their own property.[27]

We saw in Ch. 3 that the work 'viol' was apparently used in its modern sense from the time the instrument first appeared at the English court. Can the same be said of 'violin'—and its variants 'violen', 'violan', and 'violon'? It is reassuring to find that informed writers, such as the clerks

[25] *GB-Lpro*, SP4/1, no. 57; Prunières, 'La Musique de la chambre', 245; Kirk and Kirk, *Returns of Aliens*, ii. 127.
[26] Dasent, *Acts of the Privy Council*, 160; for example, *GB-Lpro*, LC5/49, 120; Dasent, *Acts of the Privy Council*, 127, 130, 474; Smythe, 'Household Expenses of the Princess Elizabeth', 38.
[27] Russell, *Harpsichord and Clavichord*, 158.

of the Treasury of the Chamber (who would have been in regular personal contact with court musicians), distinguished the violin from the viol much as we do today. By a warrant dated 31 October 1563, for instance, the Signet Office instructed the Treasury of the Chamber to pay 'Fran(ces)co de Venetia one of o(u)r vyolons, for a set of vyalls by him sold to us the sum of fiftene pounds'.[28] The variant forms of 'violin' appear to have little significance except to reflect a genuine uncertainty as to which foreign form of the root word *viola* to adopt. 'Violon' clearly comes directly from the French word *violon*, while 'violen' and 'violin' probably derive from the Italian *violino*. But, in any case, the written forms probably sounded more or less the same if, like 'pavan' (which had a similar range of written forms at the time), sixteenth-century pronunciation emphasized the first syllable.[29] 'Violeite' or 'violette', a rare form in English, presumably comes from the Italian *violetta*, an alternative to *violino* as a diminutive for *viola*. *Violetta* was used at the time in opposition to the augmentative *violone* to distinguish the violin family from the viols (see Ch. 1).

At the beginning of Edward VI's reign the string consort was re-appointed at the higher rate of 20*d*. a day, which remained a common wage for violinists and other court musicians until the Civil War and even beyond, though it was often rounded down to £30 a year. There were only two changes in the group's membership before Elizabeth's accession in 1558: 'Innocent Coming, Italian' joined it by warrant dated 28 August 1551 backdated to Christmas 1550 at the rate of 12*d*. a day, and Paul Galliardello succeeded Vincent of Venice in or shortly before October 1555.[30] Innocent of Cremona is said to have arrived in England around 1537, 1545, and 1543 in subsidy documents of 1567, 1571, and 1593 respectively; such statements, made long after the event, were often wild guesses, but we gather that he was in London for some time before he obtained a court post; he and his brother George perhaps came over in 1540 with their probable father John Maria of Cremona.[31] According to the 1593 document Innocent was an 'Italyane of Vennise', so if he was around 20 when he obtained his court post he would have been born in about 1530, which suggests that his family, like the Lupos, lived in Venice for some years before coming to London. Innocent's appointment is significant because he was given a new place, increasing the establishment of the group from six to seven, though it is unclear whether the change was primarily of musical or administrative significance.

---

[28] *GB-Lbl*, Add. MS 5750, fo. 64[r]; see Ashbee, *RECM*, vi. 12.

[29] I owe this suggestion to Paul O'Dette.

[30] *GB-Lbl*, Royal MS 18. C. xxiv, fo. 127[r]; *GB-Lpro*, E101/424/9, 196.

[31] Kirk and Kirk, *Returns of Aliens*, i. 340, ii. 132, iii. 444; George described Innocent as his brother in his will, *GB-Lpro*, PROB 11/59, q. 22, copy in PROB 11/70, q. 24.

Innocent and George were also employed by Edward Seymour, Duke of Somerset shortly before the latter's fall in the autumn of 1551: in 1556 Innocent received a lodging allowance from Somerset's estate for February to July 1551, and for 'Bourdwages being out of houshold' in that same July; 'Mr George the kinge(s) Graces musicon' was paid 4*s*. 4*d*. at the same time for 'bringing uppe a Set of vialles from London to Sion and from Sion to London againe' on 28 July 1551; this was not a court function, for on that day the king was entertaining the French ambassador at Hyde Park, some miles from Syon House, Somerset's country estate near Isleworth—another indication that the royal musicians were given considerable opportunities to undertake freelance work for members of the aristocracy.[32]

From the way that the string consort is described in court documents in the first decade of its service in England, it looks as if it used viols and violins interchangeably until the end of Mary's reign. After 1558 it is still occasionally referred to as 'viols', but mainly in establishment books, which often have inaccurate and out-of-date information about musicians, because they were not necessarily compiled in those court offices that had direct contact with musicians. The group is always referred to as 'violins' after 1558 by the clerks of the Treasury of the Chamber, which suggests that by then they played violins rather than viols on duty, though they probably continued to play viols in private.

Once again, it is difficult to know whether this is a sign of a real change in court musical taste or practice. Elizabeth was famously fond of dancing (see Ch. 5), and it may be that she preferred to hear violins and dance music in those ceremonial situations that had previously required viols and contrapuntal music. It could also be that other court musicians began to take over the string consort's viol-playing activities. Early in Elizabeth's reign, Ian Woodfield has pointed out, 'playing the viol had come to be regarded as an important element in the education of choirboys'; about the same time a group of Chapel Royal composers—among them Christopher Tye, Richard Edwards, Robert Parsons, Thomas Tallis, and William Byrd—were developing new genres with viols in mind.[33] When members of the Chapel performed In Nomines, consort songs, or verse anthems with viols, the instruments were probably played by its members,

---

[32] *GB-Lbl*, Add. MS 5755, fos. 266^r, 267^r; Jordan, *Chronicle and Political Papers of King Edward VI*, 75.

[33] Woodfield, *Early History*, 212–16; see also P. Brett, 'The English Consort Song, 1570–1625', *PRMA* 88 (1961–2), 73–88; Le Huray, *Music and the Reformation in England*, 217–26; W. Edwards, 'The Performance of Ensemble Music in Elizabethan England', *PRMA* 97 (1970–1), 113–23; P. Doe, 'The Emergence of the In Nomine: Some Notes and Queries on the Work of Tudor Church Musicians', in E. Olleson (ed.), *Modern Musical Scholarship* (Stocksfield, 1980), 79–92; J. Morehen, 'The English Consort and Verse Anthem', *EM* 6 (1978), 381–5; D. Wulstan, *Tudor Music* (London, 1985), 317–24.

boys or men; there is no sign that members of the royal string consort or any other string-players were brought in from outside to play with the Chapel until after the Restoration. The string consort, it seems, was now firmly devoted to the violin and to dance music.

As it happens, the earliest music that can be associated with violinists at the English court comes from this same period. *GB-Lbl*, Royal Appendix MSS 74–6 'began life as a set of four part-books (the Bassus is lost) containing Anglican church music of the reign of Edward VI'.[34] Later, perhaps in 1553, when the return to Catholicism under Mary would have made its liturgical music obsolete, the set passed into the library of Henry Fitzalan, Earl of Arundel. A contemporary hand wrote 'Arundel' and 'Lumley' (John, Baron Lumley, Arundel's son-in-law and heir) on the original covers, and it appears, still consisting of four volumes, as no. 2601 of the 1609 catalogue (copied from a lost catalogue of 1596) of Lumley's library, whence it passed via the library of Prince Henry and the main royal library to the collection of royal manuscripts in the British Museum.[35] At an early stage, probably soon after it was acquired by Arundel, several individuals began to collect ensemble dances on its blank pages, using the volumes as separate commonplace books instead of a set of part-books (see Table 4.2 at the end of this chapter).

The dances in Arundel's part-books are notated in several ways. A few pieces appear in ordinary score, with bars ruled or drawn through the staves; several of them have corrections to the part-writing, which suggests that the copyist was composing or arranging as he wrote them down. In one case, the 'Gallyard', MS 76, fo. 43^v (no. 110 in Doe's edition), a four-part score was evidently envisaged, but only the outer parts were written down. The author was clearly working in two stages, like masque and ballet composers of the seventeenth century: the treble and bass parts were written first (or borrowed from a version of the piece in another medium), leaving the inner parts for later. Most of the collection, however, is written in what is best described as pseudo-score: the parts appear on a single page, but are not necessarily aligned or set out in descending order of pitch. Pseudo-score was used mainly for fair copies—the galliard mentioned above, MS 76, fo. 43^v, was copied complete in pseudo-score at MS 76 INV, fo. 48^v—though in one or two cases, such as the five-part galliards, MS 74, fo. 35^r (Doe, no. 104) and MS 76, fo. 45^v (Doe, no. 111), the copyist continued to tinker with the part-writing.

Why was pseudo-score used? It was a common layout for secular music

[34] P. Doe (ed.), *Elizabethan Consort Music: I* (MB, 44; London, 1979), p. xxi; see also J. Blezzard, 'The Lumley Books', *MT* 112 (1971), 128–30.

[35] S. Jayne and F. R. Johnson (eds.), *The Lumley Library: The Catalogue of 1609* (London, 1956), 286.

in the fifteenth century, though sixteenth-century instrumental music was normally written either in ordinary score or in separate parts. Pseudo-score is inconvenient for composition or study, and cannot have been used directly for performance since four or five musicians could hardly have gathered round a single medium-size oblong page. The best explanation is that the pseudo-scores served as a bank of reference material for professional instrumentalists who, following the custom of the time, played in public from memory. Pseudo-scores would have served the purpose well, for without ruled bars or aligned parts they would have been quick to assemble and easy to use.

Little is known about music in Arundel's households—in the Strand and at Nonsuch in Surrey, the palatial country house he acquired from the Crown in 1556. A poem printed after his death mentions 'his solem Queer/By vois and Instruments so sweet to heer', and a 1596 inventory of Lumley's household includes a large array of instruments, including ten shawms, two 'bumbardes', four crumhorns, fifteen recorders, thirteen 'vyolens', forty-one viols, four sackbuts, and twelve cornetts, most of which probably came from his father-in-law.[36]

It has often been suggested that the composer Derick Gerarde was a member of Arundel's household, for many of the other manuscripts of Arundel provenance in the British Library Royal Appendix series contain his music and were apparently copied by him. Until now nothing has been known for sure about Gerarde apart from what can be deduced from his name, which sounds Flemish, and his music, which suggests that he was schooled in the Franco-Flemish idiom of the 1540s; the biography ingeniously compiled by Charles Warren for *Grove 6* is almost entirely speculation. Also, the manuscripts do not of themselves prove a direct connection with Arundel's household because they could easily have been acquired second-hand by the earl for his library, like MSS 74–6. Ian Payne, however, has recently thrown some light on this mysterious figure by showing that a 'Gerrard Direck' alias 'Direck Gerrerd' or 'Jerrit Derricke' was a member of the choir of York Minster from 1590–1 until his death in 1604; this man was a composer of conservative tastes who wrote at least one consort dance, and his appearance at York around 1590 does not conflict with employment in Arundel's household, for the earl died in 1580.[37]

The handwriting of the dances in MSS 74–6 gives an impression of total confusion: it ranges, in Doe's words 'from the meticulous to the unintelligible', and initially seems to contain the work of as many as seven

[36] C. W. Warren, 'Music at Nonesuch', *MQ* 54 (1968), 50–1.
[37] I. Payne, 'British Library Add. MSS 30826–28: A Set of Part-Books from Trinity College, Cambridge?', *Chelys*, 17 (1988), 7–8.

or eight different individuals. There is little doubt, however, that Gerarde contributed pieces in pseudo-score to the collection, and that he was also one of the people—possibly the only one—who used it for composing. The main hand of the Gerarde manuscripts is the same as Hand B in the largest section of Arundel's dance collection, at the reversed end of the original triplex part-book, MS 74. The resemblance can be seen at its clearest in the case of the short four-part alman or branle (no. 93 in Doe's edition) composed on fo. 49ᵛ (Pl. 2(a)) and fair-copied on fo. 43ᵛ; it has the distinctive treble and C clefs of the motet collection, Royal Appendix MSS 17–22, and the first section of the single part-book of French chansons, Royal Appendix MS 55, fo. 1–6. Also, the neat version of B's hand, used for four pieces in pseudo-score on MS 74, fo. 41ᵛ–40ʳ, seems to be the same as the one that occurs in a number of the Gerarde manuscripts, including the incomplete set of part-books Royal Appendix MSS 23–5. It is likely that a thorough investigation of the Gerarde manuscripts will show that some of the other seemingly different hands in MSS 74–6 are also Gerarde's work, perhaps executed at different periods with different types of pen.[38]

The activity of two other individuals can also be traced to some extent in the collection. One, Hand A, is distinguished by bold, angular C clefs and an elongated Italic literary hand; he collaborated with Gerarde on the main pseudo-score sequence in MS 74; their work alternates and they both contributed to three dances called 'desperada': 'Seconda desperada', fo. 50ᵛ (Doe, no. 80; title and music: Hand A), 'Terza desperada', fo. 50 (Doe, no. 81; title: Hand A, music: Gerarde), and '[prima] desperada', fo. 47 (Doe, no. 86; title and music: Gerarde). Hand A contributed a repertoire apparently drawn largely from Italian and Flemish sources: it includes an Italian-style pavan with harmonies related to the Passamezzo antico, fo. 49 (Doe, no. 82); 'ruger', fo. 46 (Doe, no. 87), a corrupt triple-time version of the Italian Ruggiero chord-sequence (the annotation 'by m(aste)r Rychard Pyttyns' seems to have been added by a later hand, and is probably a red herring); a 'Ronda' and a 'Brande berges', both with a related 'represa', fos. 46ʳ–44ᵛ (Doe, nos. 88–91), pieces similar to the *rondes* in Susato's 1551 dance collection; and 'Allemana d'amor', fo. 44ʳ (Doe, no. 92), a tune found in Flemish and German sources from the 1560s to the 1590s.[39]

Gerarde himself contributed a less cosmopolitan repertoire: he copied

[38] See I. Fenlon and J. Milsom, '"Ruled Paper Imprinted": Music Paper and Patents in Sixteenth-Century England', *JAMS* 37 (1984), 139–63 for a recent summary of what is known about Gerarde's manuscripts; I am grateful to John Milsom for helping me to identify Gerarde's hand in MSS 74–6.

[39] T. Susato, *Het derde musyck boexken* (Antwerp, 1551; repr. 1987); *Danserye*, ed. F. J. Giesbert (Mainz, 1935), i. 19–27; A. Curtis (ed.), *Dutch Keyboard Music of the Sixteenth and Seventeenth Centuries* (Monumenta musica neerlandica, 3; Amsterdam, 1961), 25.

three pavans, fos. 48^v–47^v (Doe, nos. 83–5), characteristically English in their use of canon; the five-part 'Pavin of Albarti' and its related 'Gallyard', fos. 41^r–40^v (Doe, nos. 97, 98); and part at least of 'galliard/Innocents', fo. 39^r (Doe, no. 102, with the *quintus* mistakenly printed separately as App. no. 3), and its related pavan, fo. 38^v (Doe, no. 101), which the writer, probably Gerarde, seems to have composed there and then, deriving it from the galliard. Doe suggests that 'Albarti' and 'Innocent' refer to Innocenzio Alberti, 'from whom Henry Fitzalan (owner of the MSS) commissioned a set of madrigals in 1566 while travelling in Italy'.[40] But it is hard to understand why a copyist should identify an individual by his first and second names within a few pages, and why Alberti, who is not known to have left Italy, should have based the 'Pavin of Albarti' on a tune that was current in northern Europe but not, as far as is known, south of the Alps: it is similar to the 'Pavanne. Si je m'en vois a5' that opens Gervaise's 1557 collection of ensemble dances, and it belongs to a family of tunes that includes the pavan 'Belle qui tiens ma vie' from Arbeau's *Orchésographie* made famous in Peter Warlock's Capriol Suite, the 'Almande du Prince', and a coranto familiar from a keyboard setting by William Byrd (Ex. 4.1).[41] Italian pavans of the time tend to be based on chord-sequences, or have tunes in the tenor rather than in the soprano, and they are not paired with thematically related galliards.[42] It makes better sense to ascribe the pieces to Albert of Venice and Innocent of Cremona, who served together in the court string consort from the latter's appointment at Christmas 1550 until Albert's death on 3 July 1559.[43] This, of course, was the period when Gerarde and his colleagues apparently began to use the collection for dance music.

The third individual, Hand C, can be distinguished most easily by his literary hand: he mixes secretary and Italic forms, and tends to leave letters such as *a* and *p* open at the top. Apart from two five-part English-style pavans in pseudo-score, MS 74, fos. 43^r and 42^v (Doe, nos. 94, 95), he also copied a set of three alto-clef single-line division parts near the end of the pseudo-score section of MS 74. No other versions of 'pavana Bryches' and the incomplete 'gallyard Bryches', fo. 37^r (Doe, App. nos. 5,

---

[40] Doe, *Elizabethan Consort Music*, 196.

[41] Gervaise, *Troisième livre*, ed. Thomas, 4; C. W. Beaumont (ed.), *Orchesography . . . by Thoinot Arbeau* (London, 1925), 58–9; see, for example, J. M. Ward (ed.), *The Dublin Virginal Book, New Edition* (London, 1983), 22–3, 48–9; *William Byrd, Keyboard Music: I*, ed. A. Brown (MB 27; London, 1969), 78; see O. Neighbour, *The Consort and Keyboard Music of William Byrd* (London and Boston, Mass., 1978), 170.

[42] See the examples in Morrow, *Italian Dances*, 1–3; F. Bendusi, *Opera nova de balli*, (Venice, 1553); ed. B. Thomas, (Italian Instrumental Music of the Renaissance, 5; London, 1974); see also C. Cunningham, 'Ensemble Dances in Early Sixteenth-century Italy: Relationships with *Villotte* and Franco-Flemish *Danceries*', *MD* 34 (1980), 160–203.

[43] *GB-Lpro*, E351/541, m. 5^v.

Ex. 4.1. Albert of Venice?, 'Pavin of Albarti', *GB-Lbl*, Royal App. MS 74 INV, fo. 41ʳ (from Doe (ed.), *Elizabethan Consort Music: I*, no. 97)

6) are known, but the 'pasemesures pavan', fo. 38ʳ (Doe, App. no. 5) consists of a single statement of the Passamezzo antico chord-sequence. A second set of divisions in the g1 clef (the French violin clef) was also copied by Hand A at the back of the tenor part-book, MS 76. Two of them are fragmentary: fos. 50ʳ–49ᵛ have been torn out, leaving six short passages of what appears to be a pavan and four of a galliard (Doe, App. nos. 12) on the stubs. The others, 'p(i)e(d) de cheval', fo. 48ʳ (Doe, App.

Ex. 4.1. *Continued*

no. 14), 'milord mark's galiarde', fo. 47ᵛ (Doe, App. no. 15), 'pavana', fos. 47ʳ–46ᵛ (Doe, App. no. 16), and 'pavana', fo. 46ʳ (Doe, App. no. 17), are complete, and all but the first are based on existing consort pieces in the pseudo-score section of MS 74, an indication perhaps that they were copied at a later stage than the pseudo-scores. Doe recognized that the last of them fits Innocent's Pavan, but missed the fact that the second and third fit the four-part galliard, MS 74, fo. 41ᵛ (Doe, no. 96), and the five-part 'Pavin', MS 74, fo. 39ᵛ (Doe, no. 100).

'Pied de cheval' has no parent consort piece in the three surviving volumes (there could, of course, have been one in the missing bass book), but is related to an alman with the same title in the Dublin Virginal Book, and in several contemporary Continental collections.[44] The resemblance is difficult to spot because the divisions are not based on the notes of the tune, and do not exactly fit its accepted harmonies, but it has the same number of bars as the other versions, and the divisions more or less fit the tune. The other French violin clef pieces show that, though the divisions are soprano-range (they do not go below d'), they are actually based on a mixture of the original alto and tenor parts transposed up an octave. In the same way, the 'Pied de cheval' divisions were probably based on the inner parts of a consort setting that harmonized the tune in an idiosyncratic fashion; it is certainly possible to produce outer parts that fit the divisions yet still sound like 'Pied de cheval'.

The French violin clef divisions use a technique that is related to that developed in late sixteenth-century Italy for viola bastarda music, involving divisions that range across all the parts of a polyphonic model; Francesco Rognoni explained in 1620 that 'one moment it moves to the alto range, the next moment to the bass, the next to the soprano; one moment it plays one part, the next moment another'.[45] Viola bastarda pieces, like other Italian pieces involving *passaggi*, were modelled on chansons, madrigals, or motets, and were accompanied by a keyboard reduction of the original; Diego Ortiz printed keyboard reductions in his *Trattato de glosas* of 1553, while later authors expected the accompanist to make up a part from a *basso seguente*.[46] A similar accompaniment was probably intended for the MS 76 pieces. A fragment of the outer parts of 'Milord marks galiarde' appears in keyboard score on MS 74, fo. 42[r]; it combines with the divisions, derived from both inner parts of the original, to make a surprisingly full texture (Ex. 4.2). The *bastarda* technique was normally associated with the viol, though it was occasionally applied to voices and other instruments, such as the piece for 'Liutto grande' written 'à modo di Viola bastarda per suonar in Concerto' by Giovanni Antonio Terzi, and the 'violone over Trombone all Bastarda' specified by Francesco Rognoni.[47] The MS 76 pieces, however, are unique in that they apply a *bastarda*-related technique to dance music and to a treble

---

[44] Ward, *Dublin Virginal Book*, 24, 49–50; Ward states that the MS 76 piece is unrelated to other versions of the alman.

[45] F. Rognoni, *Selva di varii passaggi secondo l'uso moderno per cantare e suonare con ogni sorte de stromenti* (Milan, 1620); J. Paras (ed.), *The Music for Viola Bastarda* (Bloomington, Ind., 1986), 7–8.

[46] D. Ortiz, *Trattato de glosas sobre clausulas y otros generos de puntos en la musica de violones/Glose sopra le cadenze et altre sorte de punti in la musica del violone* (Rome, 1553); ed. M. Schneider (Kassel, 1936).

[47] G. A. Terzi, *Il secondo libro de intavolatura di liuto* (Venice, 1599), 70; Paras, *Music for Viola Bastarda*, 29–32, 125–7.

Ex. 4.2. Peter Lupo?, Division on 'milord markes galiarde', *GB-Lbl*, Royal App. MS 74 INV, fos. 42ʳ, 41ᵛ; MS 76 INV, fo. 47ᵛ (from Doe (ed.), *Elizabethan Consort Music: I*, nos. 96, App. 15)

Ex. 4.2. *Continued*

instrument; by transposing the source material up an octave the composer was able to take material from alto and tenor parts, while Italian composers of *passaggi* for treble instruments were confined to material from soprano parts. The MS 76 pieces precede anything similar in English sources by about fifty years (see Ch. 9), and are nearly contemporary with the earliest Italian *bastarda* pieces, in Ortiz's *Trattado*. This means that they were almost certainly written by someone with direct experience of the Italian musical scene.

A possible clue to his identity is provided by the word 'peter' written over 'Pied de cheval' by its copyist, Hand A (Pl. 2(*b*)). An obvious candidate is Peter Lupo, the son of Ambrose. He was born in Venice, and was probably educated there, so he is likely to have been familiar with Italian diminution practice at first hand. But he also worked in Antwerp before coming to London to take up Albert of Venice's place in the violin consort around 1566 (see Ch. 5), so he would have been well placed to collect the mixture of Italian- and Flemish-style pieces that Hand A contributed to the collection. Unfortunately for such a neat theory, the surviving samples of his hand, including a letter written in Italian to the Earl of Leicester on 18 March 1578/9, are not at all similar to Hand A; the same can be said of the handwriting of his brother Joseph, who was also born in Venice and worked in Antwerp before coming to London.[48] Nevertheless, Hand A may well turn out to have been one of Peter's colleagues in the violin consort, or in another section of the royal music. If this is so, then we must reconsider the traditional notion that the dances in MSS 74–6 (and the rest of the Gerarde manuscripts, for that matter), were copied for use in Arundel's household. It is just as likely that Gerarde copied them for some other patron, in the late 1550s perhaps, and that Arundel acquired his collection of music books second-hand.[49] Either way, it now seems likely that Gerarde and his colleagues collected, copied, and composed their dances for a milieu that was closely connected with the court in general, and the string consort in particular.

What, then, can MSS 74–6 tell us about the practice of such groups? It seems, first, that the one that used the collection played regularly in five parts, for an effort seems to have been made to collect five-part pieces, or to convert four-part pieces into five parts by adding a *quintus*, often at the bottom of the pages in pseudo-score. In the 1550s four-part dance music was still the norm in Italy and much of northern Europe, though there are a few five- and six-part pieces in the Attaingnant dance books, and there are many five- and six-part adaptations of four-part dances in the

---

[48] *GB-Lbl*, Cotton Titus MS B. vii, fos. 131^r, 156^r, 329^r; *GB-Lbl*, Harley MS 1644, fo. 17^v; *GB-Lpro*, E101/430/15.

[49] I owe this idea to John Milsom.

collections published by Paulus and Bartholomeus Hessen at Breslau in 1555.[50] With the exception of a pavan for five basses (Doe, no. 106), all the MSS 74–6 consort dances use the standard sixteenth-century configuration of a single soprano, two or three inner parts, and bass, and would have been played on violin consorts using a single violin, two or three violas, and bass violin. They are written, like virtually all sixteenth-century dance music, in a neutral style equally suitable for a number of different types of instrument, and, with one exception, their parts conform to the limited ranges required by recorders and a number of other wind consorts, with the soprano kept above d', the alto and tenor above c, and the bass above F. The exception, significantly, is Albert's Pavan and Galliard, which has a soprano part that goes down to b, and a bass with optional bottom Ds, notes readily available on violin-family instruments.

It is not clear how the court violin consort, with seven members after 1550, would have played such five-part music. It may be that the outer parts were doubled; it may be that a lute or a drum was added on occasion; or it may simply be that some sort of shift system was in use. We can be fairly sure that the French violin clef divisions were not played with their parent consort pieces, for they would have produced numerous uncomfortable octaves with the inner parts. They work best with a keyboard playing the original outer parts, and they should perhaps be thought of as an early attempt to turn functional dance music into abstract 'concert' music. If some or all of them are really by Peter Lupo, then they may be intended specifically for violin, and may therefore be the earliest surviving solo music for the instrument.

---

[50] For the Hessen collections, see, for instance, B. Thomas (ed.), *Hoftanz 'Benzenhauer' (Two Settings)* (Early Music Library, 11; London, 1987); id., *Two Passamezzi* (Early Music Library, 71; London, 1990).

TABLE 4.2. *Inventory of the dances in GB-Lbl, Royal Appendix MSS 74–6*

Folio	Doe no.	Title	No. of parts	Format	Hand	Comment
MS 74 from front						
34^v	App. 8	[galliard or branle]	4	PS	C	
35^r	104	[galliard]	5	PS	D?	
MS 74 from back						
52^v	76	allemande	5	PS	A	title not in Doe
52^r	77	lero lano	5	PS	A	
51^v	78	Gaillarde	5	PS	B	crossed out
51^r	79	[branle?]	5	PS	B	related to Doe 81, 86
50^v	80	Seconda desperada	5	PS	A	crossed out; related to Doe 80, 86
50^r	81	Terza desperada	5	PS	B	crossed out; voice 2 of Doe 83
49^v	93	Canon unam mensuram [illegible word]	1	SP	B	fair copy: fo. 43^v
49^r	82	[pavan]	4	CS	B	Italian style
48^v	83	Pavane / Canon in subdiatessarum [*sic*]	5	PS	B	voice 2: fo. 49^v
48^r	84	Pavane / Canon per aliam viam reversi sunt in regionem suam	5	PS	B	
47^v	85	Canon aliud [pavan]	5	PS	B	related to Doe 80, 81
47^r	86	[prima?] desperada	5	PS	B	'by m(aste)r Rychard Pyttyns' in later hand; a
46^v	87	ruger	4	PS	A	corrupt Ruggiero

TABLE 4.2. *Continued*

Folio	Doe no.	Title	No. of parts	Format	Hand	Comment
46ʳ	88	Ronda	5	PS	A	related to Doe 88
45ᵛ	89	La represa	5	PS	A	
45ʳ	90	Brande / berges	5	PS	A	related to Doe 90
44ᵛ	91	La represa	5	PS	A	see Ch. 4 n. 39
44ʳ	92	Allemana d'amor	5	PS	A	CS; fo. 49ᵛ
43ᵛ	93	[branle?]	4	PS	B	
	App. 1	[alman?]	1	SP	A?	
43ʳ	94	pavan	5	PS	C	
42ᵛ	95	pavana	5	PS	C	
42ʳ	96	[galliard]	2	KS	B?	first strain of 96
	App. 2	[branle?]	4	CS	B?	two versions
41ᵛ	96	Gallyard	4	PS	B	division part: MS 76, fo. 47ᵛ
41ʳ	97	Pavin of Albarti	5	PS	B	by Albert of Venice?
40ᵛ	98	Gallyard	5	PS	B	related to Doe 97
40ʳ	99	Galliard	5	PS	B	
39ᵛ	100	Pavin	5	PS	B	division part: MS 76, fos. 47ʳ–46ᵛ
39ʳ	App. 3	galliard / Innocents	5	PS	B	by Innocent of Cremona? Quintus printed separately in Doe
	102	Tenor off the gallyard				
38ᵛ	101	[Innocent's pavan]	4	PS	B	some corrections; derived from galliard?
38ʳ	App. 4	pasemesures pavan	1	SP	C	division on the Passamezzo antico
37ᵛ	blank					
37ʳ	App. 5	pavana Bryches	1	SP	C	division; 'Smythes' in Doe

Folio	Doe	Title				Notes
	App. 6	gallyard Bryches	1	SP	C	incomplete division?; 'Smythes' in Doe part of Doe, App. 6?
36^v	App. 7	[galliard?]	1	SP	C	
	103	[pavan?]	5	PS	B	
MS 75 from front						
35^r	105	[galliard]	5	PS	B	
35^v	106	[pavan]	5	PS	B	
36^r	107	pav Marquese	5	PS	A	for five basses
36^v	108	[pavan]	5	PS	A	
MS 76 from front						
43^v	110	Gallard [illegible word]	2	CS	B	complete PS at fo. 48^v; related to Doe 109
44^r	109	[pavan]	4	CS	B	
45^v	111	[galliard]	5	PS	B	related to Doe 110
MS 76 from back						
50^r–49^v	App. 11	[pavan?]	1	SP	A	six? fragments of division
49^v	App. 12	galiarda	1	SP	A	four? fragments of division
48^v	110	[galliard]	4	PS	B	CS: fo. 43^v
48^r	App. 14	peter / p(i)e(d) de cheval	1	SP	A	division; see Ch. 4 n. 44
47^v	App. 15	milord markes galiarde	1	SP	A	division on Doe 96
47^r–46^v	App. 16	pavana	1	SP	A	division on Doe 100
46^r	App. 17	pavana	1	SP	A	division on Doe 101
	App. 18	vyth [pavan]	1	SP	A?	a quintus part?

Abbreviations:
CS composing score
Doe *Elizabethan Consort Music: I*, ed. P. Doe (MB 44; London, 1979)
KS keyboard score
PS pseudo-score
SP single part

5

'Musicke of Violenze'

The Elizabethan String Consort

THE accession of Elizabeth in 1558 ushered in a long period of stability for the royal violin consort. There were only nine changes of personnel in the forty-four years of her reign, a state of affairs that was partly caused by the remarkable longevity of its members: Ambrose, Peter and Joseph Lupo, Francis of Venice, Mark Anthony and Caesar Galliardello, and Innocent of Cremona all served forty years or more. But it also testifies to the strength of the relationship between the Protestant Tudor dynasty and its Jewish-Italian musicians: all Elizabeth's violinists apparently continued in her service until retirement or death, despite the fact that, with their foreign contacts, they would have been well placed to obtain lucrative employment elsewhere.

The first two changes of the reign were caused by the death of Albert of Venice on 3 July 1559 and the departure of Paul Galliardello for Italy in or shortly before May 1563; Joseph Lupo succeeded Paul a few months later by a warrant dated 16 November 1563.[1] Albert's place, however, remained unfilled until Peter Lupo was appointed by a warrant dated 20 September 1567, backdated to Lady Day (25 March) 1566; subsidy documents for 1571 show that he had been in England for four years, from 1566, and that he 'came over for that intent'—to be a court musician.[2] Joseph and Peter were brothers, sons of Ambrose Lupo and his first wife Lucia (not brothers of Ambrose as stated in *Grove 6*); they were both born in Venice and worked in Antwerp before coming to England: 'Peeter Loupez, Venetiaen' and 'Josep Lupo, Ambrosiussoone, geboren tot Venegien, speelman' joined the Antwerp musicians' guild on 17 January 1555 and 20 August 1557.[3] Peter's first wife 'Koven' or Katherine was Flemish and their daughter Elizabeth was born in Antwerp, according to a 1567 subsidy document; they were still in

---

[1] Ashbee, *RECM*, vi. 80, 86.
[2] Ibid. 95. Kirk and Kirk, *Returns of Aliens*, 10, i. 451; ii. 126.
[3] Page, *Letters of Denization*, 158; Spiessens, 'Geschiedenis van de gilde', 33.

Antwerp in 1559–60 when Peter sold a set of violins and some wind instruments to the town of Utrecht.[4]

Several of Elizabeth's musicians had connections with Antwerp. Paul Galliardello wrote his will there on 12 May 1563 before setting sail for Italy; it reveals that he had houses in Antwerp and London, that he had left his wife behind in England, and that he intended to return there: 'Thus I make and end prayinge to god to gyve me a good vyaage and good reterne'. His wish was apparently not granted, unless he can be identified with the 'Maister Galliard, dwelling over against the well not far from the Crochet Friars' who was buried on 17 August 1564 at the London church of St Olave, Hart Street.[5] Paul was not the only Galliardello with Antwerp connections: 'Franchisco Galliaerdel Jacopssoone, geboren van Bressa [Brescia]' was admitted to the guild of musicians there on 10 July 1556. The records of the Antwerp guild also contain the names of three wind-players who were later to work in London: 'Gummaer van Oisterwyck Peterssone van Rumpst, speelman', 'Segher van Pelken van Cortrycke Janssone, speelman', and 'Guillain vanden Borre Franchoyssone, geboren tot Bruessele, speelman' were admitted on 9 January 1544, 8 January 1545, and 12 January 1564.[6] The first two came to England in or around 1567, according to subsidy documents; in 1570 Gommar van Oostrewick joined the court flute consort, while van Pelken (van Pilken) became a member of the London waits. Van Pilken returned to the Continent in 1581, but van Oostrewick remained in court service, and died in England on 26 July 1592. Van den Borre succeeded Anthony Mary as a royal sackbut-player by a warrant dated 16 November 1572, and held it until his death by drowning at Windsor on 17 November 1582.[7]

The musical connections between the two cities seem to have come about in part because Antwerp had a large Jewish community that included many 'New Christians' (converted Jews from Spain and Portugal) who had settled in the Netherlands after the Inquisition was established in Portugal between 1537 and 1540.[8] Flemish Jews, afraid that the Spanish authorities in the Netherlands might persecute them as

[4] Kirk and Kirk, *Returns of Aliens*, i. 451; ii. 126; Vander Straeten, *La Musique aux Pays-Bas*, iv. 228.

[5] *GB-Lpro*, PROB 11/47, q. 5; W. B. Bannerman (ed.), *The Registers of St Olave, Hart Street, London, 1563–1700* (Harleian Society Publications, registers, 46; London, 1916), 107.

[6] Spiessens, 'Geschiedenis van de gilde', 32, 33.

[7] Kirk and Kirk, *Return of Aliens*, i. 451; ii. 126; iii. 334; Lasocki, 'Professional Recorder Players', ii. 714–16; Ashbee, *RECM*, vi. 109, 136, 138; van Oostrewick's name is found in many forms in contemporary documents, but he signed his name 'gommar van oostrewick' in *GB-Lpro*, E101/430/15.

[8] L. Wolf, 'Jews in Elizabethan England', *Transactions of the Jewish Historical Society of England*, 11 (1926), 1–91, particularly 3–5.

Marranos (New Christians who secretly retained their Judaism) often used England as a refuge, and they sometimes espoused or appeared to espouse Protestantism, which they found more congenial to the spirit of Judaism than Catholicism, and which enabled them to conceal their identity. In the light of this, it is significant that van Oostrewick was said in 1571 to have come to England 'for Religion'; he appears with van Pilken on a list dated 15 February 1570 of Protestants who were banished from Antwerp for religious reasons.[9] Van Pilken, at least, seems to have been Jewish: in 1568 he was living in the London house of John Fitzwilliams, the leader of the English Antwerp merchants, who appears to have had a Jewish wife; Dr Roger Prior points out that Seger or Segre is an Italian Jewish name.[10] More to the present purpose, the New Christian Lupo and Galliardello families are now known to have had branches in Antwerp as well as London, though there is no sign that they were actually Marranos or were engaged in politico-religious activities.

The next change in the violin consort came in 1574, with the death of George Comey of Cremona on 9 August; he made his will on the following 8 September, but it was not proved until 1587.[11] On 1 July 1579 an Italian, Agostino Dinale, petitioned the Privy Council from prison to the effect that he had been arrested and imprisoned for debt two years earlier on the complaint of Innocent Comey, who was acting as executor of Jane Comey, George's widow.[12] The petition is interesting for the unpleasant light it throws on Innocent's character: according to Dinale the violinist refused to reschedule the debt or accept any of his 'landes and goodes' in lieu; instead Dinale was imprisoned 'with all severitie', despite the fact that he was 'of great yeres, decrepite, and sickely'. George's post was left unfilled for several years, for it was not until 1 August 1578 that 'Ambrosio Grasso of Pavia' replaced him.[13] It is not known whether Grasso came directly from Italy; he is easily confused with a merchant, Ambrose Pavia, who was in London at the time—both appear in a 1582 subsidy document.[14] Ambrose Grasso may also have been Jewish, for on 24 March 1578/9 he married a Jewish girl, Elizabeth Bassano, the daughter of Anthony Bassano (see Ch. 4); her mother, Elina de Nazzi, was also probably Jewish, for de Nazzi seems to be a variant of the Jewish name Nassi or Nasi.[15] Grasso was probably the last member of

---

[9] Kirk and Kirk, *Return of Aliens*, ii. 126; Vander Straeten, *La Musique*, iv. 219.

[10] Kirk and Kirk, *Return of Aliens*, iii. 334; Prior, 'A Second Jewish Community', 146–7.

[11] Ashbee, *RECM*, vi. 108, 110; *GB-Lpro*, PROB 11/59, q. 22, copy in *GB-Lpro*, PROB 11/70, q. 24.

[12] *GB-Lpro*, SP12/131 (55).

[13] Ashbee, *RECM*, vi. 120.

[14] Kirk and Kirk, *Return of Aliens*, ii. 223, 256.

[15] Lasocki, 'Professional Recorder Players', ii. 589; see e.g. C. Roth, *The House of Nasi: The Duke of Naxos* (Philadelphia, 1948).

the violin consort who was recruited through the international network of Jewish musicians; Lupos, Comeys, and Galliardellos were still being recruited for the group well into the next century, but they were by then all first- or second-generation Englishmen.

Ambrose Grasso did not serve for long in the violin consort: on 17 November 1582 he was drowned at Windsor while attending the court there; the details are not known, but the incident also seems to have involved the court sackbut-player William van den Borre, who drowned there on the same day.[16] Thomas Browne, the singer and viol-player who worked with the violin consort in the latter part of his career (see Ch. 3), also died in the same year; to judge from an acquittance book covering the twelve months from Michaelmas 1581, in which a clerk wrote 'mortuus' after Browne had signed his name for the autumn and spring quarters, his death occurred between Lady Day and Midsummer 1582.[17] The vacancies created by the deaths of Grasso and Browne were left unfilled until 1603 and 1608 respectively, when they were given to Rowland Rubbish and Daniel Farrant (see Ch. 8). Between 1582 and 1603, therefore, the violin consort was two short of its formal establishment of eight.

This should not necessarily be interpreted as a symptom of decline, for the group was still large enough to perform the contemporary five-part dance repertoire, and it is possible that others served with it in an 'extraordinary' capacity without fee in the hope of receiving a place in the future. The next two changes of personnel show that young recruits to the group often served for several years before they received their first pay. Mark Anthony Galliardello died on 15 June 1585, and was buried two days later at the London church of Holy Trinity, Minories 'in good name and fame, and most godly Report of all his neighbors'.[18] His 16-year-old son Caesar (baptized at Holy Trinity, Minories on 1 July 1568) succeeded him at court, but had to wait more than two years for his formal appointment, a warrant dated 28 September 1587 running from Michaelmas 1587 and backdated to Midsummer 1585.[19] The warrant may have been delayed on this occasion because Caesar was too young to take the oath required of all holders of court posts: in 1641, for instance, the Lord Chamberlain ruled that the young Richard Dorney could not succeed his father in the violin band 'because the youth now in his minority is not yet lawfully capable of an Oath'.[20] Similarly, when Francis of Venice died on 26 January 1587/8 Thomas Lupo I had to wait until

[16] Ashbee, *RECM*, vi. 136.
[17] Ashbee, *RECM*, vi. 132.
[18] Ashbee, *RECM*, vi. 139; *GB-Lgc*, MS 9238.
[19] Ashbee, *RECM*, vi. 142.
[20] Ashbee, *RECM*, iii. 111.

1591 to replace him, by a warrant dated 4 May of that year; his appointment, however, was backdated to the date of Francis's death, and in a memorandum to Sir Thomas Windebank, Clerk of the Signet, the Lord Chamberlain stated that '[th]e said Tho(mas) Lupo hath bene sworne and servid in the place now allmost iii yeeres, w(ith)out any entertaynment'.[21]

For a short time, therefore, from January 1588 until Ambrose Lupo died on 10 February 1590/1, members of the Lupo family held four of the six currently active places in the violin consort, though they were evidently unable to find a relative to replace Ambrose, for his place was eventually given to William Warren by a warrant dated 4 September 1596, backdated to Lady Day 1594.[22] Warren was the first native Englishman to be given one of the regular places in the group—Thomas Browne had held one originally created for one of the 'old viols'—and his appointment marks the end of what was effectively a closed shop operated by the court's Jewish-Italian musicians; under the Stuarts it continued to recruit new members from abroad, but they came from France rather than Italy, and there is no sign that any of them were Jewish. At this period France was beginning to replace Italy as the main source of new fashions in dance and dance music. Violin consorts, too, were also beginning to be thought of as French rather than Italian; the more advanced musical circles in Italy were increasingly taken up with the cultivation of mixed ensembles.

Thomas Lupo I was Joseph's son by his first marriage to Laura, the daughter of Alvise Bassano.[23] His exact date of birth has remained unknown until now, but it seems that he should be identified with 'Thomas s(on) [of] Basanew' who was baptized on 7 August 1571 at St Olave, Hart Street, Joseph's parish church; there was a contemporary Thomas Bassano (the son of Andrea), but he was baptized on 27 February 1588/9 at All Hallows, Barking by the Tower.[24] When the clerk at St Olave recorded Thomas as a Bassano rather than a Lupo he was probably making the simple mistake of writing down his mother's maiden name rather than his father's name. Research into Thomas Lupo's life is further complicated by the existence of a cousin with the same name who also worked in the violin consort. Thomas II was the first fruit of Peter Lupo's second marriage, to the widow Katherine Wickers, celebrated at St Botolph, Aldgate on 27 October 1575; Thomas II was baptized there

---

[21] Ashbee, *RECM*, vi. 143, 148; *GB-Lbl*, Add. MS 34195, fo. 13ʳ; Ashbee, *RECM*, vi. 55.

[22] *GB-Lpro*, E351/542, m. 148; *GB-Lgc*, MS 1432/3, fo. 36ᵛ; Ashbee, *RECM*, vi. 156.

[23] The family relationship is made clear in the will of Augustine Bassano, Laura's brother, dated 18 May 1596, Greater London Record Office, Consistory Court of London, DL/C/359, fos. 301ʳ–302ᵛ.

[24] Bannerman, *Registers of St. Olave*, 5; Lasocki, 'Professional Recorder Players', ii. 560.

on 7 June 1577, and was appointed to the violin consort by a warrant dated 17 November 1599, backdated to Midsummer 1598.[25]

Some aspects of the careers of the two Thomas Lupos are almost impossible to disentangle, but it seems that only one of them, the elder, was a composer. There is never any attempt in the musical sources to distinguish two men of the same name, as there is in the case of Alfonso Ferrabosco Senior and Junior, and in the declared accounts for 1625–6 Thomas Lupo I is described as 'Thomas Lupo, senior, Composer of the violins'.[26] Three autograph 'Thomas Lupo' documents from the household of Prince Charles show that it was also the elder who was a member of the future king's important and innovative musical establishment (and also, presumably, its predecessor, in the household of Prince Henry—see Ch. 9). Two of them, a letter dated 2 September 1618 assigning salary to a third party and a receipt dated 16 October 1619, are signed by the same hand, which is different from that on a receipt for arrears dated 5 April 1647.[27] Thomas I died in or around December 1627 (he was succeeded in the violin band by his son Theophilus at Christmas that year), so the 1618/19 and 1647 documents must be autographs of Thomas I and II respectively, for the latter did not die until the Interregnum.

The handwriting of two other 'Thomas Lupo' documents, a letter dated 13 January 1627/8 asking Secretary Nicholas for a purser's place for his son in the Navy, and a chart of the Mediterranean on two hinged blocks of wood inscribed 'Mayde By Thomas Lupo in Shadwell & Neere unto the Mill', are, on the face of it, the work of a third and fourth individual with the same name. The chart could be the work of the son of Theophilus, baptized at St Giles, Cripplegate on 10 March 1646/7.[28] At least one other member of the family at the time was a sailor. A Joseph Lupo 'mariner' was among those 'strangers borne' made an English denizen on 20 June 1622; on 18 April 1633 he petitioned the king for a purser's place in one of the new ships then being built, pointing out that his father was a royal musician, and that his forebears had served at court since Henry VII's time.[29] This was, of course, an exaggeration, and the identity of his father is not clear. An obvious candidate, if we admit the possibility that the 1628 letter to Secretary Nicholas is a non-autograph copy, is Thomas Lupo I; the composer, his son Theophilus, and the sailor are all connected in documents with Gillingham in Kent and the

[25] *GB-Lgc*, MSS 9220, 9221; Ashbee, *RECM*, vi. 161.

[26] Ashbee, *RECM*, iii. 137.

[27] *GB-Lbl*, Add. MS 48590/I; *GB-Ob*, MS Autog. C. 19, fos. 148ʳ, 149ʳ; see Ashbee, *RECM*, iii. 124; iv. 218, 220–1.

[28] *GB-Lpro*, SP16/90; *GB-Lbl*, Add. MS 10041; *GB-Lgc*, MS 6419/4.

[29] *GB-Lpro*, SP38/12; Ashbee, *RECM*, v. 10.

nearby parish of Cooling; also, Joseph witnessed a document at court for Theophilus on 6 June 1629, and Joseph had a son with the unusual name Theophilus, who was buried at Cooling church on 13 April 1649, according to a 'raised stone' once in the chancel.[30]

The appointment of Thomas Lupo II in 1598 is significant in that he received a new place, the first since Thomas Browne was transferred to the group at the beginning of the reign; it increased its formal establishment to nine, and marked the beginning of a period of renewal and change that continued into the next reign. The establishment was increased again when Alfonso Ferrabosco II was given a place by a warrant dated 30 April 1602, backdated to 29 August 1601, though there are reasons for thinking that this appointment was partly a sinecure (see Ch. 9); by 1612 the group had doubled in size from the original six posts to twelve (see Ch. 8).[31] The process probably began as an administrative measure, intended perhaps to cover the demands of daily waiting at court, but it soon had the effect of turning the group into an orchestral violin band, one of the first in Europe. It is worthy of notice that the process began in the last, sombre years of Elizabeth's reign, not in the heady atmosphere at court created by the accession of James I.

Little is known about the working lives of the members of the string consort in the first decades of its residence at the English court. Some light, however, is thrown upon the subject during the second half of the century by descriptions of the court written by English diarists and foreign tourists. Dinner was the main ritual of the court day, and was therefore the focus of musical activity. One of the earliest and best accounts, showing how a formal dinner was conducted and how music fitted into the scheme of things, comes from Edward VI's own diary for 4 November 1551; it concerns a visit to Whitehall of the dowager Queen of Scotland:

At the gate there received her the Duke of Northumberland, Great Master, and the Treasurer and Comptroller and the Earl of Pembroke with all the sewers and carvers and cupbearers, to the number of thirty. In the hall I met her with all the rest of the Lords of my Council, as the Lord Treasurer, the Marquis of Northampton, etc., and from the outer gate up to the presence chamber on both sides stood the guard. The court, the hall, and the stairs were full of servingmen; the presence chamber, great chamber, and her presence chamber, of gentlemen; and so, having brought her to her chamber, I retired to mine. I went to her for dinner. She dined under the same cloth of estate at my left hand. At her reward [rearward?] dined my cousin Frances and my cousin Margaret. At mine sat the French ambassador. We were served by two services: two sewers, cupbearers,

---

[30] Ashbee, *RECM*, iii. 26, 44, 49; J. Thorpe, *Registrum Roffense* (London, 1769), 742.
[31] *GB-Lpro*, E351/543, m. 73; see Ashbee, *RECM*, vi. 164.

carvers, and gentlemen. Her maître d'hôtel came before her service, and mine officers before mine. There were two cupboards, one of gold four stages [in] height, another of massy silver six stages. In her great chamber dined at three boards the ladies only. After dinner, when she had heard some music, I brought her to the hall and so she went away.[32]

Whether dinner was taken in public in the Presence Chamber or in private in the Privy Chamber depended on the occasion and the personal preference of the sovereign. Elizabeth normally dined in the Privy Chamber; the German Lupold von Wedel witnessed an exceptional event at Greenwich on 27 December 1584: 'at no other time throughout the whole year does the Queen dine in public, and it is only on feast days that a stranger can see her at meals'.[33] The queen dined alone in the Presence Chamber, surrounded by her courtiers, all of whom had 'white staffs in their hands [their wands of office] and were handsome old gentlemen'; after describing how Elizabeth's food was served von Wedel added: 'her musicians were also in the apartment and discoursed excellent music'. On an earlier occasion von Wedel attended dinner at Hampton Court, noting that 'eight trumpeters in red uniform announced dinner with a blast very well executed', and that 'later on two drummers and a fifer made music in the English fashion'—whatever that might have been. According to Thomas Platter, who visited Nonsuch in 1599, the queen 'very seldom partakes before strangers'; as she dined in the Privy Chamber she was entertained by music 'von trommeten unndt schalmeyen' performed in the Presence Chamber.[34] The year before another traveller, Paul Hentzner, recorded that the queen dined at Greenwich to the accompaniment of 'twelve trumpets and two kettle-drums' which 'made the hall ring for half-an-hour together'.[35] Once again, the musicians evidently performed in the Presence Chamber while the food was 'conveyed into the Queen's inner and more private chamber'.

Edward VI's account of dinner at Whitehall mentions that music was performed at the end of the meal, and the writings of some Elizabethan observers suggest that it was sometimes heard in circumstances not far removed from a concert. A Venetian diplomat in 1559, for instance, commented on the quantity of music heard, though he was not impressed by its quality:

[32] Jordan, *The Chronicle and Political Papers of Edward VI*, 93–4.

[33] V. von Klarwill, *Queen Elizabeth and Some Foreigners* (London, 1928), 323, 336–7.

[34] R. Keiser (ed.), *T. Platter, Beschreibung der Reisen durch Frankreich, Spanien, England und Niederlande 1595–1600* (Auftrag der Historischen und Antiquarischen Gesellschaft zu Basel; Basle and Stuttgart, 1968), ii. 829–30; C. Williams (ed.), *Thomas Platter's Travels in England 1599* (London, 1937), 195.

[35] W. B. Rye, *England as seen by Foreigners in the Days of Elizabeth and James the First* (London, 1865), 106.

The banquet lasted till the ninth hour of the night, and I need not say that it was a stately one, as all persons may think for themselves. No one served but peers and the sons of peers. Much music was performed, but it not being remarkable, and having heard better, I will say nothing about it.[36]

The Earl of Hertford was a little more forthcoming when he recorded in his diary an account of a visit to Whitehall on 21 January 1579/80:

From Totnam Tuesday, 19 January 1579[/80], to Reding, thence on Wednesday to Hanworth and on Thursday to Canon Rowe and the Court, which I found at Whitehawll. Where at night when twelve of her Majesty's musicians were in concert, she came out and passing by saluted me, thanked me for my new year's gift, and asked me for my Lady of Pe[m] brook who she heard was sick . . . So, three or four times calling me to hear the music as she sat, saying I had judgement, she showed me the last year's new year's gift hanging at her girdle . . .[37]

The twelve, consisting perhaps of two of the six-man instrumental consorts, apparently played in the Presence Chamber while the queen dined in the Privy Chamber; after dinner she 'came out', evidently to listen to the music.

How could musicians in the Presence Chamber have entertained the queen in the Privy Chamber? We know little about the precise layout of the royal palaces, but it seems that the three chambers, Great, Presence, and Privy, were laid out in a sequence of connected areas. At Whitehall, for instance, they occupied a suite of first-floor rooms facing the Thames: the Guard Chamber opened into the Presence Chamber, which in turn opened into the Privy Chamber via a short passage.[38] A painting by Houckgeest of Charles I and Henrietta Maria dining in the Privy Chamber, though it seems to be an architectural *capriccio*, shows the royal meal in progress in an open-plan room of this sort: a flight of stairs leads through an open colonnade to a larger space, which is presumably meant to be the Presence Chamber (Pl. 1(*b*)). It is there, among the less-favoured courtiers observing the proceedings from a distance, that the instrumental consorts would presumably have been placed; indeed, the painting includes several figures behind the colonnade that appear to be carrying stringed instruments.

Tafelmusik at court was normally provided by one or more of the consorts of loud wind instruments, if the eyewitness accounts collected

[36] R. Brown and G. Cavendish-Bentinck (eds.), *Calendar of State Papers and Manuscripts, Relating to English Affairs Existing in the Archives and Collections of Venice, and in other Libraries of Northern Italy*, vii: *1558–1580* (London, 1890), 18.

[37] HMC 58, *Report on the Manuscripts of the Most Honourable the Marquess of Bath Preserved at Longleat*, iv: *Seymour Papers 1532–1686*, ed. M. Blatcher (London, 1968), 185.

[38] See the diagram in Starkey, *The English Court*, p. vi; see also G. P. V. Akrigg, *Jacobean Pageant; or, The Court of James I* (London, 1962), 279–85; Colvin, *History of the King's Works*, iv. 300–48.

above are anything to go by; they certainly would have been heard more easily than violins at a distance and over the hubbub of conversation. However, the Twenty-four Violins played regularly for Charles II's dinners (see Ch. 13), and it would be surprising if the violin consort had never fulfilled this role earlier, given the importance of the sovereign's dinner in the round of court life. A glimpse of them at work providing *Tafelmusik* for a foreign visitor to Elizabeth's court comes from an account of the visit of Frederick, Count Mömpelgard or Montbéliard, Duke of Württemberg, to the court at Reading in August 1592. He was invited to take dinner in the Earl of Essex's lodgings, where he was 'feasted most sumptuously' and entertained 'with such sweet and enchanting music (which in all probability belonged to the Queen) that he was highly astonished at it'. The cause of his astonishment seems to have been the court violin consort, for later in the year the Earl of Essex paid 'Joseph Lupo and other her Ma(jes)t(ie)s musitians' £16, apparently as a reward for their performance.[39] When Anne of Denmark visited Caversham in April 1613, 'the Queenes pleasure being that night to suppe privately, The Kings Violins attended her with their sollemnest musick, as an excellent consort in like manner did the next day at dinner'.[40]

However, the primary duty of the royal violinists was to accompany dancing. The English in general, and English courtiers in particular, were almost as famous in the sixteenth century for their love of dancing as for their gluttony. Dance music must have been required at court on virtually a daily basis, for classes and practices as well as for formal and informal dances; a Mantuan diplomat reported in August 1559 that 'every day there are dances at the Court'.[41] A hint that dance musicians were regularly assigned to members of the royal family for the purpose is given in the report of November 1541 that Anne of Cleves, recently divorced from Henry VIII, took 'no kind of pastime but kept in her chamber, whereas before she did nothing but dance and rejoice, and now when the musicians come they are told that it is no more the time to dance'.[42] Dancing appears to have followed the royal dinner more or less as a matter of course. In May 1559 a Venetian diplomat reported that supper 'lasted for two hours, with music of several sorts', and that 'after supper, the tables being removed, they danced until the eleventh hour of the night'. When Lupold von Wedel visited Greenwich in 1584, dinner was followed by a pavan and galliard:

Then a dance was begun. Men and women linked hands as in Germany. The men donned their hats or bonnets, although otherwise no one, however exalted

[39] E. M. Tenison, *Elizabethan England*, ix (Leamington, 1950), 55–6.
[40] Thomas Campion, *Works*, ed. W. R. Davis (London, 1969), 242.
[41] Brown and Cavendish-Bentinck, *Calendar of State Papers and Manuscripts . . . Venice*, vii. 80.
[42] Gairdner and Brodie, *Letters and Papers*, xvi. 614.

his rank, may put on his hat in the Queen's chamber, whether she be present or not. The dancers danced behind one another as in Germany, and all the dancers, ladies and gentlemen, wore gloves. Though the dance at first sight seemed to be of German nature, it was no German dance, for they made a few steps forward and then back again. Finally they separated. The couples changed among one another, but at the right moment each dancer returned to his or her partner. While dancing they very often courtesied to one another and every time the men bowed before their lady partners they doffed their hats. Slender and beautiful were the women who took part in this dance and magnificently robed. This dance was danced only by the most eminent who were no longer very young. But when it was over the young men laid aside their rapiers and cloaks, and clad in doublet and hose invited the ladies to dance. They danced the galliard and the Queen meanwhile conversed with those who had danced. The dancing over, the Queen waved her hand to those present and retired to her chamber.[43]

Many accounts mention Elizabeth's love of dancing. In June 1559 a Venetian diplomat wrote that 'the Queen's daily arrangements are musical performances and other entertainments (*feste*), and she takes marvellous pleasure in seeing people dance'; in 1589 it was said that 'VI or VII gallyards in a mornynge, besydes musycke & syngynge, is her ordynary exercyse'.[44] One day in January 1598 she discussed the subject with a French diplomat, Monsieur de Maisse, as they sat in a gallery watching her ladies dance:

She takes great pleasure in dancing and music. She told me that she entertained at least sixty musicians; in her youth she danced very well, and composed measures and music, and had played them herself and danced them. She takes such pleasure at it that when her Maids dance she follows the cadence with her head, hand and foot. She rebukes them if they do not dance to her liking, and without a doubt she is a mistress of the art, having learned in the Italian manner to dance high.[45]

In 1599 a diplomat reported in disgust to the Spanish court that 'on the day of Epiphany the Queen held a great feast, in which the head of the Church of England and Ireland was to be seen in her old age dancing three or four galliards'.[46] References from the end of the reign document dancing in the Presence and Privy Chambers: in January 1600 it was reported to Sir Robert Sidney that the Queen was in the Presence

[43] Brown and Cavendish-Bentinck, *Calendar of State Papers and Manuscripts... Venice*, vii. 92; Klarwill, *Queen Elizabeth and some Foreigners*, 338.
[44] Brown and Cavendish-Bentick, *Calendar of State Papers and Manuscripts... Venice*, vii. 101; D. Poulton, *John Dowland* (2nd edn., London, 1982), 405.
[45] G. B. Harrison and R. A. Jones (eds.), *André Hurault, Sieur de Maisse: A Journal of all that was Accomplished by Monsieur de Maisse, Ambassador in England from King Henri IV to Queen Elizabeth, Anno Domini 1597* (London, 1931), 94–5.
[46] M. A. S. Hume (ed.), *Calendar of Letters and State Papers Relating to English Affairs Preserved in, or originally Belonging to, the Archives of Simancas*, iv (London, 1899), 650.

Chamber almost every night over the Christmas holiday 'to see the ladies dawnce the old and new cowuntry dawnces with the taber and pipe'; in September 1602 the Earl of Worcester noted that there was much dancing of country dances in the Privy Chamber.[47]

As ever in descriptions of this sort, eyewitnesses only tend to notice musicians if they play something out of the ordinary—such as the pipe and tabor. Nor do we learn much about how dances were taught and learned at the Elizabethan court, though the French ambassador's revealing aside that the queen 'learned in the Italian manner to dance high' raises the possibility that she had been taught to dance as a child by an Italian. The profession of dancing-master had begun to separate from that of dance musician in Italy in the fifteenth century, though there was no post for one at the English court until Thomas Cardell was given an annuity of £20 a year by a warrant dated 8 December 1575 (increased to £40 a year by letters patent dated 20 December 1587). Cardell, the uncle of the lutenist Daniel Bacheler, was a musician as well as a dancing-master: Bacheler was apprenticed to him in 1579, and he is often described as a lutenist in court documents—or more accurately, he is listed among the lutenists—but he was paid 20*s*. 'for devising the daunce' for a court masque or entertainment as early as 1582–3, he is given under the heading 'To Dannce' in a subsidy document dated 19 April 1608, and in 1603 the little Princess Elizabeth asked Robert Cecil's permission to 'keep Mr. Cardell close to me, for he is teaching me to dance so well that their majesties are pleased'. In a play published in 1649, William Cavendish's *The Variety*, he is described as 'Cardell the dancing-Master in Queen Elizabeths time', and is said to have 'plaid to himself on a grave Lute, or a modest Citterne, with a politick quill, far beyond your Geofrey fiddle, or your French kit'.[48]

Before Cardell it is likely that dancing at court was taught by those who provided it with dance music. Certainly, from the middle of the sixteenth century the London Company of Musicians was authorized to regulate dancing-schools in the city, a power that was embodied in its royal charter of 1604.[49] At court the dancing-masters from the 1540s

[47] HMC 77, *Report on the Manuscripts of Lord de L'Isle and Dudley Preserved at Penshurst Place*, ed. C. L. Kingsford, ii (London, 1934), 427; D. C. Price, 'Gilbert Talbot, Seventh Earl of Shrewsbury, an Elizabethan Courtier and his Music', *ML* 57 (April, 1976), 147.

[48] A. Batchelor, 'Daniel Bacheler: The Right Perfect Musician', *The Lute*, 28 (1988), 3–12; Ashbee, *RECM*, vi. 117; *GB-Lpro*, E403/2454, fo. 57ʳ; A. Feuillerat (ed.), *Documents Relating to the Office of the Revels in the Time of Queen Elizabeth* (Materialien zur Kunde des älteren englischen Dramas, 21; Louvain, 1908; repr. 1963), 356; Ashbee, *RECM*, iv. 18; J. M. Ward, *Sprightly and Cheerful Musick: Notes on the Cittern, Gittern, and Guitar in Sixteenth- and Seventeenth-Century England*, *LSJ* 21 (1979–81), 24.

[49] Woodfill, *Musicians in English Society*, 15–16; see also J. Smith and I. Gratiss, 'What did Prince Henry Do with his Feet on Sunday 19 August 1604?', *EM* 14 (1986), 199–200.

onwards would probably have been the members of the violin consort, who as immigrants from Italy would have been well placed to teach Elizabeth to 'dance high'. It may be significant, therefore, that most of the separate posts for dancing-masters came into being at the English court shortly after 1600, at the time when the Italian-born members of the violin consort were beginning to be replaced by those born in England. Italian Jews, including Guglielmo Ebreo da Pesaro and Giuseppe Ebreo, were active in the fifteenth-century Lombard school of dancing-masters, and it may be that the name 'Galliardello' was coined with choreographic as well as musical activities in mind.[50]

Contemporary pictures of dancing are potentially important sources of information about dance musicians, if questions of their provenance can be resolved, for musicians are less often ignored in pictures than in the accounts of chroniclers and diarists. Cases in point are two paintings that show dancing accompanied by a violin consort in a setting that may or may not be the Elizabethan court. The first is the famous anonymous work at Penshurst Place in Kent that is traditionally said to represent Queen Elizabeth dancing with Robert Dudley, Earl of Leicester (Pl. 3(*a*)). Modern research has shown that it is unlikely to be an accurate depiction of an event at the English court since it is related to, and is probably derived from, a number of similar paintings of the contemporary Valois court.[51] Nevertheless, it is possible that the Penshurst picture is an English variation on a French theme, perhaps executed by an immigrant artist; the fashions shown are compatible with those worn at the French and English courts around 1580.[52]

In London immigrant artists and musicians moved in similar circles, to judge from several cases of intermarriage that have recently come to light. The miniature painter Isaac Oliver, a member of a refugee Protestant family from Rouen, was the son-in-law of Jacques Harden (James Harding), a French member of the flute consort.[53] One of his colleagues in the flute consort, Nicholas Lanier I, also came from Rouen with his family, and was probably a Protestant refugee. His grandson Nicholas Lanier II was a painter as well as a composer and a singer, and made several trips to Italy to collect paintings for Charles I. Judith Lanier, Nicholas II's sister, married Edward Norgate, a veritable Renaissance

[50] See O. Kinkeldey, 'A Jewish Dancing Master of the Renaissance', in *Studies in Jewish Bibliography . . . in Memory of Abraham Solomon Freidus* (New York, 1929), 329–72.

[51] The situation is summarized in Boyden, *History of Violin Playing*, 56–7.

[52] The fashions in the two pictures have been kindly analysed for me by Jack Edwards.

[53] M. Edmond, 'Limners and Picturemakers: New Light on the Lives of Miniaturists and Large-Scale Portrait Painters Working in London in the Sixteenth and Seventeenth Centuries', *The Forty-seventh Volume of the Walpole Society* (1978–80), 75–81; id., *Hilliard and Oliver: The Lives and Works of two Great Miniaturists* (London, 1983), particularly 161–4; R. Strong, *The English Renaissance Miniature* (2nd edn., London, 1984), 142–6.

man who exemplifies the links between the artistic and musical communities in Stuart London: he was Windsor Herald, a clerk in the Signet Office, a painter, the author of a treatise 'Miniatura; or, The Art of Limning', a keyboard-player, an instrument-maker, and tuner of the court keyboard instruments.[54] Furthermore, some of the painters working in London, such as Steven van de Meulen, Marcus Gheeraerts father and son, Hieronimus Custodis, and the de Critz family, came from Antwerp; indeed, one wonders whether there might have been Jewish 'New Christians' among them, like some of the musicians connected with the two cities.[55]

In the light of this, it is interesting that the four musicians in the Penshurst painting, who appear to be playing a violin (at the back, partly hidden), two violas (side by side) and a large bass viol or violin, are prominently painted and have more character and individuality than the figures of 'Elizabeth' and 'Dudley' and the other courtiers. The same is true of the four musicians in the other painting, entitled *Courtiers of Queen Elizabeth*, who use a small viola, a large viola held across the knees, a bass violin, and a lute to accompany seven couples dancing al fresco on a terrace (Pl. 3(*b*)).[56] It is unfortunate that the painting is known at present only from a photograph, for a dark shape on the extreme left seems to be the cloak of a fifth, standing musician, omitted presumably because the painting has been cut down or the photograph cropped; if he is (or was) a violinist, then the ensemble would be the same as the Penshurst painting—violin, two violas, and bass—with the addition of a lute. Little is known about the history of the painting, but Marcus Gheeraerts the Elder (d. 1590) has been suggested as its author—an attribution that is contradicted by the fashions of the costumes, which are from around 1600.

In view of the uncertainty that surrounds both paintings at present, it would be unwise to reach anything but the most tentative conclusions about them. However, it is possible that the artists gave the musicians prominence and individuality because they were their friends or relatives, who could easily have been painted from life or memory; it would presumably have been difficult to persuade high-ranking courtiers to sit for a small role in a group painting. If we could establish that the paintings were executed at the English court, it would raise the fascinating possibility that they contain portraits of members of the royal violin consort around 1580 and 1600 respectively. Whatever their

[54] Edmond, 'Limners and Picturemakers', 77–8; id., *Hilliard and Oliver*, 182–4.

[55] E. Waterhouse, *Painting in Britain, 1530 to 1790* (3rd edn., Harmondsworth, 1969), 19–28.

[56] Reproduced in J. Buxton, *Elizabethan Taste* (London, 1963; repr. 1983), plate 15; the late John Buxton kindly informed me that the painting was sold by Parke-Bernet of New York in the 1950s, and that he made strenuous but unsuccessful efforts at the time to discover its whereabouts.

provenance, the pictures are eloquent testimony to the fashion for violin bands at northern European courts at the time; and, in particular, they reinforce the impression already obtained from other sources that a standard dance band at the time was a four-part violin consort: violin, two violas, and a bass violin.

Royal musicians were frequently required to perform at functions outside the court, for the queen's servants were normally required to attend her everywhere she went, and her presence effectively turned any occasion into a court ceremony. Elizabeth's journeys on the Thames, London's main thoroughfare at the time, were regularly accompanied by instrumental music, as a Venetian diplomat let slip when describing her coronation day to his masters: her barge was 'towed by a long galley rowed by 40 men in their shirts, with a band of music, as usual when the Queen goes by water'.[57] Such outdoor music would presumably have been provided by wind instruments, such as the trumpets, drums, and flutes that reportedly serenaded the queen during a journey on the Thames in April 1559.[58] But the court string consort would often have been in attendance at major indoor ceremonies. Indeed, a number of descriptions of such events include lists of instruments that correspond more or less to the complete resources of the secular royal music. We must not assume, however, that they formed a single large 'orchestra'; more likely, they would have played successively, rendering the occasion the more magnificent by the aural equivalent of a procession.

In December 1561 Robert Dudley gave a banquet for the queen at the Temple; an eyewitness recorded that 'at every course the trumpetters blew the couragious blast of deadly war, with noise of drum and fyfe, with the sweet harmony of violins, sackbutts, recorders, and cornetts, with other instruments of music, as it seemed Apollo's harp had tuned their stroke'.[59] A few weeks later, on 18 January 1561/2, *The Tragedy of Ferrex and Porrex; or, Gorboduc* by Thomas Sackville and Thomas Norton was performed at the Inner Temple during another royal visit to the Inns of Court.[60] Again, the instruments mentioned correspond to sections of the royal music, though this time it is made clear that they performed successively. According to the printed text, five dumb-shows were accompanied by instrumental consorts. In the first, performed before the play began, 'the Musicke of Violenze' played while 'six wilde men clothed in leaves' demonstrated the idea that sticks are easy to break one by one, hard to break when bound in a faggot; it signified that 'a state knit

[57] Brown and Cavendish-Bentick, *Calendar of State Papers and Manuscripts . . . Venice*, vii. 12.

[58] Nichols, *Progresses and Public Processions of Queen Elizabeth*, i. 67.

[59] Ibid., i. 134.

[60] E. Creeth (ed.), *Tudor Plays. An Anthology of Early English Drama* (New York, 1966), pp. xxxiv–vi, 383–442.

in unitie doth continue strong against all force but being divided is easely destroyed'. Between the acts of the play, 'the Musicke of Cornettes' played for 'a King accompanied with a nombre of his nobilitie and gentlemen'; 'the musicke of flutes' played for 'a company of mourners all clad in blacke'; 'the musick of Howboies' accompanied three furies 'as though out of hell'; finally, 'the drommes and fluites' (fifes?) played for 'a company of Hargabusiers and of Armed men all in order of battaile'. On this occasion, the intention was not just to display the variety of sounds available in the royal music; the instruments also had a symbolic role. Frederick Sternfeld suggests that the soft sound of strings 'represented the united commonwealth according to ancient, medieval and Elizabethan beliefs', just as the flutes, shawms, and fifes and drums represented death, ill omen, and war respectively.[61] A violin consort, presumably playing dance music, would also have been an apt illustration of political unity, for the ordered patterns of the dance were seen at the time as a metaphor of cosmic harmony.

We have no idea how unusual *Gorboduc* was in its use of instruments, for only one or two texts of Elizabethan court plays and masques survive, and they contain few details of the music. But the idea that the various sections of the royal music contributed to the magnificence of public events in and out of the court clearly had a certain currency at the time, as can be seen from two related passages in a contemporary French–English conversation manual, Claudius Hollyband's *The French Schoole-Maister* (London, 1573), and a similar Spanish–English publication, *The Spanish Schoole-Master* (London, 1591).[62] The first concerns an open-air all-night celebration in the City of London on the eve of May Day, which is described to the father of the house by his friend Gossip: 'What, have you not heard the minstrels and players of instruments, which did play so sweetly before the Cities stoarehouse, from midnight even unto the breakyng of the day?' They were, he goes on, 'the minstrels of the towne [the London waits], with those of the Queenes, mingled with voyces of Italions and Englishmen, which did singe very harmoniously'. By 'Italians' Hollyband evidently meant the immigrants in the instrumental consorts, for the instruments that would have caused Father, had he been there, 'to be ravished in an yearthly paradise' were 'the Violes, Cornets, Harpes, Hobois, Trumpets, with foure Flutes the which did triumphe'—more or less a complete list of the secular royal music at the time, apart from the fifes and drums and the recorder consort. Hollyband concludes the passage with the information that the musicians had been hired by the

[61] F. W. Sternfeld, *Music in Shakespearean Tragedy* (London, 1963), 216–17.
[62] M. St Clare Byrne (ed.), *The Elizabethan Home* (3rd edn., London, 1949), 16–17; Tenison, *Elizabethan England*, ix. 54.

'best of the citie, to plant the maipole at the market place'. In *The Spanish Schoole-Master* the characters go to St Paul's Cathedral 'to see the organs and the musical instruments'. They are disappointed: 'this is nothing to the musick which I heard upon Sunday last at the Court at Richmond'. Once again the musicians are 'the Queenes minstrels mingled with the voices of Italians and Englishmen, which singed very harmoniously', though the list of the 'heavenly harmonie' is slightly different: 'you should have heard first and foremost the violes (*vihuelas* in the Spanish text), the cornets, harpes, gitarnes, and trumpets, with the flutes which did triumph'.

How frequently was the Elizabethan string consort required to attend court? No document has survived that can answer the question directly, but a certificate dated 13 February 1639/40, setting out the privileges that Ambrose Beeland would enjoy as a member of the violin band, presumably reflects established practice in stating that he was to be excused the normal parish duties of 'watching and warding' because of his 'nightly & late Attendance at Court'.[63] The Lord Chamberlain expressed himself in similar terms in a letter to the Lord Mayor of London dated 17 November 1573: 'being her servants in ordinary', the royal musicians had 'to attend daily upon her, for which reason they ought not to be chosen to any office, as Churchwarden, Constable, Scavenger, Watchmen'; in a legal document of 1564 Augustine Bassano, a member of the recorder consort, stated that he was 'one bounden to give daily attendance upon the Queen's Majesty'.[64] It seems, therefore, that the violin consort and other court instrumentalists had to be in attendance on a daily basis during the main part of the court year, corresponding to the legal terms and the sessions of Parliament, though, as evidence already brought forward suggests, they were apparently able to undertake private work for members of the aristocracy as long as it did not conflict with their court attendance.

An obvious sideline, easily combined with spells of daily attendance at court, was making and dealing in musical instruments. Members of the English branch of the Bassano family were famous at the time for making sets of wind instruments of the highest quality, which they exported to a number of European courts: forty-five instruments in a chest, shawms, flutes, cornetts, crumhorns, recorders, and a fife tuned together at organ pitch, were described as 'so beautiful and good that they are suited for dignitaries and potentates' when they were offered to the Bavarian court in 1571.[65] The Bassanos made stringed instruments as well, for the

---

[63] Ashbee, *RECM*, iii. 103–4.
[64] Overall, *Analytical Index*, 428; Lasocki, 'Professional Recorder Players', i. 95.
[65] Lasocki, 'The Anglo-Venetian Bassano Family', 120–1.

Bavarian court was also offered six of their large *viole da gamba* (two sopranos, three tenors, and a bass), and a chest of three of their lutes (soprano, tenor, and bass) in black ebony and ivory.

Members of the Lupo family are also known to have made instruments. Peter Lupo was described as 'luthier à Anvers' when he sold the town of Utrecht 'een kist met viiff vyolen' (a chest with five violins) in 1559; he also sold three 'hautbois' in the same year and a 'trompette' in 1560, though in these cases he may have been acting as a dealer.[66] Another member of the family, Francis Fransz[oon] Lupo (i.e. Francis the son of Francis Lupo), made citterns and violins in Amsterdam and founded an instrument-making dynasty there that included his son Pieter and the Kleynman family of violin-makers.[67] Francis is said in Dutch documents to have been born in London around 1582, and to have had a wife called 'Lysbet Jans', so he is probably the 'Frances Lupo' who married 'Elzabethe Benett' on 13 December 1603 at Richmond in Surrey. This in turn means that he was probably a close relative of Joseph Lupo who had settled in Richmond by July 1602 (when Joseph married the widow Margaret Allen), though no record survives of his birth, and no Francis Lupo is known in the previous generation.[68] It is possible that the sets of viols sold to the crown by Mark Anthony Galliardello in 1550 and Francis of Venice in 1565 were made by them or members of their families (see Ch. 4). Also, a 'faire lute, edged with passamayne of golde and silke' was given to Queen Mary in 1556 as a New Year's gift by its maker, one 'Browne'; the exchange of such gifts was normally confined to courtiers, so the Browne in question was probably Thomas Browne, who had recently been given one of the 'old viols' places, and was later to serve with the violin consort (see Ch. 4).[69]

The summer was the one time of the year when the string consort and other royal musicians could expect an extended period of free time, for most years the queen and a section of the court spent July and August touring great houses and towns outside the London area; the court musicians were normally left behind, and the establishments along the route had the honour and duty to entertain her, using their own servants. On a number of occasions, starting with the famous entertainment at

[66] *Bouwstenen voor een geschiedenis der toonkunst in de Nederlanden*, i (Amsterdam, 1965), 227; see Vander Straeten, *La Musique*, iv. 228; E. Closson, *La Facture des instruments de musique en Belgique* (Brussels, 1935), 58, 73; L. G. Langwill, *An Index of Musical Wind-Instrument Makers* (3rd edn., Edinburgh, 1972), 99.

[67] J. H. Giskes, 'Cornelis Kleynman (1626–1686), Vioolmaker te Amsterdam', *Amstelodamum*, 74 (1987), 11–16; according to Giskes a John Lupo is also recorded as the maker of a 'vioolbas', but no John in the English Lupo family of the period is known to have survived childhood.

[68] T. Challenor and C. Smith (eds.), *The Parish Registers of Richmond, Surrey*, i (London, 1903), 141.

[69] Ward, *A Dowland Miscellany*, 114.

Kenilworth in 1575, she heard music by groups of mixed instruments, consisting of the combination known to us as the broken or mixed consort. The role of the violin in this ensemble will be discussed in Chapter 6, but we should note here that the mixed consort was conspicuous by its absence at Elizabeth's court, so the groups concerned are unlikely to have consisted of court musicians. The mixed consort, the first English manifestation of the Continental fashion for mixed ensembles, would therefore have struck the queen and her courtiers as pleasingly novel, and would have had the effect, intended or not, of making the court consorts seem old-fashioned, made up largely as they were of complete sets of a single type of instrument.

We can take our farewell of Elizabeth's court musicians by way of a curious anecdote that circulated in seventeenth-century France; it first found its way into print in the *Histoire de la musique et de ses effets depuis son origine jusqu'à présent*, compiled by the Bonnet–Bordelet family, and published in Paris in 1715:

Queen Elizabeth of England, on her death-bed, remembered the power of music and ordered her musicians into her chamber so that, in her words, she might die as gaily as she had lived. To dispel the horror of death she listened to the music (*symphonie*) with great tranquility until her last breath.[70]

It is pleasant to imagine Elizabeth's faithful string-players, admitted to the Privy Chamber at last, softly serenading their dying queen. The reality is, as ever, a disappointment: she died in her sleep on 24 March 1603, having lost the power of speech several days earlier, so she would have been unable to call for music.

---

[70] J. Bonnet and P. Bourdelet, *Histoire de la musique et de ses effets* (Paris, 1715; repr. Amsterdam, 1725), 72–3; see Poulton, *John Dowland*, 406.

6

'Common Musicke'

The Violin outside the Court

ACCORDING to our received notions of musical history, the violin was of little importance in England until the second half of the seventeenth century. 'In England', wrote Nicholas Kenyon in 1984, 'the spread of the sonata, and of the violin, had to wait until the Restoration of Charles II in 1660.'[1] Kenyon's opinion has, at first sight, a sound basis, for it was shared by writers at the time. Roger North wrote, 'the use of chests of violls, which supplyed all instrumentall consorts, kept back the English from falling soon into the modes of forrein countrys, where the violin and not the treble viol was in use'; and again, writing of music before the Civil War: 'The violin was scarce knowne, tho' now the principall verb, and if it were any where seen, it was in the hands of a country croudero who for the portabillity served himself of it.' Anthony à Wood wrote that there was no 'complete master' of the violin in Commonwealth Oxford, 'because it had not been hitherto used in consort among gentlemen, only by common musicians, who played but two parts'; he added that the 'gentlemen in private meetings' played viol consorts, and that they 'esteemed a violin to be an instrument only belonging to a common fiddler'.[2] But Wood and North, writing over a century after the violin was first brought to England, are not necessarily reliable witnesses to its history in the sixteenth century.

To judge from the references in documents that have so far come to light, the viol first began to be used outside the court in the 1530s, two decades after it is first recorded in England. There were sets of viols in the households of the Earl of Essex in 1534, the Duke of Rutland in 1537, Lord Lisle by 1537, the Marquis of Exeter and the Earl of Hertford by 1538, the Duke of Norfolk by c.1550, and Edward Seymour, the Duke of Somerset, by 1551.[3] In the last case there is a direct

---

[1] 'The Baroque Violin', in D. Gill (ed.), *The Book of the Violin* (Oxford, 1984), 78–9.

[2] J. Wilson (ed.), *Roger North on Music* (London, 1959), 222, 342; J. D. Shute, 'Anthony à Wood and his Manuscript Wood D 19 (4) at the Bodleian Library, Oxford', Ph.D. diss. (International Institute of Advanced Studies, Clayton, Mo., 1979), ii. 99.

[3] Woodfield, *Early History*, 210–11; M. St. Clare Byrne (ed.), *The Lisle Letters*, iv (Chicago and London, 1981), 264; *GB-Lbl*, Add. MS 5755, 309, 310.

connection with the court, for the document is a payment to George of Cremona for transporting a 'set of vialles' from London to Syon House and back again; George's brother Innocent was also working in Somerset's household at the same time (see Ch. 4), so it seems that the protector's viol consort was made up, in part at least, of members of the court string consort, who of course played the violin as well as the viol.

We must be wary, in fact, of assuming that the word 'viol' was always used in its modern sense at the time, for there are cases as late as the reign of James I of non-musicians using it to mean the violin. Three, by coincidence, come from 1608: on 12 February the musician Peter Edney submitted an autograph bill for 'one base violin' to the Earl of Salisbury, but the earl's clerk endorsed it 'paid Mr Edney for a Basse vyolle'; on 11 July the violinist Jacques Bochan was listed in the accounts of Prince Henry's household as a 'frenche violer'; and in August the traveller Thomas Coryat reported that he heard 'treble viols' in Venice at the festival of San Rocco, though the payments for the occasion show that violinists actually took part.[4] As late as 1636 the court Audit Office recorded a payment to the violinist Davis Mell for a 'Treble vyoll'; in the records of the Treasury of the Chamber, an office in direct contact with musicians, it is given as a 'violin'.[5] There is no case known to me where a writer of the time can be shown to have described a viol wrongly as a violin, so it may be that 'viol' had a secondary meaning similar to, and probably derived from, *viola*, used in a generic sense in sixteenth-century Italian for all types of stringed instruments, plucked and bowed.

The earliest unambiguous references to violins outside the court are in three documents from 1557–60 relating to East Anglian waits. In an inventory of goods drawn up on the death in 1557 of Benet Pryme, a member of the Cambridge University waits from about 1546, 'vii vyalles & vyolans' are valued at £3.[6] Pryme was evidently an instrument-maker as well as a musician, for the document also refers to 'x pypes of sondry sortes & 1 shacke butt(e)s' and, 'In the shoppe', 'a nest of unp(er)fyte vyall(e)s' as well as 'unp(er)fytt regall(e)s & oth(e)r lu(m)ber'; if so, then Pryme would be by far the earliest English violin-maker so far identified. The next year, 1558, the Colchester wait John Hogg took as apprentice one Jeffrye Wood, son of Clement Wood of Calais; the indenture drawn up at the time states that Wood was to be 'enstructed, enformed and

---

[4] Library of Hatfield House, Cecil MSS, bills 14/9; *GB-Lpro*, E101/433/8; Arnold, *Giovanni Gabrieli*, 203–9.

[5] Ashbee, *RECM*, iii. 86, 152.

[6] A. H. Nelson (ed.), *Records of Early English Drama, Cambridge* (Toronto, Buffalo, and London, 1989), 203; see also I. Payne, 'Instrumental Music at Trinity College, Cambridge, c.1594–c.1615: Archival and Biographical Evidence', *ML* 68 (1987), 139.

taught' in 'the viall & viallyn'.[7] Two years later Hogg took another apprentice, Peter Sprott, son of Thomas Sprott of Blofield near Norwich, agreeing this time to teach him 'the seid science of a mynstrell, that is to say to play upon the vyall & violett, by the sight of the pricksong and so in like maner eny other thing which the said John useth or hereafter shall use'.

It is not clear to what extent these references are exceptional. We might expect to find the violin appearing outside the court first in documents relating to aristocratic households, for their musicians would surely have been in contact with royal musicians when their employers were at court. By and large, this is the pattern suggested by those references that have so far come to light. But this may be because the records of aristocratic households have been more thoroughly searched by musicologists than those relating to municipal musicians, or simply that the terminology in the latter, far from contact with the court, tended to be less precise than the former. We shall never know how many early references to the violin lie concealed in the words 'viol', 'fiddle', or just 'minstrel'.

The references to violins in aristocratic households begin with entries in Sir Henry Sidney's accounts for the period 25 February 1564/5 to 14 February 1565/6. They contain a payment of £66. 19s. 11d. for 'charges of vyolens', a large sum that perhaps represents the initial costs of establishing a violin consort in his household, and £13. 6s. 8d. for 'Redemyng the apprentyshode of two boyes for the violens'. A year or so later, in accounts dated 22 February 1566/7 to 24 November 1567 and marked 'howseholde sent to Ireland', 20s. was spent on a 'set of bookes & stringes for the violons ther'. Sidney, appointed Lord Deputy of Ireland in October 1565, arrived there in January 1566; in his accounts for 1566–7 £10. 10s. was also paid for a 'Sette of Vialles'.[8]

The next payment of this sort occurs in the accounts of Sir Thomas Kytson of Hengrave Hall in Suffolk. In December 1572 a 'treable violen' was bought for £1, while an inventory of 1602–3 includes 'one borded Chest, w(i)th locke & keye w(i)th vi vialle(s)', and 'one borded Chest with six vyolenns' valued at £4 and £3 respectively; the set of violins, at least, was already in existence by 1575, for in June of that year the instrument-maker William Lawrence was paid 6d. 'for mendying the violen cheste'.[9]

---

[7] W. G. B., '"The Science of a Mynstrell": How it was Taught in Essex in 1558', *Essex Review*, 49 (1940), 107–10.

[8] Kent Archives Office, Maidstone, U1475/A5/4, U1475/A5/6; I am grateful to Lynn Hulse for providing me with these references, and a number of others in this chapter; Woodfill, *Musicians in English Society*, 272.

[9] M. Ross, 'The Kytsons of Hengrave: A Study in Musical Patronage', M. Mus. diss. (London, 1989), esp. 6, 11–19, 20, 22, 65–70, 72, 77.

These instruments, along with recorders, cornetts, sackbuts, flutes, a set of 'three hoeboyes w(i)th a Curtall and a lysarden', several sizes of lute, five keyboard instruments, and 'one bandore and a sitherne w(i)th a dooble case', were apparently used by a group of at least four resident musicians, led by the composer Edward Johnson, who are recorded at Hengrave in a set of surviving household accounts for the years 1572–5. Johnson was still at Hengrave in 1588, when he made an agreement for twenty-one years with his employer. Their music, listed in the 1602–3 inventory, included 'v: bookes Covered w(i)th p(ar)chement w(i)th pavines galliarde(s) measures and Cuntrye daunces', 'v: bookes of levaultoes & Corrantoes', and 'v: bookes covered w(i)th p(ar)chement w(i)th pavines and galliarde(s) for the Consort', valued at 5s., 6d., and 3s. respectively.

There are a number of references to sets of viols and violins in aristocratic households over the next few decades. The Earl of Leicester's possessions at Kenilworth Castle in 1583 included 'Two chestes of Instrumentes, thone with vi vialles, thother withe fyve Violens', as well as a case of twelve flutes, three bandoras, three lutes, a claviorgan, and two 'double Virginalles'.[10] At Leicester House in London in 1580 there were 'Twoe settes of vyalles in 2 chestes', but by 1588 the same house contained 'one sett of violls and the other viollens'—perhaps the same instruments more precisely described.[11] In 1596 an inventory of Lord Lumley's household included a large collection of instruments: thirteen 'VYOLENS' and forty-one 'VYOLES', as well as ten shawms, two bombards, four crumborns, four sackbuts, twelve cornetts, fifteen recorders, eight lutes, two Irish harps, and fifteen assorted keyboard instruments; most of them had probably been bequeathed to Lumley by his father-in-law, Henry Fitzalan, Earl of Arundel (d. 1580).[12]

An account book of the household of Thomas Sackville, Earl of Dorset, for the period July 1607 to April 1608 shows that he employed ten musicians, three of whom, Horatio Lupo, Jonas Wrench, and John Myners, were later to enter royal service; Myners was paid 20s. in October 1607 for 'strings bought for yo(u)r lo(rdship's) Violls and Violins' and 43s. for 'Violl stringes of sundry sortes'.[13] A separate group, 'Thomas Cordwell . . . and the rest of his Company of violins', received £5 between them (£1 each for five players?) for work at Christmas 1607. Sackville died on 19 April 1608, and paid tribute in his will to his 'divers Musitions, some for the voice and some for the Instrument whom I have

[10] HMC 77, *Report on the Manuscripts of Lord de l'Isle*, ed. Kingsford, i. 291.
[11] Woodfield, *Early History*, 212; D. C. Price, *Patrons and Musicians of the English Renaissance* (Cambridge, 1981), 169.
[12] Warren, 'Music at Nonesuch', 50.
[13] Kent Archives Office, Maidstone, U269/A1/1; see also S. Jeans, 'Seventeenth-Century Musicians in the Sackville Papers', *MMR* 88 (1958), 182–7.

founde to be honest in their behaviour and skillful in theire profession and who have often given me, after the labors and payneful travells of the day, much recreation and contentacon with theire delightfull harmony'.[14] He requested his son Lord Buckhurst to employ them at £20 a year each.

Reading the lists of instruments in great Elizabethan households such as those of the Earls of Arundel and Leicester, it is easy to get the impression that their musical establishments were similar in size to the royal music. But the court employed about fifty instrumentalists around 1600, divided into separate groups of trumpets, fifes and drums, shawms, flutes, recorders, violins, and lutes, while at Hengrave Sir Thomas Kytson enjoyed a similar range of instrumental sound at a fraction of the cost, for it was all provided by a few versatile musicians; only the court had the resources to allow a group to specialize in a single combination. The author of the treatise 'Some Rules and Orders for the Government of an Earle', the individual known just as R. B., thought that an earl ought to employ five musicians who would undertake the following duties:

At great feastes when the Earles service is going to the table they are to play upon Shagbutts, Cornetts, Shalmes, and such other instruments going with winde. In meale times to play upon vialls, violens or other [or else] broken musicke. They are to teach the Earles children to singe and play upon the base violl the virginalls, Lute, Bandora, or Citerne.[15]

R.B., who wrote in about 1605 but was recalling the practice of households of the 1570s and 1580s, assumed that professional musicians would play all the main sets of consort instruments, but would teach the children of the house solo instruments. He did not expect them to teach consort instruments, for the more advanced skills required for playing in ensemble were still not generally found among amateurs. The earl's children might learn the bass viol to play solo pieces or to accompany their own singing, but most of them were not yet, it seems, taught to play in viol consorts; there are cases of amateur viol consorts in the late sixteenth century—the famous painting of the life of Sir Henry Unton (d. 1596) at the National Portrait Gallery in London seems to provide an example—but it seems that they only became widespread after 1600.[16] Sir Thomas Hoby's 1561 translation of Castiglione's words recom-

---

[14] *GB-Lpro*, PROB 11/113, q. 1.

[15] *GB-Lbl*, Add. MS 29262, fos. 1ʳ, 14ᵛ; see Edwards, 'The Sources of Elizabethan Consort Music', i. 50; the common attribution to Richard Braithwaite has been challenged; see M. Girouard, *Life in the English Country House* (New Haven, Conn., 1978), 323, who proposes Robert Bainbridge, a servant of the third earl of Huntingdon.

[16] This point was first made in Edwards, 'The Performance of Ensemble Music'; see also Doe, 'The Emergence of the In Nomine'; C. Monson, *Voices and Viols in England 1600–1650: The Sources and the Music* (Ann Arbor, Mich., 1982); Woodfield, *Early History*, 227, 249–50.

mending viols to courtiers—'And the music of a set of viols doth no less delight a man, for it is very sweet and artificial'—has sometimes been used to advance the case for viol-playing Elizabethan gentlemen, but it represents the practice of the northern Italian courts early in the sixteenth century, where aristocrats had played in the earliest viol consorts (see Ch. 1).[17]

We need to bear this point in mind when considering a collection such as Antony Holborne's *Pavans, Galliards, Almains, and Other Short Aeirs both Grave and Light, in Five Parts, for Viols, Violins, or Other Musicall Winde Instruments* (London, 1599). In dedicating the collection to Sir Richard Champernowne of Modbury in south Devon, a relative of Robert Cecil, Holborne wrote that part of his 'poore labors' had been 'distinctively bundled . . . into a catologue volume, accompanied with a more liberall and enlarged choice then hath at any time as yet come to your refined eares'. In other words, some of the pieces had been performed in, and were perhaps written for, Champernowne's household, while others had not been heard there and were presumably written later for other musicians; Holborne was at court from at least 1597 (he described himself as 'servant to her most Excellent Majestie' in *The Cittharn Schoole* published in that year). His dances have often been thought of as music written for amateurs, but the phrase 'come to your refined eares' suggests that Champernowne's role was as a listener rather than a performer, and we know that he maintained a regular group of musicians at Modbury. In 1595 he wrote twice to Cecil, once to deny a charge that he was 'a gelder of boys for preserving their voices', and once to dissuade him from poaching a boy singer—'lackyng hym, my whole consort for musyck, which most delytes mee, wer clean overthrown'.[18] An echo of this affair can perhaps be found in the story told by an early nineteenth-century historian of Devon that Queen Elizabeth 'contrived means' to ruin Champernowne 'in resentment of an affront he had given her by refusing the use of a band of music, on which he prided himself as the first in England'.[19]

By publishing a collection of consort dance music Holborne was not necessarily attempting to cater for the amateur market. 'Viols, violins, or other [or else] musicall winde instruments' recalls the list of instruments that R. B. recommended for professional musicians in aristocratic

---

[17] Strunk, *Source Readings in Music History*, ii. 94.

[18] HMC 9, *Calendar of the Manuscripts of the Most Hon. the Marquis of Salisbury*, ed. R. A. R[oberts], v. 155, 320, 386, 436–7; Library of Hatfield House, Cecil Papers 35/100, quoted in Edwards, 'The Sources', i. 47; C. E. Champernowne, 'The Champernowne Family', unpublished typescript in Devon County Library, Tiverton branch; B. Jeffery, 'Antony Holborne', *MD* 22 (1968), 134–5.

[19] T. Moore, *The History of Devonshire from the Earliest Period to the Present*, i (London, 1829), 530.

households; amateurs would not normally have played violins or wind instruments at the time, and in 1599 the amateur viol-playing boom was only beginning. It is equally likely that Holborne and his publisher William Barley were hoping to sell music that had been written for professional household musicians to similar groups. The option of viols, violins, and wind instruments should not be thought of as a choice between instruments played by different social classes, for household musicians would have played all three types, perhaps choosing wind instruments for outdoor work and (as R. B. suggests) processions, viols for *Tafelmusik*, and violins for the dancing that often followed Elizabethan meals. Holborne's dances seem designed to cater for these varied requirements: their restricted ranges make them equally suitable for winds or strings, and they all work perfectly well as functional dance music. Yet many of the pavans are elaborately worked and demand to be heard in a concert-like situation.

By the end of the century sets of violins began to appear in educational establishments that were training boys for possible careers as professional musicians. In 1587 John Howes drew up a comprehensive musical curriculum for Christ's Hospital in London; its children were to:

learne to singe, to play uppon all sorts of instruments, as to sounde the trumpett, the cornet, the recorder or flute, to play uppon shagbolts, shalmes, & all other instruments that are to be plaid upon, either w(i)th winde or finger.[20]

We can presume that violins were among those instruments that were to be played with the finger, and they are specifically mentioned in an educational context in the will of Sebastian Westcote, Almoner, Organist, and Master of the Children of St Paul's Cathedral, who died in April 1582; he left his 'cheste of vyalyns and vialls' to the cathedral 'to exercise and learne the children and Choristers there'.[21] Also, in 1595 the song-school at Newark-on-Trent possessed five 'violine' books and five 'violins' with a chest, as well as church music and madrigals.[22]

Unambiguous references to violins in municipal records become common around 1600. Town waits spent much of their time playing loud wind instruments outdoors, and the shawm was so closely associated with them that it was often known at the time as the 'wait' or 'wait pipe'. Violins were an indoor alternative, as was made clear when Lord Henry Clifford hired four waits of Malton in Yorkshire to entertain Lord and Lady Salisbury at Londesborough in October 1619; it was said that they

---

[20] M. C. Boyd, *Elizabethan Music and Music Criticism* (2nd edn., Philadelphia, 1962), 15.

[21] D. Scott, *The Music of St Paul's Cathedral* (London, 1972), 13; see also W. H. G. Flood, 'Master Sebastian of Paul's', *MA* 3 (1911–12), 149–57; G. E. P. Arkwright, 'Sebastian Westcote', *MA* 4 (1912–13), 187–9.

[22] Woodfill, *Musicians in English Society*, 156.

played 'at tymes with loud instruments'—presumably outdoors—'and in the great chamber with 4 violins'; they were paid 40s. for a week, and 10s. 'for their horsmeat & lodging'.[23] The Chester waits are first recorded with violins in 1591; a document relating to a dispute over the ownership of their instruments lists them as 'the how boies, the Recorders, the Cornet(e)s and violens'.[24] The Norwich waits are not known to have owned a communal set of violins in the sixteenth century; only wind instruments appear in inventories of 1584–5, 1618, and 1622. But they took a member of the cathedral to court in 1583 because, among other things, he called them 'fiddling and piping knaves'; they apparently played a mixed consort including, presumably, a violin and a viol in 1578 (see below); and in 1600 the comedian and musician William Kemp praised them in extravagant terms, mentioning 'besides their excellency in wind instruments, theyr rare cunning on the Vyoll, and Violin'—instruments that were presumably owned by individuals in the group.[25]

There is no direct evidence that the London waits, the largest and most prominent group of its type in the country, played violins until 1619, when two 'violen' players were appointed.[26] But appearances may be deceptive in this case because a set of 'vialles' had been purchased as early as 1561 (as well as 'certain new instruments' in 1576), and there is evidence that they played broken or mixed consorts with, probably, a violin by 1600 (see below). Also, if the two pairs of musicians, each consisting of a violin and a viola, who accompany dancing in Joris Hoefnagel's painting *A Fête at Bermondsey* (c.1570) are not actually intended to be members of the London waits, they certainly represent musicians of that class in the London area (Pl. 4(a)). A similar duet team, late-Elizabethan to judge from the costumes, appears in a woodcut used to illustrate seventeenth-century broadside ballads (Fig. 6.1). Nevertheless, some groups of waits do not appear to have used violins or viols until well into the seventeenth century. For instance, in the records relating to the York waits, a prominent and well-documented group, the viol (a bass) is first mentioned in the will of Richard Bradley in 1623, while violins do not appear until 1640: 'one treble violin and one tenor' were left by Thomas Girdler, who died in November of that year.[27]

---

[23] Library of Chatsworth House, Bolton MS 98, fo. 137[r].

[24] L. M. Clopper (ed.), *Records of Early English Drama, Chester* (Toronto, Buffalo, and London, 1979), 164–5.

[25] Lasocki, 'Professional Recorder Players', i. 228–41; William Kemp, *Nine Daies Wonder*, ed. G. B. Harrison (The Bodley Head Quartos, 4; London, 1923), 24.

[26] Woodfill, *Musicians in English Society*, 248–9; Lasocki, 'Professional Recorder Players', i. 223–4.

[27] J. Merryweather, *York Music: The Story of a City's Music from 1304 to 1896* (York, 1988), 94, 150, 151; see also A. F. Johnston and M. Rogerson (eds.), *Records of Early English Drama, York*, i–iii (Toronto, Buffalo, and London, 1979).

6.1. Woodcut used for English seventeenth-century broadside ballads, showing a duet team, late-Elizabethan to judge from the costumes. From C. Hindley (ed.), *The Roxburghe Ballads* (London, 1873–4), i. 303; ii. 300

The normal practice of professional groups in Elizabethan and Jacobean England was to use the various instrumental sets or families as alternatives on a musical menu, rather than as ingredients in a single dish. Charles Butler still thought that mixed consorts were the exception rather than the rule as late as 1636: 'The several kinds of Instruments ar commonly used severally by them selves: as a Set of Viols, a Set of Waits [shawms], or the like: but sometimes, upon some special occasion, many of both Sorts ar most sweetly joined in Consort', and this was at a time when the use of lutes and keyboard instruments in ensembles was greatly increasing the number and variety of mixed consorts.[28] In the sixteenth century the only established mixed consort of soft instruments (loud wind bands often mixed cornetts, shawms, sackbuts, and curtals) was the six-man group variously known as the broken consort, the English consort, the consort of six, and, to use the terminology proposed by Warwick Edwards, the mixed consort. Consisting of treble viol or violin, tenor flute or recorder, bass viol, lute, cittern, and bandora, it was the first English ensemble that was a match for the mixed consorts that had been developed in the advanced musical circles of northern Italy and southern Germany, and it was the first anywhere in Europe to have a sufficiently standardized scoring to attract a sizeable repertoire that exploited its peculiar characteristics. It also seems to have been the means

---

[28] C. Butler, *The Principles of Musik in Singing and Setting* (London, 1636), 93; see Edwards, 'The Sources', i. 40.

by which the violin was freed in England from its traditional role as the soprano member of the violin consort.

The word 'consort' is a problem. It is used today to mean a group of instrumentalists playing together, and by extension the instruments they play. For want of a better alternative I have used it in this sense in this book, and, as Edwards has pointed out in a thorough investigation of the topic, it was used thus around 1600. He cites a document in the Cecil papers recording New Year's gifts to the constituent parts of the royal music, 'the consort of veyals', (another example of 'viol' used to mean violin), 'the consort of flutes', 'the drumes', 'the trumpeters', and 'the consort of howboyes and cornets', to which can be added a document in the court Lord Steward's office relating to the provision of transport for James I's summer progresses: in 1604, 1605, and 1608 'Musicons' were allocated one cart, while 'The Consorte(s)' are allocated three; the 'musicons' are likely to be the lutenists and other miscellaneous solo instrumentalists of the Privy Chamber, while the 'consorts' can only be some or all of the four instrumental ensembles, made up respectively of shawms and trombones, flutes, recorders, and violins.[29] But Edwards's main point is undeniable: that in the earliest period of its use, from about 1575 to 1625, 'consort' was most commonly used to mean a mixed ensemble—as in the Charles Butler passage discussed above—and specifically, to mean the six-man mixed consort.

Earlier historians of the mixed consort were largely taken up with its role in the Shakespearean theatre. Thurston Dart, for instance, introduced an edition of pieces from Morley's *First Booke of Consort Lessons* with the words 'they were heard in the Shakespearean theatre, as incidental music'.[30] It has since been realized that most of the early references come from aristocratic households; that many of them relate to entertainments given for the queen on her summer progresses; and that the genre was only taken up by waits and theatre musicians several decades later. As it happens, the earliest apparent reference to a mixed consort comes from a play, *Jocasta*, published in 1566 by George Gascoigne and Francis Kinwelmershe; a dumb-show was accompanied by 'a dolefull and straunge noyse of violles, Cythren, Bandurion, and such like'.[31] But *Jocasta* was written by two students of Gray's Inn and, according to the title-page, was 'there by them presented', so it has little or no connection with the commercial theatre, such as it was at the time. Law students would probably have recruited their musicians from the households of their aristocratic friends and relations rather than from the ranks of more lowly waits or theatre musicians. The same might be said

[29] Edwards, 'The Sources', i. 36–57; *GB-Lpro*, LS13/168, 139, 184, 241.
[30] *Two Consort Lessons Collected by Thomas Morley*, ed. T. Dart (London, 1957).
[31] Ward, *Sprightly and Cheerful Musick*, 22.

of other sixteenth-century plays that contain references to a 'consort', such as *The Rare Triumphs of Love and Fortune* (1582?), *Fedele and Fortunio; or, Two Italian Gentlemen* (*c*.1584), and Robert Wilmot's *The Tragedie of Tancred and Gismund* (1591), all performed at court, the latter by 'the Gentlemen of the Inner Temple'.[32]

It may be more than a coincidence that George Gascoigne was also involved in the outdoor entertainment given for the queen by Robert Dudley, Earl of Leicester, at Kenilworth Castle in July 1575; his description of the event, published in 1576 in a pamphlet now lost, mentioned 'a consort of musicke unseene' that accompanied several songs; it is the earliest recorded use of the word 'consort' in a musical sense. It is supplemented by a more detailed account by Robert Laneham, who was greatly impressed by the 'melodious noiz, compoounded of six severall instruments', and by the 'song by a skilful artist intoo hiz parts so swaetly sorted: each part in hiz instrument so clean & sharpely toouched, every instrument again in hiz kind so excellently tunabl ... the hole armony conveyd in tyme, tune, & temper thus incomparably melodious'.[33] There is, of course, no proof that these 'six several instruments' were the six of the mixed consort, but it is significant that Edward Johnson, the leader of the Hengrave group (which possessed music 'for the Consort' and all its required instruments) was paid 10*s.* in July–August 1575 by the Kytson household 'for his charge in awayting on my Lord of Leycester', presumably in connection with the Kenilworth entertainment.[34]

Edward Johnson was also involved in some way with the entertainment given in September 1591 for the queen by the Earl of Hertford at Elvetham, his Hampshire country estate. As Elizabeth arrived she was greeted by 'a song of six parts, with the musicke of an exquisite consort, wherin was the Lute, Bandora, Base-violl, Citterne, Treble-violl, and Flute', and as she departed a 'consort of Musitions hidden in a bower' accompanied a duet; the music for both songs is ascribed to Johnson, though it survives in settings for voices and viols rather than for mixed consort.[35] During another event at Elvetham:

her Majestie graciously admitted unto her presence a notable consort of six Musitions, which my Lord of Hertford had provided to entertaine her Majestie withall, at her will and pleasure, and when it should seeme good to her highnesse. Their Musicke so highly pleased her, that in grace and favour therof,

[32] Edwards, 'The Sources', i. 56; Chambers, *The Elizabethan Stage*, iii. 514–15; *The First Book of Consort Lessons, Collected by Thomas Morley 1599 and 1611*, ed. S. Beck (New York, 1959), 14.

[33] Edwards, 'The Sources', i. 40, 55; R. Laneham, *A Letter* (London, 1575), 43.

[34] Ross, 'The Kytsons of Hengrave', 33.

[35] Edwards, 'The Sources', i. 28–9, 56; P. Brett (ed.), *Consort Songs* (MB 22; London, 1967), no. 33; see E. Brennecke, 'The Entertainment at Elvetham, 1591', in J. H. Long (ed.), *Music in Renaissance Drama* (Lexington, Ky., 1968), 32–56.

she gave a new name unto one of their Pavans, made long since by Master Thomas Morley, then Organist of Paules Church.

The identity of this piece is not known, but there are several pavans by Morley in the mixed consort repertoire.

Mixed consorts may also have been used in one or two of the other outdoor entertainments given for Elizabeth at about the same time. For instance, the month before she visited Elvetham she was 'delighted with most delicate musicke' during an outdoor banquet at Cowdray in Sussex, and at Rycote in Oxfordshire in September 1592 she heard 'sweete musicke of sundry sorts' in the garden.[36] Edward Johnson cannot be connected with these events, but his hand can perhaps be discerned in the music for Elizabeth's famous visit to Norwich in August 1578, the earliest occasion when the mixed consort can be associated with a group of town waits. One of the two chroniclers of the event, Bernard Garter, wrote that when the queen entered the city 'The Musitions within the gate upon their softe instruments used broken Musicke, and one of them did sing'; in an account of a subsequent entertainment he was more specific: 'Then entred a consorte of Musicke. viz. sixe Musitions, all in long vestures of white Sarcenet gyrded aboute them, and garlands on their heades playing very cunningly'.[37] Thomas Churchyard, the author of an outdoor entertainment that was cancelled because of the weather, wrote that there was to have been a 'noble noyse of Musicke of al kind of instruments, severally to be sounded an played upon; and at one time they shoulde be sounded all togither, that might serve for a consorte of broken Musicke'.

It has generally been assumed that the musicians concerned were the Norwich waits, but David Lasocki has pointed out that there were only five of them at the time; given that there is little or no evidence that other waits groups took up the mixed consort before the 1590s, it is likely that they had help from outside for this special event.[38] The obvious person to have supplied that help is Edward Johnson, who had already performed a similar service at Kenilworth and Elvetham, and who worked in the nearest prominent musical establishment to Norwich, about thirty miles from the city. Indeed, it may be that Johnson and his Hengrave colleagues were involved in some way with the early history of the mixed consort, and that the purchase of their treble violin in 1572 was a step in the

[36] Nichols, *The Progresses and Public Processions of Queen Elizabeth*, iii. 94, 169.

[37] Edwards, 'The Sources', i. 39, 49, 55.

[38] D. Galloway (ed.), *Records of Early English Drama, Norwich 1540–1642* (Toronto, Buffalo, and London, 1984), 157; see also Lasocki, 'Professional Recorder Players', i. 148; for the Norwich waits, see G. A. Stephen, *The Waits of the City of Norwich through Four Centuries to 1790* (Norwich, 1933); C. A. Janssen, 'The Waytes of Norwich in Mediaeval and Renaissance Civic Pageantry', Ph.D. diss. (University of New Brunswick, 1978).

process. As for the Norwich waits, they seem to have continued to play mixed consort music, for one of its members, Edward Jefferies senior, left most of the required instruments—a 'treble violyn', a violin of unspecified size, treble and bass viols, a bandora, an old lute, a flute, and two old unspecified instruments—when he died in October 1617.[39] When his colleague Thomas Quash was appointed on 13 June 1612 he promised to provide 'a treable violyn'.[40]

The four main sources of mixed consort music neatly exemplify the dissemination of the genre from the country-house circuit to the wider musical community. The earliest, now divided between England and America, consists of four 'consort Bookes' (the lute and bandora parts are lost) written by the teenage lutenist Daniel Bacheler in the household of Sir Francis Walsingham; he became Walsingham's page on 7 June 1586, and two of the pieces in the collection are dated 1588.[41] The largest source is the set of four part-books (the violin and bandora parts are lost) in *GB-Cu*; earlier writers thought that they were the repertoire of a group in the Cambridge area, but Ian Harwood showed that they were copied by Matthew Holmes, Precentor and singing-man at Christ Church, Oxford from 1588 to 1597; they were probably used there during that time by Holmes and other professional musicians.[42]

By the end of the century the mixed consort was sufficiently widespread to allow its repertoire to be published. Thomas Morley's *The First Booke of Consort Lessons, Made by Divers Exquisite Authors, for Six Instruments to Play Together* (London, 1599; 2nd edn., 1611) evidently served a double purpose. According to the title-page it was printed 'at the coast & charges of a Gentle-man, for his private pleasure, and for divers others his frendes which delight in Musicke', but Morley wrote in the dedication to the Lord Mayor of London, Sir Stephen Some, and his aldermen that 'the ancient custome of this most honorable and renowned Cittie hath beene ever, to returne and maintane excellent and expert Musitians, to adorne your Honors favors, Feasts and solemne meetings'; he recommended its contents 'to your servants carefull and skillful handling: that the wants of exquisite harmony . . . may be excused by their melodious additions'.[43]

---

[39] Galloway, *Records of Early English Drama, Norwich*, 137.
[40] Lasocki, 'Professional Recorder Players', i. 237; ii. 734–5.
[41] The Brynmor Jones Library, Hull University, MSS DDHO/20/1–3, and *US-OAm*; see W. Edwards, 'The Walsingham Consort Books', *ML*, 55 (1974), 209–14; id. (ed.), *Music for Mixed Consort* (MB 40; London, 1977), nos. 1–15; Batchelor, 'Daniel Bacheler'.
[42] MSS Dd. 3.18, 5.20, 5.21, 14.24; see I. Harwood, 'The Origins of the Cambridge Lute Manuscripts', *LSJ*, 5 (1963), 32–48; L. Nordstrom, 'The Cambridge Consort Books', *JLSA*, 5 (1972), 70–103; Edwards (ed.), *Music for Mixed Consort*, nos. 16–27.
[43] T. Dart, 'Morley's Consort Lessons of 1599', *PRMA*, 74 (1947–8), 1–9; Morley, *The First Book of Consort Lessons*, ed. Beck.

The last purely instrumental mixed consort collection, Philip Rosseter's *Lessons for Consort, Made by Sundry Excellent Authors, and Set to Six Severall Instruments* (London, 1609) was published in response to 'the good successe and francke entertainment which the late imprinted set of consort bookes [Morley's *Consort Lessons*] generally received'. Rosseter dedicated it to Sir William Gascoigne of Sedbury Hall near Richmond in Yorkshire (George Gascoigne belonged to the Bedfordshire branch of the family), making it clear that he had made the arrangements himself for the collection—'and now by mee Consorted'—and that Gascoigne maintained musicians in his house 'such as lively can express them'.[44]

I have rehearsed the early history of the mixed consort at length because it bears directly on one of the vexed questions of scoring that bedevil the genre: should the treble part be played on treble viol or violin? At first sight the viol is the preferred option: it is mentioned in *Jocasta*, in the Elvetham description, on the treble part of the Walsingham collection, and on the title-pages of the Morley and Rosseter prints. The violin is only mentioned in a single source: fos. 3 and 5 of the recorder part of the Cambridge books have the headings 'Treble violan' and (crossed out) 'The treble violan parte', suggesting that they contain some stray parts from a lost violin book. But the mixed consort in the *The Memorial Painting of Sir Henry Unton*, executed shortly after his death in 1596, shows a violin, as do all the Continental pictures of ensembles related to the mixed consort (Pl. 4(*b*); Fig. 6.2).[45] Furthermore, a description of incidental music in the Blackfriars theatre, written by Frederic Gerschow after he had visited it in the party of Duke Philip Julius of Stettin-Pomerania on 18 September 1602, seems to refer to a mixed consort with a violin: he mentioned 'delightful instrumental music of 'Orgeln', 'Lauten', 'Pandoren', 'Mandoren', 'Geigen', and 'Pfeiffen'.[46] *Geigen* was associated with the violin in Germany at the time—the English equivalent would be 'fiddles'—while *Violen* or *Fiolen* was a neutral word, like 'strings' (see Ch. 7).

It has been said that the printed mixed consort collections specify the viol rather than the violin because they were aimed at an amateur market, but equally it could be that they are further instances of 'viol' used generically to mean viol and violin. The musician who played 'treble viol' in the Elvetham entertainment was certainly a professional, as in all

---

[44] I. Harwood, 'Rosseter's *Lessons for Consort* of 1609', *LSJ*, 7 (1965), 15–23; Edwards (ed.), *Music for Mixed Consort*, nos. 28–34.

[45] Edwards (ed.), *Music for Mixed Consort*, p. xxii; W. Salmen, *Haus- und Kammermusik* (Musikgeschichte in Bildern, IV/3; Leipzig, 1982), illus. 24; van Dijck and Koopman (eds.), *The Harpsichord in Dutch Art*, illus. 60, 61, 73.

[46] Adapted from G. von Bülow, 'Diary of the Journey of Philip Julius, Duke of Stettin-Pomerania, through England in the Year 1602', *Transactions of the Royal Historical Society*, NS, 6 (1892), 28–9.

6.2. Engraving by Simon de Passe (Amsterdam, 1612) of a mixed consort with a violin. From W. Salmen, *Haus- und Kammermusik* (Musikgeschichte in Bildern, IV/3; Leipzig, 1982), 71

probability was the treble player in Walsingham's mixed consort, and Morley and Rosseter seem to have had professionals partly in mind when they put together their collections. Such musicians would have played violins as well as viols, and would have chosen whichever instrument was most appropriate to particular circumstances: dancing would have called for the violin, more refined 'chamber music' for the viol, and there must have been many occasions when either instrument would have been appropriate.

There are particular reasons for thinking that 'treble viol' should not be taken literally in the case of Morley's collection because of its connection with the London waits. Their records contain no references to violins until 1619, when Robert Parker and Henry Field were appointed, the former playing 'violen', low tenor violin and wind instruments, the latter treble 'viollen' and winds; Parker replaced Robert Salmon ('treble viol' and wind instruments), who himself had replaced Stephen Thomas (a wait from 1597) only a year before. The records of the waits do not reveal what instruments Thomas played, but he is known from another source to have been a violinist, for on 16 July 1607 he and Robert Bateman 'plaid on the treble violens' in an entertainment for James I and Prince Henry at Merchant Taylors' Hall.[47]

Taken literally, the evidence suggests that the London waits employed a violinist from 1597 until 1618, when they went back to a treble viol-player for a year before appointing two violinists; it is more likely of course that Thomas and Salmon played both instruments all along. 1597 probably marks the moment when the waits began to play mixed consort music, just as 1619 may mark the moment when they abandoned it in favour of ensembles with two violins. The waits certainly seem to have played a mixed consort for the series of events at court on 6 January 1600/1 that included, according to Leslie Hotson's theory, the first night of Shakespeare's *Twelfth Night*, for Duke Virginio Orsino, who was a guest of honour, wrote of hearing 'some instruments to my belief never heard in Italy, but miraculous ones'; the Lord Chamberlain's memorandum of the arrangements includes the note: 'To send for the Musitions of the Citty to be reddy to attend'.[48] But there is nothing to support the idea, floated by Thurston Dart, that a mixed consort was heard during Shakespeare's play.[49] Orsino wrote that the 'miraculous' instruments serenaded him in his lodgings before the show, and the Lord Chamberlain made a separate note to 'appoint Musicke severally for the Queene and some for the play in the Hall' (Orsino's description mentions 'diverse consorts of music' in the hall); it is highly unlikely that the waits would have taken precedence over the court's own consorts in the central event of the evening.

The extent to which the violin, in sets or mixed consorts, was used in the Shakespearean theatre is open to question. The commercial companies certainly employed actor-musicians such as William Kemp (described in a 1586 Danish document as 'instrumentist'), Augustine Phillips (who left a 'base viall', 'a citterne, a bandore and a lute' on his death in May 1605), and Edward Alleyn (who owned lute-books, was described as a 'musicion' in 1595, and supposedly left a bandora, a cittern, a lute, and six viols at his death in November 1626); in 1598 Alleyn's company, the Lord Admiral's Men, owned 'a trebel viall, a basse

[47] Woodfill, *Musicians in English Society*, 248–9; C. M. Clode, *The Early History of the Guild of Merchant Taylors*, 2 vols. (London, 1888), i. 290.
[48] L. Hotson, *The First Night of 'Twelfth Night'* (London, 1954), 180–1, 201–2.
[49] Dart, introduction to *Two Consort Lessons Collected by Thomas Morley*.

viol, a bandore, a sytteren', and bought several other instruments in that year and the next.[50] The English theatre companies that toured the Continent at the time are consistently described as offering music as well as drama (see Ch. 7). In 1601, for instance, a group at Münster had with them 'many different kinds of instruments on which they played, such as *luten*, *zitteren*, *fiolen*, *pipen* and the like. They danced many new and foreign dances (not customary in this country) at the beginning and end of the comedies'.[51]

But the fact remains that the references to elaborate theatre music mostly come from outside the mainstream: from court plays or those of the choirboy companies of St Paul's and the Chapel Royal (revived in 1599–1600 after some years of inactivity), or from post-1608 plays, when the King's Men inherited the Blackfriars theatre from the Chapel Royal company (by then the Queen's Revels Children), and borrowed aspects of the production style of the boy companies. In any case, the texts may record the activity of separate instrumental groups rather than musicians belonging to the companies. A good example is the passage in Dekker's *Old Fortunatus* (published in 1600) that is often cited as evidence of mixed consorts in the public theatre, since a character exclaims at the sound of 'Musicke still', 'Musicke? O delicate warble ... O delicious strings: these heavenly wyre-drawers'. However, the text as printed seems to have been prepared for a court performance in which a professional consort and one of the choirboy companies participated.[52] In Marston's *The Dutch Courtesan* (Queen's Revels, 1603–4) 'gentlemen with musicke' appear on stage at the beginning of Act II; they are presumably the same as the 'M. Creakes noyse' that plays at the end of the act.[53]

A number of plays, including Chapman's *The Gentleman Usher* (Chapel Royal Children, 1602?), Marston's *The Faun* (Queen's Revels Children, 1604 or 1605), and Middleton's *A Mad World, my Masters* (St Paul's Children, 1605), mention music played by a 'consort', though it is not

---

[50] Chambers, *The Elizabethan Stage*, ii. 272, 333–4; W. Greg (ed.), *Henslowe's Papers, being Documents Supplementary to Henlowe's Diary* (London, 1907), 38; R. A. Foakes and R. T. Rickert (eds.), *Henslowe's Diary* (Cambridge, 1961), 101, 102, 122, 318; J. P. Collier, *Memoirs of Edward Alleyn* (London, 1841), 77, which Ward, *Sprightly and Cheerful Musick*, 34, suspects is 'one of the writer's fabrications'.

[51] Translated from J. Jannsen (ed.), *Die Münsterischen Chroniken von Röchell, Stevermann und Corfey* (Münster, 1856), 174; see V. C. Ravn, 'English Instrumentalists at the Danish Court in the Time of Shakespeare', *SIMG* 7 (1905–6), 561; the date of this passage is often given wrongly as 1599; see Lasocki, 'Professional Recorder Players', i. 208.

[52] Thomas Dekker, *Dramatic Works*, ed. F. Bowers, i (Cambridge, 1962), i. 165; for the date of this play, see Chambers, *The Elizabethan Stage*, iii. 290–1, and J. H. Long, *Shakespeare's Use of Music: A Study of the Music and its Performance in the Original Production of Seven Comedies* (Gainesville, Fla. 1961), 48 n. 121.

[53] John Marston, *The Plays*, ed. H. H. Wood, ii (London, 1938), 81, 97; see also Lasocki, 'Professional Recorder Players', i. 213–4.

clear whether this still means the classic six-part mixed consort; in
Westward Ho! by Dekker and Webster (St Paul's Children, 1604) the
musicians are (or impersonate) the 'Town Consort', and are called 'a
noise of fiddlers'; in Robert Armin's *The Two Maids of Moreclacke* (King's
Revels Children, 1607–8?) a group of shawm-players are referred to as
'the waits of London', just as in Beaumont's *The Knight of the Burning
Pestle* (Queen's Revels Children, 1607) the 'shawms' of the Southwark
waits are sent for.[54] They do not appear, so Citizen and his wife Nell
have to make do with the 'scurvy music' of 'fiddlers', provided perhaps by
members of the company.

The word 'fiddle' is a problem. Clearly, it cannot have always have
been a synonym for violin since it was common in English long before the
violin arrived in England. Nor did it always mean a bowed instrument.
J. S. Manifold cites the character in Marlowe's *The Jew of Malta* (*c.*1589)
who enters disguised as a French musician with a lute, only to be
addressed repeatedly as 'Fidler'; similarly, Hortensio is referred to several
times in Acts II and III of *The Taming of the Shrew* (1593?) as a 'fidler',
though he plays the lute.[55] As late as 1673 Constantijn Huygens wrote 'I
use, as I did, to fiddle myself out of a bad humour, either upon a viol, or a
lute, or a theorbe, or a pair of virginals.'[56] Nevertheless, the constant
attribute of a fiddler was, in Manifold's phrase, 'a shabby professionalism'
combined with the use of bowed instruments; as early as the fifteenth
century word-lists translate Latin words for bowed instruments, such as
'viella', 'fidicina', 'vitula', and 'vidula', as 'fydyll', or 'fyyele'.[57] Owen
Feltham wrote in his *Resolves* (*c.*1620) that 'it is a kind of disparagement
to a man to be a common fiddler. It argues his neglect of better
employment, and that he hath spent much time on a thing unnecessarie';
to John Earle (1629) a 'poore Fidler' was 'One that rubs two sticks
together, (as the Indians strike fire) and rubs a poore living out of it';
Samuel Butler's fiddler (*c.*1667–9) has a 'magical rod, his fidlestic'; the
'roughness of his bow makes his strings speak', and 'he is very expert in
his way, and has his trade at his fingers end'.[58]

Fiddlers of this sort stalk the pages of Jacobean and Caroline plays. In
Act I, Scene ii of Dekker's *The Witch of Edmonton* (1621) a character says,
'We'll e'en have an houshold Dinner; and let the Fiddlers go scrape'; in

[54] Lasocki, 'Professional Recorder Players', i. 195, 199, 203–4, 211.

[55] J. S. Manifold, *The Music in English Drama from Shakespeare to Purcell* (London, 1956), 81; C.
Marlowe, *The Complete Works*, ed. F. Bowers, i (Cambridge, 1973), 321–2; *Mr. William Shakespeares
Comedies, Histories and Tragedies* (London, 1623), 216, 218.

[56] J. D. Roberts, 'Has the Problem Changed?', *LSJ*, 6 (1964), 27.

[57] Remnant, *English Bowed Instruments*, Appendix A.

[58] D. G. Weiss, *Samuel Pepys, Curioso* (Pittsburgh, 1957), 75; John Earle, *Micro-Cosmographie*, ed.
E. Arber (Westminster, 1904), 87–8; S. Butler, *Characters*, ed. C. W. Daves (Cleveland and London,
1970), 273–4.

Act II, Scene i of Massinger's *The Duke of Milan* (1621–2?) Gracchio, the leader of a group of 'fiddlers', says, 'You shall scrape, and Ile sing, / A scurvie Dittie to a scurvie tune'; later he says 'we poore waiters / Deale (as you see) in mirth, and foolish fyddles: / It is our element'. A group at a country wedding in Act II, Scene i of Jonson's *A Tale of a Tub* (1633?) is called 'Father Rosin, and his consort / Of fidling Boyes'; they are told to 'scrape the Gut at home'.[59] By then we can be sure that 'fiddlers' meant a group made up principally of violinists. As early as Jonson's *Poetaster* (1601) a character in Act III, Scene iv is told, 'come, we must have you turn fiddler againe, slave, get a base violin at your backe, and march in a tawnie coate, with one sleeve, to Goose-faire'; in *Bartholomew Fair* (1614) Cokes, the rustic dupe, says, 'A set of thes Violines, I would buy too, for a delicate young noise I have i' the country, that are every one a size lesse than another, just like your fiddles.'[60] And a survey of the plays in the repertoire of the King's Men has revealed that 'fiddles' and 'fiddlers' became significantly more common in the reign of Charles I: three texts out of eighty-eight up to 1625 mention them, compared with eight out of forty-three texts from 1625 to 1642; over the same period references to wind instruments decreased: shawms from twelve to one, cornetts from ten to four, and recorders from six to three.[61]

This ties in with what is known about the company's musicians over the same period. In 1624 a list of its members includes under the heading 'Musitions and other necessary attendantes' the names of the members of what appears to be a six-man instrumental consort, two of whom, Ambrose Beeland and William Saunders, later rose via the London waits to become members of the royal violin band; Beeland and a third member, Henry Wilson, were described as 'Fidlers' when they were arrested by a warrant dated 14 December 1628 'at the Complaint of Mr Hemmings', the company's manager, though Wilson was also a singer-lutenist according to a prompt copy of Massinger's *Believe as You List* (1631).[62] In 1624 the musicians of the King's Men were not members of the London waits, though they certainly were later: a list of '6 of ye Blackfriers Musique', prepared as part of the preparations for the masque *The Triumph of Peace* (1634), consists entirely of its current members; we

[59] Dekker, *Dramatic Works*, iii. 505; P. Massinger, *The Plays and Poems*, ed. P. Edwards and C. Gibson, i (Oxford, 1976), 238; C. H. Herford and P. Simpson eds., *Ben Jonson*, iii (Oxford, 1927), 27.

[60] Jonson, iv. 249; vi. 70.

[61] Lasocki, 'Professional Recorder Players', i. 269.

[62] G. E. Bentley, *The Jacobean and Caroline Stage*, 7 vols. (Oxford, 1941–68), i. 15–16; ii. 621; J. P. Cutts, 'New Findings with Regard to the 1624 Protection List', *Shakespeare Survey*, 19 (1966), 101–7; Lasocki, 'Professional Recorder Players', i. 284–90; Ashbee, *RECM*, iii. 41.

have already identified two of them, Henry Field and Ambrose Beeland, as violinists.[63]

A glimpse of their repertoire is provided by Bulstrode Whitelocke's famous coranto. Whitelocke, who oversaw the musical aspects of *The Triumph of Peace*, commissioned Simon Ives to write music for the production, and, according to his unpublished memoirs, received Ives's help with his own composition:

I was so conversant with the musitians, & so willing to gaine their favour, especially att this time, that I composed an aeir my selfe, with the assistance of Mr Ives, and called it Whitelockes Coranto, which being cryed up, was first played publiquely by the Blackefryars Musicke who were then esteemed the best of Common Musicke in all London. Whensoever I came to that house (as I did sometimes in those dayes though not often) to see a play the Musitians would presently play Whitelockes Coranto, & it was so often called for that they would have it played twice or thrice in an afternoon.[64]

Whitelocke included a two-part version of the piece in his memoirs, and a four-part setting for two trebles, tenor and bass, presumably the one used at the Blackfriars, survives in a collection of Ives's dance music.[65] Music of this type (I argue in Ch. 11) was developed at court at the beginning of Charles I's reign, and was rapidly taken up by waits and theatre musicians using (in four-part music) two violins, tenor viol (or viola), bass viol or violin, and two theorboes or (in three-part music) two violins, bass, and three theorboes; it was essentially a modernized version of the mixed consort, with a second violin replacing the flute or recorder, and theorboes replacing the lute, cittern, and bandora.

When the theatres closed in 1642 such musicians were forced to earn their living in taverns, according to the anonymous author of *The Actor's Remonstrance or Complaint* (London, 1644):

Our Musike that was held so delectable and precious, that they scorned to come to a Taverne under twentie shillings salary for two houres, now wander with their Instruments under their cloaks, I meane such as have any, into all houses of good fellowship, saluting every roome where is company, with Will you have any musike Gentlemen?[66]

The Dutch traveller Lodewijk Huygens and his companions were entertained by a typical group in a London tavern one day in January 1651/2:

---

[63] A. J. Sabol, 'New Documents on Shirley's Masque "The Triumph of Peace"', *ML*, 47 (1966), 25–6.

[64] M. Lefkowitz (ed.), *Trois masques à la cour de Charles Ier d'Angleterre* (Paris, 1970), 30; *GB-Lbl*, Add. MS 57326, 209, edited in C. Burney, *A General History of Music* (London, 1776–89), ed. F. Mercer (London, 1935), ii. 299–300.

[65] *GB-Lbl*, Add. MSS 18940–3, fos. 35^r, 35^v, 15^r, 34^r.

[66] T. W. Baldwin, *The Organization and Personnel of the Shakespearean Company* (New York, 1961), 121.

They served us with four good courses, apples for dessert with a little saucer of anise-sugar for each person. Six fiddlers ('Ses violons') came to offer their services and played the whole afternoon some very good pieces of Will. Lawes, [Charles] Colemans, [Robert?] Taylor, and also some compositions of their own. Three of them had theorboes, two of them had ordinary violins ('hand-violen'), and one had a bass with four strings.[67]

By the 1660s, when Roger North was at school at Thetford in Norfolk, even country waits were using several violins in mixed consorts: 'it is in my memory', he wrote, 'that a famous sett of Musick belonging to Thetford had few violins, but many wire instruments that made a jang or jargon to the tune'; in another passage, which seems to refer to the same group, he recalled that 'there was once a company of itinerant musicians fitted for a consort equall with any of the same numbers now celebrated: consisting of 2 violins, a base, one loud hautbois, and 2 wire pandoras'.[68]

North was presumably drawing on his childhood experience of music in Norfolk when, in the passage discussed at the beginning of this chapter, he placed the violin in the hands of his 'country croudero'. But the evidence now suggests a rather different picture. The viol and the violin were both initially used exclusively at court because they were originally brought to England by immigrants who were coming to work there; in the course of the century they were gradually taken up by professionals outside the court: by musicians in aristocratic households, theatres, and groups of waits. The class distinction between viol-players and violinists, established early on the Continent, only emerged in England in the late sixteenth century, when the viol began to be taken up by gentleman amateurs just as the violin was filtering down to the humbler sort of professional musician. Nor can we assume that the violin was never played by amateurs in the sixteenth century, for we have the late sixteenth-century wall painting at Gilling Castle in Yorkshire that shows a consort of three sizes of violin (five-string, for some reason) played by men in elegant aristocratic costume; also, for what it is worth, we have John Aubrey's report that Edward, Earl of Hertford (d. 1621) 'was wont to say, that if he were to earne his living, he had no way, but that of a Fidler: & thus were severall great persons bred in those daies'.[69]

---

[67] Translation adapted from A. G. H. Bachrach and R. G. Collmer (eds.), *Lodewijck Huygens: The English Journal 1651–1652* (Leiden and London, 1982), 62.

[68] Wilson, *Roger North on Music*, 272.

[69] J. Aubrey, 'An Idea of Education of Young Gentlemen', *GB-Ob*, MS Aubrey 26, fo. 42^r.

7

'Nach Englischer Art'

A 'Lost' Repertoire of Elizabethan Dance Music

IN studying old music it is important not to assume that the musical sources surviving from a particular time and place are representative of its musical activity. The picture will almost certainly have been distorted by the taste of later periods, by the chance survival or non-survival of particular collections, or by the fact that certain areas of the repertoire were wholly or partially improvised. Functional dance music of the sixteenth century—the material actually used by professional dance groups as opposed to copies or arrangements made for other purposes—has suffered particularly badly from the ravages of time. Changes of dance fashions soon rendered the music of particular dances obsolete; professional instrumentalists normally played without music at the time, and would have had little incentive to preserve items of their repertoire on paper once they had committed them to memory; their collections, unprepossessing documents for the most part, would have been of little interest to collectors of later times. The situation is particularly bad in England. No consort dance music was published there before Antony Holborne's *Pavans, Galliards, Almains* (London, 1599), and a survey of surviving English manuscripts produces little more than fifty pieces for the forty-odd years between the Arundel collection (*GB-Lbl*, Royal Appendix MSS 74–6; see Chapter 4) and the end of Elizabeth's reign, over half of which survive only in fragmentary sources. But the evidence of the activity of professional instrumentalists assembled in Chapter 6 suggests that this 'lost' repertoire was once large, rich, and diverse; we shall see that more of it survives in Continental sources than has previously been thought.

The earliest source is probably the group of pieces that was copied on to blank spaces of a copy at *EIRE-Dtc* of *Cantiones... sacrae* (London, 1575) by Tallis and Byrd. There are five dances: nos. 14 and 15 (following Richard Charteris's numbering), soprano and tenor parts of 'La[dy] Morleys Pavin' and 'The galy[ard]'; nos. 16 and 17, tenor parts entitled 'Dowlands Larchrimae the 5. parte' and 'Bradleys galy[ard]'; no. 19, 'Phillips pavin', the soprano part of the famous piece by Peter Philips, described as 'The first one Philips made' and dated 1580 by Francis

Tregian in the Fitzwilliam Virginal Book, *GB-Cfm*, Mu. MS 168, no. 85.[1] (No. 8, entitled 'Mr Philips', is not a galliard, as Charteris suggests, but a duple-time contrapuntal piece). Fragmentary as the source is, it provides a useful instance of how dances were arranged and rearranged for different media. Warwick Edwards drew attention to the fact that the treble part of Philips's 1580 pavan, alone among the surviving consort versions, opens with six minim rests (Ex. 7.1).[2] The implication is that the Dublin part comes from an otherwise lost setting by the composer, and that the five-part version in *D-Kl*, 4° MS mus. 125, 1–5, no. 37 (see below) and the one for mixed consort in Morley's *The First Booke of Consort Lessons* (London, 1599), no. 8 and elsewhere were derived by others from a setting in another medium, most likely the one for keyboard in the Fitzwilliam Virginal Book; the arrangers probably misconstrued its part-writing, obscuring the layout of the opening. Philips's keyboard setting need not have been derived itself from this hypothetical 'original' consort version, for he was in the habit of creating independent realizations for consort and keyboard of the same melodic and harmonic material.

The second source, *US-NH*, Filmer MS 2, is also fragmentary. It consists of three parts from a set of five or six, and it belonged to the Filmer family of Kent from the mid-seventeenth century until 1945; no detailed account of it has yet appeared in print.[3] The collection is the work of two copyists: the earlier, apparently its originator, contributed a numbered sequence of twenty-one dances and some untexted Italian vocal music; the second, who must have been connected to the Filmer family since he also contributed to other manuscripts in their collection, subsequently added five four-part fantasias by Thomas Lupo and some anonymous English songs. The dances survive in two of the volumes, providing an alto-range part (or in two cases a soprano part) and a bass part, fos. 2^r–11^r and fos. 1^r–11^v respectively, though in three cases only the bass was copied (see Table 7.1).

The collection seems to be an anthology of court composers around 1600. Edward Collard was a royal lutenist apparently only from June 1598 to September 1599; no. 19 is a consort setting of one of his lute galliards.[4] Jerome Bassano served in the court recorder consort from January 1579 until his death in August 1635.[5] J.H. is revealed as Jacques

---

[1] R. Charteris, 'Manuscript Additions of Music by John Dowland and his Contemporaries in Two Sixteenth-Century Prints', *The Consort*, 37 (1981), 399–401.

[2] Edwards, 'The Sources of Elizabethan Consort Music', 18–19; I am grateful to Warwick Edwards for providing me with transcriptions of pieces from this source.

[3] See, however, R. Ford, 'The Filmer Manuscripts, a Handlist', *Notes*, 34 (1978), 814–25.

[4] Ward, *A Dowland Miscellany*, 110–11; E. Collard, *Complete Works for the Lute*, ed. J. Duarte and H. Pratt (London, 1978), no. 6.

[5] Lasocki, 'Professional Recorder Players', ii. 559, 613–16.

Ex. 7.1. Peter Philips, 1580 Pavan, bb. 1–7, soprano part from MS additions to Tallis and Byrd, *Cantiones . . . sacrae* (London, 1575) at *EIRE-Dtc*; compared with keyboard setting in *GB-Cfm*, Mu. MS 168, no. 85

Harden (James Harding), a member of the royal flute consort from May 1575 until his death in January 1625/6, for no. 9 corresponds to the alto and bass parts of his popular galliard in the version printed by Füllsack and Hildebrand in their 1607 anthology (see below).[6] No. 18 concords with the alto and bass parts of a piece in a six-part manuscript (with one

---

[6] Edmond, 'Limners and Picturemakers', 75–81; id., *Hilliard and Oliver*, esp. 161–4.

TABLE 7.1. *Inventory of the dances in US-NH, Filmer MS 2*

No.	Title[a]	Key	Clefs	
1	Pavana de J H Nº 1	g	c2	F4
2	Pavana de A H Nº 2	G	c2	F4
3	Pavana de J H Nº 3	g	c2	F4
4	Pavana de A B Nº 4	d	c2	F4
5	Pavana Nº 5	a	c3	F4
6	Nº 6 Pavana	a	c3	F4
7	Nº 1 galiard de J H	G	c2	F4
8	Nº 2 galiard de J H	d	c2	F4
9	Nº 3 galiardo de J H	d	c2	F4
10	[galliard] Nº 4 [J H?]	d		F4
11	Nº 5 galliard de J H	G		F4
12	gailliard de Th. L Nº 6	g	c2	F4
13	[galliard] de geronnimie Bassano Nº 7	d	c2	F4
14	ga. de giero. Bassano Nº 8	a	c2	F4
15	Nº 9 gali de T L	g	g2	F4
16	gali. de W P Nº 10	d	c3	F4
17	Nº 11 Allmand de J L	G	c3	F4
18	Allmande de J H Nº 12	F	c2	F4
19	Nº 13 1 Gailliard Edward Collard	d	c2	F3
20	2 gall. Ed. Collard	g		F4
21	3 gall. of Ed. Collard	d	g2	F3

[a] titles of nos. 5, 13–16, 18 taken from alto part, rest from bass

part missing) associated with the Stuart court wind musicians, *GB-Cfm*, Mu. MS 734, section 2, no. 1.[7] A.H. is Antony Holborne, who was at court at least from 1597 until his death in November 1602; no. 2 concords with 'The Cradle', no. 5 of *Pavans, Galliards, Almains*.[8] The interpretation of the other initials is more open to question, but they fit known court musicians around 1600: A.B., Th. L., and W.P. are probably Augustine Bassano, Thomas Lupo, and Walter Piers (Pearce) respectively; Augustine, Jerome's brother, was a member of the family recorder consort from March 1550 until his death in October 1604; Thomas Lupo I joined the violin consort in 1588 (see Ch. 5); and Piers was a royal lutenist between July 1589 and 1604.[9] There were at least

[7] T. Dart (ed.), *Suite from the Royal Brass Music of King James I* (London, 1959), no. 1; see also id., 'The Repertory of the Royal Wind Music', *GSJ* 11 (1958), 70–7; R. Charteris, 'A Rediscovered Source of English Consort Music', *Chelys*, 5 (1973–4), 3–6.

[8] A. Holborne, *Pavans, Galliards, Almains*, ed. B. Thomas (London, 1980).

[9] Lasocki, 'Professional Recorder Players', ii. 558, 603–6; Ward, *A Dowland Miscellany*, 111.

four court musicians around 1600 with the initials J.L., the wind-players Innocent, John, and Jerome Lanier, and the violinist Joseph Lupo.

There are striking similarities between the early layers of Filmer MS 2 and Mu. MS 734. Both contain dances as well as Italian textless vocal music; both consist largely of music by members of the royal wind consorts; and both were probably used at court, for their copyists identified the composers only by their initials. The early layer of Mu. MS 734 also includes pieces by Augustine and Jerome Bassano, James Harding, and Thomas Lupo, though there are reasons for thinking that it was copied more than a decade later than the equivalent section of Filmer MS 2. It includes dances that come from masques performed at court in 1609 and, probably, 1613, and it generally contains a more modern repertoire, based on almans rather than pavans and galliards.[10] It is also clear that the two collections were scored differently. The Mu. MS 734 dances are six-part pieces in a six-part source, while the dances in Filmer MS 2 appear in only two of the three surviving books; the Italian vocal pieces, copied by the same individual, appear in all three books. Also, two of the Filmer MS 2 dances, Holborne's 'The Cradle' pavan and James Harding's galliard, are known five-part pieces. Filmer MS 2 was probably compiled for royal wind musicians, like Mu. MS 734, but it also apparently contains pieces drawn from the repertoire of the court violin consort—notably some dances by Thomas Lupo, otherwise unknown.

The third source, *GB-Lbl*, Egerton MS 3665, is one of the vast score-books compiled by the Catholic recusant Francis Tregian (1574–1619).[11] Most of the manuscript is taken up with motets, madrigals, and other vocal music, but at the end there are two sequences of instrumental music; one, fos. 505ʳ–511ʳ (pp. 999–1011), consists of music by Alfonso Ferrabosco II, while the other, fos. 514ʳ–523ʳ (pp. 1017–33), is entitled 'Canzone e Pavane di diversi' (see Table 7.2). Actually, 'Canzone e Pavane di diversi' is not so diverse as its title suggests, for they are all dances apart from the first piece, Richard Farrant's consort song 'Ah, alas, you salt sea gods', and all but six of them can be associated in some way with Peter Philips.

Nine pieces, the pavan and galliard pairs nos. 1–3, the galliard no. 13, the setting of the Italian chord sequence *La vecchio* no. 14, and possibly the alman no. 15 (if 'Tr[egian]' refers to its dedicatee rather than its author), seem to be original compositions by Philips, and at least six of the others were arranged for consort by him. The pavan no. 4 is said to

---

[10] See A. J. Sabol (ed.), *Four Hundred Songs and Dances from the Stuart Masque* (Providence, 1978), nos. 239, 274, and the commentary for nos. 188, 189.

[11] B. Schofield and T. Dart, 'Tregian's Anthology', *ML* 32 (1951), 205–16; E. Cole, 'L'Anthologie de madrigaux et de musique instrumentale pour ensembles de Francis Tregian', in J. Jacquot (ed.), *La Musique instrumentale de la Renaissance* (Paris, 1954), 115–26; T. Dart and W. Coates (eds.), *Jacobean Consort Music* (MB 9; 2nd edn., London, 1966), nos. 55, 71, 72, 74; A. Bassano, *Pavans and Galliards in Five Parts*, ed. P. Holman (London, 1981).

TABLE 7.2. *Inventory of 'Canzone e Pavane di diversi', GB-Lbl, Egerton MS 3665*

No.	Page	Folio	Key	Title
	1017–18	514^{r-v}	g	Abradar/Incerto
	1019–18	515^r–514^v	a	Pavana/Daniel Farant
	1020	515^v		[blank]
		516^{r-v}		[blank leaf formerly pasted on to:]
	1021	517^r	g	Pietro Philippi [short fragment of the six-part Passamezzo Pavan; see Ch. 7 n. 49]
[1]	1022–3	517^v–518^r	F	Pavana/Philippi
			F	Galiarda/Philippi
2			F	[Pa]vana/Philippi
	1023–4	518^{r-v}	F	Galiarda
3	1024–5	518^v–519^r	c	Pavana Pag.
			c	Galiarda/Philippi
[4]			d	[Pavan]a/Thomas Morley sett by P. Philip[pi]
	1026–7	519^v–520^r	d	[Galiard]a/Th. Morley. P.P.
5			g	Galiarda/Ant. Holborn. P.P.
6			g	Galiarda/Aug. Bassano. P.P.
7			F	Balla d'Amore FT [monogram]
[8]	1028–9	520^v–521^r	g	Pavana/Augustin Bassano
			g	Galiarda/Augustin Bassano
[9]			g	Pavana/Augustin Bassano
			g	Galiarda/Augustin Bassano
[10]	1030–1	521^v–522^r	g	Pavana/Alfonso Ferabosco. Sen.
[11]			g	Pavana/Josepho Lupo
[12]			G	Nowels Galiard/P.P.
[13]			g	Galiarda/P.P.
[14]	1031–2	522^{r-v}	g	La Vecha/P.P.
[15]	1032–3	522^v–523^r	d	Allemanda Tr./Pietro Philippi
[16]			G	Aria del Gran Duca Ferdinando di Toscana/P.P.
[17]			a	Pavana/Tomkins

be 'sett by P. Philip[pi]', and is based on the lute piece by Thomas Morley in Robert Dowland's *Varietie of Lute-Lessons* (London, 1610). No lute version of the galliard survives, though it has the dual ascription 'Th. Morley. P. P.'—meaning, presumably, 'Thomas Morley set by Peter Philips'—and it appears alongside the pavan in Ferdinando Richardson's keyboard setting in the Tisdale Virginal Manuscript, *GB-Cfm*, Marlay Additions no. 15.[12] Nos. 5 and 12 are similar cases, for they are galliards

---

[12] R. Dowland, *Varietie of Lute Lessons (1610)*, ed. E. Hunt (London, 1956), 19–20; A. Brown (ed.), *Tisdale's Virginal Book* (London, 1966), nos. 15, 16.

by Holborne, but in different consort settings from the ones in *Pavans, Galliards, Almains*; the Egerton MS 3665 versions were perhaps made by Philips from lute pieces before the composer's printed five-part settings became available to him.[13] No. 16 was certainly arranged by Philips from a piece in another medium, for it is an early member of the large family of pieces that descend from a recurring passage in Cavalieri's choral *ballo* in the Florentine *intermedi* of 1589.[14] No. 6 has a double ascription to Augustine Bassano and Philips, and may also be an arrangement of a lost lute piece; Bassano was a lutenist as well as a wind-player, and several lute dances by him survive.[15]

A sixteenth piece can be connected with Philips even though it does not have the secondary ascription to P. P.. No. 17 is one of several consort settings of Thomas Tomkins's famous chromatic pavan, best known from its keyboard version in the Fitzwilliam Virginal Book, *GB-Cfm*, Mu. MS 168, no. 123. The Egerton MS 3665 setting (also found in *GB-Lbl*, Add. MSS 30826–8, no. 23, and *GB-Lcm*, MS 2039, no. 5), as well as the ones in *GB-Lbl*, Add. MSS 17792–6, no. 17, and Thomas Simpson's *Opusculum newer Pavanen* (Frankfurt, 1610), no. 7, are in A minor, like the Fitzwilliam keyboard version, and may have been derived independently from it, for they share its contrapuntal outlines but differ among themselves over details of part-writing; a C minor setting, *GB-Ob*, MSS Mus. Sch. E. 415–18, no. 47, is probably a later reworking by the composer himself.[16] The Egerton MS 3665 version is connected with Philips not only because it comes at the end of the group of pieces by him, but also because the keyboard version in *S-Uu*, IMhs 408, fos. 14^v–17^r, entitled 'Pavan Anglica Thomas Tomkins. Collerirt di Pietro Philippi', seems to be a decorated intabulation of it.

Most of Philips's pieces in 'Canzone e Pavane di Diversi' also survive in keyboard settings by the composer, and some of them can help to date the collection. No. 1, the great chromatic or 'Dolorosa' pavan and galliard, is dated 1593 in the Fitzwilliam Virginal Book (nos. 80, 81), and is described as 'composta in prigione' (composed in prison) in the copy in *PL-Kj* (formerly *D-B*), Mus. MS 40316, fos. 6^r–7^v, 8^r–v. Philips was imprisoned at The Hague in the autumn of 1593 on suspicion of plotting

---

[13] Holborne, *Pavans, Galliards, Almains*, ed. Thomas, nos. 20, 40.

[14] D. P. Walker (ed.), *Musique des intermèdes de 'La Pellegrina'* (Les Fêtes du mariage de Ferdinand de Médicis et de Christine de Lorraine, Florence 1589, 1; Paris, 1963), 140–1; see also W. Kirkendale (ed.), *L'Aria di Fiorenza; id est, Il Ballo del Gran Duca* (Florence, 1972).

[15] A list is in Ward, *A Dowland Miscellany*, 110.

[16] T. Tomkins, *Keyboard Music*, ed. S. D. Tuttle (MB 5; London, 1955), no. 56; Dart and Coates (eds.), *Jacobean Consort Music*, no. 73; J. Irving, *The Instrumental Music of Thomas Tomkins* (New York and London, 1989), i. 144–5, 167–8; ii. 176–7 interprets the relationship between the sources rather differently.

against Queen Elizabeth; documents relating to the affair reveal that he was living in Antwerp at the time 'where he got his lyving by teachinge of children on instruments', that he had travelled to Holland 'onely to sie and heare an excellent ma(n) of his faculties in Amsterdam'—an unmistakeable reference to Sweelinck—and that he had been denounced to the authorities while he lay sick at Middelburg.[17]

The pavan and galliard pair no. 3 was also probably written in the Netherlands, though a few years later: 'Pag.' is shown to be an abbreviation for 'Pagget' by the title of the setting in the Fitzwilliam Virginal Book (nos. 74, 75), and Philips was in the service of the Catholic refugee Lord Thomas Paget from 1585 until the latter's death in Brussels at the beginning of 1590. The pavan may therefore have been written in Paget's memory shortly after his death, though a late copy of the keyboard setting in *S-Uu*, IMhs 408, fos. 22^v–27^r is entitled 'Pavana Scharlabaget' and 'Galliard Scharbaget', which seems to refer to Thomas's younger brother, the notorious spy Charles Paget (d. 1612). The rest of Philips's other pieces cannot be precisely dated, but the setting of Cavalieri's *ballo* must have been written after 1589, and probably post-dates Malvezzi's edition of the music for the *intermedi*, published in Florence in 1591. It may be, too, that the settings of the Holborne galliards were written in the 1590s, for the appearance of the composer's 1599 collection would have rendered them superfluous, assuming that Philips had access to it.

The six remaining pieces, nos. 8–11, form a distinct sub-group in the collection. They have no obvious collection with Peter Philips, and they seem to come from the English court of the 1570s, not the Netherlands of the 1590s. Nos. 10 and 11, pavans by Alfonso Ferrabosco I and Joseph Lupo, are based on ideas from Lassus's chanson 'Susanne un jour', published in London in 1570, or, more precisely, from Ferrabosco's own elaboration of it, published with an English text in *Musica transalpina* (London, 1588).[18] Ferrabosco presumably composed his chanson and the derived pavan between 1570 and 1578, when he left England for good, and it is likely that Lupo's pavan, composed perhaps in a spirit of friendly rivalry with Ferrabosco, dates from the same period. The same is probably true of nos. 8 and 9, the two pavan and galliard pairs by

[17] A. G. Petti, 'New Light on Peter Philips', *MMR* 87 (1957), 58–63; id. 'Peter Philips, Composer and Organist, 1561–1628', *Recusant History*, 4 (1957–8), 48–60; A. Curtis, *Sweelinck's Keyboard Music* (Leiden and Oxford, 1969), 28–31.

[18] K. Levy, 'Susanne un Jour: The History of a Sixteenth-Century Chanson', *AnnM* 1 (1953), 375–408; J. Kerman, *The Elizabethan Madrigal* (New York, 1962), 91–2; *Alfonso Ferrabosco the Elder, Opera Omnia*, ed. R. Charteris, iii, *Latin Songs, French Chansons, and English Songs* (CMM 96; Neuhausen-Stuttgart, 1984), 28–34, 64–71; J. A. Bernstein (ed.), *French Chansons of the Sixteenth Century* (University Park, Pa., 1985), no. 26; compare the opening of the first and second strains of Ferrabosco's pavan with bb. 16–18 and 65–9 of his chanson.

Ex. 7.2. Augustine Bassano, Pavan, bb. 1–16, *GB-Lbl*, Egerton MS 3665, pp. 1028–9 (from Bassano, *Pavans and Galliards*, ed. Holman, no. 1)

Augustine Bassano, since they are closer in style to the simple pavans and galliards of the early-Elizabethan Arundel collection than to Philips's own elaborate works. (Ex. 7.2).[19]

The key to understanding the circumstances surrounding the composition and arrangement of Philips's dances lies in examining the

---

[19] A point made in Neighbour, *Consort and Keyboard Music of William Byrd*, 181–3.

Ex. 7.2. *Continued*

relationship between the composer and his copyist, Francis Tregian. Many writers have postulated a personal link between the two men, for they were both Catholics, and Tregian copied a numbered sequence of nineteen Philips keyboard pieces into the Fitzwilliam Virginal Book, as well as a liberal selection of his motets and madrigals into Egerton MS 3665 and the companion volume *US-NYp*, Drexel MS 4302. Tregian's scores tend either to be the only sources of Philips's instrumental pieces, or the earliest and best source. The problem, however, has been that Philips and Tregian were not known to have been at the same place at the same time, though their lives as Catholics in exile followed similar patterns.

On leaving England in 1582 Philips stopped at Douai on his way to Rome, where he was organist of the English College until 1585. He then travelled around Europe in the service of Lord Paget until the latter's death in 1590, when he settled in Antwerp, moving in 1597 to Brussels as organist of the Archduke Albert, Regent of the Spanish Netherlands; he apparently stayed there until his death in 1628. Tregian, more than ten years younger, was sent to be educated on the Continent in 1586, first at Eu near Dieppe, then at Douai and Rheims; he followed Philips to Rome in 1592, where Cardinal Allen employed him as his secretary.[20] After a brief visit to London in 1594 he largely disappears from view until 1608, when he returned to England to retrieve his family's confiscated lands; he was convicted of recusancy the following year, was eventually imprisoned in the Fleet (he was certainly there by 1614), and died in prison in 1619.

It has been traditionally thought that Tregian copied his manuscripts during his years of enforced leisure in the Fleet prison, supposedly using material provided by a network of friends in London. Some portions of the manuscripts contain pieces that must have been collected after his return to London—Giles Farnaby's arrangements of masque dances near the end of the Fitzwilliam Virginal Book are obvious examples—but much of the material could have been acquired and copied during his years on the Continent. As far as the Philips pieces are concerned, it is significant that research into Francis Tregian the elder has revealed that his son is recorded at Brussels in 1603 and 1606, and it is likely that he lived there for some years before his return to England; Boyan and Lamb have even suggested that he was attached to Albert's court or that he served in his army. Thus the dances in 'Canzone e Pavane di diversi' could easily have been acquired direct from the composer, and may be a collection of arrangements and original compositions put together for a particular ensemble—similar to the group of six 'suonadori de violini' or 'violoni' that is known to have been employed at the Brussels court in 1589 by the Farnese governor of the Spanish Netherlands.[21] Tregian's own piece, the strange and rather earth-bound 'Balla d'Amore', may have

---

[20] A. L. Rowse, *Tudor Cornwall: Portrait of a Society* (2nd edn., London, 1969), 373–5; E. Cole, 'In Search of Francis Tregian', *ML* 33 (1952), 28–32; ead., 'Seven Problems of the Fitzwilliam Virginal Book', *PRMA* 79 (1952–3), 51–64; P. Boyan and G. R. Lamb, *Francis Tregian, Cornish Recusant* (London, 1955), 102–4, 112–23; see also the introduction to R. Vendome (ed.), *Christ Church Music MS 89: Peter Philips and Peter Cornet* (Spanish Netherlands Keyboard Music, 1; Oxford, 1983).

[21] N. Pelicelli, 'Musicisti in Parma nei secoli XV–XVI: la capella alla corte Farnese', *NA* 9 (1932), 48–9.

been written for some entertainment at the Brussels court. The older pieces by Ferrabosco I, Lupo, and Bassano could have been transmitted to Tregian in London, perhaps from a court source, or they could have formed the core of Philips's anthology of dances, perhaps acquired by the composer before he went into exile.

Whatever the truth of the matter, Philips's dances have a special place in the history of English music, for they mark the beginning of the dissemination of English consort music on the Continent. Until the middle of the sixteenth century England looked to the Continent for its dance music; the members of the court instrumental consorts were mainly recruited abroad, and doubtless brought their repertoire with them; thus the Arundel collection consists in part, if my arguments in Chapter 5 are accepted, of dances collected by immigrant members of the royal violin consort in Italy and the Netherlands. The situation began to change during Elizabeth's reign as the numbers of new immigrant musicians at court dwindled, and as the immigrant families already there became assimilated into English society; they soon produced second-generation court musicians such as Thomas Lupo I or Alfonso Ferrabosco II, who were at least as English as they were Italian in their musical outlook. In the 1580s and 1590s the pattern of musical influence went abruptly into reverse. Peter Philips established himself in religious exile in the Netherlands, and he was followed by, among others, Daniel Norcombe, John Bull, Richard Dering, and, it seems, John Dowland.[22]

There were others, not known to have been Catholic, who were probably attracted abroad by the lucrative opportunities of employment in the prosperous cities and small courts of northern Europe. William Brade and Thomas Simpson are examples of prominent Elizabethan composers of instrumental music who conducted busy and successful careers largely in Germany. Brade was already around 30 in 1594 when he is first heard of on his arrival in Copenhagen from the Brandenburg court; he spent the rest of a restless and sometimes turbulent career moving between the prominent musical centres of northern Europe, and he died in Hamburg in 1630. Simpson, a generation younger, was born in Kent in 1582, and is first heard of at Heidelberg in 1608, though he may have been earlier at the Lorraine court in Nancy, for his wife came from near there. His career was similar in its pattern to Brade's, though it was conducted at less furious a pace; he probably died in Copenhagen in 1628 (see Ch. 11). Brade and Simpson are crucial figures in the dissemination of English consort music abroad because their publications brought items from the Elizabethan

---

[22] A bibliography relating to English Catholic musicians is in Ward, *A Dowland Miscellany*, 94; for Dowland's Catholicism, see Poulton, *John Dowland*, 36–45.

consort repertoire together with their own compositions in the English style.[23]

A third group of musical expatriates was associated with the English theatre companies that began to tour the Continent in the 1580s and 1590s, following the English statute of 1572 that restricted the activities of 'Comon Players in Enterludes & Minstrels' and other 'Vacabondes'.[24] Most of the companies seem to have included musicians; indeed, they were thought of as offering musical entertainment as much as drama. When five Englishmen were appointed at the Dresden court in 1586 they were described as fiddlers (*Geiger*) and instrumentalists, and were contracted to 'entertain and play music on their fiddles (*Geygen*) and instruments of such like' during meals, as well as providing 'pleasure and amusement with acrobatics and whatever graceful things they may have learned'.[25] A company led by Robert Browne was given a passport to travel to the Netherlands in February 1591/2 'to pursue their skills of music, acrobatics, and acting comedies, tragedies, and histories'.[26] Browne was described as 'servant, comedian and musician' when he arrived at Kassel in 1594 or 1595 to enter the service of Moritz, Landgrave of Hessen-Kassel, an accomplished amateur musician; his company was to act 'all sorts of merry comedies, tragedies and other plays', and to 'perform vocal, as well as instrumental music'.[27] It left Kassel in 1598, though, when a successor led by Richard Machin replaced it in 1601, it too was noted for its music: in 1605 a Strasburg official was of the opinion that Moritz employed them largely because 'they have such musicians as can hardly be found anywhere', and an unsympathetic Kassel account of the 'damned Englishmen' refers specifically to their 'string-playing' (*Saitenspiel*).[28]

---

[23] For Brade and Simpson, see P. E. Mueller, 'The Influence and Activities of English Musicians on the Continent during the Late Sixteenth and Early Seventeenth Centuries', Ph.D. diss. (Indiana University, 1954); C. R. Huber, 'The Life and Music of William Brade', Ph.D. diss. (University of North Carolina at Chapel Hill, 1965); W. Braun, *Britannia Abundans: Deutsch-englische Musikbeziehungen zur Shakespearezeit* (Tutzing, 1977); also the introductions to W. Brade, *Pavans, Galliards, and Canzonas, 1609*, ed. B. Thomas (London, 1982) and T. Simpson, *Taffel Consort (1621)*, ed. Thomas (London, 1988). The details of Simpson's marriage and death are respectively from G. Pietzsch, *Quellen und Forschungen zur Geschichte der Musik am kurpfälzischen Hof zu Heidelberg bis 1622* (Mainz, 1963), 161, and J. Bergsagel (ed.), *Music for Instrumental Ensemble* (Music in Denmark at the Time of Christian IV, 2; Copenhagen, 1988), p. xi.

[24] A. Gurr, *The Shakespearean Stage 1574–1642* (Cambridge, 1970), 19; J. Limon, *Gentleman of a Company: English Players in Central and Eastern Europe, 1590–1660* (Cambridge, 1985), 4–6.

[25] Mueller, 'The Influence and Activities', 2; Chambers, *The Elizabethan Stage*, ii. 272–3; see also G. Sjögren, 'Thomas Bull and other "English Instrumentalists" in Denmark in the 1580s', *Shakespeare Survey*, 22 (1971), 119–23.

[26] Translated from Chambers, *The Elizabethan Stage*, ii. 274.

[27] Chambers, *The Elizabethan Stage*, ii. 277–8, translated in Mueller, 'The Influence and Activities', 6–7.

[28] Mueller, 'The Influence and Activities', 8, 9.

Machin was a musician as well as an actor. He is listed in the Kassel records as a lutenist, and two pieces by him survive in the Thysius lute manuscript (1595–1601) in *NL-Lt*, one of which turns out to be a crude version of the 'Delight Pavan' by John or Edward Johnson.[29] He may be the 'D. Richardi Anglus natione' or 'A. M. Rich. Angl.' who gave a Cologne lutenist a tuning-chart and a piece on 12 August 1600.[30] The well-known set of part-books of consort music at Kassel, *D-Kl*, 4° MS mus. 72, 1–5 may also be connected with him. Its first section, which consists largely of pieces labelled 'M.L.H.' (that is, arrangements or original compositions by the Landgrave himself), was apparently compiled while his group was at Kassel, for though it contains pieces named after aristocrats who attended a court wedding there in 1601, there is no mention of Moritz's second wife Juliana, who arrived on the scene in 1603.[31] The title of no. 51, 'Pavana de Signor Richardo', could well refer to Machin himself.

The M.L.H. pieces have attracted the most attention because of their connections with the Landgrave, and because some of them have exotic scorings—no. 27, for instance, the pavan by or for 'Francisco Segario', is for 'Flauto Corneto muto trombone sordun et Viola di gamba'. But the second section, nos. 64–86, is of particular interest in the present context because it has definite connections with English musicians: it is a sequence of five-part pavans and galliards with English titles such as 'Halfe Newe halfe olde' (no. 67), 'Goates Leape Pavin' (no. 72), and 'The shooting of the guns Pavin' (no. 76). On the other hand, there are no concordances with English sources, and some of the pieces have titles with Kassel connections such as 'Cassel Pavin' (no. 66), 'Lichtenau Pavin' (no. 68), and 'L. M. [Landgrave Moritz] Pavin' (no. 86), even though they are in an English style, recalling the pieces by Bassano, Ferrabosco I, and Joseph Lupo in Egerton MS 3665, and they all suffer from unenterprising rhythms, unconvincing harmonies, and stodgy textures. The simplest explanation is that they are all the work of a minor English composer on the spot, such as Machin himself.

A second source at Kassel of five-part dance music with English connections, *D-Kl*, 4° MS mus. 125, 1–5, was discovered recently by Warwick Edwards; it consists of a sequence of fifty-three pavans, all

[29] Curtis, *Sweelinck's Keyboard Music*, 15–16.

[30] *PL-Kj* (formerly *D-Bds*), Mus. MS 40143, fos. 20ʳ, 22ᵛ–23ʳ; I am grateful to Tim Crawford for drawing this source to my attention; a group of twelve English 'comedians and instrumentalists' was at Cologne in 1600; see Limon, *Gentlemen of a Company*, 18.

[31] Mueller, 'The Influence and Activities', 19; a selection of the pieces is in Moritz, Landgraf von Hessen, *Ausgewählte Werke*, ed. H. Birtner, i. *16 Pavanen, Gagliarden und Intraden* (EDM, ser. 2, Landschaftsdenkmale, Kurhessen; Kassel, 1936); *Four Pavans*, ed. B. Thomas (Early Music Library, 53; London, 1989).

anonymous and untitled, followed by six contrapuntal pieces.[32] The collection appears to have been drawn largely or possibly exclusively from the English repertoire: the contrapuntal pieces are by John Taverner, Brewster, Robert Parsons, Christopher Tye, and John Bull, and the thirteen pavans that have been identified so far all have concordances in English sources; among them are pieces by Richard Alison, William Byrd, John Dowland, Antony Holborne, Edward and John Johnson, Thomas Morley, Peter Philips, Richard Reade, and Nicholas Strogers. Furthermore, some of the unidentified pieces show the clear influence of well-known English pavans; four of them, for instance, follow Philips's 1580 pavan in using a plainsong-like cantus firmus in the last strain. The part-books were probably not compiled in England, for the paper was made in Eisenach, and the bindings have heraldic devices that may or may not be connected with the Munich court.[33] Whatever its origin, there is no doubt that the Kassel collection contains a portion of the Elizabethan consort dance repertoire that no longer survives in English sources, and that it was drawn from a rich and diverse manuscript tradition, for an examination of the concordances reveals a remarkable variety of relationships between its five-part settings and those in other media, principally in the mixed consort repertoire.

Three of the pavans are found in essentially the same consort settings in English sources. No. 6 is William Byrd's early C minor pavan, four parts of which are in *GB-Lbl*, Add. MSS 37402–3, 37405–6, fos. 98ᵛ, 91ᵛ, 89ᵛ, and 86ᵛ; it also exists in a keyboard setting that Francis Tregian labelled 'the first t[hat] ever hee m[ade]' in the Fitzwilliam Virginal Book, no. 167.[34] Nos. 42 and 43 are essentially the same as 'Lachrimae Antiquae', Dowland's *Lachrimae; or, Seaven Teares* (London, *c.*1604), no. 1, and 'Decrevi', Holborne's *Pavans, Galliards, Almains*, no. 35. A fourth, no. 2, can be ascribed to Edward Johnson by virtue of a concordance in Thomas Simpson's *Taffel-Consort* (Hamburg, 1621), no. 28. The Kassel setting, laid out in the classic Elizabethan five-part scoring with a single treble, three inner parts, and bass, is probably Johnson's original, or something like it, while Simpson's, laid out in four parts for two equal trebles, tenor, bass, and continuo, is clearly a later and more modern arrangement (see Ch. 11).

Eight pavans have concordances with pieces in the mixed consort

---

[32] Edwards (ed.), *Music for Mixed Consort*, 154; C. Wool, 'A Critical Edition and Historical Commentary of Kassel 4° MS Mus. 125', M. Mus. diss. (London, 1983); the contrapuntal pieces are in Dart and Coates (eds.), *Jacobean Consort Music*, no. 50; Doe (ed.), *Elizabethan Consort Music: I*, nos. 14, 25, 56; *Elizabethan Consort Music: II*, nos. 137, 141.

[33] Wool, 'A Critical Edition', 26–36.

[34] Neighbour, *William Byrd*, 180–1; Monson, *Voices and Viols in England*, 223–6; completed without the benefit of 4° MS mus. 125, 1–5 in William Byrd, *Consort Music*, ed. K. Elliott (The Collected Works of William Byrd, xvii; London, 1971), no. 14.

repertoire. Nos. 4 and 34, 'Southerne's Pavan' and the 'Sacred End Pavan' by Morley, are in Rosseter's *Lessons for Consort* (London, 1609), nos. 9 and 6; nos. 20, 37, and 49, Strogers's 'In Nomine Pavan', Philips's 1580 pavan, and Dowland's 'Piper's Pavan', are in Morley's *First Booke of Consort Lessons*, nos. 13, 8, and 4; nos. 25 and 29, the 'Delight Pavan' by John or Edward Johnson and Alison's 'Sharp Pavan', are in the Walsingham consort books, now divided between the Brnymor Jones Library, Hull University, MSS DDHO/20/1–3 and *US-Oam*, nos. 9 and 6; and no. 39 is a piece variously called Richard Reade's Sixth Pavan, the lute, bass viol, recorder, and cittern parts of which are in the Cambridge consort books, *GB-Cu*, MSS Dd. 3.18, fo. 28^r, Dd. 5.20, fo. 6^r, Dd. 5.21, fo. 8^r, and Dd. 14.24, fo. 29^v, and 'Glazers Pavan', no. 15 of Thomas Simpson's *Opusculum neuwer Pavanen* (see below).[35] The remaining concordance is between no. 3 and an anonymous lute pavan entitled 'La Sol La' in *GB-Cu*, MS Dd. 2.11, fo. 13^v.

We might expect the Kassel pavans by Reade and Alison to be arrangements of music originally written for mixed consort, since their composers were particularly associated with that medium. And indeed, the Kassel version of Alison's 'Sharp Pavan' is closely related to the mixed-consort setting: the outer parts are more or less identical, and the Walsingham flute part appears to have supplied material for the Kassel altus and quintus parts. The two settings of the Reade/Glazers pavan, however, are quite different: the Kassel and Simpson versions are in A minor and are essentially the same. But the Cambridge version is in G minor, and its recorder part (the violin part does not survive) bears no relation to any of the Kassel inner parts. It may be that both derive from a third setting now lost, which was perhaps for solo lute. The two fine pavans by Morley in Rosseter's *Lessons for Consort*, 'Southerne's Pavan' and the 'Sacred End Pavan' (so called because the imitative passage in the last strain comes from Tye's anthem 'I lift my heart to thee'), are probably cases where the Kassel version is the original and the mixed-consort setting the arrangement. Rosseter made it clear in his dedication that he had made his own arrangements (see Ch. 6), and both pieces have passages of elaborate polyphony that work better in five parts than in the inherently homophonic mixed-consort medium.

The same is probably true of Strogers's excellent 'In Nomine Pavan' (so called because its third strain refers to a famous five-part In Nomine by Robert Parsons[36]), for the composer seems to have flourished in the 1560s and 1570s before the mixed consort developed; the Morley flute

---

[35] Edwards (ed.), *Music for Mixed Consort*, nos. 29, 30; Morley, *The First Book of Consort Lessons*, ed. Beck; Edwards (ed.), *Music for Mixed Consort*, nos. 13, 2; see Nordstrom, 'The Cambridge Consort Books', 90.

[36] Doe, *Elizabethan Consort Music: II*, no. 56.

part is more or less the same as the Kassel altus part, and was probably derived from it. It is impossible to say what authority the Kassel versions of the 'Delight Pavan' and 'Piper's Pavan' have, though they are not closely related to their mixed-consort settings, nor is 'Piper's Pavan' related to a five-part setting of the piece in Konrad Hagius's *Newe künstliche musicalische Intraden* (Nuremberg, 1616), no. 25, to judge from the three surviving parts of the latter. We can be sure, however, that the Kassel setting of Philips's 1580 Pavan was not made by the composer. The top part does not start with six minims rest, as in the 'original' version discussed above; nor are its inner parts related to the flute part in Morley's *Consort Lessons* (and its variant in the Walsingham books, no. 7). Its mediocre part-writing suggests that it was cooked up from Philips's keyboard setting by an inexpert hand.

The situation is also not as straightforward as it seems in the cases of Holborne's 'Decrevi' and Dowland's 'Lachrimae Antiquae', for their texts contain significant variants from those printed in 1599 and 1604. In several places the Kassel 'Decrevi' is less polished than the printed version, and may be an early version. The counterpoint at one point in the first strain, for instance, seems to have been reorganized for the 1599 print to avoid an exposed tritone and a chord without a third (Ex. 7.3). The Kassel 'Lachrimae Antiquae' is closer to the published text, though it gives a simpler and less subtle version of the tenor line at the end of the second strain. 4° MS mus. 125, 1–5 is also the only consort source apart from *Lachrimae* to give the piece in A minor; the five-part version in *GB-Lbl*, Add. MS 17786–91, no. 30 is in D minor, the key of most of the other consort settings, including the ones for mixed consort. It is conceivable that the Kassel text came from Dowland himself, for he is known to have been there several times during the 1590s. Certainly, it is hard to believe that it was not copied until after *Lachrimae* appeared in the spring of 1604, for the Kassel collection as a whole belongs more naturally to the 1590s than to the following decade, and an obvious explanation for its presence today in a Kassel library is that some of the music at least was brought to Germany from England by a member of Machin's company.

Mention of Dowland and *Lachrimae* brings us inevitably to a discussion of that great collection in the context of what we might usefully call the Anglo-German consort repertoire. When Dowland returned to London in the summer of 1603 to supervise its publication he had been working abroad on and off for nearly a decade. In his dedication to Queen Anne, the sister of Christian IV of Denmark, his employer for the last five years, the composer made it clear that the collection was partly composed in her homeland: 'I have presumed to Dedicate this worke of Musicke to your sacred hands, that was begun where you were borne, and ended where

Ex. 7.3. Antony Holborne, Pavan 'Decrevi', bb. 1–4: (*a*) version in *D-Kl*, 4° MS mus. 125, 1–5, no. 43; compared with (*b*) *Pavans, Galliards, Almains* (London, 1599), no. 35 (from Holborne, *Pavans, Galliards, Almains*, ed. Thomas)

you raigne.' It is more than likely, indeed, that *Lachrimae* was largely written at the Danish court, and that it reflects the practice of English expatriates; among Dowland's compatriots there were William Brade, Daniel Norcombe, John Meinert (probably John Myners, not the composer John Maynard), the dancing-master Henry Sandam, the harpist 'Carolus Oralii' (an Irishman, Charles O'Reilly?) and, perhaps, 'Bendix

Ex. 7.3. *Continued*

Greebe' (also known as 'Benedictus Grep'), who may have been an
Englishman, Benedict Greave or Greaves.[37]

   Lachrimae is typical of the Anglo-German repertoire in that it is first
and foremost a collection of pavans; they take up most of the time in
a complete performance (as well as half the pages of music), and

[37] A. Hammerich, 'Musical Relations between England and Denmark in the Seventeenth
Century', *SIMG*, 13 (1911–12), 114; Ward, *A Dowland Miscellany*, 100–7; Bergsagel (ed.), *Music for
Instrumental Ensemble*, pp. ix–xiii.

attention is inevitably concentrated on the matchless variation sequence of seven 'passionate pavans' that opens the book. The five-part pavan, with or without its accompanying galliard, was the main vehicle for the dissemination of the English consort style in northern Europe. Pavans already had a more important place in the dance repertoire in England than on the Continent at the beginning of Elizabeth's reign, as a comparison between the Arundel collection and, say, the later Attaingnant dance books readily shows. By the time English musicians began to take consort music abroad in the 1580s and 1590s the pavan had come to dominate the repertoire, at a time when it was in decline in some parts of Europe; if the manuals of Negri and Caroso are anything to go by, the dance was more or less obsolete in Italy by 1600.[38]

By then the English pavan was usually too elaborate and irregular to have been used for dancing, and it was given a new lease of life in Germany as a substitute for the fantasy, which hardly figures in German collections, though it remained the backbone of the consort repertoire in England. Many Anglo-German pavans use contrapuntal devices such as canon or the 'synthetic' cantus-firmus passages made popular by Philips's 1580 pavan, and many of them rival more orthodox contrapuntal works for serious, sustained musical thought. The English instrumentalists who toured Germany, such as those in Machin's company, probably preferred the pavan to the fantasy because they were dance musicians by training and inclination, and the pavan remained a dance however complex it became. Significantly, when Brade and Simpson wrote contrapuntal music they mostly used the light and relatively homophonic Italian canzona, not the English fantasy.

We must be wary of using 4° MS mus. 125, 1–5 as evidence for the supremacy of the English pavan in Kassel around 1600—though the sight of fifty-three examples in an unbroken sequence is persuasive enough—for it is easy to imagine that sister manuscripts once existed containing galliards and other dances. Yet German consort sources over the next few years are full of pavans, many of which are English or 'nach englischer . . . Art' (in the English style) to quote from the title-page of Valerius Otto's *Newe Paduanen, Galliarden, Intraden und Currenten* (Leipzig, 1611). The prolific Valentin Haussmann, for instance, published two collections at Nuremberg in 1604, one of which, *Neue Intrade*, contains pieces labelled 'englische Paduan'—including a fine one (no. 39) with a Philips-derived cantus firmus—while the other, *Neue fünffstimmige Paduane und Galliarde*, consists largely of pavan and galliard pairs, one of which (no. 11) is based on the English tune 'Roland' or 'Lord Willoughby's Welcome Home'.[39]

---

[38] A point made by Thomas in Simpson, *Taffel Consort*, p. iv.

[39] Haussmann, *Ausgewählte Instrumentalwerke*, ed. F. Boelsche (DDT, ser. 1, 16; Leipzig, 1904), 153–4, 155–7.

The anthology *Ausserlesener Paduanen und Galliarden erster Theil*, published in Hamburg in 1607 by the local musicians Zacharias Füllsack and Christian Hildebrand, contains many English items.[40] Eight of its pavan and galliard pairs are by William Brade, the first of which, no. 2, is partly derived from 'Lachrimae antiquae'. No. 5 is a feeble work ascribed, surely wrongly, to Peter Philips, perhaps because the third strain of the pavan has a cantus firmus—but in the bass rather than the soprano. The pavan of no. 8 is credited to 'Thomas Mons. Engl.', a composer otherwise unknown; alternatively, the title could refer to Sir Thomas Monson (1564–1641), the dedicatee of a piece by Robert Dowland in *Varietie of Lute-Lessons* (London, 1610). The galliard of no. 14 is, as noted above, James Harding's famous piece, while nos. 16 and 19 are the pavans 'The image of melancholy' and 'Patientia' with their galliards 'Ecce quam bonum' and 'Hermoza', reprinted from Holborne's *Pavans, Galliards, Almains*, nos. 25–8. The pavan of no. 21, a fine piece with a cantus firmus in all three strains, is ascribed to Edward Johnson, though it does not survive in an English source. Finally, the galliard of no. 18 is an unusual setting of Dowland's 'M. Buctons Galiard' (or 'Suzanna Galliard'), quite different from the one in *Lachrimae*, no. 19 (Ex. 7.4). The soprano part has a number of florid passages, which suggests that it was derived from an ornamented lute setting; it is not related to the two ascribed to Dowland.[41] *Ander Theil ausserlesener lieblicher Paduanen*, Hildebrand's 1609 sequel, has only a few English pieces: Brade's pavan and galliard pair no. 8, Robert Bateman's galliards in nos. 10 and 4, and, possibly, the pairs nos. 3 and 11 by 'Benedict[us] Grep'. Some of the German pieces, however, have English features. No. 2, for instance, by the Lüneburg composer Johann Stephani (Steffens), has cantus firmus passages in all three strains, while his no. 18 is an extreme and bizarre example of the Elizabethan chromatic pavan, a genre popularized by the famous examples by Philips and Tomkins.[42]

A feature of the Füllsack–Hildebrand volumes is that single pavans or galliards are paired with new galliards or pavans, composed to order by local musicians. All the work for the English pieces was done by the Lüneburg cornett-player and organist Johann Sommer, an excellent composer, to judge from his witty 'James Harding's Pavan', and his own fine pavan and galliard pairs. Thomas Simpson also provided seven English pavans with his own galliards in his first collection, *Opusculum*

---

[40] *Erster Theil: Ausserlesener Paduanen und Galliarden mit fünff Stimmen*, ed. H. Mönkemeyer (Monumenta musicae ad usum practicum, 5; Celle, 1986).

[41] J. Dowland, *The Collected Lute Music*, ed. D. Poulton and B. Lam (3rd edn., London, 1981), nos. 38, 91.

[42] Hildebrand, *Ander Theil: Ausserlesener Paduanen und Galliarden mit fünff Stimmen*, ed. H. Mönkemeyer (Monumenta musicae ad usum practicum, 6; Celle, 1986).

Ex. 7.4. John Dowland, 'M. Buctons Galiard', bb. 1–8: (a) version in *Ausserlesener Paduanen und Galliarden erster Theil* (Hamburg, 1607), no. 18 (from Mönkemeyer (ed.), *Erster Theil: Ausserlesener Paduanen*); compared with (b) *Lachrimae; or, Seaven Teares*, no. 19

neuwer Pavanen (Frankfurt, 1610). Nos. 3 and 21 are Dowland's 'Lachrimae Antiquae Novae' and 'M. John Langtons Pavan', *Lachrimae* nos. 2 and 10; no. 7 is the well-known A minor piece by Tomkins mentioned earlier; nos. 13 and 17 are by Thomas Farmer, and no. 17 also exists in a keyboard setting by Giles Farnaby in the Fitzwilliam Virginal Book, no. 287; no. 11, an F major pavan by Dowland, is not

Ex. 7.4. *Continued*

known in an English source, but is found as 'La mia Barbara' in the
Schele lute manuscript, *D-Hs*, MB/2768, 49–51, and in a keyboard
setting by the Danzig organist Paul Siefert in *S-Uu*, IMhs 408, fos.
5ᵛ–7ʳ; no. 15 is the Glazers/Reade pavan discussed above.[43] The

[43] Simpson, *Opusculum neuwer Pavanen*, ed. H. Mönkemeyer (Monumenta musicae ad usum
practicum, 7; Celle, 1987); see also Dowland, *Collected Lute Music*, ed. Poulton and Lam, no. 95, and
W. Breig (ed.), *Lied- und Tanzvariationen der Sweelinck-Schule* (Mainz, 1970), no. 4.

Ex. 7.4. *Continued*

(lute part omitted)

settings of these pavans were also apparently made by Simpson, for nos. 2 and 10 are quite different from the versions in *Lachrimae*, no. 10 being transposed up a tone to G major. The desire to complete pavan-galliard pairs is best understood as part of the contemporary German fashion for grouping contrasted dances into suites, which can be observed, for instance, in Schein's *Banchetto musicale* (Leipzig, 1617), and, to some extent, in Brade's *Newe ausserlesene Paduanen* (Hamburg, 1609), and Simpson's *Opus newer Paduanen* (Hamburg, 1617).[44]

Lachrimae is also typical of the Anglo-German repertoire in that it is scored specifically for strings; the music, according to the title-page, is 'set forth for the Lute, Viols, or Violons, in five parts'. We saw in Ch. 6 that in Elizabethan England, outside the court at least, most professional instrumental groups played sets of violins or viols as alternatives to sets of wind instruments, or to the mixed consort, a state of affairs that is reflected in the specification 'Viols, Violins, or other [i.e., or else] Musicall Winde Instruments' on the title-page of Holborne's *Pavans, Galliards, Almains*. The words associated with the English musicians in Germany, however, are consistently limited to those associated with sets of bowed instruments, which suggests that the Anglo-German repertoire, at least, was specifically intended for them. The group at Dresden in 1586 were *Geiger* and played *Geygen*; Machin's group was noted for its *Saitenspiel*; William Brade was described as a *Geiger* at Berlin in 1603, and he described himself respectively as 'Violist und Musikus' and 'Fiolisten und Musicum' on the title-page of his 1609 and 1614 collections; in 1634 the poet Johann Rist described him as 'den berühmten Engländischen Violisten' (the famous English string-player); Thomas Simpson, likewise, described himself as 'Violisten und Musicum' on the title-pages of his three collections.[45]

Violen or *Fiolen* is the word mostly used to described the scoring of the Anglo-German repertoire. But it should not be translated, as it often is today, as 'viols', for it was a neutral word that covered both families of bowed instruments—like the parent Italian word *viole*; both are best rendered as 'strings'. Haussmann's *Neue Intrade* (Nuremberg, 1604), for instance, is said to be for 'Violen', but it includes several pieces with parts marked specifically for 'Un Violin'; similarly, Schein designated his *Banchetto musicale* 'for various instruments, particularly for strings' ('allerley Instumenten bevourauß auff Violen'), even though the Intrada (no. 21) has a part for 'Viglin'. Bartolomaeus Praetorius's *Newe liebliche Paduanen und Galliarden* (Berlin, 1616) is said on the title-page to be for 'der Figoli Gamba und Figoli di Braccia', and I think we can take it that much of this repertoire was thought to be equally suitable for viols and violins; professional groups in Germany, like their counterparts in England, would have played sets of both instruments, and would have chosen whichever was appropriate to the circumstances.

[44] Schein, *Banchetto musicale*, ed. D. Krickeberg in J. H. Schein, *Newe Ausgabe sämtlicher Werke*, ix (Kassel, 1967); Brade, *Pavans, Galliards, and Canzonas*, ed. Thomas; Simpson *Opus newer Paduanen, Galliarden, Intraden, Canzonen (1617)* ed. H. Mönkemeyer (Monumenta musicae ad usum practicum, 8; Celle, 1987).

[45] Huber, 'William Brade', 11, 21.

The layout of the five-part string-writing in *Lachrimae* is also characteristic of the Anglo-German repertoire. Most of it, like Holborne's
1599 collection and the rest of the Elizabethan consort dance repertoire,
uses a single soprano, three inner parts, and bass (SA for short), to be
played presumably on sets of violins using a violin, three violas, and
bass violin or the equivalent members of the viol family (whose exact
designation and pitch are at present open to question).[46] But one piece,
'M. Thomas Collier his Galiard with 2 Trebles' (no. 17), has a new
scoring in which the Quintus is raised an octave from its normal tenor
range to form a second soprano that continually crosses, echoes, and
exchanges material with the cantus (SS for short); it clearly needs two
violins, two violas, and bass, or the equivalent members of a set of viols
(Ex. 7.5).

The SS scoring was known in Elizabethan England; it occurs, for
instance, in the five- and six-part contrapuntal consort music of Robert
Parsons (d. 1570) and Christopher Tye (d. 1572?).[47] But it was not
applied to English or Anglo-German dance music until around 1600; the
earliest examples, apart from 'M. Thomas Collier his Galiard', are
probably the anonymous pavans nos. 13, 16, 30, and 31 in 4° MS mus.
125, 1–5, though there are others in the 'M. L. H.' section of 4° MS
mus. 72, 1–5. The earliest SS dances in English sources appear to be
some five-part pieces in *GB-Lbl*, Add. MS 17786–91, probably copied in
Oxford by William Wigthorpe around 1610, though five six-part SS
dances have come to light in *GB-Drc*, MS M193/1 that appear to date
from the years around 1600.[48] Oliver Neighbour has argued that an
obvious candidate in Byrd's consort music, the six-part pavan and
galliard, is a late work that dates from the reign of James I, and the same
is probably true of another six-part SS dance, Philips's great Passamezzo
Pavan.[49]

[46] See M. Morrow, 'Sixteenth-Century Ensemble Viol Music', *EM* 2 (1974), 160–3; H. M.
Brown, 'Notes (and Transposing Notes) on the Viol'; I. Harwood, 'A Case of Double Standards?
Instrumental Pitch in England *c*.1600', *EM* 9 (1981), 470–81; D. Gill, 'Plucked Strings and Pitch',
ibid. 10 (1982), 217–18; H. W. Myers, 'Instrumental Pitch in England *c*.1600', ibid. 519–22; I.
Harwood, 'Instrumental Pitch in England *c*.1600', ibid. 11 (1983), 76–7; Woodfield, *Early History*,
140–54; E. Segerman, 'English Viol Sizes and Pitches', *FoMRHI Quarterly*, 38 (Jan. 1985), 55–62;
id., 'What Praetorius wrote on English Viols', ibid. 63–5; N. Meeùs, 'Praetorius, Segerman, and the
English Viols', ibid. 39 (Apr. 1985), 28–32; Segerman, 'Praetorius, Meeùs, and the English Viols',
ibid. 40 (July 1985), 57–8; Spencer and Brown, 'How Alfonso della Viola Tuned his Viols'.
[47] See R. Bowers, 'The Vocal Scoring, Choral Balance, and Performing Pitch of Latin Church
Polyphony in England, *c*.1500–58', *JRMA* 112 (1987), 38–76, particularly 66; examples are Doe
(ed.), *Elizabethan Consort Music: I*, nos. 33, 34, 70; *Elizabethan Consort Music: II*, nos. 140, 146, 163,
173, 175, 191, 195.
[48] P. Warlock (ed.), *Eight Short Elizabethan Dance Tunes* (London, 1924); Monson, *Voices and Viols
in England*, 159–79; I. Harrison (ed.), *Three Instrumental Pieces from Durham Cathedral Library for Six
Instruments* (Early Music Library, 36; London, 1988).
[49] Neighbour, *William Byrd*, 86–8; Byrd, *Consort Music*, ed. Elliott, no. 15; Dart and Coates (eds.),
Jacobean Consort Music, no. 90.

Ex. 7.5. John Dowland, 'M. Thomas Collier his Galiard with two trebles', bb. 17–24, *Lachrimae; or, Seaven Teares*, no. 17

(lute part omitted)

The SS scoring is, however, found earlier in German dance or dance-like music: Paul Lütkeman's *Der erste Theil newer lateinischer und deutscher-Gesenge* (Stettin, 1597) includes some five- and six-part dances in a collection of vocal music and fantasias, and Alexander Orologio's

Intradae... quinque & sex vocibus... liber primus, published at Helmstedt in the same year, contains a set of five- and six-part dance-like intradas.[50] Both, significantly, are the work of wind-players, but the latter is particularly important because Orologio, an Italian cornett-player and 'trommeter', was at Kassel in 1594 with John Dowland, and later had connections with the Danish court—the *Intradae* is dedicated to Christian IV. Indeed, the SS scoring may have come into the Anglo-German string repertoire via wind music and, ultimately, Italianate vocal music. In Hans Leo Hassler's *Lustgarten neuer teutscher Gesäng* (Nuremberg, 1601), for instance, six-part intradas appear side by side with five-part German dance songs in an idiom derived from Gastoldi's *balletti*; both types use the SS scoring.[51]

In Germany SS largely replaced SA during the second decade of the century, as the collections of Brade and Simpson show, but in England itself SS was not generally used for dance music until around 1625, a change, I argue in Chapter 11, that was brought about by the arrival of Maurice Webster at the English court, who had been associated with Thomas Simpson in Germany. But even then SS was only used at court by chamber groups; the violin band itself continued to use SA at least until the 1670s, which means that its repertoire in the reigns of Charles I and Charles II can often be identified by means of its scoring. SA remained the norm for violin bands in France throughout the seventeenth century, and even enjoyed a revival in Germany in the 1680s and 1690s as composers such as Georg Muffat, Johann Caspar Ferdinand Fischer, and Johann Sigismund Kusser, inspired by Lully, took up the French orchestral style; it was to remain a common scoring there well into the eighteenth century, as some early works by J. S. Bach and Telemann show.

The Anglo-German consort repertoire deserves more attention than it has hitherto received from historians of English music, for at least three reasons. It gave rise to one of the rare moments in musical history, perhaps the only one after the *contenance angloise* of the early fifteenth century, when England briefly influenced the direction of musical events on the Continent. It produced in the figures of Peter Philips, Thomas Simpson, and William Brade three important English composers of instrumental music. (As often happens, their music has been neglected in their adopted countries because they were foreigners, and in England

---

[50] See Lütkeman, *Fantasia 'Innsbruck ich muss dich lassen'*, 1597, ed. B. Thomas (German Instrumental Music of the Late Renaissance, 1; London, 1973); Orologio, *Six Intradas, 1597* ed. Thomas (German Instrumental Music of the Late Renaissance, 4; London, 1978).

[51] Hassler, *Lustgarten neuer teutscher Gesäng (1601)*, ed. C. R. Crosby (*Sämtliche Werke*, ix; Wiesbaden, 1968); see also *Intradas and Gagliarda from Lustgarten (1601)*, ed. B. Thomas (Thesaurus Musicus, 16; London, 1979); *Six Lieder from Lustgarten (1601)*, ed. id. (Thesaurus Musicus, 26; London, 1981).

because they left home at an early age, never to return.) Most important in the present context, German sources evidently contain much of the 'lost' repertoire of Elizabethan consort dance music, and they show that that repertoire was thought of largely or even exclusively as music for sets of violins or viols.

8

'In the Arte of Musicke and Skill of Danceing'

The Jacobean Court Orchestra

SEVEN 'Violins' walked with their fellow court musicians in Elizabeth's funeral procession on 28 April 1603.[1] They were a striking testimony to the continuity of English court institutions. All but one was descended from a member of Henry VIII's string consort. Four of the seven were the children and grandchildren of Ambrose Lupo: his sons Joseph and Peter and their sons, Thomas I and II. 'Anthony Coomes' (or Comey) was probably the grandson of John Maria of Cremona, while Caesar Galliardello was the son of Mark Anthony, who had come to England from Brescia in 1545. The only member of seemingly English descent was William Warren, Ambrose Lupo's successor. Long service had always been a feature of the group. Innocent of Cremona, Anthony Comey's father and predecessor, had died just over a month earlier after over fifty years' service.[2] Mark Anthony and Caesar Galliardello between them served five monarchs for more than eighty years. Joseph and Peter Lupo served more than fifty and forty years respectively, and their sons did almost as well. In more than sixty years the group had a total of not many more than twenty members. And with an effective strength of seven it was no larger in 1603 than it had been in 1550.

The new reign brought a series of changes to the group, increasing its size and changing its character. The process began only a week after James I entered London for the first time: Rowland Rubbish (Rubidge) was sworn in with a number of his colleagues-to-be on 18 May, and by a warrant dated 23 May received the place that had been vacant ever since Ambrose Grasso's death in 1582.[3] The main changes, however, came in

[1] Ashbee, *RECM*, iv. 1.

[2] Ibid., iv. 4, 72; Innocent's place was given at first to the publisher George Eastland, according to a note dated 1 May 1603 on the back of *GB-Lpro*, SP15/33 (64); for Eastland, see Poulton, *John Dowland*, 245–52.

[3] Ashbee, *RECM*, iv. 4, 72, 231; Rubbish died on 21 Aug. 1620, and was succeeded by Leonard Mell; ibid., iii. 105; in one document (ibid., iv. 53), he was described as 'Rowland Bach', which sounds as if he was Welsh; on the other hand, Roger Prior has recently argued that his name is a version of *rybarz* or *rybiarz*, the Polish for 'fisherman', and that he was a Polish Jew; 'A Second Jewish Community', 144–5.

1607–8. By a warrant dated 23 November 1607 (with wages backdated to Lady Day) Daniel Farrant received the other dormant place in the violin consort, the one held by Thomas Browne until his death in 1582.[4] Peter Lupo evidently died early in 1608, for by a warrant dated 9 July his place was given to Alexander Chesham with wages backdated to Lady Day; Lupo had probably been ill for some time, for in February 1606/7 he was given £20 'by way of his Ma(jes)t(i)es rewarde for his service to the late quene and to his highnes, and for releif of his present necessitye'.[5] Next, Jeremy Hearne was given a place 'for the base vyoll' by a warrant dated 21 May 1608, again backdated to Lady Day; he succeeded the Elizabethan bagpiper Richard Woodward.[6] The weight of court precedence meant that the officials concerned often tried to avoid creating a new place by finding a dormant one in some recess of the labyrinthine court establishment. Finally, in February and March 1611/12 Horatio Lupo (Thomas I's younger brother) was given William Warren's place, and Thomas Warren (William's son) was given a dormant one, described as 'for the Lute', once held by the Elizabethan musician Robert Woodward.[7] Lupo served in the household of Thomas Sackville, Earl of Dorset before the earl's death in April 1608 (see Ch. 6), while Warren may be the 'Thomas Warrin' who worked at the Danish court in the 1580s.[8]

By 1612, then, the establishment of Henry VIII's string consort had been doubled from six to twelve; and the descendants of the original immigrants had been reduced within a few years to occupying only half its places. But it is difficult to work out the day-to-day size of the group. One problem is that at least two of its members, Alfonso Ferrabosco and Daniel Farrant, seem to have been viol-players rather than violinists, and formed part of a four-man viol consort at court (see Ch. 11), though they may have performed with the violins on special occasions. Another is that the court was beginning to employ individuals who are known to have been violinists, but were not members of the violin consort, at least on paper. Norman Lesley (Lisle), for instance, joined the group in 1616 in succession to Joseph Lupo by a warrant dated 8 June of that year (backdated to Lady Day), though he had actually been at court since January 1605/6, when he was given the post of 'Musitian to the Duke of Yorke', Prince Charles.[9] A year later, by a warrant dated 7 August 1617,

---

[4] Ashbee, *RECM*, vi. 132; Ashbee, *RECM*, iv. 80.

[5] Ashbee, *RECM*, iv. 22, 79, 80.

[6] Ibid. 22, 80.

[7] Ibid. 34, 88; the relationship between William and Thomas Warren is established in the administration of William's will, Feb. 1612 and Nov. 1618; M. Fitch (ed.), *Index to Administrations in the Perogative Court of Canterbury*, v: *1609–1619* (The Index Library, British Record Society, 83; London, 1968), 134.

[8] Sjögren, 'Thomas Bull and other "English Instrumentalists" in Denmark'.

[9] Ashbee, *RECM*, iv. 13, 96.

he was replaced by John Hopper, though he remained a member of Prince Charles's household until his death in 1625.[10] In the 1630s Simon Hopper was employed in the future Charles II's household to provide his young master with dance music (see Ch. 10), and it is likely that Lesley provided the same service for the future Charles I.

The picture is further complicated by the fluctuating population of court dancing-masters. Thomas Cardell had taught dancing at court ever since the 1570s (see Ch. 5), and his son Francis also held a post as 'attendant on the Lady Elizabeth' from 7 November 1604 until his death in the spring of 1606; Thomas was subsequently given his son's £40 a year, so it is likely that Francis had been teaching James I's daughter to dance.[11] Thomas Cardell was an Englishman, and seems to have played the lute and the cittern (we know nothing about his son's musical skills), but soon after James's accession English society began to demand the services of French dancing-masters; and they, it seems, all played the violin as well as its diminutive cousin, the kit or *pochette*. The association was made early in the reign in Randle Cotgrave's *Dictionarie of the French and English Tongues* (London, 1611), where the word 'poche' is defined as 'the little narrow, and long Violin (having the backe of one peece) which French dauncers, or dauncing Maisters, carrie about with them in a case, when they goe to teach their Schollers'. Indeed, the first recorded French dancing-master at the English court was one of the most famous violinists of the time, Jacques Cordier alias Bochan (Bocan).

Bochan is first heard of on 2 January 1603/4 as 'Jacques Beausem', when he was paid 40s. 'for his Chardges and paynes in bringing l(ett)res for his ma(jes)t(i)es s(e)rvice from Parrice in Fraunce sent by his ma(jes)t(i)es Embassador there'.[12] He was a member of Prince Henry's household from at least 11 July 1608 until April 1609, where he is listed once as a 'frenche violer'.[13] In June 1609 'James Bochan a violyn' was given £60 a year for life in the main royal household 'by mandate of the king', to run from the previous Lady Day; he was also employed by Queen Anne at the time of Prince Henry's death in November 1612, and he received £6 in gold from Arbella Stuart on 13 June 1610.[14] Bochan disappears from the accounts during 1614, when he probably went back to France; he returned to England in 1625 with Charles I's bride Henrietta Maria, when he was given a gift of £500.[15] In September 1627 he requested a pass to return to France, which was granted on 3 October,

[10] Ibid., iii, 16, 18, 165; iv. 108.
[11] *GB-Lpro*, E403/2454, fos. 96ʳ, 187ʳ; Ashbee, *RECM*, iv. 127; see Batchelor, 'Daniel Bacheler'.
[12] *GB-Lpro*, E351/543, m. 115.
[13] Ashbee, *RECM*, iv. 213–14.
[14] Ibid. 23–4, 36, 141; Library of Longleat House, Seymour Papers, xxii, fo. 25ᵛ.
[15] Ashbee, *RECM*, iv. 158; iii, 7.

and in November he and his servants were granted a licence to transport their luggage.[16] Nevertheless, he was in England the next year, for another pass was issued to him on 28 March 1628 'to return into France', and he continued to be showered with gifts from England: £60 from Henrietta Maria on 20 May 1630, £200 from Charles I in September 1633, and again in February 1633/4—his last appearance in English documents; he died in 1653.[17] Bochan was equally famous as a violinist and as a dancing master: he taught most of the members of the English and French royal families to dance, but he was also among those singled out by Mersenne who played the violin 'parfaictement' with 'certains tremblemens qui ravissent l'esprit'; Charles Sorel wrote in 1623 that the contemporary French violin band, the Vingt-quatre Violons, was known as 'les disciples de Bocan'.[18]

A number of other dancing-masters can be identified in contemporary court records. Thomas Giles was appointed as Prince Henry's music teacher by a patent dated 23 December 1605, but he is described as the prince's 'Teacher to Dance' in an undated list of his household; he joined the main royal household in 1614, and is described as 'instructor to the Queen' in December 1615, whereupon he disappears from the Exchequer accounts.[19] It is not known whether he was related to the church musicians Thomas and Nathaniel Giles. On 15 December 1617 Giles's place was given to Sebastian La (Le) Pierre to 'attend and instruct' Prince Charles in 'the Arte of Musicke and skill of dancing'.[20]

La Pierre had actually been at the English court as early as 1611: he was described as 'instructor to the Duke of York [Prince Charles] in dancing' by a warrant for a £30 'free gift' dated 27 July of that year, and received another gift of £36 by a warrant dated 3 November 1613 as 'instructor in dancing' to the late Prince Henry, though there are no references to him in the prince's accounts.[21] He joined the main royal household in or before July 1615, and served until August 1639, when he disappears from the accounts; however, he still appears in the accounts of Henrietta Maria's household until the end of 1641, and was presumably the 'Mounsier Sebastian, the dancing master' who received £3 from the Earl of Rutland in 1643; he was dead by 7 June 1646, when his will was

---

[16] *CSPD, Charles I, Addenda: March 1625–January 1649*, ed. W. D. Hamilton and S. C. Lomas (London, 1897), 227; J. V. Lyle (ed.), *Acts of the Privy Council of England, September 1627–June 1628* (London, 1940), 64, 254.

[17] Lyle, *Acts of the Privy Council*, 362; Ashbee, *RECM*, iii. 72, 77, 206, 245; v. 7; C. Massip, *La Vie des musiciens de Paris au temps de Mazarin (1643–1661)* (La Vie musicale en France sous les rois Bourbons, 24; Paris, 1976), 96.

[18] M. Mersenne, *Harmonie universelle*, iii: *Traité des instruments à chordes* (Paris, 1636–7), i. 11; H. Prunières, *Le Ballet de cour en France avant Benserade et Lully* (Paris, 1914), 209.

[19] Ashbee, *RECM*, iv. 12, 157, 163, 211.

[20] Ibid. 46.

[21] Ibid. 148, 156.

being proved.[22] La Pierre was also a composer: there are pieces by him in *GB-Ob*, MS Mus. Sch. D. 220 (see Table 10.1), and there are four dances among the early seventeenth-century pieces in the first Philidor manuscript (*F-Pn*, MS Rés. F. 494, third sequence, 87–98) attributed to 'Mr de la Pierre', though these may be the work of one of the many La Pierres who worked as violinists and dancing-masters in Avignon and Turin—to whom Sebastian La Pierre was probably related.[23]

The French violinist and dancing-master Adam Vallet is first heard of in England in the spring of 1616. On 3 April he shared £80 with John Tetart 'as of his Ma(jes)t(i)es free guift & reward for their attendance at Newm(ar)kett for their disport & r(e)creac(i)on of his Ma(jes)tie there, by their exercising of their Artes of fenceing & daunceing'.[24] The next January he was given £60 a year as a musician 'for the Lute untill such time as he shall have the place of a Musicon in ordinary by the next vacancy', but this was clearly another case of borrowing spare places from other parts of the royal music, for he is given as one of the 'Musicians for the Violins' in subsidy documents dated 13 July 1624 and 22 December 1625, and in the list of those given a livery for James I's funeral on 5 May 1625.[25] He is presumably the Adam Vallet who joined a group of seven of Paris's town musicians as a *dessus* player in November 1607, and who agreed to make some arrangements of ballets for his colleagues; he was still in Paris in July 1614, when he was described as 'maître joueur d'instruments'.[26] Adam Vallet was perhaps related to Bernard Vallet, 'joueur d'instruments', who married Jehanne Hérisson at Yerre near Paris on 9 November 1580, and the lutenist Nicolas Vallet, who worked in Amsterdam and published a number of collections there between 1615 and *c*.1644.[27] The title-page of Nicolas's *Regia pietas* (Amsterdam, 1620), dedicated to James I, shows the king surrounded by court musicians; the figure on the right may be intended to represent Adam Vallet (Fig. 8.1).

Adam Vallet was clearly highly regarded at the English court. In May

[22] Ibid. 162; iii, 237, 252; I. Spink, 'The Musicians of Queen Henrietta-Maria: Some Notes and References in the English State Papers', *AcM* 36 (1964), 179; a 'Guillaume La Pierre' took part in *The Triumph of Peace*, and taught Prince Charles and Princess Mary 'the Art of dancing' from 1636 to 1638; see T. Orbison and R. F. Hills (eds.), 'The Middle Temple Documents Relating to James Shirley's *The Triumph of Peace*', *Malone Society Collections*, 12 (Oxford, 1983), 61, 66, 67, 68, 71; Ashbee, *RECM*, iii. 97–8.

[23] J. Robert, 'Une famille de joueurs de violon avignonnais au XVIIe-siècle, les de La Pierre', *RMFC* 4 (1964), 54–67; M. H. Winter, *The Pre-Romantic Ballet* (London, 1974), 32.

[24] *GB-Lpro*, SO3/6; see Ashbee, *RECM*, iv. 44.

[25] *GB-Lpro*, SO3/6; see Ashbee, *RECM*, iv. 45; iv. 60, 62; iii. 3, 9.

[26] M. Jurgens (ed.), *Documents du minutier central concernant l'histoire de la musique (1600–1650)*, 2 vols. (Paris, 1967–74), i. 354–7, 610.

[27] N. Vallet, *Œuvres pour luth seul: Le Secret des muses*, ed. M. Rollin and A. Souris (Paris, 1970), pp. xi–xiv; see also L. P. Grijp, 'The Ensemble Music of Nicolaes Vallet', in L. P. Grijp and W. Mook (eds.), *Proceedings of the International Lute Symposium, Utrecht 1986* (Utrecht, 1988), 64–85.

8.1. Title-page of Nicolas Vallet, *Regia pietas* (Amsterdam, 1620), showing James I as King David with court musicians; the violinist may represent Adam Vallet. Courtesy of Robert Spencer

1622 he collaborated with several distinguished musicians, including Orlando Gibbons, Thomas Day (Master of the Children of the Chapel Royal), and William Heather (founder of the Oxford music professorship), in an unsuccessful project to obtain a monopoly to manufacture strings for musical instruments (see Ch. 2). The next month he was made an English denizen, and in March 1623/4 his court pension was increased to the unprecedented sum (for a violinist) of £110 a year 'in considerac(i)on of the faithfull service done unto us and our most deare sonne Charles Prince of Wales'—that is, he was also a member of the distinguished and innovative group of musicians in Prince Charles's household (see Ch. 9).[28] He died on 3 October 1625; his will reveals that his widow Mary was the daughter of the court violinist Caesar Galliardello.[29]

It seems, therefore, that by the time the violin consort reached its new establishment of twelve in 1612 there were as many as five extra violinists at court who could have augmented it to make an orchestral violin band of up to seventeen—besides those who could have been recruited outside the court. These changes could, of course, have had some other purpose—such as to create two one-to-a-part violin consorts for waiting at court. A shift system was certainly in operation among the wind-players in the 1630s (see Ch. 10), and the Restoration Twenty-four Violins was often divided into two groups of twelve. But there is no sign that the Jacobean violinists worked in shifts, and there is documentary evidence in the masque literature that an orchestral violin band was used at the Jacobean court.

The masque enjoyed a sudden revival at the beginning of James I's reign, after a period of neglect in Elizabeth's old age.[30] Masques were essentially vehicles for aristocratic dancing, though there was also speech and vocal music. Under James I the English court, once dependent upon Italy for its dance (see Ch. 5), turned to the increasingly fashionable and influential styles of French dance, exemplified by the complex pattern dances of the *ballet de cour*. What little is known about the formal dances in English masques shows that they, too, were choreographed in elaborate patterns, sometimes using geometric figures in the French manner.[31] So it may be that Bochan and his colleagues came over in part to train the English aristocracy in the sort of ensemble discipline that would have been needed for this sort of dancing. The French dancing-masters certainly figure prominently in the literature relating to Jacobean masques.

The earliest ones mentioned in masque texts are Thomas Giles and Jeremy Hearne. We have already encountered Hearne as a violinist, but at the time he was better known for his terpsichorean activities, and he may have been French, for he is referred to as 'Jerome Heron' as much as 'Jeremy Hearne'. At Midsummer 1615 he gave up his place in the violin band (he was succeeded by the viol-player John Friend) for a more lucrative one as a dancing-master: by letters patent dated 12 September 1616 he was promised the £140-a-year place held by Thomas Cardell, but it is not clear whether he had to wait until after Cardell's death in May 1621 (buried at St Margaret, Westminster on the 18th) to benefit

---

[28] *GB-Lpro*, SP38/12; Ashbee, *RECM*, iv. 58.

[29] Ashbee, *RECM*, iii. 165; M. Fitch (ed.), *Testamentary Records in the Archdeaconry Court of London*, i: *(1363)–1649* (The Index Library, British Record Society, 89; London, 1979), 145.

[30] See Chambers, *The Elizabethan Stage*, i. 149–70 for a survey of the Elizabethan masque.

[31] See J. M. Ward, 'Newly Devis'd Measures for Jacobean Masques', *AcM* 60 (1988), 111–42.

from it; Hearne's duties were described in January 1640/1, after his own death, as 'attending and teaching their Ma(jes)ties and the Maides of hono(u)r in the Art of danncing when he shalbe required'.[32]

Giles alone is mentioned in the texts of *Hymenai* (5 January 1605/6) and *The Masque of Beauty* (10 January 1607/8). Ben Jonson wrote in the former that the dances—one included patterns 'formed into Letters'— were 'both made, and taught by Maister THOMAS GILES', while in the latter the character of Thamesis 'was personated by Master THOMAS GILES, who made the Daunces'.[33] In *The Haddington Masque* (9 February 1607/8), Giles and Hearne 'made' two of the dances each, and 'in the persons of two Cyclopes, beat a time to them, with their hammers'.[34] Jonson's text makes it clear that the word 'made' means that on this occasion they contributed choreography rather than music, because he added that the 'tunes were M. ALPHONSO FERRABOSCO'S'. But Giles also wrote dance tunes: Thomas Campion attributed to him the fourth of the dance tunes that he published in the text of his *Lord Hay's Masque* (6 January 1606/7), and it is likely that the dancing-masters were often responsible for the tunes as well as the choreography of masque dances.[35]

The high point of the collaboration between Giles and Hearne was reached in the famous dances for Jonson's *Masque of Queens* (2 February 1608/9). One of the antimasque dances of witches was:

a magicall Daunce, full of praeposterous change, and gesticulation, but most applying to theyr property: who, at theyr meetings, do all thinges contrary to the custome of Men, dauncing, back to back, hip to hip, they[r] handes joyn'd and making they[r] circles backward, to the left hand, w(i)th strange phantastique motions of theyr heads, and bodyes.

It was, he continued, 'excellently imitated by the Maker of the Daunce, M[r]. Hierome Herne, whose right it is here to be nam'd'.[36] Giles was credited with a pattern dance 'graphically dispos'd into letters, and honoring the Name of the most sweete, and ingenious Prince, Charles, Duke of Yorke'.

Payment books sometimes reveal the contribution of dancing-masters to masques when the texts fail to mention them. Hearne, for instance, does not appear in the text of Samuel Daniel's *Tethys Festival* (5 June 1610), the masque that celebrated the creation of Prince Henry as Prince

[32] Ashbee, *RECM*, iv. 42–3, 44–5, 184; A. M. Burke (ed.), *Memorials of St Margarets Church, Westminster: The Parish Registers 1539–1660* (London, 1914), 520; Ashbee, *RECM*, iii. 106; see also Batchelor, 'Daniel Batcheler', 7, 11.

[33] *Ben Jonson*, ed. Herford and Simpson, vii. 190, 220–1, 232.

[34] Ibid. 260.

[35] Campion, *Works*, ed. Davis, 230; see Sabol (ed.), *Four Hundred Songs and Dances*, no. 5.

[36] *Ben Jonson*, vii. 301.

of Wales, but he was paid £10 by the Earl of Salisbury for teaching his son 'against the Maske when the Prince was installed'.[37] Two payments for Jonson's *Oberon* (1 January 1610/11) show that Ferrabosco, Hearne, and 'Monsieur Confesse' were paid £20 each 'for their paines having bene imployed in the Princes Maske by the space of almost six weekes', while Giles was paid £40 'for 3 dances'.[38] A bill for a masque two months later, *Love Freed from Ignorance and Folly* (3 February 1610/11), clarifies the roles of some of the participants.[39] Ferrabosco was once again paid £20 for 'making the songes', Confesse got £50 for 'teachinge all the dances', and Bochan received £20 for 'teaching the Ladies the footing of 2 dances'. In a less informative bill for Campion's *The Lords' Masque* (14 February 1612/13), Hearne and Bochan were paid £40 each, while Giles and Confesse received £30 each.[40]

Confesse is a mysterious figure: he does not seem to have been employed in any of the court households, and his first name is not given in most documents. But he was certainly a musician as well as a dancing-master, for the Board Lute Book (in the possession of Robert Spencer) contains an 'Antiq Masque p^er Mr Confesso set by Mr Taylor' that may come from the Lords' Masque, and there is a corant 'Confess' in *US-NH*, Filmer MS 3 (see Ch. 10); he is perhaps the 'Nicholas Confais' who was described as a musician of the queen of England when he acted as godfather to Madeleine Vasseur at the Paris church of Saint-Eustache on 13 May 1628, and the 'Nicholas Confene' who was described as a French musician lodging in the parish of St Martin-in-the-Fields on 16 December 1635.[41] Significantly, there are three dances attributed to 'Confais' in the Tabley Lute Book at *GB-Mr*, a collection largely of French music compiled in England *c*.1661.[42]

Violins are specifically mentioned in five Jacobean masque texts. In *Lord Hay's Masque* nine 'Violins' made up a 'consort of twelve' with three lutes, and two others played in the separate 'consort of ten' that accompanied the voices.[43] In Marston's *Ashby Entertainment* (August 1607), a masque-like work written for Ashby Castle in Leicestershire, the 'violins . . . played a new measure, to which the masquers danced', while the masquers in *The Masque of Queens* performed their first dance 'to the

[37] Library of Hatfield House, Cecil MSS, Bills 46/1, Accounts 160/1, fo. 81^v.

[38] *GB-Lpro*, E403/2730, fos. 168^v, 181^v; see *Ben Jonson*, x. 520–1.

[39] *GB-Lpro*, E407/57/1; see *Ben Jonson*, x. 528–9.

[40] Ashbee, *RECM*, iv. 233–4.

[41] R. Spencer (ed.), *The Board Lute Book* (Leeds, 1976), no. 91; Y. de Brossard (ed.), *Musiciens de Paris 1535–1792: Actes d'état d'après le fichier Laborde de la Bibliothèque Nationale* (La Vie musicale en France sous les rois Bourbons, 11; Paris, 1965), 68; I. Scouloudi (ed.), *Returns of Strangers in the Metropolis 1593, 1627, 1635, 1639* (Huguenot Society of London, quarto series, 57; London, 1985), 260.

[42] Boethius Press is preparing a facs. edn.

[43] Campion, *Works*, ed. Davis, 211.

Cornets, the second to the Violins'.[44] In Beaumont's *Masque of the Inner Temple and Gray's Inn* (20 February 1612/13) an antimasque of dancing statues was accompanied by violins and then by wind instruments:

at their comming, the Musicke changed from Violins to Hoboyes, Cornets, &c. And the ayre of the Musicke was utterly turned into a soft time, with drawing notes, excellently expressing their natures, and the Measure likewise was fitted unto the same.[45]

In William Browne's *Masque of the Inner Temple* (13 January 1614/15) 'treble violins with all the inward parts; a bass viol, bass lute, sagbut, cornemuse, and a tabor and pipe'—in effect, a violin band with exotic instruments added for grotesque effect—played for an antimasque of men transformed into animals, while the masquers danced to 'violins'.[46]

Violins are also referred to in an oblique fashion in a number of other masque texts. In Daniel's *The Vision of the Twelve Goddesses* (8 January 1603/4), the first surviving Jacobean masque, 'the Musicke of the Violls and Lutes, placed on one side of the Hall' accompanied at least one of the dances of the masquers.[47] Daniel, like other non-musicians at the time, was probably using the word 'viol' in a generic sense that covered both the families of bowed instruments, for the court string-players would hardly have used viols to accompany dancing. The author of the anonymous *Masque of Flowers* (6 January 1613/14) recorded that 'the loud music ceasing, the Masquers descend[ed] in a gallant march...to the stage, where they fell into their first measure', which implies that another ensemble—most likely the violins—took over from the wind instruments at that point.[48] Finally, in the anonymous *First Antimasque of Mountebanks* (2 and 19 February 1617/18) Paradox began a speech after the final main dance with the words 'Silence Lordings, Ladies and fiddles!'[49]

The payments to the performers for *Oberon*, *Love Freed from Ignorance and Folly*, and *The Lords' Masque* show that violins were present in masques even when they are not mentioned in the texts, and they enable the size of the band to be estimated. In *Oberon* Robert Johnson and 'Thomas Lupo' (presumably Thomas I, the composer) were paid £20 and £5 respectively for 'making the Daunces' and 'setting them to the violins'. Three 'violins', Thomas Lupo 'thelder', Alexander Chesham,

[44] J. Marston, *The Works*, ed. A. H. Bullen (London, 1887), iii. 399; *Ben Jonson*, vii. 315.

[45] F. Bowers (ed.), *The Dramatic Works in the Beaumont and Fletcher Canon*, i (Cambridge, 1966), 132–3.

[46] E. A. J. Honigman (ed.), in *A Book of Masques in Honour of Allardyce Nicoll* (Cambridge, 1970), 193.

[47] Samuel Daniel, *The Complete Works in Verse and Prose*, ed. A. B. Grosart (London, 1885), iii. 194.

[48] Honigman, *A Book of Masques*, 169.

[49] Marston, *Works*, ed. Bullen, 437; see Bentley, *The Jacobean and Caroline Stage*, v. 1376–8.

and Rowland Rubbish were given £10 between them, while £32 was spent on a 'Companie of Violins'. In *Love Freed from Ignorance and Folly* Lupo was again paid £5 for 'setting the dances to the violens', while '10 violens that contynualy practized to the Queene' (that is, that played for her dance rehearsals) and '4 more that were added att the Maske' got £20 and £4 respectively. The *Lords' Masque* document includes £10 each for Robert Johnson and Thomas Lupo, once again, presumably, in their roles as composer and arranger of the dance music, £20 for Stephen Thomas (a violin-playing London wait; see Ch. 6), £10 for '10 of the Kinges violins', and £42 for forty-two unspecified 'Musitians'. There are also payments for Jonson's masque *The Gypsies Metamorphosed*, a small-scale show that was put on three times in the summer of 1621.[50] Nicholas Lanier received the enormous sum of £200 for, presumably, writing and supervising the music, while a group of 'fiddlers' only got £12. 16s. between them. Among the performers was John Ogilby, a young London dancing-master who was later to make his mark as a translator, a printer, a surveyor, a writer on geography, and, in particular, as a map-maker.

These payments make the most sense if we suppose that the standard rate for an instrumentalist in a masque was £1 or £2, depending on the amount of time spent in rehearsal, hence the £10 for ten violins and the £42 for forty-two musicians in *The Lords' Masque*, and hence the £4 for four violins 'added att the Maske' compared with the £20 for the ten who 'contynualy practized' in *Love Freed from Ignorance and Folly*. Thus it is likely that there was a violin band of twelve in the former—ten plus Lupo and Thomas (or as many as sixteen if the dancing-masters Hearne, Bochan, Giles, and Confesse played, and were not included in the ten)—and fourteen in the latter (or seventeen if Lupo, Bochan, and Confesse played, and were not included in the fourteen). By the same token, the £12. 16s. given to fiddlers in *The Gypsies Metamorphosed* breaks down neatly into £1. 12s. apiece for eight players. The *Oberon* payments are more difficult to interpret, since it is not clear whether the three named violinists (who perhaps played for rehearsals) and the dancing-masters Hearne and Confesse were included in the 'Companie of Violins'. But if the £32 was spent on sixteen players at £2 each, the band as a whole could have been as large as twenty-one. If such a group seems improbably large, it should be remembered that it was a well-established practice for young musicians to serve for a time without payment in an 'extraordinary' capacity in the hope of receiving one of the coveted court places. Also, the Venetian diplomat Orazio Busino reported that the masquers in Jonson's *Pleasure Reconciled to Virtue* (6 January 1617/18) danced to 'violins, to the number of twenty-five or thirty'.[51] Busino may have exaggerated a little, but we can be sure that the Jacobean court danced on occasion to the sound of a sizeable orchestral violin band.

With this evidence before us, we must now reconsider the early history of the orchestra. We should first, however, be clear about what we mean by that difficult word 'orchestra'. In contemporary English it meant the space in front of the stage in the ancient Greek theatre where the chorus sang and danced—hence the title of Sir John Davies's *Orchestra; or, a Poeme of Dauncyinge* (London, 1594)—or the equivalent area of a contemporary playhouse. Musicians began to be placed in the 'orchestra' of London theatres after the Restoration, but it took time for the word to acquire any musical connotations, and it was not until the next century that it was used in the modern sense; two early examples are in Roger North's essay 'Notes of Comparison between the Elder and Later Musick and Somewhat Historicall of Both' of *c*.1726.[52] Another problem is that the word is often used today to mean any large instrumental ensemble, regardless of period or culture, as in a gamelan 'orchestra', the 'orchestras' of Florentine *intermedi*, or even the 'orchestras' of the Old Testament.[53] But in European art music it is more useful and historically appropriate to restrict the word to ensembles that are based on a body of violins playing more than one to a part, with a relatively stable personnel, instrumentation, and administrative structure; thus the ensemble for Monteverdi's *Orfeo*, regarded as a landmark of orchestral history ever since Burney's *History of Music*, belongs more properly to the *ad hoc* tradition of Renaissance festival music.[54]

Another traditional landmark of orchestral history is the French court violin band. We usually read that Baldassare de Belgioioso alias Balthasar de Beaujoyeux brought an Italian violin band to Paris in about 1555; that Andrea Amati made a complete set of thirty-eight instruments for Charles IX (reigned 1560–74); that there were twenty-two 'Violons ordinaires de la chambre du Roy' in 1609; and that Louis XIII established the group as the 'Vingt-quatre Violons du Roi' in 1626.[55] But it comes as a shock to realize that most of this is hearsay: there is no evidence that Beaujoyeux's group was of orchestral size, and the earliest documentary evidence for the Charles IX instruments seems to be a

---

[51] A. B. Hinds (ed.), *Calendar of State Papers and Manuscripts, Relating to English Affairs, Existing in the Archives and Collections of Venice, and in the other Libraries of Northern Italy*, xv: *1517–1619* (London, 1909), 113.

[52] Wilson (ed.), *Roger North on Music*, 297, 313.

[53] N. Zaslaw, 'When is an Orchestra not an Orchestra?', *EM* 16 (1988), 483–95.

[54] Burney, *A General History of Music*, ed. Mercer, ii. 519.

[55] See, for instance, Boyden, *History of Violin Playing*, 35–6, 116–17; J. R. Anthony, *French Baroque Music from Beaujoyeulx to Rameau* (2nd edn., London, 1978), 9–10; L. C. Witten, 'The Surviving Instruments of Andrea Amati', *EM* 10 (1982), 487–94; Kenyon, 'The Baroque Violin', 64.

statement in Jean-Benjamin de La Borde's *Essai sur la musique ancienne et moderne* (Paris 1780), i. 358 to the effect that 'our best violins are those that were made in Cremona by the famous Amati for Charles IX, king of France'. The references of 1609 and 1626 are repeated parrot-fashion from book to book without any documentary evidence at all. Even the 'fact' that ten violins played in *Le Balet comique de la Royne* (15 October 1581) is not quite what it seems, for the 'orchestra' on that occasion actually consisted of two separate groups of five, who played on opposite sides of the hall, so their five-part music (printed in the text) was effectively performed one to a part.[56]

In some respects the town musicians of Paris, the members of the Confrérie de St-Julien-des-Ménétriers, have a better claim to have invented the orchestra. They formed groups of orchestral size in the middle of the sixteenth century (there are instances of nine players in 1547, eight in 1551 and eleven in 1552); they often signed legal agreements that committed them to a particular group for a number of years; they frequently stipulated which parts were to be played by which musicians; and when particular instruments are mentioned in the agreements—from 1584 onwards—violins are always given as one of the options (most often as an alternative to cornetts); by then groups as large as eleven (1583) and fourteen (1584) are recorded.[57] But in the absence of adequate research into the early history of the French court violinists—a gaping hole in our knowledge that needs to be filled—the English court violin band is a contender for the title of the earliest court orchestra, for it was already a settled and permanent organization of orchestral size more than a decade before the Vingt-quatre Violons is supposed to have come into being.

We know little about the repertoire of the English court violin band in the early seventeenth century. No manuscripts survive today that can be directly associated with the group, though part-books that it used are known to have existed. In 1619 Caesar Galliardello, who was paid an annual fee at the time for providing his colleagues with strings, was given £9 for strings 'and for Bookes'; Leonard Mell received the same in 1622 for 'stringes bookes and such necessaryes', as did Galliardello in 1624 and 1626; in the next reign, by a warrant dated 28 April 1633, Stephen Nau and Davis Mell were paid £15 for 'twoe setts of Musicke Bookes for the Violins'; and by a warrant dated 6 March 1635/6 Mell was paid £6 for a violin and £3 'for a sett of books'.[58] Much of the music, particularly in the latter part of James I's reign, must have been written by Thomas

---

[56] *Balet comique de la Royne* (Paris, 1582), fos. 22^{r-v}.

[57] F. Lesure, 'Les Orchestres populaires à Paris vers la fin du XVIe-siècle', *RdM* 36 (1954), 39–54; many 17th-c. agreements are printed in Jurgens (ed.), *Documents*, i and ii.

[58] Ashbee, *RECM*, iv. 106, 112; iii. 86, 134, 136, 146.

Lupo I, for he was given 40 marks a year (£26. 8s. 4d.) by a warrant dated 16 February 1620/1 (replaced by one dated 1 April 1622 that also includes the standard livery of £16. 2s. 6d.) as 'composer for our Violins, that they might be the better furnished with variety and choise for our delight and pleasure in that kind'; Lupo's appointment actually seems to have come into force in 1619, for by a warrant dated 26 June of that year John Heydon replaced him as a rank-and-file member of the group.[59] The change was an important one, for the new post effectively involved an increase in the establishment of the band from twelve to thirteen, and it provided the model for the establishment of posts for composers in the other sections of the royal music. To judge from the activities of Lupo's sucessor, Stephen Nau, it also appears to have involved some degree of *de facto* authority and leadership over the rest of the violin players (see Ch. 10).

It is sometimes assumed that there is a connection between Lupo's appointment as composer to the violin band and his surviving output of consort music, which consists almost entirely of fantasias or fantasia-like pieces in three, four, five, and six parts. It is true that some of the three- and four-part pieces are unusually dance-like, and were probably intended for violins. But I argue in Chapter 9 that they belong to Lupo's other sphere of court activity: he received an additional £40 a year from 1611 as a member of the households of Prince Henry and Prince Charles, where there was a mixed chamber ensemble of violins, viols, and organ—the group for which Orlando Gibbons and John Coprario also wrote much of their more forward-looking consort music. A certain amount of the dance music that Lupo would have written for the violin band probably does survive, but in the mass of anonymous pieces in the central source of Jacobean masque dances, *GB-Lbl*, Add. MS 10444; the manuscript includes the two dances ascribed to him at the end of the text of *Lord Hay's Masque*, and it can certainly tell us much about the way he and his colleagues went about composing and arranging dance music.[60]

Add. MS 10444 is a mysterious and tantalizing document. It is normally thought of as a single pair of part-books, treble and bass, but it actually consists of two unrelated two-part sources of different periods brought together in a later binding. The first (the second dates from the late seventeenth century, and is of no concern here) contains two sequences of 140 and 26 Jacobean pieces described respectively as 'Masques' and 'other Tunes' on the original cover of the treble part. Pamela Willetts discovered that the treble was copied by Sir Nicholas Le Strange of Hunstanton (the bass is in another hand), and by comparing it with the opening section of his autograph collection of anecdotes,

---

[59] Ibid. iv. 50, 53, 55.   [60] Sabol, *Four Hundred Songs and Dances*, nos. 4, 6, 79, 105.

GB-Lbl, Harley MS 6395, she concluded that it was written early in his career, perhaps in the late 1620s when Le Strange was in London completing his studies at Lincoln's Inn; it was probably completed by 1629–30, when he succeeded his father as baronet, married, and settled down to the life of a country gentleman on the family estates at Hunstanton.[61]

The sequence of 'Masques' in Add. MS 10444 undoubtedly contains a major portion of the dances written for masques between 1603 and the early 1620s, and generations of scholars have tried to match their titles with the descriptions of dances in the masque texts.[62] But in most cases their arguments fail to convince, for many of the titles apply equally well to more than one surviving masque text, and we know that a number of Jacobean texts are lost. We may argue, for instance, that no. 58, 'The Pages Masque', was written for the antimasque of pages in *The Lords' Masque*, but we can never be sure that one or more of the lost Jacobean masques did not also feature groups of dancing pages.[63]

The two-part scoring of Add. MS 10444 has also baffled scholars and performers. Some have assumed that the gap between the treble and bass parts should be filled by a continuo instrument, as is the case with the two-part Locke suites 'For Several Friends' in the later section of Add. MS 10444.[64] One can easily imagine that Le Strange performed them in that way in private, with, say, treble viol, bass viol, and theorbo. But they would not have been played in two-part versions in the original masques, for the court violin band, the main vehicle for masque dances, would certainly have used settings in more than two parts, and over forty of the pieces do in fact exist in fuller versions in other sources (see Table 8.1 at the end of this chapter). Thus it is easy to see that the Add. MS 10444 pieces are somehow incomplete, but it is not so easy to work out what their original form was, or to explain how and why Le Strange obtained them in two-part versions.

Most of the concordances with the Add. MS 10444 masque dances— over 200 have been identified—are arrangements for solo instruments,

---

[61] P. Willetts, 'Sir Nicholas Le Strange's Collection of Masque Music', *British Museum Quarterly*, 29 (1964–5), 78–81; see also the introduction to H. F. Lippincott (ed.), *'Merry Passages and Jests': A Manuscript Jestbook* (Salzburg Studies in English Literature, Elizabethan and Renaissance Studies, 29; Salzburg, 1974).

[62] Sabol, *Four Hundred Songs and Dances* is the most systematic attempt to date; see also W. J. Lawrence, 'Notes on a Collection of Masque Music', *ML* 3 (1922), 49–58; J. P. Cutts, 'Jacobean Masque and Stage Music', *ML* 35 (1954), 100–25; J. E. Knowlton, 'Some Dances of the Stuart Masque Identified and Analyzed', Ph.D. diss. (Indiana University, 1966); D. Fuller, 'The Jonsonian Masque and its Music', *ML* 54 (1973), 440–52.

[63] Sabol, *Four Hundred Songs and Dances*, no. 109.

[64] P. Walls and B. Thomas (eds.), *Twenty-one Masque Dances of the Early Seventeenth Century* (English Instrumental Music of the Late Renaissance, 2; London, 1974) is a typical selection in two parts with continuo; for Locke's 'For Several Friends', see Matthew Locke, *Chamber Music: I*, ed. M. Tilmouth (MB 31; London, 1971).

and were probably made for domestic use long after the masques were given; they testify to the remarkable hold that masques had on the public mind at the time. Some of the consort settings also come into this category: examples are the delightful four-part arrangements (SSTB and continuo) in Thomas Simpson's *Taffel-Consort* (Hamburg, 1621), or the three dances from *Lord Hay's Masque* (including the two Lupo pieces mentioned above) set for mixed consort in Philip Rosseter's *Lessons for Consort* (London, 1609).[65] But the bulk of the consort concordances, a group of thirty-four pieces spread between a pair of printed sources, are more promising, for they have the uniform five-part layout with a single soprano part (SA for short) that was used by violin bands at the time (see Ch. 7).

Nineteen of them are found in William Brade's *Newe ausserlesene liebliche Branden* (Hamburg, 1617), a collection that is intended, according to the title-page, 'for all kinds of musical instruments, especially strings' ('auff allerley Musicalischen Instrumenten, insonderheit auff Fiolen zu gebrauchen').[66] Brade's remarkable career has been outlined in Ch. 7, but it is worth noticing here that there is no evidence that he returned to England after he emigrated to the Continent in the 1590s, so he probably acquired his Jacobean masque dances through an intermediary—perhaps another expatriate Englishman. This helps to explain an odd feature: that the titles in *Neue ausserlesene liebliche Branden* contradict the titles in Add. MS 10444 and other English sources in virtually every case. For example, 'The Maypole' in Add. MS 10444 (also known as 'The King's Morisco') appears as 'Der Satyrn Tantz' (The Satyr's Dance) in Brade's collection, while his 'Intrada der Jungen Princessinnen' (Intrada of the Young Princesses) is called 'The Baboons Dance' in Add. MS 10444.[67] Perhaps Brade used them in masque-like entertainments in Germany, or was working from an English manuscript that had no titles for the pieces, and devised fanciful ones of his own.

The other source is John Adson's *Courtly Masquing Ayres* (London, 1621).[68] Adson was a London wait from 1614, and would have been in a good position to acquire a set of masque dances from court sources, though he did not receive a court post himself until 1633; he dedicated it to the Duke of Buckingham, a frequent and enthusiastic masquer.[69] The

---

[65] Sabol, *Four Hundred Songs and Dances*, nos. 83, 91, 92, 107; Simpson, *Taffel Consort*, ed. Thomas, nos. 24, 32, 44, 50; Edwards (ed.), *Music for Mixed Consort*, nos. 32–4.

[66] Complete edition in *William Brade: Newe Auserlesene [liebliche] Branden, Intraden, Mascheraden, Baletten, Allmanden, Couranten, Volten, Auffzüge und Frembde Täntze*, ed. B. Thomas, i–iii (London, 1974).

[67] Sabol, *Four Hundred Songs and Dances*, nos. 78, 123, 263, 272.

[68] Complete edn. by P. Walls (English Instrumental Music of the Late Renaissance, 3–5; London, 1975–6); Walls points out that the reported edition of 1611 is a ghost.

[69] Lasocki, 'Professional Recorder Players', ii. 659–64 is the best biography of Adson.

collection consists entirely of lively masque-like dances, scored according to the title-page for 'violins, consorts [i.e. mixed ensembles] and cornets', though its organization is more complex than appears at first sight. It divides into twenty-one five-part pieces and ten six-part pieces; but there is also a distinction between nos. 1–18, which have no specific instrumentation, and nos. 19–21, which are prefaced by the rubric 'for cornets and sackbuts'; and things are further complicated by the fact that no. 21 and all the six-part pieces have two soprano parts (SS), while nos. 1–20 have the traditional SA layout.

The significance of this is not entirely clear, but the combination of six-part writing and the SS layout was certainly associated with wind instruments at the time, as a number of contemporary collections (including *GB-Cfm*, Mu. MS 734; see Ch. 7) show, so Adson probably intended the rubric 'for cornets and sackbuts' to apply to the whole of the second half of the book, including the six-part pieces. If this is so, then the five-part SA pieces nos. 1–19 may well be intended specifically for violins, a conclusion that is strengthened by the fact that fourteen of them have concordances with masque dances in Add. MS 10444, while there is only one piece, no. 19, with such a concordance in the 'cornets and sackbuts' section. By the same token, there is a distinction between the masque dances in Brade's 1617 collection, which have the SA layout and are probably intended for violins, and some of the others, which are SS pieces and may be intended more for wind instruments than strings. It is also significant that the first of the main dances for *The Masque of Queens*, printed in lute versions in Robert Dowland's *Varietie of Lute-Lessons* (London, 1610), has a six-part SS concordance in Mu. MS 734, while the second has a five-part SA concordance in Brade's 1617 collection, for Jonson wrote in the text that they were danced respectively 'to the Cornets' and 'to the Violins' (Ex. 8.1*a* and *b*).[70]

The most puzzling aspect of Add. MS 10444 is why it survives in two parts when most if not all its masque dances must have been originally performed in fuller versions. An obvious possibility is that it is the surviving fragment of a set of five or six part-books, or that Le Strange and his fellow-copyist worked from such a set, now lost. But there is no sign that this is so, and the problem with such a notion is that it is difficult to see how such a manuscript could have come into being, and what form it would have taken. The sequence of masque dances in Add. MS 10444 almost certainly includes material from dozens of ephemeral productions spread over several decades, composed by many individuals, and originally performed by a number of separate groups of court musicians, who would doubtless have created, used, and disposed of their

[70] Sabol, *Four Hundred Songs and Dances*, nos. 225, 226, 239, 315; *Ben Jonson*, vii. 315.

Ex. 8.1a. Anon., Dance from *The Masque of Queens* (1609), *GB-Cfm*, Mu. MS 734, sect. 1, no. 19

Ex. 8.1a. *Continued*

own performing material. The violin band may have been the main vehicle for masque dances, but it was not the only one: it was not uncommon for them to be scored for exotic combinations of instruments, particularly in antimasques, when some attempt would be made to match the timbre of the music to the character of the participants. In *Hymenai* the eight lady masquers danced to 'a rare and full musique of twelve Lutes'; in *Oberon* twenty lutes were paid for 'the Princes dance'— performed by Prince Henry and his fellow masquers; in Jonson's *Irish Masque* (29 December 1613 and 3 January 1613/14) footmen danced to 'the bag-pipe and other rude musique', while gentlemen in Irish cloaks danced to 'a solemn musique of harpes'; in Jonson's *The Golden Age Restored* (1 and 6 January 1615/16) Iron-age and the Evils executed a 'Phyrrick dance' to 'drummes, trumpets, and a confusion of martiall musique'.[71] The set of part-books that could have encompassed the music for even a few dances of this sort beggars the imagination.

A more likely explanation is that such a manuscript never existed, and that Add. MS 10444 was copied from a two-part collection. The dances are not incomplete in the sense that they lack something written by the composer, for that is how they were originally composed—in two parts, treble and bass. When Robert Johnson was paid for 'making the

Ex. 8.1*b*. William Brade, Dance from *The Masque of Queens*, bb. 1–8, *Neue ausserlesene liebliche Branden* (Hamburg, 1617), no. 1 (from Sabol (ed.), *Four Hundred Songs and Dances*, no. 315)

Daunces' in *Oberon* and *Love Freed from Ignorance and Folly* he was writing tunes that would have been needed weeks before the production— Ferrabosco, Hearne, and Confesse worked on the former, we have seen, for nearly six weeks before the performance. Rehearsals would have been conducted with the dancing-masters playing the tunes on their kits, or with just one or two instrumentalists helping them out: in the payment for *The Lords' Masque*, for instance, 'He that played to the boyes' was paid £6.

13*s.* 4*d.*, while '2 that paied to the Antick Maske' shared £11 between them—relatively large sums that only make sense if they are for rehearsals over an extended period.

In a Caroline masque, James Shirley's *The Triumph of Peace* (first performed on 3 February 1633/4), we have direct evidence that a single violinist was used in such a way: Davis Mell received £20 for 'service performed in attending the graund masquers practise playing to the[m] on the trible violi(n) & making some of the tunes in the antimasques'.[72] The full dance band would only have been needed near the time of the performances. Someone would then have been employed to make arrangements for the required ensemble; in the case of the violin band it was Thomas Lupo who 'set' the dances 'to the violins', which means that he added three viola parts to the existing tune and bass. We have no means of knowing whether the inner parts printed by Brade and Adson actually came from the original masque productions, or were their own work; and it matters little, for such inner parts, like the *parties de remplissage* of Lully's orchestral music, are dependent on the outer parts, serve only to fill up the harmony, and could easily have been written by any musician with a little knowledge of part-writing.

The parallel with late-seventeenth-century French orchestral music is exact and revealing. Lully left the composition of his *parties de remplissage* to assistants not because he was lazy or incompetent, as has been claimed, but because the two-stage method of composition and arrangement was a practical and efficient way of getting lengthy works into rehearsal and on to the stage. And there is plenty of evidence that the system existed long before Lully: *F-Pn*, MS Rés. F. 494, a collection of 'Vieux Aires' copied under the supervision of André Danican Philidor in the late seventeenth century, contains late-sixteenth- and early-seventeenth-century pieces in two parts side by side with others in five parts (for violins) and six parts (for various wind consorts). The two-part pieces were presumably copied in that form because Philidor and his colleagues happened across them in manuscripts like Add. MS 10444 that lacked the *parties de remplissage*. The practice of using *parties de remplissage* is, of course, related to, and was doubtless derived from, the sixteenth-century practice of composing dances successively, starting with the outer parts (see Ch. 4). It became necessary to devolve the composition of the inner parts of violin music to assistants when violin bands became involved in the production of stage works, such as French court ballets and English masques. It may be that the practice came to England from France at the beginning of James I's

---

[72] Library of Longleat House, Whitelocke Papers, Parcel II, item 9 (6); see M. Lefkowitz, 'The Longleat Papers of Bulstrode Whitelocke: New Light on Shirley's *Triumph of Peace*', *JAMS* 18 (1965), 59.

reign with Bochan and the other French dancing-masters, and its use can certainly be traced in England for much of the seventeenth century.

We can now understand what sort of source lies behind Add. MS 10444: it was probably copied from material that belonged to one of the court dancing-masters.[73] Only a dancing-master—to borrow the terminology of the detective novel—would have had the means and the motive to collect music from such diverse sources. Dancing-masters would have been supplied with dances in their two-part form to devise and teach their choreographies, and in many cases they would have composed the tunes themselves. The motive for putting together such a collection would have been partly to preserve the memory of great terpsichorean occasions, but it would also have been useful for teaching, particularly in the Inns of Court, where formal masque-like dancing flourished; Le Strange, it will be remembered, is thought to have copied the collection while he was studying at Lincoln's Inn. If his sources also contained the original choreographies of the dances, it is our loss that he did not copy them too, for our knowledge of that vital ingredient of the masque is slight. But we must be grateful for what we have, for without Nicholas Le Strange's little manuscript we would know little about Jacobean masque music, and even less about how it was composed, arranged and performed.

---

[73] Similar conclusions were reached independently by Ward in 'Newly Devis'd Measures'.

TABLE 8.1. *Consort concordances with masque dances in GB-Lbl, Add. MS 10444*

Add. MS 10444 no. and title (from soprano)	Sabol no.	concordance no. and title (from soprano)[a]	Sabol no.
4 Broxboorn berry Maske.	55	A12	241
5 Broxboorn berry Masque	56	A11	240
9 Adsonns Maske.	60	A1	279
22 The first of the Lords.	73	B19 [2nd section] Ein mal	257
23 The second of the Lordes.	74	B7 Der königinnen Intrada	258
24 The third of the Lords.	75	B8 Der jungen Prinzen Intrada	260
25 The first witches dance.	76	B49 Der Hexsen Tanz	
		W6 The wyche	247
27 The Babboons Dance.	78	B9 Intrada der Jungen Princessinnen	263
28 A Masque.	79	R22 Thomas Lupo	
32 The Cadua.	83	S50 Aria / R[obert] B[ateman]	284
36 A Masque in Flowers.	87	B3 Brand	317
39 The first of the Temple.	90	B21 Auffzug der Kauffleute	264
40 The second of the Temple.	91	B26 Der Irlender Tanz	265
		S32 Mascarada / Incert. Aut.	266
41 The third of the Temple	92	B22 Auffzug vor Grienwitsch	267
		S44 Ballet / Incert: Aut.	268
50 Cuperaree or Graysin.	101	B28 Des Rothschencken Tanz	273
		F20 Almande	274
51 The second.	102	B37 Comoedianten Tanz	275
53 The Nymphes dance.	104	B10 Mascharad der Edel Frawen	269
54 The Lord Hays his Masque.	105	R8 Thomas Lupo	412
56 The Satyres Masque.	107	S24 Robert Johnson	249
64 van=weely.	116	A15	294
70 The May=pole.	123	B18 3 mal Der Satyrn Tanz	272
73 The Cuckolds Masque.	126	B45 Rosen im Frühlinge oder Prim Rosen	282
		S31 Mascarada / Incert. Aut.	
81 The Bull Masque.	134	A19	302
83 Mr Adsons Masque.	136	A2	280
84 Adsons Masque	137	A3	281
85 The Divells dance.	138	A10	277
92 Essex Anticke Masque.	145	A4	242

TABLE 8.1. *Continued*

Add. MS 10444 no. and title (from soprano)	Sabol no.	concordance no. and title (from soprano)[a]		Sabol no.
93 The first of my Lord of Essex.	146	A5		243
94 The second.	147	A6		244
95 The Third.	148	A7		245
110 Williams his Love.	163	A13		292
122 The first of the Temple Anticke.	175	A7		300
123 The second	176	A8		301
133 Grayes Inne Masque.	186	B38	Heynen sein Tanz	276
135 The first of the Prince his.	188	F5	Almande / R[obert] J[ohnson]	
		B31	Der erste Mascharada des Pfaltzgraffen	252
136 The second.	189	F6	Almande / R[obert] J[ohnson]	
		B32	Der ander Mascharada	253
137	190	B33	Der dritte Mascharada	254
138 [in bass part only]	191	B19	Ballet	257

[a] Abbreviations:
A John Adson, *Courtly Masquing Ayres* (London, 1621)
B William Brade, *Newe ausserlesene liebliche Branden* (Hamburg, 1617)
F *GB-Cfm*, Mu. MS 734
R Philip Rosseter, *Lessons for Consort* (London, 1609)
S Thomas Simpson, *Taffel-Consort* (Hamburg, 1621)
W *GB-Lbl*, Add. MSS 17786–91; see Monson, *Voices and Viols in England*, 159–79

9

'*Coperarios Musique*'

The Households of Prince Henry and Prince Charles

IN the winter of 1609–10 the 15-year-old Prince Henry Frederick, eldest son of James I, formed his own household.[1] It was an important constitutional and social event, for there had been no adult male heir to the throne in residence at the English court for almost exactly a hundred years—since the prince's namesake became Henry VIII in 1509. In three years, from 1609 until his untimely death in the autumn of 1612, Henry became the focus of a second English renaissance. He established important collections of books, paintings, bronzes, antique gems, and medals. He patronized new developments in many of the arts and sciences, including navigation, military fortification, architecture, engraving, stage design, and gardening. His role as a patron of music has left less of a mark on history, though his household musicians formed the first new group added to the royal music since Henry VIII's reign (see Table 9.1). And they were also among the first English musicians to adopt the Italian Baroque style.

Prince Henry's first musician was Alfonso Ferrabosco II. He had been brought up at royal expense by the court flute-player Gommar van Oostrewick after his father, the composer Alfonso Ferrabosco I, returned to Italy in 1578.[2] Alfonso II continued to enjoy unusual royal favour in later life. In October 1592, shortly after van Oostrewick's death, when he was about 17, he received a salary of 40 marks (£26. 13s. 4d.) as 'musitian for the violles'.[3] In a petition to Robert Cecil, written around 1600 in 'extremity of sicknes', he requests a 'reasonable stipend by the yeare, & something to pay my debts', having only 40 marks a year: 'I was constrained to followe such as woulde helpe me (having noe freinds in the

---

[1] For a recent study, see R. Strong, *Henry Prince of Wales and England's Lost Renaissance* (London, 1986); see also T. Birch, *The Life of Henry Prince of Wales, Eldest Son of King James I* (London, 1760).

[2] HMC 9, *Calendar of the Manuscripts of the Most Hon. the Marquis of Salisbury*, iii. 362, 411; iv. 76; R. Vaught, 'The Fancies of Alfonso Ferrabosco II', Ph.D. diss. (Stanford University, 1959), i. 86–96; J. Duffy, *The Songs and Motets of Alfonso Ferrabosco the Younger (1575–1628)* (Ann Arbor, Mich., 1979–80), 17–31; R. Charteris, 'New Information about the Life of Alfonso Ferrabosco the Elder (1543–88)', *RMARC* 17 (1981), 97–114; id., *Alfonso Ferrabosco the Elder (1543–1588): A Thematic Catalogue of his Music with a Biographical Calendar* (New York, 1984).

[3] *GB-Lpro*, SO3/1, see Ashbee, *RECM*, vi. 57.

TABLE 9.1. *Musicians in the households of Prince Henry and Prince Charles (fifers, trumpeters, and drummers excluded)*

Name	Henry	Charles	probable function
Alfonso Ferrabosco II	1605–12	1617–25	viol
Thomas Giles	1605–12	died 1617	violin?/dance
Norman Lesley/Lisle		1606–25	violin/dance
Jacques Bochan	1608–12	(left England 1614)	violin/dance
John Bull	1610–12	(left England 1613)	keyboard
Thomas Lupo I	1610–12	1617–25	violin
Robert Johnson	1610–12	1617–25	lute/voice
John Myners	1610–12	(d. 1615)	lute/voice
Jonas Wrench	1610–12	1617–25	lute/voice
Thomas Day	1610–12	1617–25	lute/voice
Thomas Cutting	1610–12	(d. 1614)	lute/voice
John Sturt	1610–12	1617–25	lute/voice
Thomas Ford	1610–12	1617–25	lute/voice
Edward Wormall	1610–12	1623–5	lute/viol
Mathias Johnson	1610–12	(in Cecil's household?)	lute/voice
Valentine Sawyer	1610–12	(in Cecil's household?)	viol
John Ashby	1610–12	1617–20	unknown
Walter Quin	1610?–12		unknown
Angelo Notari	1611?–12	1617–25	lute/voice
Sebastian La/Le Pierre	1611–12?	1611–25	violin/dance
Jeremy Herne/Heron	1612	(in James I's household)	violin/dance
Orlando Gibbons		1617–25	keyboard
Richard Ball/Balls/Bales		1617–23	lute/voice
Alfonso Ball/Balls/ Bales		1617–25	lute/voice
John Coggeshall		1617–25	lute/voice
John Drew		1617–25	lute/voice
John Daniel		1617–25	lute/voice
Robert Marsh		1617–25	lute/voice
Robert Taylor		1617–25	viol
John Ballard		1622–5	lute/voice
John Coprario		1622–5	viol
John Woodington		1622–5	violin
Adam Vallet		1622?–5	violin/dance
Jacques Gaultier		1624–5	lute/voice
Nicholas Lanier		1625	lute/voice
Timothy Collins		1625?	lute/voice
John Lanier		1625?	lute/voice
Innocent Lanier		1625?	wind
Robert Bourman		1625?	unknown
Abraham Coates		1625?	unknown
James Graye		1625?	unknown
Gilbert Johnson		1625?	unknown

Court), and was rather kept hidd from her Ma(jes)t(i)es knowledge, by some whome I could never learn to knowe'.[4] The result was the second of his court appointments: a £50-a-year salary in the violin consort by a warrant dated 30 April 1602, backdated to 29 August 1601.[5]

Ferrabosco's appointment as a member of the violin consort seems to have been a sinecure. In the list of court musicians at Elizabeth's funeral he appears among the 'Lutes & others', not the violins, and in subsidy rolls for 1607–8 and 1608–9 he is listed separately from the group as 'The Viole'.[6] On 27 November 1604 he was given £20 to be 'by him bestowed and laide out in buyinge two violles w(i)th Cases and one boxe of stringes for the use and service of the Prince'; Henry was still playing the viol in August 1611, when the librarian at Richmond was paid £40 for buying him a viol and for taking it to Woodstock.[7] In 1605 Ferrabosco received a third salary, of £50 a year, 'in regard of his attendance upon the Prince, & instructing him [in] the art of musick'; the patent, dated 22 March 1604/5, also styles him an 'extraordinary groom' of the prince's Privy Chamber, a post that gave him access to the private royal apartments.[8]

A volume of Prince Henry's privy purse expenses for 1608–9 does not mention a regular group of musicians, though a fair amount was spent on music.[9] Payments include, perhaps with his future role as Prince of Wales in mind, £1. 10s. on three occasions to 'Welshe Musitians' (6 August 1608, 1 January 1608/9, and 15 August 1609), £2 to 'the player upon the harpe' (22 August 1608), and £1. 10s. to a 'blynd harper' (27 February 1608/9), as well as £1 to 'musitians at Wanstead' (20 June 1609), £1 to 'my lord hadingtons Musitians' (31 August 1609), and £1 to 'Musitians at Bagshott' (4 September 1609). Gifts were given on 1 January 1608/9 to several groups, including 'Mr Lesly and thre more with him'; at the time Norman Lesley (Lisle) was a servant of Prince Charles, Henry's younger brother, and he later joined the violin band as well (see Ch. 8). Undated bills for expenses include £176 for 'One greate Organ bought of mr Hamlett placed at St. James', £14. 5s. 'for mending the same Organ', £40 for 'Voyalls, twoe greate ons', £33. 6s. 8d. for 'twoe lutes', £5. 18s. 4d. for 'Lute and viall with other necc(essar)ies for a singinge Boy', £47. 18s. for 'Lutestringes and such like necc(essar)ies', £31 for 'songe Bookes and prickinge of songs with a guilded Coffer to keep them in', £30 to 'French Musicons', and £5. 10s. for 'Carrying the Instruments of Musicke from

[4] Library of Hatfield House, Cecil Papers 98/94, summarized in *Calendar of the Manuscripts of . . . the Marquis of Salisbury*, xiv. 242.

[5] *GB-Lpro*, E351/543, fo. 73^r, see Ashbee, *RECM*, vi. 164.

[6] Ashbee, *RECM*, iv. 2, 18, 21.

[7] *GB-Lpro*, E351/543, fo. 136^r; see Ashbee, *RECM*, iv. 76; *GB-Lpro*, E351/2793.

[8] Ashbee, *RECM*, iv. 11; *GB-Lpro*, E403/2454, fo. 123^r

[9] *GB-Lpro*, E101/433/8; see Ashbee, *RECM*, iv. 213–15.

London to woodstocke by water and back againe'.[10] By a warrant dated 5 May 1612 John Bull was paid £35 for 'sondry sortes of musick bookes provided for the Prince's use and delivered to the custody of Thomas Meller his highenes servannte'.[11]

A regular group of musicians joined Prince Henry's household in June 1610, when he was created Prince of Wales; thirteen names appear in a list of 'His Highnes Musitians' who were paid 'from the time of his creation untill the first daie of Nove(m)ber 1612'.[12] John Bull, Robert Johnson, Thomas Lupo I, John Myners (not the composer John Maynard), Jonas Wrench, Thomas Day, Valentine Sawyer, Thomas Cutting, and John Sturt received £40 a year each. Thomas Ford initially received £30 a year but was given the extra £10 in March 1611/12. John Ashby received £30 a year, and Edward Wormall and Mathias (Matthew) Johnson got £20 a year each. A later, undated list of the household adds the names of two drummers, a fifer, six trumpeters, Walter Quin, the prince's 'Techer of Musick', Jeremy Hearne, a violinist and one of the court dancing-masters (see Ch. 8), and, at the end, 'Sig(no)r° Angelo'— the Italian composer Angelo Notari.[13]

Prince Henry's group was something new in England, for it consisted mainly of those who are best described as singer-lutenists; singers at the time were expected to accompany themselves on the lute, and most lutenists were also singers. Robert Johnson, Myners, Wrench, Day, Cutting, Sturt, Ford, and Notari certainly came into that category, and Wormall and Mathias Johnson are described as 'singing boyes' who lodged with the court wind-player Peter Edney; Mathias Johnson received 6s. from the Cecil household on 13 June 1613 for lute strings.[14] John Bull and Thomas Lupo were presumably employed respectively as a keyboard-player and as a violinist, and Valentine Sawyer may also have been a string-player if he was the 'Vallentyne' who received £3 from the Cecil household to buy a viol in January 1613/14.[15] John Ashby's role is unknown.

We must be cautious about assuming that Henry's group formed a single large mixed ensemble, for we know next to nothing about how it was deployed in his household. But even if the intention was only to

[10] GB-Lpro, E351/2794; see Ashbee, RECM, iv. 215.
[11] Ashbee, RECM, iv. 212–13.
[12] Ibid. 211–12.
[13] Ibid. 211.
[14] Ibid. 212, 215; Library of Hatfield House, Cecil Papers, Acc. 13/24; for Edney, see P. Holman, '"An Addicion of Wyer Stringes beside the Ordenary Stringes": The Origin of the Baryton', in J. Paynter, R. Orton, P. Seymour, and T. Howell (eds.), Companion to Contemporary Musical Thought (London and New York, 1992), 1103–8.
[15] Library of Hatfield House, Cecil Papers, Acc. 128/1.

assemble a pool of musicians for a number of small combinations, the preponderance of lutenists suggests that they would mostly have been mixed ensembles. Mixed ensembles with a large group of plucked instruments had been a feature of progressive Italian musical circles for thirty or forty years, but English institutions mostly continued to employ 'whole' consorts of one or two instrumental families, despite the existence of the English 'broken' or mixed consort. At court the main ensembles were still the shawm and sackbut consort, the flute consort, the recorder consort, and the violin consort. So the decision to establish a mixed ensemble in Prince Henry's household should be seen in the wider context of the prince's Italianate cultural programme, and may have had its origin in his own musical taste, for 'W.H.', an early biographer and a member of his household, wrote that he 'loved Musicke, and namely good consorts of Instruments and voices joyned together'.[16]

Angelo Notari's presence in Henry's household is tangible evidence of the prince's Italianate musical interests. It is usually said, following a manuscript horoscope, that Notari was born in Padua on 14 January 1566.[17] But the portrait of him in his *Prime musiche nuove*, published with a dedication to the king's favourite Robert Carr dated 24 November 1613, gives his age as 'Di Anni 40', which gives an alternative birth-date of *c*.1573, unless, of course, the engraving was taken from a dated painting of *c*.1606. Whatever the case, Notari was certainly a Venetian citizen and a member of its Accademia degli Sprovisti, in which, for some reason, he was called 'il negligente'. We do not know how or why he came to England, but he may have arrived in the company of the prince's Florentine architect, Constantino de' Servi, who came from Paris to London in June 1611.[18] In Roy Strong's opinion Notari's portrait and the title-page of *Prime musiche nuove*, engraved by William Hole, had their origin in designs by de' Servi (Fig. 9.1).[19]

Prime musiche nuove is a typical Italian song-book of the period: it contains monodies and canzonettas for one to three voices accompanied by an unfigured *basso continuo* for 'la Tiorba, et altri Strumenti'. Notari may well have compiled it before he left Italy, but an unusual piece of evidence suggests that its contents, or at least some songs by Notari, were performed by Prince Henry's musicians. A printed pamphlet, preserved among a batch of Prince Henry's correspondence, advertises a strange musical raffle to be held a number of times during June and July 1612 at

[16] Strong, *Henry Prince of Wales*, 173.
[17] I. Spink, 'Angelo Notari and his "Prime Musiche Nuove"', *MMR* 87 (1957), 168–77; C. Egerton, 'The Horoscope of Signor Angelo Notari (1566–1663)', *The Lute*, 28 (1988), 13–18, who does not discuss the portrait.
[18] Strong, *Henry Prince of Wales*, 88–106.
[19] Ibid. 173, illus. 84, 85.

9.1. Title-page of Angelo Notari, *Prime musiche nuove* (London, 1613). British Library, Courtesy of the Trustees

'Maister Taylors house, one of the Kings Majesties servants' in Lincoln's Inn:

An Entertainment for Noblemen, Knights, and Gentlemen of worth.

PRepared of an Italian Consort of strange Musique, consisting of nine Instruments iwth [*sic*] other severall Instruments, Musically concorded with Italian voyces, very delectable for all such persons of honor, worship, and worth, as will vouchsafe their persons to hear the same. Where is also provided costly furniture, and diverse things for necessary use, and ornaments of houshould, fit for a Prince, Nobleman of any other of dignity, which are to bee Rifled [raffled], giving forty shillings a peece for three throwes with three Dice, those that throw most to gain all . . .[20]

Notari is the only Italian composer—as opposed to the descendants of Italians born in England—who is known to have been active in London at the time. And 'nine Instruments with other severall Instruments' sounds like an unusual mixed ensemble made up mainly of a single instrumental family; there were at least eight singer-lutenists in the prince's household, as well as Edward Wormall and Mathias Johnson, the two singing boys. Violins may have been among the 'other severall Instruments' in the 'Consort of strange Musique'. There were at least two violinists, Lupo and Hearne, in Prince Henry's group, and no. 17 of *Prime musiche nuove*, the duet 'Cosi di ben amar' for soprano, tenor, and continuo with a chorus of two sopranos, has a three-part 'Sinfonia Violino' laid out for two violins and continuo (Ex. 9.1). The piece is a landmark in the history of the violin in England. There are a few arrangements of vocal music and contrapuntal pieces in the mixed-consort repertoire, but Notari's duet is the earliest datable piece in an English source that uses the violin outside those repertoires that were principally associated with dance music.

There are also five solo pieces in Notari's autograph score-book, *GB-Lbl*, Add. MS 31440, scored specifically for 'Violino' and bass.[21] The volume contains vocal music from Italian prints of 1620, 1622, 1623, 1624, 1628, and 1630, and 1633, and was therefore copied much later, but at least one of the violin pieces, a set of divisions on Rore's madrigal 'Anchor che co'l partire', fos. 140^v–142^r, may be contemporary with *Prime musiche nuove*, for there is a similar piece, based on Rore's madrigal 'Ben qui si mostra', at the end of the 1613 collection, and the

[20] Library of Longleat House, Portland Papers, vol. 1, fo. 220^r; I am grateful to Kate Harris, Librarian and Archivist to the Marquess of Bath, for identifying the document from the reference in HMC 58, *Calendar of the Manuscripts of the Marquis of Bath*, ii. 61–2, and for providing me with a transcription.
[21] P. Willetts, 'A Neglected Source of Monody and Madrigal', *ML* 43 (1962), 329–39; ead., 'Autographs of Angelo Notari', *ML* 50 (1969), 124–6; I am grateful to Jonathan Wainwright for allowing me access to his unpublished research into Add. MS 31440.

Ex. 9.1. Angelo Notari, 'Sinfonia Violino' from 'Cosi di ben amar', *Prime musiche nuove* (London, 1613), no. 17

Ex. 9.1. *Continued*

vogue for divisions or *passaggi* based on vocal music had more or less
ended by 1620 (Ex. 9.2). The two pieces are laid out in the same way,
with the *passaggi* supported by a bass part derived from the lowest
sounding part of the madrigal. But the violin part of 'Anchor che co'l
partire' is based only on the soprano voice of the madrigal, while the 'Ben
qui si mostra' piece is an example of the *bastarda* idiom in that it is a
digest or 'bastard' of all the parts from soprano to bass. *Bastarda* pieces
were sometimes written for voices as well as instruments, and Notari
added the text of the madrigal to the *passaggi* with the note that it may 'as
well be sung . . . as played upon the Violl'.

The other violin pieces in Add. MS 31440, a canzona in two versions,
fos. 34ᵛ–36ʳ (the second an ornamented version of the violin part entitled
'La medesima canzone passaggiata'),[22] and three sets of variations on the
Italian ground basses *Ruggiero*, *Romanesca*, and *Monica*, fos. 21ᵛ–28ʳ, are
difficult to date. But the simple form of the canzona is similar to the
earliest Italian solo sonatas and canzonas, such as those published by
G. P. Cima in 1610, Giulio Belli in 1613, and G. B. Riccio in 1620.[23]
We cannot be sure that Notari composed them, since they are not
ascribed to him, and the manuscript contains much unattributed music
by other composers. But no concordances have come to light among the
contemporary prints of Italian instrumental music—which have mostly
appeared in recent years in facsimile reprints and editions. Even if they
are eventually shown to be by other composers, they still suggest that
Notari was an important ambassador for Italian violin music in England;
not for nothing does a *putto* with a violin adorn the title-page of *Prime
musiche nuove*.

Another manuscript collection, *GB-Ob*, MSS Mus. Sch. D. 245–7,

---

[22] Ed. P. Holman (London, 1981).
[23] See, for instance, *Cima, Drei Sonaten*, ed. K. Grebe (Hamburg, 1957); R. P. Block (ed.), *G. B.
Riccio and G. Belli: Two Canzonas, 'La Rubina' 1620 and Canzon à3 1613* (London, 1982); id., *G. B.
Riccio and G. Belli: Two Canzonas, 'La Finetta' 1620 and Canzona à2 1613* (London, 1982).

Ex. 9.2. Angelo Notari, Divisions on 'Ancor che col partire', bb. 1–19, *GB-Lbl*, Add. MS 31440, fo. 140ᵛ

contains pieces that seem to demonstrate Notari's influence on his court colleagues. It was written by the Gloucester musician John Merro (Merroe), who was a lay-clerk at the cathedral from 1609 until his death on 23 March 1635/6.[24] He was also a prolific music copyist, to judge from three large sets of part-books in his hand. D. 245–7 is probably the

---

[24] S. Eward, *No Fine but a Glass of Wine: Cathedral Life at Gloucester in Stuart Times* (Wilton, 1985), esp. 16, 336; see also P. Willetts, 'Music from the Circle of Anthony Wood at Oxford', *British Museum Quarterly*, 24 (1961), 71–5; A. Ashbee, 'Lowe, Jenkins, and Merro', *ML* 48 (1967), 310–11; J. E. Sawyer, 'An Anthology of Lyra Viol Music in Oxford, Bodleian Library, Manuscripts Music School D. 245–7', Ph.D. diss. (University of Toronto, 1972); Monson, *Voices and Viols in England*, 133–58.

latest of the three (there is a reference to a book printed in 1633 at the end of D. 245), and is mainly a source of three-part consort music and lyra viol music in tablature. But there are also solo pieces in staff-notation, including three sequences that parallel Notari's violin pieces in Add. MS 31440.

The one most easily associated with Prince Henry's musical circle is a set of seven bass viol divisions in *bastarda* style. Four of them, at least, are by an English composer, for they are based on pieces in the English vocal repertoire: Tallis's motet-fantasy 'O sacrum convivium' (D. 246, pp. 253–6; also in tablature in D. 247, fos. 69ᵛ–71ʳ), 'Sound out my voice', the English version of Palestrina's 'Vestiva i colli' in *Musica transalpina* of 1588 (two settings, D. 246, pp. 135–7, 256–9; the latter also in tablature in D. 247, fos. 67ᵛ–69ʳ), and Alfonso Ferrabosco I's 'Vidi pianger madonna', a madrigal that appears in *Musica transalpina* as 'I saw my lady weep' (D. 246, pp. 247–9).[25] The divisions on 'Sound out my voice' are both attributed to 'Alfonso', which seems to refer to the younger Ferrabosco rather than his father, for the latter left England for good before the first sizeable source of viola bastarda music, Girolamo Dalla Casa's *Il vero modo di diminuir* (Venice, 1584), had appeared in Italy. Alfonso II may well be the author of all of them, and Notari is the obvious person to have introduced him to the *bastarda* style.

Another reason for thinking that Ferrabosco's *bastarda* music dates from his time in Prince Henry's household is that it is found next to three of the earliest examples of the main English division-viol repertoire: 'Cormacks Almane by Daniell Nercum' or Norcombe (pp. 251–2) and 'S(i)r Thomas Brooks Pavin' (pp. 252–3), based on pieces by the court harper Cormack McDermott (d. 1618), and 'Cuttings Galliard' (pp. 259–62), based on a lute galliard by Francis Cutting (d. 1596).[26] The *bastarda* idiom evidently did not take hold in England, for the Merro pieces are the only English examples of the genre, though Christopher Simpson wrote that 'A Continued Ground used for Playing or Making Division upon, is (commonly) the Through-Bass of some Motet or Madrigal, proposed or selected for that purpose.'[27] But it seems to have contributed to the development of English division-viol music, via pieces

---

[25] The first of the 'Sound out my voice' pieces appears as no. 128 of the Supplementary Publications of the Viola da Gamba Society (London, 1978), ed. G. Dodd; on 'O sacrum convivium', see J. Milsom, 'A Tallis Fantasia', *MT* 126 (1985), 658–62, and the letter by M. A. O. Ham, *MT* 127 (1986), 74; see also J. Milsom, 'Tallis's First and Second Thoughts', *JRMA* 113 (1988), 209–12.

[26] Holman, 'The Harp in Stuart England', 190–1; F. Cutting, *Selected Works*, ed. M. Long (London, 1968), no. 10; L. Hulse, 'Francis and Thomas Cutting: Father and Son?', *The Lute*, 26 (1986), 73–4.

[27] C. Simpson, *The Division-Violist* (London, 1659, rev. 2/1665, repr. 1965) as *Chelys minuritionum artificio exornata/The Division-Viol; or, the Art of Playing Extempore upon a Ground*, 57.

Ex. 9.3. Anon., Divisions on an unidentified vocal piece?, bb. 1–23, VdGS
Anon. no. 361, *GB-Ob*, MS Mus. Sch. D. 246, p. 107

like the ones just mentioned that are based on complete dances. It is odd
that such sophisticated court music survives only in the manuscript of
a provincial choir-man, though the connection between Merro and
Ferrabosco is perhaps provided by the Wrench family of Gloucester,
many of whom served the cathedral as choir-men or in other capacities.[28]
Wrench is not a common name, so the Jonas Wrench in Prince Henry's
household may have been related to them, though he does not appear in
Gloucester documents.

   There are also parallels between Notari's violin *passaggi* on 'Anchor che
co'l partire' and a group of five florid single-line pieces in MS Mus. Sch.
D. 246, pp. 107–16. They have attracted little attention because they are
all anonymous and untitled, and are wrongly described in the Viola da
Gamba Society's *Thematic Index of Music for Viols* as pieces for viola
bastarda: they are soprano-range pieces with the overall range *g–a″* (Ex.
9.3). They are evidently for a stringed instrument, for they have a number
of two-note chords in sixths and thirds, though the chords are not much
help in deciding whether the composer had the violin or the treble viol in
mind, for they are equally playable on both instruments. On the violin

---

[28] Eward, *No Fine*, esp. 22, 24, 36–7; Suzanne Eward has pointed out to me that many of the
Gloucester Wrenches had Old Testament first names, and has suggested that the court musician
might have been a brother of the older Elias Wrench.

sixths and thirds often require what we think of as second or third position; we do not know whether Jacobean violinists had developed position changes, for there is nothing else like the D. 246 pieces in the English repertoire, but similar writing is certainly found in German and Italian violin music of the 1620s and 1630s.[29]

We also cannot be sure that they are divisions on vocal pieces, for no models have been found for them, and they do not have any rests: in the Notari 'Anchor che co'l partire' and other similar pieces the *passaggi* cease whenever the parent voice is silent. But the divisions do give way on occasion to long notes, as sets of *passaggi* on vocal music tend to do when they reach a new set of contrapuntal entries in the parent work. One possibility is that they are free preludes written by someone who was familiar with Italian *passaggi*; another is that they are based on vocal pieces that, for one reason or another, did not have rests in the top part. Either way, they must be among the earliest solo pieces for a treble stringed instrument in the English repertoire, and their position in D. 246 may mean that they were also written by a servant of Prince Henry. An obvious possibility is Thomas Lupo, who was a violinist of Italian descent, as well as a composer with Italianate leanings.

A third set of pieces in D. 246, pp. 140–61, parallels to some extent the variations on Italian ground basses in Add. MS 31440. There are ten in all: four pavan and galliard pairs and two single pavans. They all have a florid soprano part, and the first seven have a corresponding bass part in D. 245, pp. 92–3. Merro evidently thought of them as divisions on ground basses because he headed the first 'The first pavin to a ground', and, indeed, six are based on (or refer to) Italian chord-sequences: one pavan and galliard pair uses the Passamezzo antico, and two use the Passamezzo moderno. There can be little doubt that they were written for violin and continuo. There are one or two notes below d', the bottom note of most soprano wind instruments, and a passage like the one given in Ex. 9.4 seems to have been written with the open strings of the violin in mind. Professional string-players, who would have played both violin and viol, would doubtless have preferred the violin for such vigorous dance music. Their author, if he was a court musician, was probably an instrumentalist first and foremost, for his passage-work lacks the sophistication and variety of Notari's variations, and some of the writing is crude in places.

Prince Henry died suddenly and unexpectedly on 6 November 1612. And with his death his household was dispersed, and his musicians become difficult to trace. Eight of the singer-lutenists, Robert Johnson,

---

[29] For a discussion of the technique and some examples, see Boyden, *History of Violin Playing*, 166–70.

Ex. 9.4. Anon., 'The first pavin to a ground', bb. 72–85, VdGS Anon. no. 71, *GB-Ob*, MSS Mus. Sch. D. 245, p. 92; D. 246, pp. 140–4

Thomas Cutting, Thomas Ford, Mathias Johnson, John Sturt, 'Mr. Jonas' (Jonas Wrench), John Myners, and Thomas Day, were still performing together the following February: they formed the core of the group that was paid for Chapman's *Middle Temple and Lincoln's Inn Masque*, given as part of the celebrations for the wedding of Henry's

Ex. 9.4. *Continued*

sister, Princess Elizabeth, to Prince Frederick, the Elector Palatine.[30] After that Henry's musicians dispersed, and nothing much is heard of them until a new group was formed for Prince Charles. He was created Prince of Wales on 3 November 1616, and seventeen unnamed musicians were appointed to his household on 25 November 1617; the first surviving document with their names is dated 6 March 1617/18.[31] The new group was formed initially from the rump of the old: nine servants of Prince Henry, Ferrabosco, Lupo, Notari, Day, Wrench, Robert Johnson, Sturt, Ford, and Ashby, were still available, and were given posts. Of the rest, Cutting and Myners died in 1614 and 1615; Giles, La Pierre, and Hearne joined the main royal household in 1614, 1615, and 1616 respectively (see Ch. 8); Mathias Johnson and Sawyer had connections with Cecil's household in 1613 and 1614 (see above), and may have been employed there; Bull fled to the Continent in 1613; and Bochan apparently left England in 1614 (see Ch. 8).[32] Nothing is known of Edward Wormall's activities until he became one of Prince Charles's musicians at Christmas 1622, by a warrant dated 11 January 1622/3; La Pierre received a post at the same time, by a warrant dated 23 December 1622.[33]

Prince Charles employed even more singer-lutenists than Prince Henry. To the six he inherited from his brother (Notari, Day, Wrench, Robert Johnson, Sturt, and Ford) were added six more: Richard Ball (Balls, Bales), his nephew Alfonso, John Coggeshall (Coxall), John Drew,

---

[30] Ashbee, *RECM*, iv. 38–9; see J. Stainer, 'The Middle Temple Masque', *MT* 47 (1906), 21–4.

[31] *GB-Lpro*, E101/434/15; Ashbee, *RECM*, iii. 4–5.

[32] For Cutting, see L. Hulse, 'Hardwick MS 29: A New Source for Jacobean Lutenists', *The Lute*, 26 (1986), 63–4; Myners made his will on 12 June 1615; *GB-Lpro*, 11/125, q. 53.

[33] Ashbee, *RECM*, iv. 227.

John Daniel, and Robert Marsh. Richard Ball was paid an annual allowance of £48 by a warrant dated 26 March 1618 'for teaching and instructing in musick two of his Highnes singing boyes', a service he also performed for the London waits, while Alfonso was a singer and song composer; he received a place as one of the 'lutes and voices' after Charles I became king, as did Drew, Coggeshall, and Marsh (see Ch. 10); Daniel, of course, was a prominent composer of lute songs and lute music.[34] Only two of the new musicians played other instruments: Orlando Gibbons, who presumably inherited John Bull's place at the keyboard, and the composer and viol-player Robert Taylor. Other singer-lutenists appointed subsequently included John Ballard (by warrant dated 30 January 1621/2), and the French lutenist and composer Jacques Gaultier (by warrant dated 29 June 1624).[35] The singer and composer Nicholas Lanier is often said to have been appointed Charles's Master of the Music in 1618, but there is no record of him in the Prince's accounts until the spring of 1625 (£200 a year by two warrants dated 16 March 1624/5), and the first mention of the title 'Master of the Music' is a patent dated 11 July 1626.[36] However, it seems that Lanier was already Charles's trusted servant, for the new king sent him to Italy to buy pictures only weeks after his accession.[37] As we might expect, there are recurrent payments in the prince's accounts to Thomas Meller, keeper of the 'Lutes, Viols and musicall Bookes' (and another former servant of Prince Henry), and to Robert Johnson 'for German Strings, Roman Strings and Bases of all sortes'.[38] Johnson's partly autograph bill dated 11 February 1618/19 shows that he bought extra items in the second half of 1617, when the group was coming into being: £13. 6s. 8d. for a lute, 18s for 'three bookes', 10s. for 'mending the base lute', and 43s. (a deleted entry) 'for Carriage of the lutes to and fro'.[39]

Yet by the end of Charles's term as Prince of Wales his household had also become particularly renowned for its string-consort music. This is not too surprising, since by then he employed the four most eminent composers of consort music, Alfonso Ferrabosco, Thomas Lupo, Orlando Gibbons, and John Coprario. Some of their music for conven-

---

[34] For Richard and Alfonso Ball, see Woodfill, *Musicians in English Society*, 36, 248–9; J. P. Cutts (ed.), *La Musique de scène de la troupe de Shakespeare* (Paris, 1959), pp. xlii, 197–8.

[35] Ashbee, *RECM*, iv. 225, 228; Ballard is mentioned as a lutenist in a letter from Gaultier to Constantijn Huygens; see W. J. A. Jonckbloet and J. P. N. Land (eds.), *Musique et musiciens au XVIIᵉ siècle: correspondance et œuvres musicales de Constantin Huygens* (Leiden, 1882), pp. ccix–ccxx; for Gaultier, see M. Spring, 'The Lute in England and Scotland after the Golden Age, 1620–1750', D.Phil. thesis (Oxford, 1987), 93–112.

[36] Ashbee, *RECM*, iv. 230; iii. 19.

[37] I. Spink, 'Lanier in Italy', *ML* 40 (1959), 243.

[38] Ashbee, *RECM*, iv. 220, 222, 223, 224, 225, 227, 228, 230.

[39] In the possession of Robert Spencer; see Ashbee, *RECM*, iv. 219.

tional viol consorts was doubtless written for and played by Charles's musicians; by a warrant dated 4 June 1621 Robert Taylor was paid £23 for 'five Instrumentes'—probably viols—'boughte and delivered' for the prince's household.[40] But between them the four were also responsible for extending the English fantasia idiom to a range of new scorings, such as mixed groups of violins, viols, and organ, or consorts of lyra viols. And there are good reasons for thinking that fantasias with violins, at least, were first heard in Prince Charles's household; that they were developed there by a specially formed ensemble under Coprario's direction; and that the process was aided by the prince's personal interest and participation. Charles had a more selective cultural policy than his brother, but he had the more developed musical taste and skill, and the right musicians on hand to make the best of his patronage.

The connection between Coprario, the fantasia, the violin, and Prince Charles has always been known, for John Playford alluded to it in the prefaces to the 1664 and 1683 editions of his *Introduction to the Skill of Musick*: 'For Instrumental Musick none pleased him [Charles] like those Fantazies for one Violin and Basse Viol, to the Organ, Composed by Mr. Coperario'; and again: 'Charles I . . . could play his part exactly well on the Bass-Viol, especially of those Incomparable Fancies of Mr. Coperario to the Organ'.[41] Burney and Hawkins asserted that Coprario was a member of Prince Charles's household (Hawkins even wrote that he 'taught music to the children of James the First'), though the first hard evidence came only in 1953 when Walter Woodfill drew attention to a reference in the papers of Sir John Coke, a secretary of state to Charles I from 1625.[42] The document, notes taken at an audience at Whitehall on 12 May 1625, deals with petitions for places in the new royal household from former servants of James I, Queen Anne, and Prince Charles. Among the latter is: 'John Woodington Musition to K(ing) James 6 yeres, and to His Ma(jes)tie in Coperarios musique 3 yeres, desireth the place of John Sturt void by death.'[43]

This is a revealing sentence. It tells us that Coprario had been associated with an ensemble in Prince Charles's household since 1622; indeed, we now know that he became a servant of Prince Charles by a warrant dated 4 April 1622, and that he was associated with the prince as early as 6 March 1617/18, when he was given £50 'for his highnes

---

[40] Ibid. 224.

[41] R. Charteris, *John Coprario: A Thematic Catalogue of his Music, with a Biographical Introduction* (New York, 1977), 32–3.

[42] Woodfill, *Musicians in English Society*, 309.

[43] *GB-Lbl*, Add. MS 64883, fo. 57ʳ, a volume of the Coke papers formerly at Melbourne Hall in Derbyshire; see HMC, *Twelfth Report*, Appendix, Part I, i: *The Manuscripts of the Earl Cowper, K.G., Preserved at Melbourne Hall, Derbyshire*, (London, 1888), 195.

speciall use and service'.[44] Sturt died at the beginning of 1625: he was buried on 14 January 1624/5 at St Andrew, Holborn, when he was described as a musician of Churchyard Alley, Fetter Lane; his wages up to Lady Day 1625 were paid to his widow Elizabeth at Michaelmas 1626.[45] Most important in this context, the petition also shows us that Coprario's group included at least two violinists. Woodington did not receive Sturt's place, but he was finally given a court salary of 20*d*. a day with livery in March 1625/6, when he was described as a 'supernumerary musician to his Majesty for the violins', replacing the French violinist Adam Vallet, who died on 3 October 1625.[46] Later in the year, by a patent dated 4 July 1626, Woodington's pay was increased to £110 a year; significantly, Vallet's own pay had been increased to the same sum by a patent dated 2 March 1623/4 'in consideration(i)on of the faithfull service done unto us [King James] and our most deare sonne Charles Prince of Wales'; the patent was obtained 'by direction from the Prince his Highnes'.[47] It seems, therefore, that Woodington and Vallet doubled as members of the violin band in the main royal household, and as members of 'Coprario's Music' in Prince Charles's household. Woodington evidently served without pay in both capacities until he inherited Vallet's appointments, and it is likely that he was apprenticed to the Frenchman.

We can learn more about 'Coprario's Music' from Woodington's later activities: he continued to hold two court appointments until the Civil War, though after 1625 his place as a musician in Prince Charles's household was transferred to the 'Lutes and Voices' section of the main royal music (see Ch. 11). By a warrant dated 15 February 1634/5 he was paid £20 'for a new sett of bookes for Cooperarios Musique, by his Ma(jes)t(i)es speciall com(m)annd'; the same purchase was recorded in more detail in the declared accounts that year: 'for a whole sett of Musicke Bookes by him p(ro)vided & prickt w(i)th all Coperaries & Orlando Gibbons theire Musique, by his Ma(jes)t(ie)s speciall Comand'.[48] These documents suggest that Coprario's group was still in existence as a discrete ensemble nearly ten years after the composer's death in 1626, and they explain why Woodington was paid £8 in July 1632 for a bass viol and £12 in January 1637/8 for 'a Cremonia vyolin to play to the Organ'; he may have needed a special violin because of the high pitch of contemporary English organs.[49] Woodington's 'new sett of bookes' does not

[44] Ashbee, *RECM*, iv. 217, 226.
[45] *GB-Lgc*, MS 6673/2; Ashbee, *RECM*, v. 2.
[46] Ibid., iii. 12, 165.
[47] Ibid. 18–19; *Lpro*, SP38/12.
[48] Ashbee, *RECM*, iii. 81, 150.
[49] Ibid. 66, 96, 154; the most recent discussion of the topic is D. Gwynn, 'Organ Pitch in Seventeenth-Century England', *BIOS Journal*, 9 (1985), 65–78.

seem to have survived, but something like it (and perhaps connected with it) is represented by the collection now divided between *GB-Och*, Mus. MSS 732–5 (string parts) and *GB-Lbl*, R.M. 24.K.3 (organ). It is bound with the arms of Charles I; it has Woodington's name on the original covers; it contains most of the surviving music by Coprario and Gibbons for mixed groups of violins, viols, and organ; and, Pamela Willetts has argued, it was copied in part by John Tomkins and Stephen Bing.[50] Tomkins and Bing were colleagues of Woodington in the choir of St Paul's Cathedral, while Tomkins was also a court musician, a member of the Chapel Royal.

The set is a principal source of Coprario's fifteen fantasia suites for violin, bass viol, and organ, his eight fantasia suites for two violins, bass viol, and organ, and six of Gibbons's three- and four-part fantasias for 'The great Dooble Basse'.[51] It does not include three of the 'double bass' fantasias commonly attributed to Gibbons (MB edition, nos. 20–2). But they are anonymous in the sole complete source; one of them is ascribed to Coprario in a recently discovered fragment; and Oliver Neighbour has argued on stylistic grounds that all three of them are by Coprario rather than Gibbons.[52] He suggests that the two composers wrote them 'at the same table . . . in response to a shared commission'—a circumstance that would explain why one of the genuine Gibbons pieces and one of the disputed ones (MB, nos. 18, 22) share, in inversion, a theme based on a D minor arpeggio. The table, it seems, was provided by Prince Charles in the early 1620s. Woodington may have copied the 'new sett of bookes' to replace the original performing material used by Coprario and his colleagues in the 1620s, which had perhaps become worn out in the meantime.

Coprario's fantasia suites are the first English contrapuntal pieces to specify violins: the early sources label them variously 'Mr Coperario, with the viall and violin to the organ', 'For the Organ base viol and violin', 'Mr Coperarios Fancys for 2 Violins', '2 treble viollins the basse violl, & the Organ', 'the Songes for 2 viollins', and 'For two Treble violins one Base viol & the Organ'.[53] The precise scoring of Gibbons's 'double bass' fantasias is more in doubt. They do not have a separate organ part like the one in Coprario's fantasia suites–R.M. 24.K.3 only contains the Coprario sets—though Gibbons clearly intended an organ accompani-

[50] R. Charteris, 'Autographs of John Coprario', *ML* 56 (1975), 41–6; P. Willetts, 'John Barnard's Collections of Viol and Vocal Music', *Chelys*, 20 (1991), 28–42, esp. 34–5; for Bing, see ead., 'Stephen Bing: A Forgotten Violist', ibid. 23 (1990), 3–17.

[51] J. Coprario, *Fantasia Suites*, ed. R. Charteris (MB 46; London 1980); O. Gibbons, *Consort Music*, ed. J. Harper (MB 48; London, 1982).

[52] O. Neighbour, 'Orlando Gibbons (1583–1625): The Consort Music', *EM* 11 (1983), 355–6.

[53] Coprario, *Fantasia Suites*, ed. Charteris, p. xix.

ment. His four three-part pieces (MB, nos. 16–19) survive in three
scores, one of which, the former *GB-Lkc*, MS 3, labels them 'Fancyes . . .
to the Organ'; nos. 16 and 17 have some extra imitative entries and
fragmentary lines that do not, with a few exceptions, appear in the string
parts, though they are often essential to the music: in both they supply the
second entries of the opening point of counterpoint.[54] They are, it seems,
indications of a semi-improvised organ part, and Neighbour is surely
right to see them as a step on the path that led to Coprario's fully worked
parts.

Gibbons presumably played the organ himself in 'Coprario's Music',
for besides his £40-a-year post in Prince Charles's household he received
another £46 a year by a warrant dated 27 January 1619/20 as a virginal-
player in 'His Highnesses Privy Chamber' (that is, it seems, of Prince
Charles's household, not King James's, as is usually said) in succession to
Walter Earle; in a list relating to James I's funeral in 1625 he is placed
among the Chapel Royal—of which he was also an organist—but is
labelled 'privy organ' (i.e. chamber organ), as if that was his main role at
court.[55] There are several references to an organ (or organs) in the
prince's accounts. Matthew Goodrick was paid £13. 14*s.* in November
1621 'for paynting and guildinge the Organs at St James'; Thomas
Cradock was paid £44 for 'new making the Princes Winde Instrum(en)t at
St James', which included 'making a new stoppe of Pipes'; and Richard
Norris, joiner, was paid £40. 3*s.* in an undated bill for, among other
things, 'taking down & altering the Organ case at St James'.[56]

The main question concerning the 'double bass' fantasias is whether
they were intended just for viols, as most modern performers have
assumed (and the MB edition recommends), or for a mixture of violins
and viols. At first glance they certainly look like viol music. The violin is
not mentioned in any of the sources, as it is in Coprario's fantasia suites,
the top part is not differentiated in any way from the others, and the
bottom part, variously labelled 'Double Base' and 'The great Dooble
Basse' in MSS 732–5, is clearly for a viol—a large instrument pitched
in *A'*, a fourth lower than the normal bass in *D*. Until recently the only
known reference to such an instrument was the 'greate Base Violl' valued
at £15 in the 1638 inventory of Ingatestone Hall in Essex; in 1976, noting
a part for a 'Great Basse' in the 'Symphonia' of George Jeffreys's
madrigal 'Felice pastorella', I suggested that another might have been
owned by the Hatton family, who were patrons of Gibbons and Jeffreys.[57]

[54] *GB-Lkc*, MS 3, an item from Thurston Dart's library, was sold at Sotheby's on 27 Nov. 1987;
see *EM* 16 (1988), 251–2; see also T. Dart, 'Purcell and Bull', *MT* 104 (1963), 31.
[55] Ashbee, *RECM*, iv. 106; iii. 2.
[56] Ibid., iv. 225.
[57] Reproduced in H. E. P. Grieve (ed.), *Examples of English Handwriting 1150–1750*

We now know, however, that there were at least two great bass viols at court in the 1620s: the wind-player Jerome Lanier was paid £20 'for a greate base Vyall' by a warrant dated 24 January 1624/5, and Alfonso Ferrabosco was paid the same sum by a warrant dated 17 February 1626/7 for 'a greate Bass Vyall and a greate Lyra'.[58] Great bass viols were still in use later in the century, to judge from the large five-string instrument in Lely's *The Concert*, painted in London in the late 1640s (Pl. 6a), and the 'Double Base' part in John Blow's anthem 'Lord, who shall dwell in thy tabernacle', written around 1680 for the Chapel Royal (see Ch. 16).[59] The 'double bass' parts by Gibbons, Jeffreys, and Blow are already too low to have been played at 16' pitch, and there is little sign that bass instruments were played at anything but written pitch in England before the eighteenth century.

In considering the top parts of the Gibbons 'double bass' fantasias we cannot assume that they were written for treble viol just because they move no faster than the lower parts, and are relatively easy to play. The violin was still almost exclusively a dance instrument in England at the time, so it is not surprising that when English composers first looked around for a suitable idiom for the instrument in contrapuntal music, they settled on the use of dance rhythms and phraseology rather than virtuosity, which had already become the mainstay of the instrument in Italy. Strange as it may seem, there are grounds for thinking that virtuosity was more associated with the viol than with the violin before the 1650s, when Thomas Baltzar astonished English players with his unprecedented use of rapid passage-work, high positions, chords, and *scordatura*. John Jenkins, perhaps the first composer to develop division-like passages in the fantasia suite, appears to have written for the treble viol, at least in his earlier works. He played the treble viol himself; he worked in country houses where viols were still cultivated; and the upper parts of his fantasia suites are labelled 'treble' rather than 'violin' in the primary sources (see Ch. 11).

The upper parts of Coprario's fantasia suites were certainly conceived for violin, but they move no faster or ascend no higher than the treble viol parts of his five- and six-part fantasias. In his hands the fantasia suite is a violinistic idiom simply because it has a lively and dance-like fantasia, with a ₵ rather than C time signature, and because two dances, an alman and a galliard, are effectively enclosed within its confines—a close or

---

([Chelmsford], 1954), 30, pl. xxviii; P. Holman, 'George Jeffries and the 'Great Dooble Base'', *Chelys*, 5 (1973–4, published 1976), 79–81.

[58] Ashbee, *RECM*, iii. 134, 138.

[59] In the Lee collection at the Courtauld Institute, London; see O. Millar (ed.), *Sir Peter Lely 1618–80, Catalogue of the National Portrait Gallery exhibition, 17 November 1978 to 18 March 1979* (London, 1978), no. 11.

'drag' often returns the work at the end to the mood of the opening. In his 'double bass' fantasias Gibbons achieved a similar effect by different means. They, too, are no more virtuosic than his six-part fantasias— considerably less so than the five-part In Nomines and the six-part variations on 'Go from my window' (MB, nos. 28. 29, 40)—but they are outstandingly dance-like: all of them have sections of triple time, and a number have passages that sound like quotations from country dances. Indeed, a passage in no. 18 has been identified as a snatch of the Dutch tune 'De Rommelpot' (Ex. 9.5), while the great four-part no. 24 quotes from the second half of the English country-dance tune 'Rufty tufty'. Bearing in mind that the principal source of the 'double bass' fantasias is connected with John Woodington, we may conclude that Gibbons originally wrote them for violin with two or three viols and organ, though they were doubtless played with treble viols away from the court—just as Jenkins probably played Coprario's fantasia suites, which he helped to copy for the Le Strange household, on his own instrument.[60]

Similar arguments apply to at least some of the 'conventional' three-part fantasias by Orlando Gibbons and Thomas Lupo. The primary source of those by Gibbons is his *Fantazies of III Parts*, a mysterious publication for all its fame. It was once dated *c.*1610 because the title-page states that it was 'Cut in Copper, the like not heretofore extant'; it must, it was reasoned, pre-date the engraved keyboard book *Parthenia* of 1612–13. But Thurston Dart argued, largely because Gibbons dedicated it to Edward Wray (1589–1658), that it actually dates from about a decade later; Wray is said in the collection to be 'one of the Groomes of his Ma(jes)t(ie)s bed Chamber', a post he held between 1618 and 1622, when he was imprisoned after marrying Elizabeth, Baroness Norreys without permission.[61] Dart's revised date has been generally accepted, but his reasoning is suspect. The main problem is that the title-page describes Gibbons on the one hand as 'Batchelour of Musick', his correct title between the granting of his Cambridge B.Mus. in 1606 and his Oxford doctorate of 1622, and on the other as 'Late Organist of His MAJESTIES Chappell Royall in ordinary', which can only really mean that it was published after his death on 5 June 1625. Dart tried to argue that Gibbons gave up his Chapel Royal post in January 1619/20 when he received a post as a court virginal-player—hence the phrase 'Late Organist'—but this is not what happened: two Chapel Royal documents of 1625 describe him as organist, and I know of no other case at the time

---

[60] Coprario, *Fantasia Suites*, ed. Charteris, 175; see also P. Willetts, 'Sir Nicholas Le Strange and John Jenkins', *ML* 42 (1961), 30–43.

[61] T. Dart, 'The Printed Fantasies of Orlando Gibbons', *ML* 37 (1956), 342–9; I am indebted to Dr John Ferris for allowing me access to the material on Wray held by the History of Parliament Trust at the Institute of Historical Research, London University.

Ex. 9.5. Orlando Gibbons, 'Double bass' Fantazia, bb. 63–77, VdGS no. 3 (from Gibbons, *Consort Music*, ed. Harper, no. 18)

of a musician leaving one court group to join another.[62] Pluralism was the order of the day.

The solution to the problem seems to lie in the fact that there are two issues of the publication. The first, of which copies survive in *GB-Och* and *GB-Ge*, has no title-page, mention of publisher, or place of publication, only the dedication to Wray with the heading 'FANTAZIES OF III. PARTS'. The second issue, in *GB-Lbl* and *GB-Lcm*, has the well-known typeset title-page, with the conflicting statements just discussed, and the following location: 'LONDON, At the Bell in S^t. Pauls Churchyard', which was added to the vacant left-hand bottom corner of the dedication. The Bell in St Paul's churchyard was the address of the bookseller and publisher Thomas Adams until his death in 1620, and of his widow Elizabeth for a few years thereafter.[63] A possible explanation is that Gibbons originally published his fantasias privately for distribution in court circles during Wray's period in the Bedchamber, that is, between 1618 and 1622. The second issue may have been prepared sometime after the composer's death in 1625, perhaps to dispose of the stock. His titles 'Batchelour of Musick' and 'Late Organist' of the chapel were probably derived from the title-page of *The First Set of Madrigals and Mottetts* (London, 1612), where he appears as 'Batcheler of Musicke, and Organist of His Majesties Honorable Chappell in Ordinarie'. Elizabeth Adams would doubtless have known of his death, but may not have known that he had received a doctorate in 1622.

I make no apology for this digression if it has helped to clear up a thorny problem of Gibbons scholarship, but it is also important in the present context for the connection it provides between Gibbons and Prince Charles's circle, for Edward Wray was an 'innermost friend' of Charles's crony George Villiers, successively Earl, Marquis, and Duke of Buckingham, and owed his position at court to him. Other connections between Gibbons's three-part fantasias and Prince Charles's household are not hard to find. Six of them are in *US-LAuc*, MS fF1995M4, a set of part-books in the hand of a Jacobean scribe with court connections who also copied the first layer of the wind manuscript *GB-Cfm*, Mu. MS 734 (see Ch. 7), as well as *GB-Lbl*, Madrigal Society MSS G. 37–42.[64] MS fF1995M4 has particularly close associations with Prince Charles's household since, apart from four early works by John Jenkins, it consists entirely of music by four of his servants, Gibbons, Lupo, Coprario, and Robert Johnson.

The contents of *Fantazies of III Parts* were republished in Amsterdam

---

[62] Rimbault (ed.), *The Old Cheque-Book*, 11, 156.

[63] C. Humphries and W. C. Smith (eds.), *Music Publishing in the British Isles* (2nd edn., London, 1970), 49.

[64] Charteris, 'A Rediscovered Source'.

in 1648 in the second part of a volume that was specifically associated with Prince Charles by its publisher, Paulus Matthysz. The first part of *XX. konincklycke Fantasien*, 'Twenty Royal Fantasies, for Three Viols and other Instruments', consists of fifteen pieces by Thomas Lupo, four by John Coprario, and a stray one by William Daman, a wind-player at the English court who died in 1591.[65] Matthysz wrote in the dedication that the music was 'composed for the amusement of the greatest monarchs of Europe', and was originally selected to be performed at 'the wrecked marriage festivities between England and Spain'—that is, the wedding that would have taken place had not Prince Charles's trip to Spain in 1623 to woo the Spanish Infanta ended in failure. If his account is to be believed, and Rudolf Rasch has suggested that Matthysz obtained the music from musicians who accompanied Henrietta Maria and her daughter Mary from England to the Netherlands in 1642 (Mary married William II, the son of the Stadtholder Frederik Hendrik, in that year), it seems that the details of the wedding, including the music, had already been planned by Charles's household on the expectation of a successful outcome to the Spanish Match. Indeed, Lupo was given £20 on 8 February 1621/2 'for a Booke by him presented' to the prince, which may have been a presentation manuscript of the pieces chosen.[66]

Gibbons's nine printed fantasias divide into two groups. The first four, the more contrapuntal and conventional works, use the common treble, tenor, and bass layout. But the other five are generally more modern in style, and have two trebles. Dart suggested that they are intended for two violins, bass viol, and organ because their scoring is similar to Coprario's fantasia suites.[67] This may be so; it certainly seems that they were played with organ at the time, for there are several surviving full and short scores that were probably used as the basis of an improvised accompaniment. But, as I have argued in the case of the 'double bass' fantasias, it is their dance-like character that makes them suitable for violins rather than the two-treble scoring. Nos. 6 and 7 (MB, nos. 12, 13) are virtually in continuous three-part harmony, and are no more contrapuntal than, say, the almans of Coprario's fantasia suites. Moreover, no. 6 appears to be based on the opening motif and harmony of the popular 'Almande Bruynsmedelijn', which appears in several sixteenth-century dance songs, such as Sermisy's 'Au joly bois' and Gastoldi's 'Caro soave e desiato

---

[65] *T. Lupo, I. Coprario, W. Daman: XX Konincklycke Fantasien en noch IX Fantasien*, ed. R. Rasch (Peer, 1987), 5–11; see also Rasch, 'Seventeenth-Century Dutch Editions of English Instrumental Music', *ML* 53 (1972), 270–1; Lasocki, 'Professional Recorder Players', ii. 672–5 is the best biography of Daman.

[66] Ashbee, *RECM*, iv. 226.

[67] Dart, 'The Printed Fantasies', 345.

bene'.[68] Nos. 7, 8, and 9 (MB, nos. 13–15) also have dance-like passages of triple time.

The same is true of Lupo's three-part fantasias, though with twenty-five surviving works to Gibbons's thirteen there is inevitably a wider range of styles.[69] Some of the treble, tenor, and bass pieces—Charteris no. 11, for instance—are more conservative than any of those by Gibbons, while a batch of two-treble pieces, Charteris nos. 17–25, are so dance-like that they can hardly be described as fantasias at all; indeed, several do not even open with imitative entries, and they only differ from extended almans or airs in that section-endings are marked by fermatas rather than double bars (Ex. 9.6). Similar points can be made about Lupo's four-part fantasias: they also divide into conventional contrapuntal pieces with a single treble and modern two-treble pieces, some of which—Charteris nos. 5–7, for instance—are more like airs than fantasias.[70]

Lupo also developed a wider range of scorings than Gibbons. He was, it seems, the first composer to lay out four-part fantasias for two trebles and two equal and crossing basses; see Charteris nos. 4, 9, and 10. The three-part fantasy, Charteris no. 16, is for two tenors and bass, while four others, Charteris nos. 4–6 and 14, are for two trebles and tenor. Charteris no. 12, a fantasy for three trebles (transposed in two sources for three tenors), is of interest because it seems to relate to Charteris no. 15, for three basses, and to Robert Johnson's only surviving contrapuntal consort piece, the fantasy for three trebles, MS fF1995M4 no. 18. As with the 'double bass' fantasias, the fact that such an unusual scoring was used by two servants of Prince Charles suggests that they were working together in some way, perhaps for a particular occasion.

There is doubtless more to be learned about 'Coprario's Music', but we can begin to establish a tentative chronology for its revolutionary repertoire of music for violins, viols, and organ. It is reasonable to assume that the earliest string-consort music played in Prince Charles's household was for viols, such as the conventional contrapuntal fantasias with a single treble by Lupo, Gibbons, and Ferrabosco, whose four-part works with organ were widely distributed and imitated at the time. Gibbons and Lupo presumably introduced dance-like features into the fantasia when they first began to use violins in contrapuntal music, and that may have happened soon after Prince Charles's group of musicians was formed in 1617–18, and Coprario was first associated with it. If we can believe the preface of *XX konincklycke Fantasien*, pieces of this sort

[68] See Ward (ed.), *The Dublin Virginal Book*, 51–2; R. Hudson, *The Allemande, the Balletto, and the Tanz* (Cambridge, 1986), i. 37–8, 45.

[69] T. Lupo, *The Two- and Three-Part Consort Music*, ed. R. Charteris (Clifden, 1987); see also my review in *Chelys*, 17 (1988), 43–7.

[70] T. Lupo, *The Four-Part Consort Music*, ed. R. Charteris and J. M. Jennings (Clifden, 1983).

Ex. 9.6. Thomas Lupo, Fantasia *a 3*, bb. 1–12, VdGS no. 20 (from Lupo, *Two-and Three-Part Consort Music*, ed. Charteris, no. 19)

were in existence around 1622–3, and the first issue of Gibbons's nine fantasias must have appeared before Edward Wray lost his place in the Bedchamber. Next perhaps, Coprario and Gibbons experimented with the use of a great bass viol, possibly because they found that the sprightly violin at the top of the ensemble needed to be balanced by a deeper and more sonorous instrument at the bottom. The last stage seems to have been the development of the fantasia suite, if it is right to interpret the organ indications in the scores of the 'double bass' fantasias as a step on the road that led to Coprario's independent and fully written-out parts. By adding two formal dances to a fantasia, Coprario was able to prevent that supposedly contrapuntal form from being swamped by dance-like elements. The fantasia suite was to remain the main vehicle for the violin in serious English consort music until after the Restoration.

10

'*His Majesties Musique of Violins*'
The Caroline Court Orchestra

THE accession of Charles I to the throne on 27 March 1625 caused a crisis at court. The sizeable household that Charles had assembled while he was Prince of Wales was largely a duplicate of the one that he now inherited from his father. Indeed, a Venetian diplomat reported at the time that the subject of debate at court was 'whether the household of the dead king or that of the prince shall be the household of the present king'.[1] It was a situation that had not arisen in England for over a hundred years, since Henry VIII, the last adult Prince of Wales to inherit the throne, had succeeded Henry VII in 1509. Edward VI came to the throne as a child, without a proper household of his own; the personal households of Mary and Elizabeth were small, for they were princesses rather than princes; and though James I and his family came from Scotland with a large retinue of their countrymen, they left their less exalted servants behind, including the musicians.[2]

Charles's solution, if it can be called a solution, was to take the line of least resistance: as the Venetian diplomat put it, 'His Majesty does not wish to exclude his father's old servants or abandon his own', and it seems that most of those in both households were retained with their existing salaries, leaving the cases of duplicated posts to be resolved by natural wastage. James I's musicians were all eventually confirmed in their places, but not before some of the trumpeters took fright and petitioned the new king to be shown the same favour 'as the Musitians whoe are all continued [in their places], otherwise they are all undone'.[3] Not all Charles's former musicians were so lucky. Twenty-four 'Musitions' appear in the list of 'The Houshold of o(u)r now dread Sovereghne Lord King Charles', drawn up for the issue of livery for

---

[1] K. Sharpe, 'The Image of Virtue: The Court and Household of Charles I, 1625–1642', in D. Starkey (ed.), *The English Court, from the Wars of the Roses to the Civil War* (London, 1987), 227–8.

[2] An exception was the harper Malcolm Groat, 'Music(i)on to the late Queenes Ma(jes)tie for the Sco(t)c(h)te Musicke', who petitioned the Privy Council for relief after Queen Anne's death in 1619, claiming that he had served her 'ever since her Ma(jes)t(i)es Coming out of Scotland', *GB-Lpro*, SP14/107, fo. 108ʳ; see also Ashbee, *RECM*, iv. 49; v. 18, 22, 24.

[3] *GB-Lbl*, Add. MS 64883, fo. 62ᵛ.

James I's funeral on 5 May 1625, but seven of them, John Ballard, Robert Bourman, Abraham Coates, Thomas Hassard, John Daniel, Gilbert Johnson, and James Graye, are not encountered again in court documents, presumably because they failed to obtain posts in the new royal music.[4]

The union of the two households had a less drastic effect on musicians than on some of the other classes of royal servants because Charles's group, a mixed ensemble, or rather a pool of musicians who cultivated a range of mixed ensembles, did not duplicate the main groups of the royal music, the three wind consorts and the violin band. A miscellaneous group of this sort, it is true, had also begun to accumulate in the main royal music during James I's reign, but it was small enough to be combined with Charles's musicians to form a new group, variously called 'the Consort', the 'Lutes, Viols and Voices', or, most commonly, the 'Lutes and Voices'. Like its predecessor in Prince Charles's household, the Lutes and Voices included some violinists, and its activities impinged to some extent on the whole royal music, so we need to examine how it came into being before turning to the violin band itself.

We saw in Chapter 2 how Henry VIII's Eltham Ordinances of 1526 enforced a distinction between the majority of royal musicians, who worked in public in the Presence Chamber, and the minority, who enjoyed the privilege of access to the Privy Chamber, and tended to play soft instruments, such as the lute or the viol, that were best heard in the peace and quiet of the Privy Chamber. Nearly all these Privy Chamber posts ceased or went into abeyance during the reigns of Edward VI and Mary, and it was not until Mathias Mason and John Johnson were appointed 'musicians of the three lutes' in 1579 that they began to revive.[5] They were joined by Robert Hales—more of a singer, it seems, than a lutenist—in 1583, and places were also created (or dormant ones appropriated from other parts of the royal music) for Walter Pierce in 1589 and John Dowland in 1612, making an establishment of five in all.[6] Mason and Hales are known to have been Grooms of the Privy Chamber, an honorary title that was probably enjoyed by all the holders of these posts, though evidence is lacking in some cases.[7]

It is clear from a number of Jacobean documents that the lutenists played together in a consort, and that they were called 'musicians for the three lutes' because they played three sizes of instrument, not because

[4] Ashbee, *RECM*, iii. 4–5.

[5] 'Lists of the King's Musicians', *MA* 1, 249; Johnson succeeded the sole surviving member of Henry VIII's Privy Chamber musicians, the Spanish lutenist Anthony Conti (De County).

[6] Ibid. 251; *MA* 2, 53; Ashbee, *RECM*, iv. 89; see also Ward, 'The King's Luters, 1593–1612', in *A Dowland Miscellany*, 107–12.

[7] R. Dowland, *Varietie of Lute-Lessons*, sig. D2; Dowland, *A Musical Banquet*, sig. C2.

1. (*a*) Detail of *The Coronation of the Virgin*, fresco *c*.1510–15 attributed to Michele Coltellini or Ludovico Mazzolino. Ferrara, Church of Santa Maria della Consolazione (*b*) Gerrit Houckgeest, *Charles I Dining in Public*. By gracious permission of Her Majesty the Queen

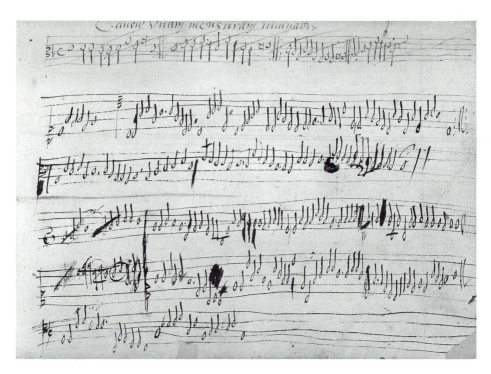

2. (*a*) The composing hand of Derick Gerarde? *GB-Lbl*, Royal Appendix MS 74, fo. 49[v]. British Library, courtesy of the Trustees

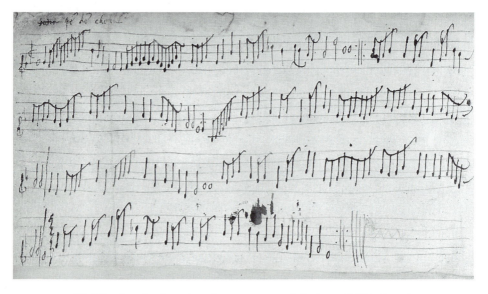

(*b*) The hand of an immigrant court violinist *c*.1560? Royal Appendix MS 76, fo. 48[r]. British Library, courtesy of the Trustees

3. (*a*) Detail of the anonymous painting *c*.1580 traditionally called *Queen Elizabeth I Dancing with Robert Dudley, Earl of Leicester*. Penshurst Place, courtesy of the Rt. Hon. Viscount de l'Isle, VC

(*b*) Detail of *Courtiers of Queen Elizabeth*, painting *c*.1600 attributed to Marcus Gheeraerts the elder. Present whereabouts unknown. Photographic archives of the National Gallery of Art, Washington DC, from a negative made by Taylor and Dull for Parke-Bernet Galleries Inc.

4. (*a*) Detail of Joris Hoefnagel, *A Fête at Bermondsey* *c*.1570. Hatfield House, courtesy of the Marquess of Salisbury

(*b*) Detail of *the Memorial Portrait of Sir Henry Unton c*.1596. National Portrait Gallery, London

5. (*a*) Peter Lely, *The Concert*, late 1640s. Courtauld Institute Galleries, London

(*b*) Painting traditionally called *The Cabal* by J. B. Medina. Nostell Priory, courtesy of Lord St Oswald

6. Jerome Janssens, *Charles II Dancing at the Hague with his Sister Mary*, late 1650s. By gracious permission of Her Majesty the Queen

7. Jerome Janssens, *Ball on a Terrace of a Palace*, late 1650s. Lille, Musée des beaux arts

8. Opening of the autograph score of Matthew Locke, 'Be thou exalted, Lord', 1666. *GB-Ob*, MS Mus. C. 23, fo. 25[r]. Bodleian Library, University of Oxford

there were originally three of them. Robert Johnson, who replaced Edward Collard (the successor of John Johnson) in 1604, was referred to as a musician 'for the base Lute' in payments for strings for the year 1610, while his colleague Philip Rosseter was also paid for lute strings, presumably for smaller sizes of instruments; in 1615 Johnson was described as 'one of the consorte of Lutes'; in 1617 it was Rosseter who was described as a musician 'for the base lute'; in 1620 Rosseter was again paid for strings 'for the base Lutes', while Johnson was paid for strings for unspecified lutes.[8] In the 1630s the group was called 'his Ma(jes)t(i)es fower Lutes', apparently because a fourth type of instrument, a theorbo, had been added: John Kelly supplied one for £8 in March 1627/8; John Coggeshall was paid for strings supplied for 'the four lutes and theorba' in 1629 and 1630, and for 'provyding & maynteyning of his Ma(jes)t(i)es Fower Lutes w(i)th Stringes at all tymes of their meetinges & practises' in 1632 and 1633.[9] It seems that a harpsichord was also used with the group on occasion: in December 1614 Andrea Bassano was paid 46s. 7d. 'for makinge of twoe settes of jackes and new stringinge of his Ma(jes)t(ie)s virginalls for the Consorte'.[10] Virtually nothing is known about the group's repertoire, but it presumably played lute trios early in its history, and it may have acted as a continuo group in secular vocal music in the 1620s and 1630s. For instance, the title-page of *Madrigales and Ayres* (London, 1632) by Walter Porter (a member of the Chapel Royal from 1617) states that they are 'To be performed with the Harpesechord, Lutes, Theorbos, Base Violl, two VIOLINS, or two VIOLS'.

A similar pattern of decline and rebirth can be observed in the history of the court viol-players. In Chapter 4 we saw that they gradually disappeared from the Privy Chamber after the arrival of the Italian string consort in 1540. Alfonso Ferrabosco's appointment as 'musitian to the violles' in 1592 (see Ch. 9) can therefore be seen as equivalent to the creation of the 'musicians for the three lutes' in 1579, and he was duly joined by three colleagues: Daniel Farrant (by a warrant dated 23 November 1607 backdated to Lady Day), Roger Major (by letters patent dated 10 January 1613/14 backdated to 27 November 1613), and John Friend (from Midsummer 1615 by letters patent dated 12 July).[11] Ferrabosco, Farrant, and Friend (we saw in Ch. 8) were nominal members of the violin band and probably played with them on occasion,

---

[8] Ashbee, *RECM*, iv. 87–8, 98, 101, 109.

[9] Ibid. iii. 54, 57, 138, 141, 146; for a consort of three lutes outside the court see Hulse, 'Hardwick MS 29', 66.

[10] Ashbee, *RECM*, iv. 95.

[11] *GB-Lpro*, LC5/50, 143; Ashbee, *RECM*, iv. 40, 80, 156; *GB-Lpro*, E351/544, m. 38; see Ashbee, *RECM*, iv. 94.

but subsidy documents, drawn up on 13 July 1624 and 8 June 1625 (and seemingly recording the actual state of the royal music on particular days, not its theoretical establishment), list them as 'Musicians for the Violls' in a separate category from the 'Musicians for the Violins'.[12] It is easy to assume that they played viol consort music, such as Ferrabosco's celebrated four-part fantasias, but we must remember that Ferrabosco and Farrant were also among those who first developed the viol as a solo instrument—the lyra viol.[13] With its chordal idiom, its tablature notation, and a repertoire of solos, duets, trios, and songs, the lyra viol was a serious rival to the lute at the time.

The list of courtiers receiving livery for the funeral of James I, marks, it seems, the first stage of the reorganization of the royal music made necessary by the accession of Charles I. The current royal lutenists, Timothy Collins, John Dowland, Robert Johnson, Nicholas Lanier (Hales's successor as 'singer'), and Maurice Webster, and the four viol-players are combined into a single ensemble called 'The Consorte' together with the harpist Philip Squire, the singer-lutenist Charles Coleman (later employed in the future Charles II's household; see Ch. 11), and Francis Cozens, whose function and subsequent history are unknown.[14] Prince Charles's musicians are still listed in a separate group in this document, as they are in the 8 June subsidy list, but in the latter they are called 'Musicians for the Lutes and Voices' for the first time, and are joined by Richard Dering, who had recently returned to England from Brussels to become organist of Henrietta Maria's Catholic chapel.

The Lutes and Voices came into being on a formal basis by means of a patent dated 11 July 1626, backdated to Lady Day 1625, when sixteen of Prince Charles's former musicians (or their heirs) received places in the main royal music, mostly with £40 a year, the prevailing wage for musicians in the prince's household.[15] The patent is headed by Nicholas Lanier, who is described as 'Master of o(u)r Musicke' with a wage of £200 a year. This appears to be the first reference to the title 'Master of the Music', and it seems that the post was created for Lanier in 1626, not in 1618 as is often said; there is no evidence that Lanier had a formal post in Prince Charles's household before the spring of 1625 (see Ch. 9). The post, whenever it was created, was a landmark in the history of music at the English court. For the first time an individual was given formal authority over all the secular musicians. In earlier times a certain amount of control seems to have been exercised by Privy Chamber musicians

[12] Ashbee, *RECM*, iv. 60–1; v. 1.

[13] For Farrant's role in the early history of the lyra viol, see Holman, '"An Addicion of Wyer Stringes"'.

[14] For Squire and the other court harpists, see Holman, 'The Harp in Stuart England'.

[15] Ashbee, *RECM*, iii. 19; the full document is in *GB-Lpro*, SP16/31 (51).

such as the lutenists Philip van Wilder and Thomas Lichfield, but the instrumental consorts seem normally to have answered to the Lord Chamberlain or members of his staff, and they probably enjoyed considerable autonomy in practice. We shall see that Lanier encountered some resistance when he tried to exert his authority over those who were not members of his own group, the Lutes and Voices.

It is difficult to be sure of the exact size of the Lutes and Voices at any one time because there are virtually no documents that give lists of all its members. Some of them were paid by the Treasury of the Chamber, while others dealt directly with the Exchequer, so they appear separately in two classes of records; names also tend to be missing from the lists of the group in subsidy documents because individuals who held more than one post usually appear only once: John Woodington, for instance, appears in a subsidy list dated 15 July 1628 just as a member of the violin band, though he also had a place as a solo violinist in the Lutes and Voices.[16] It seems, however, that the Lutes and Voices as first established consisted of twenty-nine musicians: eighteen singer-lutenists, a harpist, two keyboard-players, four viol-players, and four violinists. Of the violinists, two, Woodington and Thomas Lupo I, had been associated with 'Coprario's Music' in Prince Charles's household, the chamber ensemble that had pioneered the use of the violin in contrapuntal consort music (see Ch. 9), so they probably continued to provide the king with music of that sort. The other two posts, however, seem to have been created merely to increase the size of the violin band, and it is to the band itself that we now turn.

The subsidy documents for 13 July 1624 and 8 June 1625 list eleven 'Musicians for the Violins': Caesar Galliardello, Alexander Chesham, Anthony Comey, John Heydon, John Hopper, Horatio Lupo, Thomas Lupo I and II, Leonard Mell, Thomas Warren, and Adam Vallet. Alfonso Ferrabosco and Daniel Farrant, who appear among the viol-players, make up the establishment of thirteen, and their place was taken in the livery document for James I's funeral by Davis (David) Mell and Richard 'Dorlin' (Dorney), who were evidently serving at the time as unpaid apprentices or 'extraordinary' musicians. Mell, the son of the violinist Leonard Mell, succeeded Horatio Lupo, who died on or about 21 October 1626, and was buried two days later at St Martin-in-the-Fields.[17] Mell was a clockmaker as well as a musician, and subsequently became the

[16] Ibid. 33.

[17] Ibid. 21, 137; K. V. Kitto (ed.), *The Register of St Martins-in-the-Fields, London, 1619–1636* (Harleian Society Publications, Registers, 66; London, 1936), 225; Leonard was said to be Davis's father when he was buried at St Alfege, Greenwich on 14 Apr. 1641, register in the care of the incumbent; M. P. and P. C. Fernandez, 'Davis Mell, Musician and Clockmaker, and an Analysis of the Clockmaking Trade in Seventeenth-Century London', *Antiquarian Horology*, 16 (1987), 604–6.

most prominent English violinist of his generation. Dorney was given £20 a year with £30 boardwages as a 'supernumerary musician' by letters patent dated 14 June 1626, backdated to Lady Day; he received the Lutes and Voices place formerly held by Norman Lesley (Lisle), a violinist and dancing-master who died in the winter of 1625–6.[18]

The violin band's recorded activity under the new king began on 31 May 1625, when the court set out for Canterbury to welcome his bride-to-be, Henrietta Maria, from France. Adam Vallet and eleven of his colleagues were paid 5s. each a day by a warrant dated 27 June 1625 'for wayting and giving attendance on his Ma(jes)tie from Whitehall to Canterbury and backe again by the space of 18 days'; other documents mention a warrant dated 17 May 1625 by which Vallet was paid expenses for twenty-four musicians, but this probably includes twelve of the royal wind musicians.[19] Payments of travel expenses for groups of musicians appear regularly in the Declared Accounts of the Treasury of the Chamber during Charles I's reign, and provide valuable evidence of the actual size of the violin band on a number of specific occasions: Thomas Lupo II and Thomas Warren were paid each year from 1627 to 1633 for the expenses of the visits of a violin band of twelve to Windsor for the annual feasts connected with the Garter ceremonies on St George's day, April 23; we have no information for 1634–7, but the numbers were fifteen in 1638 and 1639.[20]

Adam Vallet's role as the recipient of the violin band's travel expenses for the trip to Canterbury suggests that he took effective control of the group when his master ascended the throne. But if so, his period of rule was short-lived: he died later the same year, on 3 October 1625.[21] Vallet's death, however, did not diminish the French element among the court violinists: Sebastian La Pierre remained at court; Jacques Bochan returned to England in 1625 with Henrietta Maria; and before long two new violinists, Etienne (Stephen) Nau and Nicholas Picart, arrived from France. A new Exchequer place of £200 a year was created for Nau by a patent dated 4 March 1626/7, backdated to Michaelmas 1626.[22] £200, the salary also enjoyed by the Master of the Music, was an unprecedented sum for a violinist, and it was increased in the winter of 1627–8 when, by a warrant dated 22 November 1628 backdated to Christmas 1627, Nau received the forty marks (£26. 8s. 4d.) with livery that Thomas Lupo II had received as the violin band's composer.[23] Picart succeeded Caesar

---

[18] Ashbee, *RECM*, iii. 16, 18, 46, 169.
[19] Ibid. 6, 134, 165.
[20] Ibid. 80, 102, 148, 154, 158.
[21] Ibid. 8, 21.
[22] Ibid. 23, 24.
[23] Ibid. 31, 39–40.

Galliardello as an ordinary member of the violin band at £30 a year by letters patent also dated 22 November 1628, backdated to Michaelmas 1627.[24]

There are signs that Adam Vallet was responsible for bringing Nau and Picart to England. Picart certainly knew Vallet in Paris, for on 2 July 1614 he witnessed a legal document in which Vallet agreed not to sue the master chef Claude Grignon and his wife for slander.[25] He seems to have been the son of Guillaume Picart master mat-maker, who had him apprenticed in Paris on 13 August 1602 for six years to the royal violinist Henri Picot; Picart was twelve at the time, and is recorded in Paris on his own account from 1608 to 1618.[26] He is listed as Henrietta Maria's 'Mr. a danser des filles' in 1625, and he may originally have come to London in that year to serve her.[27] Little is known about Stephen Nau's early life. He does not appear in any of the published documents relating to music in Paris, but Eitner reported a reference to 'Stephanus Nau', 'Gallus Aureliensis' (a Frenchman from Orleans) as 'Musikus' at the University of Leyden on 11 June 1627; significantly, he did not collect any salary from the English court between Lady Day 1627 and 11 March 1628/9.[28] Nau evidently did not arrive in England unknown or unsolicited, for he was given an enormous salary on his first appearance at court, and was promoted to the position of the violin band's composer and effective leader within the year.

If anything, the French element in the violin band was strengthened in the second half of the 1630s. Nau and Picart both served until the Civil War, when Picart apparently returned to France. In 1644 he was living in the Paris parish of Saint-Merry, and in 1646 he was one of the six French violinists who were recruited for a violin band at the Swedish court, where he remained until 1649; Nau stayed in England until his death in March 1646/7.[29] Simon Nau, who was perhaps Stephen's brother, became a member of the violin band in succession to John Heydon by letters patent dated 5 January 1638/9, backdated to Midsummer 1638; he was still in London in 1646, for he was paid £6. 13*s.* 4*d.* of 'what is due to him from his Majesty' on 4 September, but he may have left soon after, for he is not mentioned in Stephen's will.[30] Another

[24] Ibid. 39, 139.

[25] Jurgens, *Documents du minutier central*, i. 610.

[26] Ibid., ii. 336, 376; Brossard, *Musiciens de Paris 1535–1792*, 238.

[27] Spink, 'The Musicians of Queen Henrietta-Maria', 178.

[28] R. Eitner, *Biographisch-bibliographisches Quellen-Lexicon der Musiker und Musikgelehrten* (Leipzig, 1900–4; repr. 1959), vii. 150; Ashbee, *RECM*, iii. 170, 178.

[29] Jurgens, *Documents du minutier central*, ii. 327, 417–8; J. S. Mráček (ed.), *Seventeenth-Century Instrumental Dance Music in Uppsala University Library, Instr. mus. hs 409* (Musica Svecica Saeculi xvii: 5, Monumenta Musicae Svecicae, 8; Stockholm, 1976), 18–19; Ashbee, *RECM*, iii. 128; Nau's will, dated 19 Mar. 1646/7, is in *GB-Lpro*, PROB 11/199, q. 52.

[30] Ashbee, *RECM*, iii. 98, 100, 153; v. 21.

Frenchman, Francis de la France, was sworn in by a warrant dated 10 June 1635 as 'musician in ordinary for the violins, to be admitted to pay upon the next avoidance', but received instead £50 a year out of the Privy Purse by a warrant dated 22 July; he is last heard of in England in March 1637/8, when he was paid £12 for a violin.[31] By 17 November 1639 he was in The Hague: according to two statements sworn there on that day he was a dancing-master who had become entangled with an English serving-girl; she had followed him (or had been abducted, depending on who is to be believed) from England to the Netherlands.[32]

In themselves, the lives of these Frenchmen are of little importance, except to demonstrate the extent of the French influence on the affairs of the Caroline violin band. Throughout the reign there were never less than three French violinists at court, and in the later 1630s there were briefly five of them there at once. And that is without counting such shadowy figures as the 'Mr Varenn' who appears in a list of Henrietta Maria's household of c.1640, who may later have been a violinist at the French court, or the 'Nicholas Confene' listed as a French musician lodging in the parish of St Martin-in-the-Fields in a subsidy document dated 16 December 1635; he may be the same person as the Jacobean court dancing-master 'Monsieur Confesse', and the 'Nicolas Confais' who claimed to be a musician of the queen of England in 1628 (see Ch. 8).[33] By contrast, the early Restoration court, generally thought to have been especially susceptible to French influence, employed no French violinists at all. Louis Grabu, it is true, was an exponent of the French orchestral style, and arrived in England from France in 1665, but he was actually a Spaniard (see Ch. 12).

To what extent, then, was the repertoire and performing style of Charles I's violin band modelled on French practice? We can begin to answer this question by examining documents of 1630 and 1631 that concern some sort of attempted reorganization of the royal music. Some aspects of the affair are obscure, but it seems to have involved an attempt by Nicholas Lanier in his capacity as Master of the Music to extend his authority from his own group, the Lutes and Voices, to the wind musicians and the violin band. On 6 May 1630 the Lord Chamberlain issued an order to 'his Ma(jes)t(ie)s Musitions for the winde Instruments, the Musitions for the violins & all other his Ma(jes)t(ie)s Musitions and others whome it may concerne' that Lanier, who was 'by his place obliged to see the king bee well & duly served w(i)th his severall Musiques

---

[31] Ibid., iii. 83, 84, 96, 97, 154.

[32] C. Vlam and T. Dart, 'Rosseters in Holland', *GSJ* 11 (1958), 66–7.

[33] Ashbee, *RECM*, iii. 252; Spink, 'The Musicians of Queen Henrietta-Maria', 182; Scouloudi, *Returns of Strangers*, 260; Spink also connects a 'Mr Charlo' in the c.1640 document with Claude Charlot, a member of the Vingt-quatre Violons in 1657, but the entry actually reads 'Mr Charbo'.

according to the times & order of their wayting', and whose 'vigilent care & skillfall judgement in disposeing & ordering his Ma(jes)t(ie)s Musique' deserved 'great commendation & incouragement', should 'have a freedome of diet among them'.[34] He was to:

have all free Accesse and liberty to repayre unto the diett of the winde Instruments, the diett of the violins or any other of his Ma(jes)t(ie)s Musitions in Court as frequently & frely as any other of his Ma(jes)t(ie)s Musitions whatsoever. And if any of the sayd Musitions shall oppose or disrespect him therin upon his just complaint or other notice given mee thereof they shall be punished as they deserve.

The word 'diet' is normally used in court records to mean the food that royal servants received when they were on duty at court. But it is hard to understand why Lanier needed access to his colleagues at table, or why they might 'oppose or disrespect him' for claiming such access. The document makes the best sense, I suggest, if we recognize a wider secondary meaning for 'diet', which, according to the *OED*, 'might be understood to mean "daily office", and so lead to the use of [the word] for other courses, duties and occasions'—hence, by extension, 'the regular meeting of the estates of a realm or confederation'. It is easy to see that in the present context 'diet' might mean regular performances or rehearsals. Lanier clearly wished to control the day-to-day activities of groups that hitherto had enjoyed a measure of autonomy. Such a move, coming from a member of the Lutes and Voices who was by no means the longest-serving royal musician, would have been resented and resisted, hence the need for a 'freedom of diet'.

Lanier's plan to control and reform the royal wind musicians was set out in an order from the Lord Chamberlain 'for the better regulating & ordering of his Ma(jes)t(ie)s Musique of winde instruments'; it was made on the same day, 6 May 1630. The document, 'a certaine methode & order of waiting, conceived and signed by you' (Lanier), effectively reorganized the three existing consorts of wind instruments, the shawms and sackbuts, the flutes, and the recorders, into a single group. The aim of the plan, which was amplified and emended in subsequent orders dated 4 December 1633 and 22 December 1637, was partly to ensure a more reliable service—Lanier devised a rota of two groups that served alternate weeks in the Chapel Royal and 'at his Majesty's table'—and partly, it seems, to allow for the introduction of the more modern combination of cornetts and sackbuts; the changes coincided with a number of purchases of these instruments for court use.[35] The Lord Chamberlain evidently expected trouble, for he ordered Lanier to inform

[34] Ashbee, *RECM*, iii. 53.
[35] Ibid. 52–3, 56, 57, 68–9, 74, 94–5, 138, 141, 144, 146.

him if anyone 'shall refuse or neglect to conforme' to the order, 'that they may be proceeded w(i)th according to their demerits'.

It is in the context of these changes to the wind consorts that the well-known order dated 12 April 1631 'for the better regulating and ordering of his Ma(jes)t(i)es Musique of Violins' should be seen.[36] Once again the Lord Chamberlain issued a threat: 'if any of the sayd Musitions shall refuse or neglect to conforme themselves therunto' they would be 'proceeded with according to their temeritte'. But this time the order was directed not to Nicholas Lanier, but to Stephen Nau; the 'certaine methode & order of wayting' that it sets out was said to have been 'receaved & sett down by you', which suggests that Nau, as composer to the violins, was exercising *de facto* the sort of control over the group that Banister and his successors were to enjoy *de jure* over the Restoration Twenty-four Violins. It may be that Lanier's 'freedom of diet' had been successfully resisted in the case of the violins. And it is significant that the 'certaine method & order of wayting' concerns the layout of parts within the violin band, not the division of its players into a rota, for it suggests that, unlike the wind-players, it normally performed as a single orchestra. There is no mention of the band's duties, so we can presume that they remained as before.

For our purpose, the significance of the document lies principally in the unique information it provides about English orchestral practice: it is the only authenticated source of the time that tells us how many parts the group played in, and how many players were on each part. It gives fourteen names divided into five categories:

Estienne Nau	Trebles
Davis Mell	
Nichola Picart	
John Woodington	Contrat(eno)r
Theophilus Lupo	
James Johnson	Tenor
Leonard Mell	
John Heydon	
Thom(as) Lupo	Low tenor
Robert Parker	
John Hopper	Basso
Thomas Warren	
Rich(ar)d Dorney	
Rob(er)t Kindersley	

All those named held places in the group at the time, except Robert Kindersley, who was a viol-player in the Lutes and Voices; his inclusion

---

[36] *GB-Lpro*, LC5/132, 242, partly printed in Ashbee, *RECM*, iii. 59.

confirms what we have suspected in the cases of Daniel Farrant and Alfonso Ferrabosco: that viol-players served in the violin band on occasion, and were presumably expected to play the bass violin as well as the bass viol.

It seems that we are dealing here with a five-part orchestra with a single violin line. The use of the word 'contratenor' suggests that the second part was alto-range, and was played by violas, not a group of second violins, just as 'low tenor' suggests that the fourth part played a third inner part, not a first bass part. This fits in with what can be learned from the contemporary payments to members of the violin band for purchasing or making instruments. By a warrant dated 20 February 1629/30 Stephen Nau was paid £34 for four instruments, a treble violin (£10), two tenors (£6 each), and a bass (£12), which, if it was a matched set, would have made up a quartet with one treble; John Heydon and Thomas Lupo were paid £6 each for buying a 'tenor violin' by warrants dated 17 April 1630 and 21 July 1632, which suggests that even though they played in separate sections of the band, the 'tenors' and 'low tenors', they both played the same type of instrument.[37] The bass section, just 'Basso' in the document, certainly played partly on violin-family instruments, for Thomas Warren was paid £12 for a bass violin by a warrant dated 18 June 1630.[38] Thus the fourteen players were probably divided into three violins, two first violas, three second violas, two third violas, and four bass violins; there is no sign of any continuo instruments.

What is less clear, however, is to what extent the 1631 document records Stephen Nau's attempt to reform and modernize the violin band, just as the May 1630 document records Lanier's reform of the wind consorts. Today we tend to think of the five-part one-treble scoring as French, and the French violinists at the English court would certainly have been familiar with that layout, for it was embodied in the practice of the *Vingt-quatre violons*. Marin Mersenne praised the group in extravagant terms in his *Harmonie universelle* (Paris, 1636–7):

And those who have heard the Twenty-four Violins of the King avow that they have never heard anything more ravishing or more powerful. Thus it comes that this instrument is the most proper of all for playing for dancing as is experienced in the ballet and everywhere else. Now the beauties and graces that are practised on it are so great in number that it can be preferred to all the other instruments, since the strokes of the bow are so delightful sometimes that one has a great discontent to hear the end, particularly when they are mixed with ornamentation of the left hand which force the listeners to confess the violin to be king of instruments.[39]

[37] Ashbee, *RECM*, iii. 50, 51, 66, 143.
[38] Ibid. 55, 142.
[39] Marin Mersenne, *Harmonie Universelle, the Books on Instruments*, trans. R. E. Chapman (The Hague, 1957), 235.

He went on to give some details of its layout: concerts 'can be made of 500 different violins', though 'twenty-four are enough, in which are six trebles, six bass, four contratenors, four altos, and four of a fifth part'; they were played by violins, three groups of violas 'of different sizes, even though they are [tuned] in unison', and bass violins tuned $B\flat'$ F c g.[40]

We can recognize that this is similar to, if not identical with, the practice of the English violin band as revealed by the 1631 document. Nau's plan even has the characteristic French layout for dance music with more players on the essential outer parts than on the less important inner parts. The problem is that we cannot be sure whether any of this was new in England. I have argued in earlier chapters that the five-part one-treble scoring was well established in Elizabethan times, as it was everywhere in late sixteenth-century northern Europe. It only became 'French' as the violin bands of other countries gradually went over to more modern layouts with two violin parts. We can even guess that the English court violin band had used disproportionate numbers on the outer parts ever since it first began to play as an orchestra in James I's reign, for the inner parts of Jacobean masque dances were written by arrangers—like the *parties de remplissage* of French orchestral music.

Indeed, it may be that Nau's only innovation in 1631 was to specify which members of the group should play which part. The legal contracts relating to the town musicians of Paris often take care to insist that the players should not move from part to part, for this would have disrupted the performance of groups that played a composed repertoire from memory; on 23 April 1643, for instance, ten musicians, François Millot and François Lamy, 'dessus de violon', Simon Duchesne and Jerome Joubert, 'haute contre de violon', Louis Bouteville and Henri Mahieu, 'taille de violon', Christophe Hazard, 'quinte de violon', Leonard de Lorge, Jacques Bruslard, and Jean Dubois, 'basse de violon', agreed among other things that 'no one may change his part without the consent of the majority, on pain of paying four *livres*'.[41] It seems, therefore, that the presence of a number of French violinists at the Caroline court is not necessarily evidence of direct French influence on English orchestral practice. Rather, it may be a sign that the two court orchestras shared a common practice; or it may just be a reflection of the fact that Henrietta Maria's presence at the English court brought a large number of Frenchmen to Whitehall.[42] Certainly, it seems that the group was not dependent on France for its repertoire, as was, for instance, the French violin band that served at the Swedish court from 1647 until Queen

[40] Ibid. 238, 244.

[41] Jurgens, *Documents du minutier central*, ii. 403–4.

[42] For Henrietta Maria's household, see Spink, 'The Musicians of Queen Henrietta-Maria', 177–82, and Ashbee, *RECM*, iii. 244–52.

Christina's abdication in 1654, or the one that was at the Hesse court at Kassel in the 1650s and 1660s.[43]

We know surprisingly little about the repertoire of Charles I's violin band. For one thing, we have no Caroline source of masque dance music akin to the Jacobean *GB-Lbl*, Add. MS 10444 (see Ch. 8). But we know a great deal about the production of James Shirley's *The Triumph of Peace*, first performed by the combined Inns of Court on 3 February 1633/4, for the papers of the lawyer and politician Bulstrode Whitelocke relating to the musical aspects of the production have survived in the Library of Longleat House.[44] Among them is a list of 'The names of the Kinges Musitions of the Violins' who took part; it is the same as the 1631 list, except that Simon Hopper's name has been added. Hopper was not a member of the main royal household at the time, but seems to have been a servant of the young Prince Charles (the future Charles II), for in 1636 he wrote dances for the prince to perform in *The King and Queen's Entertainment at Richmond* (see Ch. 11), and in November 1638 he was given £30 a year 'to attend the Prince his highness and the Duke of York and to play on the music to them at the times of their practising to dance'.[45] Hopper was apparently brought into the violin band on this occasion as a substitute for John Woodington. As we have seen, Woodington had a second court post as a member of the Lutes and Voices, and the Whitelocke documents show that he actually took part in the masque as a member of 'the symphony', a separate group made up largely of lutenists from the Lutes and Voices that appeared on stage accompanying the singers. So the violin band that played in *The Triumph of Peace* was virtually the same as the one in the 1631 list, and there is every reason to think that it was still organized to play five-part music laid out for one violin, three violas, and bass.

This needs to be borne in mind when the dance music for *The Triumph of Peace* is considered. Whitelocke wrote in his *Memorials of the English Affairs* (London, 1682) that he 'made choice of Mr. Simon Ivy, an honest and able musician, of excellent skill in his art, and of Mr. Laws, to compose the airs, lessons, and songs for the mask, and to be master of all the music under me'.[46] William Lawes contributed most of the vocal music, for settings by him, complete or incomplete, survive for six of the

---

[43] See Mráček, *Seventeenth-Century Instrumental Dance Music*; J. Écorcheville (ed.), *Vingt suites d'orchestre du XVIIᵉ siècle français; publiées d'après un manuscrit de la Bibliothèque de Cassel* (Paris, 1906; repr. 1970).

[44] Lefkowitz, 'The Longleat Papers'; Sabol, 'New Documents on Shirley's Masque'.

[45] W. Bang and R. Brotanek (eds.), *The King and Queenes Entertainement at Richmond* (Materialen zur Kunde des älteren englischen Dramas, 2; Louvain and Leipzig, 1903; repr. 1965); *GB-Lpro*, SO3/12, printed in Ashbee, *RECM*, iii. 100.

[46] B. Whitelocke, *Memorials of the English Affairs* (London, 1682; new edn., Oxford, 1853), 54.

nine songs called for in Shirley's text.[47] Simon Ives probably wrote the remaining songs, and Sebastian La Pierre and Stephen Nau were paid £100 each for 'Composinge the tunes and settinge the figures for the graund Masque and Anti-Masques and for their services performed in their attendance on the graund Masquers in their practise and in their directions to the Anti-Masquers'; Davis Mell was paid £20 for 'making some of the tunes in the antimasques' as well as playing 'the trible violi(n)' for the rehearsals of the masquers.[48] One or two of the pieces in a sequence of twenty-five four-part dances composed and/or arranged by Ives in *GB-Lbl*, Add. MSS 18940–4 have titles that sound as if they come from *The Triumph of Peace*. 'The Fancy', no. 22, may be the music for the first antimasque, of Fancy, Opinion, Confidence, Novelty, Admiration, Jollity, and Laughter; more tenuously 'The Virgin', no. 23, may perhaps have accompanied the next antimasque, of an inn-keeper, his wife, and servants, a 'maquerelle' (a bawd, pimp, or procuress), two wenches, and two 'wanton Gamesters'. But if these pieces were used in the masque, it can hardly have been in the Add. MSS 18940–4 versions, which are four-part with two treble parts, not five-part with one treble. Indeed, Ives's set may have been assembled and arranged for the London waits (see Ch. 11)

At first sight the surviving dance music by contemporary members of the violin band is not a promising source of evidence for the practice of the group, for nearly all of it survives only in the two-part repertoire, and the sources do not seem to have court connections. The largest is *GB-Ob*, MS Mus. Sch. D. 220, a manuscript described on its 'title-page' as:

PAVANES / GALLIARDES / AYRES / ALMAINS / CORANTO'S / SARABANDS / MORISCA'S / MASKES, & / CONTRY-DANCES / Composed occasionally by Excellent moderne / Musick-Masters: And now Methodically / digested into theyre proper & distinct Keys / For the Bass & Treble Violls

Dated 1654 on the next page, this 'BASSUS' part-book—the companion treble book is lost—is a comprehensive collection of over 500 items from the mid-century dance repertoire organized and numbered by key. Robert Thompson has recently suggested that it may have been copied by a scribe working for the London publisher John Playford, perhaps for a customer who wanted a more extensive collection of two-part music than was available in existing or projected publications (Fig. 10.1).[49]

---

[47] Lefkowitz, *Trois masques*, 61–109; see also P. Walls, 'New Light on Songs by William Lawes and John Wilson', *ML* 57 (1976), 55–64.

[48] Orbison and Hill, 'The Middle Temple Documents', 58; Lefkowitz, 'The Longleat Papers', 59.

[49] R. P. Thompson, 'English Music Manuscripts and the Fine Paper Trade, 1648–1688', Ph.D. thesis (London, 1988), 221–5.

Gui: Vauchan Sculp.

10.1. Engraving by William Vaughan, apparently first used on the title-page of John Playford, *Musick's Hand-Maide* (London, 1663). It seems to show a performance of two-part dance music with violin and virginals

TABLE 10.1. *Music by Caroline court violinists in* GB-Ob, *MS Mus. Sch. D. 220*

Page	Key	No.	Title
11	G	32	A Toye / By Mr David Mell
16	G	47	A Contrydance / A Contry-dance by M^r: Ambrose Beeland
19	G	54	A Toye by A: B: / A Toye by Mr Ambrose Beeland
	G	55	Contry Dance by A: Beeland
	G	56	The Comon Hunt by A: B:
20	G	57	English / English humor By Theophilus Lupo
	G	58	French / French Humour
	G	59	Spanish / Spanish Humour:
	G	60	Irish / Irish humor
	G	61	Scotish / The End of the Suite of Languages
24	G	77	Contry Dance / A Toy A: B:
30	A	3	Almain M^r: Mell / Almaine David Mell:
30–1	A	4	Saraban / saraban M^r: David Mell.
37	A	26	Alman / M^r: Beeland
	A	27	Saraban / M^r: Beeland:
39	A	34	Ayre / M^r: Sebastian [La Pierre]
45	B♭	5	Almaine A: B:
	B♭	6	A Toye / A Toye by Am: Beeland
	B♭	7	Corant / Corant
	B♭	8	Seribran A: B / Almaine Toy Corant & seribran by Amb: Beeland
49	B♭	22	Almain / The: Lupo
	B♭	23	Corant / Theo: Lupo:
	B♭	24	Seribran / Almain Corant & Seribran by The: Lupo:
53	B♭	36	An Ayre / Theo: Lupoe Ayre
	B♭	37	Corant / Corant The: Lupo:
	B♭	38	Seribran / Arye Corant seribran By Mr: Theoph: Lupo:
57	B♭	51	An Almain by M^r: David Mell: / An Almaine by Da: Mell:
	B♭	52	Seribran D: M:
	B♭	53	Vinatorians / The: Lupoe
88	C	89	Bow bells rung backward / Ambrose Beeland
	C	90	Corant / Mr Beeland
107	D	26	Corant / Corant M^r: Lupo
	D	27	Saraban M^r: Lupo:
117	D	64	Ayre / Mr Lupoe
	D	65	Saraban / Mr Lupoe
	D	66	Lavalta / Mounsieur Noe.
143	E	16	An humour / Theoph: Lupoe
144	E	17	Almaine/Mr Lupoe
	E	18	Corant / Corant M^r: Lupoe
	E	19	Saraban / Saraban T: Lupoe
	E	20	Country dance: / 4 Ayres by M^r: Theoph: Lupoe.
169	F	62	Corant by Monsieur Sebastian

The manuscript includes over forty pieces by four members of the Caroline violin band, Theophilus Lupo, Ambrose Beeland, Davis Mell, and Stephen Nau, as well as two pieces by 'Mounsieur Sebastian', the dancing-master Sebastian La Pierre (see Table 10.1). La Pierre collaborated with Nau—and, presumably, with the violin band—on at least one other occasion in the 1630s: by a warrant dated 4 April 1637 they were paid £54 'for themselves & twelve dancers' for the Hampton Court performances of William Cartwright's play *The Royal Slave*, given on 12 January 1636/7; the production had been first seen on 30 August and 2 September 1636, during the court's visit to Oxford.[50] The warrant refers to 'Dancers and composers of Musique' in the plural, so it is likely that La Pierre was responsible for some of the dance tunes as well as the choreography.

A similar repertoire is found in several of the seventeenth-century manuscripts from the collection of the Filmer family of East Sutton in Kent, now at Yale University.[51] Filmer MS 1, a late-Elizabethan set of six part-books (but with the sixth part missing), has, among its later additions, a fragmentary D minor suite on fos. 115^v–16^r entitled '4 pt Mr Nor'; there is the cantus part of a pavan (with four bars of an altus part), an alman, and a corant; a fourth movement is announced—'the saraband follows'—but there is no music for it. Filmer MS 3 consists of three part-books, 'Treble' (Tr), 'Meane or second Treble' (M), and bass (Bs), and seems to have been compiled by the Filmer household musician Francis Block over a long period in the middle of the seventeenth century: a lyra viol setting of Bulstrode Whitelocke's famous corant, fos. 20^v–21^r in the bass book, is dated 9 May 1639, while an untitled two-part piece near the end, Tr, fo. 43^r INV, Bs, fo. 42^r INV, turns out to be a number from John Banister's suite of incidental music for Dryden's play *The Indian Queen*, first performed on 25 January 1663/4.[52] The pieces ascribed to Caroline court violinists are listed in Table 10.2; they are all in the inverted sections of the part-books.

The 'duos' for two trebles by 'Lupo' have been printed in the modern edition of Thomas Lupo's consort music as they are found in the manuscript, though these alman-like pieces are more likely to be by his son Theophilus, given the date of the source and the style of the music, and the part-writing shows that they have at least one lower part missing

[50] *GB-Lpro*, LC5/134, 165, printed in Bentley, *The Jacobean and Caroline Stage*, iii. 139; Ashbee, *RECM*, v. 13.

[51] See R. Ford, 'The Filmer Manuscripts, a Handlist', *Notes*, 34 (1978), 814–25.

[52] The second piece listed under *The Indian Queen* in the 'Catalogue of Instrumental Music in Restoration Plays, 1665–1713' in C. A. Price, *Music in the Restoration Theatre* (Ann Arbor, Mich., 1979), 181; for the date of the play, see W. B. Van Lennep (ed.), *The London Stage 1660–1800*, i: *1660–1700* (Carbondale, Ill., 1965), 74.

TABLE 10.2. *Music by Caroline court violinists in* US-NH, *Filmer MS 3*

Tr fo.	M fo.	Bs fo.	Title	Key
85^v		85^v	Confess [?Nicholas Confais] [corant]	d
85^r		85^r	M^r: Beeland [corant]	F
75^r	60^v	75^r	Almane. [Theophilus] Lupo	B♭
75^r	60^v	75^r	Corant. [Theophilus Lupo]	B♭
75^r	60^v	75^r	Saraband [Theophilus Lupo]	B♭
73^r		73^v	A duo by Lupo two trebbles	d
72^v		73^r	A duo Lupo two trebbles Lupo	g
72^r	63^r	72^r	Alman Lupo	D
72^r	63^r	72^r	Corant Lupo	D
72^r–71^v	63^r–62^v	72^r	Saraband [?Lupo]	D
71^v		71^v	M^r: Lupo [corant]	F
66^v		66^v	M^r: Noe [corant]	d

Tr = treble part-book M = mean part-book Bs = bass part-book all titles except the first taken from Bs

(Ex. 10.1).[53] Most of the other 'Lupo' pieces in Filmer MS 3, however, seem to have a part too many, for the inner parts, like most of the rest of the contents of the 'meane' part-book, are much less competently written than the outer parts and were probably added later, perhaps by Block himself. In the case of the B♭ suite, Theophilus Lupo's authorship is not in doubt, for the bass parts concord with those in MS Mus. Sch. D. 220, B♭ section nos. 22–4, which are ascribed specifically to him. Filmer MS 4 is a similar set of three part-books with music drawn from an even wider period—it has items by Cormack McDermott (d. 1618) as well as the same Banister piece from *The Indian Queen*—but it does not contain any music ascribed to members of the Caroline violin band.[54]

In Chapter 8 I argued that *GB-Lbl*, Add. MS 10444 is a two-part source not because it (or the masque music it contains) is incomplete, but because it preserves dances in the form that they were originally written—that is, before Thomas Lupo or one of the other members of the court violin band supplied them with inner parts. Much the same thing can, I believe, be said of the mid-century two-part repertoire. It is not incomplete in the sense that material essential to the function and

---

[53] *The Two- and Three-Part Consort Music*, ed. Charteris, nos. 1 and 2; see my review in *Chelys*, 17 (1988), 43–7.

[54] For McDermott's music, see Holman, 'The Harp in Stuart England', 190–1; the *Indian Queen* piece is on fo. 55^r of the treble book, fo. 53^v of the tenor book; sources not mentioned in Price, *Music in the Restoration Theatre*, 181 are *Apollo's Banquet* (London, *c*.1669), no. 159, and *GB-En*, MS 5777, fo. 27^v.

Ex. 10.1. Thomas? Lupo, 'Duo', bb. 1–9 (from Lupo, *Two- and Three-Part Consort Music*, ed. Charteris, no. 1), with a reconstructed bass part

nature of the music is missing, for dance music would have been composed at the time starting with the outer parts, which normally contained the essence of the musical argument. Additional parts would then be added to suit the ensemble at hand, sometimes by the composer, sometimes by other musicians. This explains why popular items in the two-part repertoire sometimes survive in settings with one or more extra but different parts. A case in point is John Jenkins's 'Lady Katherine Audley's Bells'. 'Of all his conceipts', wrote Roger North, none flew about with his name so universally as the small peice called his Bells. In those days the country fidlers were not so well foddered from London, as since, and a master that made new tunes for them, was a benefactor . . .

He added in another passage that 'the Bells of Mr Jenkins' was 'the first polite piece' that the waits of Thetford in Norfolk 'learnt to performe tollerably'.[55] The essential 'Lady Katherine Audley's Bells' is the version in the largest printed source of the two-part repertoire, John Playford's *Courtly Masquing Ayres* (London, 1662), no. 102, and a number of manuscript sources, including MS Mus. Sch. D. 220, D section, nos. 14–21, and Filmer MS 3, Tr and Bs, fos. 53^r–52^r INV. But there are also settings for two trebles and bass, and for 'lyra consort' (violin or treble viol, lyra viol, bass viol, and harpsichord), which were evidently made by adding an extra line—a second treble and a tenor-range lyra viol part respectively—to the existing treble and bass (Ex. 10.2).[56]

Another interesting case concerns the music by Davis Mell in *Courtly Masquing Ayres*: there are fifty-four dances seemingly grouped into twelve suites of three, four, or five movements. Many of them are also in *GB-Och*, Mus. MS 433 (a collection that can be shown to be autograph by reference to specimens of Mell's signature), but there they are without basses, and the suites are prefaced by preludes that seem to be intended specifically for unaccompanied violin: bass notes are often sketched in with chords or arpeggiated passage-work.[57] To complicate matters, some of these supposedly one-part or two-part dances were copied by Edward Lowe (Oxford professor of music 1662–82) into his continuo book *GB-Ob*, MS Mus. Sch. E. 451, pp. 326–319 INV with the comment: 'Thes 10 are Mr Davice Mell's: w(hi)ch are for 4 parts, all but the 4th w(hi)ch had noe inner parts sent. The Other two parts are in the Countertenor & Tenor of my Parchment cover Bookes.' Four of Lowe's 'Parchment cover Bookes' survive as *GB-Ob*, MSS Mus. Sch. D. 233–6, but the 'Countertenor & Tenor' parts are lost, and with them the four-part versions of Mell's dances.

We can never know what proportion of the two-part repertoire once existed with inner parts of this type, but it seems that our lack of Caroline sources of violin band music in four- or five-part settings is just an accident of survival. Certainly, sources of this sort do exist on the Continent, and two of them, *S-Uu*, IMhs 409 and *D-Kl*, mus. fol. 61,

---

[55] M. Chan and J. C. Kassler (eds.), *Roger North's The Musicall Grammarian 1728* (Cambridge, 1990), 257; Wilson, *Roger North on Music*, 272.

[56] For the sources, see G. Dodd (ed.), *The Viola da Gamba Society of Great Britain Thematic Index of Music for Viols* (London, 1980–9), 'John Jenkins'.

[57] For Mell's signature, see, for instance, Library of Longleat House, Whitelocke Papers, parcel II, item 9 (6), and *GB-Lpro*, SP29/36, no. 39; the sources of his music are collated in Dodd, *Index of Music for Viols*, 'Davis Mell'.

Ex. 10.2. John Jenkins, 'Lady Katherine Audley's Bells', bb. 1–9, with variant inner parts from *GB-Ob*, MS Mus. Sch. C. 88, no. 16, and *US-NYp*, Drexel MS 3849, p. 105

(harpsichord part in Mus. Sch. C. 88 omitted)

TABLE 10.3. *Music possibly by Stephen Nau in* S-Uu, *IMhs 409*

No.	Fo.	Title	Author	No. of parts	Key
40	20ᵛ	Allemanda	Mons: Noe:	4	B♭
41	20ᵛ	Galliard	Mons: / Nau ae.	5	d
40	22ᵛ	Allamanda	Mons: Noë	4	B♭
71	35ᵛ	Allamanda	Mons: Noa.	4	C
119	53ᵛ	Allamanda	de Mons: Noë	5	F
120	53ᵛ	Galliarde	de Mons: Noë	5	F
121	54ᵛ	1. Courante	[?Nau]	5	F
122	55ʳ	2. Courant.	[?Nau]	5	F
123	54ᵛ	3. Courant.	[?Nau]	5	F
124	54ᵛ	4. Courant.	[?Nau]	5	F
125	54ᵛ	Sarabanda	[?Nau]	5	F
140	62ᵛ	Pavan	de / Mons Nau	5	d
141	62ᵛ	Allamanda	[?Nau]	5	d
142	62ᵛ	Allamanda	[?Nau]	5	d

drawn from the repertoire of the French violin bands in Stockholm and Kassel, contain pieces attributed to members of the English violin band. IMhs 409, a tablature score largely in the hand of Gustav Düben, contains a number of pieces attributed, it seems, to Stephen Nau (see Table 10.3). In his edition of the collection, Jaroslav Mráček connects 'Noe' with Stephen Nau, but suggests that 'Nau ae' should be 'Naudé', which he tentatively identifies with Gabriel Naudé, the French bibliographer who is known to have danced in court ballets at the Swedish court in 1653.[58] However, Naudé is not known to have been a musician, let alone a composer, and the distinctive style of the pieces suggests that they are the work of a single individual, a composer of skill and imagination. The remarkable D minor pavan, no. 140, evokes the elaborate pavans of the Anglo-German repertoire with its epic scale—strains of 15, 14 and 16½ breve bars—its passages of dense counterpoint, and its brief foray into triple time in the second strain (Ex. 10.3). Also, the composer had an interest in unusual cross-rhythms, found equally in the piece Mráček assigned to Naudé, the D minor galliard no. 41, which uses three levels of triple time—in crotchets, minims, and semibreves—within a few bars, and in the alman and galliard nos. 119 and 120, in which rapid modulations combine with cross-rhythms to produce an unusually unsettling effect (Ex. 10.4).

[58] Mráček, *Seventeenth-Century Instrumental Dance Music*, 16*–18*.

Ex. 10.3. Stephen Nau, Pavan *a 5*, bb. 16–23 (from Mráček (ed.), *Seventeenth-Century Instrumental Dance Music*, no. 140)

There is little doubt that all these pieces are the work of Stephen Nau, despite the lack of concordances for them in English sources. He is the only Nau who is known to have been a composer, and no. 140 is entitled 'Pavan' in the source, which is a sign that it came from an English source. German composers and copyists at the time normally used the forms 'Paduan' or 'Paduana'—as, for example, in IMhs 409, nos. 187 and 206. A parallel case is nos. 204 and 205, entitled 'Pavin', another English form of the word. Mráček ascribed them to Pierre Verdier on the basis of a

Ex. 10.4. Stephen Nau, Galliard *a5*, bb. 14–27 (from Mráček (ed.), *Seventeenth-Century Instrumental Dance Music*, no. 120)

concordance in *S-Uu*, IMhs 9:8, but they are actually by Benjamin Rogers: they appear in *S-Uu*, IMhs 5:13a, the autograph set of parts signed 'Ben. Rogers / Windsor mai 26 / 1651' which Bulstrode Whitelocke apparently commissioned from Rogers, and took to Sweden on his diplomatic mission from the Commonwealth government to Queen

Ex. 10.4. *Continued*

Christina in 1653.[59] It is possible that Whitelocke was also responsible for taking the Nau pieces to Sweden, but a more obvious connection in their case is Nicholas Picart, who served in Queen Christina's violin band after his period in England; there is a fine five-part suite of branles by him in IMhs 409, nos. 170–7.

It is not so easy to see how a 'Ballet à5. Sr Nau' found its way to Kassel, and into *D-Kl*, mus. fol. 61, D5. Jules Écorcheville admitted that the composer had eluded him when he edited the piece in 1906; in despair, he mentioned four seventeenth-century Naus, none of whom seemed to be a musician.[60] But Jaroslav Mráček's work on IMhs 409 has shown that there are considerable connections between the repertoires of the Stockholm and Kassel violin bands, so it is possible that the piece came from England via Sweden, and is the work of Stephen Nau. The ballet, its title suggests, is probably dance music for the theatre rather than the ballroom: it consists of six movements in F major and D minor in alman or saraband rhythms, and has the sequence of strains (D = duple-time, T = triple-time): DD, DD, TD, DD, DD, TT. In general, it is simpler in style than the Nau pieces in IMhs 409, though there are enough similarities, cross rhythms included, to confirm that it is a work of the same composer. It was perhaps written for some English court masque or play of the 1630s.

[59] Shute, 'Anthony à Wood and his Manuscript', i. 257; A. Ashbee, 'A Not Unapt Scholar: Bulstrode Whitelocke (1605–1675)', *Chelys*, 11 (1982), 29; P. Holman, 'Thomas Baltzar (?1631–1663), the "Incomperable Lubicer on the Violin"', *Chelys*, 13 (1984), 7–8.

[60] Écorcheville, *Vingt suites*, i. 9.

Stephen Nau was a composer of importance whose contribution to the musical life of Charles I's court ought to be better recognized. He is certainly the earliest composer connected with the English violin band whose surviving dance music fully transcends its mundane function, and a work such as his D minor pavan deserves to be taken up by Baroque string groups today. We can only hope that more of his music will turn up as more of the contemporary sources of violin band music are investigated.

11

'The Fancy-Musick'

The Violin and Court Chamber Music 1625–1663

FOUR of England's leading composers, Orlando Gibbons, John Coprario, Thomas Lupo, and Alfonso Ferrabosco II, died between June 1625 and March 1627/8. Their premature loss—they were all in their forties or fifties—had important consequences for English music. Working in the household of the Prince of Wales, the future Charles I, they had invented or developed most of the genres and scorings of Jacobean consort music, including the lyra viol duet and trio, the air for two bass viols and organ, the madrigal-like fantasia for viol consort and organ, the fantasia with 'great double bass', and the fantasia suite for one or two violins, bass viol, and organ. But the four had no immediate successors at court, and the idioms that are associated with them were mostly taken up by composers outside the court.

This is not to say, however, that the composition of consort music ceased at court with the deaths of the four composers. Rather, the next generation abandoned the fantasia and the fantasia suite in favour of lighter and less demanding genres based on dance music. Three sources preserve a sample of the new repertoire: *GB-Och*, Mus. MSS 367–70 and 379–81, part-books from the library of John Browne (1608–91), Northamptonshire landowner and Clerk of the Parliaments 1638–49 and 1660–91, and *GB-Lbl*, Add. MS 36993, a tablature-book of single-line bass or continuo parts (one is labelled 'the continewed base') of consort music.[1] Most of the composers represented worked at court in some capacity. Coprario, Ferrabosco, Robert Johnson, and the court harper Cormack McDermott (d. 1618) represent the Jacobean generation; Nicholas Lanier, William Lawes, Thomas Ford, and Maurice Webster were members of the Caroline Lutes and Voices; Thomas Holmes and John Cobb worked in the Chapel Royal from 1633 and 1638; and William Drew and Richard Mico are known to have worked in Henrietta

---

[1] For Browne, see Ashbee, 'Instrumental Music from the Library of John Browne (1608–1691), Clerk of the Parliaments', *ML* 58 (1977), 43–59; N. Fortune, 'Music Manuscripts of John Browne (1608–91), and from Stanford Hall, Leicestershire', in I. Bent (ed.), *Source Materials and the Interpretation of Music: A Memorial Volume to Thurston Dart* (London, 1981), 155–68.

Maria's Catholic chapel from 1628 and 1629.[2] Of the four remaining composers, two, Simon Ives and William Cranford, did not have court posts (though a 'Simon Ive' became an extraordinary Groom of the Chamber on 27 April 1630), but were Londoners—members of St Paul's choir in the 1630s.[3] The early career of the third, John Jenkins, the largest contributor to MSS 367–70, is something of a mystery, but he was certainly in London for the production of the masque *The Triumph of Peace* in February 1633/4, and it is likely that he spent much of his youth in the capital.

The fourth, Charles Coleman, the largest contributor to MSS 379–81, is of particular interest in the present context. He was evidently a court musician, for Anthony à Wood described him as 'one of the private music to K. Charles I'; he was listed as a member of 'The Consorte' in a document relating to livery issued for James I's funeral (see Ch. 10); and he appears in lists of the Lutes and Voices in subsidy documents of 1628 and 1641.[4] Yet there is no record of a court appointment for him until the Restoration, and his name does not appear in any payment records. The explanation seems to be that he was a member not of the main royal household, but of the embryonic household formed at Richmond in the 1630s for Prince Charles, the future Charles II. Coleman collaborated with Simon Hopper (a servant of Prince Charles; see Ch. 10) in *The King and Queen's Entertainment at Richmond*, performed by the young prince and members of his household for his parents on 12 September 1636; Theobald Peirce, 'keeper of his Ma(jes)t(ies)s standing wardrobe at Richmond', was paid £17. 4s. in 1636 for 'making readie the Lodgings against the Prince his Masque and for ayring, brushing and making cleane such stuffe as was used there in his Charge'.[5] According to the text the music was 'excellently compos'd by Master Charles Coleman', and his setting of the dialogue 'Did not you once, Lucinda, vow' was printed by John Playford in 1652; it was sung by Lucinda and a shepherd (Coleman himself?), who accompanied on a theorbo.[6]

Charles Coleman is also connected with Richmond and Prince Charles's household by a passage in Lucy Hutchinson's biography of her husband, Colonel John Hutchinson. In 1636 Hutchinson was studying with Coleman and lodging with him at Richmond 'where the Prince's court was':

---

[2] For Henrietta Maria's chapel, see J. Bennett and P. Willetts, 'Richard Mico', *Chelys*, 7 (1977), 34–40; Ashbee, *RECM*, iii. 244–52; v. 3–19.

[3] Ashbee, *RECM*, iii. 51.

[4] Shute, 'Anthony à Wood and his Manuscript', i. 100; Ashbee, *RECM*, iii. 3, 33, 35, 38, 109.

[5] Ashbee, *RECM*, iii. 152.

[6] Bang and Brotanek, *The King and Queenes Entertainement*; I. Spink (ed.), *English Songs 1625–1660* (MB 33; London, 1971), no. 74.

The man [Coleman] being a skilful composer in music, the rest of the King's musicians often met at his house to practise new airs and prepare them for the king; and divers of the gentlemen and ladies that were affected with music, came hither to hear; others that were not, took that pretence to entertain themselves with the company.[7]

Coleman's position as a servant of Prince Charles, did not, it seems, prevent him from associating with members of the main royal music, or from performing with them—which explains why Anthony à Wood thought he was one of the Lutes and Voices, and why he is listed with them in subsidy records. The 'new airs' may, of course, have been songs or concerted vocal music, but it is perhaps more likely that they were instrumental airs of the sort that are found in MSS 367–70 and 379–81.

A novel aspect of this repertoire is its scoring. MSS 379–81 uses the 'trio sonata' layout of two equal soprano parts and bass. A tenor part is added in most of the MSS 367–70 pieces, but it acts mainly as a filler, and can easily be omitted; indeed, some of the pieces in both sources circulated in three- as well as four-part versions. The SS scoring was not new in England: it is found in some Elizabethan five- and six-part consort music (see Ch. 7), on occasion in three- and four-part Jacobean fantasias, and in Coprario's fantasia suites. But Coleman and his court colleagues were the first English composers to write dance music in the SSB or SSTB layouts, and their models apparently came not from English consort music (or from the Italian trio sonata), but from the repertoire of a small north German court, as represented by Thomas Simpson's last anthology of consort music, *Taffel-Consort* (Hamburg, 1621).[8] In 1621 Simpson was working in Bückeburg near Hanover, at the Schaumburg-Lippe court of Count Ernst III. *Taffel-Consort* can be connected with Bückeburg by virtue of the fact that most of its composers, including Nicolaus Bleyer, Christoph (Christian) Engelmann, Johann Grabbe, Johann Grosche (Krosch), Christoph Töpfer, and Maurice Webster, were working there at the time.[9] Indeed, it was probably drawn from the repertoire of a particular ensemble at Bückeburg, for all the pieces, regardless of origin or genre, use the same scoring: SSTB with a figured continuo part.

Whether or not this is so, *Taffel-Consort* is certainly one of the first collections either side of the Alps to use the 'string quartet' scoring. The label is not as anachronistic as it sounds, for the collection seems to have been intended for violins, though particular instruments are not specified.

[7] J. Hutchinson (ed.), *Memoirs of the Life of Colonel Hutchinson... Written by his Widow Lucy* (London, 1905), 55–6.

[8] Modern edn. by B. Thomas (London, 1988).

[9] F. Greissmann, 'Die Musiker am Hofe des Fürsten Ernst', unpublished paper deposited at the Staatsarchiv, Bückeburg, an item kindly drawn to my attention by Christopher Wool.

Ex. 11.1. John Dowland, arr. Thomas Simpson, 'Mistresse Nichols Almand', *Taffel-Consort* (Hamburg, 1621), no. 8

The earlier Anglo-German repertoire tends to consist of pavans and galliards, written in a neutral style equally suitable for sets of viols and violins. In *Taffel-Consort* lighter dances such as almans, corants, and voltas are in the majority, and they tend to have lively, angular writing that suits the violin better than the viol. Of course, this sort of thing is also suitable for wind instruments, but it is significant that *Taffel-Consort* contains an unusual number of pieces in D major, A major, and even E

Ex. 11.1. *Continued*

major—keys highly suitable for the open strings of the violin, but outside the traditional hexachord system.

Taffel-Consort also includes a number of settings, made presumably by Simpson himself, of English pieces. Some, such as nos. 10 and 19, Dowland's 'Were every thought an eye' and 'Lady, if you so spight me', are versions of songs. But others, such as no. 8, Dowland's 'Mistresse Nichols Almand', or no. 16, an alman by Alfonso Ferrabosco II, are updated five-part consort pieces (Ex. 11.1).[10] An odd feature of them is that the original tune is confined to the first soprano; the second soprano adds a commentary above and below it. Most of the German pieces, including those by Simpson himself, use the SSTB layout in a more sophisticated way, with the tune divided between the upper parts in a genuine dialogue. So the English arrangements in *Taffel-Consort* probably represent an early stage in the development of the medium. Bückeburg may have been a centre for experiments of this sort, for Konrad Hagius's *Newe künstliche musicalische Intraden* (Nuremberg, 1616) contains some English pieces in his own four- and five-part arrangements; Hagius was *Kapellmeister* at Bückeburg from 1609 to 1611, and retained connections with the court until his death in 1616.[11]

Taffel-Consort effectively marks the end of the Anglo-German consort repertoire. By 1621 the Thirty Year's War was taking its toll on musical

---

[10] Dowland, *Lachrimae*, no. 20; Dodd, *Thematic Index of Music for Viols*, 'Alfonso Ferrabosco', alman no. 10.

[11] No complete copy of the collection exists today, but the altus, tenor, bassus, and 'quinta et sexta vox' parts are respectively in *PL-Kj*, *F-Pn*, *GB-Lbl*, and *D-LEm*.

life in Germany, and when Count Ernst died in the next year his musicians were dispersed, and Bückeburg ceased to be an important musical centre. Simpson went from Bückeburg to Copenhagen: he held a post at the Danish court between 7 May 1622 and 4 March 1625. Nothing is known for sure of him after then, though he was dead by 20 June 1628, when the city bailiff there was asked to collect a debt from the heirs of the 'late violist'.[12] It is often said that he returned to England in the 1620s, and an apparently autograph part-book of untitled four-part 'songes', Kent Archives Office, Maidstone, MS U951/Z.23, has been cited as evidence that the composer was living there in 1630, for it is said to date from that year, and is dedicated to Sir Norton Knatchbull (1569–1636) of Mersham in Kent.[13] But there is no date on the volume itself, and Simpson calls it the 'first frutes of my unskillfull Laboures' in the dedication, which suggests that it was composed and copied before he left England as a young man. Indeed, if his 'heirs' were in Copenhagen, then he may have died in Denmark.

A more promising connection between *Taffel-Consort* and Charles Coleman and his circle is the figure of Maurice Webster, for, though he came from a expatriate family and may have been born in Germany, Webster spent more than a decade at the English court. Maurice's father George, a Bückeburg lutenist, may be the man who was a member of Robert Browne's company of English actors and musicians at Kassel in 1596, and who visited Frankfurt as the leader of the Kassel company several times between 1600 and 1603; Maurice's unusual first name is perhaps an indication that he was born in Kassel, and was named after the Landgrave Moritz of Hessen-Kassel. If so, then Maurice was perhaps related to the playwright John Webster, for E. K. Chambers has connected him with the John Webster who was with George Webster at Kassel in 1596.[14] Maurice Webster probably made the journey from Germany to England shortly after Count Ernst's death in 1622, for by letters patent dated 9 June 1623 backdated to Lady Day he succeeded Philip Rosseter as a royal lutenist; he served until his death in the winter of 1635–6, when he was succeeded by the viol-player Dietrich Stoeffken.[15]

Webster's music neatly illustrates the connection between the two

---

[12] A. Hammerich, *Musiken ved Christian den Fjerdes Hof* (Copenhagen, 1892), 70; Bergsagel (ed.), *Music for Instrumental Ensemble*, p. xi.

[13] A. Ashbee, 'Thomas Simpson', *Grove 6*; the 1630 date is given without a source in F. Hull, *Guide to the East Kent County Archives Office*, first supplement (Maidstone, 1971), 128. The volume appears to be the instrumental bass to a collection of part-songs, though the last piece, 'S(i)r Norton Knatchbull's paven', fo. 13ᵛ, is clearly instrumental.

[14] Chambers, *The Elizabethan Stage*, ii. 278–9; iii. 507; Braun, *Britannia Abundans*, 326, tentatively identifies George Webster with the 'Georg. Wesper' who contributed a 'Galliarda Engl.' for lute to G.L. Fuhrmann, *Testudo gallo-germanica* (Nuremberg, 1615), 116–17.

[15] Ashbee, *RECM*, iv. 57, 112; iii. 85, 87, 151.

repertoires. The ten consort pieces attributed to him in English sources, seven of which are in MSS 367–70 and 379–81, are similar in style to the four by him in *Taffel-Consort*, nos. 13, 33, 34, and 42.[16] In both groups the upper parts continually exchange short, often angular motives, swapping places in the texture in the process. In some of the later pieces, notably the three entitled 'An Eccho', MSS 379–81, nos. 33–5, the upper parts often converse in genuine dialogue, so that two- and three-part passages alternate (Ex. 11.2). Music of this sort marks the point at which full-voiced Renaissance dance music finally gives way to the polarized and varied textures of the Baroque.

We know little about how the idiom developed in England, but we can guess that Webster introduced it at court on his arrival in 1623; that his music provided the nucleus of the new repertoire; and that an ensemble was formed to play it within the Lutes and Voices soon after Charles I's accession in 1625. It would presumably have included the two violinists in the Lutes and Voices, Thomas Lupo (replaced by his son Theophilus at Christmas 1627) and John Woodington, as well as some of the court viol-players and lutenists—such as Webster himself and Charles Coleman. They may have enlarged the repertoire at an early stage by reducing existing five-part music to three or four parts, as Simpson had done in *Taffel-Consort*, though they did it simply by leaving out one or two inner parts. Some of the pieces by the older generation in MSS 367–70 and 379–81 are cases in point: MSS 379–81, no. 9 is a three-part version of a popular five-part alman by Ferrabosco, while nos. 40–51, by Cormack McDermott and William Drew, are also in the Jacobean layer of the largely mid-century *US-NH*, Filmer MS 4; the copyists, fortunately, chose to retain different inner parts, so four of the original five parts can be assembled.[17] In Filmer MS 4 figures were added to the bass, presumably in a crude attempt to compensate for the missing inner parts. We can guess that there are also parts missing from some of the other pieces, such as the airs by Coprario and Robert Johnson, MSS 379–81, nos. 20 and 21, for they often have chords left without thirds.[18] On the other hand, the two delightful alman-like pieces by Johnson, 'The Temporiser' and 'The Wittie Wanton', MSS 367–70, nos. 40 and 41, are in the SSTB layout and are evidently complete.[19] They are probably late works, written after Webster's arrival in England.

---

[16] See the list in Dodd, *Thematic Index of Music for Viols*, 'Maurice Webster'.

[17] Dodd, *Thematic Index of Music for Viols*, 'Alfonso Ferrabosco II', alman no. 4; Holman, 'The Harp in Stuart England', 190–1; for the Filmer collection, see Ford, 'The Filmer Manuscripts'.

[18] The piece by Johnson is in P. Holman (ed.), *Music at the Royal Court of London c.1620* (Zeitschrift für Spielmusik, 497; Celle, 1980), no. 4; see A. Ashbee, 'Towards the Chronology and Grouping of some Airs by John Jenkins', *ML* 55 (1974), 35 for an example of a five-part pavan by Jenkins cut down to three parts.

[19] Dart and Coates (eds.), *Jacobean Consort Music*, nos. 31, 32.

Ex. 11.2. Maurice Webster, 'An Eccho', bb. 1–16, *GB-Och*, MSS 379–81, no. 33

The German influence on Caroline dance music was not confined to matters of scoring, for MSS 379–81 and MS 36993 also contain the earliest extended English consort suites. The idea of ordering pieces by key was already established in the English lute, keyboard, and lyra viol repertoires; some Jacobean and Caroline sources, such as the keyboard manuscript *US-NYp*, Drexel MS 5612 (begun *c.*1620) or Lord Herbert of Cherbury's lute manuscript, *GB-Cfm*, Mu. MS 689 (possibly largely *c.*1630), were begun as collections laid out by key.[20] (Lute and lyra viol pieces were presumably grouped by key because the new tunings coming into vogue at the time required players to retune when they changed key.) Coprario, of course, had devised the three-movement fantasia suite in the early 1620s, but the extended consort suite was established first in Germany. In his *Newe ausserlesene Paduanen* (Hamburg, 1609) William Brade added almans or corants to pavan–galliard pairs, and created novel sequences such as canzona–galliard–canzona–galliard; Thomas Simpson's *Opus newer Paduanen* (Hamburg, 1617) opens with an excellent nine-movement sequence of C major pieces, progressing from the serious—pavan–intrada–ricercar–canzona—to the frivolous—corant–corant–volta–corant–alman.[21] Johann Hermann Schein's *Banchetto musicale* (Leipzig, 1617) consists mainly of suites with a standard five-movement pattern of pavan–galliard–corant–alman–tripla.[22]

Add. MS 36993 represents an early stage in the history of the English consort suite. Dances are ordered by key into suites of between four and eight movements, but each is drawn from the work of several composers. The suite in F, fos. 15^v–18^v, for instance, consists of a pavan by Richard Mico, an alman by Ferrabosco, and two by Jenkins. MSS 367–70 and 379–81 are mostly not ordered by key, though there are instances of apparent pairs such as Johnson's G minor 'The Temporiser' and G major 'The Wittie Wanton'. At the end of MSS 379–81, however, there are eleven dances in F by William Drew, nos. 41–51, six in C by Charles Coleman, nos. 52–7, and nine in F by Coleman, nos. 58–66. They are probably the earliest surviving English consort suites by single composers, but they still look as if they were assembled rather than planned. There is no sign of the orderly progression from slow to fast dances that we find in Schein's *Banchetto musicale*: corants sometimes come before almans, and sarabands (appearing here perhaps for the first time in English consort music) sometimes come before corants.

The next stage is represented by William Lawes's Royal Consort. The

---

[20] C. A. Price, 'An Organisational Peculiarity of Lord Herbert of Cherbury's Lute Book', *LSJ* 11 (1969), 5–27; J. Craig-McFeely, 'A Can of Worms: Lord Herbert of Cherbury's Lute Book', *The Lute*, 31 (1991), 20–48.

[21] Brade has been edited by Thomas, Simpson by Mönkemeyer.

[22] Schein, *Newe Ausgabe*, 9.

work has a complex history, not yet fully understood. Its earliest state seems to be preserved only in *GB-Ob*, MSS Mus. Sch. F. 568–9, the two surviving parts of a set that once consisted of '2 Trebles Tenor Bass, and through bass', according to a note on fo. 2^r of MS Mus. Sch. F. 568. It consists of over ninety pieces in fifteen suites ranging from three to ten movements, some of which are no more orderly than the Drew and Coleman works in MSS 379–81. Some were evidently discarded at an early stage, and do not appear in the other main source of the early version, *GB-Ob*, MS Mus. Sch. E. 431–6, a set of part-books that seems to have been copied by William Ellis for his Commonwealth music meetings in Oxford.[23] The Royal Consort was eventually refined so that it consisted of less than seventy pieces in ten suites of six or seven movements, laid out in an orderly progression from the most serious—pavans and fantasias—to the lightest—sarabands and other fast triple-time pieces. At the same time the scoring was changed from SSTB and continuo to '2 Violins 2 Bass Violls and 2 theorboes', to quote a heading in the autograph score, *GB-Ob*, MS Mus. Sch. B. 2, p. 50. The Oxford musician Edward Lowe, a probable associate of Lawes (they both came from Salisbury) explained why the change was made in a note on fo. 1^v of *GB-Ob*, MS Mus. Sch. D. 236, from the incomplete set of part-books Mus. Sch. D. 233–6, originally acquired by Lowe on 6 October 1636:[24]

The followinge Royall consort was first compos'd for 2 Trebles a Meane & a Base, but because the Middle part could not bee performed with equall advantage, to bee heard as the trebles were. Therfore the Author involved the Inner part in two breakeinge bases . . .

In other words, the original lower parts were redistributed so that the two bass viols divided the roles of tenor and bass between them. At the same time, as the phrase 'breakeinge basses' suggests, Lawes took the opportunity to enrich the texture by adding new divisions and contrapuntal lines.

It is not easy to date the various versions of the Royal Consort. Murray Lefkowitz suggested that the earliest might have been written around 1620, but it obviously postdates the early development of the genre by Webster and Coleman in the later 1620s. The title 'Royal Consort' suggests a date after 1635, when Lawes joined the Lutes and Voices; he succeeded the lutenist John Lawrence by letters patent dated 24 October

[23] A. Ashbee, *The Harmonious Musick of John Jenkins*, i: *The Fantasias for Viols* (Surbiton, 1992), 148; for an alternative view of the source's origin, see M. Crum, 'Early Lists of the Oxford Music School Collection', *ML* 48 (1967), 27; Ellis's hand is illustrated in J. B. Clark, 'A Re-emerged Seventeenth-Century Organ Accompaniment Book', *ML* 47 (1966), 149–52.

[24] See *William Lawes: Fantasia Suites*, ed. D. Pinto (MB 60; London, 1991), 115.

backdated to Lady Day.[25] But three of Lawes's sets of divisions for two bass viols and organ, whose autograph parts in the later section of *GB-Ob*, MSS Mus. Sch. D. 229 and 238–40 David Pinto has dated *c.*1638, are based on pieces in the Royal Consort, which suggests that the collection was well known at court by then.[26] So the first version of the Royal Consort perhaps goes back to the early 1630s, which suggests in turn that Lawes was composing for the Lutes and Voices several years before his court appointment; he would presumably have had access to the group through his brother Henry, who became a member in 1631. It was perhaps revised over a year or two in response to performances at court; the change of scoring need not have involved a change of personnel, assuming that the continuo in the early version was played on theorboes all along. Two theorboes certainly seem to have been used in performances from MSS Mus. Sch. E. 431–6, for the source includes two duplicate copies of the bass; lutenists normally read from unfigured bass at the time, while English organists either used scores or written-out parts.

We do not know what role the Royal Consort played in the court's musical life, but German collections of suites often have titles that suggest a connection with *Tafelmusik*. Schein's *Banchetto musicale* is an obvious example, and Isaac Posch wrote in the preface of his *Musicalische Ehrenfreudt* (Regensburg, 1618) that it was played at dinner, banquets, weddings, and 'other decent gatherings' in distinguished households; he suggested that his *Balletten* were suitable for the table, while the three-movement variation suites could be used either at table or for dancing later.[27] At the English court the violin band evidently provided most of the dance music, so the Royal Consort was perhaps heard during the king's dinner in the Privy Chamber—to which the Lutes and Voices alone had access. The collection is certainly ideal *Tafelmusik*, poised midway between serious consort music—which demands to be listened to in a concert-like situation—and functional dance music. The scoring seems to have been taken up quickly by professional groups outside the court. The sequence of twenty-five dances in SSTB arrangements by Simon Ives in *GB-Lbl*, Add. MSS 18940–4, for instance, may have been written for the London waits, for Ives became a wait in 1637, and it includes his setting of Bulstrode Whitelocke's Coranto, a favourite item in the repertoire of the waits (see Ch. 6).

[25] M. Lefkowitz, *William Lawes* (London, 1960), 77; Ashbee, *RECM*, iii. 82, 83, 218; Lawes's role in the Lutes and Voices is not specified in his appointment documents, but he was paid £10 for a lute 'bought and provided for his Ma(jes)t(ies) service' by a warrant dated 4 Mar. 1635/6; Ashbee, *RECM*, iii. 151.

[26] Lawes, *Fantasia Suites*, ed. Pinto, pp. xx, xxi, 115; Dodd, *Thematic Index of Music for Viols*, 'William Lawes', nos. 33, 101, 103, 107.

[27] D. Fuller, 'Suite', *Grove 6*.

Lawes's Harp Consorts seem to be products of the same environment. They can be connected with the court by virtue of the fact that they use an esoteric scoring—Lawes headed them 'For the Harpe, Base Violl, Violin, and Theorbo' in the autograph parts, MSS Mus. Sch. D 229 and 238–40—that was probably available only in the Lutes and Voices. I have argued elsewhere that Lawes wrote for a chromatic or semi-chromatic Irish harp with wire strings, an instrument cultivated at court since early in James I's reign by the Irish harpist Cormack McDermott, his pupil Philip Squire, and Squire's pupil Lewis Evans.[28] The presence of the Frenchman Jean La Flelle at the Caroline court has often been used to connect Lawes with the gut-strung triple harp, but La Flelle has no demonstrable connection with the composer: he worked in Henrietta Maria's household, not the Lutes and Voices. That Lawes was working within a tradition initiated by McDermott is indicated by the fact that Consort no. 9, a pavan in D, is based on a piece by McDermott.[29] Layton Ring has recently suggested that GB-Och, Mus. MS 5, fos. 5ᵛ–13ᵛ, seemingly the harp parts of sixteen otherwise unknown harp consorts of the Lawes type, are by Coprario.[30] If so, then the idiom was not invented by Lawes, as is usually thought, but must have been in existence by Coprario's death in 1626, and may go back to McDermott himself.

What little evidence we have suggests that Lawes's Harp Consorts were composed in the early 1630s. The set was copied by Lawes into MSS Mus. Sch. D. 238–40 in an earlier and less mature hand than the divisions for two bass viols and organ at the other end of the volume, which, Pinto has argued, can be dated c.1636–8. On the other hand, the six suites, Consorts nos. 1–6, are unlikely to be much earlier than the revised version of the Royal Consort, for they too are laid out in an ordered progression from slow to fast dances: nos. 1–3 and 5 are alman–corant–corant–saraband, while nos. 4 and 6 are respectively alman–alman–corant–saraband and alman–alman–corant–corant–saraband. The remaining five harp consorts, nos. 7–11, an air, three pavans, and a fantasia, are larger and more sophisticated pieces, and were perhaps written a little later. In most of the collection divisions are confined to the bass viol, but in Consorts nos. 9 and 10 they are extended to the violin as well (Ex. 11.3).[31] This was something new, at least in serious consort music. There are examples of divisions in the treble parts of a few pieces in the mixed consort repertoire, and there are a few

[28] Holman, 'The Harp in Stuart England', 188–203; see also M. Billinge and B. Shaljean, 'The Dalway or Fitzgerald Harp (1621)', EM 15 (1987), 175–87.

[29] Lawes, Select Consort Music, ed. M. Lefkowitz (MB 21; London, 1963), no. 10; the numbering of the consorts is that used in Lefkowitz, William Lawes, 268–9; they are nos. 162–91 in Dodd, Thematic Index of Music for Viols, 'William Lawes'.

[30] L. Ring, 'The Harp for Lawes', EM 15 (1987), 589–90.

[31] Lawes, Select Consort Music, ed. Lefkowitz, nos. 10, 11.

Ex. 11.3. William Lawes, Harp consort no. 9, based on a pavan by Cormack McDermott, bb. 141–51 (from Lawes, *Select Consort Music*, ed. Lefkowitz, no. 10)

Italianate violin *passaggi* associated with Angelo Notari and his circle (see Ch. 9). But in general, rapid passage-work is conspicuous by its absence in the English violin repertoire before Lawes, for the instrument was still strongly associated with simple dance music.

Lawes's fantasia suites were also probably written for court use, though

there is scope for argument over their date. He undoubtedly modelled them on Coprario's fantasia suites, for they use exactly the same scorings and sequence of movements as those pioneering works. All of them are laid out in the sequence fantasia–alman–galliard, and they divide into two sets, eight 'For One Violin the Basse Viole and Organ', and eight 'For 2 Violins one Basse Viol & Organ', to quote the headings in MSS Mus. Sch. D. 238 and 239. Lawes even follows and develops Coprario's

tendency to group fantasia suites in pairs, using the key-scheme g–G–a–C–d–D–d–D for each set. An obvious possibility, therefore, is that they were written in the early 1620s, when Lawes would have been studying with Coprario (Thomas Fuller wrote that he was Coprario's 'schollar'[32]), and would therefore have been in touch with 'Coprario's Music', the group in Prince Charles's household that had pioneered the use of violins in contrapuntal music (see Ch. 9). Yet it is hard to believe that the last fantasia suite of the one-violin set is a student work, for its spectacular divisions are incorporated into the fabric of the contrapuntal argument without a trace of awkwardness.[33]

Whatever the truth of the matter, it seems that the fantasia suite remained essentially a court genre during Charles I's reign. Indeed, Coprario and Lawes were probably the only composers to contribute to it before the 1640s—apart from John Jenkins, who modelled his early works on Coprario but intended them, it seems, for the treble viol (a point to which we shall return). The vehicle for the dissemination of the violin and its court repertoire into the wider musical community was, of course, the Civil War. It used to be thought that the destruction of England's main musical institutions, the royal music, the cathedral choirs, and the collegiate foundations, together with the disruption of the war

[32] Lefkowitz, *William Lawes*, 5.
[33] Lawes, *Select Consort Music*, ed. Lefkowitz, no. 14.

and the establishment of Parliamentary government, produced conditions that were wholly detrimental to its musical life. But Percy Scholes pointed out in the 1930s that the Puritans were not against music as such, only against elaborate church music, and the public exhibition of plays and dancing.[34] Some types of music, notably those that could be cultivated at home, actually flourished. As Roger North wrote:

During the troubles; and when most other good arts languished Musick held up her head, not at Court nor (in the cant of those times) profane Theatres, but in private society, for many chose to fidle at home, than to goe out, and be knockt on the head abroad . . .[35]

It is difficult to study the effect of the Civil War on the history of the violin in England because little is known of how the court violinists spent the years of the Interregnum. However, contemporary letters and diaries occasionally provide a glimpse of their activities. On 25 March 1652, for instance, Lodewijck Huygens and his companions visited Davis Mell:

We went on [from the Tower] to our destination, that is, M^r. Mell's, in order to hear some music performed. So we did. When we entered they were performing a *concert* for organ, which [Christopher] Gibbons played, bass viol and two violins, one of which was played by the master of the house, who performed admirably well. After that they played another *concert* for harpsichord, lute, theorbo, bass viol and violin. [Benjamin?] Rogers, whose compositions were being performed, played the harpsichord while his brother [John?] played the lute.[36]

The first item mentioned by Huygens was probably a fantasia or a fantasia suite by Christopher Gibbons; there are a number of surviving examples by him for two violins, bass viol, and organ.[37] Gibbons spent his youth and early adult career in the West Country, only coming to London, it seems, after he lost his post as organist of Winchester Cathedral; John Playford listed him as one of the London teachers 'for the Organ and Virginal' in his *Musicall Banquet* of 1651.[38] So it is likely that he came to write fantasia suites after his arrival in London through his contacts with Mell and other court musicians. The piece by Rogers does not seem to survive, unless it was a two-part suite played with an elaborate continuo; there are works by him of the sort in Playford's *Court Ayres* (London, 1655), and its sequel *Courtly Masquing Ayres* (London, 1662).

---

[34] P. Scholes, *The Puritans and Music in England and New England* (Oxford, 1934; repr. 1969).

[35] Wilson, *Roger North on Music*, 294.

[36] Bachrach and Collmer, *Lodewijck Huygens*, 105.

[37] Dodd, *Thematic Index of Music for Viols*, 'Christopher Gibbons', nos. 13–41.

[38] Scholes, *The Puritans and Music*, 166.

Davis Mell was also a member of the musical establishment maintained at Cromwell's Whitehall 'court' from, probably, 1654 to 1658.[39] Among his colleagues was the organist John Hingeston, the 'Master of the Music', and Richard Hudson, Thomas Blagrave, and William Howes, who were to be members of the Restoration Twenty-four Violins. The Dutch ambassador reported that Cromwell's musicians 'played all the while we were at dinner' one day in 1654, and it may be that their repertoire was drawn from the many fantasia suites for one and two violins and combinations of two to six viols with, mostly, organ in Hingeston's autograph parts, *GB-Ob*, MSS Mus. Sch. D. 205–11 and E. 382; according to Anthony à Wood, Cromwell had organs installed in Hampton Court and Whitehall palaces.[40] Blagrave and Howes were cornett-players as well as violinists, which perhaps explains why Hingeston wrote fantasia suites for the unusual combinations of one and two cornetts, sackbut, and organ; there is also a large collection of his wind music, sadly incomplete, in two autograph bass part-books bound with Cromwell's arms in the library of the Victoria and Albert Museum, Clement TT14–15.[41] Hingeston's career followed a similar pattern to that of Gibbons: he was born in York and worked for the Clifford family at Skipton Castle until it fell to a Parliamentary army in 1645, when he probably came to London; he also appears in Playford's 1651 list of music teachers. So Hingeston, too, probably came to write fantasia suites in Commonwealth London through his contacts with Mell and other former court musicians.

The best-documented instance of how the violin and its court repertoire were taken up in the wider musical community is provided by Commonwealth Oxford. William Heather endowed the university in 1627 with a music professorship, stipulating that the 'Master of Musick' and two boys should meet every Thursday afternoon in the Music School 'to receive such company as will practise Musick, and to play Lessons in three Parts, if none other come'; he provided viols and a claviorgan for the purpose.[42] The Music School ceased to function during the Civil War, but the organist William Ellis later established a weekly meeting at his house; when Anthony à Wood visited it at the beginning of 1656 he listed some eighteen amateurs and professionals who played viols, lute, and keyboard.[43] John Wilson, professor 1656–61, directed and played the

---

[39] L. Hulse, 'John Hingeston', *Chelys*, 12 (1983), 28–9; see also Scholes, *The Puritans and Music*, 142–9; R. Sherwood, *The Court of Oliver Cromwell* (London, 1977).

[40] Hulse, 'John Hingeston', 28.

[41] Hulse, 'John Hingeston', 33, 35.

[42] Crum, 'Early Lists', 23–4; see also B. Bellingham, 'The Musical Circle of Anthony Wood in Oxford during the Commonwealth and Restoration', *JVGSA* 19 (1982), 6–70; P. Gouk, 'Music in Seventeenth-Century Oxford', *History of the University of Oxford*, iv: *1603–1688* (forthcoming).

[43] Shute, 'Anthony à Wood', ii. 96–7.

lute in Ellis's meeting until, in 1657, he refurbished and reopened the Music School; the bills of his expenditure mention a harpsichord, an organ, and viols, but still no violins.[44]

Things changed rapidly in 1657–8 following visits by Davis Mell and the German virtuoso violinist Thomas Baltzar, who arrived in England from his native Lübeck in 1655 or the beginning of 1656. Wood taught himself the violin by ear, tuning it in fourths like a viol, and later took lessons from several professional Oxford musicians, but he only realized the potential of the instrument after he heard Mell and Baltzar.[45] When Mell played at Ellis's meeting in the spring of 1657 the opinion was that he had a 'prodigious hand on the violin'; no one 'could go beyond him'.[46] But when Baltzar arrived in July 1658 'they had other thoughts of Mr Mell, who though he play'd farr sweeter than Baltsar, yet Baltsar's hand was more quick and could run it insensibly to the end of the fingerboard'. The result was that 'viols began to be out of fashion and only violins used, as treble violin, tenor and bass-violin'; when Wood analysed one of Ellis's meetings in March 1658/9, four of the sixteen named amateurs now played the violin, though one, Richard Rhodes, still held it between his knees.[47]

It was at this period that John Playford began to include a short section of simple 'Instructions for the Treble Violin' in his all-purpose *Brief Introduction to the Skill of Musick* (later called *An Introduction to the Skill of Musick*). It first appears in the second edition of 1658, with a crude wood-block illustration of a violin (Fig. 11.1); in the 1664 edition it was replaced by a more elegant engraving of an instrument with a bow and a tuning diagram (Fig. 11.2).[48] Later editions included material on ornamentation ('A Table of Graces proper to the Viol or Violin'), and a small collection of tunes in tablature and staff notation.[49] By the 1650s amateur violinists would have been able to buy instruments from several London makers, including Jacob Rayman (a Tyrolese said to have worked in England 1620–50), Thomas Urquhart (said to have worked 1648–80), and Edward Pamphilon (said to have worked 1670–90).[50]

Souvenirs of the rivalry between Mell and Baltzar are probably their unaccompanied violin pieces, particularly those in *scordatura* in *GB-Och*, Mus. MSS 433, fos. 36ʳ–35ʳ INV and 1125, fo. 27ʳ—the earliest

[44] R. Poole, 'The Oxford Music School and the Collection of Portraits formerly Preserved there', *MA* 4 (1912–13), 151–2.
[45] Shute, 'Anthony à Wood', ii. 94–5.
[46] Ibid. 99–100.
[47] Ibid. 99, 101–3.
[48] Illustrated from the 1658 edn. in Scholes, *The Puritans and Music*, facing p. 280.
[49] See, for instance, the facs. edn. of the 7th edn. (London, 7/1674; repr. 1966), 109–22.
[50] W. Henley, *Universal Dictionary of Violin and Bow Makers* (Brighton, 1960), iv. 101, 188; v. 163–4.

11.1. Wood block illustrating 'Instructions for the Treble Violin', John Playford, *A Brief Introduction to the Skill of Musick* (London, 1662), 83. Courtesy of Robert Spencer

examples of the technique in English sources—and the divisions on the popular song 'John come kiss me now' (a descant to the Passamezzo moderno chord-sequence), printed side-by-side in Playford's *The Division-Violin* (London, 1684), nos. 11 and 12 (Fig. 11.3).[51] A com-

11.2. Engraved block illustrating 'Instructions for the Treble Violin', John Playford, *A Brief Introduction to the Skill of Musick* (London, 1666), 109. Courtesy of Robert Spencer

[51] For Baltzar, see Holman, 'Thomas Baltzar'; P. Walls, 'The Influence of the Italian Violin School in Seventeenth-Century England', *EM* 18 (1990), 578–80.

11.3. Title-page of John Playford, *The Division Violin* (London, 2nd edn., 1685)

parison between the two gives us an inkling of why Baltzar's playing caused such a sensation in England. It is not just that his divisions use third position and elaborate chords for perhaps the first time in English music, but also that the virtuosity is used to drive the piece to a logical and satisfying conclusion (Ex. 11.4). Mell's piece, by contrast, requires only a modest technique, and is feeble in its effect.

To cater for the new fashion for the violin in Oxford, John Wilson and his successor Edward Lowe began to acquire violin music for the Music School. Early items included a number of the sources of William Lawes's violin music already discussed: MSS Mus. Sch. B. 2, B. 3, D. 229, D. 238–40 and E. 431–6. In 1665 Lowe set up a fund for:

refurnishing the publique Musick Schoole in this university with a new organ, harpsicon, all sortes of the best authors in manuscript for vocall and instrumentall music, and other necessaryes to carry on the practicall music in that place. All

Ex. 11.4. Davis Mell, Divisions on 'John come kiss me now', bb. 95–105, compared with Thomas Baltzar, Divisions on 'John come kiss me now', bb. 117–27, Playford, *The Division Violin* (London, 1684), nos. 11, 12

the old instruments and bookes left by the founder, being either lost, broken, or imbeasled in the time of rebellion and usurpation.[52]

His purchases included '1 upright organ with 4 stopps, made by Ralph Dallans' (Dallam), and '2 violins with their bowes and cases, bought of Mr. Comer in the Strand'—probably the royal violinist Henry Comer. The bulk of the new music, seventeen sets of part-books acquired through Anthony à Wood in 1667 from the North household at Kirtling in Cambridgeshire, added more of the pre-war court violin repertoire, including the three-part fantasias of Orlando Gibbons, and fantasia suites by Coprario and Lawes.[53]

The bulk of the purchase, however, consisted of consort music by John Jenkins, who had been associated with the North family for many years, and had worked at Kirtling from 1660 to 1666 as tutor to Lord North's grandsons, Roger (the writer) and Montagu. It includes sets of fantasia suites for treble, bass, and organ, and two trebles, bass viol, and organ (MSS Mus. Sch. C. 81 and 82), as well as the fantasia and airs 'divisions' (MS Mus. Sch. C. 86), and three sets of 'lyra consorts' (MSS Mus. Sch. C. 84, 85, and 88). Jenkins's fantasia suites are as closely modelled on Coprario as those by Lawes in their style and structure, but the Kirtling copies label the upper parts just 'treble'. Indeed, Coprario's fantasia suites are said to be for 'treble' in the Kirtling copy, MS Mus.

---

[52] Printed in J. Hawkins, *A General History of the Science and Practice of Music* (London, 1776, repr. 1853 and 1963), ii. 699–700 from lost Music School documents.

[53] The volumes are listed in Crum, 'Early Lists', 28–9; see also Crum, 'The Consort Music from Kirtling, Bought for the Oxford Music School from Anthony Wood, 1667', *Chelys*, 4 (1972), 3–10; P. Willetts, 'Autograph Music by John Jenkins', *ML* 48 (1967), 124–6.

Sch. C. 101, as well as in *GB-Lbl*, Add. MS 23779, an organ-book partly in Jenkins's hand from the library of Nicholas Le Strange.[54] Jenkins, in North's words, was 'an accomplisht master of the viol', who only tried to 'compass the Violin in his old age', inspired, like Oxford's amateurs, by Baltzar's playing.[55] At Kirtling, too, Lord North 'played on that antiquated instrument called the treble viol', and the consorts there were 'usually all viols to the organ or harpsichord', for 'the violin came in late and imperfectly'.[56] So it is likely that in Jenkins's circle, at least, the treble viol replaced the violin in fantasia suites. Conversely, his fantasia suites were thought of as violin pieces in Restoration Oxford: they were listed as 'for one Base Viol & Violin to the Organ', and 'two Violins & one Base' in the 1682 catalogue of the Music School Collection.[57]

The situation is different in the case of the Kirtling copies of the Jenkins's lyra consorts—that is, suites for treble, bass, lyra viol, and harpsichord, the sort of 'Ayrey, Jocond, Lively, and Spruce' music that Thomas Mace thought should be played with a harpsichord rather than organ.[58] The first set specifies 'Vyolin', and was perhaps written or arranged (some lyra consorts are elaborated two-part pieces) for the steward at Kirtling, Francis White 'or perhaps Blanc, turned into English', as North put it, 'a brisk gay spark who had bin bredd at court', and who could 'dance, sing, and play very neatly on the violin'.[59] But even such light dances were not always played at Kirtling on the violin: the second and third sets specify 'Treble Vyole' and 'Treble' respectively. The third has elaborate divisions in the treble and bass parts, and the same is true of the fantasias and airs 'divisions' in MS Mus. Sch. C. 86, one of which has fingerings in the second treble part that are applicable to the viol rather than the violin (Ex. 11.5).[60] It is easy to imagine Jenkins playing such pieces himself on the treble viol—he is given as a treble as well as a bass player in one of Bulstrode Whitelocke's documents relating to *The Triumph of Peace*.[61]

Some of the violin music acquired by the Music School was copied by Edward Lowe himself. MS Mus. Sch. C. 102 is of particular interest: it includes three excellent extended suites for two violins and continuo by Baltzar, and five of Christopher Gibbons's fantasia suites for two violins, bass viol, and organ.[62] Lowe sold it to the Music School in 1667 for £5,

[54] Willetts, 'Sir Nicholas Le Strange and John Jenkins'.
[55] Wilson, *Roger North*, 298, 345.
[56] Ibid. 10–11.
[57] Crum, 'Early Lists', 28.
[58] T. Mace, *Musick's Monument* (London, 1676; repr. 1958), 235.
[59] Wilson, *Roger North*, 10.
[60] *John Jenkins (1592–1678): Three-Part Fancy and Ayre Divisions*, ed. R. A. Warner (The Wellesley Edition, 10; Wellesley, Mass., 1966), pp. xii, 39–40.
[61] Library of Longleat House, Whitelocke Papers, III, no. 9, on the back of item no. 12.
[62] Holman, 'Thomas Baltzar', 16–20.

Ex. 11.5. John Jenkins, Ayre from Fancy and Ayre Divisions no. 3 in B♭, bb. 15–20 (from Jenkins, *Three-Part Fancy and Ayre Divisions*, ed. Warner)

(organ part omitted)

though he copied it rather earlier: Gibbons (who received an Oxford doctorate in 1664) is styled 'Mr', and the first two Baltzar suites are labelled 'Mr. Baltzar commonly called the Swede 25 feb: 1659[/60]', and 'Given mee by the Author, Mr Tho: Baltzar. October 1662'. They were evidently used in the Music School: Lowe and an assistant copied five duplicate bass parts for the Suite in D, and three for the Suites in C minor and G in MS Mus. Sch. C. 102 and his continuo books, MSS Mus. Sch. E. 450 and 451, probably for a sizeable group of plucked instruments. One of them for the G major suite is in A, and was evidently written for an instrument—a harpsichord, perhaps—that was tuned a tone lower than the pitch of the Music School organ (and stringed instruments)—that is, presumably, at a pitch of about $a' = 415$ instead of the prevailing organ pitch of about $a' = 465$.[63] Baltzar probably wrote his suites for Lowe and the Oxford Music School, though by 1662 they had both received posts at court, so the works could have passed from composer to copyist in London. Oxford music declined after Charles II's return to England in the spring of 1660, and the repertoire of the Music School once again became dependent on the court.

At the Restoration the Lutes and Voices (now usually known as the Private Music) was revived as it stood in 1642, with new recruits replacing those who had died or retired in the Interregnum. On 16 June 1660 Davis Mell was sworn in as 'a Violin, his owne place [in the violin band] & in [John] Woodington's place for the broke[n] Consort also'; he was joined on 18 June by the violinist Humphrey Madge, who received the place formerly held by Theophilus Lupo, and on the 19th by the viol-player Henry Hawes, who took Robert Tomkins's place in 'the broken (Consort of) Musick'.[64] The Broken Consort was the successor to the pre-war groups that had played consort music with violins in the Privy Chamber; the violin band (now enlarged as the Twenty-four Violins) was still located in the Presence Chamber. The Broken Consort was also, like Coprario's Music and the Royal Consort, a mixed ensemble. The precise meaning of 'broken consort' in earlier references is obscure, but by the 1660s it had come to mean a mixed consort as opposed to one made up of a single instrumental family—witness 'Compositions for Broken, and whole Consorts', the title of Matthew Locke's autograph score-book, *GB-Lbl*, Add. MS 17801.[65]

The Broken Consort may initially have played pre-war fantasia suites until new music became available, just as the revived Chapel Royal relied at first on old anthems. A hint that this was so is provided by the scores of the Coprario and Lawes two-violin fantasia suites that were copied, along with Gibbons's three-part 'double bass' fantasias and other Jacobean music, into *F-Pn*, MS Rés. F. 770 and *US-R*, MS Vault fML96.L814 by the early-Restoration scribe 'I.A.', who has been plausibly identified as John Atkins (Atkinson), a member of the Twenty-four Violins from Midsummer 1660.[66] The first music that can definitely be associated

---

[63] For a recent account of English organ pitch, see Gwynn, 'Organ Pitch in Seventeenth-Century England'.

[64] Ashbee, *RECM*, i. 2–3.

[65] See the discussion in W. Edwards, 'The Sources of Elizabethan Consort Music', 44–57; id., 'Consort', *Grove 6*.

[66] Lawes, *Fantasia Suites*, ed. Pinto, 116; Coprario, *Fantasia Suites*, ed. Charteris, 182–3; Ashbee, *RECM*, v. 107.

with the Broken Consort is by Matthew Locke. Locke was sworn in as 'composer in the private musick in the place of Coperario (deceased)', the first of his three court posts, on 23 June 1660.[67] And the first part of his three-part two-treble collection entitled 'The Broken Consort' was in existence a little more than a year later, for I.A.'s scores of it, MS Rés. F. 770, fos. 63^v–76^v and the first item in MS Vault fML96.L814, are both dated 1661—the latter precisely to 11 October. The 'Broken Consort' belongs to the fantasia suite tradition in that each of the six suites consists of a fantasia followed by dances, though the pattern is now fantasia–corant–alman–saraband (or perhaps fantasia–alman–corant–saraband, as in I.A.'s scores) rather than fantasia–alman–galliard.[68] Also, Locke followed Lawes in grouping them in pairs by key: the set has the sequence g–G–C–C–d–D. Its sequel, the second part of the 'Broken Consort', is more loosely constructed. It consists of dance suites of four, five, and six movements headed by a pavan in the manner of Lawes's Royal Consort, though each work ends with a 'drag' or close, the short passage of duple time that rounds off many fantasia suites.

The scores of the first part of the 'Broken Consort' do not have a separate continuo part, and tell us little about its instrumentation. But the partly autograph set of parts *GB-Och*, Mus. MSS 772–6 includes four bass parts, three of which were labelled 'Theorbo' by the composer. On the evidence of this source the Broken Consort consisted of six players—two violins, bass viol, and three theorboes—though Locke may also have provided an organ accompaniment from score; there are a few figures in Add. MS 17801. But Mus. MSS 772–6 may have been copied for use in the Oxford Music School, or for an ensemble in one of the Oxford colleges, so it does not necessarily reflect the practice of the Broken Consort, though the initials 'W.G.' on MS 772, fo. 7^r probably stand for the younger William Gregory, a composer and viol-player in the Restoration Private Music.[69]

Thomas Baltzar's appointment to the Private Music in December 1661, backdated to Midsummer, was a significant event.[70] His salary of £110 was one of the highest in the royal music, and, being for a new place, it probably reflected his personal standing at court. He was also the first violinist in the Lutes and Voices or Private Music who seems never to have served in the violin band—despite numerous modern assertions that he was a prominent member of the Twenty-four Violins, or even its

---

[67] Ibid. i. 4.

[68] For the grouping of Locke's consort suites, see C. D. S. Field, 'Matthew Locke and the Consort Suite', *ML* 51 (1970), 15–25.

[69] For Gregory, see J. Riley, 'The Identity of William Gregory', *ML* 48 (1967), 236–46; id., 'Deductions from a Round', *ML* 56 (1975), 60–3.

[70] Ashbee, *RECM*, i. 27; v. 32, 108.

leader. More important, his arrival at court increased the number of violinists available to the Broken Consort from two to three, which explains why the sonorous combination of three violins and continuo, a scoring popular in northern Europe at the time, makes its first appearance in English music with Baltzar's grand and expansive ten-movement Suite in C.

The work was copied by Edward Lowe into *GB-Ob*, MSS Mus. Sch. D. 241–4 and E. 451 around 1674, but may not have been performed in Oxford, for the source has no duplicate bass parts.[71] Indeed, the exceptionally brilliant writing for all three violins in the pavan, with fourth position required for the third part (perhaps written by the composer for himself), suggests that it was composed for the Broken Consort between Baltzar's arrival at court in the summer of 1661 and his untimely death two years later (Ex. 11.6). Baltzar's three-violin writing seems to have inspired a number of imitations, including a six-movement suite in F by the London poet, apothecary, and amateur musician Valentine Oldis, and a remarkable D minor set of divisions by Nicola Matteis.[72] The tradition eventually gave rise to Purcell's matchless three-violin works, the Pavan in G minor Z752, and the divisions 'three parts upon a ground' in D Z731.

The composer most directly inspired by Baltzar seems to have been John Jenkins, who received a court post—his first—on 19 June 1660, when he was sworn in as a 'Lute (private Musicke)' succeeding John Coggeshall.[73] Jenkins and Baltzar were evidently friends: Baltzar witnessed a court document for Jenkins on 7 February 1662/3, and North wrote that Jenkins was inspired by Baltzar to take up the violin, 'which he did so farr as to performe his part, but how well handed, any one can conceive'.[74] Scholars long suspected that the ten anonymous fantasia suites for three trebles, bass, and continuo in *GB-Lbl*, Add. MS 31423, fos. 76^r—122^v were works by Jenkins, and the matter was clinched when David Pinto found an unpublished reference in North's writings to three-violin music: 'it cannot be denied that a full consort of 4. [parts] may be adapted to 3. violins (taking their turnes) & a Bass'.[75] A marginal note—

---

[71] Holman, 'Thomas Baltzar', 19–20, 36.

[72] The Oldis suite is in *GB-Ob*, MSS Mus. Sch. G. 612 INV, fos. 25^r–22^v (a, c), fos. 24^r–21^v (b), fos. 23^r–20^v (d), and *GB-Och*, Mus. MSS 382–4, nos. 31–6 (bass missing). MSS Mus. Sch. G. 612 was 'given mee by the Author 24 March 1659[/60] at the Legg in Kings-street Westminster', according to a note in Edward Lowe's hand, though it is not clear whether the suite for three trebles was copied before or after that date. The Matteis divisions are in *US-NH*, Osborn MS 515, fos. 22^v–23^r (bass only), and *GB-Ob*, MSS Mus. Sch. E. 400–3, no. 14, a source recently dated to the mid 1680s; see Thompson, 'English Music Manuscripts and the Fine Paper Trade', 458–61.

[73] Ashbee, *RECM*, i. 3.

[74] Ibid. 262; Wilson, *Roger North*, 298.

[75] See P. Holman, 'Suites by Jenkins Rediscovered', *EM* 6 (1978), 25–35, and the correspondence ibid. 481–3.

Ex. 11.6. Thomas Baltzar, Pavan from Suite in C for Three Violins and Continuo, bb. 47–60, *GB-Ob*, MSS Mus. Sch. D. 241–4, p. 51; E. 451, p. 140

Ex. 11.6. *Continued*

'of this kind I have a plain consort of Mr J. Jenkins'—is an unmistakeable reference to the Add. MS 31423 pieces, for they were written by a copyist, once thought to be Jenkins himself, who was associated with the North family. The ten fantasia suites are 'plain' in that they lack, in North's phrase, the 'high flying vein' of divisions in some of Jenkins's earlier fantasia suites.[76] In style and structure they closely resemble his late fantasia suites for two trebles and two basses, and fifteen fantasia–air sets for two trebles and bass; and, like them, they have a continuo line instead of a written-out organ part—the norm for fantasia suites until about 1660.[77] All three sets may have been written for the Broken Consort in the early 1660s.

Baltzar seems to have returned the compliment by modelling his solo violin music on the lyra viol idiom of Jenkins and his contemporaries; the German tradition of chordal violin music, to which it was once thought Baltzar belonged, only really developed in the last quarter of the seventeenth century. The crucial document here is *GB-Ob*, MS Mus. Sch. F. 573, a little-studied book of violin and bass viol music, written, it seems, by a Dutch musician in England around 1690.[78] It contains a group of fifty-five solo violin pieces, most of which are arrangements of English lyra viol pieces. They can be associated with Baltzar by virtue of the fact that the set starts on fo. 8^r with a 'Preludium T.B.', which is strikingly similar to a prelude by Baltzar in *The Division Violin*, no. 83, and by the fact that most of the arrangements are of pieces by Jenkins, Coleman, and Dietrich Stoeffken, his colleagues in the Private Music.[79] It seems that, struck by the virtuosity of his viol-playing colleagues, Baltzar made a number of arrangements of their lyra viol pieces, and then wrote his own solo violin music in the same style—just as J. S. Bach based the style of his Italian Concerto on his transcriptions of concertos by Italian composers.

I have argued elsewhere that a painting at Nostell Priory near Wakefield, conventionally called *The Cabal* and said to have been painted by Sir John Baptist Medina (1659-1710) around 1675 (see Pl. 5(*b*)), is actually a group portrait of members of the Private Music; it can be dated by the fashionable court clothes to the early 1660s, when Medina was still

[76] Wilson, *Roger North*, 347.

[77] The fantasia suites are printed complete in *John Jenkins: Consort Music in Four Parts*, ed. A. Ashbee (MB 26; London, 1969), nos. 33–40; fantasia–air sets nos. 4, 10, 14 are in *John Jenkins: Fancies and Ayres*, ed. H. Sleeper (The Wellesley Edition, 1; Wellesley, Mass., 1950), 78–100; no. 11 is in R. A. Warner (ed.), 'English Consort Music: Fancy and Ayre in G minor (*c*.1660) by John Jenkins (1592–1678)', in E. Borroff (ed.), *Notations and Editions: A Book in Honor of Louise Cuyler* (Dubuque, Ia., 1974), 106–26.

[78] See Holman, 'Thomas Baltzar', 26–9.

[79] There is a list in *Chelys*, 10 (1981), 40–1; see also G. Dodd, 'Matters Arising from Examination of Lyra Viol Manuscripts', *Chelys*, 9 (1980), 23–7.

a child.[80] It shows five musicians, four of whom—two violinists, a viola player, and a bass—are seated around a table. The fifth stands to their right with what appears to be an Italian double harp. If he is Charles Evans, Charles II's 'harper for the Italian harp', then the others may be his colleagues—perhaps Baltzar himself (the young man, front left), John Banister (the older man, front right), and Humphrey Madge (back left) with, as bass player, Henry Hawes or one of the other viol-players of the Private Music. It is significant that a small recorder or flageolet lies on the table beside 'Banister', for he was a noted player of both instruments as well as a violinist (see Ch. 14). Thus the picture appears to date from between May 1662, when Banister succeeded Mell as a member of the Private Music, and 24 July 1663 or thereabouts, when Baltzar died suddenly of drink or (Anthony à Wood recorded conflicting stories) 'the French pox and other distempers'.[81]

Thomas Baltzar's death marks the beginning of the end of the Broken Consort. On virtually the same day, 23 July 1663, Henry Hawes 'of Hadden in Derby' appointed his wife Anne as his representative at court, presumably to collect his wages in his absence, and Baltzar was not succeeded until 24 June 1667, when his post was given to the 16-year-old Thomas Fitz with the note 'He plays with the violins'—which implies that it was used to provide extra revenue for the Twenty-four Violins.[82] The same is certainly true of subsequent appointments in the Private Music, which effectively ceased to exist by the end of Charles II's reign (see Ch. 12). The king's musical taste seems to have been largely responsible for the change: according to Roger North the king had an 'utter detestation of fancys', 'could not forbear whetting his witt upon the subject of the fancy-musick', and 'could not bear any music to which he could not keep the time'.[83] It is not surprising, therefore, that nine members of the Twenty-four Violins under John Singleton were appointed 'his Ma(jes)ties Private Consort' in the winter of 1661/2, and that by June 1662 a 'select band' chosen by John Banister was attending the king 'whensoever there shall be occasion for musique' (see Ch. 12). Once members of the violin band had been granted access to the Privy Chamber, the Broken Consort lost its *raison d'être*, and its fine repertoire of 'fancy-musick' passed into history.

---

[80] Holman, 'Thomas Baltzar', 33; see also id., 'The Harp in Stuart England', 195. In these articles, written before an examination of the picture itself revealed the recorder or flageolet, I suggested that the front right figure was Davis Mell.

[81] Holman, 'Thomas Baltzar', 29.

[82] Ashbee, *RECM*, i. 80, 227.

[83] Chan and Kassler, *Roger North's The Musicall Grammarian*, 262.

12

'The Fideldedies'

Charles II and the Twenty-four Violins

ON Tuesday, 29 May 1660, Charles II entered London for the first time
as monarch. Within a month the royal household, scattered since the
outbreak of the Civil War in 1642, began to reassemble. The new Lord
Chamberlain, Edward Montagu, Earl of Manchester, was appointed on 1
June, and the swearing-in of musicians began in earnest just over two
weeks later, on Saturday 16 June. A record of the swearing-in ceremonies
conducted that day and during the following week shows that the new
royal music was based on the old: the individuals had either served
Charles I, or were replacements for those who had done so.[1] No attempt
was made to take advantage of the Interregnum to reorganize the royal
music, or to devise a logical and effective method of paying musicians.
Musicians were still divided into those who received their money from
the Treasury of the Chamber, and those who dealt directly with the
Exchequer. Rates of pay, often fixed in the previous century, still bore
little relation to the worth of the recipient, and were supplemented
haphazardly by extra payments and plural appointments. Thomas Purcell,
for instance, eventually held five or possibly six posts, two as a composer,
though he is not known to have written much music.[2] The first establishment books of the new reign show that the historic structure of the royal
music remained intact, at least on paper. It continued to be headed by the
first Master of the Music, Nicholas Lanier. Under him were the same
five groups that had served Charles I: the 'Private musick for lutes violls
and voices', the 'Wind Musick', the trumpeters, the 'Drummers and
Fifes', and the violin band.[3]

The Twenty-four Violins, as the violin band was now called, is usually
said to have been founded from scratch by Charles II. But the initial
appointments were all made using the fifteen places of the pre-war group.
Only Ambrose Beeland and Davis Mell survived the eighteen years of the
Interregnum to resume their posts. Five of their former colleagues,

---

[1] Ashbee, *RECM*, i. 2–4.
[2] Summarized in A. Ashbee (ed.), *Lists of Payments to the King's Musick in the Reign of Charles II (1660–1685)* (Snodland, 1981), 122.
[3] Ashbee, *RECM*, i. 216–24; v. 43–5.

Richard Comer, Daniel Farrant (buried 24 July 1651), Theophilus Lupo (buried July 1650), Thomas Lupo II, and Thomas Warren, were listed as dead when their replacements were appointed: Henry Comer, William Gregory II, Humphrey Madge, Philip Beckett, and Robert Strong.[4] The three Frenchmen in the pre-war group, Stephen Nau (its composer), Simon Nau, and Nicholas Picart, were also replaced, by George Hudson, Richard Hudson, and John Strong. Stephen Nau died at St Giles-in-the-Fields on 13 March 1646/7, while Picart probably left England in 1642; he was in Paris in 1644, and worked at the Swedish court from 1646 to 1649; Simon Nau is last heard of in 1646 (see Ch. 10). John Woodington was dead by 30 July 1650, when his widow Alice and his daughter Mary received £6. 13s. 4d. arrears of his salary, while Alfonso Ferrabosco III was listed as dead when his post in the wind music was reallocated in June 1660. Their places in the violin band apparently went into abeyance, though they were replaced by ones taken from elsewhere in the royal music.[5] Thomas Blagrave succeeded the flute-player Peter Guy, but the comment 'playes with the violins but his patent is for the flutes' appears against his name in an establishment book; William Howes received the place formerly held by the lutenists Robert Dowland and John Mercure.[6] John Friend died in 1643, when his place was given to the lutenist John Wilson; in 1660 Wilson petitioned Charles II to confirm the appointment.[7]

Simon Hopper was another survivor from the pre-war court. He played in the violin band as early as 1634, though his main job was to provide the future Charles II and his brother with dance music (see Ch. 10). He petitioned the king for the post in 1660, claiming that:

yo(u)r Petition(er) at the beginninge of the late unhappy wars, did waite upon yo(u)r Ma(jes)tie at Oxford, untill yo(u)r Ma(jes)tie considering his greate charge of children & the litle use there was then of your Pet(itione)r['s] Service, did gratiously give leave to yo(u)r Pet(itione)r to returne to his home, to endeavo(u)r by his labour to maintaine his family . . .[8]

He was assigned 'to his Majesty for his exercise of Dancing' in September 1660 with his salary doubled to £60.[9] Hopper's place in the Twenty-four Violins had to wait until a pre-war muddle had been sorted out. He received Richard Dorney I's place in the violin band in early 1642, but Dorney's widow pointed out in a petition dated 8 November 1641 that her son Richard had a prior claim: her husband had left 'sixe small

---

[4] Ibid., iii. 128; i. 2–3, 6.
[5] Ibid., i. 3; v. 25.
[6] Ibid., i. 9, 218, 227; iii. 111.
[7] Ibid., iii. 117; *GB-Lpro*, SP29/2, no. 58.
[8] *GB-Lpro*, SP29/33, no. 85.
[9] Ashbee, *RECM*, i. 6; v. 28.

fatherlesse Children'; he was 'an ancient servant to his Ma(jes)tye & well respected of & was 7 monethes in Spaine w(i)th his Ma(jes)tye' (Prince Charles's abortive trip in 1623 to woo the Spanish Infanta); and he 'did in his long time of sickness procure his Ma(jes)t(i)es gratious favour & promise . . . that his sonne Richard Dorney should bee admitted into his Fathers place', a claim that was endorsed by Stephen Nau and six of his colleagues.[10] The Lord Chamberlain granted Dorney junior the post, but ordered that since he was a minor he should not be sworn in, and that for the time being his place 'bee duly supplied by some able man'. At the Restoration the situation was resolved by giving Dorney the post (though technically he succeeded Hopper), and Hopper a new post—in January 1660/1 backdated to Michaelmas 1660.[11]

The decisive stage in the creation of the Twenty-four Violins came at Midsummer 1660 when new places were created for John Singleton, Theophilus Fitz, William Young, Henry Brockwell, John Atkins or Atkinson, John Yockney, William Clayton, Isaac Staggins, and Matthew Locke—who acted as a second composer and was given authority 'to order & direct them in his course of Wayting'.[12] The new recruits brought the group up to the magic number of twenty-four, though Locke probably confined his activities to directing the group and composing for it, for he is not known to have been a violinist (see Table 12.1).

There is evidence that Locke's group was to some extent independent of the main violin band, and was already in existence before its members recieved their court posts. Six of them, Young, Atkins, Staggins, Yockney, Clayton, and Brockwell, were described as 'Musitians in ordinary for the violins for his Ma(jes)ties Private Consort' in a document dated 2 December 1661, and there are two further lists of the 'private consort' from early in the next year; in the second all ten names are given and they are said to have been 'appointed by his Majesty to increase the number of his violins'.[13] They can probably be identified with the 'Singleton's Musique' that the king 'affronted' during a performance at Whitehall of Ben Jonson's *The Silent Woman* on 20 November 1660, 'he bidding them stop and bade the French Musique play', according to Samuel Pepys.[14] The activities of the group certainly seem to have caused resentment among the members of the main violin band, for in the December 1661 document just mentioned the Lord Chamberlain complained that they

[10] Ibid., iii. 114, 115; *GB-Lpro*, LC5/135, 3, printed in Ashbee, *RECM*, iii. 111, where it is dated 9 Nov.

[11] Ashbee, *RECM*, i. 218; v. 27, 28, 107.

[12] Ibid., v. 33, 107.

[13] Ibid., i. 24, 28, 29.

[14] *Diary*, ed. Latham and Matthews, i. 297–8; Van Lennep, *The London Stage 1660–1880*, i. 20–1.

TABLE 12.1. *The initial composition of the Twenty-four Violins*

Pre-war Places	New Appointments	Payment Office[a]	Wage/Livery		
			£	s.	d.
Ambrose Beeland	Ambrose Beeland	TC	46	10	10[b]
John Hopper	Edward Strong	TC	46	12	8
Nicholas Picart	John Strong	TC	46	12	8
Richard Comer	Henry Comer	TC	46	12	8
Davis Mell	Davis Mell	TC	46	10	10
″	″	TC	110		
Simon Nau	Richard Hudson	TC	46	12	8
Simon Hopper	Richard Dorney II	TC	46	10	10
Thomas Lupo II	Philip Beckett	TC	46	12	8
Thomas Warren	Robert Strong	TC	46	12	8
Stephen Nau[c]	George Hudson	TC	42	15	10
″	″	E	200		
Daniel Farrant	William Gregory II	TC	46	0	0
Theophilus Lupo	Humphrey Madge	E	40	0	0
[Peter Guy]	Thomas Blagrave	E	40	9	2[d]
[Robert Dowland]	William Howes	TC	46	12	8
	Simon Hopper	TC	46	10	10
	John Singleton	TC	46	10	10
	Theophilus Fitz	TC	46	10	10
	William Young	TC	46	10	10
	Henry Brockwell	TC	46	10	10
	John Atkins(on)	TC	46	10	10
	John Yockney	TC	46	10	10
	William Clayton	TC	46	10	10
	Isaac Staggins	TC	46	10	10
	Matthew Locke[c]	TC	46	10	10

[a] TC = Treasury of the Chamber E = Exchequer
[b] made up of 20*d.* a day and £16. 2*s.* 6*d.* livery
[c] composer
[d] made up of 16*d.* a day and £16. 2*s.* 6*d.* livery

'are not admitted or suffered to exercise in the chamber appointed for that purpose with the rest of the Musitians'; he ordered their colleagues 'forthwith to admit the said Musitians into your society in the Chamber appointed for the violins and to suffer them to exercise according to their oaths and Dutyes'.

The members of the main violin band probably objected to the Singleton–Locke group because it had been made the 'private consort', for the phrase carries the implication that it had been granted access to the Privy Chamber, which had hitherto been enjoyed only by the members of the Lutes and Voices (or the Private Music, as it was now called). Such a move, which can only have come from the king himself, would have been a particular affront to Davis Mell and Humphrey Madge, who combined a post in the Twenty-four Violins with membership of the Broken Consort, the group in the Private Music that played contrapuntal consort music with violins. I suggested in Chapter 11 that it was Charles II's musical taste—or lack of it—that was responsible for the decline and fall of the Broken Consort.

The Broken Consort was not the only group to suffer from the rise of the Twenty-four Violins. The process by which Thomas Baltzar's place in the Private Music was first left unfilled and then allocated to the Twenty-four Violins (see Ch. 11) was repeated a number of times in subsequent years, so that by the end of the reign the Private Music had effectively ceased to exist, save as a source of places for the Twenty-four Violins. Edward Hooton replaced the singer-lutenist Gregory Thorndell after the latter's death on 17 January 1670/1; Joseph Fashion and William Hall replaced the viol-players Henry Hawes and John Young on 17 February 1679/80 and 22 July 1680; and John Goodwin and Nathaniel French received two of Thomas Purcell's singer-lutenist places 'to wayte among the Violins' on 17 and 20 November 1682.[15]

The Twenty-four Violins had a similar effect on the wind consorts. Until the Civil War each of the court ensembles was a separate institution, with its own personnel, its own repertoire, and a discrete role in court life. Wind musicians, for instance, had played on occasion in the Chapel Royal since Elizabeth's reign, and on a regular basis since the early 1630s. At the Restoration they resumed this duty, but were soon in competition with members of the Twenty-four Violins; after about 1670 they were replaced permanently in the Chapel by a rota of string-players (see Ch. 16). The independence of the wind consorts was also undermined by the fact that no fewer than seven of the violinists appointed in 1660, Edward, John, and Robert Strong, Philip Beckett, Humphrey Madge, Thomas Blagrave, and William Howes, also received places as wind-players, and many of their colleagues also received them as posts fell vacant. Like the Private Music, the old royal wind music went out of existence at the end of Charles II's reign.

On the face of it, it is odd that the practice of doubling wind and stringed instruments came to the fore at the Restoration court at a time when professional musicians in general, faced with the demands of increasingly complex and virtuoso instrumental music, were beginning to specialize in a single instrument. The explanation, however, has less to do

[15] Ibid., i. 101, 188–9, 190–1, 202, 232; v. 78, 81.

with the conservatism of English court musicians than with the nature of the court as an institution. Such was the weight of tradition and precedent in the Tudor and Stuart period that the officials responsible for appointing musicians found it well-nigh impossible to change the composition of ensembles or increase the rates of pay without resorting to sleight of hand. They coped with inflation not by increasing salaries according to a logical or equitable plan, but by haphazardly handing out extra places, which were borrowed from elsewhere in the royal music. It is not clear whether the members of the Twenty-four Violins who received places as wind-players had to work twice as hard, or whether they were wind-players only in name.

However, there does seem to have been a trend at the Restoration to recruit musicians from outside the charmed circle of court musicians and their families, many of them immigrants or the descendants of immigrants, who dominated the court consorts from Henry VIII's reign to the Civil War. And many of these new recruits came from musical circles where playing several instruments had been the norm. In particular, Edward, John, and Robert Strong, three sons of Steven Strong, all had connections with the London waits, and seem to have played bass violin and bass sackbut as well as other wind instruments.[16] William Saunders, another London wait, received his place in the Twenty-four Violins after the presentation of an undated petition in which he stated that he 'hath all these late Rebellious times beene faithfull in the Loyalty to your sacred Ma(jes)tie, and your late Royall Father of ever blessed memory, For which the said Loyalty hee hath suffered much by the late Usurpers'.[17] An accompanying certificate signed by Nicholas Lanier, George Hudson, Davis Mell, Richard Hudson, and Simon Hopper testified to his ability on the sackbut, on which he was 'very fitt and able to doe Service ... in his Ma(jes)ties Chappell Royall', and on the bass violin, 'a part which there is much want of in his Ma(jes)ties Band of Violins'. He was said to be a man 'of a sober life and conversat(i)on'.

Saunders received his place in the Twenty-four Violins at the same time as John Banister and Walter Yockney; the three received warrants dated respectively May 1661, 28 March 1661, and December 1661, but they all started at the same time, Christmas 1660.[18] Their appointments have a particular importance in that they were given new places, which had the effect of increasing the establishment of the Twenty-four Violins to twenty-seven (twenty-five rank-and-file and two composers); the group seems to have consisted of twenty-four musicians for only six months,

---

[16] For the Strong family, see Lasocki, 'Professional Recorder Players', ii. 720, 765–8.

[17] *GB-Lpro*, SP29/36, no. 39; for Saunders, see Lasocki, 'Professional Recorder Players', ii. 763–5.

[18] Ashbee, *RECM*, v. 28, 29, 31, 107.

from Midsummer to Christmas 1660. It was not long before the use of extra places borrowed from the Private Music and the appointment of unpaid 'extraordinary' musicians took the number of string-players available to the group to thirty or more, as Table 12.1 shows. But we should remember that the Twenty-four Violins only performed as a single group at coronations or state occasions of similar importance; we shall see in succeeding chapters that it was often divided into two for its day-to-day work at court or in the London theatres, and when its members played in the Chapel Royal they normally did so in groups of only four, five, or six.

Under the circumstances it is remarkable that the number twenty-four was so consistently associated with Charles II's violin band. For example, as early as 5 July 1660, not much more than a month after Charles II arrived in London, '24 viols and violins' figure in a report of a banquet at the Guildhall; Samuel Pepys mentioned '24 viollins' in his description of the banquet in Westminster Hall after Charles's coronation on 23 April 1661, and again at Whitehall on 1 October 1667; Anthony à Wood wrote that the king 'would have 24 violins playing before him'; according to Roger North, Charles 'set up a band of 24 violins to play at his dinners'; and again, 'the King made an establishment, after a French model of 24 violins, and the style of the musick was accordingly'; and John Evelyn wrote in his diary for 21 December 1662 that 'a Consort of 24 Violins' had been introduced into the Chapel Royal'.[19] The point is not that Charles II was always attended by exactly twenty-four violins—that was certainly not so in the case of the Chapel Royal—but that people tended to associate the number twenty-four with the group more or less regardless of its size, to the point that in the 1690s 'Four and twenty Fidlers all in a Row' became the subject of a popular song.[20] It may even be that there is distant and confused echo of the Twenty-four Violins in the reference to twenty-four singing blackbirds in the nursery rhyme 'Sing a song of sixpence', though it must be said that Iona and Peter Opie do not include it in the five explanations of the rhyme they give in *The Oxford Dictionary of Nursery Rhymes*.[21]

Of course, the main reason why the number twenty-four was chosen was, as Wood and North implied, that the group was an imitation of the French *Vingt-quatre violons*—'always so-called even though at present they are twenty-five', to quote a description of the group in the *État de*

---

[19] HMC, *Fifth Report of the Royal Commission on Historical Manuscripts*, i (London, 1876), 154; Pepys, *Diary*, ii. 85–6; viii. 458; Shute, 'Anthony à Wood and his Manuscript', ii. 99; Wilson, *Roger North on Music*, 300; Chan and Kassler, *Roger North*, 261; J. Evelyn, *The Diary of John Evelyn*, ed. E. S. de Beer (one-volume edn., London, 1959), 449.

[20] T. D'Urfey, *Wit and Mirth: or, Pills to Purge Melancholy*, i (London, 1699), 77–8; repr. in *Songs Compleat, Pleasant and Divertive* (London, 1719; repr. 1872), iii. 61–2.

[21] (Oxford, 1951; repr. 1977), 394–5.

France for 1686.[22] Charles II, in North's words, 'had lived some considerable time abroad, where the French musick was in request'.[23] More precisely, his flight from England after the Battle of Worcester took him to France; he stayed at the French court from the winter of 1652 to the early summer of 1654. There he would doubtless have seen the 14-year-old Louis XIV and the 20-year-old Lully dancing together in the *Ballet de la nuit* on 23 February 1653, and towards the end of his stay he might have heard some of Lully's earliest ballet music; the Florentine was appointed 'Compositeur de la musique instrumentale du Roi' on 16 March 1653.

We need not, however, posit a direct connection between Lully's rise in France and the creation of the Twenty-four Violins in England. The *Vingt-quatre violons* was probably the most influential performing ensemble in Europe at the time. The universal fashion for French dances and French dance music led to the formation of violin bands staffed largely or wholly by Frenchmen at several northern European courts. We saw in Chapter 10 that the French influence on the pre-war English court violin band, exemplified by the presence of such figures as Jacques Bochan and Stephen Nau, had been considerable. Charles II was a true man of his time in his fondness for French culture in general, and for French dancing and dance music in particular (see pls. 6 and 7). 'I shall only tell Your Majesty', he wrote in August 1654 from Cologne to his aunt Elizabeth of Bohemia:

that we are now thinking how to pass our time; and in the first place of dancing, in which we find two difficulties, the one for want of the fiddlers, the other for somebody both to teach and assist at the dancing the new dances. And I have got my sister to send for Silvius as one that is able to perform both.

For the fideldedies my Lord Taafe does promise to be their convoy, and in the meantime we must content ourselves with those that make no difference between a hymn and a coranto.[24]

Roger North wrote that 'it was, and is yet a mode among the *Monseurs*, always to act the musick, which habit the King had got, and never in his life could endure any that he could not act by keeping the time; which made the comon *andante* or else the step-tripla the onely musicall styles at Court in his time'; and again, 'He could not bear any musick to which he

[22] J. R. Anthony, *La Musique en France à l'époque baroque*, trans. B. Vierne (Paris, 1981), 20, a reference brought to my attention by N. Zaslaw, 'Lully's Orchestra', unpublished paper given at the 1987 Colloque Lully in Heidelberg; see also J. de La Gorce, 'Some Notes on Lully's Orchestra', in J. Hajdu Heyer (ed.), *Jean-Baptiste Lully and the Music of the French Baroque: Essays in Honor of James R. Anthony* (Cambridge, 1989), 99–112.

[23] Wilson, *Roger North*, 299.

[24] A. Bryant (ed.), *The Letters, Speeches, and Declarations of King Charles II* (London, 1932), 51.

could not keep the time, and that he constantly did to all that was presented to him'.[25]

Charles II's musical taste may have been limited to music he could beat time to, but that does not mean that the music was necessarily French in origin or style (a point I develop in Ch. 13), or that the Twenty-four Violins was any more French than Charles I's violin band. Rather the reverse, for in the 1630s the group had a French composer, Stephen Nau, and there were as many as five or six other French violinists and dancing-masters at court. The Twenty-four Violins, on the other hand, consisted entirely of Englishmen until the Spaniard Luis or Louis Grabu arrived from France, and became Master of the Music in 1666. The thread that seems to run through Charles II's dealings with the Twenty-four Violins is a desire that the group should be as good as its counterparts abroad, not that it should necessarily imitate them in matters of style or repertoire, though it had to provide music for the latest French dances. Charles knew what he was talking about, for he was the first English monarch for generations who had experienced the cultural life of a number of Continental courts at first hand. Hence his impatience with 'Singleton's Musique' on the occasion already mentioned in November 1660, when Lord Sandwich told Pepys that the 'French Musique . . . doth much out-do all ours'.

The identity of the 'French Musique' is something of a mystery, for there is no record of an instrumental consort of Frenchmen in English court documents of the time. There was a group of six French musicians at court from, probably, October 1663 to the spring of 1668, but it seems to have been five singers and a keyboard-player, not a violin band. An undated list of the 'Noms des Musiciens Francois de sa Maiesté' gives them as:

Ferdinand de Florence	Maistre de la Musique
Claude des Granges	Bass de la musique
Eleonor Gingaut	basse taille de la musique
Nicolas Fleuri	hautecontre de la musique
Guillaume Sautre	haute taille de la musique
Jean de la Vollée	Jouëur de Clavessin de la musique[26]

Two of them, Ferdinand de Florence and Claude des Granges, were certainly singers, and *haute taille* and *basse taille* are names that were used

---

[25] Wilson, *Roger North*, 299–300; Chan and Kassler, *Roger North*, 262.

[26] *GB-Lpro*, SP29/1, no. 67; see also *CSPD, Charles II*, ed. M. A. Everett Green, *1663–1664* (London, 1862), 214; *1664–1665* (London, 1863), 227; *November 1667 to September 1668* (London, 1893), 318; *1670, with Addenda 1660 to 1670* (London, 1895), 637; Ashbee, *RECM*, i. 53, 55, 58, 63, 221; E. Boswell, *The Restoration Court Stage (1660–1702)* (Cambridge, Mass., 1932; repr. 1960), 164–6; J. A. Westrup, 'Foreign Musicians in Stuart England', *MQ*, 27 (1941), 74–5.

for inner parts in French vocal music; the equivalent parts of French violin music were labelled *taille* and *quinte*.

The trouble with the early Twenty-four Violins was that it had no single leader or director. Nicholas Lanier, as Master of the Music, had 'power to order and Convocate' all royal musicians 'at fitt time of practize and service', with penalties 'if any amongst them refuse to wayte at such convenient tymes of practize and service as he shall appoint, and for such Instruments, voyces and musick as he in reason shall thinke them fittest to serve in'.[27] But he was a member of the Private Music, and there is little sign that he controlled the day-to-day affairs of the Twenty-four Violins except to convey orders from the Lord Chamberlain, or to resolve disputes. The violin band had been run informally by its senior members and its composer, a tradition maintained when, on 31 May 1661, the Lord Chamberlain told them that 'there hath been Complaint made to mee of divers neglects' in 'practize and performance to doe his Ma(jes)ties faithfull service'.[28] George Hudson, one of the composers, and Davis Mell, one of the senior members, were to 'give orders and directions from tyme to tyme to every particular person herein concerned for their practize and performance of Musick'.

The solution was to promote John Banister as an English Lully. In the licence for his second marriage, issued on 11 January 1670/1, Banister's age was given as 46, so he was apparently born in 1624 or the beginning of 1625.[29] According to Anthony à Wood, our only source, he was 'Son of Banister, one of the musicians or public waits of S. Giles' Parish near London, and was bred up under his Father, and was one of the public waits there'.[30] He first came to public attention when he played with Thomas Baltzar in the distinguished ensemble that accompanied *The Siege of Rhodes* in the summer of 1656, and, 'his excellencies for the Violin being extraordinary he was taken into the service of His Majesty King Charles II and made on[e] of his Violins'.[31] 'Afterwards', Wood continued, 'the said King sent him to France, with the allowance of a yearly pension of 150[li] or 200[li] per annum, to see and learn the way of the French compositions'.

The evidence concerning Banister's trip to France is puzzling, and has been partially misunderstood. A passport was issued dated 2 December 1661 for him 'to goe into France upon Some speciall Service & returne

[27] Ashbee, *RECM*, i. 14.
[28] Ibid. 18.
[29] G. J. Armytage (ed.), *Allegations for Marriage Licences Issued by the Bishop of London, 1611 to 1828* (Harleian Society Publications, 26; London, 1887), 297; for Banister, see A. A. Luhring, 'The Music of John Banister', Ph. D. diss. (Stanford University, 1966).
[30] Shute, 'Anthony à Wood', i. 60.
[31] Holman, 'Thomas Baltzar', 5–6.

with all possible expedition'.[32] This document has been known from the transcript in the *Calendar of State Papers*, which omits the words 'all possible', so it has been assumed that this was the occasion when he went to 'see and learn the way of the French compositions'. Banister was certainly in London for Charles II's coronation on 23 April 1661, for he was given livery for the occasion.[33] But, 'Vacatur' is marked against his name in an acquittance book for livery collected on St Andrew's Day (30 November) 1661, and the rates on his Spur Alley house in the parish of St Martin-in-the-Fields were paid by 'Mrs Banister' in 1661 ('Mr Banister' paid in 1662 and 1663).[34] It may be that he made more than one trip to France between 1660 and the spring of 1662.

On his return to England Banister lost no time in establishing himself as the effective director of the Twenty-four Violins. On 18 April 1662 he was given the authority to choose 'twelve violins of his Ma(jes)ties servants in ordinary to attend his Ma(jes)tie in the journey to Portsmouth or elsewhere for the reception of her Ma(jes)tie his dearest consort the Queene'; Catherine of Braganza was met by Charles at Portsmouth on 19 May.[35] The same twelve players were formally constituted as a 'Select Band' shortly afterwards. On 3 May the king gave Banister 'full power for the Ordering Instructing & directing' them for the 'better performance of Our said Service without being mixed with any of Our other Violins . . . Except Wee shall please to have the twenty fower Violins to doe us Service as Wee shall from time to time give Order'.[36] At the same time he was given the £110-a-year place in the Private Music held by Davis Mell, who had conveniently died a few days before.[37] A year later Banister improved his position further: by a warrant dated 23 July 1663 he was granted £600 a year backdated to Lady Day 1662 to augment the wages of the Select Band. None of them was to 'neglect practizes, or [neglect to] performe before us in Consort upon his sumons, or mix in any Musicke w(ha)tsoever, otherwise then for Our perticular Service in Our s(ai)d Band, w(i)thout the knowledge, & allowance of the s(ai)d John Banister'.[38]

The Select Band evidently replaced the Singleton–Locke group in the Privy Chamber, for in the July 1663 document it is described as 'a select

---

[32] *GB-Lpro*, SP44/5, 62.

[33] Ashbee, *RECM*, i. 15.

[34] Ibid. 238; Westminster City Libraries, Archives Department, St Martin-in-the-Fields rate books E388-90.

[35] Ashbee, *RECM*, i. 32; *GB-Lpro*, SP44/7, 53.

[36] *GB-Lpro*, SP44/7, 37.

[37] *GB-Lpro*, SP44/7, 36–7; Ashbee, *RECM*, i. 42; v. 35–6, 41.

[38] *GB-Lpro*, SP44/15, 120–1; see also *GB-Lpro*, SP38/21, no. 287, dated 19 Aug. 1663; Ashbee, *RECM*, i. 47; v. 43; HMC, *Third Report of the Royal Commission on Historical Manuscripts* (London, 1872), 266.

Band to wait on us whensoever there shall be occasion for Musick', and Banister is said to 'give his attendance on us constantly to receive Our Comands, & to see that Our service be performed by the s(ai)d 12 persons'. Banister evidently consolidated his position by choosing its members equally from the main violin band and the Singleton–Locke group: Simon Hopper, Henry Comer, Philip Beckett, Richard Hudson, John Strong, and Robert Strong came from the former; John Singleton, William Young, William Clayton, Henry Smith (who succeeded John Yockney by a warrant dated 24 March 1661/2), Theophilus Fitz, and Isaac Staggins from the latter.[39]

Banister evidently tried to achieve 'better performance' by adopting the strategy that Lully had used at the French court in 1656, when he chose a select group from the *Vingt-quatre violons*, the sixteen-strong Petits violons, and used his exclusive control over it to achieve new standards of ensemble discipline, which he then extended to the parent group. Lully may not have invented such disciplines as synchronized bowings—the so-called 'rule of the downbow'—or the practice of beginning a piece exactly together from silence—the *premier coup d'archet*—but he certainly applied them to an unprecedented degree, and with unprecedented success.[40] Little is known of the musical aspects of Banister's reforms, but he was obviously trying to achieve a Lullian control over the Select Band by increasing the income of its members, by insisting that they rehearse properly, and by ensuring that they did not take outside work. However, if Banister's aim was to become an English Lully, he did not succeed. He did manage to keep the Select Band largely distinct from the rest of the Twenty-four Violins, to judge from eight lists of its members between 1662 and 1666.[41] But when Lanier died in 1666 the post of Master of the Music went to Louis Grabu, and Banister's control over the Select Band came to a sudden and ignominious end in the winter of 1666–7.

Trouble seems to have been brewing since the beginning of 1665. In February Henry Comer petitioned the Lord Chamberlain against Banister, and in June 'John Strong and others of the violins' followed suit; neither document seems to survive, and the details are not known.[42] Grabu probably arrived in England that same spring: he is first recorded on 2 April when 'Ludovicus Grabeu of Shalon in Catalunnia and Catherine Deluss of Paris' were married in Catherine of Braganza's Catholic chapel at St James's.[43] It has been argued that 'Shalon' is San

---

[39] Ashbee, *RECM*, i. 30–1; v. 114; Yockney was buried at St Andrew, Holborn on 19 Mar. 1661/2; GB-Lgc, MS 6673/4.

[40] The nature of Lully's orchestral discipline is discussed in Zaslaw, 'Lully's Orchestra'.

[41] GB-Lpro, SP44/7, 37, 53; Ashbee, *RECM*, i. 32, 59, 70, 72, 73, 221.

[42] Ashbee, *RECM*, i. 60, 65.

[43] J. C. M. Wade (ed.), *Registers of the Catholic Chapels Royal and the Portuguese Embassy Chapel 1662–1829*, i: *Marriages* (Publications of the Catholic Record Society, 38; London, 1941), 4.

Celoni, north-east of Barcelona, though a more likely possibility, given the habitual confusion between *n* and *u* in the script of the time, is the coastal village of Salou, just south of Tarragona.[44] Grabu had presumably met his bride (who signed herself 'Catherine de Loes') in Paris, for he seems to have been an associate of Robert Cambert and was possibly his pupil. He was probably responsible for bringing Cambert to England in 1673 (see Ch. 14), and he was certainly thought of in England as a representative of French culture.

Confusion also surrounds the date of Grabu's first court appointment. It is normally said, based on an entry in an establishment book for 1660–8, that he was appointed a royal composer in place of Nicholas Lanier on 31 March 1665, just three days before his marriage.[45] But this document is inaccurate in two respects. Lanier did not die until February 1665/6 (he was buried at Greenwich on the 24th[46]), and he did not hold an appointment as a composer. When Grabu received Lanier's £200-a-year post he was variously described as 'Master of his Ma(jes)ties Chamber musicke' and 'Master of his Majesty's Musick'; his patent is dated 17 April 1667, but he was paid from Lady Day 1666, and the warrant to swear him in is dated June 1666.[47] Establishment books tend to be inaccurate because they were often written up long after the event, or were compiled as reference works by officials who had no direct contact with musicians. In this case the date 31 March 1665 seems to be a year too early. Grabu's appointment, unfortunate for Banister, had important consequences for the whole royal music. Lanier was a singer-lutenist in the Private Music, while Grabu was a violinist in the Twenty-four Violins. As a result, the centre of power in court musical affairs moved from the former to the latter, and stayed there.

Grabu lost no time in asserting his authority. On 24 December 1666 'Mr. Bannister and the 24 violins' were ordered to 'obey the instructions of Louis Grabu, master of the private musick, both for their time of meeting to practise, and also for the time of playing in consort'.[48] On 14 March 1666/7 Grabu replaced Banister as the convener of the Select Band.[49] Finally, on 29 March 1667, the rest of the Twenty-four Violins sent in a 'Remonst(ran)ce against Mr Banister', claiming that he had embezzled most of the £600 given to the Select Band for 'extraordinary Service'; that he:

---

[44] P. H. Highfill, K. A. Burnim, and E. A. Langhans (eds.), *A Biographical Dictionary of Actors, Actresses, Musicians, Dancers, Managers, and other Stage Personnel in London, 1660–1800*, vi: *Garrick to Gyngell* (Carbondale and Edwardsville, Ill., 1978), 290–1.

[45] Ashbee, *RECM*, i. 221.

[46] Ibid. 68–9; v. 52–3.

[47] Ibid., i. 74, 75; v. 55; *GB-Lpro*, SP29/160, no. 128.

[48] Ashbee, *RECM*, i. 74.

[49] Ibid. 75; v. 55.

hath kept sometimes five or six of us out of wayting according as hee is pleased or displeased, and three of us hee hath turned out of his Band, his Ma(jes)ties pleasure not being knowne therein, nor the Lord Chamberlaines, by this meanes he thinkes to put all our Arreares [of pay] in his own purse, whereby the kings service is abused, and his poore Servants utterly ruyned.[50]

Their grievances went back to 1663: about £230 appropriated by Banister when the group played 'to the Queenes dancing which was her Birthday', which made her 'very angry' when she heard about it; £20 kept out of £50 given by 'the Queenes Ma(jes)tie at the Bath'; four gold pieces kept out of ten given by 'a person of hono(u)r'; £20 received from the Duke of Buckingham:

of which wee never had one penny, besides severall other things of that nature. And this last birthday of the Queenes hee gets a fee of 10[li] into his hands, and gives money to some, and others not a penny, neither did hee waite on the Queene himselfe . . .

Banister responded in a lost petition, and the matter was resolved in August by the Lord Chamberlain, who ordered that Grabu, not Banister, should receive arrears from the Exchequer; he reported that 'His Majesty was well pleased therewith'.[51]

Without having Banister's side of the story it is impossible to judge the rights and wrongs of the case. It seems, however, that the £600 was seriously in arrears, since he petitioned for it in July 1665, claiming he 'had spent much tyme in soliciting the payment . . . to his owne Damage & the hindrance of yo(u)r Ma(jes)t(ie)s service'; he added 'w(i)thout the constant payment of the same allowance, yo(u)r Ma(jes)t(ie)s Comands cannot effectually bee obayed'.[52] It seems, too, that the king bore him ill will for a moment of insubordination. Anthony à Wood wrote that 'for some saucy words spoken to His Majesty (viz. when he called for the Italian violins, he made answer that he had better have the English) he was turned out of his place', which is hard to believe since no Italian violinists appear in Restoration court documents.[53] Grabu was the obvious subject of Banister's 'saucy words'. Pepys wrote on 20 February 1666/7 that 'the King's viallin, Bannister, is mad that the King hath a Frenchman come to be chief of some part of the King's music—at which the Duke of York made great mirth'.[54]

Finally, we must remember that Banister's partial downfall (he kept his rank-and-file place in the Twenty-four Violins) came at a moment of

---

[50] *GB-Lpro*, SP29/195, no. 62.
[51] *CSPD, Charles II, 1666–1667*, 598; *1667*, 358.
[52] *GB-Lpro*, SP29/126, no. 29.
[53] Shute, 'Anthony à Wood', i. 60.
[54] Pepys, *Diary*, viii. 73.

crisis for the royal musicians, a moment when they could easily have turned unjustly on someone who was out of favour at court. Two months before Pepys heard the story about Banister, John Hingeston told him that:

many of the Musique are ready to starve, they being five years behindhand for their wages. Nay, [Lewis] Evens, the most famous man upon the Harp, having not his equal in the world, did the other day die for mere want, and was fain to be buried at the almes of the parish—and carried to his grave in the dark at night, without one Linke, but that Mr Hingston met it by chance and did give 12^d to buy two or three links. He says all must come to ruin at this rate, and I believe him.[55]

For some the position had been made worse by the Great Fire the previous summer. On 7 November 1666 twenty-two of the royal violinists petitioned the king for arrears of salary: their salaries were four and three-quarter years in arrears, and several of them 'have had their houses and Goods burnt by the late Fire, which hath reduced th[em] to great misery and want'.[56] Besides arrears of salary, and losing 'all he had, by the late most dreadfull fire in London', the wind-player John Gamble had contracted a debt of £120, which meant that one of his securities was 'cast a Prisoner into Newgate, where hee now remaines'.[57] He went on: 'the next Tearme, an execution wilbe obtained against him for the same, w(hi)ch wilbe the absolute ruine of him (your Pet(itione)r) and both their Families'. Under the circumstances it is not surprising that Banister was made a scapegoat.

Louis Grabu is perhaps the most derided figure in English musical history. On 15 November 1667 'little Pellam Humphrys, lately returned from France', was entertained by Pepys, who found him 'an absolute Monsieur, as full of form and confidence and vanity, and disparages everything and everybody's skill but his own'.[58] Humfrey laughed at 'all the King's music here, as Blagrave and others, that they cannot keep time nor tune nor understand anything'. He reserved especial scorn for Grabu:

how he understands nothing nor can play on any instruments and so cannot compose, and that he will give him a lift out of his place, and that he and the King are mighty great, and that he hath already spoken to the King of Grebus, would make a man piss.

Humphrey's opinion has formed the basis of Grabu's modern reputation as a dull and incompetent composer, but Pepys realized that the Spaniard was an excellent orchestral trainer, and had improved the standard of the

[55] Ibid., vii. 414.
[56] *GB-Lpro*, SP29/177, no. 105.
[57] *GB-Lpro*, SP29/173, no. 103.
[58] Pepys, *Diary*, viii. 529–30.

Twenty-four Violins within a few months. A few weeks earlier, on 1 October, he had attended a concert of Grabu's music, 'both instrumental (I think 24 violins) and vocall, an English song upon peace' in the 'Boarded-gallery' at Whitehall: 'Here was a great press of people, but I did not see many pleased with it; only, the instrumental music he had brought by practice to play very just'; on another occasion, 15 April 1668, he went to the 'fiddling concert' at Whitehall, and 'heard a practice mighty good of Grebus'.[59]

Pepys criticized Grabu's 'English song upon peace' for its word-setting. He thought that 'the manner of setting of words and repeating them out of order, and that with a number of voices, makes me sick, the whole design of vocall music being lost by it'. But it is worth remembering that the diarist was hard to please in such matters. A month later he criticized Humfrey, whose word-setting is admired today, for an anthem that was a 'very good piece of Musique' but was still nothing 'but Instrumentall music with the Voice, for nothing is made of the words at all'.[60] Also, there is no sign that the members of the Twenty-four Violins feared or resented Grabu's appointment, as Franklin Zimmerman, for one, has claimed.[61] Indeed, Banister's arrest in May 1667 for 'abusing the master of his Majesty's musick and several of his Majesty's musicians' suggests that some of them, at least, supported Grabu against him.[62]

Grabu seems to have made only one change to the structure of the Twenty-four Violins; the details are contained in an order from the Lord Chamberlain dated 29 April 1668.[63] The group—twenty-four musicians without Grabu, the two composers, and Henry Comer (who was given 'leave to travel for some years' in the spring of 1667[64])—was divided into two bands of twelve to 'wayt & attend upon his Ma(jes)ty . . . twelve one moneth & twelve the other till further ord(e)r'. Grabu consolidated his position in the same way that Banister had done: seven of the Select Band, John Singleton, Banister himself, William Young, Philip Beckett, Henry Smith, Simon Hopper, and 'Mr. Strong' (John or Robert) were placed in one group, while the other six, William Clayton, Jeffrey Banister, Theophilus and Thomas Fitz, Isaac Staggins, and Thomas Greeting (evidently deputizing for the other Strong), were placed in the other. Thus Banister's Select Band was replaced by a shift system using the entire Twenty-four Violins; and, it seems, all its members were now

[59] Ibid. 458; ix. 163.
[60] Ibid., viii. 515.
[61] F. Zimmerman, *Henry Purcell, 1659–1695: His Life and Times* (2nd edn., Philadelphia, 1983), 21.
[62] Ashbee, *RECM*, i. 78.
[63] Ibid. 83.
[64] Ibid. 76.

given access to the Privy Chamber. The Tudor distinction between the privileged few, who had access to the Privy Chamber, and the many, who waited outside in the Presence Chamber, disappeared for good.

Grabu's fall was as sudden as Banister's, and was more unexpected, for there is no sign that he did not make a success of his administrative or musical duties. On 15 August 1674 the Lord Chamberlain ordered that Nicholas Staggins be sworn 'master of his Majesty's violins'.[65] Confirmation that he had replaced Grabu as Master of the Music came with a warrant dated 29 January 1674/5, backdated to 29 September 1674, though a number of documents show that he was in effective control from the summer. Indeed, the change may have been made as early as Midsummer 1673, for on 10 May 1675 a warrant was issued to pay Staggins as Master of the Music £100 a year 'without account, for such uses as the King shall direct', and it was backdated to then.[66] Grabu was left with considerable arrears of pay, for which he petitioned the king on 5 May 1677, stating that he had 'fallen under very greivous misfortune, the greatest of which hath beene yo(u)r Ma(jes)ties willingness to receive another person into his place during pleasure'.[67] The Lord Chamberlain asked the various payment offices for particulars, and reported on 5 June that Grabu's condition was 'very poore and Miserable'; he was owed a total of £627. 9s. 6d., which was eventually paid to him.[68] On 31 March 1679, at the height of the Popish Plot, when many Catholics were fleeing the country, 'Lewis Grabu, late master of the King's music, native of France, with his wife and three small children' was issued with a passport to go to France, where he remained until his return to London in the autumn of 1683.[69]

Why did Grabu lose his post? It is often thought that it had something to do with the opera *Ariane*, produced by Cambert's French opera company, the 'Royal Academy of Music', at Drury Lane on 30 March 1674 (see Ch. 14). *Ariane* failed, and nothing more was heard of the 'Royal Academy of Music'. The Lord Chamberlain had to ask Thomas Killigrew for the return of scenery that Grabu had borrowed from the court theatre at Whitehall, but it is unlikely that Grabu would have been dismissed for this, and there is no sign that he was subsequently out of favour at court. As late as 17 January 1676/7 twelve royal violinists were ordered to 'attend to practise Mons. Grabu's musick', presumably under the direction of the composer.[70] It is more likely that Grabu was dis-

---

[65] Ibid. 140.

[66] Ibid. 147, 148, 153; *CSPD, Charles II, March 1st 1675 to February 29th 1676*, ed. F. H. B. Daniell (London, 1907), 113.

[67] Ashbee, *RECM*, i. 170–1.

[68] Ibid., 172, 290.

[69] *CSPD, Charles II, January 1st 1679 to August 31st 1680*, ed. Daniell (London, 1915), 338.

[70] Ashbee, *RECM*, i. 168.

missed because of his religion. As a Catholic—he was married in the queen's Catholic chapel—he was effectively debarred from office following the passage of the Test Act in the spring of 1673. The act evidently applied to courtiers, for a warrant book of the Lord Chamberlain's office contains a copy of the following order in council dated 14 November 1673:

No person who is a Roman Catholicke or reputed to be of the Roman Catholique Religion doe pr(e)sume after the Eighteenth day of this instant November to come into His Ma(jes)ties Royall pr(e)sence or to His Palace or to the place where his court shalbe.[71]

There are several other examples of musicians who fell foul of the Test Act. The viol-player John Smith was forced to leave the Private Music at Midsummer 1673; Francis Cruys was appointed in his place.[72] In an undated petition dealt with in December 1687 Smith pointed out that he 'was forced to quit his place in respect of his Religion and go beyond Sea', and Grabu's case was cited as a precedent that his arrears be paid.[73] The viol-player Paul Bridges seems also to have been a Catholic: he came to London from the Catholic court at Brussels in 1660, and surrendered his place in the Private Music in May 1673.[74] Around 1680 he petitioned the king for relief; a certificate signed by the Earl of Worcester and several other courtiers stated that he had 'often times brought his Comarades to make Musick for our Soveraigne the King and many times himselfe hath plaid alone before his Ma(jes)ty and did quit the said Service of the King of Spaine out of his love and duty to Serve his Majesty in England'.[75] It is likely that Grabu managed to retain his place until the winter of 1674–5 because he enjoyed the protection of an important court figure—such as the king's Breton mistress Louise de Keroualle, Duchess of Portsmouth (who certainly patronized him in the 1680s; see Ch. 15), or the Duke of York himself. Matthew Locke, another Catholic court musician, seems to have stayed out of trouble because he was the organist of Catherine of Braganza's Catholic chapel, and was therefore exempt from the provisions of the Test Act as a member of her household.

Why was Nicholas Staggins appointed Master of the Music over the heads of more distinguished candidates such as Matthew Locke and John Blow? His surviving music is not impressive, but we must remember that no extended work of his survives complete, and we have to judge him as a composer only from two- or three-part dance tunes, or strophic songs.

[71] Ibid. 131.
[72] Ibid. 129, 130.
[73] Ibid. 289–90.
[74] Ibid. 13, 36, 125.
[75] *GB-Lpro*, SP29/2, no. 57; *GB-Lpro*, SP29/442, no. 79.

Ex. 12.1. Giovanni Battista Draghi?*, Symphony, *GB-Lbl*, R.M. 20.H.9 INV, fos. 108ᵛ⁻ʳ

* I am grateful to Duncan Druce for pointing out that this is actually the first section of G. B. Vitali's sonata 'La sassatelli', from his Op. 5 (Bologna, 1669).

Ex. 12.1. *Continued*

Ex. 12.1. *Continued*

Also, the post of Master of the Music required an able administrator more than a good composer. In modern terms it combined the functions of chairman, fixer, librarian, leader, and conductor of a symphony orchestra. Composition must have been one of Staggins's lesser priorities, especially since he had four official composers working under him, two in the Twenty-four Violins and two in the Private Music. We do not know what lies behind the title of the short chromatic four-part piece in *GB-Lbl*, R.M. 20.H.9, fo. 108[v–r] INV headed 'Seignor Givana Battista [illegible word] Symphony w(hi)ch Nich(olas) Staggins produced as his owne May 29th 1679' (Ex. 12.1). But there is no sign that Staggins did not give satisfaction to his masters; indeed, he was reappointed by James II and William III, so he must have been the right man for the job.

There are signs that Staggins was chosen as Master of the Music to further Charles II's operatic ambitions. Throughout his reign the king made repeated but unsuccessful attempts to establish an Italian or French opera-house in London, beginning with the patent given to Giulio Gentileschi in October 1660.[76] Staggins's career as Master of the Music started with an elaborate and successful production of the masque-like play *Calisto*, given with his music at Whitehall in March 1674/5 (see Ch. 15). Next, he was sent on a trip to France and Italy, apparently to study the operatic practice of those countries. On 26 February 1675/6 he was issued with a pass to 'go and remain in Italy and other foreign parts for a year, with his servants &c.', and on 27 March he appointed his father Isaac as his legal attorney; Locke was appointed Master of the Music in his absence.[77] Staggins apparently returned sometime between 30 November 1678, when Charles Coleman II signed for two of his liveries, and 18 February 1678/9, when the Lord Chamberlain once again began to address orders and warrants to him.[78] In a petition dated 5 June 1695 to Sidney Godolphin, first Commissioner of the Treasury, Staggins reminded him of:

the great Charge of my Travels in France (where-unto yo(u)r Hono(u)r is no Stranger) Italy, & other Forrin Parts, to capacitate & make my self fit for the Service of His Late Ma(jes)ty K(in)g Charles the Second . . . And wheras I had before my going to France (w(hi)ch after my return to England then ceased) a very considerable Practise in teaching the young Nobility & Gentry here ab(ou)t the Town, I left & quitted all that gainfull Employment, when His said Ma(jes)ty was pleased to make me Master of His Musick . . .[79]

The fruit of Staggins's foreign trip seems to have been an operatic venture in collaboration with John Blow, who was a keyboard-player and composer in the Private Music, as well as Master of the Children of the Chapel Royal. In the spring of 1680/1 Blow and Staggins were jointly given the reversion of Thomas Purcell's place as composer for the Twenty-four Violins, a post they took up after his death on 31 July 1682.[80] In 1682, or shortly before, Blow wrote his operatic masque *Venus and Adonis* for a court production that Staggins, as Master of the Music, would presumably have overseen; I examine some of the connections between *Calisto* and *Venus and Adonis* in Chapter 15. Finally, on 4 April 1683 the king responded to a lost petition from Blow and Staggins 'for the erecting an Academy or Opera of Musick, & performing or causing to be performed therein their Musicall compositions'; the Lord Chamberlain

[76] See M. Mabbett, 'Italian Musicians in Restoration England (1660–90)', *ML*, 67 (1986), 237–47.
[77] *CSPD, Charles II, March 1st 1675 to February 29th 1676*, 581; Ashbee, *RECM*, i. 158, 171; v. 146.
[78] Ashbee, *RECM*, i, 182, 255
[79] Ibid., iii, 256–7; v. 91
[80] Ibid., i. 194, 201; Rimbault, *The Old Cheque-Book*, 17.

was asked to report on the plan, but nothing more was heard of it.[81] The death of Charles II on 6 February 1684/5 may have caused Blow and Staggins to shelve it, and the expensive fiasco later in the year of Grabu's opera *Albion and Albanius* probably ensured that their operatic ambitions remained unrealized.

[81] *GB-Lpro*, SP44/55, 248

13

'Waiters upon the Violin'

The Twenty-four Violins at Court

THE traditional round of daily attendance or 'waiting' at Court remained the prime duty of royal musicians during the Restoration period. The chroniclers of court life took the presence of music so much for granted that they rarely bothered to mention it, but it is clear that the violinists, at least, were still required to attend Whitehall daily while the court was there. On 7 November 1666 twelve of them petitioned the king for arrears of wages, pointing out that they had 'been com(m)anded to attend yo(u)r Ma(jes)tie and yo(u)r Royall Consort the Queene in all progresses, besides their dayly attendance heere'.[1] A couple of years later, when wages were between six and seven years in arrears, the musicians complained as a body that they had 'all this winter given their constant attendance morning and evening on this present mask'.[2] We saw in Chapter 12 that John Banister's Select Band had to be on hand 'whensoever there shall be occasion for Musick', and that Banister was required to attend the king 'constantly to receive our Comands'. A paragraph headed 'Musicke' in a set of ordinances or regulations drawn up for Charles II's household implies that musicians were stationed outside the royal apartments daily:

The Gentleman Usher ought to know the King's mind when it shall please him to have any musick, and without my Lord Chamberlaine, or Mr. Vice Chamberlaine, or the Gentleman Usher's order, they are not to come in.[3]

The central ceremony of the court day continued to be the sovereign's dinner. Naturally, we know most about those meals that were part of state occasions. On 5 July 1660, not much more than a month after Charles II first entered London as king, he dined at the Guildhall as the guest of the City of London. A description of the event in a letter from Andrew Newport to Sir Richard Leveson reveals that two groups of royal musicians provided the music, placed in galleries on opposite sides of the hall:

[1] *GB-Lpro*, SP29/177, no. 105.
[2] *CSPD, Charles II: Addenda*, ed. F. H. B. Daniell and F. Bickley (London, 1939), 232–3.
[3] *A Collection of Ordinances and Regulations for the Government of the Royal Household*, 371.

I am just now returned from the great entertainment the City gave the King and both Houses at Guildhall, the King sat under a state at the upper end of the hall in the middle of the table, the Duke of York at the end on the right hand, and [the] Duke of Gloucester on the left; a degree lower (divided with a rail), were four tables, two on each side of the hall for the Lords, and a degree lower than that, six tables, three on each side for the Commons, the King's own music on one side of the hall in a little gallery, and opposite to them 24 viols and violins in another, and long galleries round the hall full of women; after dinner there was some pastime by men habited like lawyers, soldiers, countrymen &c., which took up the rest of the day . . .[4]

The 'King's own music' was presumably a group from the Private Music, such as the Broken Consort, the ensemble that revived the court fantasia suite repertoire at the Restoration (see Ch. 11).

Similar arrangements were made for the feast in Westminster Hall on Charles II's coronation day, 23 April 1661. Samuel Pepys wrote that the hall was 'very fine with hangings and scaffolds, one upon another, full of brave ladies'; true to character, he 'took a great deal of pleasure to go up and down and look upon the ladies—and to hear the Musique of all sorts; but above all, the 24 violins'.[5] Later in the same year, on 15 August, the king was welcomed to a dinner at the Inner Temple with the 'loud Musick playing all the Time of his landing till he ent(e)red the Hall; where he was received with xx Violins, which continued as long as his Majesty stayed'.[6] On such occasions the 'loud music'—the royal wind musicians—would have provided an accompaniment to the royal party's journey on the Thames or through the streets of London. The violin band normally played indoors, but it ventured outside for the procession through the City of London on the eve of Charles II's coronation. Groups of musicians, drawn from the royal music and the London waits, were deployed at strategic sites along the route; the Twenty-four Violins were placed on a triumphal arch near Wood Street, and played music, now lost or unidentifiable, by Matthew Locke.[7]

Charles II was the first English monarch since Henry VIII to dine regularly in public (though he probably got the idea from Louis XIV rather than from his ancestor), and the Twenty-four Violins evidently played an important part in the ceremony. A court newsletter reported that on 8 August 1667 'their Majesties dined in public in the Queen's presence chamber, with the usual solemnities and the band of violins, and

---

[4] HMC, *Fifth Report*, i. 154.

[5] Pepys, *Diary*, ii. 84–6.

[6] R. W. Weinpahl, *Music at the Inns of Court during the Reigns of Elizabeth, James, and Charles* (Northridge, 1979), 167.

[7] E. Halfpenny, 'The "Entertainment" of Charles II', *ML* 38 (1957), 32–44.

so they intend to do three days weekly'.[8] A few weeks later Pepys saw 'the King and Queen at dinner and heard a little of their viallins music', while the author of the account of the Grand Duke of Tuscany's trip to England in 1669 wrote that the king dined in public in the Banqueting House on his birthday (29 May), and that dinner was 'enlivened with various pieces of music, performed by the musicians of the king's household'.[9] As late as 1675 Nicholas Staggins was paid for the copying of 'severall Aires that was performed at the King's dinner' by the Twenty-four Violins (see below). According to Roger North, the Twenty-four Violins was created specifically to provide *Tafelmusik* for Charles II: 'after the manner of France, he set up a band of 24 violins to play at his dinners, which disbanded all the old English musick at once', a point echoed by Anthony à Wood: 'the king, according to the French mode would have 24 violins playing before him, while he was at meales'.[10] His meals were probably enlived with violin music even when he dined in private, for members of the Twenty-four Violins were admitted to the Privy Chamber soon after the Restoration (see Ch. 12).

Dancing was perhaps the most highly prized social grace of Restoration society, and the royal family continued the pre-war practice of employing a French dancing-master. Charles and his sister Mary (the mother of the future William III) had originally been taught to dance as children by Sebastian La Pierre, and the violinist Simon Hopper had been employed to provide him with dance music—a post he retained after the Restoration.[11] La Pierre died in 1646, and his successor at the Restoration Court was Jerome (Jeremy) Gohory, who became a Groom of the queen's Privy Chamber in 1663, and is known to have taught Charles II himself, his brother James, James's wife Mary of Modena, and Princess Anne.[12] Pepys evidently had Gohory in mind when he wrote of seeing the young Princess Mary, the future queen, dance one afternoon in April 1669:

stepping to the Duchesse of York's side to speak with Lady Peterborough, I did see the young Duchess, a little child in hanging sleeves, dance most finely, so as almost to ravish me, her airs were so good—taught by a Frenchman that did heretofore teach the King and all the King's children, and the Queen-Mother herself, who doth still dance well.[13]

[8] HMC, *Twelfth Report*, Appendix, vii: *The Manuscripts of S. H. Le Fleming, Esq., of Rydal Hall* (London, 1890), 52.

[9] Pepys, *Diary*, viii. 404; L. Magalotti, *Travels of Cosmo the Third, Grand Duke of Tuscany, through England, during the Reign of King Charles the Second (1669)* (London, 1821), 364–5.

[10] Wilson, *Roger North*, 300; Shute, 'Anthony à Wood', ii. 99.

[11] Ashbee, *RECM*, iii. 97–8, 100; v. 16, 18.

[12] Spink, 'The Musicians of Queen Henrietta-Maria', 179; Ashbee, *RECM*, i. 196; ii. 121, 137, 139; v. 54, 72, 228, 229.

[13] Pepys, *Diary*, ix. 507.

The professions of dancing-master and musician were beginning to diverge at the time. The dancing-masters at the pre-war court were violinists as much as dancers, but we hear nothing of Gohory the musician. It is true that Edward Dyer, who danced at court in the 1675 masque-like play *Calisto* and was described by Anthony à Wood as a dancing-master, succeeded Matthew Locke as a composer for the Twenty-four Violins in 1677. But this was probably a sinecure, for no music by him survives (though there is a piece entitled 'MR. Dyer's Scotch Tune' in the fifth edition of Playford's *Apollo's Banquet* (London, 1687), part 3, no. 6), and he was described as a 'citizen and haberdasher' in 1676.[14]

More lowly members of society learned to dance at boarding schools, at dancing-academies, or in their own homes. Schools often advertised dancing as part of the curriculum, and were sometimes run by dancing-masters. 'John Waver, a dancing master' (the father of John Weaver, the author of *Orchesography; or, The Art of Dancing*) mentioned dancing-classes as well as 'Musick Vocal and Instrumental' when he advertised his Oxford 'school for young gentlewomen' in 1680.[15] The dancing-master Josias Priest ran a similar establishment first in Leicester Fields and then in Chelsea, and evidently used productions of Blow's *Venus and Adonis* and Purcell's *Dido and Aeneas* as shop windows for his tuition; we think of these all-sung works as operas, but they require as much dancing as most masques.[16]

'Dancing is a very common and favorite amusement of the ladies in this country', wrote the chronicler of the Grand Duke of Tuscany's London visit:

every evening there are entertainments at different places in the city, at which many ladies and citizens' wives are present, they going to them alone, as they do to the rooms of the dancing masters, at which there are frequently upwards of forty or fifty ladies. His highness had an opportunity of seeing several dances in the English style, exceedingly well regulated, and executed in the smartest and genteelest manner by very young ladies, whose beauty and gracefulness were shewn off to perfection by this exercise.[17]

Pepys saw 'good dancing' at such an establishment one evening in September 1660, 'a dancing meeting in Broadstreete, at the house that was formerly the Glasse house (Luke Channell Maister of the Schoole)',

[14] Ashbee, *RECM*, i. 146, 150, 159; v. 75; Shute, 'Anthony à Wood', i. 118.

[15] M. Tilmouth, 'A Calendar of References to Music in Newspapers Published in London and the Provinces (1660–1719)', *RMARC* 1 (1961), 4.

[16] For Priest's production of *Venus and Adonis*, see R. Luckett, 'A New Source for *Venus and Adonis*', *MT* 130 (1989), 76–9; for school masques, see N. Zaslaw, 'An English *Orpheus and Euridice* of 1697', *MT* 118 (1977), 805–8.

[17] Magalotti, *Travels of Cosmo the Third*, 315.

The English Dancing Master:

O R,

Plaine and eafie Rules for the Dancing of Country Dances, with the Tune to each Dance.

L O N D O N,

Printed by *Thomas Harper,* and are to be fold by *John Playford,* at his Shop in the Inner
Temple neere the Church doore. 1 6 5 1.

13.1. Title-page of John Playford, *The English Dancing Master* (London, 1651)

and went to 'a dancing Schoole in Fleetstreete' in November 1661, where
he 'saw a company of pretty girles dance'; he did not approve: 'I do not in
myself like to have young girles exposed to so much vanity.'[18] Typical
dancing-schools are illustrated on the title-pages of John Playford's series
The Dancing Master—volumes that contain the sort of English country
dances that the Italian visitors would have seen (Figs. 13.1, 13.2). Pepys
employed Mr Pembleton to teach his wife privately in 1663, and John
Evelyn, sorrowfully listing the virtues of his daughter Mary after her
death in March 1685, wrote that she 'daunc'd with the most grace that in
my whole life I had ever seene, & so would her Master say, who was
Monsieur Isaac'—the mysterious choreographer of a number of dances
performed at court on Queen Anne's birthdays.[19]

---

[18] Pepys, *Diary*, i. 253; ii. 212.
[19] Ibid., iv. 111 *et seq.*; Evelyn, *Diary*, 797; for Isaac, see Winter, *The Pre-Romantic Ballet*, 13, 55;
Highfill *et al.*, *A Biographical Dictionary*, viii. 103–4; Isaac's published dances are listed in W. C.
Smith, *A Bibliography of the Musical Works Published by John Walsh during the Years 1695–1720*
(London, 1948; repr. 1968).

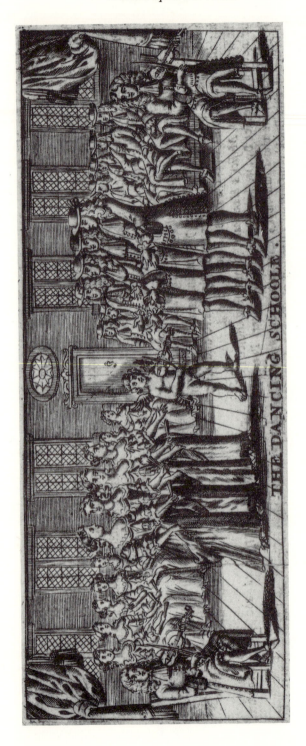

13.2. 'The Dancing Schoole', engraving on the title-pages of John Playford, *The Dancing Master* (London, 7th edn., 1686 and later editions). Bodleian Library, University of Oxford.

The skills acquired from dancing-masters were exhibited at formal balls, held regularly on royal birthdays and during the Christmas season. Such balls replaced the masque as the chief vehicle of the court's collective terpsichorean prowess, and were doubtless inspired by similar events that Charles and his courtiers had attended during their exile on the Continent. On 31 December 1662 Pepys was taken to a ball at Whitehall:

By and by comes the King and Queen, the Duke and Duchesse, and all the great ones; and after seating themselfs, the King takes out the Duchess of Yorke, and the Duke the Duchess of Buckingham, the Duke of Monmouth my Lady Castlemayne, and so the other lords other ladies; and they danced the Bransle. After that, the King led a lady a single Coranto; and then the rest of the lords, one after another, other ladies. Very noble it was, and great pleasure to see. Then to Country dances; the King leading the first which he called for; which was—says he, Cuckolds all a-row the old dance of England. Of the ladies that danced, the Duke of Monmouth's mistress and my Lady Castlemayne and a daughter of Sir Harry De Vickes were the best. The manner was, when the King dances, all the ladies in the room, and the Queen herself, stands up; and endeed he dances rarely and much better than the Duke of Yorke. Having stayed here as long as I thought fit, to my infinite content, it being the greatest pleasure I could wish now to see at Court, I went out, leaving them dancing . . .[20]

The festivities were evidently repeated several times over that Christmas season; on 7 January Evelyn 'saw the Ball, in which his Majestie daunced with severall greate Ladys', and on the 10th he saw it 'daunced againe at Court by the King, Duke & Ladys, in greate pompe &c.'.[21] Pepys attended another ball of the same type on the queen's birthday (15 November) in 1666:

Anon the house grew full, and the candles light, and the King and Queen and all the ladies set . . . Presently after the King was come in, he took the Queene, and about fourteen more couple there was, and begun the Bransles . . . then to a Corant, and now and then a French Dance; but that so rare that the Corants grew tiresome, that I wished it done. Only, Mrs. Steward danced mighty finely, and many French dances, especially one the King called the New Dance, which was very pretty.[22]

A great deal of informal dancing must have gone on at court. Anthony Hamilton, the author of the *Memoirs of the Comte de Gramont*, a semi-fictional account of a Frenchman's adventures in Restoration England, wrote that while the court was at Tunbridge Wells there was 'dancing every day at the queen's apartment—because the physicians recom-

[20] Pepys, *Diary*, iii. 300–1.
[21] Evelyn, *Diary*, 450.
[22] Pepys, *Diary*, vii. 371–2.

mended it'.[23] Such dancing was presumably accompanied by members of the Twenty-four Violins; some engagements of this sort—which attracted special payments—are listed in the 1667 'remonstrance' against John Banister (see Ch. 12). Sometimes we only know of them from mundane sources such as lists of food and drink provided 'for a Private danceing at the Maids of Hon(ou)rs Lodging' on 19 October 1686, or candles and torches for a ball at Whitehall on James II's birthday, 14 October 1686.[24] Informal dancing often attracted attention only when it caused scandal, as on the king's birthday in 1664, when Pepys was told that Charles II had been at 'my Lady Castlemaine's lodgings . . . dancing with fiddlers all night long almost, and all the world coming by taking notice of it—which I am sorry to hear'.[25] In similar vein, Evelyn was scandalized by 'the jolly blades, Racing, Dauncing, feasting & revelling, more resembling a luxurious & abandon'd rout, than a Christian Court' when he visited the court at Newmarket in October 1671. He added: 'The Duke of Buckingham was now in mighty favour, & had with him here that impudent woman, the Countesse of Shrewsbery, with his band of fidlars &c.'[26]

Eyewitness accounts provide a certain amount of information about the activities of court violinists. But by their nature they tend not to provide the sort of information we should most like to know. How, exactly, was the Twenty-four Violins constituted? What did it play? And how did it play it? Questions of this sort are best answered by the music itself, assuming that we can identify pieces written for the group in the consort repertoire at large.

Fortunately, a useful tool for the purpose is on hand in the form of the branle or brawl, the dance that opened the court balls that Pepys attended in 1662 and 1666. The branle is the only contemporary dance that was more or less confined to the dance floor. That is, it is not found in the repertoire of incidental music for Restoration plays, or in the suites that Matthew Locke and his contemporaries wrote for domestic use. Also, the branle is explicitly connected with the court and its violinists in several of Roger North's historical essays. Charles II had 'lived some considerable time abroad where the French musick was in request', he wrote in his essay 'Notes of Comparison between the Elder and Later Musick' of *c.*1726:

which consisted of an Entry (perhaps) and then Brawles, as they were called, that is motive ayres and dances. And it was, and is yet a mode among the Monseurs,

---

[23] *Memoirs of the Comte de Gramont by Anthony Hamilton, Translated by Horace Walpole*, ed. D. Hughes (London, 1965), 211.
[24] Ashbee, *RECM*, v. 233.
[25] Pepys, *Diary*, v. 164.
[26] Evelyn, *Diary*, 563.

always to act the musick, which habit the King had got, and never in his life could endure any that he could not act by keeping the time; which made the comon andante or else the step-tripla the onely musicall styles at Court in his time. And after the manner of France, he set up a band of 24 violins to play at his dinners, which disbanded all the old English musick at once.[27]

Similar ideas are found in a fuller form in a passage written *c.*1695–1700:

With Charles II came in a sort of musick after the Frenche patterne proper for dinner and a ball. Mons(ieu)r Babtist had refined his country's jejune stile of the ball, with the spirit of the Italian, and introduced a noble harmony in his overtures, and excellent aires in the branles and balletts, I thinck not equal'd by any of his imitators. Here were many instruments, all waiters upon the violin, which was predominant, a lowdness a great ingredient, together with a strong snatching way of playing, to make the musick brisk and good.[28]

And again, from North's last historical essay, 'The Musicall Grammarian' of 1728:

But during the first years of Charles 2d all musick affected by the beau-mond run into the French way, and the rather, becaus at that time the master of the court musick in France, whose name was Babtista (an Itallian Frenchifyed) had influenced the French style by infusing a great portion of the Italian harmony into it; whereby the ayre was exceedingly improved. The manner was theatricall, and the setts of lessons composed, called branles (as I take it) or braules, that is beginning with an entry, and then courants etc. And the entrys of Babtist ever were, and will be valued as most stately and compleat harmony, and all the compositions of the towne were strained to imitate Babtist's vein . . .[29]

The essential point here—that the branle was particularly associated with the court and the Twenty-four Violins—is well taken, and is borne out by the surviving sources. But not all of North's ideas can be accepted without qualification. Lully had a profound influence on English composers, but suites from his ballets and operas did not, it seems, circulate in England until around 1680, which is when the earliest English sources, such as *GB-Lbl*, Add. MSS 29283-5, *US-NH*, Filmer MS 7, and the first layer of *US-NYp*, Drexel MS 3849, were copied. Also, the branle may be an example of a theatrical manner, but it was not a theatre dance, and Charles II was not personally responsible for bringing it to England; a reference in Richard Flecknoe's *Enigmaticall Characters* (London, 1658) to a dancing-master who 'gos a Pilgrimage to Paris every year, and distributes his new Branles Gavots and Sarabands, like precious Reliques amongst his Schollars at his return' shows that it was already known in

[27] Wilson, *Roger North*, 299.
[28] Ibid. 221.
[29] Chan and Kassler, *Roger North's The Musicall Grammarian*, 261.

England before the Restoration.[30] It was dancing-masters who taught the new dances, and were the arbiters of taste in such matters, not kings or, for that matter, composers.

The pattern of branle danced at the English court is presumably the one that is found in three examples, two anonymous, and one by Jacques (James) Paisible, printed in the second part of *Apollo's Banquet* (5th edn., London, 1687), which is described as 'containing the usual Tunes of the French Dances, performed at Court, and in Dancing-Schools'. It opens with two strains of stately duple time with dotted rhythms, each made up of two six-bar phrases. Then comes a single-strain 'second brawl' of eight bars in triple time, similar in rhythm to a corant, followed by a 'leading brawl' of two six-bar strains in the same rhythm. The suite ends with a gavotte, usually in two strains. The same pattern, with the 'second brawl' and the 'leading brawl' called *branle gai* and *amener*, was also used on the Continent at the time, though in France itself a six-movement suite of branles, with a *branle double* and a *montirande* inserted after the *amener*, was more common.[31]

A possible explanation for this state of affairs is that the four-movement suite is a simplified version of the full branle. Perhaps French dancing-masters taught it to pupils outside France who had limited experience of their style of dancing. Whether or not this is so, all but one (no. 20) of the twenty-five suites of branles I have found so far in English sources conform to the four-section pattern (Table 13.1). The case for connecting the English repertoire of branles with the Twenty-four Violins is made stronger by the fact that nearly half of them are by John Banister and Matthew Locke, the two most prominent composers active in the group in the 1660s and 1670s. Further, three of the sources, *US-NYp*, Drexel MS 3976, *GB-Och*, Mus. MS 1066, and *GB-Och*, Mus. MS 1183, can be shown to contain items from the repertoire of the Twenty-four Violins, though none of the manuscripts appears to have been used by the group.

The most important of the three for the present purpose is undoubtedly Drexel MS 3976, a score of seventy-eight four-part consort pieces by Matthew Locke entitled 'The Rare Theatrical, & other Compositions'. 'The Rare Theatrical' is a much misunderstood document. It is usually said, following a written statement to that effect in the hand of an early owner, the harpist and antiquary Edward Jones (1752–1824),

---

[30] J. Harley, *Music in Purcell's London: The Social Background* (London, 1968), 35.

[31] See F. de Lauze, *Apologie de la Danse by F. De Lauze 1623*, ed. J. Wildebloode (London, 1952) for the six-movement pattern; for Continental examples of the four-movement pattern see, for instance, those by Pierre Verdier (Werdier) in Mráček (ed.), *Seventeenth-Century Instrumental Dance Music*, 185–8, and by J. C. F. Fischer in E. von Werra (ed.), *Orchestermusik des XVII. Jahrhunderts* (DDT, 1. folge, 10; Wiesbaden and Graz, 1958), 58–62.

TABLE 13.1. *Suites of branles in English sources*

No.	Composer	Source	Key	Scoring
1	J. Banister	T. Greeting, *The Pleasant Companion* (2nd edn., London, 1672), no. 48	C	flageolet
2	J. Banister	*GB-Ob*, MSS Mus. Sch. E. 447–9, fos. 27^v–48^r, 43^v–44^r, 46^v–47^r	F	a3
3	J. Banister	*GB-Och*, Mus. MS 1183, fos. 111^r–14^v	a	a4
4	J. Banister	*GB-Och*, Mus. MS 1183, fos. 115^r–21^r	C	a3
5	J. Birchensha	*GB-Lcm*, MS 2087 a/b, 380–5	B♭	a2
6	J. Birchensha	*US-NYp*, Drexel MS 3849, 101	d	a3
7	G. Diessener	*Instrumental Ayrs* (London, 1682), 38–9 *GB-Lbl*, Add. MSS 29283–5, 63–4	F	a3 a3
8	G. Diessener	*Instrumental Ayrs* (London, 1682), 66–7	A	a3
9	M. Locke	*GB-Och*, Mus. MS 1066, fos. 9^v–10^v	g	violin part
10	M. Locke	*US-NYp*, Drexel MS 3976, 1–4	A	a4
11	M. Locke	*US-NYp*, Drexel MS 3976, 13–16	B♭	a4
12	M. Locke	*US-NYp*, Drexel MS 3976, 45–8	C	a4
13	M. Locke	*US-NYp*, Drexel MS 3976, 49–53	c	a4
14	M. Locke	*US-NYp*, Drexel MS 3976, 57–60	d	a4
15	M. Locke	*US-NYp*, Drexel MS 3976, 97–100	D	a4
16	J. Paisible	*Apollo's Banquet* (5th edn., London, 1687), second part, nos. 72, 73	c	violin part
17	R. Smith	*GB-Ob*, MS Mus. 1183, fos. 15^r–17^v	D	a3
18	Anon.	*Apollo's Banquet* (5th edn., London, 1687), second part, no. 70	B♭	violin part
19	Anon.	*Apollo's Banquet* (5th edn., London, 1687), second part, no. 71	D	violin part
20	Anon.	*GB-Cu*, Add. MS 3396, nos. 1–6	C	bass part
21	Anon.	*GB-En*, MSS 9455–7, nos. 30–3	B♭	a3
22	Anon.	*GB-Mch*, MS Mus. Mun. A.2.6, fos. 7^r–8^v	g	bass part
23	Anon.	*GB-Ob*, MS Mus. Sch. C. 95, 26	c	violin part
24	Anon.	*US-NH*, Filmer MS 7, fos. 65^v–66^r	B♭	bass part
25	Anon.	*US-NYp*, Drexel MS 3849, 10	G	a3

that it was compiled by copyists working for the mid-eighteenth-century Oxford professor William Hayes. But I have argued that it actually dates from the 1680s and is the work of one individual; his identity is unknown, but he had connections with Henry Purcell and other court composers, and he may have been a member of the Isaack family of organists and choirmen—who may or may not have been related to Isaac the dancing-master.[32] 'The Rare Theatrical' is laid out in the common seventeenth-century way in an ascending sequence of keys. Sources of this type normally start with gamut (G minor and major), but the collection lacks this section as well as the ones for E and F, so it seems to be incomplete —perhaps because the copy-text had pages missing at either end. The six sets of branles in 'The Rare Theatrical' are all in different keys, and it may be that Locke wrote a cycle of branles in every common key so that the performers at court balls would always have one available to match the key of the succeeding dances. These works are certainly among the most remarkable examples of functional dance music in the history of European music. What Charles II and his courtiers thought as they danced to such wayward and essentially serious music, full of jagged melodic lines and surprising harmonic twists, is anyone's guess (Ex. 13.1).

It is not entirely clear how and why 'The Rare Theatrical' was assembled. I argue in Chapter 14 that it originally contained most if not all the incidental music Locke wrote for Restoration plays. Yet it is odd that so comprehensive and apparently authoritative a collection should be ordered in a way that distorts the composer's intentions: the theatre suites (which would normally have contained items in several keys; see below) seem to have been broken up and sorted into their respective key sections. And the musical texts are surprisingly corrupt, which suggests that there were several stages between Locke's autographs and the present collection. A possible explanation is that the copy-text of 'The Rare Theatrical' (which was probably also a score) was compiled from a disorganized collection of loose performing material, and was organized by key in an attempt to bring some sort of order out of chaos. Whether or not this is so, the uniform four-part scoring of 'The Rare Theatrical' suggests that it is drawn from the repertoire of a single performing ensemble, while its mixture of theatre music and ballroom dances is an indication that the ensemble in question was the Twenty-four Violins. In addition to its court duties, the group played regularly in the two London theatres during the 1660s and 1670s, divided into two for the purpose.

The scoring of 'The Rare Theatrical' has also been misunderstood. It has been assumed that it was intended for two equal violins, viola, and bass, the Italianate 'string quartet' scoring used by Blow and Purcell, and by Locke in his suite for *The Tempest* (1674) and in the instrumental passages of *Psyche* (1675). A few of the 'Rare Theatrical' pieces do use this SSTB layout, particularly those that have concordances with (and seem to be arrangements of) pieces for two violins and continuo from

---

[32] See M. Locke, *The Rare Theatrical, New York Public Library, Drexel MS 3976*, ed. P. Holman (MLE, series A, vol. 4; London, 1989), pp. ix–xii; for the Isaack family, see Holman, 'Bartholomew Isaack and "Mr Isaack" of Eton: A Confusing Tale of Restoration Musicians', *MT* 128 (1987), 381–5.

Ex. 13.1. Matthew Locke, Branles in C, bb. 1–12, *US-NYp*, Drexel MS 3976, p. 45

'The Broken Consort' and *Tripla concordia*.[33] But the bulk of the collection uses the earlier SATB layout; that is, the second part does not cross the top part, and does not go higher than *f''*, the normal top note for viola parts at the time (being a fourth-finger extension on the top string in first position). Also, there are numerous instances where the second part is a third too high in the manuscript, a mistake that is best explained by supposing that the copyist was changing from soprano clef to treble clef as he went along. The soprano is the standard clef for the upper viola parts of French violin band music, and *US-NYp*, Drexel MS 5061, a score of consort music in the same hand as 'The Rare Theatrical', opens with a fifteen-movement set of four-part dances by Locke in G minor, pp. 1–13, the first six of which have the second part in the soprano clef; indeed, the set may be drawn from the missing G section of 'The Rare Theatrical'.[34]

It seems, therefore, that most of the pieces in 'The Rare Theatrical' were intended for one violin, two violas, and bass, and that this was how the Twenty-four Violins was first constituted—a conclusion supported by a document, now untraceable, that described the group as consisting in 1660 of 'six violins, six counter-tenors, six tenors, and six basses'.[35] The violin, two-viola layout had not, it seems, been used by the English court violin band before—the group played in five parts before the Civil War—but it was common abroad. It is found in the repertoires of French violin bands that worked at Kassel and at the Swedish court, in Viennese court ballet music, in many mid-century German and Austrian publications, and even in a few Italian sources, such as some of Stradella's orchestral music and Gasparo Zannetti's *Il scolaro* (Milan, 1645).[36] Matthew Locke's orchestral music suggests that the Twenty-four Violins went over to the string-quartet scoring in the early 1670s. Court orchestral music was still occasionally written in five parts with two or three violas, but none of the four-part dance music of Blow, Purcell, or their contemporaries seems to be intended for the one-violin two-viola layout.

A last point raised by 'The Rare Theatrical' concerns the range of the bass part. It frequently descends to *B♭'*, which indicates that Locke was writing for the large bass member of the violin family, tuned a tone lower than the violoncello; the *B♭'*, *F*, *c*, *g* tuning is given for it from 1683 to at least 1697 in successive editions of Playford's *An Introduction to the Skill of Musick*, as well as in James Talbot's manuscript, written during the

---

[33] See *The Rare Theatrical*, ed. Holman, pp. xxii–xxiv for a list of concordances.

[34] Edited in *Matthew Locke: Eight Suites in Four Parts from 'Consort Music'*, ed. S. Beck (New York, n.d.), 14–24.

[35] Quoted in Boyden, *History*, 230, from W. Sandys and S. A. Forster, *The History of the Violin* (London, 1864), 146, which gives no source for the reference.

[36] G. Zannetti, *Il Scolaro* (Milan, 1645), ed. J. Tyler (Early Dance Music, 5, 6; London, 1983, 1985).

1690s.[37] Bb' and B', unobtainable on the violoncello and the six-string English bass viol, are frequently found in Restoration orchestral music, and appear as late as the 1690s; for instance, there are Bbs in Purcell's Ode for the Duke of Gloucester's Birthday, first performed on 24 July 1695, and Bps in John Eccles's 1701 setting of *The Judgement of Paris*.[38] The violoncello, the small solo version of the Italian *violone* or bass violin, seems to have been rare in England until the first decade of the eighteenth century; it was probably popularized by Nicola Haym and the other Italian cellists who came to London at that time to work for the newly established opera company at the Queen's Theatre in the Haymarket.[39]

GB-Och, Mus. MS 1066 also contains some court orchestral music. The manuscript, a small oblong part-book entitled 'first Treble' and 'Cantus primus' on the cover, is the work of two copyists. It opens with a numbered sequence of twenty-four pieces consisting of: (1) a five-movement suite in D minor by Matthew Locke, fos. 1ʳ–2ʳ, also in 'The Rare Theatrical', nos. 60–4; (2) a four-movement suite in G minor by 'Senior Mich: de Ferara', fos. 2ᵛ–3ʳ; (3) a twelve-movement suite in Bb by Philip Beckett, fos. 3ᵛ–7ʳ; (4) three pieces by Lully, fos. 7ᵛ–9ʳ, from *Ballet d'Alcidiane* (1658) and *Hercule amoreux* (1662).[40] Then come three items by Locke in the second hand: a G minor suite of branles (fos. 9ᵛ–10ᵛ), a G minor 'roundo' (fos. 10ᵛ–11ʳ), set for keyboard in *Melothesia* (London, 1673), p. 12, and a Bb 'curtain tune' (fos. 11ᵛ–12ʳ), also in 'The Rare Theatrical', no. 18. Most if not all these pieces must have been in four parts, for items 1 and 3 are labelled 'A: 4' at several points, and all but one of the Locke concordances are with four-part pieces in 'The Rare Theatrical'. The rest of the manuscript, copied (with the exception of one piece) by the first scribe, consists largely or entirely of trios by the French keyboard-player Jean la Volée.[41]

---

[37] H. Playford, *An Introduction to the Skill of Musick* (10th edn., London, 1683), 108; (13th edn., London, 1697), 64; R. Donington, 'James Talbot's Manuscript: Bowed Strings', *Chelys*, 6 (1975–6), 45, 46, 56.

[38] Purcell, *A Song for the Duke of Gloucester's Birthday*, ed. I. Spink (The Works of Henry Purcell, 4; London, 1990), pp. viii, 7, 22, 25; Eccles, *The Judgement of Paris*, ed. R. Platt (MLE, series C, vol. 1; Tunbridge Wells, 1984), 7, 8.

[39] For the meaning of the word *violone*, see Bonta, 'From Violone to Violoncello'; id., 'Terminology for the Bass Violin'; for early Italian opera in London, see C. A. Price, 'The Critical Decade for English Music Drama, 1700–1710', *Harvard Library Bulletin*, 26 (1978), 38–76; J. Milhous and R. D. Hume, *Vice Chamberlain Coke's Theatrical Papers 1706–1715* (Carbondale and Edwardsville, Ill., 1982).

[40] H. Schneider (ed.), *Chronologisch-thematisches Verzeichnis sämtlicher Werke von Jean-Baptiste Lully* (Tutzing, 1981), LWV 17/23, 9/79, 17/30.

[41] Many of them have concordances in *B-Bc*, MS Litt. XY24.910, and *GB-Lbl*, Add. MS 31424, where they are attributed respectively to 'La Volée' and 'L. V.'; item no. 44 in the sale catalogue of Thomas Britton's library was 'Three sets by Orl. Gibbons, Mons. la Voles, and Lock, 3 parts'; see Hawkins, *A General History*, ii. 792.

Nearly all the music in the manuscript can be connected with the Restoration court in one way or another. The Locke pieces clearly come from the same orchestral repertoire as 'The Rare Theatrical', as does the suite by Philip Beckett; Beckett was a member of the Twenty-four Violins from 1660 until he surrendered his place in the summer of 1674.[42] Jean la Volée also worked at the Restoration Court. He was sworn into the Private Music on 18 October 1661, was the harpsichordist for a group of French singers at court from, probably, 1663 to 1668 (see Ch. 12), and can probably be identified with the 'John Vollett' who became an English denizen in May 1673.[43] The identity of 'Senior Mich: de Ferara' is a problem, for no one of that name is known in English documents of the time. A possibility, admittedly remote, is that it refers to the French violinist Michel Farinel, who worked in England in the 1670s; his set of divisions on *La folia*, 'Farinel's Ground', was published in Playford's *The Division Violin* and became quite popular.[44] Farinel was born in Grenoble, but spent much of his career in Italy: he studied in Rome, and worked at the Savoy court in Turin.

Philip Beckett's suite is of interest since it is apparently the sort of thing that the Twenty-four Violins played for court ceremonies. It has no overture or curtain tune (all twelve movements are dances), and is in B♭ throughout, so it does not seem to have been written for the theatre. It was not necessary to keep to a single key in theatre suites because the movements were not heard in a single sequence—some were played before the play began, others between the acts. Also, Purcell and his contemporaries seem to have associated particular keys with specific emotions, and they used changes of key in the theatre to mirror changes of mood in the action.[45] Nor do extended suites of this sort belong to the domestic consort repertoire. The fantasia suite was outmoded by the 1660s, but composers such as Matthew Locke, William Gregory, Benjamin Rogers, and John Hingeston continued to write domestic consort suites most often with three, four, or five movements. Extended suites in a single key may be connected with public or semi-public performance—such as the appearances of the Twenty-four Violins at the king's public dinner. Indeed, some of them, such as the three- and four-part works by Thomas Baltzar, seem to have been written for the music meetings in Commonwealth and Restoration Oxford (see Ch. 11).

---

[42] Ashbee, *RECM*, i. 3, 140–1; v. 107, 139.

[43] Ibid., i. 220; v. 62.

[44] For Farinel, see Westrup, 'Foreign Musicians', 77; J. M. Ward, 'Apropos *The British Broadside Ballad and its Music*', *JAMS* 20 (1967), 37–41; there is a suite attributed to 'Ferera' among the 'L. V'. pieces in *GB-Lbl*, Add. MS 31424.

[45] For a recent discussion of this point, see C. A. Price, *Henry Purcell and the London Stage* (Cambridge, 1984), 21–6.

On 31 October 1666 the Lord Chamberlain ordered nine members of the Twenty-four Violins to 'meet and practise with Mr. Becket, his Lessons'.[46] Most likely, the purpose was to rehearse his B♭ suite (or a similar work, now lost) for performance at some court ceremony.

The third source, *GB-Och*, Mus. MS 1183, is not a single manuscript but twenty separate sets of parts in at least five hands; they were evidently kept loose in a pile over a long period, folded in half in some cases, and were only bound together at a late stage (Table 13.2). Apart from a chaconne from Purcell's music for *Dioclesian* (1690), added by a later hand to a blank leaf of Set 1, all the music seems to come from the 1660s or the 1670s. It is a major source of John Banister—Sets 10–20, thirteen suites and a ground, all seem to be by him—and it forms the largest and most accurate corpus of his music.[47] It shows that he was a better composer than is suggested by the corrupt printed sources of his music, such as *Tripla concordia*, and the successive editions of *The Division Violin*.

Many of the composers represented in Mus. MS 1183 worked at court. Banister, Thomas Farmer, and John Twist were colleagues in the Twenty-four Violins in the late 1670s, while Robert Smith was briefly a member of the Private Music from 1673 until his early death in the autumn of 1675; 'Mr Evans' and 'H. Mountagu' can perhaps be identified with Charles Evans, harper in the Private Music from 1660 to 1685, and Henry Montagu, a choirboy who left the Chapel Royal in 1669.[48] Yet the collection was clearly assembled outside Whitehall. One of the copyists has recently been identified as Francis Withey, singing man at Christ Church, Oxford, from June 1670 until his death in December 1727, and there are a number of pieces by non-court composers, such as Christopher Simpson (an autograph copy of a set of divisions), and the Dublin city musicians George and Thomas Tollett; 'Mr Holt' may be Richard Holt, also a Dublin musician.[49] It may be that the collection was compiled for the use of an instrumental group in Oxford; Set 5, a composite suite by Robert Smith and Thomas Farmer, has the label 'made in Oxford'.

The fact remains, however, that the connections that have been made between 'The Rare Theatrical' and the Twenty-four Violins apply equally

[46] Ashbee, *RECM*, i. 73.

[47] *Dioclesian*, ed. J. F. Bridge and J. Pointer, rev. M. Laurie (The Works of Henry Purcell, 9; London, 1961), 57–9; sets nos. 10–20 are edited respectively in Luhring, 'The Music of John Banister', 381–97, 506–12, 348–56, 434–9, 414–27 and 455–63, 470–85, 464–9, 495–505, 398–413, 440–54, 428–33.

[48] Holman, 'The Harp in Stuart England', 195; Ashbee, *RECM*, i. 87, 89; v. 133–4.

[49] R. P. Thompson, '"Francis Withie of Oxon" and his Commonplace Book, Christ Church, Oxford MS 337', *Chelys*, 20 (1991), 3–27; M. Urquhart, 'The Handwriting of Christopher Simpson', *Chelys*, 15 (1986), 62–3; W. H. G. Flood, 'Dublin City Music from 1456 to 1789', *SIMG* 11 (1909–10), 33–42.

TABLE 13.2. *Summary of the contents of* GB-Och, *Mus. MS 1183*

Set	Folio	Key	Title/description
1	1ʳ–14ᵛ	various	[a collection of 10 grounds a3 by Anon., John Banister, Michel Farinel, Robert Smith, George Tollett, and (added later) Henry Purcell]
2	15ʳ–17ᵛ	D	Mʳ Rob: Smith's Brawls in D sol re [a3]
3	18ʳ–21ᵛ	C/d	Mʳ Robartt Smith in C fa utt [a4, 8-movt. suite]
4	22ʳ–25ᵛ	g/B♭	Mʳ Robartt Smith in Gamutt key [a4, 6-movt. suite]
5	26ʳ–27ᵛ	F/A	Mʳ Rob Smyth / made in Oxford [at end:] Mʳ Farmor [vn. 1 part, composite 9-movt. suite]
6	28ʳ–29ᵛ	C	Division Treble and Bass / Chr. Simpson [autograph]
7	30ʳ–31ᵛ	D/F/G	Mʳ John: Twist [vn. 1 part, 12-movt. suite]
8	32ʳ–33ᵛ	d	Polwheele [bass viol divisions]
9	34ʳ–69ᵛ	various	[a numbered sequence of 55 pieces a3 and a4 by Anon., (Charles?) Evans, (Richard?) Holt, 'H. Mountagu' (Henry Montagu?), George Tollett, and Thomas Tollett]
10	70ʳ–73ᵛ	g/B♭	Gamut / John Banister [9-movt. suite a4]
11	74ʳ–75ᵛ	B♭	Trumpet [vn. 1 and bass parts of 5-movt. suite, anon. but probably by Banister]
12	76ʳ–81ᵛ	B♭	Mʳ Jo: Banisters Ground / in Be mi [a3, with some fragments]
13	82ʳ–84ᵛ	c	[5-movt. suite a3, anon. but probably by Banister]
14	85ʳ–90ᵛ	g/d	Mʳ Banister in Gamut / Mʳ B: De sol re [6- and 7-movt. suites a3]
15	91ʳ–96ᵛ	d/C	Mʳ Banisters Ground in D sol re [a3, with a 5-movt. suite]
16	97ʳ–102ᵛ	d	[6-movt. suite a3, anon. but probably by Banister]
17	103ʳ–110ᵛ	B♭	The Musick att the Bath 2: Pᵗˢ / Mʳ John Banister [12-movt. suite a2]
18	111ʳ–114ᵛ	a/F	A:4 A re Bralls Mʳ John Banister [a4, with a 4-movt. suite]
19	115ʳ–121ᵛ	C/d/F	Branles in C fa ut [a3, with a 7-movt. suite]
20	124ʳ–126ᵛ	G/g	Mʳ J: Banister [4-movt. suite a3]

to much of Mus. MS 1183, and, in particular, to the music by John Banister. There are two suites of branles; the three- and four-part pieces divide into those that are clearly written for two violins and those that have the characteristics of the violin, two-viola scoring; and many of the bass parts descend to $B\flat'$. Also, one of the Banister suites can be connected with some confidence to a particular performance of the Twenty-four Violins. In September 1663 the queen visited Bath to take the waters, and a section of the Twenty-four Violins went with her; Banister and six colleagues were paid their travelling expenses to the city, and when the group complained about Banister's conduct in March 1667 they claimed that he 'received 50^{li} from the Queenes Ma(jes)tie at the Bath, and paid to those that attended onely 5^{li} each keeping 20^{li} for himselfe' (see Ch. 12).[50] Among the pieces they played on that occasion was presumably Set 17 of Mus. MS 1183, Banister's 'The Musick att the Bath'. Significantly, the work consists of twelve movements, all dances and all in B♭—the type of suite that has been connected with public or semi-public occasions. The other Banister suites in Mus. MS 1183 are either much shorter, or contain movements in several keys—which does not mean, of course, that they were not written for the Twenty-four Violins.

Why is 'The Musick att the Bath' in only two parts, treble and bass? The copyist evidently thought that it was complete since he wrote '2: P(ar)ts' at the top of fo. 103^v, and the music, with its imitative writing, works well enough as it stands (Ex. 13.2). However, it is difficult to believe that Banister and his six colleagues would have played the work with a yawning gap between the treble and bass; it clearly needs inner parts or, to use the French term, *parties de remplissage*. French seventeenth-century composers often wrote only the outer parts of their orchestral music, leaving the time-consuming inner parts to assistants; I argued in Chapter 8 that the composers of English masque dances did the same thing, and the existence of such a system would certainly help to explain why so much English dance music by court composers survives in only two parts. Music of this sort is not incomplete in the sense that the sources are defective—though some undoubtedly are. The outer parts were presumably preserved more often than the others because they contain the essence of the music; also, some copyists and librarians would have known that they were the only ones written by the original composers.

More of the repertoire of the Twenty-four Violins can be identified in some of the three-part manuscripts copied for domestic use. A good example is *US-NYp*, Drexel MS 3849, a set of part-books compiled during the 1670s by the composer and theorist John Birchensha, who died in May 1681; it was later owned and added to by Thomas Britton, who presumably used it in his famous concerts.[51] Drexel MS 3849 is not

---

[50] Ashbee, *RECM*, i. 48.

[51] A facsimile edition is scheduled to appear in the series Music in London Entertainment; I identified Birchensha's hand in Drexel MS 3849 by comparing it with a partly autograph copy of his composition rules, *GB-Lbl*, Add. MS 4910, fos. 39^r–56^v; see L. E. Miller, 'John Birchensha and the

Ex. 13.2. John Banister, Air, no. 1 of 'The Musick att the Bath', *GB-Och*, Mus. MS 1183, fos. 103ᵛ, 107ᵛ

a good source. The texts tend to be corrupt, and it is organized by key, which means that the theatre suites in more than one key are broken up. For instance, a separate piece entitled 'Mʳ Banisters Divell' on p. 74 also appears as the last number of the six-movement Set 15 in Mus. MS 1183; the complete work was probably written for Ben Jonson's play *The Devil is an Ass*, produced a number of times in the early 1660s (see Table 14.1). Also, some pieces clearly have a viola part missing; for instance, four-part versions of the seven G minor pieces by Robert Smith on pp. 15 and 17–18 are found in *US-NYp*, Drexel MS 5061, pp. 42–7. Nevertheless, the Birchensha layer of Drexel MS 3849 undoubtedly contains a good deal of court orchestral music. Much of it is by court composers such as Banister, Locke, and Smith, and it includes a suite by Nicholas Staggins which, I argue in Chapter 15, comes from his music for the masque-like play *Calisto*, produced at court in February 1675.

The clearest case is the eight-movement suite by Robert Smith entitled 'New Years Day', Drexel MS 3849, pp. 47–50. It was probably written for the annual New Year ceremony at court that featured the series of odes by Humfrey, Blow, Purcell, and others (see Ch. 17). Little is known about these events, but it is clear from a document of January 1675/6, when Staggins was paid for the 'fayre writeing' of 'a song for New Yeares day & other Aires performed at the same tyme', that orchestral suites were sometimes heard as well as the New Year odes.[52] Assuming that it was a court work, Smith's suite must have been written either for 1 January 1673/4 or 1674/5, the only two New Year's days that fell within the short period that he was a court musician. The work certainly conforms to the profile that we have established for court ceremonial music. It is an extended suite of eight movements, all in B♭ except for a short but remarkable prelude that dives unexpectedly into B♭ minor (Ex. 13.3). The bass part descends to *B♭'*, and a viola part seems to be needed to complete the harmonies.

In general, the sources of Restoration music improve in quantity and quality as we move from the 1670s to the 1680s, and from the generation of Locke and Banister to that of Blow and Purcell. The number of surviving court odes increases markedly after the late 1670s, and the same is true to an even greater extent of Restoration theatre suites; more than a hundred have been identified for plays produced between 1660 and 1710, yet only a handful come from the first twenty years of that period (though others must lurk incognito in manuscripts such as 'The Rare Theatrical' and Mus. MS 1183; see Ch. 14).

Early Royal Society: Grand Scales and Scientific Composition', *JRMA* 115 (1990), 63–79; for Britton, see C. A. Price, 'The Small-Coal Cult', *MT* 119 (1978), 1032–4.

[52] Ashbee, *RECM*, i. 156.

Ex. 13.3. Robert Smith, Prelude from 'New Years Day', *US-NYp*, Drexel MS 3849, p. 47

It is odd, therefore, that the reverse is true for the day-to-day repertoire of the Twenty-four Violins: much more of it survives from the 1660s and 1670s than the 1680s and 1690s. There are, of course, a few pieces by John Blow and Henry Purcell that might come into this category, such as Blow's remarkable four-part Chaconne in G, or Purcell's Chacony in G minor and the recently discovered 'Staircase Overture'—perhaps his earliest surviving instrumental work.[53] But there is no particular reason to think that they were written for the Twenty-four Violins. Indeed, the elaborate fugal passages and complex rhythmic patterns in the Blow suggest that it was intended to be played one to a part. It has a separate continuo part, which is needed at times to complete the harmonies; there is precious little evidence that the Twenty-four Violins played with continuo instruments, except when voices were present for concerted vocal works. Purcell and Blow were given places as composers for the Twenty-four Violins, from September 1677 and August 1682 respectively, but to judge from their surviving output, their contribution to the group's repertoire was largely confined to odes and anthems.[54] Purcell, of course, also wrote a great deal of orchestral music for the theatre, though nearly all of it was for productions in the 1690s, when the Twenty-four Violins had ceased playing in the commercial theatres, and the composer had loosened his ties with the court.

One explanation for this state of affairs is that less court orchestral music was composed in the 1680s and 1690s than in previous decades, as accumulating arrears of salary forced royal musicians to seek work outside Whitehall—which, presumably, curtailed musical activity at court. Another is that the Master of the Music, Nicholas Staggins, seems to have been responsible for the composition of court orchestral music, particularly after the deaths of Locke and Banister in 1677 and 1679. We know of a number of orchestral pieces by Staggins from bills of 1675–6 relating to the copying of parts for the Twenty-four Violins. In May 1675 he was paid for 'several Airs of Musick for the selected Band of violins at Windsor', in July for 'a Chaccon with several others that was played at Scaramoucha' (evidently for a performance by the *commedia dell'arte* company that played at Whitehall in 1673, 1674, and 1675), in November for 'the Aires composed for the Maske', in December for 'severall Aires that was performed at the King's dinner', and in January 1676 for the New Year's ode and suite discussed above.[55] In a later bill, from

---

[53] Blow, *Chaconne for String Orchestra*, ed. W. Shaw (London, 1958); Purcell, *Fantasias and Miscellaneous Instrumental Music*, ed. T. Dart, rev. M. Tilmouth (The Works of Henry Purcell, 31; 2nd edn., London, 1990), 61–7, 76–8.

[54] Ashbee, *RECM*, i. 173, 201.

[55] Ibid. 155–6; v. 147; for the *commedia dell'arte* company, see Boswell, *The Restoration Court Stage*, esp. 118–22.

November 1686, Staggins was paid £19. 11s. 9d. for the copying of a piece for the coronation of James II on 23 April 1685: 'for faire writeing of a composition for his Majesty's coronation day from the originall in score the 6 parts, for drawing the said composition into forty severall parts for trumpetts, hautboyes, violins, tennors, bases'.[56] Staggins was also paid for 'faire writing & pricking several sorts of Musicke' in 1679, 1680, 1689–94, and 1698–1701; the details are not given, but he probably wrote a great deal of orchestral music in his twenty-five years as Master of the Music.[57]

Staggins's orchestral pieces are conspicuous by their absence in the surviving sources. Indeed, his *Calisto* suite is just about his only composition of any size that has come down to us in more than fragments. The reason seems to be that he was not rated highly by his contemporaries as a composer (which is not to say that he was not an efficient and valued administrator; see Ch. 12). Staggins's music was evidently ignored by the circle of pupils and admirers of Blow and Purcell—among them William Croft, John Church, and William Isaack—who preserved so much of the Restoration court repertoire in score. Much of it probably only existed in the sets of parts made for the original performances at Whitehall, which, if they were kept there, would have been consumed in the devastating fire of January 1697/8 that destroyed nearly all the old palace. The same fate probably befell the rest of the performing-material used by the Twenty-four Violins, but not, luckily, before 'The Rare Theatrical' had been assembled, or before some of Banister's orchestral music found its way into the repertoire of groups outside the court, and into collections such as Mus. MS 1183.

Before we leave Staggins and his lost orchestral music we need to sort out a confusion concerning the piece for James II's coronation. Franklin Zimmerman suggested that the copying bill relates to an arrangement of Purcell's 'My heart is inditing', one of the coronation anthems performed in Westminster Abbey.[58] But there is no mention of voices in the bill, and the piece in question was in six parts, while Purcell's anthem is in twelve parts—eight voices and four-part strings. Also, the bill mentions trumpets, yet there is no trumpet-like writing in the anthem, and no obvious place where trumpets might be inserted. It is more likely that Staggins was paid for an orchestral work of his own that was played not in the coronation service, but at the feast afterwards in Westminster Hall. We know from a plate in Francis Sandford's published account of the event that the Twenty-four Violins was there (see Ch. 16). The engraving,

[56] Ashbee, *RECM*, ii. 12, 138.
[57] Ibid., i. 191; ii. 141–2; v. 158.
[58] Zimmerman, *Henry Purcell*, 124–5.

13.3 Detail of 'A Prospect of the Inside of Westminster Hall', Francis Sandford, *The History of the Coronation of James II* (London, 1687), pl. 4, showing members of the Twenty-four Violins playing during the coronation banquet. The Pepys Library, Magdalene College, Cambridge, courtesy of the Master and Fellows.

the only known picture of the group, seems to show a string band of twenty in a side gallery, consisting of ten violins and/or violas and ten basses (Fig. 13.3). Actually, we know from Sandford's text that thirty-six instrumentalists took part in the ceremonies, and that 'Trumpets and Kettle-Drums' were present in Westminster Hall, placed in a 'Gallery over the Portico, at the great North-Door'.[59] The piece was evidently played by a group of forty, for it was copied into 'forty severall parts', and

[59] F. Sandford, *The History of the Coronation of the Most High, Most Mighty, and Excellent Monarch, James II* (London, 1687), 29–30, 116.

the 1676 copying bills show that it was the practice to give 'every man a part to himselfe'. If, as is likely, the orchestral writing was four-part, and was played by the thirty-six musicians (with, presumably, oboes doubling the strings), then it may be that four trumpeters played the two remaining parts two to a part.

14

'By Intervals Design'd'
Music for the London Stage

ONE evening in February 1667 Samuel Pepys had a conversation with the theatre manager Thomas Killigrew. After a while Killigrew began to compare conditions in the London theatres before and after the Civil War:

That the stage is now by his pains a thousand times better and more glorious then ever heretofore. Now wax-candles, and many of them: then, not above 3 lb. of tallow. Now, all things civil, no rudeness anywhere; then, as in a bear garden. Then, two or three fiddlers; now, nine or ten of the best. Then, nothing but rushes upon the ground and everything else mean; and now, all otherwise. Then, the Queen seldom and the King would never come; now, not the King only for state, but all civil people do think they may come as well as any.[1]

Killigrew and Sir William Davenant, the leading survivors of the pre-war London theatre, were the managers of the two 'patent' theatres, formed at the Restoration under the respective patronage of the king and his brother, James, Duke of York. Yet Pepys should have known better than to believe Killigrew's boast that the innovations of the Restoration stage had been made 'by his pains'. As Killigrew let slip, the decisive agent of change was Charles II himself. Unlike his father, who was said never to have set foot in a commercial theatre, the new king took an interest in the affairs of the two theatres, and regularly patronized them in person.

The character of Restoration theatre music, too, was determined by the king's play-going. Royal musicians had traditionally accompanied the monarch on his journeys outside the court, and would have expected to perform at functions he attended, even if they were organised and paid for by his hosts. The Twenty-four Violins and other royal musicians played at the banquet thrown by the City of London at the Guildhall on 5 July 1660, for example, and in the pageant put on to welcome the king into the City on the eve of his Coronation (see Ch. 13). Thus, royal musicians probably first began to work for the patent companies because Charles II had taken to attending their theatres, but it soon became a regular arrangement that clearly did not depend on the king's presence;

[1] Pepys, *Diary*, viii. 55–6.

Killigrew and Davenant could count on 'nine or ten of the best' fiddlers because they had members of the Twenty-four Violins at their disposal.

An instrumental ensemble formed part of the establishment of the Duke's Company from the time it was reconstituted at the Restoration: when Davenant concluded an agreement with his colleagues on 5 November 1660, provision was made for a 'band of musicians' who were to be paid not more than 30 s. daily out of the gross receipts.[2] We know nothing of who played in this group, or how large it was, but most actors were paid between 10 s. and 50 s. for a six-day week in the 1690 s, so, given that Killigrew told Pepys that the theatres consisted of 'nine or ten of the best', the daily 30 s. was perhaps divided between nine musicians, giving them £1 a week each.[3] £1 was still thought to be a suitable weekly wage for musicians when a plan was drawn up for a proposed United Company in, probably, the 1702–3 season.[4]

Pepys's diary for 8 May 1663 provides the first clear sign that an ensemble of orchestral size was in use in one of the theatres, the King's Company's new playhouse in Bridges Street, Covent Garden. According to him, the 'musique' for the play that night, Fletcher's *The Humorous Lieutenant*, was sufficiently large to have 'trebles' and 'basses' in the plural:

The house is made with extraordinary good contrivance; and yet hath some faults, as the narrowness of the passages in and out of the pit, and the distance from the stage to the boxes, which I am confident cannot hear. But for all other things it is well. Only, above all, the Musique being below, and most of it sounding under the very stage, there is no hearing of the bases at all, nor very well of the trebles, which must sure be mended.[5]

It was an innovation for an English theatre to be laid out with the instrumentalists in front of the stage; the normal practice had been to place them in a small gallery above the proscenium arch or at the side of the stage.[6] Killigrew probably adopted this arrangement, which he would have seen while he was on the Continent during the Interregnum, because the ensemble was now too large to be placed in a gallery. 'Fiddlers' and other instrumentalists frequently appeared on stage in Restoration plays, though it is not clear whether they worked independently, or were drawn from the main band.[7]

---

[2] L. Hotson, *The Commonwealth and Restoration Stage* (New York, 1962), 207.

[3] Van Lennep, *The London Stage*, i, p. ciii.

[4] A. Nicoll, *A History of English Drama*, ii: *Early Eighteenth-Century Drama* (3rd edn., Cambridge, 1961), 276–8; see J. Milhous, 'The Date and Import of the Financial Plan for a United Theatre Company in P. R. O. LC 7/3', *Maske und Kothurn*, 21 (1975), 81–8.

[5] Pepys, *Diary*, iv. 128.

[6] Price, *Music in the Restoration Theatre*, 82–7.

[7] H. Love, 'The Fiddlers on the Restoration Stage', *EM* 6 (1978), 391–9; C. A. Price, 'Restoration Stage Fiddlers and their Music', *EM* 7 (1979), 315–22.

A French visitor to London in the same year, Samuel de Sorbière, singled out the music of the Bridges Street theatre for praise: 'The Musick with which you are entertained diverts your time till the Play begins, and People chuse to go in betimes to hear it.'[8] Another Frenchman, Samuel Chappuzeau, wrote in 1667 that the music at Bridges Street was 'excellent and the dancing marvellous; there are no fewer than twelve violins to play both the preludes and the entr'actes'.[9] An account of the visit to London in 1669 by the Grand Duke of Tuscany also praises the music at the Bridges Street theatre: 'before the comedy begins, that the audience may not be tired with waiting, the most delightful symphonies are played; on which account many persons come early to enjoy this agreeable entertainment'.[10]

Members of the Twenty-four Violins were presumably present when Charles II made his first visit to a commercial theatre; the occasion was 28 June 1661 when the Duke's Company opened their new house in Lincoln's Inn Fields with Davenant's *The Siege of Rhodes*.[11] John Downes, later the company's prompter, was in the cast that night and had reason to remember it:

I must not forget my self, being Listed for an Actor in Sir William Davenant's Company in Lincoln-Inn-Fields: The very first Day of opening the House there, with the Siege of Rhodes, being to Act Haly; (The King, Duke of York, and all the Nobility in the House, and the first time the King was in a Publick Theatre); The sight of that August presence, spoil'd me for an Actor too.[12]

Direct evidence that the orchestras of both theatres were made up of members of the Twenty-four Violins is found in several court documents of 1664–5. At the beginning of 1663/4 the Great Wardrobe was ordered to supply the King's company with £40 worth of 'silkes for to cloath the Musick for the play called the Indian Queene to be acted before their Ma(jes)ties Jan(uary) 25th 1663[/4]'.[13] *The Indian Queen*, by John Dryden and his brother-in-law Sir Robert Howard, was first performed on that day, and John Banister was probably among those who played in the band, for he wrote a popular suite of incidental music for the play.[14] We cannot be sure that his music was written for the original production, but pieces from it occur in the early manuscripts *US-NH*, Filmer MSS 3 and

[8] T. Prat (ed.), *A Voyage to England* (London, 1709), 69; translated from *Relation d'un voyage en Angleterre* (Paris, 1664), 167; see Price, *Music in the Restoration Theatre*, 54, 259.

[9] Price, *Music in the Restoration Theatre*, 267, translated from *L'Europe vivante, ou relation nouvelle* (Paris, 1667), 215.

[10] Magalotti, *Travels of Cosmo the Third*, 191.

[11] Van Lennep, *The London Stage*, 29; see also J. Protheroe, 'Not so much an Opera...a Restoration Problem Examined', *MT* 106 (1965), 666–8.

[12] John Downes, *Roscius Anglicanus*, ed. J. Milhous and R. D. Hume (London, 1987), 73.

[13] A. Nicoll, *A History of Restoration Drama 1660–1700* (4th edn., Cambridge, 1952), 316.

[14] Van Lennep, *The London Stage*, 74; Price, *Music in the Restoration Theatre*, 181–2.

4 (see Ch. 10), and it was in existence by the late 1660s, for the tune of the third movement is found in the first edition of Playford's *Apollo's Banquet* (London, *c.*1669), no. 159; Henry Purcell's music for *The Indian Queen* was written for an operatic revival in 1695.[15]

Banister was certainly working for the King's Company by the end of 1664, for on 20 December of that year the Lord Chamberlain ordered John Singleton, William Clayton, William Young, Theophilus Fitz, Richard Hudson, John Strong, Isaac Staggins, Jeffrey Banister, and Henry Brockwell, all members of his Select Band, to 'attend at his Majesty's theatre whenever Thomas Killigrew shall desire them', and six days later Thomas Fitz, 'lately sworn a violin in ordinary', was ordered to 'wait in the band of violins under the direction of John Bannister when they play before his Majesty and the Queen and at the Theatre Royal'.[16] By the following March the other half of the Twenty-four Violins had been assigned to the Duke's Company, for the Wardrobe was ordered to make up:

habits of several coloured silks for 24 violins, 12 of them being for his Majesty's service in the Theatre Royal, and the other 12 habits for his Majesty's service in his Highness the Duke of York's Theatre; and also 24 garlands of several coloured flowers to each of them after the same manner as those that were delivered to Mr. Killigrew for his Majesty's extraordinary service.[17]

Members of the Twenty-four violins were still playing in the London theatres in the 1670s. The complete group evidently played in Shadwell's operatic version of *The Tempest*, first performed by the Duke's Company on, probably, 30 April 1674, to judge from a passage at the beginning of the printed text: 'The Front of the Stage is open'd, and the Band of 24 Violins, with the Harpsicals and theorbo's which accompany the Voices, are plac'd between the Pit and the Stage.'[18] In May 1677 the Lord Chamberlain was petitioned by five royal violinists, John Singleton, Theophilus Fitz, Henry Brockwell, Edmund Flower, and Joseph Fashion, to prevent Charles Killigrew 'dismissing them their attendance at the play house'.[19] The dispute may have had something to do with the difficulties that the King's Company was experiencing at the time, caused by a series of disagreements between Charles Killigrew and his father Thomas. Alternatively, it could indicate that the connection between the Twenty-four Violins and the King's Company was severed around then.[20]

---

[15] Price, *Henry Purcell and the London Stage*, 125–43.
[16] Ashbee, *RECM*, i. 59.
[17] Ibid. 61.
[18] Price, *Music in the Restoration Theatre*, 79.
[19] Ashbee, *RECM*, i. 171.
[20] See Van Lennep, *The London Stage*, 247.

More light is shed on the subject by the theatrical connections of some of the Twenty-four Violins. William Clayton married Elizabeth Wintershall, the daughter of the King's Company actor William Wintershall, on 3 August 1663.[21] They set up house in the parish of St Paul, Covent Garden, convenient for the Bridges Street theatre. When his father-in-law died in June 1683, Clayton acted as his executor and inherited four shares of the recently formed United Company; the two patent companies amalgamated in 1682 and operated as a single entity until 1695.[22] When Clayton died in January 1697 he left his house in Little Bridge Street alias Vinegar Yard 'wherin I now dwell, and all my rent, shares and interest in the Theatre or playhouse' to his son, the composer Thomas Clayton.[23] A reference in Act III, scene 1 of Shadwell's *Bury Fair* (1689) suggests that William Clayton appeared in a King's Company production with his fellow-violinist John Singleton. The Thetford waits, the 'best Musick in England', are said to have sung 'Charon, Oh, gentle Charon' and 'Come my Daphne' 'better than Singleton and Clayton did'. Both of these pieces are by William Lawes. The first is a setting of Robert Herrick's dialogue between Charon and the Nightingale, while the second, the dialogue 'Come my Daphne, come away', comes from Act V, scene 3 of Shirley's *The Cardinal* (1641); the play was performed a number of times in the 1660s, and was assigned to the King's Company in 1669.[24]

There is another possible reference to John Singleton as an actor: Dryden's satirical poem *Mac Flecknoe* (London, 1682) has the lines: 'That, pale with envy, Singleton foreswore/The Lute and Sword which he in Triumph bore,/And vow'd he ne'er would act Villerius more'.[25] Villerius, the Grand Master of Rhodes, a character in *The Siege of Rhodes*, was shared by Gregory Thorndell and Dubartus Hunt in the original 1656 production. Thomas Lilleston played it after the Restoration (when Davenant's 'opera' seems to have been given as a spoken play), but Singleton may have taken it over after he left the stage in the middle of the 1660s; the work was still in the repertoire in May 1667.[26] Like Clayton, Singleton lived near the King's Theatre in Bridges Street, and

[21] Highfill *et al.*, *A Biographical Dictionary*, iii. 315–17.

[22] Hotson, *The Commonwealth and Restoration Stage*, 258–82.

[23] Ashbee, *RECM*, ii. 57–8.

[24] Bentley, *The Jacobean and Caroline Stage*, v. 1084–7; Van Lennep, *The London Stage*, 38, 52, 56, 101, 112, 134, 152; 'Come my Daphne, come away' is available in J. Playford, *The Treasury of Musick* (London, 1669; repr. 1966), 74–5.

[25] J. Dryden, *Works*, ed. H. T. Swedenberg and V. A. Dearing, ii: *Poems 1681–1684* (Berkeley, 1972), 55.

[26] Highfill *et al.*, *A Biographical Dictionary*, ix. 295–6; Van Lennep, *The London Stage*, 108–9.

was buried at St Paul, Covent Garden on 7 April 1686.[27] Samuel Pepys was much taken with *The Siege of Rhodes*, and on 22 January 1666/7 asked 'Darnell the Fidler, one of the Duke's House' to obtain a copy of its music, 'which he tells me he can get me, which I am mighty glad of'.[28] 'Darnell'—most likely the royal violinist Richard Dorney II—had obtained Pepys 'a set of lessons, all three parts' that had been played 'to the Duke of York this Christmas at his lodgings'.

Matthew Locke and John Banister, the two main composers of the early-Restoration Twenty-four Violins, were heavily involved with the commercial theatres. We have some evidence of the authorship of the music in the case of twenty-three plays produced between 1660 and 1669 (see Table 14.1 at the end of this chapter): Banister contributed to ten, Locke to seven, Alfonso Marsh to three, Pelham Humfrey to two, and William Howes and Robert Smith to one. Marsh, Humfrey, Howes, and Smith are only credited with songs; all the instrumental music is ascribed to Banister or Locke, a situation that obtains until 1674, when the Duke's Company produced Shadwell's version of *The Tempest* with incidental music by Locke, Giovanni Battista Draghi, and, it seems, Robert Smith (see below). The first theatre suite by a member of the younger generation seems to be the one by William Turner in *US-NYp*, Drexel MS 3849, pp. 39–41 for Settle's *Pastor Fido; or, The Faithful Shepherd*, produced by the Duke's Company in the winter of 1676.[29]

The conclusion is unmistakable. Locke and Banister composed most if not all the incidental music for the London theatres from 1660 until the mid 1670s because this was the period when groups from the Twenty-four Violins were working regularly for the patent companies. They both began by writing for the Duke's Company, which is not surprising since Davenant had pioneered the public performances of operatic works in the 1650s with *The First Day's Entertainment* and *The Siege of Rhodes*. Once the Select Band was allocated to the King's Company in 1664 Banister began to write for their plays—such as *The Indian Queen*. After the spring of 1667, when Grabu replaced him as the leader of the Select Band, Banister was evidently free to work again for the Duke's Company, though he continued his association with the King's Company: he wrote at least one song for its production of Sedley's *The Mulberry Garden* in May 1668. Locke, on the other hand, stayed loyal to the Duke's Company almost until the end of his life: he wrote for at least ten of its productions between Davenant's *Love and Honour* (21 October 1661), and D'Urfey's *Madam Fickle* (4 November 1676), though for some reason his last-known

[27] W. H. Hunt (ed.), *The Registers of St Paul's Church, Covent Garden, London*, iv: Burials, *1653–1752* (Harleian Society Publications, Registers, 36; London, 1908), 111.
[28] Pepys, *Diary*, viii. 24–5.
[29] Price, *Music in the Restoration Theatre*, 209; Van Lennep, *The London Stage*, 252.

work for the theatre, a song for D'Urfey's *The Fool Turn'd Critic* (18 November 1676), was for the King's Company.[30]

Where are all the suites of incidental music that Banister and Locke must have written for the commercial theatre? Only one by each composer, Banister's for *The Indian Queen* and Locke's for *The Tempest*, feature in the catalogue compiled by Curtis Price of over 100 surviving suites for plays produced between 1660 and 1713. This led him to suggest, not unreasonably, that the 'practice of providing each play with its own incidental music was probably encouraged by the amalgamation of the two principal theatre companies ... in 1682', which carries the implication that incidental music was not normally written especially for plays before then.[31] But the eyewitness descriptions of the London Theatres in the 1660s show that the essential elements of later theatre suites—the preliminary first and second music, the 'curtain tune' or overture, and the interval 'act tunes'—were heard in plays at the time. Indeed, in his essay *Of Dramatick Poesie* (1668) Dryden likened the effect of mixing tragedy with comedy to the contrast that 'musick betwixt the Acts' brought to a spoken play.[32]

A little-known bass part-book, *US-NH*, Filmer MS 7, provides additional evidence of a sizeable repertoire of pre-1682 theatre suites. It contains over twenty works, all apparently theatre suites, including Locke's *Tempest* music, fos. 21^v–24^r, a complete ten-movement version of Turner's *Pastor Fido* suite, fos. 54^r–57^r, and a hitherto unknown six-movement suite for Banister's semi-opera *Circe*, fos. 72^r–74^r, given by the Duke's Company in May 1677.[33] It is unfortunate that the other parts are lost, and that the collection mostly contains untitled and apparently unique works, for it is clearly an important early source of theatre suites. It preserves them in the sequence in which they would have been heard in the theatre, with the curtain tune or overture placed after the first and second music; in most sources the overtures come first, so that the suites make sense as concert works. Another piece of evidence that connects Filmer MS 7 with the theatre is a note on a flyleaf: 'all Mr Banisters things that were made for the new house; & Mr Smiths things in gamut only'. The 'new house' was the Dorset Garden theatre, opened by the Duke's Company in 1671 (see below), so the manuscript presumably contains suites written by Banister after then for the company. It has recently been suggested that the pieces from Lully's music for Molière's *George Dandin* (1668) on fos. 38^v–39^r labelled 'J. Banister' are in his

---

[30] For a list of Locke's contributions to Restoration plays, see Locke, *The Rare Theatrical*, ed. Holman, pp. xx–xxi.

[31] Price, *Music in the Restoration Theatre*, 53.

[32] Ibid. 51–2.

[33] Van Lennep, *The London Stage*, 256–7.

autograph, and it may be that the whole collection was put together by musicians working for the company.[34]

'The Rare Theatrical', *US-NYp*, Drexel MS 3796 (see Ch. 13), undoubtedly contains the bulk of Locke's incidental music for Restoration plays, but it is a particularly frustrating source because it is organized by key. The composers of theatre suites did not normally keep to a single key because the items were not heard in a continuous sequence, and they were then free to use traditional key associations to mirror the changing moods of the parent play.[35] Thus, to include complete suites in the collection, the compiler would have had to dismember them, sorting the movements into the respective key sections. This is why six of the eight pieces labelled 'Curtain Tune' occur in a sequence of thirteen pieces on pp. 23-44; in collections like Filmer MS 7 that contain theatre suites as they were originally composed, the curtain tunes would have been separated by about eight to ten other movements.[36]

But it is possible to estimate how many theatre suites are lurking in 'The Rare Theatrical', since a play required only one curtain tune, which was heard as the curtain was drawn for Act 1. In addition to the eight pieces labelled 'Curtain Tune', there are four others of a similar type, one of which is called 'The Fantastick', pp. 4-5. If, as I argued in Chapter 13, the collection has three key sections missing, and they were similar in size and character to the ones that survive, then it may contain material drawn from twenty or more suites—which suggests that it was originally a comprehensive collection of Locke's music for the Restoration theatre. The famous *Tempest* suite, his only one that can be identified with a particular play, is not in 'The Rare Theatrical', presumably because its first seven movements would have been in the lost G minor and F major sections, while the last four, in B♭, D minor and G minor, are probably not by Locke; they are missing from some copies of the printed score, *The English Opera: or, The Vocal Music in Psyche... To which is Adjoyned the Instrumental Musick in the Tempest* (London, 1675), and three of them are attributed to Robert Smith in Filmer MS 7, fos. 23ᵛ–24ʳ.[37]

Locke's curtain tunes are important for the light they throw on the early history of the French overture in England. The word *ouverture* is found as early as 1640 in French court ballets to describe an introductory piece in two contrasted sections, the first in a stately duple time with

---

[34] C. B. Schmidt, 'Newly Identified Manuscript Sources for the Music of Jean-Baptiste Lully', *Notes*, 43 (1987), 27.

[35] The significance of key in Restoration music has been examined recently in Price, *Henry Purcell*, esp. 21–6.

[36] For an inventory of the manuscript, see Locke, *The Rare Theatrical*, ed. Holman, pp. xxii–xxiv.

[37] Edited most recently in M. Locke, *Dramatic Music*, ed. M. Tilmouth (MB 51; London 1986), 19–31, 47–8, 63, 65–7, 84–6.

dotted rhythms, the second in a dance-like triple time.[38] Fugal writing appeared as early as 1658—in the overture to Lully's ballet *Alcidiane*—but Marc-Antoine Charpentier and other composers continued to write homophonic second sections for several more decades.[39] The overture seems to have been introduced to England just after the Restoration, perhaps as a result of Banister's experience of French music in 1660-2 (see Ch. 12). Examples of overture-like pieces called 'symphony' can be found in several of Pelham Humfrey's verse anthems—for instance 'Haste thee O God', written in 1663 or 1664.[40] In the theatre the term 'curtain tune' was used during the 1660s and 1670s, even for pieces that have some features of the French overture. Confusingly, Locke's curtain tune for *The Tempest*, which does not conform to the French pattern at all, was described in Shadwell's text as an 'overture', while in Filmer MS 7 both terms are used for what look like true French-style overtures; for instance, the 'Curtaine tune' in Turner's *Pastor Fido* music, fos. 56^v–57^r, and an 'Overture' by Thomas Farmer, fo. 60^v.

Some of the curtain tunes in 'The Rare Theatrical' are similar to French overtures in that a duple-time passage using at least some dotted notes is followed by a passage in saraband or jig rhythm. In some cases, such as 'The Fantastick', there is a return at the end to dotted rhythms in duple time. But the most interesting of Locke's curtain tunes are those, like the one in *The Tempest*, that do not conform to the French pattern because they are apparently intended to reinforce the atmosphere of the opening scene of a play. In the one in C, pp. 39-42, for instance, a passage that sounds like a musical sunrise leads to a calm central passage reminiscent of tolling bells; it could be wonderfully evocative if only we knew what scene it was evoking (Ex. 14.1). The word 'overture' only became established during the 1680s, when Lully's mature examples of the form became known in England through manuscript copies, and the next generation of English theatre composers began to imitate them.[41]

London's theatres and their orchestras went through a period of change in the early 1670s. Both companies acquired new premises: the Duke's moved from Lincoln's Inn Fields to a splendid new building at Dorset Garden in November 1671, while the King's lost the Bridges

---

[38] For the early history of the overture, see H. Prunières, 'Notes sur les origines de l'ouverture française', *SIMG* 12 (1910–11), 565–85; G. G. Waterman, 'French Overture', *Grove 6*; P. Dennison, *Pelham Humfrey* (Oxford, 1986), 21–7.

[39] See, for instance, Charpentier's *Circé* (1675) and *Les Fous divertissants* (1680); I am grateful to Andrew Parmley for providing me with transcriptions of Charpentier's theatre works.

[40] See P. Humfrey, *Complete Church Music, I*, ed. P. Dennison (MB 34; London, 1972), 22–4, 140.

[41] Suites of music by Lully are found mixed with English theatre music in many sources, including *EIR-Dtc*, MS 413, *GB-Ckc*, MS 122, *GB-LEc*, MS Q784.21 L969, *GB-Lbl*, Add. MSS 24889, 29283–5, *GB-Lcm*, MS 1172, *US-NYp*, Drexel MS 3849, *US-NH*, Filmer MSS 6, 7, 9.

Ex. 14.1. Matthew Locke, Curtain Tune in C, bb. 1–26, *US-NYp*, Drexel MS 3976, pp. 39–41

Ex. 14.1. *Continued*

Street theatre in a fire in January 1671/2; its replacement, in Drury Lane, was opened on 26 March 1674. With new theatres and better facilities for scenic effects, the companies vied with each other to put on lavish operatic shows, featuring French dancers and musicians and spectacular scenic effects. John Dryden wrote, in lines spoken at the opening of Drury Lane, that 'Scenes, Machines, and empty Opera's reign', and 'Troops of famisht Frenchmen hither drive', while Roger North explained the trend as a response to the emergence of public concerts: 'It had bin strange if the gentlemen of the theaters had sate still all this while, seeing as they say a pudding creep, that is a violent inclination in the towne to follow musick, and they not serve themselves of it.'[42]

The first hungry Frenchmen arrived in August or September 1673 with Robert Cambert. Cambert's operatic career in Paris had ended in the spring of the previous year when Pierre Perrin, his librettist and partner, sold the royal privilege to run the *Académies d'opéra* to Lully.[43] Cambert seems to have come to London with at least the nucleus of an opera company, including some instrumentalists. In January or February 1674 it gave a court performance of the *Ballet et musique pour le divertissement du roy de la Grand-Bretagne*; it had a text by Sebastien Brémond and music, now lost, by Cambert and a certain Favier.[44] The preface to the text is signed by 'M. de Bream', 'musicien français de la chapelle royale de violons et hautbois'. De Bream or De Bresmes was one of the four French musicians who played the oboe and the recorder in the court production of Crowne's *Calisto* in February 1675 (see Ch. 15), and David Lasocki has argued that the four, led by the young Jacques (James) Paisible, were members of Cambert's party, and that they introduced the newly remodelled Baroque oboe and recorder to England. Cambert had already used the oboe in *Pomone* and *Les Peines et plaisirs de l'amour*, both performed in Paris in 1671, and in July 1676 he played the harpsichord at a dinner given by the Duchess of Portsmouth with 'two Frenchmen who play the flute extremely well'.[45]

Cambert's next opera production was *Ariane, ou le mariage de Bacchus*,

---

[42] Van Lennep, *The London Stage*, 209; Chan and Kassler, *Roger North's The Musical Grammarian*, 266.

[43] Anthony, *French Baroque Music*, 62–4.

[44] A. Tessier, 'Robert Cambert à Londres', *ReM* 9 (1927–8), 101–22; W. H. G. Flood, 'Quelques précisions nouvelles sur Cambert et Grabu à Londres', ibid. 351–61; E. P. Grobe, 'S. Bre., French Librettist at the Court of Charles II', *Theatre Notebook*, 9 (1954), 20–1; P. Danchin, 'The Foundation of the Royal Academy of Music in 1674 and Pierre Perrin's *Ariane*', *Theatre Survey*, 25 (1984), 53–67; C. Bashford, 'Perrin and Cambert's *Ariane, ou le mariage de Bacchus* Re-examined', *ML* 72 (1991), 1–26.

[45] Lasocki, 'Professional Recorder Players', i. 318–21; id., 'The French Hautboy in England, 1673–1730', *EM* 16 (1988), 339–40; Danchin, 'The Foundation of the Royal Academy of Music', 64; see also E. Halfpenny, 'The English Debut of the French Hautboy', *MMR* 79 (1949), 149–53.

produced at the new Drury Lane theatre on 30 March 1674; his company is referred to in the printed text as the 'Royall Academy of Musick', which suggests that he was hoping for, or had obtained, royal protection similar to that enjoyed by the Académie royale de musique. The 1674 text of *Ariane*, printed in French and English, states it was 'Now put into Musick' by Louis Grabu, the Master of the Music and a disciple of Cambert. However, the opera was actually an expanded version of the Paris *Ariane* written by Perrin for Cambert in 1659 and revised in 1671-2, so Grabu's contribution, if he made one, may have been confined to some extra scenes.[46] No music survives for either work, but the 1674 text suggests that all four of Cambert's wind-players took part, playing *haubois* and *flutes*—'hoboyes' and 'flutes' in the English version. For instance, in the first scene, set in Bacchus' palace, 'Several Hoboyes belonging to Bacchus' appear on stage, and a little later a 'Band of Corybants, some singing, others dancing' is accompanied by 'Hoboyes, Flutes, and Violins'.

Nothing more was heard of the Royal Academy, except that four 'French Dancers in the late Opera' joined the King's Company at the beginning of May 1674, once some difficulties concerning their obligations to Grabu had been sorted out.[47] The French wind-players followed suit soon after, to judge from an anonymous manuscript prologue for Ben Jonson's *Volpone; or, The Fox* entitled 'Prologue at the Fox, when a Consort of Hautboyes were added to the Musick'.[48] *Volpone* was assigned to the King's Company in 1669, and it is known to have been performed on 17 January 1675/6, though there is nothing to suggest that the prologue was written for that day.[49] Indeed, the wind-players may have made their debut in *Volpone* at the beginning of the 1674-5 season, for September and October were often given over to the revivals of old plays. The prologue was evidently written by someone who felt that the musical ambitions of the theatres were getting out of hand:

> Did Ben now live, how would he fret, and rage,
> To see the Musick-room outvye the stage?
> To see French Haut-boyes charm the listning Pitt
> More than the Raptures of his God-like wit!
> Yet 'tis too true that most who now are here,
> Come not to feast their Judgement, but their Ear.
> Musick, which was by Intervals design'd

---

[46] Danchin, 'The Foundation of the Royal Academy of Music', 63; Bashford, 'Perrin and Cambert's *Ariane*', 20–2.

[47] Ashbee, *RECM*, v. 67.

[48] R. G. Noyes, 'A Manuscript Restoration Prologue for *Volpone*', *Modern Language Notes*, 42 (1937), 198–200.

[49] Van Lennep, *The London Stage*, 242.

To ease the weary'd Actors voice and mind,
You to the Play judiciously prefer,
'Tis now the bus'ness of the Theatre . . .

It has been argued recently that the prologue relates to a Dublin production of *Volpone*, because it survives in a collection of texts that relate to its
Smock-Alley theatre.[50] But it is difficult to believe that Dublin's one
theatre had the sort of musical life that would provoke these lines, and
there is certainly no evidence that the French oboists ever travelled to
Ireland.

The King's Company's French wind-players are also mentioned in
Etherege's play *The Man of Mode; or, Sir Fopling Flutter*, first given by the
Duke's Company in March 1676. In Act II, scene 1 Emilia is asked
'What, are you of the number of the Ladies whose Ears are grown so
delicate since our Operas, you can be charm'd with nothing but Flute
doux and French Hoboys?', and in Act IV, scene 1 Sir Fopling offers an
entertainment provided by his servants, 'whom I pickt out of the best in
France and brought over, with a Flutes deux or two'; significantly, since
this was a Duke's Company production, they are not required to play.[51]
The introduction of oboes and recorders into the Drury Lane orchestra
evidently enabled the King's Company to compete for a time on its rival's
home ground; under Davenant's management the Duke's Company had
always been the more musical of the two.

The Duke's Company had been planning its response to Cambert's
company with the help of a troupe of French dancers ever since the
summer of 1673. On 22 August James Vernon reported to Sir Joseph
Williamson in Cologne that:

The Duke's house are preparing an Opera and great machines. They will have
dansers out of France, and St. André comes over with them, who is to have a
pension of the King, and a patent of master of the compositions for ballets;
further, the King hath granted them what boys of his Chappell they shall have
occasion for to sing.[52]

The work in question was Thomas Shadwell's *Psyche*, set to music
by Matthew Locke with dances by Giovanni Battista Draghi and choreography by the French dancing-master Saint-André; it was the first
specially written example of the genre that Roger North christened

[50] P. Danchin (ed.), *The Prologues and Epilogues of the Restoration, 1660–1700*, I, ii (Nancy, 1981), 206.

[51] G. Etherege, *The Dramatic Works*, ed. H. F. B. Brett-Smith (Oxford, 1927), ii. 209, 253.

[52] W. D. Christie (ed.), *Letters Addressed from London to Sir Joseph Williamson while Plenipotentiary at the Congress of Cologne in the Years 1673 and 1674* (Camden Society Publications, NS, 8; London, 1874), 180–1.

'semi-opera', a spoken play produced with spectacular scenic effects and episodes of masque-like music.[53]

The date of the first performance of *Psyche* has been a matter for debate ever since John Downes wrote in 1708 that the 'long expected Opera of Psyche, came forth in all her Ornaments' in February 1673—that is, presumably, February 1673/4.[54] 1673 or 1674 was accepted until 1922, when Allardyce Nicoll drew attention to a reference in the Lord Chamberlain's records to the 'first acting' of *Psyche* on 25 February 1674/5.[55] Later scholars mostly favoured 1675, but Murray Lefkowitz has recently advocated a return to 1674, pointing out that Locke states in his score, *The English Opera; or, The Vocal Music in Psyche...* (London, 1675), that the music was 'now Printed' after being 'so long expos'd'; that the Lord Chamberlain issued an order dated 18 May 1674 giving permission for members of the Chapel Royal to sing in Shadwell's version of *The Tempest*, first heard in March or April 1674, adding that they could 'also perform the like service in the Opera in the said Theatre'; and that the texts of plays were published on average six months to a year after the first performance.[56]

To take the last point first: according to Judith Milhous and Robert Hume the average delay between première and publication was six months in the middle of the 1670s, but operas were an exception: they 'tended to get printed exceptionally quickly, even simultaneously with the première'.[57] Lefkowitz's second point is also less than conclusive, for the Lord Chamberlain's order can easily be taken to mean that the unnamed opera had not yet been performed, or perhaps even put into rehearsal. *Psyche* was a complex production, with, in Downes's words, 'new Scenes, new Machines, new Cloaths, new French Dances', and was a long time in preparation: it was 'long expected', and Shadwell stated that his text had been written 'Sixteen moneths since'—that is, in about October 1673. If the delay was caused by production difficulties, as Milhous and Hume suggest, then Locke's remark about the music being 'so long expos'd' might refer to the gap between public or semi-public rehearsals and the actual performances. But the most compelling reason for rejecting 1674 is that it is hard to see how the Duke's Company could have found the time and the resources to mount two complex and expensive semi-opera productions within a few months; Downes added that *Psyche* 'was

---

[53] Chan and Kassler, *Roger North*, 266–7; Wilson, *Roger North*, 306–7; *Psyche* was edited by Tilmouth in Locke, *Dramatic Music*, 87–229.

[54] Downes, *Roscius Anglicanus*, ed. Milhous and Hume, 36.

[55] *The Times Literary Supplement*, 21 Sept. 1922; see M. Lefkowitz, 'Shadwell and Locke's *Psyche*, the French Connection', *PRMA* 106 (1979–80), 55.

[56] Ibid. 50–2; Ashbee, *RECM*, i. 138.

[57] J. Milhous and R. D. Hume, 'Dating Play Premières from Publication Data, 1660–1700', *Harvard Library Bulletin*, 22 (1974), esp. 381, 383–4, 394, 398, 402–3.

Splendidly set out, especially in Scenes; the Charge of which amounted to above 800*l*'.

Shadwell's immediate model for *Psyche* was *Psyché*, the *tragédie-lyrique* by Molière, Pierre Corneille, Quinault, and Lully, produced in Paris in 1671. Lefkowitz argued that Locke owned a copy of a suite from *Psyché*, but if that is so, which is debatable, there is no sign that Lully's music influenced his own score.[58] Indeed, Locke entitled the published edition *The English Opera*, and proudly compared it in the preface to Italian opera rather than French opera. Lefkowitz suggested more plausibly that the chauvinist tone of the preface should be seen in the context of the rivalry between the pro- and anti-French factions at court, led respectively by the Dukes of York and Monmouth. Monmouth was the dedicatee of the score and the text of *Psyche*, and was responsible for bringing Saint-André to England, according to the anonymous author of *A Comparison between the Two Stages* (London, 1702).[59] The orchestral writing in *Psyche* can certainly be seen as Locke's response to Cambert and his wind-players. There is no mention of wind instruments in the text of the 1674 *Tempest*, despite the presence of a sizeable ensemble: a 'Band of 24 Violins, with the Harpsicals and Theorbo's which accompany the Voices'. Yet in *Psyche*, less than a year later, the strings were joined by an astonishing array of wind and brass: 'Flajolets', 'Recorders', 'Flutes', 'Pipes', 'Hoboys', 'Cornets', 'Sackbuts', 'Trumpets', as well as 'Kettle Drums', and 'Organ and Harpsicals', according to Shadwell's text.

Not all of them were played by separate groups of musicians. The chorus 'How happy are those that inhabit this place' in Act I is labelled 'Chorus of all the Voices and Instr[uments]' in Locke's score, and more precisely in Shadwell's text as 'Voices, Flajolets, Violins, Cornets, Sackbuts, Hoa-boys'. Yet in Act V, scene 3 an instrumental group, seated in 'several Semi-circular Clouds, of the breadth of the whole House', accompanies Apollo's descent from his own cloud; they play the chorus 'With his immortal Psyche' on 'Flagellets and Recorders', and then play a symphony successively on 'Pipes', 'Hoboys', and 'Recorders'. The chorus for the Followers of Mars 'He turns all the horrors of war to delight' later in the act is accompanied by 'Trumpets, Kettle-Drums, Flutes and Warlike Musick', while the succeeding Bacchic chorus 'But Love's great debauch is lasting and strong' uses 'Hoboys and Rustick Musick of Maenades and Aegipanes'. The implication is that some of the instruments mentioned in Act V, such as the flutes, the recorders, the 'pipes', the 'Warlike Musick', and the 'Rustick Musick' (whatever that might have been), were played by the same musicians who played the flageolets, cornetts, sackbuts, and 'hoboys' in Act I. It is not always clear from the

[58] Lefkowitz, 'Shadwell and Locke's *Psyche*', 44–5.   [59] Ibid. 47, 50.

compressed score in *The English Opera* exactly what each instrument played. It is unfortunate, for instance, that Locke did not print separate instrumental parts for 'He turns all the horrors of war to delight', for this chorus is the first clearly documented instance in England of the use of trumpets and drums in concerted music (see Ch. 17).[60]

At first glance the scoring of *Psyche* is a great advance on anything produced hitherto by an English composer, though it actually looks backwards rather than forwards. We must remember that Locke did not 'orchestrate' his work as a later composer would have done. He would have chosen his instruments more for their traditional symbolic associations than for any expressive possibilities they might offer. 'Flutes' (evidently the transverse instruments, because 'recorders' are also specified) were used for a warlike scene because they had ancient associations with death and military music.[61] Similarly, trumpets and drums had been associated with royalty and war since time immemorial. An extra layer of associations came into play when a composer set a work based on a classical subject. Locke used 'hoboys' in a Bacchic scene for the same reason that oboes were used in *Ariane*: they represented the double-reed aulos, which was associated with the Dionysian cult. Other wind instruments were also thought of as aulos substitutes, particularly since the Greek word was frequently translated into Latin as *tibia*, and then into English as 'flute'—hence the use of 'flutes' (meaning recorders; see below) with the oboes in the Bacchic scenes of *Ariane*.[62] Composers only began to 'orchestrate' when they started writing for full orchestra outside the theatre and independent of vocal music. In England this only happened in the 1690s, and the scoring of Henry Purcell and his contemporaries still needs to be considered in the context of the older symbolic tradition.

On a practical level, too, Locke's use of instruments is conservative. He seems to have used the older consorts of woodwind instruments in *Psyche*, not the new remodelled French instruments. Cambert's four wind-players were probably the only oboists in England for a few years after their arrival, and, as David Lasocki has pointed out, the French term *flûte douce* (usually shortened to 'flute') quickly displaced the old English word 'recorder' once the new instrument was established.[63] Thus, Locke's 'hoboys' were probably shawms, just as his 'flutes' and 'recorders' are likely to have been transverse and end-blown consort instruments of a

---

[60] P. Downey, 'What Samuel Pepys Heard on 3 February 1661: English Trumpet Style under the Later Stuart Monarchs', *EM* 18 (1990), 417–28 surveys Restoration trumpet music, but does not mention *Psyche*.

[61] See Manifold, *The Music in English Drama*, 69–70 for further examples in Jacobean drama.

[62] J. Hollander, *The Untuning of the Sky* (Princeton, NJ, 1961), 46.

[63] Lasocki, 'Professional Recorder Players', i. 324.

pre-Baroque type. There is no evidence of the Baroque transverse flute in England before James Talbot included it in his notes on musical instruments, compiled in the 1690s, and Eccles included a 'Flute D. Almagne' part in the score of his *Judgement of Paris* (London, 1702), 28-31; a 'Flute allemande' is also called for in Jakob Kremberg's 'New Fram'd Entertainment', *GB-Lcm*, MS 2231, fo. 1ʳ, written at about the same time.[64] The wind instruments in *Psyche* are also used in an old-fashioned way. For instance, the four-part 'Simphonie' in Act V, scene 3, played successively by 'pipes', shawms, and recorders, needs a complete consort of three or four sizes of each instrument, from a single treble to bass—or in the case of the recorders, great bass (Ex. 14.2). Those English works of the 1680s and 1690s that have wind parts usually call just for pairs of treble recorders or oboes.

More light can be thrown on the orchestral writing in *Psyche* by John Banister's concert activities. Banister's concerts are first recorded in December 1672, though they may have been in existence earlier, and they can be traced through newspaper advertisements until January 1679, less than a year before his death.[65] There are also several descriptions of them in Roger North's writings, which give the impression that they were cheap, informal, and unpretentious:

The first attempt [at public concerts] was low: a project of old Banister, who was a good violin, and a theatricall composer. He opened an obscure room in a publik house in White fryars; filled it with tables and seats, and made a side box with curtaines for the musick. 1ˢ. a peice, call for what you please, pay the reckoning and Welcome gentlemen. Here came most of the shack-performers in towne, and much company to hear . . .[66]

A rather different impression is given by a printed word-book of one of Banister's concerts; this remarkable document has not, to my knowledge, been described in print before. On 11 December 1676 'the first part of the Parley of Instruments, composed by Mr John Banister, and perform'd by eminent masters' was advertised in *The London Gazette* to run nightly at the 'Academy in Lincoln's Inn Fields' from 14 December. The word-book is a fourteen-page pamphlet with the following title-page:

MUSICK: / OR A / PARLEY / OF / Instruments. / [rule] / *The First Part*. / [rule] / Licensed, / *Roger L'estrange*. / *Octob*. 30. 1676. / [rule] / [ornamental device] / [rule] / *London*, Printed in the Year 1676.

---

[64] A. Baines, 'James Talbot's Manuscript (Christ Church Library, Music MS 1187). I: Wind Instruments', *GSJ* (1948), 16–17.

[65] Tilmouth, 'A Calendar of References to Music', 2–4; the best account of early concerts, and Banister's role in them, is Tilmouth, 'Chamber Music in England, 1675–1720', Ph.D. thesis (Cambridge, 1959), 13–17.

[66] Wilson, *Roger North*, 302–3.

Ex. 14.2. Matthew Locke, 'Simphonie' from *Psyche*, Act V, scene 3, *The English Opera; or, The Vocal Music in Psyche* (London, 1675), 54

Ex. 14.2. *Continued*

The British Library copy, apparently unique, does not mention Banister by name, which probably explains why it has not come to light before. The text features Pallas, Alexis, Strephon, Corydon, and 'assistant Voices'. In the first 'entertainment' Pallas sings of the power of music to unite souls in a 'general Quire', whereupon the others resolve to debate the merits of three classes of instruments: Strephon takes the part of the 'Harp, the Harpsicons, Guittar and Lute', Corydon the 'Wind-Musicks Excellence', and Alexis instruments played by the 'charming bow'; after another appearance by Pallas in the third entertainment they agree to 'mix and make one great Compound'. On the last page there is an address to the 'Courteous Reader':

These three forgoing Odes were design'd for one Days Entertainment: But finding by the Composition it exceeded the time limited for the performance, beginning at six a clock in the Evening, he could present but one at a time, by reason of the Scholars Teaching; and more especially being required by some persons of Quality, to have a Ball after the Musick, for which all such as are desirous, shall have twenty Violins to attend them till ten a clock at Night. As the Parts shall fall out to be perform'd, you shall hereafter by Bills or otherwise be informed.

The Arts and Sciences taught and practis'd in the Academy are these.

All sorts of Instruments, Singing, and Dancing.
French, and Italian.
The Mathematicks.
Grammar, Writing and Arithmetick.
Painting and Drawing.
Fencing, Vaulting and Wrastling.

Or any young Gentleman design'd for Travel, there are persons of several Nations fit to instruct him in any Language. Like wise any one that hath a desire

to have any New Songs or Tunes, may be furnish'd by the same Person that
serves his Majesty in the same Imployment.

We gather from this that Banister's 'Academy in Lincoln's Inn Fields'
was indeed a school, and that his court colleagues were helping him to
run it. They presumably provided the 'twenty Violins' for the ball, helped
with the music-teaching and dancing-lessons, and perhaps taught other
subjects as well; after all, there was a ready supply of 'persons of several
Nations' in the royal music who could have supplied the necessary foreign
languages.

The strongest evidence that *A Parley of Instruments* was a mass exercise
in moonlighting by court musicians is provided by the text itself. Although
it is laid out like a play, and Pallas makes her appearances 'as from
above', it is far from clear that it was actually staged; indeed, the entertainments are referred to as 'musick' and 'odes' that were 'perform'd by
eminent masters'; stage productions at the time would have been referred
to as 'acted' or 'represented'. The text reads more like an ode in praise of
music than a dramatic work, and it was obviously written mainly as
a vehicle for the extraordinary instrumental ensemble that Banister
assembled for the work. At the beginning of the third entertainment a
dialogue between Strephon and Corydon is prefaced by a 'Symphony of
Theorboes, Lutes, Harps, Harpsicons, Guittars, Pipes, Flutes, Flagellets,
Cornets, Sackbutts, Hoboys, Rechords, Organs, and all sort of Wind-
Instruments ... with assistant Voices, and Violins', and even this does
not exhaust the catalogue of instruments present, for viols appear in a
'Consort of Lutes, Theorboes, Guittars, Harpsicons, Violins, Viols and all
other Instruments struck with the Finger or Bow' at the beginning of the
second entertainment, and citterns are mentioned a little later, in a
'Consort of Theorboes, Lutes, Harps, Harpsicons, Guittars, Citterns,
&c.'. There must have been about fifty instrumentalists, even if all
the instruments mentioned in the plural in Banister's musical ark were
present only in pairs.

The parallels between *A Parley of Instruments* and *Psyche* are obvious.
Like Locke, Banister combined a violin band with some of the pre-
Baroque consorts of wind instruments. Once again flutes were contrasted
with recorders, and cornetts and sackbuts were present, making virtually
their last appearance in English music. It is also significant that both
works used 'pipes' and flageolets; the exact nature of the former is in
doubt, but the latter, the small recorder-like instrument with four finger-
holes and two thumb-holes, was particularly associated with two members
of the Twenty-four Violins, John Banister and Thomas Greeting.

According to Roger North the flageolet was 'one of Banister's perfec-
tions'; one of the 'musicall curiositys' of his concerts was 'a flageolett in

consort, which was never heard before nor since, unless imitated by the high manner upon the violin'; and again, 'Banister himself (inter alia) did wonders upon a flageolett to a thro base'.[67] Anthony à Wood wrote that Banister played 'on the flageolet on which he was excellent', and recorded an occasion at the Oxford Music School on 11 January 1665/6 when 'Mr Banister of London and divers of the king's musicians gave us a very good meeting at the Schooles in Musick, where he played on a little pipe or flagellet in consort which hath bin about seven yeares in fashion.'[68] In the masque *Beauty's Triumph*, produced in 1676 at the boarding school run by Jeffrey Banister and James Hart in Chelsea (in the building later occupied by Josias Priest's school), Thomas Duffett's text mentions 'a flourish of Violins, Rechorders, Flajolets &c.', and a dance with 'Rechorders and Flajolets playing'; to judge from the surviving songs, John Banister wrote the music.[69] Greeting taught Pepys the flageolet, published a tutor for it, *The Pleasant Companion*, in the late 1660s, and is apparently pictured on its title-page playing it; his other instruments, the recorder and violin (or viola?), are also displayed (Fig. 14.1).[70]

Thus, Banister and Greeting probably played the flageolet in *Psyche*, and may have helped Locke to devise its scoring and recruit its instrumentalists. In turn, Locke, the most prominent royal composer, was presumably the person whose services were offered in *A Parley of Instruments*: 'Like wise any one that hath a desire to have any New Songs or Tunes, may be furnish'd by the same Person that serves his Majesty in the same Imployment.' More generally, the two works can be seen as part of a concerted attempt by the royal musicians to cope with the recurrent financial crises at court. By 1666 their wages were four or five years in arrears, and were not finally paid in some cases until the early 1690s (see Ch. 12). An obvious solution was to make up large orchestras in concerts and in the theatre; *A Parley of Instruments* could easily have used every available member of the royal wind consorts, the Private Music, and the twenty-four Violins, though with so many performers it cannot have brought them much return. Banister might also have been angling to write the music for the next semi-opera at Dorset Garden by demonstrating that he could handle even larger forces than those used by Locke. In the event, he was given his chance with Charles Davenant's *Circe*, produced in May 1677. Davenant's text calls for nearly as much music as *Psyche*, though it gives few details of the instruments, and nothing survives

[67] Ibid. 303; Chan and Kassler, *Roger North*, 265.
[68] Shute, 'Anthony à Wood', i. 61; ii. 109.
[69] Van Lennep, *The London Stage*, 238; Price, *Henry Purcell*, 226.
[70] Pepys, *Diary*, viii. 87 *et seq.*; T. E. Warner, *An Annotated Bibliography of Woodwind Instruction Books, 1600–1830* (Detroit Studies in Music Bibliography, 11; Detroit, 1967), 2; S. Godman, 'Greeting's "Pleasant Companion for the Flagelet"', *MMR* 86 (1956), 20–6.

14.1. Engraving on the title-page of Thomas Greeting, *The Pleasant Companion* (London, 2nd edn., 1673). It is presumably intended to represent the author with his instruments, flageolet, recorder, and ?viola

of the music apart from three songs and the bass part of the incidental music; Purcell reset a scene in Act I for a later revival, probably during the 1680s.[71]

Roger North wrote of the composer of *Psyche* that 'wee may say, as the Greeks sayd of Cleomenes, that he was ultimus Heroum'.[72] Indeed, the old court-dominated musical establishment of the London theatres began to break up in the spring of 1677, if we can interpret the dismissal of five court violinists from the King's Company at that time (see above) as a sign of significant and permanent change. Locke and Banister died in August 1677 and October 1679, and with their deaths the regular relationship between the Twenty-four Violins and the two patent companies may have ceased. The King's Company was severely weakened by a series of internal disputes, and by the turmoil surrounding the Popish Plot of 1679; the events of 1679 even affected the much stronger Duke's Company, and a single United Company was eventually created in November 1682.

We know virtually nothing about the effects of these changes on London's theatre musicians, but it is significant that a new and distinctive

---

[71] Van Lennep, *The London Stage*, 256–7; Price, *Henry Purcell*, 97–105.
[72] Wilson, *Roger North*, 306–7.

repertoire of theatre suites emerged in the early 1680s. They are found in a new group of sources, such as *US-NH*, Filmer MS 6, which seems to be mainly a chronological collection of incidental music for plays produced by the Duke's Company between January and April 1682, and *GB-Lb1*, Add. MSS 29283-5, mostly a chronological collection covering 1682-4, but less focused on theatre music. The composers represented, such as John Lenton, Solomon Eccles, Thomas Farmer, Francis Forcer, and Raphael Courteville, also belong to a new generation—one that was less closely connected with the Twenty-four Violins than their predecessors. Only Farmer (joined 1675) and Lenton (joined 1681) were members of the group at the time.[73] Their suites, too, tend to be in three parts rather than four, and are much simpler and less enterprising than Locke's theatre music. For one reason or another, the 1680s were depressed years for music in the commercial theatre, the more so after Grabu's opera *Albion and Albanius* failed disastrously in June 1685. Operatic productions on the scale of the 1670s were only resumed with Purcell's *Dioclesian*, produced by the United Company in June 1690. By then the centre of London's musical life had shifted away from the court, and the theatres no longer relied on the Twenty-four Violins for their orchestras.

[73] Ashbee, *RECM*, i. 151–2, 195, 196, 230, 232.

TABLE 14.1. *Attributed music for plays in the commercial theatre, 1660–1669*

Date	Title	Author	Evidence of composer
Productions by the Duke's Company, Lincoln's Inn Fields			
21/10/61	*Love and Honour*	Davenant	*PC*, no. 15, 'Love & Honour a Dance / M. L.'
15/2/62	*The Law against Lovers*	Davenant	song 'Wake all ye dead what ho' by Marsh, *TM*, 60, *DM*, no. 3561
8/1/63	*The Adventures of Five Hours*	Tuke	song 'Can Luciamira so mistake' by Banister, *CA* 1673, 24, *DM*, no. 470
23/2/63	*The Slighted Maid*	Stapylton	1663 edn.: 'The Instrumental, Vocal, and Recitative Musick, was composed by Mr Banister'
?/10/63	*The Step-Mother*	Stapylton	1664 edn.: 'The Instrumental, Vocal, and Recitative Musick, was compos'd by Mr Lock'
22/12/63	*Henry VIII*	Shakespeare/ ?Davenant	song 'Orpheus with his lute' by Locke, *CCC*, 174–5, *DM*, no. 2645
7/3/64	*The Unfortunate Lovers*	Davenant	song 'Run to love's lottery' by Marsh, *CA* 1673, 5–7, *DM*, no. 2838
?/3/64	*The Comical Revenge/Love in a Tub*	Etherege	*PC*, no. 8, 'Love in a Tubb: a dance / M. L.'
10/9/64	*The Rivals*	Davenant	song 'My lodging it is on the cold ground' sung in the play; see *RA*, 55; ascribed to Locke in Chappell, 526 on unknown evidence
5/11/64	*Macbeth*	Shakespeare/ Davenant	*AB*, no. 11, 'The Dance in the Play Macbeth'; also in *PC*, no. 7, 'Mackbeth / M. L.'
15/8/67	*Feign'd Innocence/ Sir Martin Marall*	Dryden	*PC*, no. 29, 'Sr Martin Maralls Jigg by M^r. J. B.'
7/11/67	*The Tempest*	Shakespeare/ Davenant/ Dryden	at least one of Banister's songs, 'Go thy way', *DM*, no. 1157, was written for this production; see Pepys, 189

TABLE 14.1. *Continued*

Date	Title	Author	Evidence of composer
6/2/68	*She Would if She Could*	Etherege	*AB*, no. 64, 'She would if she could', four-part setting by Locke, *RT*, 88–9
26/3/68	*The Man's the Master*	Davenant	song 'The bread is all baked' by Banister, *GB-Och*, Mus. MS 23
19/10/68	*The Queen of Arragon*	Habington	song 'Fine young folly though you wear' by Howes, *CCC*, 182, *DM*, no. 1008
25/2/69	*The Royal Shepherdess*	Shadwell	song by Banister, 'Thus all our lives long', *CA* 1673, 13, *DM*, no. 3347

Productions by the King's Company, Bridges Street Theatre

Date	Title	Author	Evidence of composer
25/1/64	*The Indian Queen*	Howard/ Dryden	incidental music by Banister in several sources; see Price, 181–2
?/4/65	*The Indian Emperor*	Dryden	song 'Ah fading joy' by Humfrey, *CA* 1675, 70–1, *DM*, no. 45; he was abroad 1664–7, so it may be for a revival
25/9/67	*The Storm/The Sea Voyage*	Fletcher/ Massinger	songs 'Hark the storm grows loud' by Smith, and 'Cheer up my mates' by Humfrey, *CA* 1673, 1–3, *DM*, nos. 1268, 538
18/5/68	*The Mulberry Garden*	Sedley	song, 'Ah, Chloris now that I could sit' by Banister; see Pepys, 189
12/6/68	*An Evening's Love/ The Mock Astrologer*	Dryden	songs 'After the pangs of a desperate lover' and 'Calm was the evening' by Marsh, *CA* 1673, 8, 9, *DM*, nos. 17, 468

Company and theatre unknown

Date	Title	Author	Evidence of composer
?5/63	*Pompey*	Phillips	songs by Banister probably for a London production, *GB-Och*, Mus. MS 350, 93–4; see Price, 62–4, 262

TABLE 14.1. *Continued*

Date	Title	Author	Evidence of composer
?	*The Devil is an Ass*	Jonson	piece entitled 'Divell', *US-NYp*, MS Drexel 3849, 74 is the last movement of a suite by Banister in *GB-Och*, Mus. MS 1183, fos. 91^r– 96^v; the play was popular around 1663, and was assigned to the King's Company in January 1669

Abbreviations

AB 1669	J. Playford, *Apollo's Banquet* (London, *c*.1669)
CA 1673	J. Playford, *Choice Songs and Ayres*, 1 (London, 1673)
CA 1675	J. Playford, *Choice Ayres, Songs and Dialogues*, 2 (London, 1675)
CCC	J. Playford, *Catch that Catch Can* (London, 1667)
Chappell	W. Chappell, *Popular Music of the Olden Time* (London, 1859)
DM	C. L. Day and E. Boswell Murrie (eds.), *English Song Books 1651–1702: A Bibliography* (London, 1940)
PC	T. Greeting, *The Pleasant Companion* (2nd edn., London, 1672)
Pepys	Samuel Pepys, *The Diary of Samuel Pepys*, ed. R. Latham and W. Matthews, ix: *1668–1669* (London, 1976)
Price	C. A. Price, *Music in the Restoration Theatre* (Ann Arbor, Mich., 1979)
RA	J. Downes, *Roscius Anglicanus*, ed. J. Milhous and R. D. Hume (London, 1987)
RT	M. Locke, *The Rare Theatrical, New York Public Library, Drexel MS 3976*, ed. P. Holman (Music for London Entertainment, series A, vol. 4; London, 1989)
TM	J. Playford, *The Treasury of Musick*, book 2 (London, 1669)

Unless otherwise stated, information is taken from W. B. Van Lennep (ed.), *The London Stage*, i: *1660–1700* (Carbondale, Ill., 1965); dates are of first known performances in a commercial theatre.

15

'Infinitely Gallant'

Court Masque and Opera

ON the morning of Tuesday, 20 November 1660 Samuel Pepys waited on the Earl of Sandwich in his apartment at Whitehall:

I found my Lord in bed late, he having been with the King, Queene, and Princesse at the Cockpitt all night, where Generall Monke treated them; and after supper, a play—where the King did put a great affront upon Singleton's Musique, he bidding them stop and bade the French Musique play—which my Lord says doth much out-do all ours.[1]

Pepys's diary entry has a triple significance. It seems to be the first reference to the performance of a play at the newly restored court; the play in question was *The Silent Woman* by Ben Jonson, and was given at the Cockpit in Court, the private theatre in Whitehall Palace.[2] It is an early reference to members of the Twenty-four Violins; John Singleton evidently led the group of violinists who were 'appointed by his Majesty to increase the number of his violins' at Midsummer 1660, and who formed a 'private consort' that played in the Privy Chamber until succeeded by Banister's Select Band in 1662 (see Ch. 12). It is also the first sign that Charles II envisaged a role for his violinists as theatre musicians.

The royal violin band had, of course, appeared in court masques and entertainments before the Civil War, though they were special events, and the group's role in them was essentially an extension of its day-to-day activities at court: it accompanied the dancing of courtiers. At the Restoration Charles had the sense not to revive the masque as a regular form of court entertainment. After all, the masques of the 1630s, lavish expositions of the theory of absolute monarchy, had provided the Puritans with obvious symbols of the court's decadence, and had contributed not a little to Charles I's financial difficulties. Instead, his son relied on the commercial theatre. Command performances were sometimes given at the Cockpit in Court or, after 1665, in the Hall Theatre. More often, the king patronized the two patent companies by visiting them in their own theatres, and by lending them court equipment and personnel; the

[1] Pepys. *Diary*, i. 297–8.
[2] Boswell, *The Restoration Court Stage*, 10–21; Van Lennep, *The London Stage*, i. 20–1.

Twenty-four Violins, divided into two for the purpose, seems to have played regularly in the commercial theatres in the 1660s and 70s (see Ch. 14).

Nevertheless, a surprising number of masques were given at Whitehall in the 1660s. John Evelyn witnessed a 'greate Masque at Court' on 2 July 1663.[3] Waller's *Pompey the Great*, performed at court in January 1663/4, concluded with a 'grand Masque ... Danc'd before Caesar and Cleopatra, made (as well as the other Dances and the Tunes to them) by Mr John Ogilby'—the dancing-master, writer, translator, printer, surveyor, and map-maker.[4] Another 'fine Mask' was given on 2 February 1664/5, performed, according to Evelyn, by '6 Gent(lemen) & 6 Ladys surprizing his Majestie, it being Candlemas day'.[5] Pepys was told about the 'Masquerade' the following day while on a visit to Lady Sandwich: 'six women (my Lady Castlemayne and Duchesse of Monmouth being two of them) and six men (the Duke of Monmouth and Lord Aron and Monsieur Blanfort being three of them) in vizards, but most rich and antique dresses, did dance admirably and most gloriously'.[6] The next year, on 19 February 1666/7, Evelyn 'saw a magnificent Ball or Masque in the Theater at Court, where their Majesties & all the greate Lords & Ladies daunced infinitely gallant: the Men in their richly imbrodred, most becoming Vests'.[7] Masque-like entertainments were also given in the Hall Theatre a year later, on 4 February 1667/8 between the acts of a performance of Katherine Philips's tragedy *Horace*. Evelyn, there once again, wrote that ''twixt each act a Masque & Antique: daunced: The excessive galantry of the Ladies was infinite'; the production was described as a 'great mask at Court' by Thomas Rugge in his public journal.[8]

There is direct evidence later in Charles II's reign of the role of the Twenty-four Violins in theatrical performances at court. On 4 July 1674 twelve violins were ordered to:

meete in his Ma(jes)ties Theatre within his Ma(jes)ties pallace of Whitehall on Wednesday morning next by seaven of the clock, to practise after such manner as Mons(ieu)r Combert shall enforme them, which things are hereafter to be pr(e)sented before his Ma(jes)tie at Windsor upon Saterday next.[9]

What the 'things' were is not known, but the composer Robert Cambert had come to London the previous year with a French opera company (see Ch. 14). On 22 May 1677 the Lord Chamberlain ordered:

---

[3] Evelyn, *Diary*, 453.
[4] Van Lennep, *The London Stage*, 73–4.
[5] Evelyn, *Diary*, 470.
[6] Pepys, *Diary*, vi. 29.
[7] Evelyn, *Diary*, 506.
[8] Ibid. 520; Boswell, *The Restoration Court Stage*, 137.
[9] Ashbee, *RECM*, i. 140.

That all his Ma(jes)ties musitians doe attend to practice in the Theatre at Whitehall at such tymes as Madame Le Roch and Mr. Paisible shall appoynt for the practiceing of such musick as is to be in the French comedy to be acted before his Ma(jes)tie on the 29 May instant.[10]

The comedy was *Rare en tout* by Madame de La Roche-Guilhen. The text has operatic scenes between the acts that were presumably set to music by Jacques (James) Paisible, the oboist and recorder-player who probably came to England with Cambert's group; the music is lost, but John Verney thought that, while the play was 'most pitifully done, so ill that the king was aweary on't', the 'dances and voices were pretty well performed'.[11] On 18 February 1678/9 Nicholas Staggins was ordered to ensure that the Twenty-four Violins should 'attend his Majesty every night that a play is acted at Court'; suspension was threatened for those 'neglecting the duty', a measure carried out in the case of four violinists in November 1681.[12] Near the end of the reign, on 26 January 1684/5, ten violinists were ordered to 'attend at his Majesty's Theatre Royal to practise music for a ball which is to be before his Majesty there'.[13]

The musical aspects of two court masques can be reconstructed in more detail. They have been little studied by musicians, yet they shed light on many aspects of Restoration theatre music, so I will not confine myself to those matters that concern the Twenty-four Violins. The first was given in the Hall Theatre a number of times in February 1670/1. Evelyn saw it on the 9th and described it as 'the greate Ball danced by the Queene & greate Ladies at White hall Theater', while the author of a court newsletter, referring to a performance on the 20th, wrote 'This evening was danced over the grand ballet at Whitehall, wherein the Court appeared in their greatest gallantry imaginable, and the time spent in songs, the chiefest dances and musick the town could afford.'[14] The most detailed account occurs in a letter to Katherine Noel from her friend Lady Mary Bertie, who also went on the 20th:

I was on Munday at Court to see the grane ballett danced. It was so hard to get room that wee were forced to goe by four a clocke, though it did not begin till nine or ten. The[y] were very richly [dressed] and danced very finely, and shifted their clothes three times. There was also fine musickes and excellent sing[ing of] some new song[s] made [on] purpose for it. After the ballet was over, several others danced, as the King, and Duke of Yorke, and Duke of Somerset, and Duke of Buckingham. And the Dutchesse of Cleveland was very fine in a riche

[10] Ibid. 172.

[11] Boswell, *The Restoration Court Stage*, 122–3.

[12] Ashbee, *RECM*, i. 182, 196.

[13] Ibid. 214.

[14] Evelyn, *Diary*, 550; *The Collection of Autograph Letters and Historical Documents Formed by Alfred Morrison*, 2nd ser., *1882–1893, The Bulstrode Papers*, i: *1667–1675* (London, 1895), 173–4.

petticoat and halfe shirte, and a short man's coat very richly laced, a per[i]wig cravatt and a hat: her hat and maske was very rich.[15]

Despite that fact that it is referred to as a ball or ballet, the work was clearly a masque. The king only danced after it was over, and when carpenters altered the Hall Theatre for the production they did not lay a dancing-floor over the pit, as they would have done for an ordinary ball.[16] The payments for these alterations, preserved in the accounts of the Office of Works, provide some information about the musicians who took part in the production.[17] There were evidently three separate groups, placed in different parts of the hall, for the work included 'Cutting out part of the stage & fitting a place there for the Queens musick, w(i)th railes about it & bourded', putting up 'one square & ½ Bourding w(i)th slitt deale about the Musick seate in the Clowds', and 'Incloseing a roome for the Italian musitions'. The 'music seat in the clouds' seems to be the same as the 'large seat w(i)th severall degrees in it for the musick' mentioned in the accounts for the construction of the Hall Theatre in the spring of 1665; an elevation of the stage drawn by John Webb at the time shows four tiers of seats marked 'Musick' raised up at the back of the stage so that the occupants could be revealed through a set of 'Ovall Shutt(e)rs' (Fig. 15.1).[18] Eleanore Boswell suggested that the Italians were placed 'at one side of the pit, immediately below the stage', and the queen's musicians were probably placed on the opposite side, at or near the front of the stage.[19]

Mention of French and Italian musicians in a Whitehall masque brings to mind Roger North's well-known account of a court entertainment, found in its fullest form in the c.1726 version of 'The Musicall Grammarian':

Once he [Charles II] took a fancy to have a sort of opera in his theater at Whitehall; and the designe was, that every nation should shew upon the stage a peice of their best musick, after the manner of their severall countrys. So there came Germanes, Spaniards, Italians and French; the English brought up the 'rere. A peice of the Italian consort I procured and as an example of the excellence of comon air in musick, I have added it in score. I presume Sig(no)r Babtista Draghe was the composer of it. But the English, who came with a few slight songs as—I pass all my hours in a shady old grove,—A wife I doe hate for either she's false or she's jealous—and the like, after the others made a poor appearance. And so proceeded the Court, in the weighty affair of musick.[20]

[15] Boswell, *The Restoration Court Stage*, 139.
[16] Ibid. 138.
[17] Ibid. 250.
[18] Ibid. 243–4.
[19] Ibid. 47.
[20] Wilson, *Roger North*, 300.

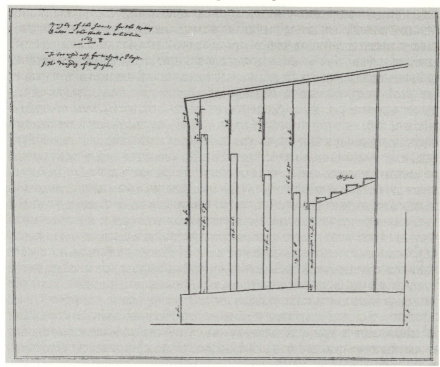

15.1. John Webb, elevation of the stage of the Hall Theatre, Whitehall, 1665 'for the Queens Ballet in the Hall at Whitehall / To be used also for masques & Playes'. Library of Chatsworth House, courtesy of His Grace the Duke of Devonshire

North added in the 1728 version of 'The Musicall Grammarian' that the king chose 'I pass all my hours in a shady old grove' as the best song, though 'others were not of his opinion'.[21]

The English songs mentioned by North are by Pelham Humfrey, and were published in John Playford's *Choice Songs and Ayres*, i (London, 1673), 15, and *Choice Ayres and Songs*, v (London, 1684), 38–9. Copies of the texts confirm that North's passage is an account of the 1671 masque—albeit garbled, for the Office of Works documents do not mention groups of Spaniards or Germans, and none is recorded in England at the time. The first is in *Westminster Drollery*, i (London, 1671) under the title 'The first Song in the Ball at Court', along with 'A lover I'm born and a lover I'll be', 'A second Song in the Masque at Court';

---

[21] Chan and Kassler, *Roger North*, 262.

this is also by Humfrey, and is in *Choice Songs and Ayres*, i. 12.[22] Further, the text of 'I pass all my hours in a shady old grove' has the title '1st Song in the Masque 1670[/1]' in *GB-Lbl*, Harley MS 3991, fo. 155[r].

North wrote out the 'peice of the Italian consort', 'Amante, che dite', at the end of 'The Musicall Grammarian' with the title 'Sung at a muster of voices in the theater at White hall [in the] reign [of] Charles 2'.[23] It is not by the harpsichordist Giovanni Battista Draghi, as he thought, but is the last movement of Carissimi's popular serenata 'I Naviganti'.[24] Neverthe-less, the attribution is revealing, for Draghi was a member of Charles II's group of Italian musicians. The Italians, a vocal consort directed by Vincenzo Albrici, apparently came to England in 1663 to establish an opera company in London.[25] In one court document it is said that they 'could serve in the chamber and the theatre', and on 12 February 1666/7 Pepys heard Draghi sing an act of his own 'play in Italian for the Opera'; Thomas Killigrew, who was present, told the diarist that he intended to put on operas 'some times of the year' in the two London theatres.[26] Pepys added: 'Baptista tells me that Jiacomo Charissimi is still alive at Rome, who was maister to Vincentio, who is one of the Italians the King hath here, and the chief composer of them.' The identity of the 'Queens musick' is more of a problem. Catherine of Braganza arrived in England in 1662 with a group of Portuguese musicians, who were replaced, in part at least, by the Italians in the late 1660s.[27] But there would have been little point to Charles II's international singing contest if the Italians also doubled as the queen's musicians. Some of Charles II's French singers (see Ch. 12) were still at Whitehall in 1671, but there is no sign that they were members of the queen's household.

Some of the instrumental music for the masque survives in *GB-En*, MS 5777, a violin tune-book from the library of the Ker family of Newbattle Abbey, Midlothian; it was mostly written by someone who also wrote manuscripts for the Maule family of Panmure House in Angus. More research needs to be done on the Panmure and Newbattle violin books, but MS 5777, at least, was probably written in London in the 1670s or 1680s, perhaps by a teacher employed by the families while they were resident in the capital.[28] It contains music by a number of

---

[22] Dennison, *Pelham Humfrey*, 83, 113.

[23] Edited in Chan and Kassler, *Roger North*, 273–8.

[24] See G. Dixon, *Carissimi* (Oxford, 1986), 65.

[25] W. J. Lawrence, 'Foreign Singers and Musicians at the Court of Charles II', *MQ*, 9 (1923), 217–25; Westrup, 'Foreign Musicians in Stuart England', 72–3, 77–80; Mabbett, 'Italian Musicians in Restoration England', 237–47.

[26] Mabbett, 'Italian Musicians', 238, 244; Pepys, *Diary*, viii. 54–7.

[27] Westrup, 'Foreign Musicians', 72; Mabbett, 'Italian Musicians', 239.

[28] C. McCart, 'The Kers and the Maules: Music in the Lives of Two Seventeenth-Century Scottish Aristocratic Families', B. A. diss. (Colchester Institute, 1988), especially 53–6.

court composers, such as Matthew Locke (including two of the 'Rare Theatrical' pieces, fos. 5ᵛ–6ʳ²⁹), Robert Smith, Louis Grabu (including a probable theatre suite with a dance for 'Marcury', fos. 33ᵛ–38ʳ), William Clayton, John Singleton, and John Jenkins. A clue to the identity of the copyist is provided by a Panmure violin book in the same hand, Scottish Record Office, Edinburgh, MS GD 45/26/104. It opens with a suite by 'Jafery Bannester', the only composer in the manuscript not to be given the title 'Mr.'; further, his name appears on the second page in an elaborate, signature-like form (Fig. 15.2). Jeffrey Bannister, John's supposed brother, was a member of the Twenty-four Violins from 1662 until 1684, when he was given permission to travel 'beyond the Seas for the space of Six Moneths, or longer if his Occasions shall require'. He was dead by 13 October 1684, when his will, dated 29 August, was proved.³⁰

There are at least three suites by John Banister in MS 5777, including a portion of his widely distributed music for *The Indian Queen* by Sir Robert Howard and John Dryden, first produced by the King's Company in January 1663/4.³¹ The music that seems to come from the 1671 masque is a suite in B♭, fos. 41ᵛ–42ʳ, 43ᵛ–44ᵛ; the six movements are entitled 'Ballet 1 entre/B(aniste)r', '2 entre', 'B(aniste)r/Entry: 3', 'queens Gigue B(aniste)r', 'Entry queens Ballett. 1671. whitthall B(aniste)r', and 'queens aire. B(aniste)r'. The masque was given in February 1670 according to the way dates were reckoned in Restoratian England, but in Scotland (and possibly in Scottish households temporarily based in London) the year had been reckoned from 1 January since 1600. Without a text or a detailed description we cannot know whether the suite contains all the dance music for the masque; 'The Queen's Mask' and a 'Saraband', a pair of D major dances added to the 1678 edition of Playford's keyboard collection *Musicks Hand-Maide*, may come from the same production.³²

A little more light can be thrown on the 1671 masque by a well-known episode in the semi-fictional *Mémoires du Comte de Gramont*, written by Anthony Hamilton, published in French at Cologne in 1713, and best known in English in Horace Walpole's translation, published in 1772.³³ Hamilton includes a long and rambling account of the intrigues surrounding an undated 'splendid masquerade' which the queen had

---

²⁹ Locke, *The Rare Theatrical*, ed. Holman, p. xxiv.
³⁰ Ashbee, *RECM*, i. 37, 211, 222; *GB-Lpro*, PROB 11/377, q. 123.
³¹ Van Lennep, *The London Stage*, 74; Price, *Music in the Restoration Theatre*, 181–2.
³² Playford, ed. T. Dart, *The First Part of Musick's Hand-Maid Published by John Playford* (London, 1969), nos. 57, 58.
³³ *Memoirs of the Comte de Gramont by Anthony Hamilton, Translated by Horace Walpole*, ed. D. Hughes (London, 1965), 89–99.

15.2. The hand of Jeffrey Banister? Scottish Record Office, Edinburgh, GD45/126/104, 2. By permission of the Earl of Dalhousie and with the approval of the keeper of the Records of Scotland.

devised 'to represent different nations'. He tells how Lady Muskerry was tricked into dressing for the occasion 'in the Babylonian fashion', and how Gramont himself had promised the king that he would dress 'in the French manner'. His servant was sent to Paris for a costume, only to lose it in a quicksand near Calais. Much of this is probably fiction, but it is possible that Hamilton based it on real events surrounding the production of the 1671 masque: the queen's plan to represent the manners of different countries would have complemented the king's for an international singing contest. The result would have been not unlike those French stage works, such as Campra's *L'Europe galante* of 1697, that portrayed the humours of different nations in music and dance.

It is a pity that so many aspects of the 1671 masque are still obscure, for it was clearly an event of some importance. We are more fortunate in the case of the 1675 masque, John Crowne's *Calisto; or, The Chaste Nymph*, given in the Hall Theatre with music by Nicholas Staggins a number of times in February of that year.[34] *Calisto*, in fact, is only like a pre-war court masque in that characters from myth and allegory sing and dance, and the performers were led by prominent courtiers; rather, it is a lively spoken play based on the story of how Jupiter, disguised as the goddess Diana, tried to rape the chaste nymph. The music is confined to an allegorical prologue and four pastoral interludes between the acts. Reversing the way roles were traditionally allocated in the masque, the spoken parts were taken by courtiers, including the young Princesses Mary and Anne, while the dances were mostly performed by professionals—though 'several sarabands with castanets' were danced by 'the Princesses and the other Ladies', and the Duke of Monmouth danced a minuet.

Two lists of performers survive for *Calisto*. The first is labelled 'These are the Names of such as are admitted to come in at the Dore behind the Sceenes & none other', and was evidently designed to restrict access to the backstage area during rehearsals and performances.[35] Apart from the names of the dancers, amateur and professional, and the singers, it lists fifty-one instrumentalists: two harpsichords, three bass viols, two theorboes, four recorders, four 'Gittars', four trumpets, a 'Kettle Drummer', and thirty-one 'Violins'. The second list, dated 27 May 1675, is a warrant to pay a number of them for 'theire service & attendance in the Maske at Whitehall', including seven 'French Violins and Hoboyes', a harpsichordist, a theorbo-player, and nine of the violinists.[36] The harpsichordist, 'Mr. Bartholomew' (Bartolomeo Albrici), and the theorbo-player, 'M^r [Alfonso] Marsh Sen(ior)', were paid £10 for 'Extraord[ina]ry Attendance'—presumably for extra continuo rehearsals that were thought to be over and above their normal duties as court musicians. The rest were paid £5 or £3 each, and were evidently on the list because they were not salaried court musicians. The four French oboists (listed as 'Recorders' in the first list), Jacques Paisible, Maxent De Bresmes (De Breame), Pierre Guiton, and (?Jean) Boutet (Boutell), had only recently arrived in England; they probably came in the summer of 1673 with Robert Cambert and his opera company (see Ch. 14).[37] The three 'French Violins', Bejard (Basrier), Violett (Viblett, possibly the French harpsichordist Jean la Volée), and Cornelius (who only appears in the second list), may have come at the same time.

More than fifty instrumentalists took part in *Calisto*, but they did not form one large orchestra, as has been assumed. Eleanore Boswell drew attention to two documents relating to alterations to the Hall Theatre for

[34] Van Lennep, *The London Stage*, 225–9; see also Boswell, *The Restoration Court Stage*, especially 177–227; O. Baldwin and T. Wilson, 'An English *Calisto*', *MT*, 112 (1971), 651–3.

[35] Ashbee, *RECM*, i. 145–6; Boswell, *The Restoration Court Stage*, 200–2.

[36] Ashbee, ibid. 149–50; Boswell, ibid. 222–3.

[37] For Boutet, see Lasocki, 'Professional Recorder Players', ii. 830.

the production.[38] One instructs Christopher Wren to 'enclose the front of the pitt next the stage for the musick the whole breadth of the house', while the other is a payment for 'takeing downe the Musicke seats & layeing two large floores & rayseing another floore with severall degrees for the Musicke'. She suggests that the 'severall degrees' were tiers of seats raised up behind the shutters at the back of the stage, as shown on Webb's elevation plan of the Hall Theatre; they were described as 'the Musick seate in the Clowds' in the payments for the alterations for the 1671 masque.

Boswell was surely right to conclude that the instrumentalists in *Calisto* were divided into two groups, one placed in front of the stage, the other behind the scenes. She cited a bill for special costumes for twenty of the violins, two of the oboes, the four guitars, and the five-man trumpet and drum band.[39] But her suggestion that the costumed group played in front of the stage while the rest—two harpsichords, two theorboes, three bass viols, twelve violins, and the other pair of oboes—were behind the scenes, cannot be right. It must have been the other way round. The theorbo-players and the harpsichordists would have needed to sit in front of the stage to see the singers, and it is unlikely that two harpsichords could have been fitted into the 'music seat in the clouds'. Also, the group behind the scenes would have needed costumes because the shutters in front of them would have opened from time to time, revealing them to the audience.

It looks, in fact, as if the orchestras in *Calisto* had separate functions, and may not even have played together—as was the case in most pre-war court masques. The orchestra in front of the stage, with its continuo instruments, would have accompanied the vocal music; its 'violins' (that is, violin-family instruments) and oboe/recorder-players presumably played introductions and interludes to the songs. The bass viols may have had a continuo function, though they were not paid 'extraordinary attendance', so they were probably not used in the solo vocal sections. The orchestra behind the scenes probably accompanied the dances, with the shutters open so that the dancers could hear the music and the musicians see the dancers. The guitarists may have played continuo, or they may have played some of the dances by themselves. Spanish dances were often accompanied by on-stage guitars and castanets in the Restoration theatre. In Dryden's *The Indian Emperor* (1667) 'two Spaniards arise and Dance a Saraband with Castanieta's', while there is a dance with 'Gittars and Castanietta's' in Shadwell's *The Royal Shepherdess* (1669).[40]

---

[38] Boswell, *The Restoration Court Stage*, 204.
[39] Ibid. 304–6.
[40] Price, *Music in the Restoration Theatre*, 36, 257.

So the guitarists probably played the 'several sarabands with castanets' that were danced in the prologue of *Calisto*. They may also have played in the 'Entry of Gipsies' at the end of Act II, and the 'Entry of Africans' at the end of Act V; guitars had been in the hands of stage gypsies ever since Jonson's masque *The Gypsies Metamorphosed* (1621), while the dances with guitars mentioned in the 1689 libretto of *Dido and Aeneas* are obvious instances of the connection between Africans and the instrument.

Staggins evidently composed all the music for *Calisto*. Crowne wrote in the preface to the text that he was 'the Composer of all the Musick both vocal and instrumental', and praised him in extravagant terms: 'Mr. Staggins has not only delighted us with his excellent Composition, but with the hopes of seeing in a very short time a Master of Musick in England equal to any France or Italy had produced.'[41] In January 1675/6 he submitted a bill for £13. 10s. for the 'faire writeing of the Aires composed for the Maske from the fowle originall on score', and £10 for 'drawing the said musick for the voyces, with the instrumentall musick composed at the same time'; it is not clear whether this document refers to *Calisto*.[42]

More music for *Calisto* survives than has been thought. The voice parts of seven songs are in *GB-Lbl*, Add. MS 19759, fo. 18^{r-v}, and most if not all the instrumental pieces can be identified in two manuscripts of consort music. The connection between *Calisto* and one of them, *EIRE-Dtc*, MS 413, has been made several times, and is mentioned by Watkins Shaw in his article on Staggins in *Grove 6*. The manuscript is a set of three part-books, dating probably from the 1680s, of music by Lully, Grabu, Banister, and Robert Smith, as well as the obscure composer Thomas Bullamore, who might well have been the copyist. There are four pieces by 'Si(g)n(o)r Callisto', an air in F minor, p. 6, and a three-movement suite in E minor, p. 7. 'Callisto' could be an inaccurate reference to the Roman composer Lelio Colista, who was known in Restoration England as a composer of trio sonatas, but it is perhaps more likely that the name of the play in a copy source was wrongly taken to be an Italian surname.[43] On the other hand, *US-NYp*, Drexel MS 3849 has not hitherto been thought of as a source of music from *Calisto*. On pp. 122‑4 the original compiler, the composer John Birchensha (see Ch. 13), copied a nine-movement F major suite by Staggins; a comparison between its titles and the passages relating to the music in Crowne's text strongly suggests that the work derives from *Calisto* (Table 15.1).

---

[41] John Crowne, *The Dramatic Works*, ed. J. Maidment and W. H. Logan, i (Edinburgh, 1872), 219–342.

[42] Ashbee, *RECM*, i. 155.

[43] See P. Allsop, 'Problems of Ascription in the Roman *Simfonia* of the Late Seventeenth Century: Colista and Lonati', *MR*, 50 (1989), 34–44.

TABLE 15.1. *The instrumental music in* Calisto

1675 text	US-NYp, Drexel MS 3849, pp. 122–4 (titles from first treble)
Prologue	
'The Curtain is drawn up'	1: 'Mr Staggin's Overture at the drawing up of the Curtaine'
'An Entry of Shepherds and Nymphs, Dancing round the Thames, &c'	2: 'Jigg'
'Here the Princesses and the other Ladies danced several Sarabands with Castanets'	[improvised pieces played by the guitars?]
'A Minouet was also danced by his Grace the Duke of Monmouth'	3: 'Entry danc't by the Duke, & minutes together'
'Two Entries are danc'd: One of Sea-gods, and the other of Warriors'	[pieces from *EIRE-Dtc*, MS 413?]
'An Entry of Rural Gods and Nymphs'	[piece from *EIRE-Dtc*, MS 413?]
'An Entry of Carpenters'	[piece from *EIRE-Dtc*, MS 413?]
Act I	
'An Entry of Basques'	4: 'Minutte for the flageoletts' / 'Act 1'
Act II	
'An Entry of Cupids, and Winds'	5: 'Scotch tune' / 'Act 2^d'
Act III	
'An Entry of Gipsies'	[improvised piece played by the guitars?]
'An Entry of Satyrs'	6: [minuet] / 'Act 3^d'
Act IV	
'An Entry of Bacchusses'	7: 'Countrey Dance' / 'Act 4th'
Act V	
'Enter Spirits'	8: 'The Entry' / 'The Witches'
'Calisto and Nyphe enter under a Canopy, supported by Africans'	
'The whole concludes with an Entry of Africans'	9: 'The young Ladies dance for the flageolets' / 'Finis Mr Staggyns'

A couple of the identifications need to be discussed. In Act V Crowne's spirits are not witches, but they are referred to as 'fierce, tempestuous Spirits of the air', and are ordered by Juno to tear a group of rebellious nymphs limb from limb; it is easy to understand how such fearsome airborne beings might have been thought of as witches. Also, the final dance of 'young Ladies' does not seem compatible with an 'Entry of Africans', until it is realized that Calisto and Nyphe were played by the two princesses; perhaps they started a dance that was joined by the Africans. If the four 'Sinr Callisto' pieces really are the four dances in the Prologue that are missing in Drexel MS 3849, then we have all the instrumental music required by Crowne's text, except for two pieces that might have been improvised by the guitarists.

Staggins's music for *Calisto* is not a great discovery. Some of the short dances are effective enough, but the thin-textured and short-winded overture seems to be barely competent in places. We must remember, however, that there would have been at least one more inner part—a viola entry seems to be missing at the beginning of the fugue—and that the source gives little idea of how the pieces would originally have sounded. Could the successive phrases marked 'loud' and 'soft' in the fugue have been played in antiphonal fashion, with the soft passages taken by the orchestra behind the scenes? (see Ex. 15.1.) What is meant by the reference to 'flageolets' in nos. 4 and 9? Paisible and his colleagues are listed as recorder-players in one of the *Calisto* documents, and the range of the parts, which do not go below f', suggests alto recorders rather than flageolets. How were the wind instruments used? Did they play by themselves, did they double the strings, or were they given independent parts in an orchestral texture? In short, we can get little idea of how Staggins's music sounded from such a poor source.

Used with caution, the *Calisto* documents are a useful guide to the performance of other masques and operas of the time. John Blow's *Venus and Adonis* is a case in point. Nothing is known about the circumstances of its original production, apart from what can be deduced from the main source of its first version. In *GB-Lbl*, Add. MS 22100, copied by the reliable and well-connected Eton musician John Walter, the work is entitled 'A Masque for the Entertainment of the King', and the parts of Venus and Cupid are said to have been taken by Charles II's mistress Moll Davies and their small daughter Lady Mary Tudor, born in 1673. The manuscript is labelled 'Mr Dolbins Book Anno Domini 1681/2', and includes court odes written by Blow in 1680–1, so it has been generally assumed that *Venus and Adonis* dates from around then, and was written for an unrecorded court performance. The later history of the work is obscure, but evidence has now come to light of a production in 1684 at Josias Priest's school in Chelsea (which lends substance to the

Ex. 15.1. Nicholas Staggins, 'Overture at the drawing up of the Curtaine' from
Calisto, US-NYp, Drexel MS 3849, p. 122

Ex. 15.1. *Continued*

idea that it was the model for *Dido and Aeneas*, performed at Chelsea in 1689); there are several sources of a revised version of the score, which is not known to have been put on the stage.[44]

Those who have written about *Venus and Adonis* in modern times have tended to compare it with *Dido and Aeneas*, a strategy that tells us more about the latter than the former. *Venus and Adonis* is more usefully compared with *Calisto*, the more so since Staggins collaborated with Blow on an abortive operatic project in 1683 (see Ch. 12), and would doubtless have had a hand in a court production of the opera as Master of the Music. Also, the anonymous librettist seems to have had at least half an eye on Crowne's masque: they are both based on stories from Ovid, treated in a lively, semi-satirical fashion; and they have masque-like dance entries concentrated in the prologue and at the end of the acts.

Calisto certainly throws light on the instrumental writing in *Venus and Adonis*. Blow calls for two 'flutes' as well as four-part strings. By 'flute' he meant the Baroque alto recorder, most likely introduced to England by Paisible and his colleagues and used by them in *Calisto* (see Ch. 14). The Frenchmen played the oboe as well as the recorder in *Calisto*, so oboes may have doubled the violins in the tutti passages of *Venus and Adonis*, even though they are not specified in the score. At any rate, Blow's use of wind instruments in *Venus and Adonis* may be a sign that it was conceived for larger forces than, say, *Dido and Aeneas*, which seems to have been written just for strings.

Another sign that Blow wrote for a group of orchestral size is provided by a detail of his string-writing. Most of it, including the overture and the dances, is in four parts, but there are two passages in the vocal sections of Acts I and III that are laid out in three parts, for two trebles and bass. The same feature can be found in *The Fairy Queen*, and in other semi-operas of the 1690s, and it also occurs in works written for the Paris Opéra, the Académie royale de musique: in Lully's operas the *ritournelles* that punctuate the vocal sections are mostly in three parts, two trebles and bass, while the overture, the dances, and the other instrumental passages are in five parts. This is because two instrumental groups were used: the full orchestra, the *grand chœur*, would have played the five-part passages, while the *petit chœur*, a group that consisted in 1704 (the earliest year for which we have detailed information) of two solo violins, a harpsichord, two theorbes, two bass viols, and three bass violins (or, possibly, two bass violins and *contrebasse*), would have accompanied the solo vocal sections, with the solo violins taking the three-part *ritournelles*.[45]

[44] For the 1684 production, see Luckett, 'A New Source for *Venus and Adonis*', 76–9; see also Blow, *A Masque for the Entertainment of the King: Venus and Adonis*, ed. C. Bartlett (Wyton, 1984).

[45] J. de La Gorce, 'L'Académie Royale de Musique en 1704, d'après des documents inédits conservés dans les archives notariales', *RdM*, 65 (1979), 178–82; see also Anthony, *French Baroque*

Unfortunately, we do not know to what extent French orchestral practice can be applied to the Twenty-four Violins. We may reasonably conclude that the three- and four-part passages in *Venus and Adonis* were played respectively by solo strings and an orchestra. This makes particularly good sense for the three-part 'Hunter's Musick' in Act I that imitates the distant sound of the hunting horn. When the same horn imitations recur later at the end of the act in the 'Dance by a Huntsman', the huntsmen are on stage, and the music is four parts—played, presumably, by the full orchestra. However, many questions remain. How large was the orchestra? Was the continuo group placed with it, as in French operas, or was it in another part of the theatre, as in *Calisto* and pre-war English masques? Was the bass of the solo vocal sections doubled by a bowed instrument, as in Lully's operas? A low *G* at the end of the singing lesson in Act II suggests that it was not, or not throughout, for the note was available on theorboes and English keyboard instruments, but not on bass violins or English six-string bass viols; it is not in the revised version of the score. We are unlikely to find answers to all these questions simply because only a few sources of English operatic works survive, and they tend to be incomplete or uninformative. The situation is much better in France, for most French operas were published in authoritative full scores, and a certain amount of original performing material survives for them.

Venus and Adonis is unusually informative in one respect. In Add. MS 22100 the first recorder part of the 'Tune for flutes' that precedes Act I is covered with the ornament signs x and ⟍ (Ex. 15.2). They seem to correspond to the 'shakes' and 'beats' illustrated in short extracts of dance tunes in John Lenton's violin tutor *The Gentleman's Diversion* (London, 1694, 13 (Fig. 15.3).[46] Taken together, the two sources suggest that English dance music was played with more ornamentation than is usual in modern performances, and that the ornaments were graces—trills and appoggiaturas—rather than florid divisions. Lenton is a particularly valuable witness, for he was a member of the Twenty-four Violins from 1681, wrote a number of theatre suites of his own, and must have played often in orchestras directed by Blow or Purcell; indeed, he could have played in the first performance of *Venus and Adonis*.

The best English sources of information about orchestral practice in the theatre are two works by Louis Grabu. They were published in full score, and are virtually the last products of the court tradition of masques

Music, 92–5; P. Holman, 'An Orchestral Suite by François Couperin?', *EM*, 14 (1986), 71–6; La Gorce, 'Some Notes on Lully's Orchestra', 99–112.

[46] See M. Boyd and J. Rayson, '*The Gentleman's Diversion*: John Lenton and the First Violin Tutor', *EM*, 10 (1982), 329–32; I am grateful to Malcolm Boyd for providing me with a copy of Lenton's work.

Ex. 15.2. John Blow, first treble part of 'Tune for the flutes' from *Venus and Adonis*, Act I, *GB-Lbl*, Add. MS 22100, fo. 128ᵛ

and masque-like plays. *Valentinian*, Fletcher's bloodthirsty tragedy about a Roman emperor's rape of his general's wife, was adapted by the poet John Wilmot, Earl of Rochester, during the 1670s; an early version was evidently more or less ready for production by the King's company in the 1675–6 season, though it does not seem to have been performed before Rochester's death in July 1680.[47] The first known performance was given in the Hall Theatre at Whitehall by the United Company on 11 February 1683/4. Theatre historians have presumed that the Whitehall production was preceded by a run in a commercial theatre, since only masques like *Calisto* normally had their premières at court; plays were given there from repertoire. But there is no evidence of a prior commercial production of *Valentinian*, and the play has masque-like scenes that demand the resources of royal musicians—including the Twenty-four Violins. The 1684 production may have been organized by a group of literary courtiers as a tribute to Rochester's memory; the prologue for the first night was written by his friend, the playwright Aphra Behn.

The music for *Valentinian* is all by Grabu (apart from a song by Robert King, a later addition), and was evidently written on his return to London

---

[47] The music in Rochester's *Valentinian* is discussed in more detail in P. Holman, '*Valentinian*, Rochester and Louis Grabu', in J. Caldwell, E. Olleson, and S. Wollenberg (eds.), *The Well Enchanting Skill: Music, Poetry, and Drama in the Culture of the Renaissance: Essays in Honour of F. W. Sternfeld* (Oxford, 1990), 127–41.

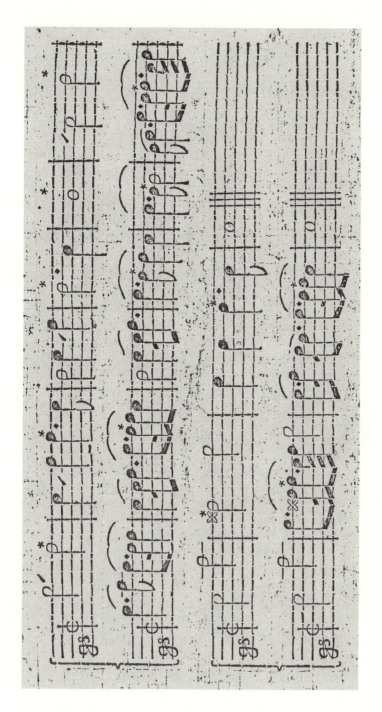

15.3. John Lenton, illustration of ornaments in *The Gentleman's Diversion* (London, 1694), 13

in the winter of 1683–4; he had been hounded out of England along with other Catholics during the Popish Plot crisis of 1679. It consists of two songs and eight instrumental pieces, and appears in Grabu's little-studied publication *Pastoralle* (London, 1684). Nowhere in the volume is it revealed that the pieces are for Rochester's play; indeed, Grabu referred to them merely as 'other Aires & some English Songs' on the title-page. I have argued that this was because his dedicatee, the Duchess of Portsmouth (Charles II's Breton mistress Louise de Keroualle), had been the subject of some satires attributed to Rochester. The songs certainly come from the play—the words are in the 1685 printed text— and there is a strong case for associating the instrumental movements with it, as will be shown.

In most respects Rochester's *Valentinian* is a typical Restoration adaptation of a Jacobean play, though it is unusual in that music is used to advance the action—something that was normally confined to masques and all-sung operas. The crucial episode straddles Act III, scenes 2 and 3: the heroine Lucina, asleep in a grove, dreams of the misfortune that is to befall her. Rochester evidently planned a dumb-show to represent this on stage, but the 1685 text only contains a reference to a 'Dance of Satyrs'. However, when Lucina awakes, she gives a detailed account of her dream:

> In what Fantastique new world have I been?
> What Horrors past? what threatning Visions seen?
> Wrapt as I lay in my amazing Trance,
> The Host of Heav'n and Hell did round me Dance:
> Debates arose betwixt the Pow'rs above
> And those below: Methought they talkt of love
> And nam'd me often; but it could not be
> Of any Love that had to do of me.
> For all the while they talk'd and argu'd thus,
> I never heard one word of Maximus . . .
> Mishapen Monsters round in Measures went
> Horrid in Form with Gestures insolent;
> Grinning throu' Goatish Beards with half clos'd Eyes,
> They look'd me in the face . . .

A six-movement suite in G, pp. 46–52 of *Pastoralle*, is evidently the music used for the dumb-show. Its single-section prelude consists largely of tranquil rising and falling scales, a classic seventeenth-century way of portraying sleep. The 'Host of Heav'n' is represented by a stately duple-time 'Air pour Jupiter', and a triple-time 'Air pour les suivans de Jupiter'; they correspond to the first two movements of the suite of branles, and for good reason: in England and France the King opened court balls by dancing the branle, which was then taken up by prominent courtiers (see Ch. 13). The 'Mishapen Monsters' evidently danced to an air for 'frightening dreams' ('songes affreux'), full of the rushing scales that were associated with demons in French opera, and an 'Air pour les satires', a suitably rustic loure (Ex. 15.3). The suite ends with a minuet, intended perhaps to represent a resolution of the 'love debate'.

The other masque-like scene in *Valentinian* is the extraordinary comic episode, Act IV, scenes 2 and 3, in which the eunuch Lycinius arranges a rehearsal of a masque to distract attention from Lucina's rape:

[Scene] *Opens and discovers 5 or 6 Dancing-masters practising.*
1 DAN[CER]. That is the damn'st shuffling Step, Pox on't.
2 DAN. I shall never hit it.
    Thou hast naturally
    All the neat Motions of a merry Tailor,
    Ten thousand Riggles with thy Toes inward,
    Cut clear and strong: let thy Limbs play about thee;
    Keep time, and hold thy Back upright and firm:
    It may prefer thee to a waiting Woman.
1 DAN. Or to her Lady, which is worse.

Enter Lycinius.   [*Ten dance.*

LYCIN. Bless me, the loud Shrieks and horrid Outcries
    Of the poor Lady! Ravishing d'ye call it?
    She roars as if she were upon the Rack:
    'Tis strange there should be such a difference
    Betwixt half-ravishing, which most Women love,
    And thor[o]ugh force, which takes away all Blame,
    And should be therefore welcome to the vertuous.
    These tumbling Rogues, I fear, have overheard 'em;
    But their Ears with their Brains are in their Heels.
    Good morrow Gentlemen:
    What is all perfect? I have taken care
    Your Habits shall be rich and glorious.
3 DAN. That will set off. Pray sit down and see,
    How the last Entry I have made will please you.

Second Dance.

LYCIN. 'Tis very fine indeed.
2 DAN. I hope so Sir—

[*Ex. Dancers*

The dances called for are probably the two remaining ones in *Pastoralle*. The first, an 'Air pour les haubois', pp. 37–9, an unusual rondeau with a gavotte-like theme and triple-time episodes, is a perfect vehicle for the 'shuffling step' of the dancing-masters. The second, an elegant saraband entitled 'Air pour les flutes', pp. 39–40, would serve well as the dance that the dancing-masters demonstrate for Lycinius.

The instrumental pieces for *Valentinian* are in five parts, for violin, three violas (the second is in the soprano clef and does not go above e''),

Ex. 15.3. Louis Grabu, 'Air pour les songes affreux', bb. 1–7, for *Valentinian, Pastoralle* (London, 1684), 49

and bass. This scoring was common in northern Europe earlier in the century: I argued in earlier chapters that the English court band used it until the Civil War, but in 1660 it went over to a four-part layout, and by the 1680s five-part one-treble music was more or less confined to the French court, and was thought of as exclusively French; it occurs in only one piece by an English Restoration composer, Matthew Locke's anthem 'Be thou exalted Lord' of 1666 (see Ch. 16). The *Valentinian* pieces as

Ex. 15.3. *Continued*

printed in *Pastoralle* do not specify wind instruments, but the titles 'Air pour les haubois' and 'Air pour les flutes' were added by a contemporary hand, perhaps that of the composer, to the unique copy of the print, owned by Samuel Pepys and now in the Pepys Library, Magdalene College, Cambridge. These movements are no different from the others and are apparently written just for five-part strings. It is not immediately clear what the wind instruments played—they may have doubled one or

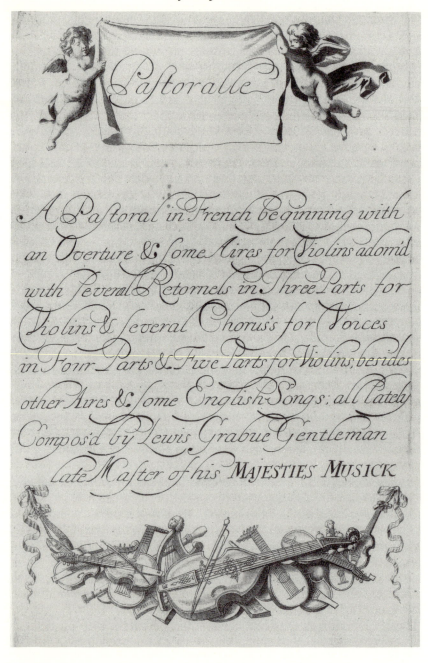

15.4. The title-page of Louis Grabu, *Pastoralle* (London, 1684). The Pepys Library, Magdalene College, Cambridge, courtesy of the Master and Fellows.

more of the string parts—but the titles show that wind-players were present in the orchestra, presumably playing recorders as well as oboes— which supports the idea that the wind-players in *Venus and Adonis* played both instruments.

Grabu's last major work for the stage was *Albion and Albanius*, Dryden's partriotic and allegorical opera that was disastrously produced in the period of upheaval following the death of Charles II and the Monmouth rebellion in the spring and early summer of 1685.[48] The unfortunate history of *Albion and Albanius* is well known and need not be repeated here, save to point out that, though the work was finally performed in public at Dorset Garden by the United Company, it was instigated by Charles II, and was produced under court patronage with the assistance of the court. Roger North wrote that 'The King resolved to have a very solemne opera and gave the subject, which was *Albanus*', and Charles II certainly sent the actor Thomas Betterton to Paris in the summer of 1683 to recruit a French opera company; on 22 September Lord Preston, an English ambassador at the French Court, wrote that:

Mr Betterton coming hither some Weeks since by his Majestyes command to endeavour to carry over the opera, & finding that impracticable, did treat with Mons(ieu)r Grabue to go over to represent something at least like an Opera in England for his Majestyes diversion.[49]

The 'something at least like an Opera', *Albion and Albanius*, was evidently complete by the end of 1684, for Edward Bedingfield wrote to the Countess of Rutland on 1 January 1684/5 that it had been 'soe well performed at the repetition that has been made before his Majesty at the Duchess of Portsmouth's'; Grabu wrote in the dedication to the full score, published in 1687, that Charles II had 'more than once condescended to be present at the Repetition, before it came into the publick View'.[50]

The score of *Albion and Albanius* gives much more detailed information about the orchestral writing than most English sources. As befits what is best described as an English *tragédie-lyrique*, the type-set score even imitates the appearance of the Ballard full scores of Lully's operas—a feature copied by Purcell in the full score of *Dioclesian*, just as he

---

[48] For the background to *Albion and Albanius*, see the edn. by E. Milner and G. R. Guffey, *The Works of John Dryden*, xv: *Plays: Albion and Albanius, Don Sebastian, Amphitryon* (Berkeley, Calif., 1976), 323–55; P. Hammond, 'Dryden's *Albion and Albanius*: The Apotheosis of Charles II', in D. Lindley (ed.), *The Court Masque* (Manchester, 1984), 169–83.

[49] *GB-Lbl*, Add. MS 63759, 91; the complete letter is transcribed in Holman, '*Valentinian*, Rochester and Louis Grabu', 127; Wilson, *Roger North*, 311.

[50] HMC, *Twelfth Report*, Appendix, v: *The Manuscripts of his Grace the Duke of Rutland, K. G., Preserved at Belvoir Castle*, ii (London, 1889), 85.

borrowed some superficial features of Grabu's music.[51] As we might expect in such a Lullian work, Grabu uses the French five-part one-treble string scoring; and once again wind instruments are specified: a pair of 'flutes' have a number of solos, and their players doubtless doubled orchestral passages on oboes, as they had done in *Valentinian*. In view of the discussion of *Venus and Adonis*, it is of interest that Grabu maintains the distinction between three-part writing in the solo vocal sections, often marked 'violins', and five-part writing elsewhere. The 'Concert of Venus' in Act III, pp. 284–7, is particularly significant because the two solo violins engage in complex interplay with the recorders and the orchestra (Ex. 15.4). This memorable piece, probably the earliest concerto-like movement written in England, would have required the solo violins and recorders to be placed in or near the orchestra—which suggests that the divided layout of *Calisto* was not used in *Albion and Albanius*.

The score of *Albion and Albanius* also contains important information about Grabu's continuo practice. The bass line of the solo vocal sections, the choruses, and some of the orchestral movements is repeatedly marked 'The BASS continued', a translation of the phrase *basse continue* that appears in the scores of French operas; there is a separate continuo part in the choruses, which often differs from the bass of the orchestra. But the bass parts of the dances tend not to be marked 'the bass continued', and have no figures. Grabu is not always consistent in his use of the system, but in general the pattern is close to that used in Lully's full scores, and seems to mean that the continuo instruments were present in his operas principally to accompany the voices, and did not necessarily play in the dances or other purely instrumental movements.[52]

We cannot be sure that the same thing happened in other English operas and masques. It probably did in works where the dance band and the continuo group were physically separated, as in *Calisto*, and it is perhaps implied in the well-known sentence in Shadwell's 1674 adaptation of *The Tempest*: 'the Band of 24 Violins, with the Harpsicals and Theorbo's which accompany the Voices, are plac'd between the Pit and the Stage'.[53] Even the best English sources, such as the printed score of *Dioclesian*, are of little help in this respect: they do not have such useful labels as 'the bass continued', and contain too few figures for any conclusions to be drawn from the pattern of figuring. Nevertheless, a recent

[51] For the connection between *Albion and Albanius* and *Dioclesian*, see Price, *Henry Purcell*, 263–70.

[52] G. Sadler, 'The Role of the Keyboard Continuo in French Opera, 1673–1776', *EM*, 8 (1980), 148–57; see also M. Cyr, '*Basses* and *Basse Continue* in the Orchestra of the Paris *Opéra*, 1700–1764', *EM*, 10 (1982), 155–70.

[53] A point made in Sadler, 'The Role of the Continuo', 157.

Ex. 15.4. Louis Grabu, 'Concert of Venus', bb. 1–24, *Albion and Albanius, an Opera* (London, 1687), 284–7

study of the provision and use of harpsichords in the commercial theatres in the early eighteenth century has shown that they 'were used exclusively to accompany the voices', and there is little evidence for the use of continuo instruments in English theatre suites (see Ch. 14).[54]

[54] J. Milhous and C. A. Price, 'Harpsichords in the London Theatres, 1697–1715', *EM*, 18 (1990), 38–46.

Ex. 15.4. *Continued*

Albion and Albanius was a failure. John Downes wrote that 'being perform'd on a very Unlucky Day, being the Day the Duke of Monmouth, Landed in the West: The Nation being in a great Consternation, it was perform'd but Six times, which not Answering half the Charge they were at, Involv'd the Company very much in Debt'; according to Roger North it 'proved the ruin of the poor man [Grabu], for the King's death supplanted all his hopes, and so it dyed'.[55] It is true that the United Company fought shy of putting on another opera for the rest of the decade—until *Dioclesian* in June 1690—but there is no sign that this was because Grabu was an inept composer, or that *Albion and Albanius* was thought to be a poor work, as Edward Dent and other modern writers have maintained.[56] In fact, Downes and North merely made the point that Grabu had the bad luck to put the work on at a time of national crisis. Many copies of the score survive in British and American libraries, so the work was held in some esteem. It is easy to poke fun at Grabu's setting of English, but his part-writing is always competent; if anything, as Curtis Price has pointed out, it is too polished.[57] His inner parts sound bland compared with, say, those in Locke's orchestral dance music, but that is because they belong to a tradition that valued elegant melody, used relatively little dissonance, and concentrated most of the musical interest in the outer parts. Indeed, it is easy to imagine that Locke's magnificently angular, dissonant, and contrapuntal part-writing would have struck Grabu

[55] Downes, *Roscius Anglicanus*, ed. Milhous and Hume, 84; Wilson, *Roger North*, 311.
[56] Summarised in Price, *Henry Purcell*, 266–7.
[57] Ibid. 268–9.

as being barbarous and old-fashioned, an unsuitable idiom for fashionable dance music. The best of Grabu's orchestral dance music, such as the suite from *Valentinian*, is capable of making a considerable effect in the hands of the sort of orchestra he would have known.

16

'The French Fantastical Light Way'

Violins in the Chapel Royal

THE Chapel Royal, the royal choir, was the oldest and largest musical institution at court. Originally, it provided the king with choral services wherever he happened to be, but the Eltham Ordinances of 1526 restricted its travels, and after the Restoration its activities were concentrated almost entirely on the chapel in Whitehall Palace, at least during the working part of the year. The Chapel Royal was not, of course, just a musical organization. At its head were the Dean of the Chapel, often a bishop, and the sub-Dean, who was sometimes a prominent clergyman with musical interests—such as the composer and author William Holder, sub-Dean 1674–89. Among the non-musical officials were the royal chaplains, and the Serjeants, Yeomen, and Grooms of the Vestry. Nevertheless, the choir made up the bulk of the Chapel's members: on paper there were twelve boys and twenty gentlemen during the Restoration period, though the gentlemen were augmented by a variable number of unpaid 'extraordinary' members, and in practice they operated a rota for day-to-day services. From the ranks of the Gentlemen were chosen the three organists, the Master of the Children, the Clerk of the Cheque (effectively, the Chapel's secretary), and the 'Recorder of Songs', its music librarian.[1]

Little is known about the building that was the Chapel Royal's home from the 1520s until it was destroyed with most of the rest of Whitehall in the fire of January 1697/8. No detailed descriptions or reliable pictures of its interior exist, and the surviving plans of Whitehall tell us little beyond the fact that it was situated on a north-south axis in the north-east corner of the palace between the great hall and the Thames (more or less where Horseguards Avenue now meets Whitehall Court), and that it was a small building, roughly 75 feet by 30.[2] With carpets and wall hangings the

---

[1] For the Chapel Royal, see Woodfill, *Musicians in English Society*, 161–76; Le Huray, *Music and the Reformation*, 57–89; D. Baldwin, *The Chapel Royal*.

[2] G. Vertue, *A Survey and Ground Plot of the Royal Palace of Whitehall* (London, 1747); W. L. Spiers, 'An Account of the View of the Palace of Whitehall from the River, 1683', *London Topographical Record*, 7 (1912), 26–30; id., 'Explanation of a Plan of Whitehall', ibid. 56–66; G. S. Dugdale, *Whitehall through the Centuries* (London, 1950).

16.1. Anonymous German engraving of the ratification of the Spanish marriage treaty in the chapel at Whitehall, 20 July 1623. British Library, courtesy of the Trustees

acoustics would have been domestic rather than ecclesiastical in character.

A possible glimpse of the interior of the chapel is provided by a German engraving of James I's ratification of the abortive Spanish marriage treaty on 20 July 1623 (Fig. 16.1). It shows two galleries side by side along the west wall; the one nearest the altar is lined with spectators, and the one next to it is filled with an organ, the organist, and ten or eleven other figures, at least four of whom are playing instruments. The picture is clearly not entirely realistic, for the side-chapel on the left, to which the king is being guided, seems to represent the Catholic church—or, more precisely, the Catholic chapel that was being built at St James's under the provisions of the treaty. But there certainly were galleries of that sort at Whitehall. James I watched the christening of his daughter Mary in May 1605 'in his clossett above'; at Prince Henry's confirmation in April 1607 James remained 'in his greate Closett'; and when Princess Elizabeth was confirmed in March 1610/11 the king and queen were in 'their greate closettes'.[3] This seems to mean that there were separate galleries for the king and queen opening into the chapel at first-floor level; the king's closet, at least, was separated from the chapel by a glazed partition, for workmen were paid in 1635–6 for 'Coullering and guilding with fine gold the Lead of five Cazements on both sides in the windowe in the King's Clozett that looketh into the Chappell'.[4]

The chapel largely escaped damage during the Civil War, though the organ was removed and the stained glass and other religious pictures were destroyed. But it was evidently still in use during the Commonwealth, for on Sunday, 31 December 1651 Lodewijck Huygens went to a service there:

Captain Morgan and Mr. Temple had dinner with us at noon, and afterwards we went with them and Dr. Johnson and one or two others to the Chapel Royal in Whitehall. It is about as large as the French church in The Hague and panelled round almost up to the roof. The people are mostly seated in a gallery, which runs around the upper part of the church. The pulpit is oblong but divided into two parts, and behind the minister stood two or three men who wrote down his sermon. More than 20 others, both men and women, including a handsome, rather bejewelled young lady, were doing the same thing.[5]

The passage is of interest in that it suggests that the seemingly separate galleries referred to in other documents were actually part of a continuous structure that ran around several sides of the chapel, a common feature of seventeenth- and eighteenth-century churches in England and on the Continent. The title-page of John Weldon's *Divine Harmony* (London, 1716) shows an imaginary Chapel Royal of this sort, with two stories of galleries running the length of the side walls.

The chapel was quickly refurbished at the Restoration. Thomas Rugge noted in his diary for 17 June 1660 that 'his majesty's chappell att whithall was fitted w(i)th organs and all other things fitt for his majesty, which was the first day that his majesty was att his devocetion theire', while Samuel Pepys wrote on the same day that 'the Organs did begin to play at White-hall before the King'.[6] In 1673 John Playford claimed in a petition to Charles II that 'at the time of your Majesties most happy Restauration' he rescued 'both the Organ and Books belonging to your Majesties Chappel Royal' which 'had bin embezled' during the Civil War; part of the organ is said to survive at Stanford-on-Avon in

---

[3] Rimbault, *The Old Cheque-Book*, 168, 171, 172.

[4] Baldwin, *The Chapel Royal*, 101.

[5] Bachrach and Collmer, (eds.), *Lodewijck Huygens: The English Journal*, 42.

[6] *GB-Lbl*, Add. MS 10116, fo. 103ʳ; see W. L. Sachse (ed.), *The Diurnal of Thomas Rugge, 1659–1661* (Camden Third Series, 91; London, 1961), 92; Pepys, *Diary*, i. 176.

Northamptonshire.[7] Pepys went to the chapel several times later that year: on Sunday 8 July he 'heard very good Musique, the first time I remember ever to have heard the Organs and singing-men in Surplices in my life'; on 14 October he heard 'an anthemne, ill sung, which made the King laugh', and noticed that the Duke of York and Barbara Palmer 'did talke to one another very wantonly through the hangings that parts the King's closet and the closet where the ladies sit'; two weeks later a member of the Chapel Royal got him into the closet for Sunday service when the king was away, which he thought 'a great honour'.[8]

It is often said that Bernard Smith provided a new organ for the chapel in 1662, but the 'faire Double Organ' was actually built by Robert Dallam; it was ready for Easter 1664, and while it was under construction a 'new Stopp with Conveyances and another sett of keyes' was added, possibly to allow it to be played from two separate positions.[9] The new instrument required some alterations to the building. A 'large organ loft' was put up 'in the place where formerly the great Double organ stood', and two stories of 'roomes over the bellowes roome' were rebuilt, providing a room for the sub-Dean, and, above it, rooms for the organist and for John Hingeston, the 'keeper and repayrer' of the court keyboard instruments; the rooms had 'a Chymney, and Boxes and shelves for keeping the materials as belonging to the organ, and the organ-books'. References to a 'music room' in the chapel first appear about the time the work was finished: Henry Cooke, the Master of the Children, was paid £20 by a warrant dated 3 March 1663/4 for 'fire in the music room at the Chapel, and also for strings for the bass viol and other instruments belonging to the Chapel', a payment made each year to Cooke and his successors Pelham Humfrey and John Blow until the end of the reign.[10] More changes were made in the spring of 1671. On 8 February 1670/1 Christopher Wren was ordered to have 'the music room in his Majesty's Chapel Royal' enlarged '3½ feet in length towards his Majesty's closet', and a few weeks later 'three crimson damask curtains' were delivered 'for the music room in the Chapel, the music room being enlarged'.[11]

Baffling as these documents seem at first sight, we can make sense of them by supposing that the 'music room' was another name for the room allocated to John Hingeston; that it was actually the rear portion of a

[7] A. Freeman, 'Organs Built for the Royal Palace of Whitehall', *MT* 52 (1911), 720–1; B. Owens, 'The Early Seventeenth-Century Organ in St Nicholas's Church, Stanford-on-Avon', *The Organ Yearbook*, 19 (1988), 5–30.

[8] Pepys, *Diary*, i. 195, 265–6, 276.

[9] See, for instance, A. Freeman, *Father Smith* (2nd edn., rev. J. Rowntree, London, 1977), 2; Ashbee, *RECM*, i. 47–8, 69–70; *RECM*, v. 38.

[10] Ashbee, *RECM*, i. 53, 56, 57, 62, 82, 90, 98, 105, 114, 120–1, 124–5, 130, 142, 151, 166, 176, 182–3, 187, 212.

[11] Ibid. 102, 104.

gallery that opened into the chapel at first-floor level; and, similarly, that the organist's room was the rear portion of the organ loft. The curtains for the music room (and those ordered for the organ loft in July 1662 and March 1664/5[12]) were presumably put up to prevent the rooms at the rear, with their shelves, instruments, and fireplaces, being seen from the chapel. It is not clear exactly where they were situated, but they were evidently next to each other, since they were both built over the bellows room of the organ, and they were probably near the king's closet/gallery, since the music room was enlarged in 1671 'towards his Majesty's closet'. Perhaps they were ranged along the west wall, as the galleries are in the 1623 picture. Perhaps, also, the music room replaced the queen's closet of the 1611 document, for Charles II's Catholic queen, Catherine of Braganza, had her own chapel at St James's and did not attend the Chapel Royal.

I have discussed the geography of Whitehall chapel at some length because the subject has been neglected in accounts of the Chapel's music, and because I believe that an understanding of how musicians were deployed there can throw new light on the performance of Restoration verse anthems. First, however, we need to examine the role of instrumentalists in the chapel. References to wind consorts can be found as early as Elizabethan times. At St George's day in 1597, for instance, 'princely music of voices, organs, cornets and sackbuts' was heard at the Garter ceremony; at Princess Mary's christening on 5 May 1605 an anthem was performed 'the Chorus wherof was filled with the help of musicall instrumentes'; at the ceremony of the queen's churching a fortnight later, on 19 May, the Chapel Royal sang 'sundry anthems . . . with organ, cornets, sagbot, and other excellent instruments of musicke'; and as Prince Henry's coffin lay at St James's prior to his funeral on 7 November 1612 'the gentlemen of the King's chapel, with the children belonging to it, sung several anthems to the organs and other wind-instruments'.[13] In 1633 the three court wind consorts were reorganized into two companies 'for waiting in the Chapel and at his Majesty's table', and twelve surplices were provided for wind musicians 'at times of their service in the Chapel'.[14]

Wind consorts were heard in the chapel once again at the Restoration. Indeed, some of the wind-players combined service there with membership of the Twenty-four Violins. For example: the violinists Thomas

[12] Ibid. 34, 37, 61, 62, 68.

[13] G. B. Harrison (ed.), *A Second Elizabethan Journal* (London, 1931), 184; Rimbault, *The Old Cheque-Book*, 185; J. Nichols, *The Progresses, Processions, and Magnificent Festivities, of King James the First* (London, 1823), i. 514; Birch, *The Life of Henry Prince of Wales*, 361–2; see also A. Parrott, '"Grett and Solompne Singing": Instruments in English Church Music before the Civil War', *EM* 6 (1978), 182–7.

[14] Ashbee, *RECM*, iii. 74, 81, 94.

Blagrave and William Howes were said by Anthony à Wood to have played the cornett in the chapel; in 1660 William Saunders petitioned Charles II for a place as a bass violinist in the 'Band of Violins', pointing out that he was 'alsoe willing and ready to doe service on the Sagbutt in your Ma(jes)ties Chappell Royall', and by a warrant dated 2 September 1661 he received £30 'for a Base Violin for the Chamber and a double Sackbutt for his Ma(jes)t(y')s Chappell Royall'; on the same day Philip Beckett was paid £18 'for a Vyolin to be used in the Chamber of Vyolins and for a Cornett to be used in his Ma(jes)ties Chappell Royall'.[15] The twelve surplices used by wind-players in the chapel before the Civil War were replaced by an order dated 4 May 1663; and on 22 May 1665 the Lord Chamberlain ordered those 'Musitians for the Wind Instruments' who give 'theire Attendance in his Majesty's Chappell Royal' not to neglect their duty; as late as 15 April 1668 Samuel Pepys attended the chapel 'expecting wind music'.[16] In the successive editions of Edward Chamberlayne's *Angliae notitiae; or, The Present State of England* from the first (1669) to the ninth (1676) 'Saickbuts and Cornets belonging to the King's Private Musick' are said to play on 'Sundayes, Collar-dayes, and other Holy-dayes' to make 'the Chappel Musick more full and compleat'; from 1679 the reference is just to a 'Consort of the King's Musick'.[17]

It is not clear what role the wind-players played in the chapel. One function was to reinforce or even replace voices, particularly in the early 1660s before a new generation of boys was fully trained. Matthew Locke wrote in *The Present Practice of Musick Vindicated* (London, 1673; repr. 1974), p. 19 that for 'above a Year after the Opening of His Majesties Chappel, the Orderers of the Musick there, were necessitated to supply the superiour Parts of their Musick with Cornets and Mens feigned Voices, there being not one Lad, for all that time, capable of singing his Part readily'. The wind-players probably spent most of their time doubling the choir, but there is one unambiguous pre-war reference to them playing independent instrumental parts in a verse anthem: William Lawes's 'Before the mountains were brought forth' is described as an 'anthem with Verses for Cornetts and Sagbutts' in a 1635 collection of the texts of Chapel Royal anthems; the work is lost, but Andrew Parrott has argued that it was not an isolated experiment.[18]

Three of Matthew Locke's verse anthems also seem to be for cornetts and sackbuts rather than strings. The pieces in question, 'I will hear what the Lord God will say' (and its unpublished first part 'Lord, thou hast

[15] Shute, 'Anthony à Wood', i. 77, 173; *GB-Lpro*, SP29/36, no. 39; Ashbee, *RECM*, i. 109, 110.

[16] Rimbault, *The Old Cheque-Book*, 92–3; Ashbee, *RECM*, i. 64; Pepys, *Diary*, ix. 163.

[17] Ashbee, *RECM*, v. 280.

[18] 'The Chapel Royal Anthem Book of 1635', *MA* 2 (1910–11), 113; Parrott, 'Grett and Solompne Singing', 186.

been gracious'), 'The Lord hear thee in the day of trouble', and 'When the son of man shall come in his glory', are unusual in that they combine features of the pre-war and Restoration types of verse anthem.[19] Like Jacobean anthems, they tend to move at a dignified walking pace, and the solo passages are mostly supported by a web of intricate instrumental counterpoint. Yet they also have more modern features: some of the solos are declamatory in style, and are accompanied only by continuo; on occasion the instruments alternate with the voices in the Restoration manner. At least one of them, 'Lord, thou hast been gracious' / 'I will hear what the Lord God will say', was apparently in the repertoire of the Restoration chapel, for its text appears in James Clifford's *The Divine Services and Anthems usually Sung in his Majestie's Chappel* (2nd edn., London, 1664, 400–1). Yet the instrumental writing in all three is grave and largely contrapuntal, and there is a striking lack of the dance-like passages that appear in virtually all Restoration anthems with violins, including Locke's 'Be thou exalted Lord' and 'O be joyful in the Lord, all ye lands'.[20]

Several details of their instrumental writing also suggest cornetts and sackbuts. The top parts of 'When the son of man' have the same tessitura and use the same sort of rapid stepwise motion as the cornett parts of Locke's music 'For his Majesties Cornetts and Sackbuts'.[21] 'The Lord hear thee in the day of trouble' opens with a symphony laid out for the three upper parts without bass, a texture that works well on two cornetts and sackbut, but not so well on violins and viola or treble viols and tenor viol. Also, 'Lord, thou hast been gracious' / 'I will hear what the Lord God will say' has three instrumental parts, treble, tenor, and bass. Three-part string-writing is common in Restoration verse anthems, but it always has two treble parts, and is clearly intended for two violins and continuo. The STB layout is never found in Restoration violin music; it suggests viols or, more likely at this period, wind instruments. Cornett and two sackbuts is the obvious combination (Ex. 16.1).

It is not clear exactly when violins were first used in Whitehall chapel. John Evelyn thought it was on 21 December 1662:

[one] of his Majesties Chaplains preachd: after which, instead of the antient grave and solemn wind musique accompanying the Organ was introduced a Consort of 24 Violins betweene every pause, after the French fantastical light way, better suiting a Tavern or Play-house than a Church: This was the first

---

[19] Locke, *Anthems and Motets*, ed. P. Le Huray (MB 38; London, 1976), nos. 9, 13, 15; 'Lord, thou hast been gracious' is identified as the first part of 'I will hear what the Lord God will say' in B. Wood, 'John Blow's Anthems with Orchestra', Ph.D. thesis (Cambridge, 1976), 432–3; see also R. Harding, *A Thematic Catalogue of the Works of Matthew Locke* (Oxford, 1971), 16.

[20] *Anthems and Motets*, ed. Le Huray, nos. 7, 12.

[21] Locke, *Music for his Majesty's Sackbuts and Cornetts*, ed. A. Baines (London, 1951).

Ex. 16.1. Matthew Locke, 'Lord, thou hast been gracious', bb. 1–9, *GB-Lbl*, Add. MS 31444, fos. 184ʳ–188ᵛ

time of change, & now we no more heard the Cornet, which gave life to the organ, that instrument quite left off in which the English were so skilfull...[22]

Evelyn's memorable passage appears in every study of Restoration church music, but it contains several errors of fact. As we have seen, the 'antient grave and solemn wind musique' actually played in the chapel until the end of the 1660s, and Pepys had already heard 'Captain Cookes new Musique' at Whitehall three months earlier; he thought Sunday 14 September 1662 was 'the first day of having Vialls and other Instruments to play a Symphony between every verse of the Anthem'.[23] Also, Pepys had already heard 'a most excellent Anthem (with Symphony's between) sung by Captain Cooke' the previous Sunday, 7 September.[24]

It may be, of course, that this last piece was a verse anthem with wind instruments, though there is evidence that the viol-player William Gregory and the violinist Humphrey Madge were working in the chapel as early as the spring of 1662. By a warrant dated 7 February 1664/5 they were paid £20 each 'for their attendance in his Majesty's Chapel from Easter 1662 to Christmas 1664'.[25] At the same time Gregory was paid £12 for a bass viol and Madge £24 for two violins 'all brought for his Majesty's service in the Chapel'; they may have needed special instruments because of a discrepancy between the chapel organ, which would have been at least a semitone above modern pitch, and the pitch used by the court instrumentalists in secular music, which was probably considerably lower.[26] The violinist William Yockney also seems to have played in the chapel with Madge and Gregory: he was suspended on 22 March 1664/5 because he had 'neglected and refused to attend his Majesty's service in his Chapel Royal upon notice given him by Henry Cooke'.[27]

There is no sign that any other string-players worked in the Chapel before 4 April 1667, when a quartet, Theophilus Fitz, William Clayton, Humphrey Madge, and John Mayer, was appointed 'to attend at his Majesty's Chapel Royal at Whitehall so often as they shall be appointed by Capt. Cooke for his Majesty's service'.[28] Many early verse anthems, such as those by Henry Cooke or Pelham Humfrey's first setting of 'Have mercy upon me, O God' (heard by Pepys in the chapel on 22 November 1663), have three-part instrumental writing, and were probably written for Madge, Yockney, and Gregory; indeed, the bass part of 'Have mercy

---

[22] Evelyn, Diary, 449.
[23] Pepys, *Diary*, iii. 197.
[24] Ibid. 190.
[25] Ashbee, *RECM*, i. 60.
[26] See Gwynn, 'Organ Pitch', 65–78; also E. H. Jones, *The Performance of English Song, 1610–1670* (New York and London, 1989), 43–7, 157–69, and my review in *EM* 18 (1990), 295–7.
[27] Ashbee, *RECM*, i. 61.
[28] Ibid. 76.

upon me, O God' seems to be intended for bass viol, for it goes up to g' in the 'overture', beyond the normal range of the bass violin tuned Bb', F, c, g (see Ch. 13).[29] Anthems with four-part strings became more common in the 1670s and 1680s, but at least one, Locke's 'O be joyful in the Lord, all ye lands', was written in the early 1660s, for its text appears in the 1664 edition of Clifford's *Divine Services and Anthems*, pp. 399–400.[30]

Violins seem to have replaced wind instruments in the chapel for good in 1670. On 6 May a roster entitled 'Musitians to attend the Chapell' was issued; it consists of three groups of five names who were ordered to 'wayte & attend in his Ma(jes)ties Chappel Royall as they are here set downe, five in one moneth & five in another'.[31] A similar list , also of three groups of five names, covers October to December 1671, while a third, with six in each group, covers March to May 1672.[32] It took time to establish the new regime. The Lord Chamberlain had to threaten the musicians in May and June 1672 with suspension if 'they shall refuse or neglect their attendance' in the chapel; the second time he told them that 'his Majesty is Displeased that the violins neglect theire Duty in attending in his Chappell Royall'.[33] There are no other surviving rosters, but by a warrant dated 17 October 1673 backdated to Lady Day Thomas Purcell was given £400 a year for twenty musicians 'in Consideracon of their Extraordinary attendance in his Maj(es)t(ie)s Chappell'; John Blow received it after Purcell's death in 1682, and it evidently ceased at the end of the reign, though arrears were paid until 1692.[34] The twenty musicians were probably divided into four groups of five, to serve for a quarter of the year each—a standard way of organizing rosters in other parts of the royal household.

Thus, it seems that there were never more than six in the groups that attended Whitehall chapel. Indeed, they may have been limited to that number by the size of their performing space. According to Hawkins, Restoration verse anthems 'were sung to violins, [or?] cornets, and sacbuts, the performers on which were placed in the organ-loft'.[35] This may have been so in pre-Civil War anthems, which used instrumental consorts to support the solo voices. But in Restoration anthems the

---

[29] Pepys, *Diary*, iv. 393–4; Humfrey, *Complete Church Music: I*, ed. Dennison, no. 4a; for Cooke's anthems, see J. C. Bridge, 'A Great English Choir Trainer, Captain Henry Cooke', *MA* 2 (1910–11), 61–79; H. W. Shaw, 'A Collection of Musical Manuscripts in the Autograph of Henry Purcell and other English Composers, *c*.1665–85', *The Library*, 14 (1959), 126–31; I. Cheverton, 'Captain Henry Cooke (*c*.1616–72): The Beginnings of a Reappraisal', *Soundings*, 9 (1982), 74–86.

[30] Dennison, *Pelham Humfrey*, 18, 111.

[31] Ashbee, *RECM*, i. 98.

[32] Ibid. 109–10, 113.

[33] Ibid. 115–16.

[34] Ibid., ii. 203–6, 209, 210, 212, 215, 217; v. 64, 200, 203, 207.

[35] Hawkins, *A General History*, ii. 693.

instruments mostly have an antiphonal relationship with the soloists, who are accompanied separately by the continuo, so it made sense to separate them. The voices presumably stayed in the organ loft, and were accompanied by the organ, while the strings, I suggest, played in the music room. Significantly, the music room was constructed at about the time the new verse anthem came into being; also, its gallery was enlarged in February 1671, soon after groups of five, rather than three or four, had become the norm.

The organ loft was frequently used to seat visitors during the Restoration period. On Sunday 23 April 1665 Pepys took his wife and her maid 'to Whitehall chapel and set them in the Organ loft' before going off to the tavern for a pre-service drink; he was there again on 3 April 1667, meeting 'Mr. Cartaret and my Lady Jemimah and Sir Tho. Crew's two daughters', and listening to William Child play the organ.[36] By the 1680s some of the court ladies had their own seats there. On 8 January 1686/7 John Blow was ordered to let 'Mrs. Kingdon have the seate in the Organ loft (w(hi)ch Mrs. Crofts lately had) wholely for herselfe & whome shee allowes to sitt in, & none others'.[37] She was to have libertie to put her owne lock on the doore of the seate'. Things evidently got out of hand, for in May the Lord Chamberlain ordered that 'noe person pr(e)sume to goe into the Organ roome in his Ma(jes)t(ie)s Chappell Royall but the Musick who are to Officiate their'.[38] By the 1690s the visitors were back: Blow was told several times to keep seats for named individuals, and to appoint one of the choirboys to prevent others from taking them.[39] It may be that there was room for visitors in the organ loft because the solo singers had moved into the music room; as we shall see, William and Mary banned instrumentalists from the chapel in 1689.

Wherever they were placed, it certainly looks as if the chapel string-players played one to a part, a conclusion that is supported by an eye-witness, Thomas Tudway, a Chapel Royal choirboy in the 1660s. In later life he wrote in the anthology of anthems he assembled for the Earl of Oxford that Charles II 'Order'd the Composers of his Chappell, to add Symphonys &c. w(i)th Instruments to their Anthems', and added that the king 'thereupon Establis[h]'d a *select number* of his private music, to play the Symphonys, & Retornellos, w(hi)ch he had appointed' (my italics).[40] It is possible to argue, of course, that pieces with three-part strings were

[36] Pepys, *Diary*, vi. 87; viii. 145.
[37] Ashbee, *RECM*, ii. 13.
[38] Ibid. 14.
[39] Ibid. 32–3, 42, 50.
[40] C. Hogwood, 'Thomas Tudway's History of Music', in C. Hogwood and R. Luckett (eds.), *Music in Eighteenth-Century England: Essays in Honour of Charles Cudworth* (Cambridge, 1983), 25; see also E. Turnbull, 'Thomas Tudway and the Harleian Collection', *JAMS* 7 (1955), 203–7.

played two to a part by six instrumentalists. But it is likely that at least one of the group actually played the theorbo, even though they were drawn from the Twenty-four Violins. Edmund Flower is a case in point: he received £15 in March 1673 for 'a theorbo bought by him for his Majesty's service in the Chapel Royal'.[41] Several of his violinist colleagues, such as Henry Brockwell, William Clayton, and John Singleton, also held places in the Private Music as lutenists. And, in January 1676 Nicholas Staggins was paid for the copying of a verse anthem that included parts for lutes:

For the faire writeing of an Anthem, composed for the voyces of the Chappell & lutes & violls & other instrum(en)ts in score, from the fowle draft, the prickers dyet included   £5. 9s.

For drawing the said Anthem for the voyces & Instruments into severall parts, one for every man, the prickers chamber rent, fire, candle, ruled paper, Inke and pens   £4. 2s.[42]

Thus the groups of five may well have consisted of string quartet and theorbo in anthems with four-part strings, or two violins and bass with two theorboes for anthems with three-part strings.

Larger forces, of course, could be used when the Chapel Royal performed outside Whitehall chapel. The best-documented instances are the coronations of Charles II and James II. Like succeeding coronations up to modern times, they took place in Westminster Abbey, and featured anthems performed by the combined Chapel Royal and Westminster Abbey choirs, accompanied by a large orchestra. In Charles's coronation, on 23 April 1661, verse anthems with strings by Cooke (one of which, 'Behold, O Lord, our defender', is in *GB-Bu*, MS 5001, pp. 118–25), were performed in a polychoral manner, with the main choir in a gallery on the north side of the Abbey, the 'Violins, and other Instrumental Musick' in a gallery next to them, and a small choir of 'twelve Gentlemen, four Children, and one Organist' (who presumably took the verse passages) in 'a Gallery, raised on the South-side of the Upper Quire, peculiarly appointed for them'.[43] All the Twenty-four Violins and eight of the royal wind musicians took part in their scarlet liveries, but Pepys complained of 'so great a noise, that I could make but little of the Musique; and endeed, it was lost to everybody'.[44]

---

[41] Ashbee, *RECM*, i. 124.

[42] Ibid. 155.

[43] E. Ashmole, 'A Brief Narrative of the Solemn Rites and Ceremonies Performed upon the Day of the Coronation of our Sovereign Lord King Charles II', 172, 186, appended to the *GB-Lgc* copy of J. Ogilby, *His Majesties Entertainments Passing through the City of London to his Coronation* (London, 1662); see also A. Hughes, 'Music of the Coronation over a Thousand Years', *PRMA* 79 (1952–3), 81–100.

[44] Ashbee, *RECM*, i. 15–17; Pepys, *Diary*, ii. 83–4.

The arrangements were similar for James II's coronation on 23 April 1685, though this time there were no fewer than thirty-five instrumentalists in addition to the royal trumpeters. They were nearly all string-players, though a piece by Staggins that was probably performed during the coronation feast in Westminster Hall had oboe parts (see Ch. 13), and the list also includes Blow and Purcell, who may have played continuo in the anthems; two organs were certainly used for William and Mary's coronation in 1689—Purcell was paid £32 for 'providing an Organ & other necessarys'—and it is likely that a portable instrument played in the verse passages while the abbey organ supported the main choir.[45] Among the works performed in 1685 were Blow's 'God spake sometime in visions' and Purcell's 'My heart is inditing', both scored for eight solo voices, eight-part choir, and four-part strings.[46] They are among the handful of verse anthems that we know were performed with an orchestra rather than single strings (Fig. 16.2).

The Chapel Royal also ventured outside Whitehall when the court moved to Windsor for the Garter ceremonies, held each year either on St George's Day, 23 April, or in late May; during the 1670s it often stayed there for much of the summer. We know of the presence of violinists in Windsor mainly from the payment of travel expenses, though it is usually not clear whether they were there to play in the chapel or to provide the king with secular music. In 1671, however, four 'violins' and two bass viol-players seem to have been in Windsor from 24 May to 15 July specifically to play in verse anthems, for they are twice listed with members of the Chapel Royal.[47] In 1674 fourteen string-players were in Windsor between 18 May and 3 September; twelve others were there from 11 July to 1 September.[48] The group of fourteen is said to have attended 'his Majesty at Windsor in the Chapel', and is often cited as evidence for the use of orchestras in verse anthems. But two of them, William Gregory and John Lilly, were bass viol players, not violinists; and the remaining twelve probably worked a roster divided into three, producing at any one time groups of four 'violins' and two bass viols, the same as in 1671. According to Elias Ashmole, present at the 1674 Garter ceremony as Windsor Herald, anthems were performed by 'the Kings Vocall & Instrumentall Musick', placed 'in a scaffold made on the North side of the Altar short of King Ed(ward) the 4ths: Tombe'.[49]

[45] Sandford, *The History of the Coronation*, 29–30, 82–101; Ashbee, *RECM*, v. 276; see also Zimmerman, *Henry Purcell*, 117–25.
[46] Blow, *Coronation Anthems, Anthems with Strings*, ed. A. Lewis and H. W. Shaw (*MB* 7; 2nd edn., London, 1969), 1–45; Purcell, *Sacred Music III: Seven Anthems with Strings*, ed. H. E. Wooldridge, G. E. P. Arkwright, and N. Fortune (The Works of Henry Purcell, xvii; London, 1964), 69–118.
[47] Ashbee, *RECM*, i. 108–9; v. 141.
[48] Ibid. i. 142–3, 147.
[49] C. H. Jossen (ed.), *Elias Ashmole (1617–1692), iv: Texts 1673–1701* (Oxford, 1966), 1377–83.

A Perspective of WESTMINSTER-ABBY from the High-Altar to the West end shewing the manner of His Majesties CROWNING.

16.2 'A Perspective of Westminster Abbey from the High-Altar to the West end', Sandford, *The History of the Coronation of James II*, pl. 1, showing members of the Twenty-four Violins playing during the coronation service. The Pepys Library, Magdalene College, Cambridge, courtesy of the Master and Fellows

Pairs of bass viol-players occasionally appear in Chapel Royal documents. For instance, Robert Strong and Edward Strong were ordered to
'attend with their double Curtolls in his Majesty's Chappell Royall at
Whitehall, and Thomas Bates and William Gregory with their violls,
every Sunday and Holy day' from 30 August 1662.[50] It is often said that
the viols formed part or all of the bass section of the chapel string groups,
but this is to misunderstand the use of the word 'violins' in court
documents: it will be evident from earlier chapters that it meant a consort
of several sizes of the violin family—just as the word 'recorders' meant a
complete consort from soprano to bass. So it is perverse to suggest that
the 1671 Windsor group consisted of four upper strings and two bass
viols. It is more likely that the 'violins' were a complete consort, with a
bass violin, and that the viols had some discrete function. They may, for
instance, have doubled the bass of the Decani and Cantoris sections of
the choir, as curtal- and sackbut-players seem to have done in outdoor
processions. Ashmole wrote in his account of the 1661 Garter ceremony
that the combined Chapel Royal and Windsor choirs sang a processional
hymn by Henry Cooke:

by whose direction some instrumental loud musick was at that time introduced,
namely, two double sackbuts and two double courtals, and placed at convenient
distance among the classes of the Gentlemen of both choirs, to the end that all
might distinctly hear, and consequently keep together in both time and tune: for
one sackbut and courtal was placed before the four petty canons who began the
hymn, and the other two immediately before the prebends of the college.[51]

An orchestra is known to have performed in Whitehall chapel on only
one occasion: the service held on 14 August 1666 to celebrate Albemarle's
naval victory over the Dutch. Pepys was there, and wrote of hearing 'a
special good Anthemne before the king after sermon'.[52] The work in
question is Locke's great anthem 'Be thou exalted, Lord', described in
the autograph score, *GB-Ob*, MS Mus. C. 23, fos. 25^r–34^r, as 'A song of
Thanksgiving for his Majesty's Victory over the Dutch on St. James his
day 1666 And perform'd befoer his Majesty on the 14th of August
following' (pl. 8).[53] The work is worth studying with care, since Locke
clearly wrote it with the geography of the chapel in mind, and its scoring
is partially misunderstood in the modern edition. It consists of two
movements: a 'Grand Chorus', scored for three four-part choirs, a five-
part 'Band of Violins', and a separate four-part 'Consort', is heard before
and after the 'Song of Thanksgiving', which has a central symphony for

[50] Ashbee, *RECM*, i. 35.
[51] Rimbault, *The Old Cheque-Book*, 216.
[52] Pepys, *Diary*, vii. 245.
[53] Locke, *Anthems and Motets*, ed. Le Huray, no. 7.

the violin band but is otherwise scored just for eight solo voices and a group of 'Violins, theorbos, and viols, to the Organ'.

It is assumed in the edition that the 'consort' in the Grand Chorus should consist of four viols, and that the indication 'Violins, theorbos, and viols, to the Organ' means that the upper viols should be doubled by violins and a viola. But it makes better sense to think of the 'consort' and the 'Violins, theorbos, and viols' as two labels for the same thing: a group of two violins, two bass viols, and two theorboes, the combination used by William Lawes in his 'Royal Consort', and by other mid-century composers. Locke uses it rather as French composers used the *petit chœur* in their *grands motets*: it is contrasted with the violin band, and it provides ritornelli for the solo vocal passages. Also, the first choir in the Grand Chorus seems to be intended for a solo quartet, since it is accompanied by the consort at one point, and shares staves with it in Locke's score; and all four of its voices are given solos in the 'Song of Thanksgiving'. The five parts of the violin band are allocated in the edition to three violins, viola, and bass viol, but Locke clearly intended one violin, three violas, and bass violin, the French orchestral layout. The clefs of the inner parts—C1, C2, and C3—are the same as those used in French orchestral music; the range of the second part does not go above f'', the highest note of the viola in first position and the normal limit of orchestral viola parts; and the bass part goes down to $B\flat'$, the bottom note of the bass violin. The work was written only a few months after Grabu took control of the Twenty-four Violins, and it may have been intended to demonstrate the group's mastery of the French orchestral idiom; it is the only surviving piece by an English Restoration composer that has the violin, three-viola scoring.

Where were the performers of 'Be thou exalted, Lord' placed in the chapel? The second and third choirs of the Grand Chorus were presumably the Chapel Royal choir, placed on the floor of the building in their Decani and Cantoris choir stalls. The 'Band of Violins' must have been on that level too, if anything like the complete Twenty-four Violins took part. The six-man 'consort' was presumably placed in the music room, since it is similar in size and composition to the groups that played in ordinary verse anthems. The obvious remaining location for the four solo voices of the first choir is the organ loft. Thus Locke's magnificent spatial effects would have had an extra dimension that is not immediately apparent from the score.

'Be thou exalted, Lord' is clearly an exceptional work, but rubrics in more modest scores suggest that all verse anthems were performed in a polychoral manner at Whitehall. The anonymous 'O clap your hands together' has been attributed to Locke, presumably because a note in the score, *GB-Ob*, MS Mus. C. 23, fos. 2^r–9^r, wrongly claims that it is in his autograph. It is not the same as his setting of the text in William Tucker's fragmentary Chapel Royal part-books, or the one by Edward Lowe, but it could be the unidentified one by Henry Cooke listed in the 1664 edition of Clifford's *Divine Services and Anthems*, pp. 369–70.[54] A passage on p. 3 marked 'verse above' is 'to be sung in the Gallery by 4 voices to the violls without the organ', while on p. 5 there are the instructions 'above in the Gallereye' and 'still to the soft organ both above and below'. We cannot be sure that the rubrics relate to Whitehall chapel, but it is clear that the piece was performed with four solo voices in a gallery with the choir below; the viols are not given separate parts, and are perhaps meant to double the solo voices.

Similar conclusions can be drawn from a work that was almost certainly written for Whitehall, Blow's 'O give thanks unto the Lord'. It dates from about 1680 and survives in a score copied by William Isaack of Eton, *GB-Cfm*, Mu. MS 117, fos. 258^v–263^r.[55] It is effectively laid out for five groups of voices and instruments: SSB soloists marked 'Above', ATB soloists also marked 'Above', SATB soloists marked 'Below', four-part choir, and an instrumental group of two violins and bass. To clarify matters Isaack added the comment: 'This anthem is to be sung some part in the singing loft & som part below in the Quire.' It is not clear whether the phrase 'singing loft' refers to the organ loft or the music room, but Blow's antiphonal use of two solo trios marked 'Above' may mean that he made use of at least two galleries; the SATB soloists marked 'Below' were presumably placed with the choir in the choir-stalls. 'O give thanks unto the Lord' is exceptional in the number of separate groups it requires rather than its use of a polychoral disposition; it suggests that all verse anthems were performed with the soloists separated horizontally from the strings and vertically from the choir—which was also divided into Decani and Cantoris. Modern performances with the soloists, choir, and instruments in a single mass, are, so to speak, two-dimensional realizations of three-dimensional works.

The polychoral nature of Restoration verse anthems is also reflected in an important feature of their continuo scoring. It seems that the solo vocal sections were performed without a bass violin or viol doubling the continuo. In other words, the bass of the string consort only played when the upper strings played, in the instrumental passages and tutti sections, presumably in part because the player was physically separated from the

[54] For Tucker's part-books, see M. Laurie, 'The Chapel Royal Part-Books' in *Music and Bibliography: Essays in Honour of Alec Hyatt King* (New York and London, 1980), 28–32; Lowe's incomplete anthem is edited in G. Middleton, 'A Profile of Edward Lowe *c.*1610–1682: His Life and Work in the University of Oxford', BA diss. (Colchester Institute, 1989), ii. 1–8; for Cooke's anthem, see Bridge, 'Henry Cooke', 71.

[55] I am grateful to Bruce Wood for providing me with a transcription of the piece; for Isaack, see Holman, 'Bartholomew Isaack'.

continuo players. This was a feature of much concerted church music on the Continent: in sets of performing material, manuscript and printed, of composers ranging from Grandi to Buxtehude, the bowed bass parts almost invariably have rests in the solo vocal sections.[56]

The problem with the sources of Restoration verse anthems is that they are nearly all scores, which tend not to indicate precisely when the bowed bass should play. Only two contemporary sets of parts survive for anthems with strings, neither of which seems to derive from a Whitehall performance. They are both in the same source: *GB-Och*, Mus. MSS 1188–9 contains an incomplete set of parts (the second violin is missing) in Edward Lowe's hand for Locke's 'O be joyful in the Lord, all ye lands', and a partly autograph set for Purcell's 'My song shall be alway'. The 'O be joyful in the Lord' set was almost certainly prepared for the Oxford Music School (where Lowe was Professor 1662–82) in the 1660s or 1670s; the lower string parts are marked 'Countertenor viol' and 'Bass viol', probably because there were no viola or bass violin-players among Oxford's amateurs. The 'My song shall be alway' set may have been copied for a performance, possibly the first, at Windsor in 1690. The work is usually dated *c*.1688, but an early score in the hand of Francis Withey, *GB-Ob*, MS Mus. Sch. C. 61, fos. 73^r–64^r INV, is endorsed 'H.P. Sep: 9/90'; on that day William III entered Windsor in triumph after the Siege of Limerick, an event that is likely to have called for a celebratory anthem.[57] In both cases there are only single string parts, and the bowed bass plays only when the upper strings play.

The same feature is also found in the sets of parts of concerted works performed at the Oxford Music School, such as Christopher Gibbons's doctoral act music of 1664, or Locke's motet 'Ad te levavi oculos meos', written, Lowe wrote on one of the parts, 'to carry on the Meetinge at the musick schoole. Thursday the 16th Novem(ber) 1665'.[58] The latter, copied by Lowe and the composer, is a particularly interesting case. There are four bass parts. One is probably for organ, since it is laid out on two staves, is partially figured, and has fragments of a right-hand realization. It is continuous, as is the second, which is probably for theorbo, since it has a few figures but is on only one stave. The third is

[56] See N. Fortune, 'Continuo Instruments in Italian Monodies', *GSJ* 6 (1953), 10–13; T. Borgir, 'The Performance of the Basso Continuo in Seventeenth-Century Italian Music', Ph.D. diss. (University of California, Berkeley, 1971); P. Allsop, 'The Role of the Stringed Bass as a Continuo Instrument in Italian Seventeenth-Century Instrumental Music', *Chelys*, 8 (1978–9), 31–7; G. Dixon, 'Continuo Scoring in the Early Baroque: The Role of Bowed Bass Instruments', *Chelys*, 15 (1986), 38–53; for Buxtehude, see K. Snyder, *Dieterich Buxtehude, Organist in Lübeck* (New York and London, 1987), 368–73, 377–82.

[57] B. Wood, 'A Newly Identified Purcell Autograph', *ML* 59 (1978), 329–32.

[58] *GB-Ob*, MSS Mus. Sch. C. 138–9, C. 44, fos. 1^r–15^v; the Locke is edited by Le Huray, in *Anthems and Motets*, no. 1; facsimiles of the bass parts appear as illus. nos. 3–6.

unfigured, and includes all the passages that the violins play; the fourth, also unfigured, has only the opening symphony and the last chorus. The last two are probably for the two bass viols that played in the work that Locke wrote for the same occasion, the so-called 'Oxford Suite' for two violins and two bass viols.[59]

The Oxford sources, then, suggest that the bass parts of Restoration verse anthems were laid out in the following way. The organ played throughout, as did any theorbo-players who were present—placed, perhaps, in the organ loft. A bass violin or a bass viol played whenever the upper strings played, and was presumably placed with them in the music room. Two extra bass viols may have doubled the bass of the two sides of the choir, placed near them on the floor of the chapel. This type of continuo scoring appears in the performing material of Oxford act music as late as Richard Goodson's 'Janus did ever to thy wond'ring eyes' of 1705.[60] The practice of using a continuous bowed bass in concerted vocal music probably began in England in the early eighteenth century when the cello, popularized by Italian players through the medium of florid continuo arias in Italian operas and cantatas, began to supersede the bass viol and the bass violin.

The Baroque oboe and recorder seem to have been introduced to England in 1673 by four Frenchmen led by James Paisible (see Ch. 14). The first evidence of them in the chapel is a certificate dated 8 June 1678 naming three 'Frenchmen who serve as musicians in the Chapel Royal': Maxent De Bresmes and Pierre Guiton, two of the four who came in 1673, and 'Cir Felix alias La Montagu Cir'.[61] De Bresmes had already described himself as 'musicien français de la chapelle royale de violons et hautbois' when he published Cambert and Favier's *Ballet et Musique pour le Divertissement du Roi de la Grand Bretagne* in 1674 (see Ch. 14), so he may have served in the chapel from soon after his arrival in London— if the phrase *chapelle royale* means the Chapel Royal rather than the royal music in general. In September 1675 'Mr. Beale'—probably the trumpeter and trumpet-maker Simon Beale—was paid £2 for 'mending & altering two recorders', and David Lasocki has suggested that he was 'changing Renaissance recorders into the new Baroque types'.[62] Another possibility is that Beale was trying to reconcile discrepancies between the low pitch of French wind instruments and the high pitch of English organs.[63] He may have retuned them so that they were exactly a minor or

[59] Locke, *Chamber Music: II*, ed. Tilmouth, 100–4.
[60] *GB-Ob*, MS Mus. Sch. C. 135.
[61] Ashbee, *RECM*, i. 179.
[62] Ashbee, *RECM*, i. 157; Lasocki, 'Professional Recorder Players', i. 321.
[63] B. Haynes, 'Johann Sebastian Bach's Pitch Standards: The Woodwind Perspective', *JAMIS* 2 (1985), 55–114.

major third lower than the organ, which would have allowed the players to transpose their parts.

Two anthems by John Blow, 'Lord, who shall dwell in thy tabernacle?' and 'Sing unto the Lord, O ye saints of his', seem to have been written for the three Frenchmen. The former uses '2 Flutes' (i.e. treble recorders) and 'Base Flute', and the latter two low-pitched 'Hoboys'—*tailles* or tenor oboes (the parts are in C3 clefs with the range *f–b'*)—alternating with two treble recorders.[64] Bruce Wood dates the latter to between 1681 and 1683, and the former, which he thinks a revision of an earlier piece, to after 1680. The anthems are more similar in their instrumentation than the scores immediately suggest. Most of 'Lord, who shall dwell in thy tabernacle?' is laid out for pairs of recorders and violins supported respectively by a 'bass flute' and a 'double bass'—which share a single bass line in the score. Pairs of oboes and violins alternate in a similar fashion in 'Sing unto the Lord, O ye saints of his', though the bass instruments are not specified. But it may be that Blow intended a viol to play with the violins and a bassoon with the 'hoboys'. According to James Talbot, the bassoon was introduced to England in the early 1680s; he wrote that the sackbut was 'left off towards the latter end of K(ing) Ch(arles) 2d & gave place to the 'Fr(ench) basson'.[65]

The example of 'Sing unto the Lord, O ye saints of his' also throws light on a problem in 'Lord, who shall dwell in thy tabernacle?'. The former requires the players to change between oboes and recorders several times, and they may also have changed instruments in the latter at b. 184, where the recorders stop and a viola suddenly appears in the string group. Bruce Wood thinks the work a 'patchwork of disparate movements' of different dates, and suggests that Blow revised it up to that point working in recorder parts; the rest of the work is less mature in style, and he probably left it unrevised, expecting the wind-players to double the string parts on oboes and bassoon. It may be, too, that the entry of the viola signals the introduction of a larger body of strings (Ex. 16.2). We can imagine a performance of the work in the chapel laid out like Locke's 'Be thou exalted, Lord', with the solo voices and the trios of recorders and strings in the galleries, and an orchestral 'band of violins' below with the choir.

There is also a problem with the identity of the bass instruments in 'Lord, who shall dwell in thy tabernacle?' The 'bass flute' part goes down to *C*, so it is presumably intended for the largest size of Baroque recorder,

[64] Blow, *Anthems II: Anthems with Orchestra*, ed. B. Wood (*MB* 50; London, 1984), nos. 3, 6; 'Sing unto the Lord, O ye saints of his' was once thought to be by Locke; see Harding, *Matthew Locke*, 8; *Anthems*, ed. Wood, 180.
[65] Baines, 'James Talbot's Manuscript', 19; W. Waterhouse, 'Bassoon', *Grove 6*; J. B. Kopp, 'Notes on the Bassoon in Seventeenth-Century France', *JAMIS* 17 (1991), 100–2.

Ex. 16.2. John Blow, 'Lord, who shall dwell in thy tabernacle', bb. 178–87 (from Blow, *Anthems II*, ed. Wood, no. 3)

called 'Double Bass' by Talbot; Purcell used the same instrument in a similar way—a single bass line alternates a 'bass flute' and a bass violin under pairs of treble recorders and violins—in 'Hark each tree' from his 1692 St Cecilia ode 'Hail bright Cecilia'.[66] The problem is that recorders sound (or, at least, are usually perceived to sound) an octave higher than written, while the bowed 'Double Base' might be thought to be an instrument sounding an octave lower than written—an unsatisfactory state of affairs since they frequently exchange phrases. But Blow's 'Double Base' is probably the instrument that earlier composers called 'great bass' or 'great double bass' (see Ch. 9): a large viol pitched in A' or G', a fourth or a fifth below the normal bass viol in D, which was used to play low-lying bass parts at written pitch. Thus 'Double Base' means an instrument a size larger than the normal bass, just as Talbot used it to mean a recorder one size larger than the ordinary bass in F. Blow presumably chose it rather than an ordinary bass viol or bass violin for its rich yet delicate sonority. These anthems with oboes and recorders are experimental works, evidently written for sophisticated and well-equipped players. After the Frenchmen left England, perhaps in 1682, there was a

---

[66] *Ode on St Cecilia's Day 1692*, ed. P. Dennison (The Works of Henry Purcell, 8; London, 1978), 8.

lull in the use of oboes and recorders in court works until after 1685, when Paisible and several other wind-players were brought into the royal music (see Ch. 17). They do not seem to have been used again with the Chapel Royal until the eighteenth century, even at the coronation services of 1685 and 1689.

According to Thomas Tudway, the practice of using strings in the chapel on a regular basis was discontinued after 1685:

After the death of King Charles, symphonys, indeed, w(i)th Instruments in the Chappell, were laid aside; But they continu'd to make their Anthems w(i)th all the Flourish, of interludes, & Retornellos, w(hi)ch are now perform'd by the Organ.[67]

It is true that the annual payments of £400 for twenty violinists to serve in the chapel were not continued by James II, though Blow did not receive all the arrears until 3 March 1691/2.[68] Yet the Chapel Royal continued to function during his reign, despite the fact that the king did little to disguise his Catholic sympathies, and attended the Catholic chapel at St James's, opened on Christmas Day 1686 (Fig. 16.4). Princess Anne, at least, still attended Whitehall chapel: on 21 October 1687 Nicholas Staggins, who had 'neglected to give Order to the Violins to attend at the Chappell at Whitehall where Her Royal Highnesse the Princesse Ann of Denmarke is pr(e)sent', was ordered to 'give notice to them that they give theire attendance there upon Sunday next & soe continue to doe so as formerly they did'.[69] No payments for these duties appear to survive.

A group of verse anthems in the Gostling Manuscript, an important score-book of Restoration church music now at the University of Texas at Austin, have dates in James II's reign: William Turner's 'Preserve me O God', pp. 86–94, is dated 24 August 1686; Purcell's 'Behold, I bring you glad tidings', pp. 95–104, has the rubric 'For Christmas day 1687'; Purcell's 'Blessed are they that fear the Lord', pp. 105–9, was 'Composed by Mr Henry Purcell. Jan: 12. 1687[/8]'; Purcell's 'Praise the Lord, O my soul', pp. 110–18, and 'Thy way, O God, is holy', pp. 119–23, are dated 1687; his 'O sing unto the Lord', pp. 124–37, is dated 1688; and Turner's 'O sing praises unto our God', pp. 138–45, is dated 1687.[70]

An instrumental group was also employed in the Catholic chapel. Nine instrumentalists were among those appointed by a warrant dated 5 July

---

[67] Hogwood, 'Thomas Tudway's History of Music', 26.

[68] Ashbee, *RECM*, ii. 217.

[69] Ibid. 15–16.

[70] F. Zimmerman, 'Anthems of Purcell and Contemporaries in a Newly Rediscovered "Gostling Manuscript"', *AcM* 41 (1969), 55–70; id. (ed.), *The Gostling Manuscript, Compiled by John Gostling*, facs. (Austin, Tex., and London, 1977).

16.3. Anonymous engraving of the Catholic chapel at St James's in 1687. The Pepys Library, Magdalene College, courtesy of the Master and Fellows

1687.[71] The nine consisted of six members of Charles II's Twenty-four Violins, William Hall, Thomas Farmer, Edward Hooton, John Crouch, John Goodwin, and Robert Carr, with the oboist, recorder-player, and bass violinist James Paisible (see Ch. 17), the Moravian composer and bass viol-player Gottfried or Godfrey Finger, and 'Mᵣ Neydenhanger'; they all received £50 a year except for the last two, who got £40, perhaps because they were recent arrivals. A list dated 20 March 1687/8 is more informative: by then the group had increased to twelve with the addition of John Caspar Keiling, 'Tennor', Edmund Flower, theorbo, and 'Seign(o)r Francisco Lodie Theorbo'; everyone now received £50 a year, and £20 was set aside for 'one to distribute and collect the music papers', as well as £15 for 'one to tune the harpsichords'.[72] A final list, a warrant dated 20 October 1688 paying travel expenses to Windsor that summer, is harder to interpret, since the instrumentalists are mixed up with the singers.[73] But one addition to the group can be identified: François La Riche, who, like Paisible, played oboe, recorder, and bass violin.

Not much is known about the music performed in the Catholic chapel. Evelyn, who visited it on 29 December 1686, wrote of 'a world of mysterious Ceremony the Musique pla(y)ing & singing', but none of the concerted vocal and instrumental music performed there can be identified.[74] However, Finger dedicated his *Sonatae XII, pro diversis instrumentis* (London, 1688) to James II, stating that the contents—three sonatas for violin, bass viol, and continuo, three for two violins, bass viol, and continuo, three for three violins and continuo, and three for string quartet and continuo—were played in the Catholic chapel—'haec musica Capellae Regiae'.[75] Sonatas were presumably used in its liturgy as they were in courtly chapels in Italy—or in Finger's native Moravia. There is no evidence, incidentally, that independent consort works such as Purcell's trio sonatas were played in the Anglican Chapel Royal, as has been suggested.[76]

The Glorious Revolution put an end to the Catholic chapel and its group of instrumentalists, and the practice of using groups of instrumentalists in the Anglican chapel ended soon after. In 1691 William III ordered that the 'King's Chappell shall be all the year through kept both morning and evening with solemn musick like a collegiate church', which carries the implication that violins were to be excluded, for they were not

---

[71] Ashbee, *RECM*, ii. 16–17; v. 84, 274; W. A. Shaw (ed.), *Calendar of Treasury Books Preserved in the Public Record Office*, viii, pt. 3 (London, 1923), 1441–2.

[72] Ashbee, *RECM*, v. 86–7; Shaw, *Calendar of Treasury Books*, viii, pt. 3, 1822–3.

[73] Ashbee, *RECM*, ii. 21.

[74] Evelyn, *Diary*, 857–8.

[75] Pointed out in Lasocki, 'Professional Recorder Players', i. 324.

[76] For instance, T. Dart, 'Purcell's Chamber Music', *PRMA* 85 (1958–9), 87.

used in collegiate foundations outside the court.[77] Thereafter, by and large, the Chapel Royal was accompanied by orchestras only on great state occasions.

[77] Lafontaine, *The King's Musick*, 407; the significance of this document was pointed out to me by Bruce Wood. I am grateful to Paul Hopkins for pointing out that Queen Mary issued an order on 23 February 1689 banning instruments in the chapel, *GB-Lpro*, RG 8/110, fos. 24ʳ–25ᵛ.

17

'A Mighty Musique Entertainment at Court'

Reform and Retrenchment in the Royal Music, 1685–1690

THE news of Charles II's death on 6 February 1685 was received by his people with mixed feelings. He had endeared himself by his wit, intelligence, and charm; yet his fickleness, debauchery, and double-dealing had reduced Whitehall to 'a dissolute annexe to Versailles', in the words of David Ogg.[1] John Evelyn expressed the thoughts of many when he wrote in his diary:

Thus concluded this sad, & yet Joyfull day: I am never to forget the unexpressable luxury, & prophanesse, gaming, & all dissolution, and as it were total forgetfullnesse of God (it being Sunday Evening) which this day sennight, I was witnesse of; the King, sitting & toying with his Concubines Portsmouth, Cleaveland, & Mazarine: &c: A french boy singing love songs, in that glorious Gallery, whilst about 20 of the greate Courtiers & other dissolute persons were at Basset round a large table, a bank of at least 2000 in Gold before them, upon which two Gent(lemen) that were with me made reflexions with astonishment, it being a sceane of utmost vanity; and surely as they thought would never have an End: six days after was all in the dust.[2]

The new king, Charles's brother James, was no saint—he had had his share of amorous intrigue—but he was determined to bring order, economy, and decency to the British court, as his father had tried to do in 1625. He began with a thorough reform of the overgrown, ramshackle, and hidebound royal household, the first since the reign of Henry VIII.

When James came to the throne there were places for more than sixty instrumentalists in the royal household, according to the 1684 edition of Edward Chamberlayne's *Angliae notitiae*:

Musicians in Ordinary, sixty two, which are ranked in these three degrees, viz.
Private Musick,
Wind Music, and

---

[1] D. Ogg, *England in the Reigns of James II and William III* (2nd edn., Oxford, 1969), 139.
[2] Evelyn, *Diary*, 791.

twenty-four Violins

Of all which, as also of the Instrumental Musick of the Chappel, Dr. Nicholas Staggins Esq. is Master.

Trumpeters in Ordinary are sixteen, and one Kettle Drummer, of whom Gervas Pryce, Esq; is the Sergeant Trumpeter.

John Maugridge Drum-Major, four other Drummers, and a Fife.[3]

The actual number of individuals was smaller than this, for some of the places were held by pluralists, and the situation was further confused by the archaic system by which they were paid variously from the Treasury of the Chamber, the Exchequer, or the Privy Purse, at annual rates ranging from £20 to £200—sums that had been fixed more by precedent and historical accident than by an assessment of the worth of the recipient. The process of reform was aided by the fact that most musicians held appointments 'during pleasure', which had automatically lapsed at the end of the previous reign; the minority who held life pensions from the Exchequer were required to surrender them before the new scheme could come into being.[4] The new royal music consisted of the Master of the Music, Nicholas Staggins, who continued to receive £200 a year, and a single group of 'Private Music', who were paid a standard rate of £40 a year from the Treasury of the Chamber. At the same time a determined attempt was made to pay the enormous arrears of salary that had accumulated in Charles II's time. The details are missing from the records of the Treasury of the Chamber, but the Exchequer was concerned with it until the spring of 1692, by which time many of the individuals concerned were dead.[5]

James II's reforms had several important consequences for musical life at court. The first was that the instrumentalists were no longer divided into a number of separate consorts, each with an autonomous role in the daily round at Whitehall, as they had been ever since the reign of Henry VIII. To some extent theory was just catching up with practice, for the old system broke down in Charles II's reign, as the violin band grew in size and importance, and places in the wind consorts and the Private Music were gradually given to violinists. We saw in earlier chapters that the pace of change was forced by Charles II's own musical taste: he preferred dance music to fantasias, and ordered violins to replace the 'ancient grave and solemn wind musique' in verse anthems. As a result violin bands invaded the Privy Chamber and the Chapel Royal, territory previously held by the Private Music and the wind consorts. The Twenty-four Violins expanded its empire further when its members began to play

---

[3] Ashbee, *RECM*, v. 284.

[4] Ibid. ii, p. vii; Shaw (ed.), *Calendar of Treasury Books*, viii, pt. 1, 378–9.

[5] Ashbee, *RECM*, ii. 199–218.

in the London theatres, and again when a new genre, the court ode, developed. In Charles II's reign the Twenty-four Violins had played in the private areas of the court on a *de facto* basis; now all the court instrumentalists (with the exception of the trumpeters and the fife- and drum-players) were listed under the heading 'Private Music', and seemingly enjoyed the privilege *de jure*, though no order to that effect seems to survive.

A second consequence of the reforms was to turn the Twenty-four Violins from a violin band into an up-to-date Baroque orchestra of strings, wind, and continuo. The first list of the new Private Music, dated 31 August 1685, shows how the changes were made:[6]

Thomas Farmer
Jeoffrey Ayleworth   } These were
Edmund Flower   at sea
James Peasable
Joseph Fashion, his father drowned at sea
Edward Greeting, his father drowned at sea
John Twist
Robert King
John Crouch
John Bannister
William Clayton
William Hall
Robert Carr
Nathaniel French
Richard Tomlinson
John Goodwyn
Edward Hooton
Henry He[a]lle
Theophilus Fitz
Charles Staggins, junior
John Lenton
John Abell   } The vocall part   Countertenors
William Turner
Bases: [John] Gosling
        [John] Bowman
For the flute: Monsieur Mario [François Mariens]
Tenor: Thomas Heywood
Base Viol: [Charles] Coleman [the younger]
Harpsicall: Henry Purcell
Composer: Dr. [John] Blow

---

[6] Ibid. 2–3; in Lafontaine, *The King's Musick*, 371–2, the word 'Countertenors', wrongly placed at the head of the document, gave rise to the entertaining notion that James II's Private Music had included twenty-one countertenors; see also Ashbee, *RECM*, ii. 122; *CSPD, James II, February–December 1685*, ed. E. K. Timings (London, 1960), 360–1.

Bases: [Balthazar] Reading
       Henry Eagles [actually Solomon Eccles]
       Mons. Le Rich [François La Riche]
Keeper of the Instruments: Henry Brockwell

At the end of Charles II's reign there were thirty-four places available to the Twenty-four Violins (see Appendix C): fourteen from the pre-Civil War violin band, thirteen places created in 1660, two created in 1672 and 1679 by dividing existing places, and six borrowed from the Private Music. Thus the new Private Music was clearly the direct successor of the Twenty-four Violins, for it too consisted of thirty-five musicians with the Master of the Music, Nicholas Staggins.

The first twenty-one names on the list were the rump of Charles II's Twenty-four Violins. Nine of their colleagues were dropped in 1685, in most cases, it seems, because they were past active service. Four of those who disappeared had served since 1660, and Robert Strong and Simon Hopper went back respectively to 1640 and 1641. Strong made a comeback in 1689 and served William and Mary until his death in June 1694 at the age of 72, but his wife Mary signed for his wages each year from 1689, so he was probably living in retirement away from the court.[7] In the document of 21 October 1685 that confirmed the appointment of the new Private Music Balthazar Reading, Solomon Eccles, and François La Riche are described as 'three New Bases' who replaced 'three disabled by Age'.[8] By a bill dated 3 May 1686 Henry Brockwell was paid £2 for strings 'for the Base Violins', and £6 for '3 New cases for the Base violins'; the three brought the string-players in the Private Music up to the familiar number of twenty-four.[9]

The mysterious references to musicians being 'at sea' and drowning have been explained by Harold Love.[10] It seems that they were aboard the frigate *Gloucester* when it was wrecked off the Norfolk coast on the morning of 6 May 1682; the ship was taking James (then Duke of York) to Scotland to collect his wife Mary of Modena, with more than 250 courtiers and seamen, nearly 150 of whom perished. Edward Greeting's father Thomas, the Duke's personal musician and Pepys's flageolet teacher, was certainly one of the victims.[11] It was said in 1688 that he had been 'cast away in the Gloucester frigate'; his widow Joyce was given compensation from Secret Service funds, was recommended for a place at Chelsea Hospital, and her son Edward was given a place in the new

---

[7] Lasocki, 'Professional Recorder Players', ii. 776; Ashbee, *RECM*, ii. 51, 124, 163–5.
[8] Ashbee, *RECM*, ii. 5.
[9] Ibid. 8.
[10] H. Love, 'The Wreck of the *Gloucester*', *MT*, 125 (1984), 194–5.
[11] For Greeting in the Duke of York's household, see Ashbee, *RECM*, ii. 121.

Private Music.[12] The case of Joseph Fashion is more complex, for a man of that name appears in court records before and after 1682. Love puts this down to an error in the 1685 list, but there were actually two Joseph Fashions, father and son. They are both mentioned in the will of Thomas Fitz dated 24 March 1675/6, and in the elder Fashion's will, proved on 16 March 1685/6, the younger was given £100 with the proviso that it be divided among his family should he obtain a court post.[13] Love points out that a Joseph Fashion was required to surrender his Exchequer life pension in 1685, but he was not among those who replied with a consenting letter, and there is no sign that anything but arrears was paid on his account after 1682.[14] Most likely, the father's place was held open until the son was old enough to succeed him—which was in 1685.

Jacques (James) Paisible also seems to have been on the *Gloucester*. He was one of the four French wind-players who came to England in, probably, 1673 (see Ch. 14), though he did not hold a post in the main royal music until 1685. A few weeks after the shipwreck, however, on 15 July 1682, Nicholas Staggins was paid £25 'being intended for Mr. Peceable'.[15] David Lasocki suggests that the money was compensation for losses incurred, and points out that Paisible is not recorded in London between 1679, when the Duke of York settled in Edinburgh in the aftermath of the Popish Plot, and the shipwreck in 1682.[16] Lasocki's conclusion is that Paisible was a member of James's household during those years, and there is support for this in two recently published Exchequer documents. Paisible, François Mariens, and two otherwise unknown musicians, James Arneau and Lewis Brunot, were paid £100 a year each for service from midsummer 1678 to Christmas 1684 with money raised on customs dues from tobacco, sugar, and French linen.[17] They are said to be 'four of his late Majesty's private musick', but their absence in documents relating to Charles II's royal music, and the unorthodox method of payment, suggests that James was rewarding former members of his personal household. Those affected by the 1682 shipwreck presumably appear at the head of the 1685 list because the intention was to compensate them for their loss by choosing them first for the new Private Music.

Paisible played the bass viol, the bass violin, and the violoncello as well as the oboe and the recorder. A bass violin belonging to him was examined by James Talbot in the 1690s; he is listed variously as a cellist,

---

[12] Shaw, *Calendar of Treasury Books*, viii, pt. 4, 1958; Ashbee, *RECM*. ii. 4; v. 274–7.
[13] *GB-Lpro*, PROB 11/354, q. 91; PROB 11/377, q. 123.
[14] Shaw, *Calendar of Treasury Books*, viii, pt. 1, 379; Ashbee, *RECM*, ii. 201; v. 214, 215, 217, 218.
[15] Shaw, *Calendar of Treasury Books*, vii, pt. 1, 543.
[16] Lasocki, 'Professional Recorder Players', ii. 784–5.
[17] Ashbee, *RECM*, ii. 205, 214.

a bass viol-player, or simply as one of the 'Bases' in documents relating to the Italian opera company at the Haymarket in the years 1707-13; and he left three bass violins and a bass viol in his will.[18] He presumably spent much of his time at court playing the bass violin, but it is hard to believe that he never played wind instruments there, particularly since François Mariens is listed in the 1685 document as a 'flute', and recorder parts in court orchestral music of the period nearly always come in pairs. The same thing can be said of three of Paisible's string-playing colleagues: François La Riche was also a famous oboist like Paisible; John Banister II was a recorder-player and the author of the first English oboe tutor (see below); and Robert King was a recorder-player and a composer of recorder music.[19] Thus, at least five members of the new Private Music seem to have been woodwind-players, and their presence allowed court composers to use oboes and recorders on a regular basis in their orchestral scores.

The best guide to the changing orchestral practice of the English court is the series of odes that were performed at the New Year, on royal birthdays, and on special occasions from soon after the Restoration until the early nineteenth century.[20] The information they offer is particularly useful because most of them can be dated exactly, and we can be sure that they were written for performance at court by court musicians. By James II's reign they had assumed considerable importance in musical life at Whitehall, in part because older types of ceremonial music had declined in importance, in part because the odes themselves were becoming ever longer, more elaborate, and more fully scored. Indeed, one reason for retaining 'The vocall part' in the Private Music—a vestige of Charles II's singer-lutenists—was probably to provide soloists for court odes; among them were the famous soloists John Abell and John Gostling, the composer William Turner, and the tenor Thomas Heywood (a 'Page of the Back-stairs' to James while he was Duke of York[21]). The younger Charles Coleman (bass viol) and Henry Purcell (harpsichord) are listed in the 1685 document immediately below the singers, and may have acted as their continuo team.

Surprisingly little is known about how court odes were performed. The best general description of a royal birthday is in the account of the Grand Duke of Tuscany's visit to England in 1669:

---

[18] Donington, 'James Talbot's Manuscript'; Milhous and Hume (eds.), *Vice Chamberlain Coke's Theatrical Papers*, 31, 38, 69, 119, 127, 151, 158, 159, 192; Lasocki, 'Professional Recorder Players', ii. 805.

[19] Lasocki, 'Professional Recorder Players', ii. 816–29, 835–7, 957–9; see also id., 'The French Hautboy in England', 353–4.

[20] The repertoire is surveyed in R. McGuinness, *English Court Odes 1660–1820* (Oxford, 1971).

[21] Ashbee, *RECM*, ii. 121.

This day [Charles II's birthday, 29 May] is no otherwise solemnized in London than by keeping the shops shut, and by the king's going to chapel with his court, and dining in public, with the princes of the blood, in the banquetting room at Whitehall, which is hung with tapestry in the more elevated part of it, under the canopy, and is traversed by a balustrade, to prevent the people who resort thither from flocking round the royal table. The dinner is enlivened with various pieces of music, performed by the musicians of the king's household.[22]

The earliest specific description of an ode concerns Blow's 'Up, shepherds, up', given on the king's birthday in 1681. The report is in *The Loyal Protestant and True Domestic Intelligence* for 4 June:

Windsor—May 29 1681 This day (being His Majesty's Birthday) all the usuall Ceremonies were performed; as ringing of Bells, sounding of Trumpets, beating of Drums, with variety of other Musick. At His Majesty's up-rising a Song was sung in the Privy Chamber, concerning the Birth, Restauration, and Coronation, much to the satisfaction of His Majesty . . .[23]

There is evidence, however, that several of James II's odes were performed in the evening. Pepys wrote to Sir Robert Southwell on 10 October 1685 that 'To night we have had a mighty Musique-Entertainment at Court for the welcomeing home the King and Queene.'[24] According to Evelyn the king's birthday celebrations a few days later, on 15 October, preceded a court ball, which would have been held in the evening:

Being the Kings birth-day, was a solemn Ball at Court; And Musique of Instruments & Voices before the Ball: At the Musique I happen(ed) (by accident) to stand the very next to the Queene, & the King, who ta(1)ked with me about the Musick.[25]

Similarly, the Lord Steward's department delivered '12 White wax lights' for 'the singing' on New Year's day 1686/7.[26] However, three years later, on New Year's day 1689/90, Narcissus Luttrell recorded that:

the king and queen came to Whitehall, where many of the nobility and gentry came to wish them a happy new year; and there was a great consort of musick, vocal and instrumental, and a song composed by the poet laureat.[27]

On this occasion the ode followed formal New Year greetings, so it was probably performed in the morning. The same thing probably happened on 1 January 1695/6, when courtiers went to call on the king at Kensington Palace. According to *The Flying Post*:

[22] Magalotti, *Travels of Cosmo the Third*, 364–5.
[23] McGuinness, *English Court Odes*, 10.
[24] Pepys, *Letters and the Second Diary*, ed. R. G. Howarth (London, 1932), 171.
[25] Evelyn, *Diary*, 829.
[26] Ashbee, *RECM*, v. 233.
[27] N. Luttrell, *A Brief Relation of State Affairs from September 1678 to April 1714* (Oxford, 1857; repr. 1969), ii. 1.

all the Nobility, Judges, Gentlemen &c., went to Kensington and wished His Majesty many joyful and happy years, the Trumpets, Kettle-Drums, &c., made that performance, as did also his Majesty's Musicianers, and a curious Ode, being composed on this occasion was sung and plaid to.[28]

All in all, there seems to have been no fixed time and place for the performance of court odes.

Among the Lord Chamberlain's accounts relating to the Office of Works is one, from January 1684/5, that seems to be concerned with preparations for the performance of Blow's New Year ode 'How does the new-born infant year rejoice?' in the Hall Theatre at Whitehall. Carpenters were paid for:

taking downe and removing the Kings old Throne in the Hall & carrying it out and placing it over the enclosure in the Lobby and setting up three boxes and seats in the place of the Throne and enlarging and setting up a new flo(o)r forward over the pit for his Ma(jes)t(ie)s Chairs 10 fo(o)t long and about 8 fo(o)t wide and enclosing it with railes and boards about 3 fo(o)t ½ high and making two desk boards for the Musick 8 fo(o)t long a peice, and setting up two bearers for the Harpsicall ...[29]

It seems that the musicians were on stage, and that the royal family sat in a railed-off area constructed over the pit. Sixteen feet of 'desk boards' (continuous music stands?) would have accommodated about eight violinists or viola-players, so there might have been about eleven or twelve strings if there were three or four bass-players who had their own stands or looked over the shoulder of the harpsichordist; Blow's ode is scored for four-part strings and continuo. Other payments of a similar nature show that carpenters were kept busy altering the Hall Theatre back and forth from a theatre to a ballroom or to a concert hall for the performance of court odes. Carpenters, for instance, were paid in May 1678 for:

fitting & laying a floore Joysted bridged & bourded over the pitt at the Theater in Whitehall Cont(aining?) about 5 squares, Cutting fitting & setting severall formes uppon the stage & makeing 4 new formes to be used there Carryeing & recarryeing 4 musick formes from the Queenes pr(e)sence to & from the said Theater ...[30]

Perhaps this bill relates to preparations for the performance of Blow's 'The birth of Jove', written that year for the king's birthday.

A survey of the thirty-seven surviving court odes from Locke's 'Welcome, welcome, royal May' (29 May 1661?) to Purcell's 'Arise my muse' (30 April 1690) shows that their scoring went through five distinct

---

[28] McGuinness, *English Court Odes*, 52.
[29] Boswell, *The Restoration Court Stage*, 264.
[30] Ibid. 256.

phases.[31] The earliest odes, it seems, were accompanied only by a small group. The two by Locke, the one just mentioned and 'All things their certain periods have' (1 January 1665/6), are scored just for voices and continuo, while the three by Henry Cooke, 'Good morrow to this year' (also probably 1 January 1665/6). 'Rise, thou best and brightest morning', and 'Come, we shepherds' (both for royal birthdays pre-1672), have simple preludes and ritornelli for two violins and continuo. They were probably intended for single strings, and would have been within the resources of the early-Restoration Private Music.

The second phase, which probably marks the beginning of the regular association of the Twenty-four Violins with the court ode, starts with the three surviving odes by Pelham Humfrey, 'See, mighty Sir, the day appears' (1 January 1671/2), 'When from his throne the Persian god displays' (29 May 1672), and 'Smile, smile again twice happy morn' (29 May 1673?).[32] They are now longer and more complex works, and use three, four, or five solo voices and choir with four-part strings and continuo. Some of them, such as Blow's 1678 birthday ode 'Dread Sir, the prince of light', have the type of string-writing—with low-lying second lines in C1 or C2 clefs—that has been associated in earlier chapters with the use of violin, two violas, and bass, though most of the odes of the 1680s are clearly written with two equal violin parts.

Little is known about the size of the orchestras for the odes of the 1670s and early 1680s. The whole Twenty-four Violins was evidently in attendance on 1 October 1667, when Pepys wrote of hearing music by Louis Grabu at Whitehall: 'both instrumental (I think 24 violins) and vocall, an English song upon peace'.[33] On the other hand, the fact that Blow's 'Up, shepherds, up' was performed in the Privy Chamber at Windsor may mean that only small forces took part. But these works may be atypical. The former was evidently performed on an exceptional occasion—perhaps a belated celebration of the end of the second Dutch war—and may have been written for five-part strings in the one violin–three viola layout—like *Albion and Albanius* and *Pastoralle* (see Ch. 15), while the latter does not survive with string parts, and may never have had them. The evidence relating to 'How does the new-born infant year rejoice?' is admittedly rather tenuous, but an orchestra of about twelve—half the Twenty-four Violins—is certainly plausible for the ordinary odes with four-part strings, and it is all we have to go on at present.

---

[31] I am grateful to Dr Rosamond McGuinness for making her unpublished transcriptions of court odes available to me; there is a checklist of the repertoire in McGuinness, *English Court Odes*, 12–61; another incomplete ode, possibly by Purcell, is discussed in N. Fortune, 'A New Purcell Source', *MR*, 25 (1964), 109–13.

[32] See Dennison, *Pelham Humfrey*, 76–81.

[33] Pepys, *Diary*, viii. 458.

The third phase mainly concerns two welcome odes by Purcell, 'Swifter, Isis, swifter flow', and 'What, what shall be done in behalf of the man?'. The former was probably written for the king's return to Whitehall from Windsor on 27 August 1681, while the latter greeted the Duke of York on 27 May 1682, the day he eventually reached the court after the *Gloucester* debacle.[34] Both require two 'flutes' (i.e. recorders) in addition to four-part strings and continuo, and one instrumental passage in 'Swifter, Isis, swifter flow' has an extra line marked in one source 'Hoboy 3rd treble'. Both should probably be associated with the three French wind-players who worked in the Chapel Royal around 1680, and for whom, I argued in Chapter 16, Blow wrote his two experimental verse anthems with oboes and recorders. The short 'hoboy' passage in 'Swifter, Isis, swifter flow' is presumably a sign that Purcell expected one of his recorder-players to double on oboe, and it is likely that they both changed freely between the two instruments, using oboes for the tutti passages. A third wind-player is not specified in these odes, though it is easy to imagine that one was present, accompanying the oboes with a bassoon and the treble recorders with a great bass—as happened in Blow's 'Lord, who shall dwell in thy tabernacle?'.

'Swifter, Isis, swifter flow' and 'What, what shall be done in behalf of the man?' are the first items in the reversed portion of Purcell's scorebook, *GB-Lbl*, R.M. 20.H.8. This sequence of more than forty odes, songs, and dialogues, the main autograph of his non-theatrical secular vocal music, has a particular importance in that the pieces seem to have been entered more or less in order of composition: those that can be dated precisely, from 'Swifter, Isis, swifter flow' of August 1681 to 'Arise my muse', written for Queen Mary's birthday on 30 April 1690, occur in sequence.[35] The point is that after the third item, the ode 'The summer's absence unconcerned we bear' (21 October 1682), there are four undated 'symphony songs' with instruments, three of which, 'How pleasant is this flowery plain', the incomplete 'We reap all the pleasures', and 'Hark, Damon, hark', have parts for two recorders. There is then a gap of more than three years and more than thirty pieces before wind parts reappear in 'Ye tuneful Muses' (perhaps 1 October 1686), with the exception of the duet 'Soft notes and gently raised', which comes in the sequence soon after pieces written in the autumn of 1683. In the same way, no Chapel Royal anthems have wind parts after the works written by Blow around 1680, just as none of Blow's odes has wind parts before 'Ye sons of Phoebus', written for the New Year 1688. A possible explanation for this

[34] Purcell, *Welcome Songs, Part 1*, ed. R. Vaughan Williams (The Works of Henry Purcell, 15; London, 1905), 24–51, 52–82; see Zimmerman, *Henry Purcell*, 84, 87.

[35] For a list of contents, see N. Fortune and F. B. Zimmerman, 'Purcell's Autographs', in I. Holst (ed.), *Henry Purcell 1659–1695: Essays on his Music* (London, 1959), 112–15.

pattern is that the three French wind-players in the Chapel Royal left England sometime in late 1682 or early 1683, leaving Purcell and other court composers without readily available oboe- or recorder-players until Paisible and his colleagues were appointed to the Private Music in 1685.

To understand the fourth phase we must turn to the parallel series of works written for St Cecilia's Day, 22 November.[36] The English St Cecilia celebrations are first documented in 1683. Purcell's 'Welcome to all the pleasures' was published in score by John Playford in 1684 with the title *A Musical Entertainment Perform'd on November XXII. 1683*, and his Latin ode 'Laudate Ceciliam' is headed 'A Latine Song made upon St Cecilia, whos day is comm[em]erated yearly by all Musitians, made in the year 1683' in R.M. 20.H.8.[37] It is not known whether the two works were performed together (G. E. P. Arkwright suggested that 'Laudate Ceciliam' was written for the queen's Catholic chapel), nor is it certain that 'Welcome to all the pleasures' was the first of the main series. As Bruce Wood has pointed out, Playford's statement that St Cecilia is 'annually honour'd by a public Feast made on that Day by the Masters and Lovers of Music, as well in England as in Foreign Parts' could be taken to mean that the celebrations did not begin in 1683; indeed, Purcell's undated St Cecilia ode 'Raise, raise the voice' is shorter and more modestly scored than 'Welcome to all the pleasures' (STB, 2 violins, and continuo against SSATB solo, SATB chorus, four-part strings, and continuo), and may have preceded it.[38] It is not known where 'Welcome to all the pleasures' was performed, but the 1684 ode, Blow's 'Begin the song', was given at Stationers' Hall, which became the venue for succeeding years. 'Begin the song' was also published in score by Playford, but only the words for the 1685 and 1686 odes ever got into print; their music, by William Turner and Isaac Blackwell, is lost.[39]

Eyewitness descriptions of the early St Cecilia odes are few and far between. Goodwin Wharton, second son of Philip, Lord Wharton, dedicatee of John Carr's collection of three-part dance music *Tripla concordia* (London, 1677), and religious maniac, was present at the 1687 celebrations to hear Giovanni Battista Draghi's setting of Dryden's 'From harmony, from heavenly harmony'.[40] Unfortunately, the Lord appeared to him during the performance, so he failed to mention the music in his

[36] The best survey of the subject is still W. H. Husk, *An Account of the Musical Celebrations on St Cecilia's Day* (London, 1857).

[37] Purcell, *Three Odes for St Cecilia's Day*, ed. B. Wood (The Works of Henry Purcell, 10; London, 1990), 1–35, 63–88.

[38] Ibid., pp. ix–x, 36–62.

[39] Husk, *An Account*, 18–20; I am grateful to Bruce Wood for informing me that there is a copy of the printed text of Blackwell's ode at *GB-Cu*.

[40] *GB-Lbl*, Add. MS 20007, fo. 58ʳ; see Locke, *Suite in G Minor from Tripla Concordia*, ed. P. Holman (London, 1980); J. K. Clark, *Goodwin Wharton* (Oxford, 1984).

diary: 'Being also att St Cecilias feast of musick in honor of her & the Lord told me, th(a)t she was mighty glad I honor[e]d her so farr & would wate upon me, therefore as soon as she could: &c.' Peter Motteux's account of the 1691 celebrations in *The Gentleman's Journal* for January 1690/1 is more useful, at least to mere mortals:

On that day or the next, when it falls on a Sunday, as it did last time, most of the lovers of music, whereof many are persons of the first rank, meet at Stationers' Hall in London . . . A splendid entertainment is provided, and before it is always a performance of music by the best voices and hands in town; the words, which are always in the patronesses praise, are set by some of the greatest masters in town.[41]

'This feast', he added, is 'one of the genteelest in the world; there are no formalities nor gatherings, like as at others, and the appearance there is always very splendid.'

The St Cecilia ode was initially based on the court ode, in the manner of its performance as well as the style of its composition. Court musicians composed most of the early odes, and they figure frequently among the stewards appointed each year to oversee the proceedings—Nicholas Staggins, for instance, officiated in 1684. Court musicians also predominate in those cases where the names of individual performers are known. For instance, West Sussex Record Office, Cap. VI/1/1, fos. 24^r–63^r, a volume largely in the hand of the Eton copyist John Walter, containing a carefully annotated early score of the 1687 ode, gives the cast for, probably, the first performance. It mentions seven singers by name: William Turner, John Abell, and Anthony Robert II (countertenors), Alfonso Marsh (tenor), John Gostling, Leonard Woodson, and John Bowman (basses), all but one of whom were court musicians at the time. Turner, Abell, Gostling, and Bowman were in the 'vocall part' of the Private Music, while Turner, Abell, Marsh, Gostling, and Woodson were in the Chapel Royal.[42] Anthony Robert (not to be confused with his namesake and probable relative, the French singer, who died in 1679) received a court post in 1689.[43]

'From harmony, from heavenly harmony' was a turning-point in the development of the ode. It is on a much larger scale than its predecessors; it opens with a descriptive, Italianate prelude rather than the traditional French overture; it has massive choruses based, for the first time, on Italianate counterpoint rather than French dance patterns; and its solos are more florid and extended than anything written up to that time in England. The work was clearly the model for Purcell's next St

[41] Husk, *An Account*, 26–9.
[42] Baldwin, *The Chapel Royal*, 424–5.
[43] Ashbee, *RECM*, i. 172–3, 185; ii. 27, 28, 126.

Cecilia ode, 'Hail, bright Cecilia' of 1692, and it was highly regarded by English musicians, to judge from the number of surviving contemporary scores.[44] Anyone who has heard it would find it hard to agree with Franklin Zimmerman that Draghi's 'poetic sensibilities and musical powers were not such as to take full and imaginative advantage of the opportunity Dryden had provided'.[45] The work has its rough edges, but it has a vividness and a grandeur that was matched by Purcell only in his most ambitious odes.

More to the present purpose, several aspects of Draghi's orchestral writing were new in 1687, and influenced the subsequent development of English orchestral music. 'From harmony, from heavenly harmony' is the first ode to use five-part strings with two violins, two violas, and bass. Draghi would have known this scoring (not to be confused with the one-violin, three-viola layout) in his native Italy: it often occurs in the concerted works of such composers as Giovanni Legrenzi, Pietro Andrea Ziani, Giovanni Battista Vitali, Domenico Gabrielli, Giovanni Bononcini, and Antonio Caldara. 'From harmony, from heavenly harmony' evidently created a vogue for it in England: it was used by Purcell in 'Now does the glorious day appear', the ode for Queen Mary's birthday (30 April 1689), by Blow in 'With cheerful hearts let all appear', the 1690 New Year ode, and by Purcell again in 'Arise my muse', Queen Mary's 1690 birthday ode.[46] There is also a fine G minor overture by Purcell that has been generally thought of as an early work, presumably because of its scoring; I suggest that it also belongs to this period, and is the overture to a lost ode.[47] Five-part writing with two violas is occasionally found in later English orchestral music—for instance, in Gottfried (Godfrey) Finger's music for Settle's semi-opera *The Virgin Prophetess* of 1701.[48]

Several rubrics in the score of 'From harmony, from heavenly harmony' throw light on the way the orchestra was laid out. Two brief passages for two trebles and continuo near the beginning of the work are marked 'One single viol[in]', 'one single 2. viol[in]', and 'One Single Basse' (or, in the second case, 'two basses'), and they are contrasted with

---

[44] The other sources are *GB-Lbl*, Add. MS 33287, *GB-Lcm*, MSS 1097, 1106, and *GB-Ob*, Tenbury MS 1226. MS 1106 seems to be derived from a performance in 1694 or 1695, for among the twelve solo singers named are the countertenor Josias Bourchier, who died in Dec. 1695, and the tenor John Church, who was only born in 1675; see Rimbault, *The Old Cheque-Book*, 21, 241. For Draghi and his ode, see Husk, *An Account*, 22–4; E. Brennecke, 'Dryden's Odes and Draghi's Music', *Proceedings of the Modern Language Association of America*, 49 (1934), 1–36.

[45] Zimmerman, *Henry Purcell*, 147; the first modern performance, recorded by the Playford Consort and The Parley of Instruments, was broadcast on BBC Radio 3 on 22 Nov. 1987.

[46] Purcell, *Birthday Odes for Queen Mary, Part 1*, ed., G. E. P. Arkwright (The Works of Henry Purcell, 11; London, 1902), 2–35, 36–71; see Zimmerman, *Henry Purcell*, 170, 177–8.

[47] Purcell, *Fantasias and Miscellaneous Instrumental Music*, 85–8.

[48] R. Fiske, *English Theatre Music in the Eighteenth Century* (2nd edn., Oxford, 1986), 8, 10, 11; Finger does not write for 'a string band like Lully's', as Fiske states.

a five-part passage marked 'here enter all the viol[ins] and other instruments'. This is another indication that the solo vocal passages of English concerted works were accompanied by a small group of instruments that was to some extent distinct from the orchestra, as the *petit chœur* in French court orchestras was distinct from the *grand chœur*. The 'other instruments' were probably oboes, played in the tutti passages by the two musicians who were required for the recorders in the superb ground bass 'The soft complaining flute'.

Draghi also broke new ground in 'From harmony, from heavenly harmony' by writing for two trumpets. The trumpet first began to appear in concerted instrumental music around 1650; hitherto it had been used for improvised fanfares in trumpet and drum bands, and played only a peripheral role in art music, though Schütz, Praetorius, and other German composers had experimented with it in church music. Maurizio Cazzati's *Suonate à due, trè, quattro, e cinque, con alcune per tromba* Op. 35 (Bologna, 1665) may contain the earliest music for solo trumpet and strings, as Don Smithers suggested, but Johann Heinrich Schmelzer had already published a sonata for two trumpets and strings in his *Sacro-profanus concentus musicus* (Nuremberg, 1662), and there is a 'Sonata a5. 2 Violini e 2 Trombette con Fagotto' by Vincenzo Albrici that seems to date from the 1650s.[49] The source, *S-Uu*, IMhs 1:3, is part of the collection of performing material assembled by Swedish court musicians; Albrici was the director of a group of Italian musicians there between 1652 and 1654, and another instrumental piece by him, the 'Sinfonia a6. Primo Tono', *S-Uu*, IMhs 1:1, is dated 1654. Albrici's trumpet sonata, short and unsophisticated as it is, is important because its author later worked at the Restoration court, where he collaborated with Draghi in an abortive plan to establish Italian opera in London.[50]

Trumpets certainly seem to have been used in English orchestral music long before the early 1690s, when Purcell and Blow wrote the first imitations of Bolognese trumpet sonatas: Locke used trumpets in a chorus of *Psyche* (1675; see Ch. 14), and a piece for trumpets and orchestra was evidently heard at James II's coronation banquet in 1685, though it is known only from a bill for copying the score and parts (see Ch. 13). The earliest surviving or partially surviving English instrumental work with trumpets seems to be the 'Concerto di trombe a tre trombette con violini e flauti' by Nicola Matteis, published in *Other Ayrs and Pieces*, the fourth part of his *Ayrs for the Violin* (London, 1685), and in a fuller,

---

[49] D. Smithers, *The Music and History of the Baroque Trumpet before 1721* (London, 1973), 95–8; J. H. Schmelzer, *Sacroprofanus concentus musicus (1662)*, ed. E. Schenk (DTÖ, 111/112; Graz and Vienna, 1965), no. 1; A. Schering (ed.), *Geschichte der Musik in Beispielen* (Leipzig, 1931), no. 214.

[50] Mabbett, 'Italian Musicians in Restoration England'.

Ex. 17.1. Giovanni Battista Draghi, Chorus 'As from the power of sacred lays', bb. 54–6, from 'From harmony, from heavenly harmony', West Sussex Record Office, Cap. VI/1/1, 24–63

Trumpetts & Violins

revised form when the second treble of the collection was published in 1687.[51]

The trumpets in 'From harmony, from heavenly harmony' are notated in a way that suggests that they were still a relative novelty in 1687. They are called for twice, once at the words 'The trumpet's loud clangour excites us to arms', and once in the last chorus at the words 'The trumpet shall be heard on high'. On both occasions the music swings into C major (the prevailing key is C minor), and the brass parts are written on the violin staves so that it is not always obvious what notes they should play or when they should stop. Should they play in the C major 'Cho[rus] of all' at the words 'Charge, charge, 'tis too late to retreat'? What notes should the second trumpet play in the last chorus at the point marked 'trumpets & violins', where the second violin part has some non-harmonic tones? (Ex. 17.1)[52] Drums are not mentioned in the score; should they be used

---

[51] Matteis, *Concerto in C*, ed. P. Holman (London, 1982); see also Downey, 'What Samuel Pepys Heard'; A. Pinnock and B. Wood, 'A Counterblast on English Trumpets', *EM* 19 (1991), 436–43, and my response, ibid. 443.

[52] Downey, 'What Samuel Pepys Heard', 424, interprets these non-harmonic tones as evidence of the use of an advanced lipping technique among English trumpeters, a view disputed, rightly in my view, in Pinnock and Wood, 'A Counterblast'.

when the trumpets are playing? In particular, are the bars of repeated bass Cs at the words 'The double, double, double beat of the thund'ring drum' actually the vestige of a timpani part? Whatever the answers to these questions, the fact that they are posed by such a well-annotated score suggests that Draghi did not find writing for trumpets an easy task. Perhaps he had never written for them before; perhaps he did not know what his players, accustomed to ceremonial fanfares, could achieve; perhaps he relied on them to some extent to devise or improvise their parts.

Similar questions are raised by two of Purcell's odes, 'Ye tuneful muses' and 'Sound the trumpet, beat the drum'.[53] They are usually said to have been written for James II's birthday, 14 October, in 1686 and 1687, but both texts have clear references to the king arriving home, and the autographs in R.M. 20.H.8 are headed 'Welcome Song 1686' and 'Welcome Song 1687'. They may have been written respectively for James's return to Whitehall from Windsor on 1 October 1686, and his return from Oxford on 11 October 1687. In 'Ye tuneful muses' a four-part ritornello in C major introduces the chorus 'From the rattling drums and the trumpet's loud shouts'. Its top part uses only notes in the harmonic series, the bass looks like a drum part and uses only tonic and dominant notes, and it is easy to imagine trumpets and drums more or less doubling the strings; there is a plausible reconstruction along these lines in Peter Downey's article.[54]

On the other hand, as Andrew Pinnock and Bruce Wood have pointed out, Purcell could easily have been imitating trumpets and drums in string-writing of this sort, and Downey certainly weakens his case by going on to claim that a verse anthem by Humfrey and one by William Turner should have trumpet parts; there is no evidence that trumpets and drums were ever used in anthems at Whitehall.[55] There is a better case of missing trumpets in the famous D major opening solo and chorus of 'Sound the trumpet, beat the drum'. Again, the fanfare-like string parts can either be thought of as imitations of trumpets or as providing evidence for their presence, according to the point of view. In this case, however, an early eighteenth-century score, *GB-Lbl*, R.M. 24.E.7, fos. 1ʳ–39ᵛ, provides effective separate parts for two trumpets and timpani.[56] Their absence in R.M. 20.H.8 shows that they were not part of Purcell's original conception, though it is conceivable that the composer added them after hearing 'From harmony, from heavenly harmony'.

[53] Purcell, *Welcome Songs, Part 2*, ed. R. Vaughan Williams (The Works of Henry Purcell, 18; London, 1910), 80–120, 121–63.

[54] Downey, 'What Samuel Pepys Heard', 426.

[55] Pinnock and Wood, 'A Counterblast', 442.

[56] Edited in Purcell, *Welcome Songs, Part 2*, pp. vii–ix, x–xi.

With Purcell's 1690 birthday ode for Queen Mary, 'Arise, my muse', the fifth and final phase of the development of the Restoration court orchestra was reached. It is the first score of a court ode that clearly specifies and exploits a complete Baroque orchestra: it calls for two trumpets (to which, presumably, was added timpani), two oboes doubling recorders, strings, and continuo—which would probably have included at least one bassoon. For the first time the scores (which include the non-autograph portion of R.M. 20.H.8 and the late-seventeenth-century *GB-Ob*, MS Mus. C. 26) have separate staves for the trumpets and oboes, and the instruments are given elaborate obbligato parts. Its opening 'symphony' is one of the earliest examples of an Italianate trumpet sonata by an Englishman. 'Arise, my muse', together with the orchestral music in *Dioclesian*, first heard at Dorset Garden not much more than a month later, established a new pattern of orchestral writing in England, typified by brilliant, antiphonal writing for wind, brass, and strings. It was in tune with the martial spirit of the 1690s, and was still current when Handel arrived in London in 1710. By an extraordinary coincidence, 'Arise, my muse' was performed 150 years almost to the day after a Jewish string consort, the ancestor of the Twenty-four Violins, was taken on at Henry VIII's court.

The spring of 1690 also marks a turning-point in the fortunes of the royal music. In 1689 William and Mary initially accepted the thirty-four-man establishment of James II's Private Music and slightly expanded it: a list of those sworn in between 4 and 27 July contains forty names under the heading 'Musitians for the private Musick'.[57] But on 2 May 1690, two days after 'Arise, my muse' was performed, the king ordered the Lord Chamberlain to reduce the size of the Household: among others, the Grooms of the Chamber were reduced to ten, the messengers from forty to thirty, and the post of Physician of the Household was abolished. It was also ordered that the 'musicians be presently reduced to 24 and an instrument keeper', though provision was made 'for paying the rest for the time they have served'.[58]

The main casualties among the musicians were the five solo singers, the bass viol-player and the harpsichordist—James II's 'vocall part'. The harpsichordist, of course, was Henry Purcell, who was henceforth retained at court only as a member of the Chapel Royal, and, on paper at least, as 'tuner of the regals, organs, virginals, flutes and recorders'—the first post he received after ceasing to be a Chapel Royal choirboy at the age of fourteen.[59] There was probably nothing personal in the decision.

[57] Ashbee, *RECM*, ii. 23–4, 28.
[58] Shaw, *Calendar of Treasury Books*, ix, pt. 2, 609–10.
[59] Ashbee, *RECM*, i. 126, 132; ii. 56.

Purcell continued to write birthday odes for Queen Mary, and the solo singers sang in them. When the king went to Holland at the beginning of 1691 for the Congress of the Allies at The Hague, the lists of musicians accompanying him were drawn up according to the pre-1690 establishment, though scholars have argued whether Purcell actually went or not.[60] He was still called on by Queen Mary to serve as a court harpsichordist on an informal basis, if a charming anecdote printed by Hawkins can be believed:

The queen having a mind one afternoon to be entertained with music, sent to Mr. Gostling, then one of the chapel, and afterwards subdean of St. Paul's, to Henry Purcell and Mrs. Arabella Hunt, who had a very fine voice, and an admirable hand on the lute, with a request to attend her; they obeyed her commands; Mr. Gostling and Mrs. Hunt sang several compositions of Purcell, who accompanied them on the harpsichord; at length the queen beginning to grow tired, asked Mrs. Hunt if she could not sing the old Scots ballad 'Cold and Raw', Mrs. Hunt answered yes, and sang it to her lute. Purcell was all the while sitting at the harpsichord unemployed, and not a little nettled at the queen's preference of a vulgar ballad to his music; but seeing her majesty delighted with this tune, he determined that she should hear it upon another occasion: and accordingly in the next birthday song, viz. that for the year 1692, he composed an air to the words, 'May her bright example chace Vice in troops out of the land,' the bass whereof is the tune to Cold and Raw...[61]

Nevertheless, 1690 was a watershed in Purcell's career. Before, he was essentially a court composer, writing anthems for the Chapel Royal, court odes, and other secular music for the Private Music. After 1690 he was mainly a theatre composer: he wrote music for nearly fifty plays in little more than five years, and cannot have attended court on more than an occasional basis.

What of those who remained in the Private Music? The court orchestra stayed in existence, but its role in court life suffered from changing fashions, and from William III's musical taste—which, so far as it can be identified, favoured martial instruments. John Banister II evidently had the king in mind when he wrote of the oboe in *The Sprightly Companion* (London, 1695), the first English treatise for the instrument:[62]

besides its Inimitable charming Sweetness of Sound (when well play'd upon) it is also Majestical and Stately, and not much Inferiour to the Trumpet; and for that

    [60] Ibid., ii. 38–41; see also Zimmerman, *Henry Purcell*, 183–90, and the review by M. Tilmouth in *ML*, 48 (1967), 368–9; J. Buttrey, 'Did Purcell Go to Holland in 1691?', *MT*, 110 (1969), 929–31.
    [61] Hawkins, *A General History*, ii. 564; the piece in question is in 'Love's goddess sure was blind', ed. G. Shaw in *Birthday Odes for Queen Mary, Part 2* (The Works of Henry Purcell, 24; London, 1926), 19–21.
    [62] Warner, *An Annotated Bibliography*, 4–5; E. Halfpenny, 'A Seventeenth-Century Tutor for the Hautboy', *ML*, 40 (1949), 355–63.

reason the greatest Heroes of the Age (who sometimes despise Strung-Instruments) are infinitely pleased with This for its brave and sprightly Tone.

The Dutch hero of the age began to equip his regiments with oboe bands, and had them play at court balls instead of 'strung instruments'. By a warrant dated 23 November 1692 Thomas Chavile, John Ober, and 'four other hautboyes' were paid £3. 4s. 6d. each 'for playing twice at the practice and once at the Ball on his Majesty's Birthday at night, the 4 November last'; the same group was paid similar sums for balls on the king's birthday in 1693 and 1694.[63] Another group, from Princess Anne's household, played at 'two balls and a play at Whitehall' on the king's birthday in 1699.[64] This group included at least one trumpeter, John Shore, and bands of oboes and trumpets were also thought proper to accompany ambassadors abroad, according to a memorandum written by Sir Joseph Williamson in 1697:

Memorandum. That six hautboys with the trumpets will be more significant than twice the number of any other instruments in a consort.

That there may be either a whole set borrowed, which will be best, or otherwise one or two out of a set either from the Princess [Anne], Lord Romney, Lord Cutts, Lord Essex, or the Fusiliers.

These are in the King's pay.

That I know of two very useful men, that may be hired. They all play upon the flute [recorder], and most upon the violin.

That if there be separate tables [at a banquet], it cannot be done well without four trumpets.[65]

Trumpets and oboes played at the 1691 St Cecilia Day celebrations. 'Whilst the company is at table', Motteux wrote, 'the hautboys and trumpets play successively', and he added:

Mr. Showers hath taught the latter of late years to sound with all the softness imaginable; they plaid us some flat tunes made by Mr. Finger with a general applause, it being a thing formerly thought impossible upon an instrument designed for a sharp key.[66]

'Mr. Showers' is normally taken to be the young John Shore, but by 'hath taught the latter' Motteux seems to mean the players of the oboes and trumpets rather than the instruments themselves (throughout this study we have constantly encountered musicians named after the instruments they played). This in turn seems to mean that the individual concerned

---

[63] Ashbee, *RECM*, ii. 47, 52, 55.
[64] Ibid. 65, 69.
[65] *CSPD, William III 1 January–31 December 1697*, ed. W. J. Hardy (London, 1927), 10.
[66] Husk, *An Account*, 28–9.

was the Sergeant Trumpeter Matthias Shore, who by virtue of his office had jurisdiction over all trumpeters, at court or outside.

Also, it has been assumed too readily that Finger's 'flat tunes' were played by 'flat trumpets', the slide instruments that Purcell wrote for in *The Libertine* and the music for Queen Mary's funeral.[67] But English composers, like their contemporaries in Austria, also wrote for trumpets in 'flat' (i.e. minor) keys using notes available on the ordinary instrument. Vejvanovský and Biber wrote sonatas in G minor for the C trumpet, while Finger (who came from Olomouc in Moravia and may have been a pupil of Vejvanovský) included the trumpet in a C minor passage of his Sonata in C for trumpet or oboe, violin, and continuo, *GB-Lbl*, Add. MS 49599, no. 8.[68] The example of the Vejvanovský and Biber sonatas suggests that Finger could have written his 'flat tunes' in G minor for an ordinary trumpet band, exploiting the little-used bb' and cb'' harmonics on the C trumpet.

The subsequent history of the royal band need not detain us long. Superseded at court by oboe bands, overshadowed outside by London's burgeoning concert life, by 1700 it seems already to have become a part-time institution, with duties not far removed from those that were summarized in an article in *The Daily Graphic* for 20 July 1903:

Throughout the eighteenth century, besides their ordinary duties [court balls?], the band was employed, together with the gentlemen and children of the Chapel Royal, in the performance of odes, annually composed for their Majesties birthdays, for New Year's Day, and to celebrate victories, but since the discontinuance of the production of such odes their duties have been reduced to attendance on Royal Weddings, baptisms, State banquets, and State concerts.[69]

The twenty-four places of Charles II's violin band remained in existence in the royal household throughout the eighteenth century, though by the time William Parke published his memoirs in 1830, many of them were sinecures, held by non-musicians:

It [the band] consists of twenty-four musicians, attached to the King's household. The salary of each is forty pounds a year, and the wardrobe fees that they receive in lieu of clothes makes it up to fifty. The salary of the master of the band is two hundred pounds if he composes the odes only, the three hundred if he composes the odes and minuets. This establishment gave birth to the well-

[67] Purcell, *Dramatic Music, Part 2*, ed. A. Gray (The Works of Henry Purcell, 20; London, 1916), 55–63; *Fantasias and Miscellaneous Instrumental Music*, ed. Dart and Tilmouth, 97–8; for the slide trumpet, see A. Pinnock, 'A Wider Role for the Flat Trumpet', *GSJ*, 42 (1989), 105–111; C. Steele-Perkins, 'Practical Observations on Natural, Slide, and Flat Trumpets', ibid. 122–7; D. Rycroft, 'Flat Trumpet Facts and Figures', ibid. 134–42.

[68] Finger, *Sonata in C for Oboe/Trumpet in C (Descant Recorder), Violin, and Basso Continuo*, ed. P. Holman (London, 1979).

[69] J. Harley, 'Music at the English Court in the Eighteenth and Nineteenth Centuries', *ML*, 50 (1969), 341–2.

known burlesque song, 'Four and twenty fidlers all in a row'. It has by some been considered a grievance that a former Lord Chamberlain gave the places frequently to nobleman's butlers and valets, nay, in one instance even to a huntsman! But if the musical professors considered the appointment of the latter, who was a sort of horn player, derogatory to their art, the same nobleman amply soothed their wounded feelings by filling up a following vacancy with an alderman![70]

Despite several attempts at reform towards the end of Victoria's reign, the band went out of existence during the Great War; it gave its last performance at court in 1913, though its members were listed in the *British Imperial Calendar* until 1920. In the words of John Harley, 'rather than being formally dissolved, the royal band seems simply to have faded away'.[71]

[70] W. T. Parke, *Musical Memoirs* (London, 1830), ii. 129.
[71] Harley, 'Music at the English Court', 338.

Appendix A
Succession of Places for String-Players at the Early Tudor Court

(← = first heard of   → = last heard of   ··· = conjectural succession)

REBECS

1. Thomas Evans 1514–44→—Robert Woodward ('musician') 1553–99
2. John Savernake (also a flautist) 1518–57—James Foeinyart (flautist) 1558–
3. John Pyrot ←1525–9 ··· Thomas Bowman ('minstrel') 1530–40
4. ?William De Troches ←1537–61 and/or William Devayt ←1537–73 (latterly flautists)

'OLD VIOLS'

1. Matthew van Wilder 1516–17 (also a lutenist)
2. Peter van Wilder 1519–59 (also a singer)
3. Philip van Wilder ←1525–53 (principally a lutenist)
4. Hans Hossenet ←1525–54—Thomas Browne 1554–82 (latterly a violinist)
5. Hans Highorne ←1525–42—Thomas Kent 1549–55→ (also a singer)

Appendix B
Succession of Places for Court Violinists
1540–1642

(← = first heard of   → = last heard of)

ORIGINAL PLACES 1540

1. Albert of Venice 1540–59—Peter Lupo 1566–1608—Alexander Chesham 1608–25—James Johnson 1625–39—Ambrose Beeland 1639–42
2. Vincent of Venice 1540–55—Paul Galliardello 1555–63—Joseph Lupo 1563–1616—Norman Lesley/Lisle 1616–17 (also no. 20)—John Hopper 1617–42
3. Alexander of Milan 1540–4→—Mark Anthony Galliardello 1545–85—Caesar Galliardello 1585–1627—Nicholas Picart (from no. 25) 1627–42
4. John Maria of Cremona/Coimbra 1540–2—Paul of Venice 1543–4→—George Comey/of Cremona 1545–74—Ambrose Grasso/of Pavia 1578–82—Rowland Rubbish 1603–20—Leonard Mell 1620–41—Richard Comer/Comey? 1641–2
5. Ambrose de Almaliach/Lupo/of Milan 1540–91—William Warren 1594–1612—Horatio Lupo 1612–26—Davis/David Mell 1626–42
6. Romano of Milan 1540–2—Francis Kellim/of Venice 1543–88—Thomas Lupo I 1588–1619 (then to no. 14)—John Heydon 1619–38—Simon Nau 1638–42

NEW PLACE 1550

7. Innocent Comey/of Cremona 1550–1603—Anthony Comey 1603–29—Richard Dorney 1629–41—Simon Hopper 1641–2

REVIVAL OF HANS HOSSENET'S 'OLD VIOLS' PLACE 1554

8. Thomas Browne 1554–82—Daniel Farrant 1607–42

NEW PLACE 1598

9. Thomas Lupo II 1598–1642

NEW PLACE 1601

10. Alfonso Ferrabosco II 1601–28—Alfonso Ferrabosco III 1628–42

REVIVAL OF RICHARD WOODWARD'S PLACE 1608

11. Jeremy Hearne/Heron 1608–15 (then to no. 16)—John Friend 1615–42

REVIVAL OF ROBERT WOODWARD'S PLACE 1612

12. Thomas Warren 1612–42

NEW PLACE 1616

13. Adam Vallet 1616–25—John Woodington 1625–42

NEW PLACE 1619, COMPOSER TO THE VIOLINS

14. Thomas Lupo I (from no. 6) 1619–27—Stephen Nau 1627–42

NEW PLACE 1629, OBTAINED BY DIVIDING NO. 7

15. Robert Parker 1629–40—Robert Strong 1640–2

DANCING-MASTERS AND/OR SUPERNUMERARY VIOLINISTS

16. Thomas Cardell 1588–1618—Jeremy Hearne (from no. 11) 1618–40
17. Jacques Bochan/Cordier 1604–14, 1625–34→
18. Francis Cardell 1604–6 (place given to Thomas Cardell)
19. Thomas Giles 1605–15
20. Norman Lesley/Lisle 1606–25 (also no. 2)
21. Sebastian La/Le Pierre 1611–39→
22. 'Monsieur Confesse'/Nicholas Confais? ←1611–13→, 1625?–1635→
23. Stephen Nau 1626–7 (then with no. 14)
24. Francis de La France 1635–8→
25. Nicholas Picart 1625–7? (then to or with no. 3)
26. 'Mr Varenn'/Nicholas Varin? ←1640→

Appendix C
Succession of Places in the Twenty-four Violins
1660–1685

All years reckoned from 1 January. Square brackets indicate duplicate places. Dates in parentheses are for 'extraordinary' appointments without pay.

→ = last heard of * = Composer to the Violins

EXISTING VIOLIN BAND PLACES

1. Ambrose Beeland 1660–71—Edmund Flower 1671–1712
2. Edward Strong 1660–3—Jeffrey Banister (1662) 1663–84 ⋯ Richard Lewis 1685–96
3. John Strong 1660–75—Thomas Farmer (1671?) 1675–88
4. Henry Comer 1660–76—James Banister 1676–85
5. Davis/David Mell 1660–2—William Yockney 1662–8—John Myer (1662) 1668–83—Henry Heale 1683–1709
6. Richard Hudson 1660–8—Thomas Fitz (1664) 1668–77—[John Twist 1677–87]
7. Richard Dorney II 1660–81—John Lenton 1681–1719
8. William Gregory II 1660–85
9. Philip Beckett 1660–74—Henry Dove 1674–6—Giles Stevens 1676–85
10. Robert Strong 1660–85, 1689–94
*11. George Hudson 1660–72—Pelham Humfrey 1672–4—[Nicholas Staggins 1682–1700]

PLACE FROM THE FLUTE CONSORT

12. Thomas Blagrave 1660–88

PLACE FROM THE LUTES AND VOICES

13. William Howes 1660–76—Richard Tomlinson 1676–91

NEW PLACES 1660

14. Simon Hopper 1660–85
15. John Singleton 1660–85
16. Theophilus Fitz 1660–1708
17. William Young 1660–70—Nicholas Staggins 1670–1700
18. Henry Brockwell 1660–87
19. John Atkins/Atkinson 1660–71—Thomas Finell (1665) 1671–85
20. John Yockney 1660–2—Henry Smith 1662–70—Joseph Fashion I 1670–82 ··· Joseph Fashion II 1685–9
21. William Clayton 1660–97
22. Isaac Staggins 1660–84—Charles Staggins 1684–9
*23. Matthew Locke 1660–77—Henry Purcell 1677–89
24. John Banister I 1660–79—John Banister II 1679–1736
25. Walter Yockney 1660–5—Edmund Tanner (1663) 1665–71—John Twist 1671–87
26. William Saunders 1660–74—Thomas Greeting 1674–82—John Crouch 1682–9

PRIVATE MUSIC VIOLIN PLACES

27. Davis Mell 1660–2—John Banister 1662–79—Thomas Farmer 1679–88
28. Humphrey Madge 1660–79—Jeffrey Ayleworth 1679–87
29. Thomas Baltzar 1661–3—Thomas Fitz 1667–77—Edward Hooton 1677–1703

NEW PLACE 1672, OBTAINED BY DIVIDING NO. 11

*30. Thomas Purcell 1672–82—John Blow 1682–1708

NEW PLACE 1679, OBTAINED BY DIVIDING NO. 27

31. Robert King 1679–1728→

NEW PLACE 1680, BORROWED FROM THE PRIVATE MUSIC

32. William Hall 1680–1700

NEW PLACE 1681, OBTAINED BY DIVIDING NO. 7

33. John Abell 1681–9

NEW PLACES 1682, BORROWED FROM THE PRIVATE MUSIC

34. Nathaniel French 1682–9
35. John Goodwin 1682–93

EXTRAORDINARY PLACES

William Ayleworth 1662
William Pagett 1664
Richard Browne 1670
John Spicer 1670
William Kidwell 1671
Francis Garrard 1673

Appendix D
Some Sizes of English Court Violin Bands in
Performance 1607–1685

(* = years reckoned from 1 January → = an unknown period beginning on the date given)

Date*	Occasion	Size	Remarks
6 Jan. 1607	*Lord Hay's Masque*	12	9 violins, 3 lutes
1 Jan. 1611	masque: *Oberon*	16?	or 19, 21 with dancing-masters?
3 Feb. 1611	masque: *Love Freed from Ignorance and Folly*	14?	or 17 with dancing-masters?
14 Feb. 1613	*The Lords' Masque*	12?	or 16 with dancing-masters?
6 Jan. 1618	masque: *Pleasure Reconciled to Virtue*	'25 to 30'	
Aug.–Sept. 1621	masque: *The Gypsies Metamorphosed*	9?	
June 1625	trip to Canterbury to welcome Henrietta Maria	12	
23 Apr. 1627	Garter ceremonies at Windsor	12	same for 1628–33
12 Apr. 1631	waiting at court?	14	breakdown given: 4–2–3–2–4
3 Feb. 1634	masque: *The Triumph of Peace*	14	
23 Apr. 1638	Garter ceremonies at Windsor	15	same for 1639
5 July 1660	banquet at Guildhall	24	
5 Nov. 1660→	theatre band for Duke's Company	9?	
24 Apr. 1661	coronation banquet in Westminster Hall	24	

Date	Event	Number	Note
15 Aug. 1661	banquet at Inner Temple	20	
1662→	Chapel Royal at Whitehall	3	2 violins, bass viol
Sept. 1663	visit of queen to Bath	7	
1664→	theatre bands for King's Company	12	
1665→	theatre bands for Duke's Company	12	
31 Oct. 1666	rehearsal	9	music by Philip Beckett
4 Apr. 1667→	Chapel Royal at Whitehall	4	a roster of 3 groups
6 May 1670→	Chapel Royal at Whitehall	5	and 2 bass viols
May–July 1671	Chapel Royal at Windsor	4	a roster of 3 groups
Mar.–May 1672	Chapel Royal at Whitehall	6	20 listed—a roster of 4 groups?
Sept. 1673→	Chapel Royal at Whitehall	5?	'with Harpsicals and Theorbo's which accompany the voices'
Mar.–Apr. 1674	*The Tempest*, Duke's Company	24	12 violinists and 2 bass viols listed—a roster of 3 groups?
May–Sept. 1674	Chapel Royal at Windsor	4?	
Feb. 1675	masque: *Calisto*	21	orchestra 1: 12 violins, 2 oboes, 2 harpsichords, 2 theorboes, 3 bass viols
		26	orchestra 2: 20 violins, 2 oboes, 4 guitars
1 Jan. 1685	court ode	about 12?	Blow's 'How does the new-born infant year rejoice?'

Bibliography

BOOKS AND ARTICLES

AGRICOLA, M., *Musica instrumentalis deudsch* (Wittenberg, 1528; 2nd edn., 1529; repr. 1969; 6th edn., 1545); quasi-facsimile in R. Eitner (ed.), Publikationen älterer praktischer und theoretischer Musikwerke, 20 (Leipzig, 1896).

AKRIGG, G. P. V., *Jacobean Pageant; or, The Court of James I* (London, 1962).

ALLSOP, P., 'Problems of Ascription in the Roman *Simfonia* of the Late Seventeenth Century: Colista and Lonati', *MR* 50 (1989), 34–44.

—— 'The Role of the Stringed Bass as a Continuo Instrument in Italian Seventeenth-Century Instrumental Music', *Chelys*, 8 (1978–9), 31–7.

ANGLÉS, H., 'Un manuscrit inconnu avec polyphonie du xve siècle conservé à la cathédrale de Ségovie (Espagne)', *AcM* 8 (1936), 6–17.

ANGLO, S., 'The Court Festivals of Henry VII: A Study Based upon the Account Books of John Heron, Treasurer of the Chamber', *Bulletin of the John Rylands Library*, 43 (1960), 12–45.

ANTHONY, J. R., *French Baroque Music from Beaujoyeulx to Rameau* (2nd edn., London, 1978); trans. B. Vierne as *La Musique en France à l'époque baroque* (Paris, 1981).

ANZELEWSKY, F., *Dürer* (London, 1980).

ARKWRIGHT, G. E. P., 'Sebastian Westcote', *MA* 4 (1912–13), 187–9.

ARMYTAGE, G. J. (ed.), *Allegations for Marriage Licences Issued by the Bishop of London, 1611 to 1828* (Harleian Society Publications, 26; London, 1887).

ARNOLD, D., *Giovanni Gabrieli and the Music of the Venetian High Renaissance* (London, 1979).

ASHBEE, A., 'Lowe, Jenkins, and Merro', *ML* 48 (1967), 310–11.

—— 'Towards the Chronology and Grouping of some Airs by John Jenkins', *ML* 55 (1974), 30–44.

—— 'Instrumental Music from the Library of John Browne (1608–1691), Clerk of the Parliaments', *ML* 58 (1977), 43–59.

—— 'A Not Unapt Scholar: Bulstrode Whitelocke (1605–1675)', *Chelys*, 11 (1982), 24–31.

—— (ed.), *Lists of Payments to the King's Musick in the Reign of Charles II (1660–1685)* (Snodland, 1981).

—— (ed.), *Records of English Court Music*, i: *1660–1685* (Snodland, 1986).

—— (ed.), *Records of English Court Music*, ii: *1685–1714* (Snodland, 1987).

—— (ed.), *Records of English Court Music*, iii: *1625–1649* (Snodland, 1988).

—— (ed.), *Records of English Court Music*, iv: *1603–1625* (Snodland, 1991).

—— (ed.), *Records of English Court Music*, v: *1625–1714* (Aldershot, 1991).

—— (ed.), *Records of English Court Music*, vi: *1558–1603* (Aldershot, 1992).

—— *The Harmonious Musick of John Jenkins*, i: *The Fantasias for Viols* (Surbiton, 1992).

ASHLEY, M., *England in the Seventeenth Century (1603–1714)* (The Pelican History of England, 6; (3rd edn., Harmondsworth, 1961).

ASHMOLE, E., 'A Brief Narrative of the Solemn Rites and Ceremonies Performed upon the Day of the Coronation of our Sovereign Lord King Charles II', appended to the *GB-Lge* copy of J. Ogilby, *His Majesties Entertainments Passing through the City of London to his Coronation* (London, 1662).

ASPLAND, A. (ed.), *Triumph of the Emperor Maximilian I* [commentary volume] (London, 1875).

ATLAS, A., 'On the Identity of some Musicians at the Brescian Court of Pandolfo III Malatesta', *CMc* 36 (1983), 14–16.

AYLMER, G. E., *The State's Servants: The Civil Service of the English Republic 1649–1660* (London, 1973).

—— *The King's Servants: The Civil Service of Charles I 1625–1642* (2nd edn., London, 1974).

B., W. G., '"The Science of a Mynstrell": How it was Taught in Essex in 1558', *Essex Review*, 49 (1940), 107–10.

BACHRACH, A. G. H., and COLLMER, R. G. (eds.), *Lodewijck Huygens: The English Journal 1651–1652* (Leiden and London, 1982).

BAINES, A., 'James Talbot's Manuscript (Christ Church Library, Music MS 1187). I: Wind Instruments', *GSJ* 1 (1948), 9–26.

—— 'Fifteenth-Century Instruments in Tinctoris's *De Inventione et Usu Musicae*', *GSJ* 3 (1950), 19–26.

BALDWIN, D., *The Chapel Royal, Ancient and Modern* (London, 1990).

BALDWIN, O., and WILSON, T., 'An English *Calisto*', *MT* 112 (1971), 651–3.

BALDWIN, T. W., *The Organization and Personnel of the Shakespearean Company* (New York, 1961).

BANG, W., and BROTANEK, R. (eds.), *The King and Queenes Entertainement at Richmond* (Materialen zur Kunde des älteren englischen Dramas, 2; Louvain and Leipzig, 1903; repr. 1965).

[BANISTER, J.], *Musick; or, A Parley of Instruments, the First Part* (London, 1676).

BANNERMAN, W. B. (ed.), *The Registers of St Olave, Hart Street, London, 1563–1700* (Harleian Society Publications, registers, 46; London, 1916).

BASHFORD, C., 'Perrin and Cambert's *Ariane, ou le Mariage de Bacchus* Re-examined', *ML* 72 (1991), 1–26.

BATCHELOR, A., 'Daniel Bacheler: The Right Perfect Musician', *The Lute*, 28 (1988), 3–12.

BEAUJOYEUX, B. de, *Balet comique de la Royne* (Paris, 1582; repr. 1965).

BEAUMONT, C. W. (ed.), *Orchesography . . . by Thoinot Arbeau* (London, 1925).

BELLINGHAM, B., 'The Musical Circle of Anthony Wood in Oxford during the Commonwealth and Restoration', *JVGSA* 19 (1982), 6–70.

BENNETT, J., and WILLETTS, P., 'Richard Mico', *Chelys*, 7 (1977), 24–46.

BENTLEY, G. E., *The Jacobean and Caroline Stage*, 7 vols. (Oxford, 1941–68).

BERGENROTH, G. A. (ed.), *Calendar of Letters, Despatches, and State Papers, Relating to the Negotiations between England and Spain, Preserved at the Archives at Simancas and Elsewhere*, ii (London, 1866).

BERNSTEIN, J., 'Philip van Wilder and the Netherlandish Chanson in England', *MD* 33 (1979), 55–75.

BILLINGE, M., and SHALJEAN, B., 'The Dalway or Fitzgerald Harp (1621)', *EM* 15 (1987), 175–87.

BIRCH, T., *The Life of Henry Prince of Wales, Eldest Son of King James I* (London, 1760).

BLEZZARD, J., 'The Lumley Books', *MT* 112 (1971), 128–30.

BONNET, J., and BOURDELET, P., *Histoire de la musique et de ses effets* (Paris, 1715; repr. Amsterdam, 1725; repr. 1966).

BONTA, S., 'From Violone to Violoncello: A Question of Strings?', *JAMIS* 3 (1977), 64–99.

—— 'Terminology for the Bass Violin in Seventeenth-Century Italy', *JAMIS* 4 (1978), 5–42.

—— 'Catline Strings Revisited', *JAMIS* 14 (1988), 38–60.

—— 'The Use of Instruments in Sacred Music in Italy, 1560–1700', *EM* 18 (1990), 519–35.

BORGIR, T., 'The Performance of the Basso Continuo in Seventeenth-Century Italian Music', Ph.D. diss. (University of California, Berkeley, 1971).

BOSWELL, E., *The Restoration Court Stage (1660–1702)* (Cambridge, Mass., 1932; repr. 1960).

Bouwstenen voor een geschiedenis der toonkunst in de Nederlanden, i (Amsterdam, 1965).

BOWERS, F. (ed.), *The Dramatic Works in the Beaumont and Fletcher Canon*, i (Cambridge, 1966).

BOWERS, R., 'The Vocal Scoring, Choral Balance, and Performing Pitch of Latin Church Polyphony in England, *c.*1500–58', *JRMA* 112 (1987), 38–76.

BOWLES, E. A., '*Haut* and *Bas*: The Grouping of Musical Instruments in the Middle Ages', *MD* 8 (1954), 115–40.

—— 'Iconography as a Tool for Examining the Loud Consort in the Fifteenth Century', *JAMIS* 3 (1977), 100–13.

BOYAN, P., and LAMB, G. R., *Francis Tregian, Cornish Recusant* (London, 1955).

BOYD, M., and RAYSON, J., '*The Gentleman's Diversion*: John Lenton and the First Violin Tutor', *EM* 10 (1982), 329–32.

BOYD, M. C., *Elizabethan Music and Music Criticism* (2nd edn., Philadelphia, 1962).

BOYDELL, B., *The Crumhorn and other Renaissance Windcap Instruments* (Buren, 1982).

BOYDEN, D., 'Monteverdi's *Violini Piccoli alla Francese* and *Viole da Brazzo*', *AnnM* 6 (1958–63), 388–401.

—— 'The Tenor Violin: Myth, Mystery, or Misnomer?', in W. Gerstenberg, J. La Rue, and W. Rehm (eds.), *Festschrift Otto Erich Deutsch* (Kassel, 1963), 273–9.

—— *The History of Violin Playing from its Origins to 1761* (London, 1965).

BRAUN, W., *Britannia Abundans: Deutsch-englische Musikbeziehungen zur Shakespearezeit* (Tutzing, 1977).

BRENNECKE, E., 'Dryden's Odes and Draghi's Music', *Proceedings of the Modern Language Association of America*, 49 (1934), 1–36.

—— 'The Entertainment at Elvetham, 1591', in J. H. Long (ed.), *Music in Renaissance Drama* (Lexington, Ky., 1986), 32–56.

BRETT, P., 'The English Consort Song, 1570–1625', *PRMA* 88 (1961–2), 73–88.

BREWER, J. S. (ed.), *Letters and Papers, Foreign and Domestic, of the Reign of Henry VIII*, i, part 3, *1509–1513* (London, 1920; repr. 1965); i, part 2, *1513–1514* (London, 1864; repr. 1965).

BRIDGE, J. C., 'A Great English Choir Trainer, Captain Henry Cooke', *MA* 2 (1910–11), 61–79.

BROSSARD, Y, DE (ed.), *Musiciens de Paris 1535–1792: Actes d'état d'après le fichier Laborde de la Bibliothèque Nationale* (La Vie musicale en France sous les rois Bourbons, 11; Paris, 1965).

BROWN, H. M., *Instrumental Music Printed before 1600: A Bibliography* (Cambridge, Mass., 1965).

—— *Sixteenth-Century Instrumentation: The Music for the Florentine Intermedii* (MSD, 30; Rome, 1973).

—— 'Instruments and Voices in the Fifteenth-Century Chanson', in J. W. Grubbs (ed.), *Current Thought in Musicology* (Austin, Tex., 1976), 89–137.

—— 'Notes (and Transposing Notes) on the Viol in the Early Sixteenth Century', in I. Fenlon (ed.), *Music in Mediaeval and Early Modern Europe: Patronage, Sources, and Texts* (Cambridge, 1981), 61–78.

—— 'St. Augustine, Lady Music, and the Gittern in Fourteenth-Century Italy', *MD* 38 (1984), 25–65.

—— 'Notes (and Transposing Notes) on the Transverse Flute in the Early Sixteenth Century', *JAMIS* 12 (1986), 5–39.

—— 'The Trecento Fiddle and its Bridges', *EM* 17 (1989), 308–29.

BROWN, R. (ed.), *Four Years at the Court of Henry VIII* (London, 1854).

—— and CAVENDISH-BENTINCK, G. (eds.), *Calendar of State Papers and Manuscripts, Relating to English Affairs Existing in the Archives and Collections of Venice, and in other Libraries of Northern Italy*, vii: *1558–1580* (London, 1890).

BRYANT, A. (ed.), *The Letters, Speeches, and Declarations of King Charles II* (London, 1932).

BUCKLAND, N., 'Styll Shalmes', *FoMRHI Quarterly*, 19 (Apr. 1980), 42–57.

—— 'Further to the "Styll Shalmes"', *FoMRHI Quarterly*, 25 (Oct. 1981), 24–5.

BULLOCK-DAVIES, C., *A Register of Royal and Baronial Domestic Minstrels 1272–1327* (Woodbridge and Dover, NH, 1986).

BÜLOW, G. VON, 'Diary of the Journey of Philip Julius, Duke of Stettin-Pomerania, through England in the Year 1602', *Transactions of the Royal Historical Society*, NS, 6 (1892), 1–67.

BURKE, A. M. (ed.), *Memorials of St Margarets Church, Westminster: The Parish Registers 1539–1660* (London, 1914).

BURNEY, C., *A General History of Music* (London, 1776–89), ed. F. Mercer (London, 1935; repr. 1957).

BUTLER, C., *The Principles of Musik in Singing and Setting* (London, 1636; repr. 1970).

BUTLER, S., *Characters*, ed. C. W. Daves (Cleveland and London, 1970).

BUTTREY, J., 'Did Purcell Go to Holland in 1691?', *MT* 110 (1969), 929–31.

BUXTON, J., *Elizabethan Taste* (London, 1963; repr. 1983).

CALDWELL, J., *English Keyboard Music before the Nineteenth Century* (Oxford, 1973).

—— 'Two Polyphonic *Istampite* from the Fourteenth Century', *EM* 18 (1990), 371–80.

Calendar of the Patent Rolls Preserved in the Public Record Office, Edward VI, iii: *1549–1551* (London, 1925).

CAMPION, T., *Works*, ed. W. R. Davis (London, 1969).

CARTER, T., 'A Florentine Wedding of 1608', *AcM* 55 (1983), 89–107.

CHALLENOR, T., and SMITH, C. (eds.), *The Parish Registers of Richmond, Surrey*, i (London, 1903).

CHAMBERS, E. K., *The Elizabethan Stage*, 4 vols. (Oxford, 1923; repr. 1974).

CHAMPERNOWNE, C. E., 'The Champernowne Family', unpublished typescript in Devon County Library, Tiverton branch.

CHAN, M., and KASSLER J. C. (eds.), *Roger North's The Musicall Grammarian 1728* (Cambridge, 1990).

'The Chapel Royal Anthem Book of 1635', *MA* 2 (1910–11), 108–13.

CHAPPELL, W., *Popular Music of the Olden Time* (London, 1859; repr. 1965).

CHARLTON, J., *The Banqueting House, Whitehall* (London, 1964).

CHARTERIS, R., 'A Rediscovered Source of English Consort Music', *Chelys*, 5 (1973–4), 3–6.

—— 'Autographs of John Coprario', *ML* 56 (1975), 41–6.

—— *John Coprario: A Thematic Catalogue of his Music, with a Biographical Introduction* (New York, 1977).

—— 'Manuscript Additions of Music by John Dowland and his Contemporaries in Two Sixteenth-Century Prints', *The Consort*, 37 (1981), 399–401.

—— 'New Information about the Life of Alfonso Ferrabosco the Elder (1543–1588)', *RMARC* 17 (1981), 97–114.

—— *Alfonso Ferrabosco the Elder (1543–88): A Thematic Catalogue of his Music with a Biographical Calendar* (New York, 1984).

CHEVERTON, I., 'Captain Henry Cooke (*c*.1616–72): The Beginnings of a Reappraisal', *Soundings*, 9 (1982), 74–86.

CHRISTIE, W. D. (ed.), *Letters Addressed from London to Sir Joseph Williamson while Plenipotentiary at the Congress of Cologne in the Years 1673 and 1674* (Camden Society Publications, NS, 8; London, 1874).

CLARK, J. B., 'A Re-emerged Seventeenth-Century Organ Accompaniment Book', *ML* (1966), 149–52.

CLARK, J. K., *Goodwin Wharton* (Oxford, 1984).

CLIFFORD, J., *The Divine Services and Anthems usually Sung in his Majestie's Chappel* (2nd edn., London, 1664).

CLODE, C. M., *The Early History of the Guild of Merchant Taylors*, 2 vols. (London, 1888).

CLOPPER, L. M. (ed.), *Records of Early English Drama, Chester* (Toronto, Buffalo, and London, 1979).

CLOSSON, E., *La Facture des instruments de musique en Belgique* (Brussels, 1935).

COLE, E., 'In Search of Francis Tregian', *ML* 33 (1952), 28–32.

—— 'Seven Problems of the Fitzwilliam Virginal Book', *PRMA* 79 (1952–3), 51–64.

—— 'L'Anthologie de madrigaux et de musique instrumentale pour ensembles de Francis Tregian', in J. Jacquot (ed.), *La Musique instrumentale de la Renaissance* (Paris, 1954), 115–26.

The Collection of Autograph Letters and Historical Documents Formed by Alfred Morrison, 2nd ser., *1882–1893*, *The Bulstrode Papers*, i: *1667–1675* (London, 1895).

A Collection of Ordinances and Regulations for the Government of the Royal Household (Society of Antiquaries; London, 1790).

COLLIER, J. P., *Memoirs of Edward Alleyn* (London, 1841).

COLVIN, H. M. (ed.), *The History of the King's Works*, 6 vols. (London, 1963–82).

CORDERO DI PAMPARATO, S., 'Emanuele Filiberto di Savoia, protettore dei musici', *RMI* 34 (1927), 229–47, 555–78; *RMI* 35 (1928), 29–49.

COTGRAVE, R., *Dictionarie of the French and English Tongues* (London, 1611; repr. 1950).

CRAIG-MCFEELY, J., 'A Can of Worms: Lord Herbert of Cherbury's Lute Book', *The Lute*, 31 (1991), 20–48.

CRANE, F., *Materials for the Study of the Fifteenth-Century Basse Dance* (Brooklyn, 1968).

CREETH, E. (ed.), *Tudor Plays: An Anthology of Early English Drama* (New York, 1966; repr. 1972).

CROWNE, J., *The Dramatic Works*, ed. J. Maidment and W. H. Logan, 4 vols. (Edinburgh, 1872–4).

CRUM, M., 'Early Lists of the Oxford Music School Collection', *ML* 48 (1967), 23–34.

—— 'The Consort Music from Kirtling, Bought for the Oxford Music School from Anthony Wood, 1667', *Chelys*, 4 (1972), 3–10.

CSPD, Charles I, Addenda: March 1625–January 1649, ed. W. D. Hamilton and D. C. Lomas (London, 1897).

—— *Charles II, 1663–1664*, ed. M. A. Everett Green (London, 1862); *1664–1665* (London, 1863); *1666–1667* (London, 1864); *1667* (London, 1866); *November 1667 to September 1668* (London, 1893); *1670, with Addenda 1660 to 1670* (London, 1895); *March 1st 1675 to February 29th 1676*, ed. F. H. B. Daniell (London, 1907); *January 1st 1679 to August 31st 1680* (London, 1915); *Charles II: Addenda*, ed. F. H. B. Daniell and F. Bickley (London, 1939).

—— *James II, February–December 1685*, ed. E. K. Timings (London, 1960).

—— *William III, 1 January–31 December 1697*, ed. W. J. Hardy (London, 1927).

CUDDY, N., 'The Revival of the Entourage: The Bedchamber of James I, 1603–1625', in D. Starkey (ed.), *The English Court, from the Wars of the Roses to the Civil War* (London, 1987), 173–225.

CUNNINGHAM, C., 'Ensemble Dances in Early Sixteenth-Century Italy: Relationships with *Villotte* and Franco-Flemish *Danceries*', *MD* 34 (1980), 160–203.

CURTIS, A., *Sweelinck's Keyboard Music* (Leiden and Oxford, 1969).

CUTTS, J. P., 'Jacobean Masque and Stage Music', *ML* 35 (1954), 110–25.

—— 'New Findings with Regard to the 1624 Protection List', *Shakespeare Survey*, 19 (1966), 101–7.

CYR, M., '*Basses* and *Basse Continue* in the Orchestra of the Paris *Opéra*, 1700–1764', *EM* 10 (1982), 155–70.

DANCHIN, P., 'The Foundation of the Royal Academy of Music in 1674 and Pierre Perrin's *Ariane*', *Theatre Survey*, 25 (1984), 55–67.

—— (ed.), *The Prologues and Epilogues of the Restoration, 1660–1700*, I, ii (Nancy, 1981).

DANIEL, S., *The Complete Works in Verse and Prose*, ed. A. B. Grosart, 5 vols. (London, 1885).

DANN, E., 'Martin Agricola and the Early Three-Stringed Fiddles', in E. Strainchamps, M. R. Maniates, and C. Hatch (eds.), *Music and Civilization: Essays in Honor of Paul Henry Lang* (New York and London, 1984), 232–42.

DANNER, P., 'Before Petrucci: The Lute in the Fifteenth Century', *JLSA* 5 (1972), 4–17.

DART, T., 'Morley's Consort Lessons of 1599', *PRMA* 74 (1947–8), 1–9.

—— 'The Printed Fantasies of Orlando Gibbons', *ML* 37 (1956), 342–9.

—— 'The Repertory of the Royal Wind Music', *GSJ* 11 (1958), 70–7.

—— 'Purcell's Chamber Music', *PRMA* 85 (1958–9), 81–93.

—— 'The Viols', in A. Baines (ed.), *Musical Instruments through the Ages* (Harmondsworth, 1961), 184–90.

—— 'Purcell and Bull', *MT* 104 (1963), 30–1.

—— 'Two New Documents Relating to the Royal Music, 1584–1605', *ML* 45 (1964), 16–21.

DASENT, J. R. (ed.), *Acts of the Privy Council of England*, NS, iii: *1550–1552* (London, 1891); viii: *1571–1575* (London, 1894).

DAVIES, J., *Orchestra; or, a Poeme of Dauncyinge* (London, 1594).

DAY, C. L., and BOSWELL MURRIE, E., *English Song Books 1651–1702: A Bibliography* (London, 1940).

DEKKER, T., *Dramatic Works*, ed. F. Bowers, i (Cambridge, 1962); iii (Cambridge, 1958).

DENNISON, P., *Pelham Humfrey* (Oxford, 1986).

DIJCK, L. VAN, and KOOPMAN, T. (eds.), *The Harpsichord in Dutch Art before 1800 (Het klavicimbel in de Nederlandse kunst tot 1800)* (Amsterdam and Zutphen, 1987).

DISERTORI, B., 'Pratica e tecnica della lira da braccio', *RMI* 45 (1941), 150–75.

DIXON, G., *Carissimi* (Oxford, 1986).

—— 'Continuo Scoring in the Early Baroque: The Role of Bowed Bass Instruments', *Chelys*, 15 (1986), 38–53.

DODD, G., 'Matters Arising from Examination of Lyra Viol Manuscripts', *Chelys*, 9 (1980), 23–7, and the list in *Chelys*, 10 (1981), 40–1.

—— (ed.), *The Viola da Gamba Society of Great Britain Thematic Index of Music for Viols* (London, 1980–9).

DOE, P., 'The Emergence of the In Nomine: Some Notes and Queries on the Work of Tudor Church Musicians', in E. Olleson (ed.), *Modern Musical*

Scholarship (Stocksfield, 1980), 79–82.

DONINGTON, R., 'James Talbot's Manuscript: Bowed Strings', *Chelys*, 6 (1975–6), 43–60.

DOWNES, J., *Roscius Anglicanus*, ed. J. Milhous and R. D. Hume (London, 1987).

DOWNEY, P., 'The Renaissance Slide Trumpet: Fact or Fiction?', *EM* 12 (1984), 26–33.

—— 'What Samuel Pepys Heard on 3 February 1661: English Trumpet Style under the Later Stuart Monarchs', *EM* 18 (1990), 417–28.

DRYDEN, J., *Works*, ii: *Poems 1681–1684*, ed. H. T. Swedenberg and V. A. Dearing; xv: *Plays: Albion and Albanius, Don Sebastian, Amphitryon*, ed. E. Milner and G. R. Guffey (Berkeley, Calif., 1972, 1976).

DUFFETT, T., *Beauty's Triumph* (London, 1676).

DUFFIN, R. W., 'The *Trompette des Menestrels* in the Fifteenth-Century *Alta Capella*', *EM* 17 (1989), 397–402.

DUFFY, J., *The Songs and Motets of Alfonso Ferrabosco the Younger (1575–1628)* (Ann Arbor, Mich., 1979–80).

DUGDALE, G. S., *Whitehall through the Centuries* (London, 1950).

DUNLOP, I., *Palaces and Progresses of Elizabeth I* (London, 1962).

EARLE, J., *Micro-Cosmographie*, ed. E. Arber (Westminster, 1904).

EDMOND, M., 'Limners and Picturemakers: New Light on the Lives of Miniaturists and Large-Scale Portrait Painters Working in London in the Sixteenth and Seventeenth Centuries', *The Forty-seventh Volume of the Walpole Society* (1978–80), 60–242.

—— *Hilliard and Oliver: The Lives and Works of two Great Miniaturists* (London, 1983).

EDWARDS, W., 'The Performance of Ensemble Music in Elizabethan England', *PRMA* 97 (1970–1), 113–23.

—— 'The Sources of Elizabethan Consort Music', Ph.D. thesis (Cambridge, 1974).

—— 'The Walsingham Consort Books', *ML* 55 (1974), 209–14.

—— 'The Instrumental Music of "Henry VIII's Manuscript" ', *The Consort*, 34 (1978), 274–82.

EGERTON, C., 'The Horoscope of Signor Angelo Notari (1566–1663)', *The Lute*, 28 (1988), 13–18.

EITNER, R., *Biographisch-bibliographisches Quellen-Lexicon der Musiker und Musikgelehrten* (Leipzig, 1900–4; repr. 1959).

ELSNER, E., 'Untersuchung der instrumentalen Besetzungspraxis der weltlichen Musik im 16. Jahrhundert in Italien', Ph.D. diss. (Berlin, 1935).

ELTON, G. R., *The Tudor Revolution in Government* (Cambridge, 1953; repr. 1979).

ETHEREGE, G., *The Dramatic Works*, ed. H. F. B. Brett-Smith (Oxford, 1927).

EVELYN, J., *The Diary of John Evelyn*, ed. E. S. de Beer (one-volume edn., London, 1959).

EWARD, S., *No Fine but a Glass of Wine: Cathedral Life at Gloucester in Stuart Times* (Wilton, 1985).

FALLOWS, D., 'Fifteenth-Century Tablatures for Plucked Instruments: A Summary, a Revision, and a Suggestion', *LSJ* 19 (1977), 7–33.

—— 'Specific Information on the Ensembles for Composed Polyphony, 1400–1474', in S. Boorman (ed.), *Studies in the Performance of Late Medieval Music* (Cambridge, 1983), 109–44.

FENLON, I., *Music and Patronage in Sixteenth-Century Mantua* (Cambridge, 1980).

—— (ed.), *The Renaissance* (Man and Music; London, 1989).

—— and MILSOM, J., ' "Ruled Paper Imprinted": Music Paper and Patents in Sixteenth-Century England', *JAMS* 37 (1984), 139–63.

FERNANDEZ, M. P. and P. C., 'Davis Mell, Musician and Clockmaker, and an Analysis of the Clockmaking Trade in Seventeenth-Century London', *Antiquarian Horology*, 16 (1987), 602–17.

FEUILLERAT, A. (ed.), *Documents Relating to the Office of the Revels in the Time of Queen Elizabeth* (Materialien zur Kunde des älteren englischen Dramas, 21; Louvain, 1908; repr. 1963).

FIELD, C. D. S., 'Matthew Locke and the Consort Suite', *ML* 51 (1970), 15–25.

FISKE, R., *English Theatre Music in the Eighteenth Century* (2nd edn., Oxford, 1986).

FITCH, M. (ed.), *Index to Administrations in the Perogative Court of Canterbury*, v: *1609–1619* (The Index Library, British Record Society, 83; London, 1968).

—— ed., *Testamentary Records in the Archdeaconry Court of London*, i: *(1363)–1649* (The Index Library, British Record Society, 89; London, 1979).

FLOOD, W. H. G., 'Dublin City Music from 1456 to 1789', *SIMG* 11 (1909–10), 33–42.

—— 'Master Sebastian of Paul's', *MA* 3 (1911–12), 149–57.

—— 'Quelques précisions nouvelles sur Cambert et Grabu à Londres', *ReM* 9 (1927–8), 351–61.

—— (ed.), 'Entries Relating to Music in the English Patent Rolls of the Fifteenth Century', *MA* 4 (1912–13), 225–35.

FOAKES, R. A., and RICKERT, R. T. (eds.), *Henslowe's Diary* (Cambridge, 1961).

FORD, R., 'The Filmer Manuscripts, a Handlist', *Notes*, 34 (1978), 814–25.

FORTUNE, N., 'Continuo Instruments in Italian Monodies', *GSJ* 6 (1953), 10–13.

—— 'A New Purcell Source', *MR* 25 (1964), 109–13.

—— 'Music Manuscripts of John Browne (1608–91), and from Stanford Hall, Leicestershire', in I. Bent (ed.), *Source Materials and the Interpretation of Music: A Memorial Volume to Thurston Dart* (London, 1981), 155–68.

—— and ZIMMERMAN, F. B., 'Purcell's Autographs', in I. Holst (ed.), *Henry Purcell 1659–1695: Essays on his Music* (London, 1959), 106–21.

FREEMAN, A., 'Organs Built for the Royal Palace of Whitehall', *MT* 52 (1911), 521–3, 585–7, 720–1.

—— *Father Smith*, rev. J. Rowntree (2nd edn., London, 1977).

FULLER, D., 'The Jonsonian Masque and its Music', *ML* 54 (1973), 440–52.

GAI, V., *Gli strumenti musicali della corte medicea e il museo del Conservatorio "Luigi Cherubini" di Firenze* (Florence, 1969).

GAIRDNER, J., and BRODIE, R. H. (eds.), *Letters and Papers, Foreign and Domestic, of the Reign of Henry VIII*, xiv, part 1: *January–July 1539* (London, 1894; repr. 1965); xvi: *September 1540–December 1541* (London, 1898).

GALLOWAY, D. (ed.), *Records of Early English Drama, Norwich 1540–1642*

GALLOWAY, D. (ed.), *Records of Early English Drama, Norwich 1540–1642* (Toronto, Buffalo, and London, 1984).

GALPIN, F. W., *Old English Instruments of Music*, rev. T. Dart (4th edn., London, 1965).

GANASSI, S. DI, *Lettione seconda* (Venice, 1543; repr. 1970).

GAYANGOS, P. DE (ed.), *Calendar of Letters, Despatches, and State Papers, Relating to the Negotiations between England and Spain, Preserved at the Archives of Simancas, Vienna, Brussels, and Elsewhere*, vi, part 1 (London, 1890).

GEISER, B., *Studien zur Frühgeschichte der Violine* (Berne and Stuttgart, 1974).

GERLE, H., *Musica teusch* (Nuremberg, 1532; repr. 1977).

GILL, DOMINIC (ed.), *The Book of the Violin* (Oxford, 1984).

—— DONALD, 'Vihuelas, Violas, and the Spanish Guitar', *EM* 9 (1981), 455–62.

—— 'Plucked Strings and Pitch', *EM* 10 (1982), 217–18.

GIROUARD, M., *Life in the English Country House* (New Haven, Conn., 1978; repr. 1980).

GISKES, J. H., 'Cornelis Kleynman (1626–1686), Vioolmaker te Amsterdam', *Amstelodamum*, 74 (1987), 11–16.

GIUSTINIANI, V., *Discorso sopra la Musica (1628)*, trans. C. MacClintock (MSD 9; Rome, 1962).

GODMAN, S., 'Greeting's "Pleasant Companion for the Flagelet"', *MMR* 86 (1956), 20–6.

GODT, I., 'A Major Angel Concert in Ferrara', *Musei ferraresi, bollettino annuale*, 12 (1982 [actually 1984]), 209–17.

GODWIN, J., 'The Renaissance Flute', *The Consort*, 28 (1972), 70–81.

GOODWIN, P., 'Venice Preserved', *Philharmonia Year Book* (London, 1986–7), 59–63.

GOUK, P., 'Music in Seventeenth-Century Oxford', *History of the University of Oxford, iv: 1603–1688* (forthcoming).

GREG, W. (ed.), *Henslowe's Papers, being Documents Supplementary to Henslowe's Diary* (London, 1907).

GREISSMANN, F., 'Die Musiker am Hofe des Fürsten Ernst', unpublished paper deposited at the Staatsarchiv, Bückeburg.

GRIEVE, H. E. P. (ed.), *Examples of English Handwriting 1150–1750* ([Chelmsford], 1954).

GRIJP, L. P., 'The Ensemble Music of Nicolaes Vallet', in L. P. Grijp and W. Mook (eds.), *Proceedings of the International Lute Symposium, Utrecht 1986* (Utrecht, 1988), 64–85.

GROBE, E. P., 'S. Bre., French Librettist at the Court of Charles II', *Theatre Notebook*, 9 (1954), 20–1.

Guide to the Contents of the Public Record Office, 3 vols. (London, 1963, 1968).

GURR, A., *The Shakespearean Stage 1574–1642* (Cambridge, 1970).

GWYNN, D., 'Organ Pitch in Seventeenth-Century England', *BIOS Journal*, 9 (1985), 65–78.

HAAR, J., 'Munich at the Time of Orlande de Lassus', in I. Fenlon (ed.), *The Renaissance* (Man and Music; London, 1989), 243–62.

HAJDECKI, A., *Die italienische Lira da Braccio* (Mostar, 1892; repr. 1965).

HALFPENNY, E., 'The English Debut of the French Hautboy', *MMR* 79 (1949), 149–53.

—— 'A Seventeenth-Century Tutor for the Hautboy', *ML* 30 (1949), 355–63.

—— 'The "Entertainment" of Charles II', *ML* 38 (1957), 32–44.

HAM, M. A. O., letter in *MT* 127 (1986), 74.

HAMILTON, A., *Memoirs of the Comte de Gramont by Anthony Hamilton, Translated by Horace Walpole*, ed. D. Hughes (London, 1965).

HAMMERICH, A., *Musiken ved Christian den Fjerdes Hof* (Copenhagen, 1892).

—— 'Musical Relations between England and Denmark in the Seventeenth Century', *SIMG* 13 (1911–12), 114–19.

HAMMOND, P., 'Dryden's *Albion and Albanius*: The Apotheosis of Charles II', in D. Lindley (ed.), *The Court Masque* (Manchester, 1984), 169–83.

HARDING, R., *A Thematic Catalogue of the Works of Matthew Locke* (Oxford, 1971).

HARLEY, J., *Music in Purcell's London: The Social Background* (London, 1968).

—— 'Music at the English Court in the Eighteenth and Nineteenth Centuries', *ML* 50 (1969), 332–51.

HARRISON, G. B. (ed.), *A Second Elizabethan Journal* (London, 1931).

—— and JONES, R. A. (eds.), *André Hurault, Sieur de Maisse: A Journal of all that was Accomplished by Monsieur de Maisse, Ambassador in England from King Henri IV to Queen Elizabeth, Anno Domini 1597* (London, 1931).

HART, G., *The Violin: Its Famous Makers and their Imitators* (London, 1875).

HARWOOD, I., 'The Origins of the Cambridge Lute Manuscripts', *LSJ* 5 (1963), 32–48.

—— 'Rosseter's *Lessons for Consort* of 1609', *LSJ* 7 (1965), 15–23.

—— 'A Case of Double Standards? Instrumental Pitch in England *c*.1600', *EM* 9 (1981), 470–81.

—— 'Instrumental Pitch in England *c*.1600', *EM* 11 (1983), 76–7.

HAWKINS, J., *A General History of the Science and Practice of Music* (London, 1776; repr. 1853 and 1963).

HAYES, G., *Musical Instruments and their Music 1500–1700*, ii, *The Viols and other Bowed Instruments* (London, 1930; repr. 1969).

—— *King's Music: An Anthology* (London, 1937; repr. 1979).

HAYNES, B., 'Johann Sebastian Bach's Pitch Standards: The Woodwind Perspective', *JAMIS* 2 (1985), 55–114.

HEARTZ, D., 'The Basse Dance: Its Evolution *c*.1450–1550, *AnnM* 6 (1958–63), 287–340.

—— *Pierre Attaingnant, Royal Printer of Music* (Berkeley and Los Angeles, 1969).

HENLEY, W., *Universal Dictionary of Violin and Bow Makers* (Brighton, 1960).

HIBBERD, L., 'On "Instrumental Style" in Early Melody', *MQ* 32 (1946), 107–30.

HIGHFILL, P. H., BURNIM, K. A, and LANGHANS, E. A. (eds.), *A Biographical Dictionary of Actors, Actresses, Musicians, Dancers, Managers, and other Stage Personnel in London, 1660–1800*, 16 vols. in progress (Carbondale and Edwardsville, Ill., 1973–).

HILL, A. F., 'Thomas Evans', *MA* 4 (1912–13), 262.

HINDLEY, C. (ed.), *The Roxburghe Ballads* (London, 1873).

HINDS, A. B. (ed.), *Calendar of State Papers and Manuscripts, Relating to English*

Affairs, Existing in the Archives and Collections of Venice, and in the other Libraries of Northern Italy, xv: *1517–1619* (London, 1909).

HITZLER, D., *Extract aus der neuen Musica oder Singkunst* (Nuremberg, 1623).

HMC, *Third Report of the Royal Commission on Historical Manuscripts* (London, 1872).

—— *Fifth Report of the Royal Commission on Historical Manuscripts*, i (London, 1876).

—— *Twelfth Report*, Appendix, Part I, i: *The Manuscripts of the Earl Cowper, K. G., Preserved at Melbourne Hall, Derbyshire* (London, 1888).

—— *Twelfth Report*, Appendix, v: *The Manuscripts of his Grace the Duke of Rutland, K. G., Preserved at Belvoir Castle*, ii (London, 1889).

—— *Twelfth Report*, Appendix, vii: *The Manuscripts of S. H. Le Fleming, Esq., of Rydal Hall* (London, 1890).

—— *Calendar of the Manuscripts of the Most Hon. the Marquis of Salisbury . . . Preserved at Hatfield House, Hertfordshire*, 9, iii (London, 1889); iv (London, 1892); v (London, 1894); xiv (London, 1923).

—— *Calendar of the Manuscripts of the Marquis of Bath Preserved at Longleat, Wiltshire*, 58, ii (Dublin, 1907); iv: *Seymour Papers 1532–1686*, ed. M. Blatcher (London, 1968).

—— *Report of the Manuscripts of the Earl of Ancaster Preserved at Grimsthorpe*, ed. S. C. Lomas, 66 (Dublin, 1907).

—— *Report on the Manuscripts of Lord de L'Isle and Dudley Preserved at Penshurst Place*, ed. C. L. Kingsford, 77, i (London, 1925); ii, (London, 1934).

HOGWOOD, C., 'Thomas Tudway's History of Music', in C. Hogwood and R. Luckett (eds.), *Music in Eighteenth-Century England: Essays in Honour of Charles Cudworth* (Cambridge, 1983), 19–47.

HOLLANDER, J., *The Untuning of the Sky* (Princeton, NJ, 1961).

HOLMAN, P., 'George Jeffries and the "Great Dooble Base" ', *Chelys*, 5 (1973–4, published 1976), 79–81.

—— 'Suites by Jenkins Rediscovered', *EM* 6 (1978), 25–35, and the correspondence ibid. 481–3.

—— 'Thomas Baltzar (?1631–1663), the "Incomparable Lubicer on the Violin" ', *Chelys*, 13 (1984), 3–38.

—— 'An Orchestral Suite by François Couperin?', *EM* 14 (1986), 71–6.

—— 'Bartholomew Isaack and "Mr Isaack" of Eton: A Confusing Tale of Restoration Musicians', *MT* 128 (1987), 381–5.

—— 'The Harp in Stuart England: New Light on William Lawes's Harp Consorts', *EM* 15 (1987), 188–203.

—— Review of R. Charteris (ed.), *Thomas Lupo: The Two- and Three-Part Consort Music*, in *Chelys*, 17 (1988), 43–7.

—— Review of E. Huws Jones, *The Performance of English Song*, in *EM* 18 (1990), 295–7.

—— '*Valentinian*, Rochester and Louis Grabu', in J. Caldwell, E. Olleson, and S. Wollenberg (eds.), *The Well Enchanting Skill: Music, Poetry, and Drama in the Culture of the Renaissance: Essays in Honour of F. W. Sternfeld* (Oxford, 1990), 127–41.

—— Response to P. Downey, 'What Samuel Pepys Heard on 3 February 1661', in *EM* 19 (1991), 443.

—— '"An Addicion of Wyer Stringes beside the Ordenary Stringes": The Origin of the Baryton', in J. Paynter, R. Orton, P. Seymour, and T. Howell (eds.), *Companion to Contemporary Musical Thought* (London and New York, 1992), 1098–1115.

HONIGMAN, E. A. J. (ed.), *A Book of Masques in Honour of Allardyce Nicoll* (Cambridge, 1970).

HOTSON, L., *The First Night of 'Twelfth Night'* (London, 1954).

—— *The Commonwealth and Restoration Stage* (New York, 1962).

HUBER, C. R., 'The Life and Music of William Brade', Ph.D. diss. (University of North Carolina at Chapel Hill, 1965).

HUDSON, R., *The Allemande, the Balletto, and the Tanz* (Cambridge, 1986).

HUGHES, A., 'Music of the Coronation over a Thousand Years', *PRMA* 79 (1952–3), 81–100.

HULL, F., *Guide to the East Kent County Archives Office*, first supplement (Maidstone, 1971).

HULSE, L., 'John Hingeston', *Chelys*, 12 (1983), 23–42.

—— 'Francis and Thomas Cutting: Father and Son?', *The Lute*, 26 (1986), 73–4.

—— 'Hardwick MS 29: A New Source for Jacobean Lutenists', *The Lute*, 26 (1986), 63–72.

HUME, M. A. S. (ed.), *Calendar of Letters and State Papers Relating to English Affairs Preserved in, or originally Belonging to, the Archives of Simancas*, iv (London, 1899).

HUMPHREYS, D., 'Philip van Wilder: A Study of his Work and its Sources', *Soundings*, 9 (1979–80), 13–36.

HUMPHRIES, C., and SMITH, W. C. (eds.), *Music Publishing in the British Isles* (2nd edn., London, 1970).

HUNT, W. H. (ed.), *The Registers of St Paul's Church, Covent Garden, London*, iv: *Burials, 1653–1752* (Harleian Society Publications, Registers, 36; London, 1908).

HUSK, W. H., *An Account of the Musical Celebrations on St Cecilia's Day* (London, 1857).

HUTCHINSON, J. (ed.), *Memoirs of the Life of Colonel Hutchinson . . . Written by his Widow Lucy* (London, 1905).

IRVING, J., *The Instrumental Music of Thomas Tomkins* (New York and London, 1989).

JACQUOT, A., *La Musique en Lorraine* (Paris, 1882; repr. 1971).

JANNSEN, C. A. (ed.), 'The Waytes of Norwich in Medieval and Renaissance Civic Pageantry', Ph.D. diss. (University of New Brunswick, 1978).

JANNSEN, J. (ed.), *Die Münsterischen Chroniken von Röchell, Stevermann und Corfey* (Münster, 1856).

JAYNE, S., and JOHNSON, F. R. (eds.), *The Lumley Library: The Catalogue of 1609* (London, 1956).

JEANS, S., 'Seventeenth-Century Musicians in the Sackville Papers', *MMR* 88 (1958), 182–7.

JEFFERY, B., 'Antony Holborne', *MD* 22 (1968), 129–205.

JOHNSTON, A. F., and ROGERSON, M. (eds.), *Records of Early English Drama, York*, 3 vols. (Toronto, Buffalo, and London, 1979).

JONCKBLOET, W. J. A., and LAND, J. P. N. (eds.), *Musique et musiciens au XVIIe siècle: correspondance et œuvres musicales de Constantin Huygens* (Leiden, 1882).

JONES, E. H., *The Performance of English Song, 1610–1670* (New York and London, 1989).

JONSON, BEN, *Ben Jonson*, ed. C. H. Herford and P. and E. Simpson, 11 vols. (Oxford, 1925–62).

JORDAN, W. K. (ed.), *The Chronicle and Political Papers of King Edward VI* (London, 1966).

JOSSEN, C. H. (ed.), *Elias Ashmole (1617-1692)*, iv: *Texts 1673–1701* (Oxford, 1966).

JURGENS, M. (ed.), *Documents du minutier central concernant l'histoire de la musique (1600–1650)*, i (Paris, 1967); ii (Paris, 1974).

KEISER, R. (ed.), *T. Platter, Beschreibung der Reisen durch Frankreich, Spanien, England und Niederlande 1595-1600* (Auftrag der Historischen und Antiquarischen Gesellschaft zu Basel; Basle and Stuttgart, 1968).

KEMP, W., *Nine Daies Wonder*, ed. G. B. Harrison (The Bodley Head Quartos, 4; London, 1923).

KEMP, W. H., ' "Votre trey dowce", a Duo for Dancing', *ML* 60 (1979), 37–44.

KENYON, N., 'The Baroque Violin', in D. Gill (ed.), *The Book of the Violin* (Oxford, 1984).

KENYON DE PASCUAL, B., 'Bassano Instruments in Spain?', *GSJ* 40 (1987), 74–5.

KERMAN, J., *The Elizabethan Madrigal* (New York, 1962).

KINKELDEY, O., 'A Jewish Dancing Master of the Renaissance', in *Studies in Jewish Bibliography . . . in Memory of Abraham Solomon Freidus* (New York, 1929), 329–72.

KINNEY, G. J., 'Viols and Violins in the *Epitome Musical* (Lyon, 1556) of Philibert Jambe de Fer', *JVGSA* 4 (1967), 14–20.

KIRK, R. E. G., and E. F. (eds.), *Returns of Aliens Dwelling in the City, and Suburbs of London from the Reign of Henry VIII to that of James I* (The Publications of the Huguenot Society of London, 10, i–iii; Aberdeen, 1900, 1902, 1907).

KITTO, K. V. (ed.), *The Register of St Martins-in-the-Fields, London, 1619–1636* (Harleian Society Publications, Registers, 66; London, 1936).

KLARWILL, V. VON, *Queen Elizabeth and Some Foreigners* (London, 1928).

KNOWLTON, J. E., 'Some Dances of the Stuart Masque Identified and Analyzed', Ph.D. diss. (Indiana University, 1966).

KÖCHEL, L. VON, *Die kaiserliche Hof-Musikkapelle in Wien von 1543 bis 1867* (Vienna, 1869).

KOPP, J. B., 'Notes on the Bassoon in Seventeenth-Century France', *JAMIS* 17 (1991), 85–111.

LA BORDE, J. B. DE, *Essai sur la musique ancienne et moderne* (Paris, 1780; repr. 1972).

LAFONTAINE, H. C. DE (ed.), *The King's Musick: A Transcript of Records Relating to Music and Musicians (1460–1700)* (London, 1909; repr. 1973).

LA GORCE, J. DE, 'L'Académie Royale de Musique en 1704, d'après des documents inédits conservés dans les archives notariales', *RdM* 65 (1979), 178–82.

—— 'Some Notes on Lully's Orchestra', in J. Hajdu Heyer (ed.), *Jean Baptiste*

Lully and the Music of the French Baroque: Essays in Honor of James R. Anthony (Cambridge, 1989), 99–112.

LANEHAM, R., *A Letter* (London, 1575; repr. 1968).

LANFRANCO, G. M., *Scintille di musica* (Brescia, 1533; repr. 1970).

LANGWILL, L. G., *An Index of Musical Wind-Instrument Makers* (3rd edn., Edinburgh, 1972).

LASOCKI, D., 'Professional Recorder Players in England, 1540–1740', Ph.D. diss. (University of Iowa, 1983).

—— 'The Anglo-Venetian Bassano Family as Instrument Makers and Repairers', *GSJ* 38 (1985), 112–32.

—— 'The Bassanos: Anglo-Venetian and Venetian', *EM* 14 (1986), 558–60.

—— 'The French Hautboy in England, 1673–1730', *EM* 16 (1988), 339–57.

LAURIE, M., 'The Chapel Royal Part-Books', in *Music and Bibliography: Essays in Honour of Alec Hyatt King* (New York and London, 1980), 28–50.

LAUZE, F. DE, *Apologie de la Danse by F. De Lauze 1623*, ed. J. Wildeblood (London, 1952).

LAWRENCE, W. J., 'Notes on a Collection of Masque Music', *ML* 3 (1922), 49–58.

—— 'Foreign Singers and Musicians at the Court of Charles II', *MQ* 9 (1923), 217–25.

LEE, B., 'Giovanni Maria Lanfranco's *Scintille de Musica* and its Relation to Sixteenth-Century Music Theory', Ph.D. diss (Cornell University, 1961).

LEFKOWITZ, M., *William Lawes* (London, 1960).

—— 'The Longleat Papers of Bulstrode Whitelocke: New Light on Shirley's *Triumph of Peace*', *JAMS* 18 (1965), 42–60.

—— 'Shadwell and Locke's *Psyche*, the French Connection', PRMA, 106 (1979–80), 42–55.

LE HURAY, P., *Music and the Reformation in England 1549–1660* (London, 1967).

LELAND, J., *De rebus Britannicis collectanea*, ed. T. Hearn (London, 1770).

LESURE, F., 'Les Orchestres populaires à Paris vers la fin du XVIᵉ siècle', *RdM* 36 (1954), 39–54.

—— 'L' *Épitome musical* de Philibert Jambe de Fer (1556)', *AnnM* 6 (1958–63), 341–86.

LEUCHTMANN, H. (ed.), *Die Münchner Fürstenhochzeit von 1568. Massimo Troiano: Dialoghe* (Munich, 1980).

LEVY, K., 'Susanne un Jour: The History of a Sixteenth-Century Chanson', *AnnM* 1 (1953), 375–408.

LIBIN, L., 'Early Violins: Problems and Issues', *EM* 19 (1991), 5–6.

LIMON, J., *Gentlemen of a Company: English Players in Central and Eastern Europe, 1590–1660* (Cambridge, 1985).

LINDEN, A. VANDER, 'Les Aveugles de la cour de Bourgogne', *RBM* 4 (1950), 74–6.

LIPPINCOTT, H. F. (ed.), *'Merry Passages and Jests': A Manuscript Jestbook* (Salzburg Studies in English Literature, Elizabethan and Renaissance Studies, 29; Salzburg, 1974).

'Lists of the King's Musicians, from the Audit Office Declared Accounts', *MA* 1 (1909–10), 56–61, 119–24, 182–7, 249–53; *MA* 2 (1910–11), 51–5, 114–

18, 174–8, 235–40; *MA* 3 (1911–12), 54–8, 110–15, 171–6, 229–34.

LITTERICK, L., 'Performing Franco-Netherlandish Secular Music of the Late Fifteenth Century', *EM* 8 (1980), 474–85.

—— 'On Italian Instrumental Ensemble Music in the Late Fifteenth Century', in I. Fenlon (ed.), *Music in Medieval and Early Modern Europe: Patronage, Sources, and Texts* (Cambridge, 1981), 117–30.

LOCKE, M., *The Present Practice of Musick Vindicated* (London, 1673; repr. 1974).

LOCKWOOD, L., *Music in Renaissance Ferrara 1400–1505* (Oxford, 1984).

LONG, J. H., *Shakespeare's Use of Music: A Study of the Music and its Performance in the Original Productions of Seven Comedies* (Gainesville, Fla., 1961).

LOVE, H., 'The Fiddlers on the Restoration Stage', *EM* 6 (1978), 391–9.

—— 'The Wreck of the *Gloucester*', *MT* 125 (1984), 194–5.

LUCKETT, R., 'A New Source for *Venus and Adonis*', *MT* 130 (1989), 76–9.

LUHRING, A. A., 'The Music of John Banister', Ph.D. diss. (Stanford University, 1966).

LUTTRELL, N., *A Brief Relation of State Affairs from September 1678 to April 1714* (Oxford 1857; repr. 1969).

LYLE, L. V. (ed.), *Acts of the Privy Council of England, September 1627–June 1628* (London, 1940).

LYNDON-JONES, M., 'The Bassano/HIE(RO).S./!!/Venice Discussion', *FoMRHI Quarterly*, 47 (April 1987), 55–61.

MABBETT, M., 'Italian Musicians in Restoration England (1660–90)', *ML* 67 (1986), 237–47.

MACCAFFREY, W. T., 'Place and Patronage in Elizabethan Politics', in S. T. Bindoff, J. Hurstfield, and C. T. Williams (eds.), *Elizabethan Government and Society: Essays Presented to Sir John Neale* (London, 1961), 95–126.

McCART, C., 'The Kers and the Maules: Music in the Lives of Two Seventeenth-Century Scottish Aristocratic Families', B.A. diss. (Colchester Institute, 1988).

MACCLINTOCK, C., *Giaches de Wert (1535–1596)* (MSD 17; Rome, 1966).

—— and L. (eds.), *Le Balet comique de la Royne, 1581* (MSD 25; [Rome], 1971).

MACE, T., *Musick's Monument* (London, 1676; repr. 1958).

McGEE, T. J., 'Instruments and the Faenza Codex', *EM* 14 (1986), 480–90.

—— with MITTLER, S. E., 'Information on Instruments in Florentine Carnival Songs', *EM* 10 (1982), 452–61.

McGUINNESS, R., *English Court Odes 1660–1820* (Oxford, 1971).

MACKERNESS, E. D., *A Social History of English Music* (London, 1964).

MADDEN, F. (ed.), *The Privy Purse Expenses of the Princess Mary* (London, 1831).

MAGALOTTI, L., *Travels of Cosmo the Third, Grand Duke of Tuscany through England, during the Reign of King Charles the Second (1669)* (London, 1821).

MANIFOLD, J. S., *The Music in English Drama from Shakespeare to Purcell* (London, 1956).

MANDY, W. H., 'Notes from the Assize Rolls and other Documents Relating to the Hundred of Blackheath', *Transactions of the Greenwich and Lewisham Antiquarian Society*, 1/5 (1913), 282–312, 1/6 (1914), 373–96.

MARIX, J., *Histoire de la musique et des musiciens de la cour de Bourgogne sous la règne de Philippe le Bon (1420–1467)* (Strasburg, 1939; repr. 1974).

MARLOW, R., 'Sir Ferdinando Heybourne alias Richardson', *MT* 115 (1974), 736–9.

MARLOWE, C., *The Complete Works*, ed. F. Bowers, i (Cambridge, 1973).

MARSTON, J., *The Works*, ed. A. H. Bullen (London, 1887; repr. 1970).

—— *The Plays*, ed. H. H. Wood, ii (London, 1938).

MASSINGER, P., *The Plays and Poems*, ed. P. Edwards and C. Gibson, i (Oxford, 1976).

MASSIP, C., *La Vie des musiciens de Paris au temps de Mazarin (1643–1661)* (La Vie musicale en France sous les rois Bourbons, 24; Paris, 1976).

MEEÙS, N., 'Praetorius, Segerman, and the English Viols', *FoMRHI Quarterly*, 39 (Apr. 1985), 28–32.

MERRYWEATHER, J., *York Music: The Story of a City's Music from 1304 to 1896* (York, 1988).

MERSENNE, M., *Harmonie universelle*, iii: *Traité des instruments à chordes* (Paris, 1636–7; repr. 1963); trans. R. E. Chapman, *Marin Mersenne: Harmonie Universelle, the Books on Instruments* (The Hague, 1957).

METCALFE, W. C. (ed.), *The Visitations of Essex* (Harleian Society Publications, 13; London, 1878).

MIDDLETON, G., 'A Profile of Edward Lowe *c*.1610–1682: His Life and Work in the University of Oxford', BA diss. (Colchester Institute, 1989).

MILHOUS, J., 'The Date and Import of the Financial Plan for a United Theatre Company in P.R.O. LC 7/3', *Maske und Kothurn*, 21 (1975), 81–8.

—— and HUME, R. D., 'Dating Play Premières from Publication Data, 1660–1700', *Harvard Library Bulletin*, 22 (1974), 374–405.

—— (eds.), *Vice Chamberlain Coke's Theatrical Papers 1706–1715* (Carbondale and Edwardsville, Ill., 1982).

—— and PRICE, C. A., 'Harpsichords in the London Theatres, 1697–1715', *EM* 18 (1990), 38–46.

MILLAR, O. (ed.), *Sir Peter Lely 1618–80: Catalogue of the National Portrait Gallery Exhibition, 17 November 1978 to 18 March 1979* (London, 1978).

MILLER, L. E., 'John Birchensha and the Early Royal Society: Grand Scales and Scientific Composition', *JRMA* 115 (1990), 63–79.

MILSOM, J., 'A Tallis Fantasia', *MT* 126 (1985), 658–62.

—— 'Tallis's First and Second Thoughts', *JRMA* 113 (1988), 209–12.

MOENS, K., 'Der frühe Geigenbau in Süddeutschland', in F. Hellwig (ed.), *Studia organologica: Festschrift für John Henry van der Meer zu seinem fünfundsechzigsten Geburtstag* (Tutzing, 1987), 349–88.

MONSON, C., 'Consort Song and Verse Anthem: A Few Performance Problems', *JVGSA* 13 (1976), 4–11.

—— *Voices and Viols in England 1600–1650: The Sources and the Music* (Ann Arbor, Mich., 1982).

MOORE, T., *The History of Devonshire from the Earliest Period to the Present* (London, 1829).

MOREHEN, J., 'The English Consort and Verse Anthem', *EM* 6 (1978), 381–5.

MORROW, M., 'Sixteenth-Century Ensemble Viol Music', *EM* 2 (1974), 160–3.

MUELLER, P. E., 'The Influence and Activities of English Musicians on the Continent during the Late Sixteenth and Early Seventeenth Centuries', Ph.D.

diss. (Indiana University, 1954).

MYERS, H. W., 'The Construction of a Fifteenth-Century Fiddle', unpublished paper (1977).

—— 'Instrumental Pitch in England *c*.1600', *EM* 10 (1982), 519–22.

—— 'The *Mary Rose* "Shawm"', *EM* 11 (1983), 358–60.

—— 'Slide Trumpet Madness: Fact or Fiction?', *EM* 17 (1989), 383–9.

—— 'Renaissance Flute', in J. T. Kite-Powell (ed.), *A Practical Guide to Historical Performance: The Renaissance* (New York, 1989), 37–41.

NAGEL, W., 'Annalen der englischen Hofmusik von der Zeit Heinrichs VIII. bis zum Tode Karls I. (1509–1649)', *MMg* 26, Beilage (1894).

NEDDEN, O. ZUR, *Quellen und Studien zur oberrheinischen Musikgeschichte im 15. und 16. Jahrhundert* (Kassel, 1931).

NEIGHBOUR, O., *The Consort and Keyboard Music of William Byrd* (London and Boston, Mass., 1978).

—— 'Orlando Gibbons (1583–1625): The Consort Music', *EM* 11 (1983), 351–7.

NELSON, A. H. (ed.), *Records of Early English Drama, Cambridge* (Toronto, Buffalo, and London, 1989).

NEWCOMB, A., *The Madrigal at Ferrara 1579–97* (Princeton, NJ, 1980).

NICHOLS, J., *The Progresses and Public Processions of Queen Elizabeth* (2nd edn., London, 1823).

—— *The Progresses, Processions, and Magnificent Festivities, of King James the First* (London, 1823).

NICOLAS, N. H. (ed.), *Privy Purse Expenses of King Henry the Eighth* (London, 1827).

NICOLL, A., item in *The Times Literary Supplement*, 21 Sept. 1922.

—— *A History of Restoration Drama 1660–1700* (4th edn., Cambridge, 1952).

—— *A History of English Drama*, ii: *Early Eighteenth-Century Drama* (3rd edn., Cambridge, 1961).

NORDSTROM, L., 'The Cambridge Consort Books', *JLSA* 5 (1972), 70–103.

NOYES, R. G., 'A Manuscript Restoration Prologue for *Volpone*', *Modern Language Notes*, 42 (1937), 198–200.

OED, The Compact Edition of the Oxford Dictionary (London, 1979).

OGG, D., *England in the Reigns of James II and William III* (2nd edn., Oxford, 1969).

OGILBY, J., *The Entertainment of his Most Excellent Majestie Charles II* (London, 1662).

ONGARO, G. M., 'Sixteenth-Century Venetian Wind Instrument Makers and their Clients', *EM* 13 (1985), 391–7.

OPIE, I., and P., *The Oxford Dictionary of Nursery Rhymes* (London, 1951).

ORBISON, T., and HILL, R. F. (eds.), 'The Middle Temple Documents Relating to James Shirley's *The Triumph of Peace*, 12 (Oxford, 1983), 31–84.

OVERALL, W. H., and H. C. (eds.), *Analytical Index to the Series of Records known as the Remembrancia Preserved among the Archives of the City of London, 1579–1664* (London, 1878).

OWENS, B., The Early Seventeenth-Century Organ in St Nicholas's Church, Stanford-on-Avon', *The Organ Yearbook*, 19 (1988), 5–30.

PAGE, C., 'Machaut's "Pupil" Deschamps on the Performance of Music: Voices or Instruments in the Fourteenth-Century Chanson?', *EM* 5 (1977), 484–91.

—— 'The Performance of Songs in Late Medieval France: A New Source', *EM* 10 (1982), 441–50.

—— *Voices and Instruments of the Middle Ages* (London, 1987).

—— *The Owl and the Nightingale: Musical Life and Ideas in France 1100–1300* (London, 1989).

PAGE, W. (ed.), *Letters of Denization and Acts of Naturalisation for Aliens in England 1509–1603* (The Publications of the Huguenot Society of London, 8; Lymington, 1893).

PARKE, W. T., *Musical Memoirs* (London, 1830).

PARKS, E. W., *Sidney Lanier, the Man, the Poet, the Critic* (Athens, Ga., 1968).

PARROTT, A., '"Grett and Solompne Singing": Instruments in English Church Music before the Civil War', *EM* 6 (1978), 182–7.

PASQUÉ, E., 'Die Weimarer Hofkapelle im XVI. Jahrhundert', *MMg* 29 (1897), 137–44.

PAYNE, I., 'Instrumental Music at Trinity College, Cambridge, *c*.1594–*c*.1615: Archival and Biographical Evidence', *ML* 68 (1987), 128–39.

—— 'British Library Add. MSS 30826–28: A Set of Part-Books from Trinity College, Cambridge?', *Chelys*, 17 (1988), 3–15.

PELICELLI, N., 'Musicisti in Parma nei secoli XV–XVI: la capella alla corte Farnese', *NA* 9 (1932), 41–52.

PEPYS, S., *Letters and the Second Diary of Samuel Pepys*, ed. R. G. Howarth (London, 1932).

—— *The Diary of Samuel Pepys*, ed. R. Latham and W. Matthews, 11 vols. (London, 1970–83).

PERCY, T. (ed.), *The Regulations and Establishment of the Household of Henry Algernon Percy, the Fifth Earl of Northumberland, at his Castles of Wresslle and Leckonfield in Yorkshire* (London, 1770; new edn., London, 1905).

PERRIN, P., *Ariane, ou le mariage de Bacchus/Ariadne; or, the Marriage of Bacchus* (London, 1674).

PETTI, A. G., 'New Light on Peter Philips', *MMR* 87 (1957), 58–63.

—— 'Peter Philips, Composer and Organist, 1561–1628', *Recusant History*, 4 (1957–8), 48–60.

PHILIPPS, G. A., 'Crown Musical Patronage from Elizabeth to Charles I', *ML* 58 (1977), 29–42.

PIETZSCH, G., *Quellen und Forschungen zur Geschichte der Musik am kurpfälzischen Hof zu Heidelberg bis 1622* (Mainz, 1963).

PINNOCK, A., 'A Wider Role for the Flat Trumpet', *GSJ* 42 (1989), 105–111.

—— and WOOD, B., 'A Counterblast on English Trumpets', *EM* 19 (1991), 436–43.

PLAYFORD, J., and H., *A Breif (Brief) Introduction to the Skill of Musick/An Introduction to the Skill of Musick* (2nd edn., London, 1658; 3rd edn., 1660; 1662; 4th edn., 1664; 1666; 1667; 1670; 6th edn., 1672; 7th edn., 1674; repr. 1966; 8th edn., 1679; 10th edn., 1683; 11th edn., 1687; 12th edn., 1694; repr. 1972; 13th edn., 1697.

POLK, K., 'Wind Bands of Medieval Flemish Cities', *Brass and Woodwind*

Quarterly, 1 (1966–8), 93–118.

—— 'Municipal Wind Music in Flanders in the Late Middle Ages', *Brass and Woodwind Quarterly*, 2 (1969), 1–15.

—— 'Instrumental Music in the Urban Centres of Renaissance Germany', *EMH* 7 (1987), 159–86.

—— 'The Trombone, the Slide Trumpet, and the Ensemble Tradition of the Early Renaissance', *EM* 17 (1989), 389–97.

—— '*Vedel* and *Geige*—Fiddle and Viol: German String Traditions in the Fifteenth Century', *JAMS* 42 (1989), 504–46.

—— 'Voices and Instruments: Soloists and Ensembles in the Fifteenth Century', *EM* 18 (1990), 179–98.

POOLE, R., 'The Oxford Music School and the Collection of Portraits formerly Preserved there', *MA* 4 (1912–13), 143–59.

POULTON, D., *John Dowland* (2nd edn., London, 1982).

PRAETORIUS, M., *Syntagmatis musici tomus secundus* (Wolfenbüttel, 1618–19; repr. 1958); trans. D. Z. Crookes, *Michael Praetorius: Syntagma Musicum II. De Organographia Parts I and II* (Oxford, 1986).

PRAT, T. (ed.), *A Voyage to England* (London, 1709).

PRICE, C. A., 'An Organisational Peculiarity of Lord Herbert of Cherbury's Lute Book', *LSJ* 11 (1969), 5–27.

—— 'The Critical Decade for English Music Drama, 1700–1710', *Harvard Library Bulletin*, 26 (1978), 38–76.

—— 'The Small-Coal Cult', *MT* 119 (1978), 1032–4.

—— *Music in the Restoration Theatre* (Ann Arbor, Mich., 1979).

—— 'Restoration Stage Fiddlers and their Music', *EM* 7 (1979), 315–22.

—— *Henry Purcell and the London Stage* (Cambridge, 1984).

PRICE, D. C., 'Gilbert Talbot, Seventh Earl of Shrewsbury, an Elizabethan Courtier and his Music', *ML* 57 (1976), 144–51.

—— *Patrons and Musicians of the English Renaissance* (Cambridge, 1981).

PRIOR, R., 'Jewish Musicians at the Tudor Court', *MQ* 69 (1983), 253–65.

—— 'A Second Jewish Community in Tudor London', *Jewish Historical Studies (Transactions of the Jewish Historical Society of England)*, 31 (1988–90), 137–52.

PRIZER, W. F., *Courtly Pastimes: The Frottole of Marchetto Cara* (Ann Arbor, Mich., 1980).

—— 'Lutenists at the Court of Mantua in the Late Fifteenth and Early Sixteenth Centuries', *JLSA* 13 (1980), 5–34.

—— 'Bernardo Piffaro e i pifferi e tromboni a Mantova: strumenti a fiato in una corte italiana', *RIM* 16 (1981), 151–84.

—— 'Isabella d'Este and Lorenzo da Pavia, "Master Instrument Maker"', *EMH* 2 (1982), 87–127.

—— 'The Frottola and the Unwritten Tradition', *Studi musicali*, 15 (1986), 3–37.

—— 'North Italian Courts, 1460–1540', in I. Fenlon (ed.), *The Renaissance* (Man and Music; London, 1989), 133–55.

PROTHEROE, J., 'Not so much an Opera . . . a Restoration Problem Examined', *MT* 106 (1965), 666–8.

PRUNIÈRES, H., 'Notes sur les origines de l'ouverture française', *SIMG* 12 (1910–11), 565–85.

—— 'La Musique de la chambre et de l'écurie sous la règne de François Ier', *L'Année musicale*, 1 (1912), 215–51.

—— *Le Ballet de cour en France avant Benserade et Lully* (Paris, 1914).

RASCH, R., 'Seventeenth-Century Dutch Editions of English Instrumental Music', *ML* 53 (1972), 270–3.

RASTALL, R., 'The Minstrels of the English Royal Households, 25 Edward 1–1 Henry VIII: An Inventory, *RMARC* 4 (1964), 1–41.

—— 'Some English Consort Groupings of the Late Middle Ages', *ML* 55 (1974), 179–202.

RAVN, V. C., 'English Instrumentalists at the Danish Court in the Time of Shakespeare', *SIMG* 7 (1905–6), 550–63.

REESE, G., *Music in the Renaissance* (rev. edn., New York, 1959).

REMNANT, M., *Musical Instruments of the West* (London, 1978).

—— *English Bowed Instruments from Anglo-Saxon to Tudor Times* (Oxford, 1986).

RICHARDSON, W. C., *Tudor Chamber Administration 1485–1547* (Baton Rouge, La., 1952).

RILEY, J., 'The Identity of William Gregory', *ML* 48 (1967), 236–46.

—— 'Deductions from a Round', *ML* 56 (1975), 60–3.

RILEY, M., 'The Teaching of Bowed Instruments from 1511 to 1756', Ph.D. diss. (University of Michigan, 1954).

RIMBAULT, E. F. (ed.), *The Old Cheque-Book or Book of Remembrance of the Chapel Royal from 1561 to 1744* (London, 1872; repr. 1966).

RING, L., 'The Harp for Lawes', *EM* 15 (1987), 589–90.

RIPIN, E. M., 'A Re-evaluation of Virdung's *Musica Getutscht*', *JAMS* 29 (1976), 189–223.

ROBERT, J., 'Une famille de joueurs de violon avignonnais au XVIIe siècle, les de La Pierre', *RMFC* 4 (1964), 54–67.

ROBERTS, J. D., 'Has the Problem Changed?', *LSJ* 6 (1964), 27–8.

ROSENFIELD, M. C., 'The Disposal of the Property of Monastic Houses, with a Special Study of Holy Trinity, Aldgate', Ph.D. thesis (London, 1961).

ROSS, M., 'The Kytsons of Hengrave: A Study in Musical Patronage', M. Mus diss. (London, 1989).

ROTH, C., *The House of Nasi: The Duke of Naxos* (Philadelphia, 1948).

—— *A History of the Jews in England* (3rd edn., Oxford, 1964; repr. 1978).

—— 'The Middle Period of Anglo-Jewish History (1290–1655) Reconsidered', *Transactions of the Jewish Historical Society of England*, 19 (1960), 1–12.

ROWSE, A. L., *Tudor Cornwall: Portrait of a Society* (2nd edn., London, 1969).

RUSSELL, R., *The Harpsichord and Clavichord* (London, 1959).

RYCROFT, D., 'Flat Trumpet Facts and Figures', *GSJ* 42 (1989), 134–42.

RYE, W. B., *England as seen by Foreigners in the Days of Elizabeth and James the First* (London, 1865).

RYLANDS, W. H. (ed.), *Grantees of Arms Named in Docquets and Patents to the End of the Seventeenth Century* (Harleian Society Publications, 66; London, 1915).

SABOL, A. J., 'New Documents on Shirley's Masque "The Triumph of Peace"', *ML* 47 (1966), 10–26.

SACHSE, W. L. (ed.), *The Diurnal of Thomas Rugge 1659–1661* (Camden Third Series, 91; London, 1961).

SADIE, S. (ed.), *The New Grove Dictionary of Music and Musicians [Grove 6]*, 20 vols. (London, 1980).

SADLER, G., 'The Role of the Keyboard Continuo in French Opera, 1673–1776', *EM* 8 (1980), 148–57.

ST CLARE BYRNE, M. (ed.), *The Elizabethan Home* (3rd edn., London, 1949).

—— (ed.), *The Lisle Letters*, iv (Chicago and London, 1981).

SALMEN, W., *Haus- und Kammermusik* (Musikgeschichte in Bildern, IV/3; Leipzig, 1982).

SANDBERGER, A., *Beiträge zur Geschichte der bayerischen Hofkapelle unter Orlando di Lasso* (Leipzig, 1894–5).

SANDFORD, F., *The History of the Coronation of the Most High, Most Mighty, and Excellent Monarch, James II* (London, 1687).

SANDYS, W., and FORSTER, S. A., *The History of the Violin* (London, 1864).

SANUTO, M., *I diarii*, ed. F. Stefano, G. Berchet, and N. Berozzi, xix (Venice, 1887); xxiv (Venice, 1889); xxix (Venice, 1890).

SAWYER, J. E., 'An Anthology of Lyra Viol Music in Oxford, Bodleian Library, Manuscripts Music School D. 245–7'. Ph.D. diss. (University of Toronto, 1972).

SCHMID, E. F., *Musik an den schwäbischen Zollerhöfen der Renaissance* (Kassel, 1962).

SCHMIDT, C. B., 'Newly Identified Manuscript Sources for the Music of Jean-Baptiste Lully', *Notes*, 43 (1987), 7–39.

SCHNEIDER, H. (ed.), *Chronologisch-thematisch Verzeichnis sämtlicher Werke von Jean-Baptiste Lully* (Tutzing, 1981).

SCHOFIELD, B., and DART, T., 'Tregian's Anthology', *ML* 32 (1951), 205–16.

SCHOLES, P., *The Puritans and Music in England and New England* (Oxford, 1934; repr. 1969).

SCOTT, D., *The Music of St Paul's Cathedral* (London, 1972).

SCOULOUDI, I. (ed.), *Returns of Strangers in the Metropolis 1593, 1627, 1635, 1639* (Huguenot Society of London, quarto series, 57; London, 1985).

SEGERMAN, E., 'Hizler's [*sic*] Tenor Violin', *FoMRHI Quarterly*, 27 (Apr. 1982), 38.

—— 'English Viol Sizes and Pitches', *FoMRHI Quarterly*, 38 (Jan. 1985), 55–62.

—— 'What Praetorius Wrote on English Viols', *FoMRHI Quarterly*, 38 (January 1985), 63–5.

—— 'Praetorius, Meeùs, and the English Viols', *FoMRHI Quarterly*, 40 (July 1985), 57–8.

SELFRIDGE-FIELD, E., *Venetian Instrumental Music from Gabrieli to Vivaldi* (Oxford, 1975).

SENN, W., *Musik und Theater am Hof zu Innsbruck* (Innsbruck, 1954).

[SHAKESPEARE], *Mr. William Shakespeares Comedies, Histories and Tragedies* (London, 1623; repr. 1954).

SHARPE, K., 'The Image of Virtue: The Court and Household of Charles I, 1625–1642', in D. Starkey (ed.), *The English Court, from the Wars of the Roses to the Civil War* (London, 1987).

SHAW, H. W., 'A Collection of Musical Manuscripts in the Autograph of Henry Purcell and other English Composers, *c.*1665–85', *The Library*, 14 (1959), 126–31.

SHAW, W. A. (ed.), *Calendar of Treasury Books Preserved in the Public Record Office*, vii: *1681–1685* (London, 1916); viii: *1685–1689* (London, 1923); ix: *1689–1692* (London, 1931).

SHERWOOD, R., *The Court of Oliver Cromwell* (London, 1977).

SHUTE, J. D., 'Anthony à Wood and his Manuscript Wood D 19 (4) at the Bodleian Library, Oxford', Ph.D. diss. (International Institute of Advanced Studies, Clayton, Mo., 1979).

SILBIGER, A., 'The First Viol Tutor: Hans Gerle's *Musica Teusch*', *JVGSA* 6 (1969), 34–48.

SJÖGREN, G., 'Thomas Bull and other "English Instrumentalists" in Denmark in the 1580s', *Shakespeare Survey*, 22 (1971), 119–23.

SLAUGHTER, T. P. (ed.), *Ideology and Politics on the Eve of Restoration: Newcastle's Advice to Charles II* (Philadelphia, 1984).

SLAVIN, D., 'In Support of "Heresy": Manuscript Evidence for the *a cappella* Performance of Early Fifteenth-Century Songs', *EM* 19 (1991), 178–90.

SMITH, D. A., 'The Musical Instrument Inventory of Raymund Fugger', *GSJ* 33 (1980), 36–44.

SMITH, J., and GRATISS, I., 'What did Prince Henry Do with his Feet on Sunday 19 August 1604?', *EM* 14 (1986), 198–207.

SMITH, W. C., *A Bibliography of the Musical Works Published by John Walsh during the Years 1695–1720* (London, 1948; repr. 1968).

SMITHERS, D., *The Music and History of the Baroque Trumpet before 1721* (London, 1973).

SMYTHE, P. C. S. (Viscount Strangford) (ed.), 'Household Expenses of the Princess Elizabeth during her Residence at Hatfield, October 1, 1551, to September 30, 1552', *The Camden Miscellany*, ii (Publications of the Camden Society, os, 55; London, 1853).

SNYDER, K., *Dieterich Buxtehude, Organist in Lübeck* (New York and London, 1987).

SOLERTI, A., *Musica, ballo e drammatica alla corte medicea dal 1600 al 1637* (Florence, 1905; repr. 1969).

SPENCER, K. M., AND BROWN, H. M., 'How Alfonso della Viola Tuned his Viols, and how he Transposed', *EM* 14 (1986), 520–33.

SPIERS, W. L., 'An Account of the View of the Palace of Whitehall from the River, 1683', *London Topographical Record*, 7 (1912), 26–30.

—— 'Explanation of a Plan of Whitehall', *London Topographical Record*, 7 (1912), 56–66.

SPIESSENS, G., 'Geschiedenis van de gilde van de Antwerpse spellieden (Deel 1: xvide eeuw)', *RBM* 22 (1968), 5–50.

SPINK, I., 'Angelo Notari and his "Prime Musiche Nuove"', *MMR* 87 (1957), 168–77.

—— 'Lanier in Italy', *ML* 40 (1959), 242–52.

—— 'The Musicians of Queen Henrietta-Maria: Some Notes and References in the English State Papers', *AcM* 36 (1964), 177–82.

SPRING, M., 'The Lute in England and Scotland after the Golden Age, 1620–1750', D.Phil. thesis (Oxford, 1987).

STAINER, J., 'The Middle Temple Masque', *MT* 47 (1906), 21–4.

STARKEY, D., *The Reign of Henry VIII: Personalities and Politics* (London, 1991).

—— (ed.), *The English Court, from the Wars of the Roses to the Civil War* (London, 1987).

—— (ed.), *Henry VIII: A European Court in England* (London, 1991).

STEELE-PERKINS, C., 'Practical Observations on Natural, Slide, and Flat Trumpets', *GSJ* 42 (1989), 122–7.

STEPHEN, G. A., *The Waits of the City of Norwich through Four Centuries to 1790* (Norwich, 1933).

STERNFELD, F. W., *Music in Shakespearean Tragedy* (London, 1963).

STEVENS, J., *Music and Poetry in the Early Tudor Court* (2nd edn., London, 1979).

STROHM, R., *Music in Late Medieval Bruges* (Oxford, 1985).

STRONG, R., *Holbein and Henry VIII* (London, 1967).

—— *The English Renaissance Miniature* (2nd edn., London, 1984).

—— *Henry Prince of Wales and England's Lost Renaissance* (London, 1986).

STRUNK, O. (ed.), *Source Readings in Music History*, 5 vols. (London, 1965; repr. 1981).

TENISON, E. M., *Elizabethan England*, 9 vols. (Leamington, 1932–51).

TESSIER, A., 'Robert Cambert à Londres', *ReM* 9 (1927–8), 101–22.

THOMAS, B., 'The Renaissance Flute', *EM* 3 (1975), 2–10.

THOMPSON, R. P., 'English Music Manuscripts and the Fine Paper Trade, 1648–1688', Ph.D. thesis (London, 1988).

—— '"Francis Withie of Oxon" and his Commonplace Book, Christ Church, Oxford MS 337', *Chelys*, 20 (1991), 3–27.

THORPE, J., *Registrum Roffense* (London, 1769).

TILMOUTH, M., 'Chamber Music in England, 1675–1720', Ph.D. thesis (Cambridge, 1959).

—— Review of Zimmerman, *Henry Purcell* in *ML* 48 (1967), 368–9.

—— (ed.), 'A Calendar of References to Music in Newspapers Published in London and the Provinces (1660–1719)', *RMARC* 1 (1961); *RMARC* 2 (1962), 1–15.

TURNBULL, E., 'Thomas Tudway and the Harleian Collection', *JAMS* 7 (1955), 203–7.

URQUHART, M., 'The Handwriting of Christopher Simpson', *Chelys*, 15 (1986), 62–3.

VAN LENNEP, W. B. (ed.), *The London Stage 1660–1800*, i: *1660–1700* (Carbondale, Ill., 1965).

VANDER STRAETEN, E., *La Musique aux Pays-Bas avant le XIXe siècle*, 8 vols. (Brussels, 1867–88; repr. 1969).

VAUGHT, R., 'The Fancies of Alfonso Ferrabosco II', Ph.D. diss. (Stanford University, 1959).

VERTUE, G., *A Survey and Ground Plot of the Royal Palace of Whitehall* (London, 1747).

VIELLA, M., 'The Violeta of S. Caterina de' Vigri', *GSJ* 28 (1975), 60–70.

VIGI, B. G., *Ferrara: chiese-palazzi-musei* (Ferrara, 1991).

VIRDUNG, S., *Musica getutsch* (Basel, 1511; repr. 1970).

VLAM, C., and DART, T., 'Rosseters in Holland', *GSJ* 11 (1958), 63–9.

WADE, J. C. M. (ed.), *Registers of the Catholic Chapels Royal and the Portuguese Embassy Chapel 1662–1829*, i: *Marriages* (Publications of the Catholic Record Society, 38; London, 1941).

WAGNER, R., *Kurtze doch gegründete beschreibung des . . . Hochzeitlichen Ehren Fests* (Munich, 1568).

WALDNER, F., 'Zwei Inventarien aus dem XVI. und XVII. Jahrhundert über hinterlassene Musikinstrumente und Musikalien am Innsbrucker Hofe', *SMz* 4 (1916), 128–47.

WALLS, P., 'New Light on Songs by William Lawes and John Wilson', *ML* 57 (1976), 55–64.

—— 'The Influence of the Italian Violin School in Seventeenth-Century England', *EM* 18 (1990), 575–87.

WARD, J. M., 'The Lute Music of MS Royal Appendix 58', *JAMS* 13 (1960), 117–25.

—— 'Apropos *The British Broadside Ballad and its Music*', *JAMS* 20 (1967), 28–85.

—— 'The Maner of Dauncying', *EM* 4 (1976), 127–42.

—— *A Dowland Miscellany*, *JLSA* 10 (1977).

—— *Sprightly and Cheerful Musick: Notes on the Cittern, Gittern, and Guitar in Sixteenth- and Seventeenth-Century England*, *LSJ* 21 (1979–81).

—— 'The English Measure', *EM* 14 (1986), 15–21.

—— 'Newly Devis'd Measures for Jacobean Masques', *AcM* 60 (1988), 111–42.

WARNER, T. E., *An Annotated Bibliography of Woodwind Instruction Books, 1600–1830* (Detroit Studies in Music Bibliography, 11; Detroit, 1967).

WARREN, C. W., 'Music at Nonesuch', *MQ* 54 (1968), 47–57.

WATERHOUSE, E., *Painting in Britain, 1530 to 1790* (3rd edn., Harmondsworth, 1969).

WEINPAHL, R. W., *Music at the Inns of Court during the Reigns of Elizabeth, James, and Charles* (Northridge, 1979).

WEINREB, B., and HIBBERT, C., (eds.), *The London Encyclopaedia* (London, 1983; repr. 1987).

WEISS, D. G., *Samuel Pepys, Curioso* (Pittsburgh, 1957).

Westminster Drollery, i (London, 1671).

WESTRUP, J. A., 'Foreign Musicians in Stuart England', *MQ* 27 (1941), 70–89.

WHITELOCKE, B., *Memorials of the English Affairs* (London, 1682; new edn., Oxford, 1853).

WILLETTS, P., 'Music from the Circle of Anthony Wood at Oxford', *British Museum Quarterly*, 24 (1961), 71–5.

—— 'Sir Nicholas Le Strange and John Jenkins', *ML* 42 (1961), 30–43.

—— 'A Neglected Source of Monody and Madrigal', *ML* 43 (1962), 329–39.

—— 'Sir Nicholas Le Strange's Collection of Masque Music', *British Museum Quarterly*, 29 (1964–5), 78–81.

—— 'Autograph Music by John Jenkins', *ML* 48 (1967), 124–6.

—— 'Autographs of Angelo Notari', *ML* 50 (1969), 124–6.

—— 'Stephen Bing: A Forgotten Violist', *Chelys*, 23 (1990), 3–17.

—— 'John Barnard's Collections of Viol and Vocal Music', *Chelys*, 20 (1991), 28–42.

WILLIAMS, C. (ed.), *Thomas Platter's Travels in England 1599* (London, 1937).

WILLIAMS, P., *The Tudor Regime* (Oxford, 1973).

WILSON, J. (ed.), *Roger North on Music* (London, 1959).

WINTER, M. H., *The Pre-Romantic Ballet* (London, 1974).

WINTERNITZ, E., 'The School of Gaudenzio Ferrari and the Early History of the Violin', in G. Reese and R. Brandel (eds.), *The Commonwealth of Music: Writings on Music in History, Art, and Culture in Honor of Curt Sachs* (New York and London, 1965), 182–200.

—— *Musical Instruments and their Symbolism in Western Art* (London, 1967).

WITTEN, L. C., 'Apollo, Orpheus and David: A Study of the Crucial Century in the Development of Bowed Strings in North Italy 1480–1580, as seen in Graphic Evidence and some Surviving Instruments', *JAMIS* 1 (1975), 5–55.

—— 'The Surviving Instruments of Andrea Amati', *EM* 10 (1982), 487–94.

WOLF, L., 'Jews in Elizabethan England', *Transactions of the Jewish Historical Society of England*, 11 (1926), 1–91.

WOLFF, A. S., 'The Chansonnier Biblioteca Casanatense 2856: Its History, Purpose, and Music', Ph.D. diss. (North Texas State University, 1970).

WOOD, B., 'John Blow's Anthems with Orchestra', Ph.D. thesis (Cambridge, 1976).

—— 'A Newly Identified Purcell Autograph', *ML* 59 (1978), 329–32.

WOODFIELD, I., 'The Origin of the Viol', Ph.D. thesis (London, 1977).

—— *The Early History of the Viol* (Cambridge, 1984).

WOODFILL, W. L., *Musicians in English Society from Elizabeth to Charles I* (Princeton, NJ, 1953; repr. 1969).

WOODLEY, R., 'The Printing and Scope of Tinctoris's Fragmentary Treatise *De Inuentione et Usu Musice*', *EMH* 5 (1985), 239–68.

WOOL, C., 'A Critical Edition and Historical Commentary of Kassel 4° MS Mus. 125', M. Mus. diss. (London, 1983).

WRIGHT, C., 'Voices and Instruments in the Art Music of Northern France during the Fifteenth Century: A Conspectus', in D. Heartz and B. Wade (eds.), *Report on the Twelfth Congress* [of the International Musicological Society] *Berkeley 1977* (Kassel, 1981), 643–9.

WRIGHT, L., 'The Medieval Gittern and Citole: A Case of Mistaken Identity', *GSJ* 30 (1977), 8–42.

WRIGHT, R., *Dictionnaire des instruments de musique* (London, 1941).

WULSTAN, D., *Tudor Music* (London, 1985).

ZACCONI, L., *Prattica di musica* (Venice 1592; repr. 1967).

ZASLAW, N., 'An English *Orpheus and Euridice* of 1697', *MT* 118 (1977), 805–8.

—— 'Lully's Orchestra', unpublished paper given at the 1987 Colloque Lully in Heidelberg.

—— 'When is an Orchestra not an Orchestra?', *EM* 16 (1988), 483–95.

ZIMMERMAN, F., 'Anthems of Purcell and Contemporaries in a Newly Rediscovered "Gostling Manuscript"', *AcM* 41 (1969), 55–70.

—— *Henry Purcell, 1659–1695: His Life and Times* (2nd edn., Philadelphia, 1983).

MUSIC

ADSON, J., *Courtly Masquing Ayres* (London, 1621), ed. P. Walls (English Instrumental Music of the Late Renaissance, 3–5; London, 1975–6).

ATTAINGNANT, P., *Six gaillardes et six pavanes avec treze chansons musicales a quatre parties* (Paris, 1530), ed. B. Thomas (The Attaingnant Dance Prints, 1; London, 1989).

—— *Neuf basses dances deux branles vingt et cinq pavennes avec quinze gaillardes en musique a quatre parties* (Paris, 1530), ed. B. Thomas (The Attaingnant Dance Prints, 1; London, 1989).

BANISTER II, J., *The Sprightly Companion* (London, 1695; repr. 1984).

BASSANO, A., *Pavans and Galliards in Five Parts*, ed. P. Holman (London, 1981).

BENDUSI, F., *Opera nova de balli* (Venice, 1553), ed. B. Thomas (Italian Instrumental Music of the Renaissance, 5; London, 1974).

BERGSAGEL, J. (ed.), *Music for Instrumental Ensemble* (Music in Denmark at the Time of Christian IV, 2; Copenhagen, 1988).

BERNSTEIN, J. A. (ed.), *French Chansons of the Sixteenth Century* (University Park, Pa., 1985).

BLOCK, R. P. (ed.), *G. B. Riccio and G. Belli: Two Canzonas, 'La Finetta' 1620 and Canzona à2 1613* (London, 1982).

—— (ed.), *G. B. Riccio and G. Belli: Two Canzonas, 'La Rubina' 1620 and Canzona à3 1613* (London, 1982).

BLOW, J., *Chaconne for String Orchestra*, ed. W. Shaw (London, 1958).

—— *Coronation Anthems, Anthems with Strings*, ed. A. Lewis and H. W. Shaw (MB 7; 2nd edn., London, 1969).

—— *Anthems II: Anthems with Orchestra*, ed. B. Wood (MB 50; London, 1984).

—— *A Masque for the Entertainment of the King: Venus and Adonis*, ed. C. Bartlett (Wyton, 1984).

BOROFF, E. (ed.), *Notations and Editions: A Book in Honor of Louise Cuyler* (Dubuque, Ia., 1974).

BRADE, W., *Newe ausserlesene Paduanen* (Hamburg, 1609); *Pavans, Galliards, and Canzonas*, ed. B. Thomas (London, 1982).

—— *Newe ausserlesene liebliche Branden* (Hamburg, 1617): ed. B. Thomas, 3 vols. (London, 1974).

BREIG, W. (ed.), *Lied- und Tanzvariationen der Sweelinck-Schule* (Mainz, 1970).

BRETT, P. (ed.), *Consort Songs* (MB 22; London, 1967).

BROWN, A. (ed.), *Tisdale's Virginal Book* (London, 1966).

BYRD, W., *Consort Music*, ed. K. Elliott (*The Collected Works of William Byrd*, xvii; London, 1971).

—— *Keyboard Music: I*, ed. A. Brown (MB 27; London, 1969).

CARR, J., *Tripla concordia* (London, 1677).

CIMA, G. P., *Concerti ecclesiastici* (Milan, 1610); ed. K. Grebe, *Drei Sonaten* (Hamburg, 1957).

COLLARD, E., *Complete Works for the Lute*, ed. J. Duarte and H. Pratt (London, 1978).

COPRARIO, J., *Fantasia Suites*, ed. R. Charteris (MB 46; London, 1980).

CURTIS, A. (ed.), *Dutch Keyboard Music of the Sixteenth and Seventeenth Centuries* (Monumenta musica neerlandica, 3; Amsterdam, 1961).

CUTTING, F., *Selected Works*, ed. M. Long (London, 1968).

CUTTS, J. P. (ed.), *La Musique de scène de la troupe de Shakespeare* (Paris, 1959).

DALLA CASA, G., *Il vero modo di diminuir, libri I et II* (Venice, 1584; repr. 1970).

DALZA, J. A., *Intabolatura de lauto* (Venice, 1508; repr. 1980).

DART, T. (ed.), *Suite from the Royal Brass Music of King James I* (London, 1959).

—— and COATES, W. (eds.), *Jacobean Consort Music* (MB 9; 2nd edn., London, 1966).

DAWES, F. (ed.), *Ten Pieces by Hugh Aston and Others* (Early Keyboard Music, 1; London, 1951).

DIESSENER, G., *Instrumental Ayrs* (London, 1682).

DOE, P. (ed.), *Elizabethan Consort Music: I, II* (MB 44, 45; London, 1979, 1988).

DOWLAND, J., *Lachrimae; or, Seaven Teares* (London, *c.*1604; repr. 1974); ed. E. Hunt in *John Dowland: Complete Consort Music* (London, 1985).

—— *Collected Lute Music*, ed. D. Poulton and B. Lam (3rd edn., London, 1981).

DOWLAND, R., *A Musicall Banquet* (London, 1610; repr. 1969).

—— *Varietie of Lute-Lessons* (London, 1610; repr. 1958); ed. E. Hunt (London, 1956).

D'URFEY, T., *Wit and Mirth; or, Pills to Purge Melancholy* (London, 1699), repr. in *Songs Compleat, Pleasant and Divertive* (London, 1719; repr. 1872).

ECCLES, J., *The Judgement of Paris* (London, 1702); ed. R. Platt (MLE, series C, vol. 1, facs.; Tunbridge Wells, 1984).

ÉCORCHEVILLE, J. (ed.), *Vingt suites d'orchestre du XVIIe siècle français, publiées d'après un manuscrit de la Bibliothèque de Cassel* (Paris, 1906; repr. 1970).

EDWARDS, W. (ed.), *Music for Mixed Consort* (MB 40; London, 1977).

ESTRÉES, Jean d', *Tiers livre de danseries* (Paris, 1559).

FERRABOSCO I, A., *Latin Songs, French Chansons, and English Songs*, ed. R. Charteris (*Opera Omnia*, iii; CMM 96; Neuhausen-Stuttgart, 1984).

[?FERRABOSCO II. A.], 'Sound out my voice', ed. G. Dodd (Supplementary Publications of the Viola da Gamba Society, 128; London, 1978).

FINGER, G., *Sonatae XII pro diversis instrumentis*, Op. 1 (London, 1688).

—— *Sonata in C for Oboe/Trumpet in C (Descant Recorder), Violin, and Basso Continuo*, ed. P. Holman (London, 1979).

FISCHER, J. C. F., *Le Journal de printems*, Op. 1 (Augsburg, 1695); ed. E. von Werra in *Orchestermusik des XVII. Jahrhunderts* (DDT, 1. folge, 10; Wiesbaden and Graz, 1958).

FUHRMANN, G. L., *Testudo gallo-germanica* (Nuremberg, 1615; repr. 1975).

FÜLLSACK, Z., and HILDEBRAND, C., *Ausserlesener Paduanen und Galliarden, erster Theil* (Hamburg, 1607); ed. H. Mönkemeyer (Monumenta musicae ad usum practicum, 5; Celle, 1986).

GERVAISE, C., *Troisième livre de danceries à quatre et cinq parties* (Paris, 1557); ed. B. Thomas (The Attaingnant Dance Prints, 3; London, 1972).

—— *Sixième livre de danceries, mis en musique à quatre parties* (Paris, 1555); ed. B. Thomas (The Attaingnant Dance Prints, 6; London, 1972).

GIBBONS, O., *The First Set of Madrigals and Mottets* (London, 1612); ed. E. H. Fellowes, rev. T. Dart (The English Madrigalists, 5; 2nd edn., London, 1964).

—— *Fantazies of III Parts* (London, *c.*1620).

—— *Consort Music*, ed. J. Harper (MB 48; London, 1982).

GRABU, L., *Pastoralle* (London, 1684).

—— *Albion and Albanius, an Opera* (London, 1687).

GREETING, T., *The Pleasant Companion* (2nd edn., London, 1673).

HAGIUS, K., *Newe künstliche musicalische Intraden* (Nuremberg, 1616).

HARRISON, I. (ed.), *Three Instrumental Pieces from Durham Cathedral Library for Six Instruments* (Early Music Library, 36; London, 1988).

HASSLER, H. L., *Lustgarten neuer teutscher Gesäng* (Nuremberg, 1601); ed. C. R. Crosby (*Sämtliche Werke*, ix; Wiesbaden, 1968); ed. B. Thomas, *Intradas and Gagliarda from Lustgarten (1601)* (Thesaurus Musicus, 16; London, 1979); ed. id., *Six Lieder from Lustgarten (1601)* (Thesaurus Musicus, 26; London, 1981).

HAUSSMANN, V., *Neue fünffstimmige Paduane und Galliarde* (Nuremberg, 1604).

—— *Neue Intrade* (Nuremberg, 1604).

—— *Ausgewählte Instrumentalwerke*, ed. F. Boelsche (DDT, series 1, 16; Leipzig, 1904).

HILDEBRAND, C., *Ander Theil ausserlesener lieblicher Paduanen* (Hamburg, 1609), ed. H. Mönkemeyer (Monumenta musicae ad usum practicum, 6; Celle, 1986).

HOLBORNE, A., *The Cittharn Schoole* (London, 1597; repr. 1973); ed. M. Kanazawa in *Complete Works*, ii (Cambridge, Mass., 1973).

—— *Pavans, Galliards, Almains* (London, 1599); ed. B. Thomas (London, 1980).

HOLMAN, P. (ed.), *Music at the Royal Court of London c.1620* (Zeitschrift für Spielmusik, 497; Celle, 1980).

—— (ed.), *Seven Dances from the Court of Henry VIII* (Corby, 1983).

HUMFREY, P., *Complete Church Music; I*, ed. P. Dennison (MB 34; London, 1972).

JENKINS, J., *Fancies and Ayres*, ed. H. Sleeper (The Wellesley Edition, 1; Wellesley, Mass., 1950).

—— *Three-Part Fancy and Ayre Divisions*, ed. R. A. Warner (The Wellesley Edition, 10; Wellesley, Mass., 1966).

—— *Consort Music in Four Parts*, ed. A. Ashbee (MB 26; London, 1969).

—— 'Fancy and Ayre in G minor', ed. R. A. Warner in E. Boroff (ed.), *Notations and Editions: A Book in Honor of Louise Cuyler* (Dubuque, Ia., 1974), 106–26.

KIRKENDALE, W. (ed.), *L'Aria di Fiorenza; id est, Il Ballo del Gran Duca* (Florence, 1972).

LAWES, W., *Select Consort Music*, ed. M. Lefkowitz (MB 21; London, 1963).

—— *Fantasia Suites*, ed. D. Pinto (MB 60; London, 1991).

LEFKOWITZ, M. (ed.), *Trois masques à la cour de Charles Ier d'Angleterre* (Paris, 1970).

LENTON, J., *The Gentleman's Diversion* (London, 1694).

LOCKE, M., *Melothesia* (London, 1673; repr. 1975); ed. C. Hogwood (Oxford, 1987).

—— *The English Opera; or, The Vocal Music in Psyche . . . To which is Adjoined the Instrumental Musick in the Tempest* (London, 1675); ed. M. Tilmouth in *Matthew Locke: Dramatic Music* (MB 51; London, 1986).

—— *Music for his Majesty's Sackbuts and Cornetts*, ed. A. Baines (London, 1951).

—— *Chamber Music: I, II*, ed. M. Tilmouth (MB 31, 32; London, 1971–2).

—— *Anthems and Motets*, ed. P. Le Huray (MB 38; London, 1976).

—— *Suite in G Minor from Tripla Concordia*, ed. P. Holman (London, 1980).

—— *The Rare Theatrical, New York Public Library, Drexel MS 3976*; ed. P. Holman (MLE, series A, vol. 4; London, 1989).

—— *Eight Suites in Four Parts from 'Consort Music'*, ed. S. Beck (New York, n.d.).

LUPO, T., *The Four-Part Consort Music*, ed. R. Charteris and J. M. Jennings (Clifden, 1983).

——*The Two- and Three-Part Consort Music*, ed. R. Charteris (Clifden, 1987).

LÜTKEMAN, P., *Der erste Theil newer lateinischer und deutscher Gesenge* (Stettin, 1597); *Fantasia 'Innsbruck ich muss dich lassen' 1597*, ed. B. Thomas (German Instrumental Music of the Late Renaissance, 1; London, 1973).

MARTINI, J., *Secular Pieces*, ed. E. G. Evans (Recent Researches in the Music of the Middle Ages and Early Renaissance, 1; Madison, Wisc., 1975).

MATTEIS, N., *Other Ayrs and Pieces . . . the Fourth Part* (London, 1685; repr. 1966; 2nd edn., 1687; repr. 1966).

—— *Concerto in C*, ed. P. Holman (London, 1982).

MATTHYSZ, P., *XX Konincklycke Fantasien* (Amsterdam, 1648; ed. R. Rasch in *T. Lupo, I. Coprario, W. Daman: XX Konincklycke Fantasien en noch IX Fantasien* (Peer, 1987).

MORITZ, Landgraf von Hessen, *Ausgewählte Werke*, i: *16 Pavanen, Gagliarden und Intraden*, ed. H. Birtner (EDM, series 2, Landschaftsdenkmale, Kurhessen; Kassel, 1936).

—— *Four Pavans*, ed. B. Thomas (Early Music Library 53; London, 1989).

MORLEY, T., *The First Book of Consort Lessons* (London, 1599, rev. 2nd edn., 1611); ed. S. Beck (New York, 1959).

—— *Two Consort Lessons Collected by Thomas Morley*, ed. T. Dart (London, 1957).

MORROW, M. (ed.), *Italian Dances of the Early Sixteenth Century* (Dance Music of the Middle Ages and Renaissance, 1–3; London, 1976–8).

MRÁČEK, J. S. (ed.), *Seventeenth-Century Instrumental Dance Music in Uppsala University Library, Instr. mus. hs. 409* (Musica Svecica Saeculi xvii: 5, Monumenta Musicae Svecicae, 8; Stockholm, 1976).

NOTARI, A., *Prime musiche nouve* (London, 1613).

—— *Canzona Passaggiata*, ed. P. Holman (London, 1981).

OROLOGIO, A., *Intradae . . . quinque & sex vocibus . . . liber primus* (Helmstedt, 1597); ed. B. Thomas, *Six Intradas, 1597* (German Instrumental Music of the Late Renaissance, 4; London, 1978).

ORTIZ, D., *Trattado de glosas sobre clausulas y otros generos de puntos en la musica de violones/Glose sopra le cadenze et altre sorte di punti in la musica del violone* (Rome, 1553; repr. 1984); ed. M. Schneider (Kassel, 1936).

OTTO, V., *Newe Paduanen, Galliarden, Intraden und Currenten, nach englischer und frantzösicher Art* (Leipzig, 1611).

PARAS, J. (ed.), *The Music for Viola Bastarda* (Bloomington, Ind., 1986).

PLAMENAC, D. (ed.), *Keyboard Music of the Late Middle Ages* (CMM 57; Rome, 1972).

PLAYFORD, J., *The English Dancing Master* (London, 1651; repr. 1957).

—— *A Musicall Banquet* (London, 1651).

—— *Court Ayres* (London, 1655).

—— *Courtly Masquing Ayres* (London, 1662).

—— *Musick's Hand-Maide* (London, 1663); ed. T. Dart, (London, 1969).

—— *Catch that Catch Can; or, The Musical Companion* (London, 1667).

—— *The Treasury of Musick* (London, 1669; repr. 1966).

—— *Apollo's Banquet* (London, *c.*1669; 5th edn., 1687).

—— *Choice Songs and Ayres/Choice Ayres, Songs and Dialogues*, 1, 2 (London, 1673, 1675; repr. 1989).

—— *The Division Violin* (London, 1684; repr. 1984; 2nd edn., 1685).

PORTER, W., *Madrigales and Ayres* (London, 1632; repr. 1969).

PRAETORIUS, B., *Newe liebliche Paduanen und Galliarden* (Berlin, 1616).

PURCELL, H., *Birthday Odes for Queen Mary, Part 1*, ed. G. E. P. Arkwright (The Works of Henry Purcell, 11; London, 1902).

—— *Welcome Songs, Part 1*, ed. R. Vaughan Williams (The Works of Henry Purcell, 15; London, 1905).

—— *Welcome Songs, Part 2*, ed. R. Vaughan Williams (The Works of Henry Purcell, 18; London, 1910).

—— *Dramatic Music, Part 2*, ed. A. Gray (The Works of Henry Purcell, 20; London, 1916).

—— *Birthday Odes for Queen Mary, Part 2*, ed. G. Shaw (The Works of Henry Purcell, 24; London, 1926).

—— *Dioclesian*, ed. J. F. Bridge and J. Pointer, rev. M. Laurie (The Works of Henry Purcell, 9; London, 1961).

—— *Sacred Music III: Seven Anthems with Strings*, ed. H. E. Wooldridge, G. E. P. Arkwright, and N. Fortune (The Works of Henry Purcell, 17; 2nd edn., London, 1964).

—— *Ode on St Cecilia's Day, 1692*, ed. P. Dennison (The Works of Henry Purcell, 8; London, 1978).

—— *Fantasias and Miscellaneous Instrumental Music*, ed. T. Dart, rev. M. Tilmouth (The Works of Henry Purcell, 31; 2nd edn., London, 1990).

—— *Three Odes for St Cecilia's Day*, ed. B. Wood (The Works of Henry Purcell, 10; London, 1990).

—— *A Song for the Duke of Gloucester's Birthday*, ed. I. Spink (The Works of Henry Purcell, 4; London, 1990).

ROGNONI, F., *Selva di varii passaggi secondo l'uso moderno per cantare e suonare con ogni sorte de stromenti* (Milan, 1620; repr. 1970).

ROSSETER, P., *Lessons for Consort* (London, 1609).

SABOL, A. J. (ed.), *Four Hundred Songs and Dances from the Stuart Masque* (Providence, 1978).

SCHEIN, J. H., *Banchetto musicale* (Leipzig, 1617); ed. D. Krickenberg in *Newe Ausgabe sämtlicher Werke*, ix (Kassel, 1967).

SCHERING, A. (ed.), *Geschichte der Musik in Beispielen* (Leipzig, 1931).

SCHMELZER, J. H., *Sacro-profanus concentus musicus* (Nuremberg, 1662); ed. E. Schenk (DTÖ, 111/112; Graz and Vienna, 1965).

SIMPSON, C., *The Division-Violist* (London, 1659; rev. edn., 1665; repr. 1965) as *Chelys minuritionum artificio exornata/The Division Viol; or, The Art of Playing Extempore upon a Ground*.

SIMPSON, T., *Opusculum neuwer Pavanan* (Frankfurt, 1610); ed. H. Mönkemeyer (Monumenta musicae ad usum practicum, 7; Celle, 1987).

—— *Opus newer Paduanen* (Hamburg, 1617); ed. H. Mönkemeyer (Monumenta musicae ad usum practicum, 8; Celle, 1987).

—— *Taffel-Consort* (Hamburg, 1621); ed. B. Thomas (London, 1988).

SPENCER, R. (ed.), *The Board Lute Book*, facs. (Leeds, 1976).

SPINK, I. (ed.), *English Songs 1625–1660* (MB 33; London, 1971).

STAINER, J. F. R. and C. (eds.), *Dufay and his Contemporaries* (London, 1898).

STEVENS, J. (ed.), *Music at the Court of Henry VIII* (MB 18; 2nd edn., London, 1969).

—— (ed.), *Early Tudor Songs and Carols* (MB 36; London, 1975).

SUSATO, T., *Het derde musyck boexken* (Antwerp, 1551; repr. 1987); *Danserye*, ed. F. J. Giesbert, 2 vols. (Mainz, 1935).

TERZI, G. A., *Il secondo libro de intavolatura di liuto* (Venice, 1599; repr. 1981).

THOMAS., B. (ed.), *Six Dances from the Court of Henry VIII* (London, 1989).

—— (ed.), *Hoftanz 'Benzenhauer' (Two Settings)* (Early Music Library, 11; London, 1987).

—— (ed.), *Two Passamezzi* (Early Music Library, 71; London, 1990).

—— and GINGELL, J. (eds.), *The Renaissance Dance Book* (London, 1987).

TINCTORIS, J., *Opera Omnia*, ed. W. Melin (CMM 18; Rome, 1976).

TOMKINS, T., *Keyboard Music*, ed. S. Tuttle (MB 5; London, 1955).

VALLET, N., *Regia pietas* (Amsterdam, 1620; repr. 1986).

—— *Œuvres pour luth seul: Le Secret des muses*, ed. M. Rollin and A. Souris (Paris, 1970).

VENDOME, R. (ed.), *Christ Church Music MS 89: Peter Philips and Peter Cornet* (Spanish Netherlands Keyboard Music, 1; Oxford, 1983).

WALKER, D. P., *Musique des intermèdes de 'La Pellegrina'* (Les Fêtes du mariage de Ferdinand de Médicis et de Christine de Lorraine, Florence 1589, 1; Paris, 1963).

WALLS, P., and THOMAS, B. (eds.), *Twenty-one Masque Dances of the Early Seventeenth Century* (English Instrumental Music of the Late Renaissance, 2; London, 1974).

WARD, J. M. (ed.), *The Dublin Virginal Book, New Edition* (London, 1983).

—— (ed.), *Music for Elizabethan Lutes* (Oxford, 1992).

WARLOCK, P. (ed.), *Eight Short Elizabethan Dance Tunes* (London, 1924).

WELDON, J., *Divine Harmony: Six Select Anthems* (London, 1716).

WILDER, P. VAN, *Fantasia con Pause et senza Pause*, ed. P. Holman (Corby, 1983).

YONGE, N., *Musica transalpina* (London, 1588; repr. 1972).

ZANNETTI, G., *Il scolaro* (Milan, 1645); ed. J. Tyler (Early Dance Music, 5, 6; London, 1983, 1985).

ZIMMERMAN, F. (ed.), *The Gostling Manuscript, Compiled by John Gostling*, facs. (Austin, Tex., and London, 1977).

Index